The Makings of America:

The United States and the World

The Makings of America:
The United States and the World
Volume I: To 1865

D. C. HEATH AND COMPANY
Lexington, Massachusetts Toronto

Address editorial correspondence to:

D. C. Heath and Company
125 Spring Street
Lexington, MA 02173

Acquisitions Editor: James Miller
Developmental Editor: Sylvia Mallory
Production Editor: Heather Monahan
Cover Designer: Jan Shapiro
Production Coordinator: Lisa Merrill
Permissions Editor: Margaret Roll

Cover: Detail from "Plan of the City of New York, 1776," a Cartouche from Faden, *North American Atlas* (London, 1777). Library of Congress.

Published simultaneously in Canada.

Printed in the United States of America.

International Standard Book Number: 0-669-33251-8

10 9 8 7 6 5 4 3 2

ACKNOWLEDGMENTS

pp. 395–406; 416–428: From *Major Problems in the History of American Workers*, edited by Eileen Boris and Nelson Lichtenstein, pp. 84–95; 124–136. © 1991 by D. C. Heath and Company.

pp. 215–247: From *Major Problems in the Era of the American Revolution, 1760–1791*, edited by Richard D. Brown, pp. 465–497. © 1992 by D. C. Heath and Company.

pp. 187–196; 429–461: From *Major Problems in the History of the American South, Volume I: The Old South*, edited by Paul D. Escott and David R. Goldfield, pp. 41–50; 256–263; 292–317. © 1990 by D. C. Heath and Company.

pp. 103–125; 141–177: From *Major Problems in American Colonial History*, edited by Karen Ordahl Kupperman, pp. 1–2; 9–17; 39–51; 83–100; 117–135. © 1993 by D. C. Heath and Company.

pp. 5–30; 95–102; 125–140; 256–293; 342–358; 496–509; 558–569: From *The Heath Anthology of American Literature, Volume 1*, edited by Paul Lauter et al., pp. 40–66; 80–88; 99–114; 685–687; 694–728; 1467–1471; 1499–1511; 1873–1886; 2709–2713; 2810–2817. © 1990 by D. C. Heath and Company.

pp. 31–95: From *1492: Discovery, Invasion, Encounter*, edited by Marvin Lunenfeld, pp. 13–32; 35–50; 63–74; 259–272; 294–298. © 1991 by D. C. Heath and Company.

pp. 1–4; 294–320: From *Major Problems in the History of the American West*, edited by Clyde A. Milner II, pp. 35–38; 131–142; 211–255. © 1989 by D. C. Heath and Company.

pp. 178–186; 248–255; 407–415: From *Major Problems in American Women's History*, edited by Mary Beth Norton, pp. 18–26; 82–89; 171–179. © 1989 by D. C. Heath and Company.

pp. 197–214; 510–531: From *Major Problems in American Foreign Policy, Volume I: To 1914*, Third Edition, edited by Thomas G. Paterson, pp. 27–44; 254–265; 305–314. © 1989 by D. C. Heath and Company.

pp. 462–495; 532–557: From *Major Problems in the Civil War and Reconstruction*, edited by Michael Perman, pp. 118–125; 202–215; 353–365; 400–414; 474–484. © 1991 by D. C. Heath and Company.

pp. 321–341; 359–394: From *Major Problems in the Early Republic, 1787–1848*, edited by Sean Wilentz, pp. 188–212; 423–443; 471–479; 482–484. © 1992 by D. C. Heath and Company.

Contents

Native American Traditions
Page 1

Europe on the Eve of Contact
Page 31

Contact in Meso-America
Page 78

Two Worlds Discover Each Other
Page 103

British Colonies in the Seventeenth and Eighteenth Centuries
Page 141

THE CHESAPEAKE: ENGLAND'S FIRST SUCCESSFUL COLONIZATION   141

NEW ENGLAND: THE SETTLEMENT OF THE PURITAN COLONIES   159

The New Nation
Page 215

African Americans in the Revolutionary Age
Page 256

Movement West
Page 294

Antebellum Reform and Reformers
Page 321

The Industrial Revolution in the United States
Page 370

THE RISE OF NORTHERN CAPITALISM   370

FROM THE ARTISAN'S REPUBLIC TO THE FACTORY

SYSTEM   395

WORK AND PROTEST IN ANTEBELLUM NEW ENGLAND

407

Slavery and the Old South
Page 416

The Civil War
Page 462

Two Views of the War's Meaning
Page 496

Diplomatic Issues in the Civil War Era
Page 510

Walt Whitman Remembers President Lincoln
Page 558

Native American

Traditions

Scholars may disagree about whether to view the West historically as a frontier or a region, but for the native peoples of North America, this continent has been a homeland for thousands of years. Misnamed "Indians" by the European newcomers, these native peoples had established an "old world" of their own long before 1492. The interaction between native Americans and European newcomers is the first major story of both American and western history. Understanding the profound changes that occurred when Europeans swept into these native homelands is a formidable challenge to the student of the American past. Evidence from a wide range of disciplines, such as archaeology, anthropology, folklore, linguistics, climatology, and epidemiology, has been used by historians to recapture the early era of Indian-white contact. The full story may be impossible to reconstruct, but most recent scholarship is demonstrating that American Indians are very much actors and survivors in this postcontact history, not passive victims of an overwhelming invasion.

Y D O C U M E N T S

The oral traditions of many native American tribes contain clear memories of the first contact with Europeans. These stories were written down by white visitors who came later. The first two documents indicate how truly foreign these newcomers appeared to native people. The events described in the first document, a Chippewa narrative first written down in 1855, occurred in the Great Lakes region. The second document, a Chinook story recorded in 1894, took place near the mouth of the Columbia River in what today is Oregon.

The next two documents are accounts of the Pueblo revolt of 1680 in colonial New Mexico. The third document is a report to the king of Spain by the recently arrived viceroy of New Spain, the count of Paredes, who learned of this rebellion on the northern frontier before he reached Mexico City to take up his post. The testimony before his Spanish inquisitors of Pedro Naranjo, an imprisoned Pueblo Indian, indicates how traditional religious beliefs and one native leader helped launch the revolt. This event remains a vivid memory in the minds of present-day Pueblo Indians—as significant to them as the American Revolu-

1

tion for Anglo-Americans. Although New Mexico would be reconquered after the revolt, Spanish domination would never be as intense as before 1680.

The final two documents, written over two hundred years apart, demonstrate the deadliest aspect of the European "invasion" of America—the introduction of epidemic diseases, especially smallpox. The first account, concerning an epidemic in 1633, was written by William Bradford, the governor of Plymouth Colony in Massachusetts. The second is from the 1837 journal of Francis Chardon, a trader at Fort Clark, located on the Missouri River some fifty-five miles above present-day Bismarck, North Dakota. In 1633 in many of the native villages of southern New England, up to 95 percent of the Indians died. Similar catastrophic rates of death occurred in 1837 in villages of the Arikaras, Mandans, Hidatsas, Assiniboins, and Blackfeet.

A Chippewa Narrative, Recorded in 1855

For a long time before this story began, my people had lived on a small promontory on Lake Superior. It is called the Point of the Old Village.

One night one of my grandfathers, a prophet of the tribe, had a dream which had a strange effect on him. For days he busied himself very earnestly, as a result of this dream. He fasted, he took sweat baths every day, he shut himself alone in his prophet lodge.

His penance was so thorough, so unusual, that the people of the village were curious. What was about to happen? Was there to be a great famine or an unusually successful hunting season? Was there to be a serious war with the Sioux? Or was something else of equal importance about to take place?

At last when the prophet had considered everything carefully, and after he had the whole story of his dream clear in his mind, he called together the other prophets and the chiefs of his people. He had astonishing news for them.

"Men of strange appearance have come across the great water," he told them. "They have landed on our island. Their skins are white like snow, and on their faces long hair grows. These people have come across the great water in wonderfully large canoes which have great white wings like those of a giant bird. The men have long and sharp knives, and they have long black tubes which they point at birds and animals. The tubes make a smoke that rises into the air just like the smoke from our pipes. From them come fire and such terrific noise that I was frightened, even in my dream."

Half a day it took the prophet to tell his dream. He described the sails and the masts of the ships, the iron corslets, the guns and cannon. The other prophets and the chiefs listened in amazement. When he finished speaking, all agreed at once that they should prepare a fleet of several canoes and send it eastward along the Great Lakes and the great river. There at the big water, their messengers should find out about these strange people and, on their return home, should make a report to the tribe.

Canoes were made ready for the long journey, and trusted men were selected. For many suns and several moons they travelled over the waters of the lakes and down the great river, through the lands of friendly tribes. These people knew nothing yet of the white strangers, for they had no gifted dreamer and prophet among them.

At last the travellers from the Point of the Old Village came to the lower part of the great river. One evening they found a clearing in the forest, where even the largest trees had been cut down quite smoothly. The Indians camped there and examined the stumps closely. Giant beavers with huge, sharp teeth had done the cutting, the men thought.

"No," said the prophet. "These trees were probably cut by the long knives I saw in my dream. The white strangers must have camped here."

His companions were filled with awe, and with terror also. Using their own stone-headed axes, they could not cut down such large trees or cut anything so smoothly. Then they found some long, rolled-up shavings that puzzled them, and also some pieces of bright-coloured cloth. The shavings they stuck in their hair and in their ears; the cloth they wound around their heads.

Wearing these decorations, the travellers went on. Soon they came to the camp of the strangers. The men had white faces and bushy beards, just as the prophet had said. They had long knives, thundering fire-tubes, and giant canoes with white wings, just as the prophet had said. Now we know that these first white men were Frenchmen.

When the travellers had finished their visit, they made the long journey back to their home on Lake Superior and reported what they had seen. They were excited, and their story excited all the village. Everyone crowded round, to see the things the men had brought back: the shavings, the pieces of wood cut with sharp tools, the gaily-coloured cloth. This cloth was torn into small pieces, so that each person might have one.

To impress other chiefs and other tribes, the Chippewas followed an old custom. In former days they had bound the scalps of their enemies on long poles and sent them from one tribe to another; now they fastened splinters of wood and strips of calico to poles and sent them with special messengers.

And so these strange articles were passed from hand to hand around the whole lake. In this way the people of Lake Superior gained their first knowledge of the white men from Europe.

A Chinook Story, Recorded in 1894

An old woman in a Clatsop village near the mouth of Big River mourned because of the death of her son. For a year she grieved. One day she ceased her wailing and took a walk along the beach where she had often gone in happier days.

As she returned to the village, she saw a strange something out in the water not far from shore. At first she thought it was a whale. When she came nearer, she saw two spruce trees standing upright on it.

"It is not a whale," she said to herself. "It is a monster."

When she came near the strange thing that lay at the edge of the water, she saw that its outside was covered with copper and that ropes were tied to the spruce trees. Then a bear came out of the strange thing and stood on it. He looked like a bear, but his face was the face of a human being.

"Oh, my son is dead," she wailed, "and now the thing we have heard about is on our shore."

The old woman returned to her village, weeping and wailing. People hearing her called to each other, "An old woman is crying. Someone must have struck her."

The men picked up their bows and arrows and rushed out to see what was the matter.

"Listen!" an old man said.

They heard the old woman wailing, "Oh, my son is dead, and the thing we have heard about is on our shore."

All the people ran to meet her. "What is it? Where is it?" they asked.

"Ah, the thing we have heard about in tales is lying over there." She pointed toward the south shore of the village. "There are two bears on it, or maybe they are people."

Then the Indians ran toward the thing that lay near the edge of the water. The two creatures on it held copper kettles in their hands. When the Clatsop arrived at the beach, the creatures put their hands to their mouths and asked for water.

Two of the Indians ran inland, hid behind a log awhile, and then ran back to the beach. One of them climbed up on the strange thing and entered it. He looked around inside it. He saw that it was full of boxes, and he found long strings of brass buttons.

When he went outside to call his relatives to see the inside of the thing, he found that they had already set fire to it. He jumped down and joined the two creatures and the Indians on shore.

The strange thing burned just like fat. Everything burned except the iron, the copper, and the brass. The Clatsop picked up all the pieces of metal. Then they took the two strange-looking men to their chief.

"I want to keep one of the men with me," said the chief.

Soon the people north of the river heard about the strange men and the strange thing, and they came to the Clatsop village. The Willapa came from across the river, the Chehalis and the Cowlitz from farther north, and even the Quinault from up the coast. And people from up the river came also—the Klickitat and others farther up.

The Clatsop sold the iron, brass, and copper. They traded one nail for a good deerskin. For a long necklace of shells they gave several nails. One man traded a piece of brass two fingers wide for a slave.

None of the Indians had ever seen iron and brass before. The Clatsop became rich selling the metals to the other tribes.

The two Clatsop chiefs kept the two men who came on the ship. One stayed at the village called Clatsop, and the other stayed at the village on the cape.

Changing Woman and the Hero Twins after the Emergence of the People (Navajo)[1]

The Navajos now removed to White Standing Rock, where, a few days after they arrived, they found on the ground a small turquoise image of a woman; this they preserved. Of late the monsters had been actively pursuing and devouring the people, and at the time this image was found there were only four persons remaining alive; these were an old man and woman and their two children, a young man and a young woman. Two days after the finding of the image, early in the morning, before they rose, they heard the voice of the Talking God, crying his call of "Wuʻhuʻhuʻhú" so faint and far that they could scarcely hear it. After a while the call was repeated a second time, nearer and louder than at first. Again, after a brief silence, the call was heard for the third time, still nearer and still louder. The fourth call was loud and clear, as if sounded near at hand; as soon as it ceased, the shuffling tread of moccasined feet was heard, and a moment later Talking God stood before them.

He told the four people to come up to the top of *Tsolíhi* after twelve nights had passed, bringing with them the turquoise image they had found, and at once he departed. They pondered deeply on his words, and every day they talked among themselves, wondering why Talking God had summoned them to the mountain.

On the morning of the appointed day they ascended the mountain by a holy trail, and on a level spot, near the summit, they met a party that awaited them there. They found there Talking God, Calling God, White Body (who came up from the lower world with the Navajos), the eleven brothers (of Maid Who Becomes a Bear), the Mirage Stone People, the Daylight People standing in the east, the Blue Sky People standing in the south, the Yellow Light People standing in the west, and the Darkness People standing in the north. White Body stood in the east among the Daylight People, bearing in his hand a small image of a woman wrought in white shell, about the same size and shape as the blue image which the Navajos bore.

Talking God laid down a sacred buckskin with its head toward the west. The Mirage Stone People laid on the buckskin, heads west, the two little images,—of turquoise and white shell,—a white and a yellow ear of corn, the Pollen Boy, and the Grasshopper Girl. On top of all these Talking God laid another sacred buckskin with its head to the east, and under this they now put Wind.

Then the assembled crowd stood so as to form a circle, leaving in the east an opening through which Talking God and Calling God might pass in and out, and they sang the sacred song of Blessingway. Four times the gods entered and raised the cover. When they raised it for the fourth time, the images and the ears of corn were found changed to living beings in human form: the turquoise image had become the Woman Who Changes (or rejuvenates herself); the white shell image had become the White Shell Woman; the white ear of corn had become the White Corn Boy and the yellow ear of corn, the Yellow Corn Girl. After the ceremony, White Body took Pollen Boy, Grasshopper Girl, White Corn Boy, and Yellow Corn Girl with him into *Tsolíhi*; the rest of the assembly departed, and the two divine

---

[1] The Navajo Indians of the southwest United States migrated from northwestern Canada by about 1200 A.D. They came to the Southwest as a hunting and gathering people; they learned agri- culture from the pueblo peoples and in the sixteenth century acquired livestock from the Spanish. Their religious customs are thus somewhat similar to the Hopi people.

sisters, Changing Woman and White Shell Woman,[2] were left on the mountain alone.

The women remained here four nights; on the fourth morning Changing Woman said: "Younger Sister, why should we remain here? Let us go to yonder high point and look around us." They went to the highest point of the mountain, and when they had been there several days Changing Woman said: "It is lonely here; we have no one to speak to but ourselves; we see nothing but that which rolls over our heads (the sun), and that which drops below us (a small dripping water-fall). I wonder if they can be people. I shall stay here and wait for the one in the morning, while you go down among the rocks and seek the other."

In the morning Changing Woman found a bare, flat rock and lay on it with her feet to the east, and the rising sun shone upon her. White Shell Woman went down where the dripping waters descended and allowed them to fall upon her. At noon the women met again on the mountain top and Changing Woman said to her sister: "It is sad to be so lonesome. How can we make people so that we may have others of our kind to talk to?" White Shell Woman answered: "Think, Elder Sister; perhaps after some days you may plan how this is to be done."

Four days after this conversation White Shell Woman said: "Elder Sister, I feel something strange moving within me; what can it be?" and Changing Woman answered: "It is a child. It was for this that you lay under the waterfall. I feel, too, the motions of a child within me. It was for this that I let the sun shine upon me." Soon after the voice of Talking God was heard four times, as usual, and after the last call he and Water Sprinkler[3] appeared. They came to prepare the women for their approaching delivery.

In four days more they felt the commencing throes of labor, and one said to the other: "I think my child is coming." She had scarcely spoken when the voice of the approaching god was heard, and soon Talking God and Water Sprinkler were seen approaching. The former was the accoucheur of Changing Woman, and the latter of White Shell Woman. To one woman a drag-rope of rainbow was given, to the other a drag-rope of sunbeam, and on these they pulled when in pain, as the Navajo woman now pulls on the rope. Changing Woman's child was born first. Talking God took it aside and washed it. He was glad, and laughed and made ironical motions, as if he were cutting the baby in slices and throwing the slices away. They made for the children two baby-baskets, both alike; the foot-rests and the back battens were made of sun-beam, the hoods of rainbow, the side-strings of sheet lightning, and the lacing strings of zigzag lightning. One child they covered with the black cloud, and the other with the female rain.[4] They called the children grandchildren, and they left, promising to return at the end of four days.

When the gods returned at the end of four days, the boys had grown to be the size of ordinary boys of twelve years of age. The gods said to them: "Boys, we have come to have a race with you." So a race was arranged that should go all around a neighboring mountain, and the four started,—two boys and two gods. Before the long race was half done the boys, who ran fast, began to flag, and the gods, who

---

[2] Changing Woman represents Nature as cyclical— the seasons, the parts of a day, the ages of an individual life. White Shell Woman is not a separate individual, but Changing Woman in another form. In this version of the story, each conceives a son; yet, Changing Woman alone has conceived twins.

[3] A holy being responsible for rain.

[4] The fundamental principle of the Navajo world is complementarity. All things can be termed male or female and are associated with colors and the cardinal directions. Male rain is the dark thunderstorm; female rain is the light shower.

were still fresh, got behind them and scourged the lads with twigs of mountain mahogany. Talking God won the race, and the boys came home rubbing their sore backs. When the gods left they promised to return at the end of another period of four days.

As soon as the gods were gone, the Wind whispered to the boys and told them that the old ones were not such fast runners, after all, and that if the boys would practice during the next four days they might win the coming race. So for four days they ran hard, many times daily around the neighboring mountain, and when the gods came back again the youths had grown to the full stature of manhood. In the second contest the gods began to flag and fall behind when half way round the mountain, where the others had fallen behind in the first race, and here the boys got behind their elders and scourged the latter to increase their speed. The elder of the boys won this race, and when it was over the gods laughed and clapped their hands, for they were pleased with the spirit and prowess they witnessed.

The night after the race the boys lay down as usual to sleep; but hearing the women whispering together, they lay awake and listened. They strained their attention, but could not hear a word of what was uttered. At length they rose, approached the women, and said: "Mothers, of what do you speak?" and the women answered: "We speak of nothing." The boys then said: "Grandmothers, of what do you speak?" but the women again replied: "We speak of nothing." The boys then questioned: "Who are our fathers?" "You have no fathers," responded the women; "you are illegitimate." "Who are our fathers?" again demanded the boys, and the women answered: "The round cactus and the sitting cactus are your fathers."[5]

Next day the women made rude bows of juniper wood, and arrows, such as children play with, and they said to the boys: "Go and play around with these, but do not go out of sight from our hut, and do not go to the east." Notwithstanding these warnings the boys went to the east the first day, and when they had travelled a good distance they saw an animal with brownish hair and a sharp nose. They drew their arrows and pointed them toward the sharp-nosed stranger; but before they could shoot he jumped down into a canyon and disappeared. When they returned home they told the women—addressing them as "Mother" and "Grandmother"— what they had seen. The women said: "That is Coyote which you saw. He is a spy for the monster *Téelgĕt*.". . .[6] Alas, our children! What shall we do to make you hear us? What shall we do to save you? You would not listen to us. Now the spies of the *alien gods* in all quarters of the world have seen you. They will tell their chiefs, and soon the monsters will come here to devour you, as they have devoured all your kind before you."

The next morning the women made a corncake and laid it on the ashes to bake. Then White Shell Woman went out of the *hogán*, and, as she did so, she saw *Yéitso*,[7] the tallest and fiercest of the alien gods, approaching. She ran quickly back and gave the warning, and the women hid the boys under bundles and sticks. *Yéitso* came and sat down at the door, just as the women were taking the cake out of the ashes.

[5] The mystery of the boys' paternity is linked to that of the monsters they will slay, for they will discover that the Sun is the father of both the slayers and the slain.

[6] This edition of the story eliminates three repetitions of this episode in which the Twins, who should be hiding from the monsters who are terrorizing the people, play in the open where they are observed by spies for the monsters. *Téelgĕt* is a monstrous, horned quadruped.

[7] The name means "the Great Fear." The monsters were conceived unnaturally in the underworld by women who had turned away from men. Each monster or obstacle the Twins overcome can be understood to represent certain kinds of fears.

"That cake is for me," said *Yéitso*. "How nice it smells!" "No," said Changing Woman, "it was not meant for your great maw." "I don't care," said *Yéitso*. "I would rather eat boys. Where are your boys? I have been told you have some here, and I have come to get them." "We have none," said Changing Woman. "All the boys have gone into the paunches of your people long ago." "No boys?" said the giant. "What, then, has made all the tracks around here?" "Oh! these tracks I have made for fun," replied the woman. "I am lonely here, and I make tracks so that I may fancy there are many people around me." She showed *Yéitso* how she could make similar tracks with her fist. He compared the two sets of tracks, seemed to be satisfied, and went away.

When he was gone, the White Shell Woman went up to the top of a neighboring hill to look around, and she beheld many of the anáye hastening in the direction of her lodge. She returned speedily, and told her sister what she had seen. Changing Woman took four colored hoops, and threw one toward each of the cardinal points,—a white one to the east, a blue one to the south, a yellow one to the west, and a black one to the north. At once a great gale arose, blowing so fiercely in all directions from the *hogán* that none of the enemies could advance against it.

Next morning the boys got up before daybreak and stole away. Soon the women missed them, but could not trace them in the dark. When it was light enough to examine the ground the women went out to look for fresh tracks. They found four footprints of each of the boys, pointing in the direction of the mountain of *Dsilnáotil,* but more than four tracks they could not find. They came to the conclusion that the boys had taken a holy trail, so they gave up further search and returned to the lodge.

The boys travelled rapidly in the holy trail, and soon after sunrise, near *Dsilnáotil,* they saw smoke arising from the ground. They went to the place where the smoke rose, and they found it came from the smoke-hole of a subterranean chamber. A ladder, black from smoke, projected through the hole. Looking down into the chamber they saw an old woman, the Spider Woman,[8] who glanced up at them and said: "Welcome, children. Enter. Who are you, and whence do you two come together walking?" They made no answer, but descended the ladder. When they reached the floor she again spoke to them, asking: "Whither do you two go walking together?" "Nowhere in particular," they answered; "we came here because we had nowhere else to go." She asked this question four times, and each time she received a similar answer. Then she said: "Perhaps you would seek your father?" "Yes," they answered, "if we only knew the way to his dwelling." "Ah!" said the woman, "it is a long and dangerous way to the house of your father, the Sun. There are many of the monsters dwelling between here and there, and perhaps, when you get there, your father may not be glad to see you, and may punish you for coming. You must pass four places of danger,—the rocks that crush the traveller, the reeds that cut him to pieces, the cane cactuses that tear him to pieces, and the boiling sands that overwhelm him. But I shall give you something to subdue your enemies and preserve your lives." She gave them a charm, the feather of the alien gods, which consisted of a hoop with two life-feathers (feathers plucked from a living eagle) attached, and another life-feather to preserve their existence. She taught them also this magic formula, which, if repeated to their enemies, would subdue their anger: "Put your feet down with pollen. Put your hands down with pollen. Put your head

[8] In southwestern Native literatures, Spider Woman is a grandmotherly figure whose great wisdom is often placed at the service of humanity.

down with pollen. Then your feet are pollen; your hands are pollen; your body is pollen; your mind is pollen; your voice is pollen. The trail is beautiful. Be still."[9]

Soon after leaving the house of Spider Woman, the boys came to the rocks that crush.[10] There was here a narrow chasm between two high cliffs. When a traveller approached, the rocks would open wide apart, apparently to give him easy passage and invite him to enter; but as soon as he was within the cleft they would close like hands clapping and crush him to death. These rocks were really people; they thought like men; they were monsters. When the boys got to the rocks they lifted their feet as if about to enter the chasm, and the rocks opened to let them in. Then the boys put down their feet, but withdrew them quickly. The rocks closed with a snap to crush them; but the boys remained safe on the outside. Thus four times did they deceive the rocks. When they had closed for the fourth time the rocks said: "Who are ye; whence come ye two together, and whither go ye?" "We are children of the Sun," answered the boys. "We come from *Dsilnáotil,* and we go to seek the house of our father." Then they repeated the words the Spider Woman had taught them, and the rocks said: "Pass on to the house of your father." When next they ventured to step into the chasm the rocks did not close, and they passed safely on.

The boys kept on their way and soon came to a great plain covered with reeds that had great leaves on them as sharp as knives. When the boys came to the edge of the field of reeds, the latter opened, showing a clear passage through to the other side. The boys pretended to enter, but retreated, and as they did so the walls of reeds rushed together to kill them. Thus four times did they deceive the reeds. Then the reeds spoke to them, as the rocks had done; they answered and repeated the sacred words. "Pass on to the house of your father," said the reeds, and the boys passed on in safety.

The next danger they encountered was in the country covered with cane cactuses. These cactuses rushed at and tore to pieces whoever attempted to pass through them. When the boys came to the cactuses the latter opened their ranks to let the travellers pass on, as the reeds had done before. But the boys deceived them as they had deceived the reeds, and subdued them as they had subdued the reeds, and passed on in safety.

After they had passed the country of the cactus they came, in time, to the land of the rising sands. Here was a great desert of sands that rose and whirled and boiled like water in a pot, and overwhelmed the traveller who ventured among them. As the boys approached, the sands became still more agitated and the boys did not dare venture among them. "Who are ye?" said the sands, "and whence come ye?" "We are children of the Sun, we came from *Dsilnáotil,* and we go to seek the house of our father." These words were four times said. Then the elder of the boys repeated his sacred formula; the sands subsided, saying: "Pass on to the house of your father," and the boys continued on their journey over the desert of sands.

Soon after this adventure they approached the house of the Sun. As they came near the door they found the way guarded by two bears that crouched, one to the right and one to the left, their noses pointing toward one another. As the boys drew near, the bears rose, growled angrily, and acted as if about to attack the intruders; but the elder boy repeated the sacred words the Spider Woman had taught him, and when he came to the last words, "Be still," the bears crouched down again and

---

[9] This is a prayer for life and peace, symbolized by pollen, which serves to bless their journey.
[10] These mythical places are also identified with real locales in the Navajo world, so that the story accounts for how the landscape came to assume its present form.

lay still. The boys walked on. After passing the bears they encountered a pair of sentinel serpents, then a pair of sentinel winds, and, lastly, a pair of sentinel lightnings. As the boys advanced, all these guardians acted as if they would destroy them; but all were appeased with the words of prayer.

The house of the Sun God was built of turquoise; it was square like a pueblo house, and stood on the shore of a great water. When the boys entered they saw, sitting in the west, a woman; in the south, two handsome young men; and in the north, two handsome young women. The women gave a glance at the strangers and then looked down. The young men gazed at them more closely, and then, without speaking, they rose, wrapped the strangers in four coverings of the sky, and laid them on a shelf.

The boys had lain there quietly for some time when a rattle that hung over the door shook and one of the young women said: "Our father is coming." The rattle shook four times, and soon after it shook the fourth time, the Sun Bearer entered his house. He took the sun off his back and hung it up on a peg on the west wall of the room, where it shook and clanged for some time, going "tla, tla, tla, tla," till at last it hung still.

Then the Sun Bearer turned to the woman and said, in an angry tone: "Who are those two who entered here to-day?" The woman made no answer and the young people looked at one another, but each feared to speak. Four times he asked this question, and at length the woman said: "It would be well for you not to say too much. Two young men came hither to-day, seeking their father. When you go abroad, you always tell me that you visit nowhere, and that you have met no woman but me. Whose sons, then, are these?" She pointed to the bundle on the shelf, and the children smiled significantly at one another.

He took the bundle from the shelf. He first unrolled the robe of dawn with which they were covered, then the robe of blue sky, next the robe of yellow evening light, and lastly the robe of darkness. When he unrolled this the boys fell out on the floor. He seized them, and threw them first upon great, sharp spikes of white shell that stood in the east; but they bounded back, unhurt, from these spikes, for they held their life-feathers tightly all the while. He then threw them in turn on spikes of turquoise in the south, on spikes of haliotis in the west, and spikes of black rock in the north; but they came uninjured from all these trials and the Sun Bearer said: "I wish it were indeed true that they were my children."

He said then to the elder children—those who lived with him,—"Go out and prepare the sweat-house and heat for it four of the hardest boulders you can find. Heat a white, a blue, a yellow, and a black boulder." When the Winds heard this they said: "He still seeks to kill his children. How shall we avert the danger?" The sweat-house was built against a bank. Wind dug into the bank a hole behind the sudatory, and concealed the opening with a flat stone. Wind then whispered into the ears of the boys the secret of the hole and said: "Do not hide in the hole until you have answered the questions of your father." The boys went into the sweat-house, the great hot boulders were put in, and the opening of the lodge was covered with the four sky-blankets. Then the Sun Bearer called out to the boys: "Are you hot?" and they answered: "Yes, very hot." Then they crept into the hiding-place and lay there. After a while the Sun Bearer came and poured water through the top of the sweat-house on the stones, making them burst with a loud noise, and a great heat and steam was raised. But in time the stones cooled and the boys crept out of their hiding-place into the sweat-house. The Sun Bearer came and asked again: "Are you hot?" hoping to get no reply; but the boys still answered: "Yes, very hot." Then he took the coverings off the sweat-house and let the boys come out. He greeted them in a friendly way and said: "Yes, these are my children," and yet he was thinking of other ways by which he might destroy them if they were not.

The four sky-blankets were spread on the ground one over another, and the four young men were made to sit on them, one behind another, facing the east. "My daughters, make these boys to look like my other sons," said the Sun Bearer. The young women went to the strangers, pulled their hair out long, and moulded their faces and forms so that they looked just like their brethren. Then Sun bade them all rise and enter the house. They rose and all went, in a procession, the two strangers last.

As they were about to enter the door they heard a voice whispering in their ears: "St! Look at the ground." They looked down and beheld a spiny caterpillar, who, as they looked, spat out two blue spits on the ground. "Take each of you one of these," said Wind, "and put it in your mouth, but do not swallow it. There is one more trial for you,—a trial by smoking." When they entered the house the Sun Bearer took down a pipe of turquoise that hung on the eastern wall and filled it with tobacco. "This is the tobacco he kills with," whispered Wind to the boys. The Sun Bearer held the pipe up to the sun that hung on the wall, lit it, and gave it to the boys to smoke. They smoked it, and passed it from one to another till it was finished. They said it tasted sweet, but it did them no harm.

When the pipe was smoked out and the Sun Bearer saw the boys were not killed by it, he was satisfied and said: "Now, my children, what do you want from me? Why do you seek me?" "Oh, father!" they replied, "the land where we dwell is filled with monsters, who devour the people. There are Yéitso and the Horned Monster, the Giant Eagle, Those-Who-Slay-With-Their-Eyes, and many others. They have eaten nearly all of our kind; there are few left; already they have sought our lives, and we have run away to escape them. Give us, we beg, the weapons with which we may slay our enemies. Help us to destroy them."

"Know," said the Sun Bearer, "that Yéitso who dwells at *Tsótsil* is also my son, yet I will help you to kill him. I shall hurl the first bolt at him, and I will give you those things that will help you in war." He took from pegs where they hung around the room and gave to each a hat, a shirt, leggings, moccasins, all made of flint,[11] a chain-lightning arrow, a sheet-lightning arrow, a sunbeam arrow, a rainbow arrow, and a great stone knife or knife club. "These are what we want," said the boys. They put on the clothes of flint, and streaks of lightning shot from every joint.

Next morning the Sun Bearer led the boys out to the edge of the world, where the sky and the earth came close together, and beyond which there was no world. Here sixteen wands or poles leaned from the earth to the sky; four of these were of white shell, four of turquoise, four of haliotis shell, and four of red stone. A deep stream flowed between them and the wands. As they approached the stream, the Wind whispered: "This is another trial;" but he blew a great breath and formed a bridge of rainbow, over which the brothers passed in safety. Wind whispered again: "The red wands are for war, the others are for peace;" so when the Sun Bearer asked his sons: "On which wands will ye ascend?" they answered: "On the wands

---

[11] Actually, armor, like arrow points and knife blades, made from flint.

of red stone," for they sought war with their enemies. They climbed up to the sky on the wands of red stone, and their father went with them.

They journeyed on till they came to the sky-hole which is in the centre of the sky. The hole is edged with four smooth, shining cliffs that slope steeply downwards,—cliffs of the same materials as the wands by which they had climbed from the earth to the sky. They sat down on the smooth declivities,—the Sun Bearer on the west side of the hole, the brothers on the east side. The latter would have slipped down had not the Wind blown up and helped them to hold on. The Sun Bearer pointed down and said: "Where do you belong in the world below? Show me your home." The brothers looked down and scanned the land; but they could distinguish nothing; all the land seemed flat; the wooded mountains looked like dark spots on the surface; the lakes gleamed like stars, and the rivers like streaks of lightning. The elder brother said: "I do not recognize the land, I know not where our home is." Now Wind prompted the younger brother, and showed him which were the sacred mountains and which the great rivers, and the younger exclaimed, pointing downwards: "There is the Male Water (San Juan River), and there is the Female Water (Rio Grande); yonder is the mountain of *Tsisnadzini;* below us is *Tsótsil;* there in the west is *Dokoslid;* that white spot beyond the Male Water is *Depentsa;* and there between these mountains is *Dsilnáotil,* near which our home is."[12] "You are right, my child, it is thus that the land lies," said the Sun Bearer. Then, renewing his promises, he spread a streak of lightning; he made his children stand on it,—one on each end,—and he shot them down to the top of *Tsótsil* (Mt. Taylor).

They descended the mountain on its south side and walked toward the warm spring at *Tósato.* As they were walking along under a high bluff, where there is now a white circle, they heard voices hailing them. "Whither are you going? Come hither a while." They went in the direction in which they heard the voices calling and found four holy people,—Holy Man, Holy Young Man, Holy Boy, and Holy Girl. The brothers remained all night in a cave with these people, and the latter told them all about Yéitso. They said that he showed himself every day three times on the mountains before he came down, and when he showed himself for the fourth time he descended from *Tsótsil* to *Tósato* to drink; that, when he stooped down to drink, one hand rested on *Tsótsil* and the other on the high hills on the opposite side of the valley, while his feet stretched as far away as a man could walk between sunrise and noon.

They left the cave at daybreak and went on to *Tósato,* where in ancient days there was a much larger lake than there is now. There was a high, rocky wall in the narrow part of the valley, and the lake stretched back to where Blue Water is to-day. When they came to the edge of the lake, one brother said to the other: "Let us try one of our father's weapons and see what it can do." They shot one of the lightning arrows at *Tsótsil;* it made a great cleft in the mountain, which remains to this day, and one said to the other: "We cannot suffer in combat while we have such weapons as these."

Soon they heard the sound of thunderous footsteps, and they beheld the head of Yéitso peering over a high hill in the east; it was withdrawn in a moment. Soon

---

[12] These rivers and the sacred boundary mountains (*Depentsa,* Hesperus Peak, in the north; *Tsisnadzini,* the Sangre de Cristo Mountains in the east; *Tsótsil,* Mt. Taylor, in the south; and *Dokoslid,* the San Francisco Peaks, in the east) mark Navajo land, of which *Dsilnáotil,* or Gobernador Knob, is the Center.

after, the monster raised his head and chest over a hill in the south, and remained a little longer in sight than when he was in the east. Later he displayed his body to the waist over a hill in the west; and lastly he showed himself, down to the knees, over *Tsótsil* in the north. Then he descended the mountain, came to the edge of the lake, and laid down a basket which he was accustomed to carry.

Yéitso stooped four times to the lake to drink, and, each time he drank, the waters perceptibly diminished; when he had done drinking, the lake was nearly drained. The brothers lost their presence of mind at sight of the giant drinking, and did nothing while he was stooping down. As he took his last drink they advanced to the edge of the lake, and Yéitso saw their reflection in the water. He raised his head, and, looking at them, roared: "What a pretty pair have come in sight! Where have I been hunting?" (*i. e.,* that I never saw them before). "Throw (his words) back in his mouth," said the younger to the elder brother. "What a great thing has come in sight! Where have we been hunting?" shouted the elder brother to the giant. Four times these taunts were repeated by each party. The brothers then heard Wind whispering quickly, "Akó'! Akó'! Beware! Beware!" They were standing on a bent rainbow just then; they straightened the rainbow out, descending to the ground, and at the same instant a lightning bolt, hurled by Yéitso, passed thundering over their heads. He hurled four bolts rapidly; as he hurled the second, they bent their rainbow and rose, while the bolt passed under their feet; as he discharged the third they descended, and let the lightning pass over them. When he threw the fourth bolt they bent the rainbow very high, for this time he aimed higher than before; but his weapon still passed under their feet and did them no harm. He drew a fifth bolt to throw at them; but at this moment the lightning descended from the sky on the head of the giant and he reeled beneath it, but did not fall. Then the elder brother sped a chain-lightning arrow; his enemy tottered toward the east, but straightened himself up again. The second arrow caused him to stumble toward the south (he fell lower and lower each time), but again he stood up and prepared himself to renew the conflict. The third lightning arrow made him topple toward the west, and the fourth to the north. Then he fell to his knees, raised himself partly again, fell flat on his face, stretched out his limbs, and moved no more.

When the arrows struck him, his armor was shivered in pieces and the scales flew in every direction. The elder brother said: "They may be useful to the people in the future."[13] The brothers then approached their fallen enemy and the younger scalped him. Heretofore the younger brother bore only the name, Child of the Water; but now his brother gave him also the warrior name of He Who Cuts Around. What the elder brother's name was before this we do not know; but ever after he was called Monster Slayer.

They cut off his head and threw it away to the other side of *Tsótsil,* where it may be seen to-day on the eastern side of the mountain.[14] The blood from the body now flowed in a great stream down the valley, so great that it broke down the rocky wall that bounded the old lake and flowed on. Wind whispered to the brothers: "The blood flows toward the dwelling of Those-Who-Slay-With-Their-Eyes; if it reaches them, Yéitso will come to life again." Then Monster Slayer took his flint club, and drew with it across the valley a line. Here the blood stopped flowing and

[13] By providing the Navajo with flint for blades and arrow points.
[14] Forty miles northeast of Mt. Taylor is Cabezon ("The Head") Peak. Yéitso's blood coagulated into The Malpais, an extensive lava flow south of Mt. Taylor.

piled itself up in a high wall. But when it had piled up here very high it began to flow off in another direction, and Wind again whispered: "It now flows toward the dwelling of the Bear that Pursues; if it reaches him, Yéitso will come to life again." Hearing this, Monster Slayer again drew a line with his knife on the ground, and again the blood piled up and stopped flowing. The blood of Yéitso fills all the valley to-day, and the high cliffs in the black rock that we see there now are the places where Monster Slayer stopped the flow with his flint club.

They then put the broken arrows of Yéitso and his scalp into his basket and set out for their home near *Dsilnáotil.* When they got near the house, they took off their own suits of armor and hid these, with the basket and its contents, in the bushes. The mothers were rejoiced to see them, for they feared their sons were lost, and they said: "Where have you been since you left here yesterday, and what have you done?" Monster Slayer replied: "We have been to the house of our father, the Sun. We have been to *Tsótsil* and we have slain Yéitso." "Ah, my child," said Changing Woman, "do not speak thus. It is wrong to make fun of such an awful subject." "Do you not believe us?" said Monster Slayer; "come out, then, and see what we have brought back with us." He led the women out to where he had hidden the basket and showed them the trophies of Yéitso. Then they were convinced and they rejoiced, and had a dance to celebrate the victory. . . .[15]

"Surely all the monsters are now killed," said Changing Woman. "This storm must have destroyed them." But Wind whispered into Monster Slayer's ear, "Old Age still lives." The hero said then to his mother: "Where used Old Age to dwell?" His mother would not answer him, though he repeated his question four times. At last Wind again whispered in his ear and said: "She lives in the mountains of *Depentsa.*"

Next morning he set out for the north, and when, after a long journey, he reached *Depentsa,* he saw an old woman who came slowly toward him leaning on a staff. Her back was bent, her hair was white, and her face was deeply wrinkled. He knew this must be Old Age. When they met he said: "Grandmother, I have come on a cruel errand. I have come to slay you." "Why would you slay me?" she said in a feeble voice, "I have never harmed any one. I hear that you have done great deeds in order that men might increase on the earth, but if you kill me there will be no increase of men; the boys will not grow up to become fathers; the worthless old men will not die; the people will stand still. It is well that people should grow old and pass away and give their places to the young. Let me live, and I shall help you to increase the people." "Grandmother, if you keep this promise I shall spare your life," said Monster Slayer, and he returned to his mother without a trophy.

When he got home Wind whispered to him: "Cold Woman still lives." Monster Slayer said to Changing Woman: "Mother, grandmother, where does Cold Woman dwell?" His mother would not answer him; but Wind again whispered, saying: "Cold Woman lives high on the summits of *Depentsa,* where the snow never melts."

Next day he went again to the north and climbed high among the peaks of *Depentsa,* where no trees grow and where the snow lies white through all the summer. Here he found a lean old woman, sitting on the bare snow, without cloth-

[15] This is the first Scalp Dance, which celebrates victory over the enemy while it cleanses the warrior from the effects of contact with enemy dead. After this initial victory, the Twins slay many other monsters and return home after a storm, presuming to have made the world safe and habitable for humankind. In the remarkable encounters which follow, people learn that, although they might have power over some things, it may not always be wise to use it.

14

ing, food, fire, or shelter. She shivered from head to foot, her teeth chattered, and her eyes streamed water. Among the drifting snows which whirled around her, a multitude of snow-buntings were playing; these were the couriers she sent out to announce the coming of a storm. "Grandmother," he said, "a cruel man I shall be. I am going to kill you, so that men may no more suffer and die by your hand," and he raised his knife-club to smite her. "You may kill me or let me live, as you will. I care not," she said to the hero; "but if you kill me it will always be hot, the land will dry up, the springs will cease to flow, the people will perish. You will do well to let me live. It will be better for your people." He paused and thought upon her words. He lowered the hand he had raised to strike her, saying: "You speak wisely, grandmother; I shall let you live." He turned around and went home.

When Monster Slayer got home from this journey, bearing no trophy, Wind again whispered in his ear and said: "Poverty still lives." He asked his mother where Poverty used to live, but she would not answer him. It was Wind who again informed him. "There are two, and they dwell at *Dsildasdzini.*

He went to *Dsildasdzini* the next day and found there an old man and an old woman, who were filthy, clad in tattered garments, and had no goods in their house. "Grandmother, grandfather," he said, "a cruel man I shall be. I have come to kill you." "Do not kill us, my grandchild," said the old man: "it would not be well for the people, in days to come, if we were dead; then they would always wear the same clothes and never get anything new. If we live, the clothing will wear out and the people will make new and beautiful garments; they will gather goods and look handsome. Let us live and we will pull their old clothes to pieces for them." So he spared them and went home without a trophy.

The next journey was to seek Hunger, who lived, as Wind told him, at White Spot of Grass. At this place he found twelve of the Hunger People. Their chief was a big, fat man, although he had no food to eat but the little brown cactus. "I am going to be cruel," said Monster Slayer, "so that men may suffer no more the pangs of hunger and die no more of hunger." "Do not kill us," said the chief, "if you wish your people to increase and be happy in the days to come. We are your friends. If we die, the people will not care for food; they will never know the pleasure of cooking and eating nice things, and they will never care for the pleasures of the chase." So he spared also Hunger, and went home without a trophy.

When Monster Slayer came back from the home of Hunger, Wind spoke to him no more of enemies that lived. The Monster Slayer said to his mother: "I think all the monsters must be dead, for every one I meet now speaks to me as a relation; they say to me, 'my grandson,' 'my son,' 'my brother.'" Then he took off his armor—his knife, moccasins, leggings, shirt, and cap—and laid them in a pile; he put with them the various weapons which the Sun had given him, and he sang this song:—

> Now Monster Slayer arrives
> Here from the house made of the dark stone knives.
> From where the dark stone knives dangle on high,
> You have the treasures, holy one, not I.
>
> The Child of the Water now arrives,
> Here from the house made of the serrate knives.
>
> From where the serrate knives dangle on high,
> You have the treasures, holy one, not I.

He who was Reared beneath the Earth arrives,
Here from the house made of all kinds of knives.
From where all kinds of knives dangle on high,
You have the treasures, holy one, not I.

The hero, Changing Grandchild, now arrives,
Here from the house made of the yellow knives.
From where the yellow knives dangle on high,
You have the treasures, holy one, not I.[16]

1897

The Coming of the Spanish and the Pueblo Revolt (Hopi)[1]

It may have taken quite a long time for these villages to be established. Anyway, every place was pretty well settled down when the Spanish came.[2] The Spanish were first heard of at Zuni and then at Awatovi. They came on to Shung-opovi, passing Walpi. At First Mesa, Siky-atki was the largest village then, and they were called Si-kyatki, not Walpi. The Walpi people were living below the present village on the west side. When the Spaniards came, the Hopi thought that they were the ones they were looking for—their white brother, the Bahana, their savior.[3]

The Spaniards visited Shung-opovi several times before the missions were established. The people of Mishongovi welcomed them so the priest who was with the white men built the first Hopi mission at Mishongovi. The people of Shung-opovi were at first afraid of the priests but later they decided he was really the Bahana, the savior, and let him build a mission at Shung-opovi.

Well, about this time the Strap Clan were ruling at Shung-opovi and they were the ones that gave permission to establish the mission. The Spaniards, whom they called Castilla, told the people that they had much more power than all their chiefs and a whole lot more power than the witches. The people were very much afraid of them, particularly if they had much more power than the witches. They were so

[16] In this song, the Twins bring the story full circle by acknowledging that Changing Woman is really the most powerful being, the one for whom the Sun's weapons have been used, the one whose treasures benefit everyone.

[1] The Hopi Indians, descendants of the Anasazi who had occupied cliff dwellings, occupy a number of pueblos in northeastern Arizona. Agricultural in their culture and economy, they had their own complex social and religious customs when they were subjected to the missionary efforts of the Spanish in 1629; Coronado had visited them in 1540. They joined the Pueblo Revolt of 1680.

[2] The first Spaniard to visit the Hopi was Coronado in 1540. Other expeditions followed. The Catholic missions, staffed by Franciscan priests, were established there in the beginning of the seventeenth century.

[3] The Hopis, like the Aztecs, believed that a fair-skinned culture hero would return from exile in the East to establish peace and prosperity. This belief in the *Bahana* had been greatly influenced by Christianity by the time the present narrative was published in 1936, but it is clear from available evidence that both Cortez in Mexico and the Spanish priests at Hopi used it as a means of entrance into the community.

16

scared that they could do nothing but allow themselves to be made slaves. Whatever they wanted done must be done. Any man in power that was in this position the Hopi called *Tota-achi,* which means a grouchy person that will not do anything himself, like a child. They couldn't refuse, or they would be slashed to death or punished in some way. There were two *Tota-achi.*

The missionary did not like the ceremonies. He did not like the Kachinas and he destroyed the altars and the customs. He called it idol worship and burned up all the ceremonial things in the plaza.

When the Priests started to build the mission, the men were sent away over near the San Francisco peaks to get the pine or spruce beams. These beams were cut and put into shape roughly and were then left till the next year when they had dried out. Beams of that size were hard to carry and the first few times they tried to carry these beams on their backs, twenty to thirty men walking side by side under the beam. But this was rather hard in rough places and one end had to swing around. So finally they figured out a way of carrying the beam in between them. They lined up two by two with the beam between the lines. In doing this, some of the Hopis were given authority by the missionary to look after these men and to see if they all did their duty. If any man gave out on the way he was simply left to die. There was great suffering. Some died for lack of food and water, while others developed scabs and sores on their bodies.

It took a good many years for them to get enough beams to Shung-opovi to build the mission. When this mission was finally built, all the people in the village had to come there to worship, and those that did not come were punished severely. In that way their own religion was altogether wiped out, because they were not allowed to worship in their own way. All this trouble was a heavy burden on them and they thought it was on account of this that they were having a heavy drought at this time. They thought their gods had given them up because they weren't worshiping the way they should.[4]

Now during this time the men would go out pretending they were going on a hunting trip and they would go to some hiding place, to make their prayer offerings. So to-day, a good many of these places are still to be found where they left their little stone bowls in which they ground their copper ore to paint the prayer sticks. These places are called *Puwa-kiki,* cave places. If these men were caught they were severely punished.

Now this man, Tota-achi (the Priest)[5] was going from bad to worse. He was not doing the people any good and he was always figuring what he could do to harm them. So he thought out how the water from different springs or rivers would taste and he was always sending some man to these springs to get water for him to drink, but it was noticed that he always chose the men who had pretty wives. He tried to

---

[4] The Hopi religion, like that of the Zunis and other pueblos, uses mask dancing to invoke the assistance of the ancestral dead and the kachinas in securing life-giving rain for the crops. Spanish missionary policy was to destroy native religion by disrupting ceremonies and by destroying all ritual objects, especially masks, which they identified with the Devil.

[5] The precise identity of this priest is unclear. Several priests served at Shungopovi prior to the Pueblo Revolt. Fr. José Trujillo, who came to the Hopi from service in the Philippines, was a charismatic, intense, religious zealot. Fr. Salvador de Guerra, who preceded him, was transferred from Shungopovi to Jemez, much farther east, as discipline for having tortured the Indians in his charge. It is likely that this Tota-achi is a corporate figure, whose image conflates the memory of the misdeeds of several individuals.

send them far away so that they would be gone two or three days, so it was not very long until they began to see what he was doing. The men were even sent to the Little Colorado River to get water for him, or to Moencopi. Finally, when a man was sent out he'd go out into the rocks and hide, and when the night came he would come home. Then, the priest, thinking the man was away, would come to visit his wife, but instead the man would be there when he came. Many men were punished for this.

All this time the priest, who had great power, wanted all the young girls to be brought to him when they were about thirteen or fourteen years old. They had to live with the priest. He told the people they would become better women if they lived with him for about three years. Now one of these girls told what the Tota-achi were doing and a brother of the girl heard of this and he asked his sister about it, and he was very angry. This brother went to the mission and wanted to kill the priest that very day, but the priest scared him and he did nothing. So the Shung-opovi people sent this boy, who was a good runner, to Awatovi to see if they were doing the same thing over there, which they were. So that was how they got all the evidence against the priest.

Then the chief at Awatovi sent word by this boy that all the priests would be killed on the fourth day after the full moon. They had no calendar and that was the best way they had of setting the date. In order to make sure that everyone would rise up and do this thing on the fourth day the boy was given a cotton string with knots in it and each day he was to untie one of these knots until they were all out and that would be the day for the attack.[6]

Things were getting worse and worse so the chief of Shung-opovi went over to Mishongnovi and the two chiefs discussed their troubles. "He is not the savior and it is your duty to kill him," said the chief of Shung-opovi. The chief of Mishongnovi replied, "If I end his life, my own life is ended."

Now the priest would not let the people manufacture prayer offerings, so they had to make them among the rocks in the cliffs out of sight, so again one day the chief of Shung-opovi went to Mishongnovi with tobacco and materials to make prayer offerings. He was joined by the chief of Mishongnovi and the two went a mile north to a cave. For four days they lived there heartbroken in the cave, making *pahos*. Then the chief of Mishongnovi took the prayer offerings and climbed to the top of the Corn Rock and deposited them in the shrine, for according to the ancient agreement with the Mishongnovi people it was their duty to do away with the enemy.

He then, with some of his best men, went to Shung-opovi, but he carried no weapons. He placed his men at every door of the priest's house. Then he knocked on the door and walked in. He asked the priest to come out but the priest was suspicious and would not come out. The chief asked the priest four times and each time the priest refused. Finally, the priest said, "I think you are up to something."

---

[6]The Pueblo Revolt of August 13, 1680, was a concerted, successful effort of the Pueblo Indian communities to throw off Spanish military and religious oppression. Many soldiers and perhaps as many as 28 priests were killed in the uprising. The remaining colonists retreated south to El Paso del Norte and did not re-establish control over the northern frontier until Vargas's reconquest in 1692. The present narrative views the events at Hopi as a solution to a particular problem and not as part of a larger action.

The chief said, "I have come to kill you." "You can't kill me," cried the priest, "you have no power to kill me. If you do, I will come to life and wipe out your whole tribe."

The chief returned, "If you have this power, then blow me out into the air; my gods have more power than you have.[7] My gods have put a heart into me to enter your home. I have no weapons. You have your weapons handy, hanging on the wall. My gods have prevented you from getting your weapons."

The old priest made a rush and grabbed his sword from the wall. The chief of Mishongnovi yelled and the doors were broken open. The priest cut down the chief and fought right and left but was soon overpowered, and his sword taken from him.

They tied his hands behind his back. Out of the big beams outside they made a tripod. They hung him on the beams, kindled a fire and burned him.

1936

[7] The debate between the Mishongnovi and Shungopovi chiefs indicates that the core of the Hopi interest in this narrative is religious, not military, conflict. Christianity fails because a drought follows the suppression of the kiva religion and because the priest fails to live up to his own culture's Christ-like ideal and the Hopi's ideal of the *Bahana*.

Iroquois or Confederacy of the Five Nations (Iroquois)[1]

By the tradition of the Five Nations it appears that in their early history, they were frequently engaged in petty wars one with another, as well also with tribes living north of the lakes. The Five Nations, on account of their small numbers, suffered more by these wars than their neighbors, until there sprang up among the Onondagas a man more formidable in war than a whole tribe or nation. He consequently became the terror of all the surrounding nations, especially of the Cayugas and Senecas. This man, so formidable and whose cabin was as impregnable as a tower, is said to have had a head of hair, the ends of each terminating in a living snake; the ends of his fingers, and toes, his ears, nose & lips, eye brows & eye lashes all terminated in living snakes. He required in war, no bow and arrow, no battle axe or war club, for he had but to look upon his enemies, & they fell dead—so great was the power of the snakes that enshrouded him. He was a warrior by birth, and by his great power he had become the military despot of all the surrounding nations. And when he marched against his enemies they fled before his fatal sight.

Among the Onondagas there lived a man renowned for his wisdom, and his great love of peace. For a long time he had watched with great anxiety the increasing power of this military despot who on account of his snakey habilaments, was known by the applicable name Tadodahoh, or Atotahoh, signifying tangled because the snakes seemed to have tangled themselves into his hair; he saw bands of noble warriors fall before his fatal look. He revolved in his mind by what means he could take from the Tadodahoh his power, and also to divest him of his snakey appendages. He well knew that he could not wrest his power from him, unless he could put into his hands some means by which he could still exercise power and influence. He therefore concluded to call a general council, of the Five Nations, and to invite to this council the Tadodahoh, at which council he proposed to lay before the wise men a plan of Union that would secure not only amity and peace among themselves, and a perpetual existence as a confederacy but they would render themselves formidable & superior in power to any nation on the Continent. He accordingly called a council to be held upon the east bank of the Onondaga Lake, and to this council the Tadodahoh was invited, who it is said lived near the shores of Lake Ontario a short distance from Irondequoit Bay. He accepted the invitation and proceeded to the place. He occupied the council grounds alone, for no one would approach near to him, although great numbers had come to attend. The projector of the alliance alone proceeded to the grounds and into the presence of the Tadodahoh. He proceeded to divulge his plan when he was informed that his daughter had died whom

---

[1] The Iroquois were a confederacy of five nations— the Cayuga, Mohawk, Oneida, Onondaga, and Seneca Indians. These five Indian groups, later joined by the Tuscarora, joined together about 1450 under the legendary leadership of Dekanawida (probably a Huron) and Hiawatha (a Mohawk). Because they lived in what is now the Northeast, largely in present-day New York state, the Iroquois confederacy successfully slowed the westward expansion of the Europeans until nearly the middle of the eighteenth century.

Parker Papers "Iroquois, or the Confederacy of the Five Nations" (Senaca, Ely S. Parker). Reprinted by permission of the Buffalo and Erie County Historical Society.

he had left at home sick. He drew his robe about him, covering himself completely, and mourned for her. (His style of mourning was afterwards adopted by the Confederacy as the custom to mourn for sachems just before another was to be installed in his place.) He mourned night and day, and in his mourning which he did in a kind of song, he repeated the whole plan of Union. And when he had finished, no one of the wise men seemed to understand or comprehend his meaning and objects. Daganowedah, the projector of the plan of alliance, being provoked at their dullness of comprehension, which resulted more from their ignorance of civil matters than dullness of comprehension, arose in the night and travelled towards the east. He had not travelled far when he struck a small lake, and anyone could go around it sooner than to cross it in a canoe. Yet he chose to make a canoe of bark and go across it. It seems that he did not wish to deviate from a straight line. While he was crossing the lake, his canoe ran upon what he supposed to be a sand bar; he put his paddle down into the water to ascertain the cause of the stopping of the boat; in taking out his paddle he found a quantity of small shells, he took pains to put a sufficient quantity into his canoe, and after going ashore, he made a pouch of a young deer skin, and put these shells into it, after having first made a number of belts, and put the rest into strings of equal lengths. To this he gave the name of wampum, and the belts and strings he had made of the shells, he converted into the records of his wise sayings & the entire plan of his project of alliance.

He then proceeded on his journey, and he had not travelled far when he came to an Indian castle.[2] Without calling a council he began to rehearse his plan of alliance, by means of his belts and strings of wampum. But the people of this castle were unable to comprehend the benefits of his project, and talked of him as crazy. When he heard what they were saying concerning him, he proceeded on his journey, sorrowing that he could not find a people who would listen to the words of wisdom. He at length came to another settlement, which was one of the Mohawk castles. Here again he rehearsed his plan of Union. Still his sayings were incomprehensible to that people. They however listened carefully for the purpose of ascertaining what it was that he could talk so long upon. All that they could understand of it, was the manner in which councils were to be called. A council was accordingly called and he invited to attend. They invited him for the purpose of giving him an opportunity to say in council and before a large number what he had been so long saying in the open fields. But after he had taken his seat in council and nothing was said or done, no exchange of wampum belts (for he had lent them a belt with which to call a council), he arose and again went into the fields and there repeated his speeches. He concluded by saying that they too were ignorant, and knew nothing about transacting civil matters. This was reported to the Grand Chief of the Mohawks and again he called another council and invited Daganowedah. When the council was opened and the wise man had taken his seat, the Mohawk Chief presented to him a belt of wampum, with a request that whatever he should have to say, should be said in open council. If he was a messenger from another tribe, they would hear in open council what were their wishes. He merely replied that he was the messenger of no one; that he had conceived a noble plan of alliance, but had not

---

[2] A settlement.

found a nation wise enough to comprehend its benefits, and thus he had travelled and should continue so to travel until he found support. He then rehearsed in open council his plan of Union, which though they could not comprehend it, was pronounced by all to be a noble project. Daganowedah the Onondaga wise man was immediately adopted into the Mohawk Nation, nor could the Onondagas afterwards claim him, since they first rejected his project of Alliance. He was also made a chief of the Mohawk Nation, and was to exercise equal power with the original Mohawk chief. They were to live in the same lodge, and to be, in every respect, equals.

But he had lived with the original chief but a short time, when he was ordered about as though he had been a mere servant. To this a free spirit will ever revolt, he therefore left him, and again went into the fields. He was asked why he left the house of his friend. He replied that he had not been treated as a friend or visitor, but as a slave. The original chief begged his pardon, and solicited him to return. He did, and was thenceforth treated with great regard. Daganowedah at length suggested the propriety of sending runners to the west, from whence he had come, to ascertain what may be doing from whence he had come. He wanted runners to go and seek the smoke of the council fire. The chief of the Mohawks at once called upon some runners to go towards the west in search of the smoke of a council fire. The guardian bird of the runners was the heron; they accordingly took upon themselves the form of herons. They went towards the west, but flying too high they did not see the smoke of the council fire of Onondaga. They proceeded as far west as Sandusky in Ohio, where they were unable to transform or change themselves again into men. Another set of runners were then sent out, who took upon them the form or shape of crows. They found the smoke of the council fire at Onondaga and so reported.

Daganowedah then proposed to send a few runners to the council to inform them that they had found a wise man of the Onondaga nation, who had conceived a plan of Union, and to request that he might be heard before the Great Tadodahoh. This was done; and as soon as the council at Onondaga heard where their wise man had gone, they sent a deputation to recall him. Daganowedah had in the mean time made arrangement with the Mohawk Chief to act as his spokesman when they should be in council. He was also to take the lead in the file, and to perform all the duties necessary to the completion of the Alliance, but he was to act as Daganowedah should direct. His reason for choosing a spokesman, was that he had not been heard when the council first opened, and that probably they might listen to a wise man of the Mohawks. To this arrangement the Mohawk agreed. He agreed also to divest Tadodahoh of his snakes, and to make him as other men, except that he should clothe him in civil power as the Head of the Confederacy that should be formed. They then proceeded with a delegation of the Mohawks to the council grounds at Onondaga. When they had arrived they addressed Todadahoh the great military despot. The Mohawk divested him of his snakes, and for this reason he was styled Hayowenthah, or one who takes away or divests.

The plan of alliance was at first simple. It provided for the establishment of a confederacy, enjoying a democratic form of government. The civil and legislative power was to be vested in a certain number of wise men who should be styled civil sachems, and the military and executive power in another set of men who should be styled military sachems. The Union was to be established as a family organization, the Mohawks, Onondagas and Senecas to compose the Fathers and the Cayugas and Oneidas the children. This plan was adopted.[3]

Raven and Marriage (Tlingit)[1]

Next Raven married the daughter of a chief named Fog-over-the-salmon. It was winter, and they were without food, so Raven wanted salmon very much. His wife made a large basket and next morning washed her hands in it. When she got through there was a salmon there. Both were very glad, and cooked and ate it. Every day afterward she did the same thing until their house was full of drying salmon. After that, however, Raven and his wife quarreled, and he hit her on the shoulder with a piece of dried salmon. Then she ran away from him, but, when he ran after her and seized her, his hands passed right through her body. Then she went into the water and disappeared forever, while all of the salmon she had dried followed her. He could not catch her because she was the fog. After that he kept going to his father-in-law to beg him to have his wife come back, but his father-in-law said, "You promised me that you would have respect for her and take care of her. You did not do it, therefore you can not have her back."

Then Raven had to leave this place, and went on to another town where he found a widower. He said to this man, "I am in the same fix as you. My wife also has died." Raven wanted to marry the daughter of the chief in that town, so he said, "Of course I have to marry a woman of as high caste as my first wife. That is the kind I am looking for." But *TsAgwâ'n*, a bird, who was also looking for a high-caste wife, followed Raven about all the time. He said to the people, "That man is telling stories around here. His first wife left him because he was cruel to her." For this reason they refused to give the girl to him. Then he said to the chief, "If I had

[3] This text was transcribed about 1850 by Ely S. Parker, a full Seneca born on the Tonawanda Seneca Reservation in New York state. Educated at a mission school and then sent to Canada, Parker eventually returned to New York, learned English, and studied law, only to be denied legal practice because he was Indian. He worked on the Genesee Valley canal as an engineer until he was appointed superintendent of construction of the custom house and marine hospital at Galena, Illinois. Parker entered into Civil War conflict in 1863, serving as secretary to General Grant, whom he had known at Galena. Having remained in the army after the war until 1869, Parker served until 1871 as President Grant's commissioner of Indian affairs. When Parker died in 1895, he was a member of the New York City police department.

Parker wrote about this narrative, "I cannot tell how much reliance can be placed upon this tradition, which is more of an allegory than real. The main facts of its origin may be embodied in the allegory, while it has been painted up by the imagination of the Indians."

[1] The Tlingit Indians were a northwest coastal group that occupied the southeastern coast of Alaska from Yakutat Bay to Cape Fox. Their abundant food supply from hunting, fishing, and gathering afforded the Tlingits ample time in winter to develop complex social systems and religious ceremonies. They lived in cedar plank dwellings, and they traded freely with the Russians, Americans, and English.

married your daughter you would have had a great name in the world. You will presently see your daughter take up with some person who is a nobody, and, when they speak of you in the world, it will always be as Chief-with-no-name. You may listen to this *TsAgwâ'n* if you want to, but you will be sorry for it. He is a man from whom no good comes. Hereafter this *TsAgwâ'n* will live far out at sea. And I will tell you this much, that neither *TsAgwâ'n* nor myself will get this woman." This is why *TsAgwâ'n* is now always alone. Raven also said to the chief, "You will soon hear something of this daughter of yours." All the high-caste men wanted to marry this woman, but she would not have them.

Going on again, Raven came to an old man living alone, named *DAmnā'djî*, and said to him, "Do you know the young daughter of the chief close by here?" "Yes, I know her." "Why don't you try to marry her?" "I can't get her. I know I can't, so I don't want to try." Then Raven said, "I will make a medicine to enable you to get her." "But I have no slave," said the old man; "to get her a man must have slaves." "Oh!" said Raven, "you do not have to have a slave to get her. She will take a liking to you and nobody can help it. She will marry you. Her father will lose half of his property." Then he made the old man look young, got feathers to put into his hair and a marten-skin robe to put over him so that he appeared very handsome. But Raven said to him, "You are not going to look like this all of the time. It is only for a day or so."

After this the rejuvenated man got into his skin canoe, for this was well to the north, and paddled over to where the girl lived. He did not ask her father's consent but went directly to her, and she immediately fell in love with him. Although so many had been after her she now said, "I will marry you. I will go with you even if my father kills me for it."

When the chief's slaves found them in the bedroom at the rear of the house, they said to the chief, "Your daughter is married." So her mother looked in there and found it was true. Then her father said, "Come out from that room, my daughter." He had already told his slaves to lay down valuable furs on the floor for his daughter and her husband to sit on. He thought if she were already married it was of no use for him to be angry with her. So the girl came out with her husband, and, when her father saw him he was very glad, for he liked his looks, and he was dressed like a high-caste person.

Then the chief related to his son-in-law how a fellow came along wanting to marry his daughter, and how *TsAgwâ'n* had come afterward and told him that he had been cruel to his first wife. Said the chief, "This man had a wife. His first wife is living yet. I don't want to hurt his wife's feelings."

After that his son-in-law said, "My father told me to start right out after him to-day in my canoe." He was in a hurry to depart because he was afraid that all of his good clothing would leave him. He said to his wife, "Take only your blanket to use on the passage, because I have plenty of furs of every description at home." So she took nothing but her marten-skin robe and a fox robe.

As she lay in the canoe, however, with her head resting on his lap she kept feeling drops of water fall upon her face, and she said many times, "What is that dripping on my face?" Then he would say, "It must be the water splashing from my paddle," but it was really the drippings that fall from an old man's eyes when he is very filthy. Her husband had already become an old man again and had lost his fine clothing, but she could not see it because her face was turned the other way. When the woman thought that they were nearly at their destination she raised herself to look out, glanced at her husband's face, and saw that he was an altogether different man. She cried very hard.

After they had arrived at his town the old man went from house to house asking the people to take pity on him and let him bring his wife to one of them, because he knew that his own house was not fit for her. These, however, were some of the people that had wanted to marry this woman, so they said, "Why don't you take her to your own fine house? You wanted her." Meanwhile she sat on the beach by the canoe, weeping. Finally the shabby sister of this old man, who was still older than he, came down to her and said, "See here, you are a high-caste girl. Everybody says this man is your husband, and you know he is your husband, so you better come up to the house with me." Then she saw the place where he lived, and observed that his bed was worse than that of one of her father's slaves. The other people also paid no attention to her, although they knew who she was, because she had married this man. They would eat after everybody else was through, and, while he was eating, the people of the town would make fun of him by shouting out, "DAmnā' djî's father-in-law and his brothers-in-law are coming to his grand house to see him." Then he would run out to see whether it were so and find that they were making fun of him. Every morning, while he was breakfasting with his wife, the people fooled him in this way.

Although he had not said so, the father-in-law and the brothers-in-law of DAmnā' djî thought that he was a very high-caste person because he was dressed so finely. So they got together all their expensive furs to visit him, and they had one canoe load of slaves, which they intended to give him, all dressed with green feathers from the heads of mallard drakes. One morning the people again shouted, "DAmnā' djî's father-in-law and his brothers-in-law are coming to see him." Running out to look this time, he saw canoe after canoe coming, loaded down deep. Then he did not know what to do. He began to sweep out the house and begged some boys to help him clean up, but they said, "You clean up yourself. Those are your people coming." The people of the place also began hiding all of their basket-work pots, and buckets.

As they came in, the people in the canoes sang together and all of them were iridescent with color. They were very proud people. Then the old man begged the boys to carry up the strangers' goods, but they replied as before, "You carry them up yourself. You can do it." So the strangers had to bring up their own things into the house and sit about without anyone telling them where. The old man's sister was crying all the time. Then the strangers understood at once what was the matter and felt very sorry for these old people.

After that the old man kept saying to the boys who came in to look at his visitors, "One of you go after water," but they answered, "Go after water yourself. You can do it." He tried to borrow a basket for his guests to eat off of, but they all said, "Use your own basket. What did you go and get that high-caste girl for? You knew that you couldn't afford it. Why didn't you get a poor person like yourself instead of a chief's daughter? Now you may know that it isn't fun to get a high-caste person when one is poor." His brothers-in-law and his father-in-law felt ashamed at what they heard, and they also felt badly for him. Then the old woman gave her brother a basket that was unfit for the chief's slaves to eat out of, and he ran out to get water for his guests.

When he got there, however, and was stooping down to fill his basket, the creek moved back from him and he followed it. It kept doing this and he kept running after it until he came to the mountain, where it finally vanished into a house. Running into this, he saw a very old woman sitting there who said to him, "What are you after? Is there anything I can do for you?" He said, "There is much that you can do for me, if you can really do it. My friends are very mean to me. My father-in-law and the other relations of my wife have all come to my place to visit me. I married a very high-caste woman, and the people of my place seem to be very mean about it. I am very poor and have nothing with which to entertain them." He told all of his troubles to her from the beginning, and, when he was through, she said, "Is that all?" "Yes, that is all." Then the woman brushed back his hair several times with her hand, and lo! he had a head of beautiful hair, while his ragged clothes changed into valuable ones. He was handsomer and better clothed than at the time when he first obtained his wife. The old basket he had also turned into a very large beautiful basket. Then she said to him, "There is a spring back in the corner. Go there and uncover it and dip that basket as far down as you can reach." He did so and, when he drew it out, it was full of dentalia.

Now *DAmnā'djî* returned home very quickly, but nobody recognized him at first except his wife and those who had seen him when he went to get her. Afterward he gave water to his guests, and they could see dentalia shells at the bottom. The house was now filled with spectators, and those who had made fun of him were very much ashamed of themselves. After he had given them water, he gave them handfuls of dentalia, for which his father-in-law and his brothers-in-law gave him slaves, valuable furs, and other property. So he became very rich and was chief of that town. That is why the Indians do the same now. If a brother-in-law gives them the least thing they return much more than its value.

Now he had a big house built, and everything that he said had to be done. The people that formerly made fun of him were like slaves to him. He also gave great feasts, inviting people from many villages. But, after he had become very great among them, he was too hard upon the people of his town. His wife was prouder than when she was with her father and if boys or anyone else displeased her they were put to death.

As they were now very proud and had plenty of people to work for them, the husband and wife spent much time sitting on the roof of their house looking about. One spring the woman saw a flock of swans coming from the southeast, and said, "Oh! there is a high-caste person among those birds that I was going to marry." Another time they went up, and a flock of geese came along. Then she again said to her husband, "Oh! there is the high-caste person I was going to marry." By and by some sand-hill cranes flew past, and she repeated the same words. But, when the brants came over, and she spoke these words, they at once flew down to her and carried her off with them. Her husband ran after the brants underneath as fast as he could, and every now and then some of her clothing fell down, but he was unable to overtake her.

When the birds finally let this woman drop, she was naked and all of her hair even was gone. Then she got up and walked along the beach crying, and she made a kind of apron for herself out of leaves. Continuing on along the beach, she came upon a red snapper head, which she picked up. She wandered on aimlessly, not knowing what to do, because she was very sad at the thought of her fine home and her husband. Presently she saw smoke ahead of her and arrived at a house where was an old woman. She opened the door, and the old woman said, "Come in." Then she said to the old woman, "Let us cook this red snapper head." "Yes, let us cook it," said the latter. After they had eaten it, the old woman said to her, "Go along the beach and try to find something else." So she went out and found a sculpin. Then she came back to the house and cooked that, but, while they were eating, she heard many boys shouting, and she thought they were laughing at her because she was naked. She looked around but saw no one. Then the old woman said to her, "Take the food out to that hole." She went outside with the tray and saw an underground sweathouse out of which many hands protruded. This was the place from which the shouting came. She handed the tray down and it was soon handed up again with two fine fox skins in it. Then the old woman said to her, "Make your clothing out of these furs," and so she did.

After she had put the skins on, this old woman said, "Your father and mother live a short distance away along this beach. You better go to them. They are living at a salmon creek." So the girl went on and soon saw her father and mother in a canoe far out where her father was catching salmon. But, when she ran down toward the canoe to meet them, her father said to his wife, "Here comes a fox." As he was looking for something with which to kill it, she ran back into the woods.

Then she felt very badly, and returned to the old woman crying. "Did you see your father?" said the latter. "Yes." "What did he say to you?" "He took me for a fox. He was going to kill me." Then the old woman said, "Yes, what else do you think you are? You have already turned into a fox. Now go back to your father and let him kill you."

The woman went to the same place again and saw her father still closer to the shore; and she heard him say, "Here comes that big fox again." Then she ran right up to him, saying to herself, "Let him kill me," and he did so. Years ago all the high-caste people wore bracelets and necklaces, and each family had its own way of fixing them. Now, as this woman was skinning the fox, she felt something around its foreleg. She looked at it and found something like her daughter's bracelet. Afterward she also cut around the neck and found her daughter's necklace. Then she told her husband to come and look saying, "Here on this fox are our daughter's necklace and bracelet." So they cried over the fox and said, "Something must have made her turn into a fox." They knew how this fox ran toward them instead of going away.

Now they took the body of the fox, placed it upon a very nice mat, and laid another over it. They put eagle's down, which was always kept in bags ready for use, on the body, crying above it all the time. They also began fasting, and all of her brothers and relations in that village fasted with them. All cleaned up their houses and talked to their Creator. One midnight, after they had fasted for many days, they felt the house shaking, and they heard a noise in the place where the body lay. Then the father and mother felt very happy. The mother went there with a light and saw that her daughter was in her own proper shape, acting like a shaman. Then the woman named the spirits in her. The first she mentioned was the swan spirit, the next the goose spirit, the next the sand-hill-crane spirit, the next the brant spirit. Another spirit was the red-snapper-head spirit which called itself Spirit-with-a-*labret*-in-its-chin, and another the fox spirit. Now the father and mother of this woman were very happy, but her husband lost all of his wealth and became poor again.[2]

1909

Raven Makes a Girl Sick and Then Cures Her (Tsimshian)[1]

Raven went on, not knowing which way to turn.[2] He was very hungry, staying in a lonely place. After a while he came to the end of a large town. He saw many people walking about, and he was afraid to let himself be seen. Raven sat down there; and on the following day, while he was still sitting there, he saw a large canoe being launched on the beach. Aboard were many young women who went to pick blueberries. Then Raven thought how he could enter the great town. Finally it occurred to him to catch a deer. He went into the woods and caught a deer, skinned it, put on the skin, and then swam in front of the large canoe which was full of young women who were going to pick blueberries.[3] Among them was a young princess, the daughter of the master of that large town. Raven saw that she was among the young women. She was sitting near the middle of the large canoe, between two women. Now, they saw the stag swimming along in front of the canoe. Then the princess said to her companions, "Let us pursue him!" They did so. They paddled along, and soon they caught and killed the stag, and took him into the canoe. Raven thought, "Let them put me down in front of the princess!" and then they took him into the canoe and placed him in front of the princess, as Raven had wished them to do. Then they paddled along toward the place where the blueberries were. Before they reached the blueberry-patch, the deer moved his hind leg and kicked the princess in the stomach. Then he leaped out of the canoe and ran into the woods. The princess fainted when she received the wound, and therefore the young women turned back and went home. The princess became worse as they went along.

Finally they reached the beach in front of the house of the head chief. They told

---

[2] The complex social systems of the Tlingits usually kept young men from marrying women of higher social standing.

[1] The Tsimshian Indians lived on the northwest coast, along the Nass and Skeena Rivers and the islands that now form western British Columbia. Their abundant food supply from gathering, fishing, and hunting enabled them to live in stationary cedar plank dwellings and develop arts and crafts related to their complex ceremonial life. They traded with the Russians, Americans, and English.

[2] The Trickster is often figured as a wanderer who lacks foresight and self-consciousness but who is an opportunist in satisfying his appetites.

[3] Women and food are the perpetual objects of Trickster's attention. The references throughout this tale to "princess," "master," and "slaves" reflect the nature of Tsimshian society, which was stratified according to kinship and status. The Tsimshians fostered competition for status and accumulation of wealth.

the people what had happened to them on their journey. Then they took the princess up to her father's house. A great number of people were following them. The chief was very sorrowful because his only daughter was hurt. He called together all the wise men, and asked them what he should do to cure his daughter. The wise men told him to gather all the shamans, and let them try to cure her wound. There was a wound under her ribs made by the hind leg of the deer. Then the chief ordered his attendants to call all the shamans. The attendants went and called all the shamans. They gathered in the chief's great house. Then the shamans worked over her with their supernatural powers, but they all failed. The wound could not be cured by the supernatural powers of the shamans. The girl became worse and worse, until she was very ill. Still the shamans worked on, day and night. Three days had passed, and the many shamans had been working in vain. On the fourth day, behold! before the evening set in a canoe filled with young men came to town. They came ashore, and some people went down to meet them. Then the people who were going down saw a shaman sitting in the middle of the canoe. They went up quickly and told the chief that a shaman had come to town. Therefore the chief sent to him, asking him to cure his only daughter. (This shaman was Raven and the crew of his canoe were his grandchildren the Crows.)

In the evening, when he came in, he saw the princess lying there very ill, for he had hurt her a few days before; and all the shamans who had failed before were sitting along the wall on one side of the house. Raven pretended to be a shaman. He sat down near the head of the princess, who was lying down; and all the young men followed him, carrying a large box which contained his magic powers. He took charcoal and rubbed it on his face, and rubbed ashes over it. He put on the crown of bears' claws, placed a ring of red-cedar bark around his neck, and put on his shaman's dancing-apron, and took up his large shaman's rattle. He started with beating of the drum; and after the drumming and beating, he began his song; and when they were singing, they pronounced these words:

"Let the mighty hail fall on the roof of this chief's house,
   On the roof of this chief's house,
   On the roof of this chief's house!"

and as the singers pronounced these words, hail beat on the roof of the chief's house terribly. (Before Raven arrived in the town, he had ordered some of his grandchildren the Crows to take each a small white stone in his mouth, and said, "When we pronounce the words of our song, then drop the stones on the roof of the chief's house." Thus had Raven spoken to his grandchildren the Crows, and they had done so.) When the mighty hail ceased, Raven said, "Bring me a mat of cedar bark." They brought him the mat, and he spread it over the princess to cover her. He himself also went under it with the girl,[4] touched the wound, said, "Be cured, wound under the right ribs!" and so it happened.

Then the chief was very glad because his daughter had been cured of her illness. He gave Raven all kinds of food. Now, the chief spoke to the shaman after he had fed him, and said, "Ask me whatever you wish, and I will give it to you." Then he made a promise unto him: "Whatever you may ask me, I will give it to you,

---

[4]Trickster's sexual relations with the girl, which are euphemistically glossed over here, are made explicit in other texts. He does, nevertheless, cure her.

my dear, good, and true supernatural man,—you, who are possessed of supernatural powers,—for you have succeeded in restoring my only daughter." Then Raven looked around and smiled. He said, "What I want is that you should move, and leave for me all the provisions you have; for my young men have nothing, because we have no time to obtain our own provisions, for we are going around all the time healing those who need us." Then the chief ordered his slaves to go out, and ordered the people to move on the next day. Then the slaves ran out, crying, "Leave, great tribe, and leave your provisions behind!"[5] The people did so. They left in the morning, and left all their food, according to the order of their master. Raven was very glad, because now he had much food.

On the following day he took a walk; and while he was absent, his grandchildren assembled, opened many boxes of crabapples mixed with grease, and ate them all. When Raven came home from his walk, behold! he saw all the empty boxes, and he knew that his grandchildren had done this.[6]

1916

---

[5] Given what the audience knows of Trickster, the chief's assessment of his character and his willingness to move the village reflect a lack of wisdom, which will be charged against him.

[6] Trickster figures seldom realize an enduring benefit from their tricks.

Europe on the Eve of Contact

Iberian Initiatives

Portugal

At Christopher Columbus's birth, the outline of a European's view of the world was dramatically smaller than it had been in the thirteenth century, when the new Mongol empire provided security on the trading roads in a vast area from China to the Black Sea. Marco Polo's visit of 1271–1295 is the most famous only because he wrote of his travels (Document 11). Colonies of Italian merchants, mostly Genoese, were established at the southwestern terminals of the "silk roads" to Tabriz [Afghanistan], Samarkand [Turkestan], and Ormuz [Iran], and thence to China or the spice-producing regions of Southeast Asia. Malacca became an enormous international port, with shipping of spices to China and the Malabar cities of India.

> "the logic of its geohistory dictated Atlantic expansion."

Displacement of the Mongols in the fourteenth century by the isolationist native Ming Dynasty closed up the roads and, along with increased Islamic hostility toward Christians, reduced European trade through Alexandria [Egypt] to a minimum. Payment at Alexandria for Asian luxury goods was required in gold or silver, and this stimulated a search for precious metals. The nearest gold mines were in the Niger region of Africa, and Italian merchants, such as the Genoese Malfante, tried to reach these sources directly by traveling across the dangerous Sahara Desert. The merchants had more success when they allied Italian finance to Portuguese navigation in a methodical search along Africa's west coast for a reliable contact with gold traders via ship.

Other motives besides a search for gold impelled the elite and the seamen of Portugal to look to the coast of Africa for new wealth. These included shortages at home of grain and fish, and, unfortunately, a search for slave labor to work sugar plantations. Many other European kingdoms considered a seafaring solution to their internal problems, but only Portugal

SOURCE From *The Modern World-System, Capitalist Agriculture and the Origins of the European World-Economy in the Sixteenth Century*, pp. 49–52 by Immanuel Wallerstein, 1974. Reprinted with permission of Academic Press.

was ready, for reasons discussed in this selection, to put in the consistent effort that was required.

Why was Portugal, of all the polities of Europe, most able to conduct the initial thrust? One obvious answer is found on any map. Portugal is located on the Atlantic, right next to Africa. In terms of the colonization of Atlantic islands and the exploration of the western coast of Africa, it was obviously closest. Furthermore, the oceanic currents are such that it was easiest, especially given the technology of the time, to set forth from Portuguese ports (as well as those of southwest Spain).

In addition, Portugal already had much experience with long-distance trade. Here, if Portugal cannot match the Venetians or the Genoese, recent research had demonstrated that their background was significant and probably the match of the cities of northern Europe.

A third factor was the availability of capital. The Genoese, the great rivals of the Venetians, decided early on to invest in Iberian commercial enterprise and to encourage their efforts at overseas expansion. By the end of the fifteenth century, the Genoese would prefer the Spaniards to the Portuguese, but that is largely because the latter could by then afford to divest themselves of Genoese sponsorship, tutelage, and cut in the profit. Verlinden calls Italy "the only really colonizing nation during the middle ages." In the twelfth century when Genoese and Pisans first appear in Catalonia, in the thirteenth century when they first reach Portugal, this is part of the efforts of the Italians to draw the Iberian peoples into the international trade of the time. But once there, the Italians would proceed to play an initiating role in Iberian colonization efforts because, by having come so early, "they were able to conquer the key positions of the Iberian peninsula itself." As of 1317, according to Virginia Rau, "the city and the port of Lisbon would be the great centre of Genoese trade. . . ." To be sure, in the late fourteenth and early fifteenth centuries, Portuguese merchants began to complain about the "undue intervention [of the Indians] in the *retail* trade of the realm, which threatened the dominant position of national merchants in that branch of trade." The solution was simple, and to some extent classic. The Italians were absorbed by marriage and became landed aristocrats both in Portugal and on Madeira.

There was one other aspect of the commercial economy that contributed to Portugal's venturesomeness, compared to say France or England. It was ironical that it was least absorbed in the zone that would become the European world-economy, but rather tied in a significant degree to the Islamic Mediterranean zone. As a consequence, her economy was relatively more monetized, her population relatively more urbanized.

It was not geography nor mercantile strength alone, however, that accounted for Portugal's edge. It was also the strength of its state machinery. Portugal was in this regard very different from other west European states, different that is during the fifteenth century. She knew peace when they knew internal warfare. The stability of the state was important not only because it created the climate in which entrepreneurs could flourish but because it encouraged nobility to find outlets for their energies other than in internal or inter-European warfare. The stability of the state was crucial also because it itself was in many ways the chief entrepreneur. When the state was stable, it could devote its energies to profitable commercial ventures. For Portugal, as we have seen, the logic of its geohistory dictated Atlantic expansion as the most sensible commercial venture for the state.

Why Portugal? Because she alone of the European states maximized will and possibility. Europe needed a larger land base to support the expansion of its economy, one which could compensate for the critical decline in seigniorial revenues and which could cut short the nascent and potentially very violent class war which the crisis of feudalism implied. Europe needed many things: bullion, staples, proteins, means of preserving protein, foods, wood, materials to process textiles. And it needed a more tractable labor force.

But "Europe" must not be reified. There was no central agency which acted in terms of these long-range objectives. The real decisions were taken by groups of men acting in terms of their immediate interests. In the case of Portugal, there seemed to be advantage in the "discovery business" for many groups—for the state, for the nobility, for the commercial bourgeoisie (indigenous and foreign), even for the semiproletariat of the towns.

For the state, a *small* state, the advantage was obvious. Expansion was the most likely route to the expansion of revenue and the accumulation of glory. And the Portuguese state, almost alone among the states of Europe of the time, was not distracted by internal conflict. It had achieved moderate political stability at least a century earlier than Spain, France, and England.

It was precisely this stability which created the impulse for the nobility. Faced with the same financial squeeze as European nobles elsewhere, they were deprived of the soporific and financial potential (if they won) of internecine warfare. Nor could they hope to recoup their financial position by internal colonization. Portugal lacked the land. So they were sympathetic to the concept of oceanic expansion and they offered their "younger sons" to provide the necessary leadership for the expeditions.

The interests of the bourgeoisie for once did not conflict with those of the nobility. Prepared for modern capitalism by a long apprenticeship in long-distance trading and by the experience of living in one of the most highly monetized areas of Europe (because of the economic involvement with the Islamic Mediterranean world), the bourgeoisie too sought to escape the confines of the small Portuguese market. To the extent that they lacked the capital, they found it readily available from the Genoese who, for reasons of their own having to do with their rivalry with Venice, were ready to finance the Portuguese. And the potential conflict of the indigenous and foreign bourgeoisie was muted by the willingness of the Genoese to assimilate into Portuguese culture over time.

Finally, exploration and the consequent trade currents provided job outlets for the urban semiproletariat, many of whom had fled to the towns because of the increased exploitation consequent upon the seigniorial crisis. Once again, a potential for internal disorder was minimized by the external expansion.

And if these conjunctures of will and possibility were not enough, Portugal was blessed by the best possible geographic location for the enterprise, best possible both because of its jutting out into the Atlantic and toward the south but also because of the convergence of favorable oceanic currents. It does not seem surprising thus, in retrospect, that Portugal made the plunge.

Round Africa to India

The Portuguese gained a toehold in Muslim North Africa with King John I's conquest of Ceuta in 1415. His son Henry ("the navigator," as he was labeled in the nineteenth century) withdrew from court after an unsuccessful attempt to capture Tangiers so that he might direct expeditions along the west coast of Africa, where Muslims held no sway. Although the contemporary chronicler Gomes Eannes de Azura, whose work is excerpted below, presents the prince's motives in a way appropriate to the time in which he writes, modern historians point out that Henry was likely interested principally in increasing his income from fishing and maritime activities. Also, he was not the only patron of exploration, since during his lifetime two-thirds of the trips were sponsored by the king, aristocrats, or merchants.

"no mariners or merchants would ever dare to attempt it."

Contrary to early historical speculation, Henry appears to have had no master plan to explore the coastline, much less to try to reach India. Because he gathered together a "think tank" of geographers and navigators in the far south of Portugal at Sagres, however, he set the pattern of systematic exploration that would guide the royal house thereafter. His principal achievement was to support many tries, at last successful in 1434, to round Cape Bojado ("Bulging Cape"). Today the cape is a mere bump on the part of Africa then called Guinea, but it was an actual and psychological barrier blocking entry to the fabled "Sea of Darkness." By Henry's death in 1460, a fleet had reached as far as Sierra Leone.

King John II was the first Portuguese monarch to put into play a comprehensive plan of systematic discovery. He founded a series of trading colonies supported by forts, of which the principal was São Jorge da Mina ("the Mine") at the Gulf of Guinea. By 1482 his ships reached the mouth of the Congo River.

Christopher Columbus tried his luck in Portugal because the Genoese had a well-established trading and banking presence there. Possibly he was a commercial agent for a firm interested in Portugal's commerce with Africa. Whether or not he ever took an actual navigational role in a voyage has not been established, but he did learn enough about the sea to offer a plan for a great oceangoing "enterprise" to King John II in 1483 or 1484.

When Columbus presented his proposal to the court to sail west to the riches of the Orient, he drastically underestimated the size of the globe. The men appointed by the king to review the proposal rejected it on the sensible grounds that the estimate of distance was impossibly small. His wishful belief that only 2,500 miles lay between the Azores and Japan mistakenly placed the latter kingdom approximately on the longitude of the Virgin Islands—a shortfall of 8,000 miles. It is difficult to tell, in view of the committee's rejection, if King John II would have had any sensible reason to act in the underhanded manner about which Columbus's son reports in the second selection.

The final blow to the foreigner's hopes came when Bartolomew Dias rounded the Cape of Good Hope, returning in 1488 with news that an eastern passage to India was feasible. There was nothing for Columbus to do but look for another patron. When Castile took up the challenge and gave Columbus his three ships, the race for Asia was on in earnest. During the reign of King Manuel I, appropriately nicknamed "the Fortunate," his servant Vasco da Gama returned to Lisbon from India in 1499. In the final selection, the king of Portugal cheerfully, but diplomatically, informs Ferdinand and Isabella of this feat and, coincidentally, sets out Portugal's legal claims to a monopoly in trade in the area.

Henry "the Navigator" and the Exploration of the Coast of Africa, 1451–1460

In which five reasons appear why the Lord Infant [Henry] was moved to command the search for the lands of Guinea [Africa].

We imagine that we know a matter when we are acquainted with the doer of it and the end for which he did it. And since in former chapters we have set forth the Lord Infant as the chief actor in these things, giving as clear an understanding of him as we could, it is meet that in this present chapter we should know his purpose in doing them. And you should note well that the noble spirit of this Prince [Henry], by a sort of natural constraint, was ever urging him both to begin and to carry out very great deeds. For which reason, after the taking of Ceuta [1415] he always kept ships well armed against the Infidel [Muslims], both for war, and because he had also a wish to know the land that lay beyond the isles of Canary and that Cape called Bojador ["Bulging"], for that up to his time, neither by writings, nor by the memory of man, was known with any certainty the nature of the land beyond that Cape. Some said indeed that Saint Brandan [legendary Irish explorer] had passed that way; and there was another tale of two galleys rounding the Cape, which never returned. But this doth not appear at all likely to be true, for it is not to be presumed that if the

SOURCE Gomes Eannes de Azura, *Chronicle of the Discovery and Conquest of Guinea*, ed. and trans. C. R. Beazley and Edgar Prestage, 2 vols. (London: Hakluyt Society, 1896–1898), pp. 27–30.

said galleys went there, some other ships would not have endeavoured to learn what voyage they had made. And because the said Lord Infant wished to know the truth of this,—since it seemed to him that if he or some other lord did not endeavour to gain that knowledge, no mariners or merchants would ever dare to attempt it—(for it is clear that none of them ever trouble themselves to sail to a place where there is not a sure and certain hope of profit)—and seeing also that no other prince took any pains in this matter, he sent out his own ships against those parts, to have manifest certainty of them all. And to this he was stirred up by his zeal for the service of God and of the King Edward his Lord and brother, who then reigned. And this was the first reason of his action. . . .

The second reason was that if there chanced to be in those lands some population of Christians, or some havens, into which it would be possible to sail without peril, many kinds of merchandise might be brought to this realm, which would find a ready market, and reasonably so, because no other people of these parts traded with them, nor yet people of any other that were known; and also the products of this realm might be taken there, which traffic would bring great profit to our countrymen.

The third reason was that, as it was said that the power of the Moors [Muslims] in that land of Africa was very much greater than was commonly supposed, and that there were no Christians among them, nor any other race of men; and because every wise man is obliged by natural prudence to wish for a knowledge of the power of his enemy; therefore the said Lord Infant exerted himself to cause this to be fully discovered, and to make it known determinately how far the power of those infidels extended.

The fourth reason was because during the one and thirty years that he had warred against the Moors, he had never found a Christian king, nor a lord outside this land, who for the love of our Lord Jesus Christ would aid him in the said war. Therefore he sought to know if there were in those parts any Christian princes, in whom the charity and the love of Christ was so ingrained that they would aid him against those enemies of the faith.

The fifth reason was his great desire to make increase in the faith of our Lord Jesus Christ and to bring to him all the souls that should be saved,— understanding that all the mystery of the Incarnation, Death, and Passion of our Lord Jesus Christ was for this sole end—namely the salvation of lost souls—whom the said Lord Infant by his travail and spending would fain bring into the true path. . . .

But over and above these five reasons I have a sixth that would seem to be the root from which all the others proceeded: and this is the inclination of the heavenly wheels [astrology]. For, as I wrote not many days ago in a letter I sent to the Lord King, that although it be written that the wise man shall be Lord of the stars, and that the courses of the planets (according to the true estimate of the holy doctors) cannot cause the good man to stumble; yet it is manifest that they are bodies ordained in the secret counsels of our Lord God and run by a fixed measure, appointed to different ends, which are revealed to men by his grace, through whose influence bodies of the lower order are inclined to certain passions. . . . And that was because his ascendent was Aries, which is the house of Mars and exaltation of the sun, and his lord in the XIth house, in company of the sun. And because the said

Mars was in Aquarius, which is the house of Saturn, and in the mansion of hope, it signified that this Lord should toil at high and mighty conquests, especially in seeking out things that were hidden from other men and secret, according to the nature of Saturn, in whose house he is. And the fact of his being accompanied by the sun, as I said, and the sun being in the house of Jupiter, signified that all his dealings and his conquests would be loyally carried out, according to the good pleasure of his king and lord.

Why ships had not hitherto dared to pass beyond Cape Bojador.

So the Infant, moved by these reasons, which you have already heard, began to make ready his ships and his people, as the needs of the case required; but this much you may learn, that although he sent out many times, not only ordinary men, but such as by their experience in great deeds of war were of foremost name in the profession of arms, yet there was not one who dared to pass that Cape of Bojador [in West Africa] and learn about the land beyond it, as the Infant wished. And to say the truth this was not from cowardice or want of good will, but from the novelty of the thing and the wide-spread and ancient rumour about this Cape, that had been cherished by the mariners of Spain from generation to generation. And although this proved to be deceitful, yet since the hazarding of this attempt seemed to threaten the last evil of all, there was great doubt as to who would be the first to risk his life in such a venture. How are we, men said, to pass the bounds that our fathers set up, or what profit can result to the Infant from the perdition [loss] of our souls as well as of our bodies—for of a truth by daring any further we shall become wilful murderers of ourselves? Have there not been in Spain other princes and lords as covetous perchance of this honour as the Infant? For certainly it cannot be presumed that among so many noble men who did such great and lofty deeds for the glory of their memory, there had not been one to dare this deed. But being satisfied of the peril, and seeing no hope of honour or profit, they left off the attempt. For, said the mariners, this much is clear, that beyond this Cape there is no race of men nor place of inhabitants: nor is the land less sandy than the deserts of Libya, where there is no water, no tree, no green herb—and the sea so shallow that a whole league from land it is only a fathom deep, while the currents are so terrible that no ship having once passed the Cape, will ever be able to return.

Therefore our forefathers never attempted to pass it: and of a surety their knowledge of the lands beyond was not a little dark, as they knew not how to set them down on the charts, by which man controls all the seas that can be navigated. . . .

Columbus in Portugal,
1477–1485

inding himself near Lisbon, and knowing that many of his Genoese countrymen lived in that city, he [Columbus] went there as soon as he could. When they learned who he was, they gave him such a warm welcome that he made his home in that city and married there.

As he behaved very honorably and was a man of handsome presence and one who never turned from the path of honesty, a lady named Doña Felipa Moniz, of noble birth and superior of the Convent of the Saints, where the Admiral [Columbus] used to attend Mass, had such conversation and friendship with him that she became his wife. His father-in-law, Pedro Moniz Perestrello, being dead, they went to live with his widow, who, observing the Admiral's great interest in geography, told him the said Perestrello, her husband, had been a notable seafarer; and she told how he and two other captains had gone with license from the King of Portugal to discover new lands, agreeing to divide all they discovered into three parts and cast lots for the share that should fall to each. Sailing to the southwest, they discovered the islands of Madeira and Pôrto Santo [in 1418]. Since the island of Madeira was the larger of the two, they made two parts of it, the third being the island of Pôrto Santo, which fell to the share of the Admiral's father-in-law, Perestrello, who governed it till his death.

Seeing that her stories of these voyages gave the Admiral much pleasure, she gave him the writings and sea-charts left by her husband. These things excited the Admiral still more; and he informed himself of the other voyages and navigations that the Portuguese were then making to [São Jorge da] Mina and down the coast of Guinea, and greatly enjoyed speaking with the men who sailed in those regions. To tell the truth, I do not know if it was during this marriage that the Admiral went to Mina or Guinea, but it seems reasonable that he did so. Be that as it may, one thing leading to another and starting a train of thought, the Admiral while in Portugal began to speculate that if the Portuguese could sail so far south, it should be possible to sail as far westward, and that it was logical to expect to find land in that direction. . . .

In due time, the Admiral, convinced of the soundness of his plan, proposed to put it into effect and sail over the Western Ocean in search of new lands. But he knew that his enterprise required the cooperation and assistance of some prince; and since he resided in Portugal, he decided to offer it to the king of that country. Although King João [John II] listened attentively to the Admiral, he appeared cool toward the project, because the discovery and conquest of the west coast of Africa, called Guinea, had put the prince to great expense and trouble without the least return. At that time the Portuguese had not yet sailed beyond the Cape of Good Hope [in 1488], which name according to some was given that cape in place of its proper one, Agesingua, because it marked the end of those fine hopes of conquest and discovery; others claim it got that name because it gave promise of the discovery of richer lands and of more prosperous voyages.

Be that as it may, the King was very little inclined to spend more money on discovery; and if he paid some attention to the Admiral, it was because of the strong arguments that the latter advanced. These arguments so impressed the King that the launching of the enterprise waited only upon his

Source From *The Life of the Admiral Christopher Columbus by His Son Ferdinand*, trans. and annotated by Benjamin Keen, 1959, pp. 14–36, passim. Reprinted by permission of the translator.

acceptance of the conditions laid down by the Admiral. The latter, being a man of noble and lofty ambitions, would not covenant save on such terms as would bring him great honor and advantage, in order that he might leave a title and estate befitting the grandeur of his works and his merits.

So the King, counseled by a Doctor Calzadilla in whom he placed much trust, decided to send a caravel secretly to attempt what the Admiral had offered to do, thinking that if those lands were discovered in this way, he would not have to give the Admiral the great rewards he demanded. With all speed and secrecy, then, the King outfitted a caravel on the pretext of sending provisions and reinforcements to the Cape Verde, and dispatched it whither the Admiral had proposed to go. But because the people he sent lacked the knowledge, steadfastness, and ability of the Admiral, they wandered about on the sea for many days and returned to the Cape Verde and thence to Lisbon, making fun of the enterprise and declaring that no land could be found in those waters.

When he learned of this, the Admiral, whose wife had meantime died, formed such a hatred for that city and nation that he resolved to depart for Castile with his little son Diego—who after his father's death succeeded to his estate.

Letter from Manuel I
to Ferdinand and Isabella, 1499

Most high and excellent Prince and Princess, most potent Lord and Lady!

Your Highnesses already know that we had ordered Vasco da Gama, a nobleman of our household, and his brother Paulo da Gama, with four vessels to make discoveries by sea, and that two years have now elapsed since their departure. And as the principal motive of this enterprise has been with our predecessors, the service of God our Lord, and our own advantage, it pleased Him in His mercy to speed them on their route. From a message which has now been brought to this city by one of the captains, we learn that they did reach and discover India and other kingdoms and lordships bordering upon it; that they entered and navigated its sea, finding large cities, large edifices and rivers, and great populations among whom is carried on all the trade in spices and precious stones, which are forwarded in ships (which these same explorers saw and met with in good numbers and of great size) to Mecca, and thence to Cairo, whence they are dispersed throughout the world. Of these [spices, etc.] they have brought a quantity including cinnamon, cloves, ginger, nutmeg, and pepper, as well as other kinds, together with the boughs and leaves of the same; also many fine stones of all sorts, such as rubies and others. And they also came to a country in which there are mines of gold, of which [gold], as of the spices and precious stones, they did not bring as much as they could have done, for they took no merchandise with them.

SOURCE *A Journal of the First Voyage of Vasco da Gama,* ed. and trans. E. G. Ravenstein (London: Hakluyt Society, 1898), pp. 77–79.

As we are aware that your Highnesses will hear of these things with much pleasure and satisfaction, we thought well to give this information. And your Highnesses may believe, in accordance with what we have learnt concerning the Christian people whom these explorers reached, that it will be possible notwithstanding that they are not as yet strong in the faith or possessed of a thorough knowledge of it, to do much in the service of God and the exaltation of the Holy Faith, once they shall have been converted and fully fortified in it. And when they shall have thus been fortified in the faith, there will be an opportunity for destroying the Moors [Muslims] of those parts. Moreover, we hope, with the help of God, that the great trade which now enriches the Moors of those parts, through whose hands it passes without the intervention of other persons or peoples, shall, in consequence of our regulations, be diverted to the natives and ships of our own kingdom, so that henceforth all Christendom, in this part of Europe, shall be able in a large measure to provide itself with these spices and precious stones.

QUESTIONS

1. Why was Portugal, of all the European kingdoms, the most likely candidate for expansion?
2. What were the principal factors that pushed a small European state into exploration and colonization?
3. What social groups in Portugal were the most interested in the push to expand?
4. What five reasons does the chronicler of the exploits of Henry "the Navigator" give for Henry's desire to explore the west coast of Africa?
5. In what ways does the list of motivations set out for Henry "the Navigator" (from Question 4) differ from those enumerated by a modern historian (Document 2)?
6. Why had European sailors not passed beyond the Cape of Bojador?
7. Why did Columbus decide to remain in Portugal?
8. Why was Columbus's plan to sail west rejected by the king of Portugal?
9. List the advantages to Portugal, and to all Christians, that Manuel I saw in the successful voyage to India.

Spain During the Reconquest

In 711 A.D., Muslims from North Africa landed on the Iberian Peninsula. Generals Tariq and Musa proceeded to conquer its Visigothic Christian leadership within seven years. Quickly enough, the bulk of the population converted.

In the least productive lands to the far north, at small rural areas in the Asturian mountains, tiny Christian realms survived as heirs to the half-forgotten tradition of Visigothic sovereignty. From these remnants, grew the kingdoms of León, Castile, Aragón, and Portugal. During an early stage of the conflict, Christians came to believe the apostle St. James the Younger, on his white horse, took part in the fighting. A belief that God was on their side endured.

"a society organized for war, . . ."

The process of "reconquering" land that once belonged to Christians was complex because much of the fighting on the borders was undertaken by aristocrats operating on their own, with royal approval after the fact. This set a pattern for the conquest of the New World, where independent conquistadores, sometimes with and often without specific authorization from the crown, put into practice the negotiating and fighting techniques their ancestors evolved over centuries. Islands of the Caribbean, the plains of Mexico, and the heights of the Andes would resound with the crusading war cry of the Reconquest: "St. James and at them!"

I t is hardly surprising that a process lasting seven centuries should have given rise to innumerable differences of interpretation, especially since terms like Reconquest, Holy War and Crusades have been used with considerable ambivalence, since some periods have been but little studied and since source material is generally patchy. However, it is already possible to indicate the main lines of development and some of the problems yet to be solved.

If one defines the Reconquest as the transfer of political power over the Peninsula from Muslim to Christian hands, then it is clear that this really occurred between 718 and 1492. What is also clear is that most of the characteristics of this transfer already existed by the time of Alfonso III [866–911], rather than being inventions of the eleventh century. The chronicles of his reign show that the policy of reconquering the whole of Spain had already been formulated and adopted, that one motive for this policy was the desire to recover the heritage which the Muslims had allegedly usurped from the rightful successors of the Visigothic [Germanic tribal] monarchy, and that the other motives included religious hatred of the

SOURCE *The Reconquest of Spain*, pp. 173–178, by D. W. Lomax. Reprinted by permission of The Peters Fraser & Dunlop Group Ltd.

enemy: the Christians were already fighting against the Muslims, not only as "usurpers" but also as "infidels." On the other hand, there is simply no earlier evidence for deciding how far this religious motivation and the adoption of this policy preceded their formulation in the texts of Alfonso III's reign. There is a similar lack of evidence about such questions for 910–1035; and in both periods the safest course is to suspend judgment rather than to argue from the silence of our scanty texts. In contrast, the whole tradition of Frankish [Germanic tribal] military involvement is fairly well documented from Charlemagne down to the reconquest of Granada; it was by no means a novelty in the age of Alfonso VI [1065–1109].

What then was new in the eleventh century? With the collapse of the caliphate, there ended any chance of a powerful independent monarchy among the Spanish Muslims, and the balance of political power tipped decisively away from them and towards the Christians, although the reasons for this decisive change are still obscure. On the Christian side, there now appeared for the first time, not foreign expeditionaries nor the concept of the Holy War—both had existed for centuries—but the idea of the Crusade, that is, a Holy War entered into for religious motives (among others, no doubt), authorized by the Church and conferring on its participants a specific juridical status, no matter whether they were French, English or Spanish. And, of course, Frankish expeditions increased in frequency, size, recruiting-areas and effectiveness . . . most of them went to the Ebro valley and provided essential assistance in its reconquest. . . .

One must discount the view that the peaceful co-existence of the ordinary people was occasionally disturbed by warfare provoked by the religious and political establishment; it would be truer to say that the kings made occasional ineffectual attempts to limit the endless warfare enjoyed by their subjects. This was natural enough: as in medieval Russia, though to a lesser extent, the ease with which peasants could acquire land and freedom on an open frontier meant that it was difficult for the civil and military authorities to control them. Consequently, they were left within the framework of frontier townships and militias to do very much as they liked, and what they liked was plundering Muslim villages. The concepts of Reconquest and Crusade may have originated among the leaders of Christendom; the practice of permanent warfare against the Muslims was a creation of the people. And, despite the gaps in our evidence, it seems clear that even these concepts of Reconquest, Holy War and Crusade became widely diffused and accepted among the lower levels of society. . . .

Even with what is known now, however, it ought to be possible to reach some tentative conclusions. The Reconquest was a lengthy process and a continuous one in the sense that fighting rarely stopped for long, but it was not, as is often implied, a slow, steady and gradual one. The Christians did not advance steadily, step-by-step; they took great leaps forward, to the Duero [River], the Tagus [River], the Guadalquivir [River] and the south coast, and after each leap they waited for centuries to consolidate their position before making the next one. Rather than gradual, the Reconquest was spasmodic; it proceeded not by townships but by great regions such as Aragón, New Castile or Andalusia, and one of its results was to emphasize the importance of such regions as the basic units of Spanish national life.

Other results have aroused more polemical discussion. Sánchez Albornoz has argued that the Muslim Conquest diverted Spain from its natural development as a European country and that though the Reconquest corrected this diversion, its slowness placed Spain several centuries behind Europe on the path of progress. Though this theory does not define Europe or progress, it implicitly identifies both with France, and on its own terms is unanswerable. Not even Spain, where most things are possible, can be as French as France—but this is not the fault of Tariq [Muslim general] or Pelayo [Germanic Christian warrior].

Other historians argue that Spanish civilization reached its zenith in the tenth century and then declined because its Muslim rulers were replaced by Christians; but this is hardly supported by the history of civilization in neighbouring Morocco, where no Reconquest occurred. The case of Spain is more complex and unusual than, for example, the decline of Italy in the seventeenth century or the rise of England in the nineteenth; for between 1050 and 1250 Spain *transferred* from one culture, the Islamic, which was passing its zenith, to another, western Christendom, which was rising. Her exceptional case cannot therefore be measured by the simpler standards of Morocco or France, for unlike them she has mixed two cultures, the Islamic and the Latin Christian, in a process which has here been called the Muslim Conquest and the Reconquest.

The mixture was strongest between 1000 and 1250 when political forces reinforced nobler motives making for religious toleration. Spain was then a land of several religions, and not until 1492 did it adopt the European pattern of religious uniformity which before 1250 would have been as disastrous for the Christians as it proved for the Almoravids and Almohads [North African Muslim groups]. Under a regime of religious pluralism this society was intellectually very productive: The science of ancient Greece and medieval Persia and India was translated into Arabic in Syria, imported into Spain by the scholars of Ummayad Córdoba, augmented by Spanish scholars like Averroes and then translated into Latin by Christian scholars who spread the knowledge to the rest of Europe. Astronomy, physics, medicine, optics, mathematics, alchemy and magic suddenly burst upon a world which had known little beyond Bede and Isidore [of Seville]. So too did stories from Asian bazaars, new types of mysticism, new legends about the after-life and new philosophical theories. Thanks to the translators, both Spanish and foreign, doctors throughout Europe learned new cures for diseases, merchants and administrators could calculate accounts with positioned Hindu numbers and overseas discoverers could rely on tables of the stars for the voyages to Africa, Asia and America. It was the Reconquest which provided suitable conditions for these translations, for only in reconquered territory did Christians have the opportunity and interest to make them. None were made in Muslim Africa, where all educated men read Arabic, and even in Sicily such translations were fewer and dependent on capricious royal patronage.

In Spain these translations crowned a political, economic, social and cultural revolution as profound as any in medieval Europe. This had been achieved because the Christians had learnt several lessons in the twelfth century. The first and most important was the value of unity: realizing that their former quarrels had led to defeat at the hands of the Almohads, the Christians collaborated with each other after 1224 and, in their turn, exploited Muslim disunity. Secondly, recognizing the ineffectiveness of foreign crusaders and of the international military Orders, they learned to rely on themselves alone and to create their own Orders of Santiago, Calatrava and Alcántara. Thirdly, the resettlement of the south with Christians ensured that the next African invasion would face not merely Christian garrisons in a Muslim country but a solid line of Christian cities, prosperous and belligerent, with their own militias and castles. The social revolution which this implied led briefly to a wide distribution of property in Andalusia; but this did not last. Emigration from north to south probably impoverished the northern nobles, driving them into rebellion, whilst southern land was so cheap that noble families could buy up farms and amass great estates, and whenever the monarchy was weak they enriched themselves, and rewarded their vassals, at the expense of crown, Church and cities.

Indeed, they were almost forced to do so by the nature of Spanish society. For though capable leaders' unity, self-reliance and resettlement all helped to achieve the Reconquest, the most important factor was probably the willingness of Christian Spaniards to transform their society for this purpose. This transformation was extremely thorough. Late medieval Castile became essentially a society organized for war, a dynamic military machine which would fuction well so long as it had more lands to conquer. It might be disconcerted by military defeats, but it could survive them. What threw it into complete confusion was the end of the attempt at conquest, and when the kings stopped leading their armies against Granada they implicitly invited their barons to find a new role which could only be that of fighting each other. Just as the English barons of Edward III or Henry V united to plunder the French, so the Castilian barons would unite under Alfonso XI [1312–1350] to plunder Granada, the France of Castile; but, just as peace with France led to civil wars within England under Richard II and Henry VI, so peace with the Muslims led to civil wars within Castile under Fernando IV [1295–1312] and Juan II [1406–1454]. Fernando and Isabel [Ferdinand and Isabella] could cure one crisis in 1481 simply by setting the war-machine to work once more, to conquer Granada; but after 1492, there was no more Muslim territory to be conquered inside Spain. The machine was running out of land, and more crises loomed ahead.

It might of course have been sent against the Maghrib [in North Africa], and raids were made on Melilla (1497), Oran (1509) and Algiers (1510), and perhaps it might have conquered Morocco. Or it might have been turned back against northern Europe, with incalculable effects on the sixteenth-century religious wars. However, in thanksgiving for the fall of Granada, Isabel equipped Columbus's exploratory expedition and in 1492 his discovery of America opened up a virtually limitless stretch of conquerable territory. Castilian society rose to the occasion. Within fifty years it conquered most areas from Texas to Argentina and established the framework of political, religious, social and economic life within which they would henceforth live.

No other European society could have done this at that date. Explorers from England, for example, discovered Nova Scotia in 1497, but no permanent English settlement was made in America until the seventeenth century. Only Spain was able to conquer, administer, Christianize and Europeanize the populous areas of the New World precisely because during the previous seven centuries her society had been constructed for the purpose of conquering, administering, Christianizing and Europeanizing the inhabitants of al-Andalus [Muslim Spain]. Thus if the Reconquest is important in Old World history because it is the primary example of the reversal of an Islamic conquest and because it fostered the transfer of Greek and Asian culture to western Europe, in the general sweep of world history it is vital because it prepared the rapid conquest and Europeanization of Latin America and thereby spared it most of the religious and imperialist wars which would henceforth afflict almost all the rest of mankind.

Conquest of the Canary Islands

The logical progress of the Christian southward sweep across the Iberian Peninsula would, by the sixteenth century, have taken their war across the narrow stretch of water separating the Spanish kingdoms from Muslim North Africa. Instead, Castile followed the example of Portugal, which settled the Azores and Madeira, far out in the Atlantic.

To head off the Portuguese, Ferdinand and Isabella launched a preemptive strike on the little-known island of Gran Canaria, arriving just before their Portuguese rivals. The use of sword, cannon, musket, horse, and dog to subdue the unclothed Stone Age Canary islanders was copied by Columbus during his Caribbean assault. It should be noted that Felipe Fernández-Armesto, author of this selection, refers to all native populations as "savages," an unfortunate bit of outdated terminology.

"the crucial similarity between the Canarians and Indians."

The Iberian islands formed stepping-stones for exploration in the midst of what one scholar has called the "Atlantic Mediterranean." Fortunately for Columbus, the Canaries (which take their name not from birds, but from the Spanish for the dogs found there) sit in the southern wind zone of westerlies, which made his first voyage feasible.

I n the Treaty of Alcaçovas of 1479, Ferdinand and Isabella expressly reserved to Castile the conquest of the stretch of coast opposite the Canary Islands, where their subjects established a garrison at Santa Cruz de la Mar Pequeña, and continued to make raids and attempts at

SOURCE *Ferdinand and Isabella*, pp. 146–161, passim, by Felipe Fernández-Armesto, 1975. Taplinger Publishing Co. Inc.

conquest in a sporadic and individual fashion. In 1492 the monarchs commissioned the conquistador Alonso de Lugo to organize these efforts, but the vastness of the area and the strength of resistance confined him to raiding and the maintenance of coastal footholds. The fall of Granada in 1492 released energies for assaults elsewhere on the mainland. In 1495 the Pope confirmed Castile's rights—for although these had long been assumed, pontifical clarification was useful in the face of conflicting Portuguese claims—and in 1497 a major and successful expedition, which conserved many elements of organization and personnel from the time of the Granada war, seized Melilla for the monarchs. But the same years saw the rise of the Barbary corsairs and, correspondingly, the difficulties of making more than local North African conquests increased. In that area of expansion Ferdinand and Isabella were limited to a coastal, military presence and could not establish settled colonies.

But already before the completion of the Reconquest, when Castilian expansion overseas could be launched in earnest like the ships that bore it, settlers from Andalucia had begun the colonization of the Canary Islands. . . .

The decisive phase came with the reign of Ferdinand and Isabella, who completed the conquest of the Canary Islands, encouraged their "peopling" with colonists by means of fiscal exemptions, and imposed a policy of land- and water-sharing, which encouraged sugar production. Madeiran and Valencian personnel were deliberately introduced to run the irrigation and refining industries. Genoese capitalists were brought in with sufficient money concentrations to set up the waterways and mills, and Negro slaves imported to supplement the indigenous and colonial labour-force. As well as sugar, corn was cultivated on dry lands by poorer settlers; and other Spanish crops like grapes, quince and saffron were introduced and nurtured in a garden economy of the Andalucian type, which grew up in the hinterlands of the growing townships. Cattle, pigs and sheep were imported to supplement the goats, while Castilian co-operative pastoral methods were promoted. The indices of the rapidity and extent of change are clear. Before the monarchs' reign, sugar was unknown on Gran Canaria; but within a few years Bernáldez could call it "a land of many canes." A clergyman who visited La Laguna in 1497, within a year of its foundation, found "only two or three shanties"—but by the end of the reign it had some 6,000 inhabitants. To a great extent, the architect of the new kind of colonial economy was Alonso Fernández de Lugo, who had served in the conquest of Gran Canaria and took command for the wards in Tenerife and La Palma: he seems to have realized that because of the distribution of rainfall in the archipelago, the western islands could be adapted for sugar-farming in a way that had not been possible in the earlier conquests. He introduced the sugarcane in 1484, as soon as the conquest of Gran Canaria was completed, and risked controversy and unpopularity during his governorship of Tenerife by favouring foreign technicians and capitalists. . . .

For the monarchs particularly desired that the soil of the Indies should be divided among the colonists, and a new agronomy introduced, just as was being effected by their command at the same time in the Canary Islands.

They repeated the same policy, based on land grants and fiscal exemptions, for encouraging immigration, as had been used in the Canaries. Lastly, the elements of the new agronomy were not to be cultivated to the exclusion of the pastoral sector, which the monarchs were determined to favour in their new as in their old realms. Within a few years, as in the Canaries, the labour force of the new colonies was expanded by the importation of Negroes, though the paganism and indiscipline of black slaves so perturbed the early governors, and the Portuguese monopoly of the trade was so strong, that the supply was only intermittent under the Catholic monarchs. Isabella was personally opposed to the employment of Negroes because she was afraid that their pagan practices would impede Spanish efforts to evangelize the Indians. Even though after her death Ferdinand removed all restrictions on the trade in blacks, the labour force of the New World colonies remained far more heavily dependent on indigenous sources than did that of the Canary Islands; as Columbus insisted, "The Indians are the wealth of Hispaniola—for they perform all labour of men and beasts." . . .

To exacerbate the efforts of their relative remoteness, the methods of finance employed in the conquests of the Canaries and the New World displayed ominous features for the future of royal government there. In the Canary Islands from 1477, the monarchs had placed the burden of financing the conquest on the royal exchequer [treasury], and indeed the first expeditions relied heavily on public finance: the methods of finance and recruiting of these early days were largely borrowed from the *Reconquista* [Reconquest]. But as the conquest wore on and more expeditions were dispatched, private sources of finance and means of recruiting tended increasingly to displace public ones. Instead of wages, the *conquistadores* would receive the promise of *repartimiento* or a share of the soil; instead of the yield from the sale of indulgences or the direct use of the royal fifth to meet the expenses of war, fifths yet uncollected were pledged as rewards to conquerers who could raise the necessary finance elsewhere. In other words, the conquest of the islands was begun with the financial arrangements of the *Reconquista*, and terminated with those of the conquest of the New World. . . .

In many ways the crucial similarity between the Canarians and Indians was that they were naked: that was the first fact Columbus noticed about the Indians and the first which Europeans had observed about the Canarians; indeed for every European observer of primitive peoples till well into the sixteenth century, clothes were the measure of difference between primitivism and civilization; conformity of dress was a sign of conformity of manners. The promotion of European *couture* was a major preoccupation of the proselytizers of the Moors and the Spanish settlers among the Indians. Beatriz de Bobadilla, heiress of the isle of Gomera and enslaver of its people, argued before Ferdinand and Isabella that the Gomerans could not be considered truly Christian on the ground that "they go about naked." Hieronymus Münzer at about the same time displayed the same state of mind when he wrote of the Canarians. "They all used to go naked, but now use clothes like us." Then he added, very characteristically of his epoch, "Oh, what doctrine and diligence can do, that can turn beasts in human shape into civilized men!" But in terms of the two cultural traditions of which men in the late

Middle Ages disposed—that of Christianity and that of classical antiquity—social nakedness had a profound significance: it evoked in the context of the first idea of primitive innocence, in that of the second, the legend of the age of gold.

Both these concepts were of great importance in the formation of European ideas about the Canary Islanders and Indians. Accounts of the Canary Islanders influenced notions of the age of gold; Peter Martyr and his correspondents thought the Indians a model of sylvan innocence. Of both peoples, it was thought that their uncorrupt state peculiarly fitted them to hear the gospel and helped to create the widespread impression that the existing and often harsh juridical norms for the treatment of pagans were unsuited to them. . . .

In 1477, however, a new factor intervened which acted as a catalyst around which the prevailing doctrine on savages' rights was altered. In October of that year, Ferdinand and Isabella took the conquest of the three still unsubdued Canary Islands under their own wing, out of the hands of the local seigneurs and private adventurers, whose efforts had been so unproductive in the preceding years. On the question of whether the islanders should be enslaved, the Catholic monarchs upheld the cautious doctrines of Pope Eugenius and the missionaries. In 1477, their liberation of "certain Canarians who are Christians and others who are on the road to conversion" on the grounds that "it would be a source of bad example and give cause why none should wish to be converted," may be compared with the aim expressed by Eugenius forty-three years previously when he spoke of the danger of pagans being deterred from joining the faith. No doubt the monarchs' attitude was not uncoloured by the exigencies of power: enslavement would have involved a change in the natives' status from royal vassals to personal chattels, whereas the monarchs' aim was as far as possible to exclude intermediate lordship from the institutions by which they ruled their monarchy (or at least to limit it where it existed already). In this respect, their ordinances against enslavement of the Canary Islanders were motivated in a way akin to those by which they protected the Indians of the New World. Columbus's first plans for enslaving the Indians aroused the monarchs' immediate disapproval. "What does he think he is doing with my vassals?" Isabella is traditionally said to have asked. They commissioned a "junta of theologians" to examine the proposed enslavement, and when they pronounced unfavourably, ordered Fonseca to have the slaves liberated and their owners compensated. This was almost a re-enactment of their reaction to the enslavement of the Gomerans in 1489.

It was equally in the interests of extending their own power that the monarchs insisted on their right to make war against the savages. This was made clear by their attitude to the bulls of indulgence for the conversion of the Canarians, promulgated by Sixtus IV in 1478. The Pope, continuing the traditions of peaceful evangelization and apparently sharing the common opinion that to make war on the islanders was unlawful, designated the funds expressly for the conversion of the natives and the erection of religious houses. By an insidious abuse of language, however, the monarchs' writs on this subject described the bulls as "for the said conversion and conquest" or with equivalent phrases. Antonio Rumeu de Armas has recently shown that this early case of "double-think" caused a rift between the monarchs and some of their clergy, in which opponents of the use of violence actually attempted to suspend the collection of funds. At the end of the day, the success of the monarchs' policy brought their expansionist and evangelistic aims into perfect harmony: it would be but a short step now to Alexander VI's bulls [Document 27] on the New World, where the duty of evangelization would be seen as making the Castilian conquest just. This was an important moment in the elaboration of the canonistic doctrine of just war: conversion had never in itself been generally considered a sufficient pretext (though it had been advocated by individuals) up to that time.

In the remainder of the monarchs' reign one final development was still to come. Most clerics and religious continued to espouse exclusively peaceful methods of conversion. And Ferdinand and Isabella were not ill-disposed towards attempts along those lines, provided obedience to themselves was among the objects to which the missionaries sought to persuade their congregations: for instance, the mission of Fray Antón de Quesada, whom the monarchs dispatched to Tenerife in 1485, involved a brief both to convert the natives and reduce them to royal authority. Meanwhile, peaceful conversion revived in peninsular Spain when Granada was conquered and proselytization of the new community began. The tenacity of the pacific point of view about conversion during these wars led to the separation in doctrine of a war of conversion from a war waged in order to subject the heathen and so render by peaceful means possible conversion. This was not a point contrary to existing doctrines but merely a question which earlier jurists had left in doubt. Under this new doctrinal distinction, Ferdinand and Isabella were free to make war on the Indians and Canarians as on rebel subjects, theoretically without prejudice to the question of peaceful conversion. . . .

QUESTIONS

1. How did the Spanish shape their society around war?
2. What were the main aspects of the Christian Reconquest and Crusade against Iberia's Muslims?
3. Which lessons in conquest did the Christian kingdoms of Iberia learn in the twelfth century?
4. Sometimes it is maintained that Castile stumbled by luck into supporting Columbus. Why was Spain, based upon its history and location, a good candidate to carve out an overseas empire?
5. Locate the Canary Islands on a map.
6. What similarities would Columbus have noted between the islanders in the Canaries and in the Caribbean?
7. Why were black slaves brought to both the Canaries and the Caribbean?
8. What were the key elements in the varying policies of the monarchs toward the native peoples in each location?

Motivating Factors

Wonders of the Ocean Sea

Stories of the marvels and wonders to be found in distant parts of the world have always had an audience. This immensely popular travel guide was created by attaching a fanciful collection of tales about distant realms, culled from many sources, to a reasonably accurate account of a trip to the Holy Land. The vision of a world that one could circumnavigate given enough time certainly had its appeal to Columbus. Ordinary readers were more attracted by outrageous tales of life on Asian islands, like those of one-legged men who screen the sun by means of their broad foot (which might be a distorted memory of East Indians carrying parasols), or one-eyed giants taken right out of Homer's *Odyssey.*

> "*diverse folks,
> . . . of diverse
> manners and
> laws . . .*"

Sir John presents to his readers a magical world where anything is possible. The harassed European, encouraged to be chaste, limited to one marriage partner, kept in poverty by private property, and likely to regard women as subordinate to men, could find here less deprived lands. To his credulous audience, Sir John carried as much authority as Marco Polo (Document 11).

Despite the real wonder, after 1492, of an entire hemisphere being newly uncovered, people continued to look for tales like Sir John's. In Carlo Ginzburg's *The Cheese and the Worms: The Cosmos of a 16th Century Miller* (1980), old Menocchio talks about the intellectual ferment stirred in his acute mind by "having read that book of Mandeville about many kinds of races and different laws that sorely troubled me" (p. 42).

The first European arrivals in the New World spent time chasing after phantoms, such as the Golden Man *(El Dorado),* who was coated afresh every day with gold dust by his subjects. Columbus hoped to find the wealthy Seven Cities of Cíbola (allegedly founded by a Spanish monk who fled the Muslims) or at least locate the island of the Amazons, as evidenced in the second selection. He eagerly misinterprets gestures and half-understood words in the expectation that what he wants is around the next bend. The islanders were probably happy to tell Columbus anything to send him on his way. He alternated between belief and skepticism. An entry in his logbook, dated 9 January 1493, relates how he convinced himself that he saw three mermaids *(sirenas)* standing high out of the water: "They had faces something similar to those of human beings, but were not so handsome as it was customary to represent them." He had likely encountered manatees, tame sea cows that feed on herbs near shore.

Mandeville, *The Travels*

I John Mandeville, Knight although I be not worthy, that was born in England, in the town of St. Albans, and passed the sea in the year of our Lord Jesus Christ, 1322, in the day of St. Michael; and hitherto have been long time over the sea, and have seen and gone through many diverse lands, and many provinces and kingdoms and isles and have passed throughout Turkey, Armenia the little and the great; through Tartary, Persia, Syria, Arabia, Egypt the high and the low; through Lybia, Chaldea, and a great part of Ethiopia; through Amazonia, India the less and the more, a great part; and throughout many other Isles, that be about India; where dwell many diverse folks, and of diverse manners and laws, and of diverse shapes of men. . . .

Beside the land of Chaldea [Babylonia] is the land of Amazonia, that is the land of women. And in that realm is all women and no man; not, as some men say, that men may not live there, but for because that the women will not suffer no men among them to be their sovereigns. . . . And then they have loves that use them; and they dwell with them an eight days or ten, and then go home again. And if they have any male child they keep it a certain time, and then send it to the father when he can go alone and eat by himself; or else they slay it. And if it be a female they do away with one breast with an hot iron. And if it be a woman of great lineage they do away the left breast that they may the better bear a shield. And if it be a woman on foot they do away the right breast for to shoot with bow turkeys: for they shoot well with bows.

In that land they have a queen that governs all that land, and all they be obedient to her. And always they make her queen by election that is most worthy in arms; for they be right good warriors and brave, and wise, noble and worthy. And they go oftentime in soldiering to help other kings in their wars, for gold and silver as other soldiers do; and they maintain themselves right vigourously. This land of Amazonia is an isle, all surrounded with the sea save in two places, where be two entries. And beyond that water dwell the men that be their paramours and their loves, where they go to solace them when they will. . . .

There is another land, that is full great, that men call Lamary [Sumatra]. In that land is full great heat. And the custom there is such, that men and women go all naked. And they scorn when they see any strange folk going clothed. And they say, that God made Adam and Eve all naked, and that no man should be ashamed to show himself such as God made him, for nothing is foul that is of human nature. And they say that they that be clothed be folk of another world, or they be folk that believe not in God. And they say,

SOURCE From *The Travels of Sir John Mandeville* (1499 edition, from 1725 text), ed. A. W. Pollard (London: Macmillan & Co., 1900; reprinted New York: Dover Publications, Inc., 1964), pp. 5–131, passim. Text modernized. Reprinted by permission of Dover Publications, Inc.

that they believe in God that formed the world, and that made Adam and Eve and all other things. And they wed there no wives, for all the women there be common and they forsake no man. And they say they sin if they refuse any man; and so God commanded to Adam and Eve and to all that come of him, when he said, "Be fruitful and multiply and replenish the earth." And therefore may no man in that country say, This is my wife; nor no woman may say, This my husband. And when they have children, they may give them to what man they will that has companied with them. And also all the land is common; for all that a man holds one year, another man has it another year; and every man takes what part that he likes. And also all goods of the land be common, grains and all other things: for nothing there is kept in close, nor nothing there is under lock, and every man there takes what he will without any contradiction, and as rich is one man there as is another. . . .

But in that country there is a cursed custom, for they eat more gladly man's flesh than any other flesh; and yet is that country abundant of flesh, of fish, of grains, of gold and silver, and of all other goods. There go merchants and bring with them children to sell to them of the country, and they buy them. And if they be lean they feed them till they be fat, and then they eat them. And they say, that it is the best flesh and the sweetest of all the world. . . .

I say securely that a man might go all the world about, both above and beneath, and come again to his own country, so that he had his health, good shipping and good company, as I said before. And always he should find men, lands, isles and cities and towns, as are in their countries. For you know well that those men that dwell even under the Pole Antartic are foot against foot, to those that dwell even under the Pole Artic, as well as we and those men that dwell against us are foot against foot; and right so it is of other parts of the world. For that a part of the earth and of the sea has his contrary of things which are even against him. And you shall understand that, as I conjecture, the land of Prester John [see Document 9], emperor of India, is even under us. For if a man shall go from Scotland or England unto Jerusalem, he shall go always upward. For our land is the lowest part of the west and the land of Prester John is in the lowest part of the east. And they have day when we have night, and night when we have day. And, so much as a man ascends upward out of our countries to Jerusalem, so much shall he go downward to the land of Prester John; and the cause is for the earth and the sea are round.

For it is the common word that Jerusalem is in midst of the earth; and that may well be proved thus. For, and a man there take a spear and set it even in the earth at midday, when the day and the night are both alike long, it makes no shadow. And David also bears witness thereof, when he says, "God our king before the beginning of the word wrought health in midst of the earth." And therefore they that go out of our countries of the west toward Jerusalem, so many journeys as they make to go there upward, so

MACROBIUS, GLOBAL MAP (1483) *This is an example of "deductive" map making. A fifth-century Greek grammarian living in Rome created a model of what the earth should look like. He emphasized the need to keep to a theoretical symmetry by placing a landmass in the north and south of each hemisphere. Only the Eastern Hemisphere is shown because the other half of the map was dropped over the centuries. We still divide the globe as he did into two frigid, two temperate, and one hot equatorial zone, and continue to place north at the top. Columbus relied on the map for arguments in favor of his voyage. It seemed to demonstrate that it was possible to use the world ocean to pass from area to area, and that he was likely to find populated landmasses.*

many journeys shall they make to go into the land of Prester John downward from Jerusalem. And so he may go into those isles going round all the roundness of the earth and of the sea till he come even under us.

And therefore I have oft-times thought on a tale that I heard, when I was young, how a worthy man of our country went on a time for to see the world; and he passed India and many isles beyond India, where are more than five thousand isles, and he went so long by land and by sea, going round the world, that he found an isle where he heard men speak his own language. For he heard one drive beasts, saying to them such words as he heard men say to oxen in his own country going at the plough; of which he had great marvel, for he knew not how it might be. But I suppose he had so long went on land and on sea, going round the world, that he was come in to his own marches; and, if he had passed furthermore he should have come even to his own country.

Columbus's Letter About the First Voyage

In these islands I have so far found no human monstrosities, as many expected, but on the contrary the whole population is very well formed, nor are they negroes as in Guinea [Africa], but their hair is flowing and they are not born where there is intense force in the rays of the sun. . . .

As I have found no monsters, so I have had no report of any, except in an island "Quaris," which is the second at the coming into the Indies, and which is inhabited by a people who are regarded in all the islands as very fierce and who eat human flesh. They have many canoes with which they range through all the islands of India and pillage and take whatever they can. They are no more malformed than are the others, except that they have the custom of wearing their hair long like women, and they use bows and arrows of the same cane stems, with a small piece of wood at the end, owing to their lack of iron which they do not possess. They are ferocious among these other people who are cowardly to an excessive degree, but I make no more account of them than of the rest. These are they who have intercourse with the women of "Martinio," which is the first island met on the way from Spain to the Indies, in which there is not a man. These women engage in no feminine occupation, but use bows and arrows of cane, like those already mentioned, and they arm and protect themselves with plates of copper, of which they have much.

SOURCE Columbus's Letter to the Sovereigns on His First Voyage, 15 February–4 March 1493 in *Journals and Other Documents on the Life and Voyages of Christopher Columbus*, trans. and ed. S. E. Morison (New York: The Heritage Press, 1963), pp. 182–186, passim.

In another island, which they assure me is larger than Española [Hispaniola], the people have no hair. In it there is gold incalculable, and from it and from the other islands I bring with me Indians as evidence.

QUESTIONS

1. Why would an author make up a pseudo-travelbook filled with wild tales, and what would keep Europeans believing these stories for two centuries?
2. In what ways would the stories about the people of "Lamory" fulfil the deepest hopes of the common people and the greatest fears of the aristocratic and clerical elite?
3. Why would Columbus, having found no "monsters" in his first voyage, still expect to locate Amazons, cannibals, and hairless men on other islands?

The Craze for Spices

Spices once had many uses that are now unnecessary or forgotten. Today they hardly seem worth the effort once invested in crossing deserts by caravan or in spending months in leaky ships. Yet from a medical standpoint, they once performed an invaluable role similar to today's chemical drugs. Small amounts of the more exotic varieties, like opium, balm of mithridate, or lemnian earth, could cost a fortune, thus providing a powerful economic motive to get to the sources.

"the West sacrificed its precious metals for them [spices]."

During an age when fresh food was available only in the summer, spices preserved. They also enlivened dried foods and dreary "brewetts" of creamy sauced meat, poultry, or fish. Since starchy ingredients reduce the intensity of salt or spice, a large quantity was required. Cooks also threw handfuls of black pepper into dishes because that was the rage. Readers addicted to hot sauces for their tacos will understand.

Columbus was aware that the Portuguese had located a profitable pepper substitute called *malaguetta* in Africa. He hoped to use Castilian resources to beat the Portuguese to Asian spice islands for the real thing. The promise of gaining direct access to spice sources controlled by Arab intermediaries was a powerful argument that Columbus used during his negotiations with Ferdinand and Isabella. Over and over in his logbook, he mentions gold and spices as though they were of equal value. He brought along samples of spices, which he constantly and anxiously compared with whatever he culled from the islands. Upon his return, his enemies at court made much of his failure to bring back the expensive spices he had boasted that he would locate. Since the New World blocked Columbus's way to the Orient, Portugal won the race.

Culinary and Medicinal Uses

Pepper occupies a peculiar position in the history of food. An ordinary seasoning we are far from considering indispensable today, it was for many centuries associated with spice, the primary object of trade with the Levant. Everything depended on it, even the dreams of the fifteenth-century explorers. "As dear as pepper" was a common saying.

Europe had had a very old passion for pepper and spices—cinnamon, cloves, nutmeg and ginger. We must not be too quick to call it a mania. Islam, China and India shared the taste, and every society has its crazes for particular foods that become almost indispensable. They express the need to break the monotony of diet. A Hindu writer said: "When the palate revolts against the insipidness of rice boiled with no other ingredients, we dream of fat, salt and spices."

It is a fact that the poorest and most monotonous diets in underdeveloped countries today are those which most readily resort to spices. By spices we mean all types of seasoning in use in our period (including pimento, which came from America under many names) and not merely the glorious spices of the Levant. There were spices on the tables of the poor in Europe in the middle ages: thyme, marjoram, bay leaves, savory, aniseed, coriander and particularly garlic, which Arnaud de Villeneuve, a famous thirteenth-century doctor, called the peasants' theriac [snake bite antidote]. The only luxury product amongst these local spices was saffron. . . .

The West inherited spices and pepper from Rome. It is probable that both were later in short supply, in Charlemagne's time, when the Mediterranean was all but closed to Christianity. But compensation followed rapidly. In the twelfth century the craze for spices was in full swing. The West sacrificed its precious metals for them and engaged in the difficult Levant trade which meant travelling half-way round the world. The passion was so great that along with black and white pepper (both genuine peppers, the colour depending on whether or not the dark coating was left on) Westerners bought "long pepper," also from India, and a substitute product like the bogus pepper or *malaguetta* which came from the Guinea coast from the fifteenth century onwards. Ferdinand of Spain tried in vain to prevent the importing of cinnamon and pepper from Portugal (it meant letting silver out of the country in return) arguing that *"buena especia es el ajo"*—garlic is a perfectly good spice.

Cookery books show that the mania for spices affected everything: meat, fish, jam, soup, luxury drinks. Who would dare cook game without using "hot pepper," as Douet d'Arcy counselled as early as the beginning of the fourteenth century? The advice of *Le Ménagier de Paris* (1393) was to "put in the spices as late as possible." Its recipe for black pudding ran as follows: "take ginger, clove and a little pepper and crush together." In this booklet, *oille*, "a dish brought back from Spain" and consisting of a mixture of various meats, duck, partridge, pigeon, quail and chicken (to all appearances the popular *olla podrida* of today), also becomes a mixture of spices, "aromatic drugs," eastern or otherwise, nutmeg, pepper, thyme, ginger and basil. Spices were also consumed in the form of preserved fruits and elaborate powders to treat any disease medicine might diagnose. They were all reputed "to drive off wind" and "favour the seed." In the West Indies, black pepper was often replaced by red pepper, "axi or chili," which was so liberally sprinkled over meat that new arrivals could not swallow a mouthful.

In fact there was nothing in common between this spice-orgy and the late and moderate consumption known to the Roman world. It is true that the Romans ate little meat (even in Cicero's time it was the object of sumptuary laws). The medieval West, on the other hand, was carnivorous. We might assume that the badly preserved and not always tender meat cried out for the seasoning of strong peppers and spicy sauces, which disguised its poor quality. Some doctors argue today that the sense of smell has some curious psychological features. They claim that there is a sort of mutual exclusion between the taste for seasonings "with a bitter smell, like garlic and onion . . . and the taste for more delicate seasonings with sweet and aromatic smells, reminiscent of the scent of flowers." In the middle ages, the former may have predominated.

Things were probably not so simple. In any case consumption of spice increased in the sixteenth century (until then, it had been a great luxury) with the sharp rise in deliveries following Vasco da Gama's voyage. The increase was particularly marked in the north, where purchases of spices far exceeded those in the Mediterranean regions. The spice-market shifted from Venice and its *Fondaco dei Tedeschi* [a center for German merchants] to Antwerp (with a short sojourn at Lisbon) and then to Amsterdam, so the trade was not governed by simple considerations of commerce and navigation. Luther, who exaggerated, claimed that there was more spice than grain in Germany. The large consumers were in the north and east. In Holland, in 1697, it was thought that after coin, the best merchandise "for cold countries" was spice, consumed "in prodigious quantities" in Russia and Poland. Perhaps pepper and spices were more sought after in places where they had been late arrivals and were still a new luxury. When Abbé Mably reached Cracow he was served with wine from Hungary and "a very plentiful meal which might have been very good if the Russians and the Confederates had destroyed all those aromatic herbs used in such quantities here, like the cinnamon and nutmeg that poison travellers in Germany." It would seem therefore that in eastern Europe the taste for strong seasoning and spices was still medieval in style at that date, while the ancient culinary customs were to some extent disappearing in the West. But this is conjecture and not fact.

It seems at any rate that when spices began to fall in price and to appear on all tables, so that they were no longer a symbol of wealth and luxury, they were used less and their prestige declined. Or so a cookery book of 1651 (by François-Pierre de La Varenne) would suggest, as does Boileau's satire (1665) ridiculing the misuse of spices.

As soon as the Dutch reached the Indian Ocean and the Indian Archipelago they did their utmost to restore and then maintain for their own profit the monopoly in pepper and spices against the Portuguese (whose trade was gradually eliminated) and soon against English competition and later French and Danish. They also tried to control supplies to China, Japan, Bengal and Persia, and were able to compensate for a slack period in Europe by a sharp rise in their trade with Asia. The quantities of pepper reaching Europe via Amsterdam (and outside its market) probably increased, at least until the middle of the seventeenth century, and then were maintained at a high level. Annual arrivals in about 1600 before the Dutch success were possibly of the order of 20,000 present-day quintals [one quintal = 101.42 pounds], hence an annual quota of 20 grams per inhabitant for 100 million Europeans. Consumption may well have been of the order of 50,000 quintals in about 1680, more than double the figure at the time of the Portuguese monopoly. The sales of the *Oost Indische Companie* [a Dutch East India Company] from 1715 to 1732 suggest that a limit was reached. What is certain is that pepper ceased being the dominant spice-trade commodity it was in the days of Priuli and Sanudo and the undisputed supremacy of Venice. Pepper still held first place in the trade of the Company in Amsterdam in 1648–1650 (33% of the total). It fell to fourth in 1778–1780 (11%) after textiles (silk and cotton, 32.66%), spices (24.43%) and tea and coffee (22.92%). Was this a typical case of the ending of a luxury consumption and the beginning of a general one? Or the decline of excessive use?

For this decline the popularity of new luxuries—coffee, chocolate, alcohol and tobacco—can legitimately be blamed; perhaps also the spread of new vegetables which gradually began to vary Western diet (asparagus, spinach, lettuce, artichokes, peas, green beans, cauliflower, tomatoes, pimentoes, melons). These vegetables were mostly the product of European, and especially Italian, gardens. (Charles VIII brought the melon back from Italy.) Some, like the cantaloupe, came from Armenia, others, like the tomato, haricot bean and potato, from America.

One last but rather unconvincing explanation remains. A general decrease in meat consumption took place after 1600 or even earlier, which meant a break with former diet. Concurrently the rich adopted a simpler style of cooking, in France at least. German and Polish cooking may have been behindhand and have also had better supplies of meat and therefore a greater need for pepper and spices. But this explanation is only conjectural and those given before will have to satisfy us until fuller information is available.

Columbus's Logbook, 1492

Friday 19 October 1492

It is an island [Crooked Island] of many very green and very large trees. And this land is higher than the other islands found, and there are on it some small heights; not that they can be called mountains, but they are things that beautify the rest; and it seems to have much water. There in the middle of the island, from this part northeast, it forms a great bight [cove] and there are many wooded places, very thick and of very large extent. I tried to go there to anchor in it so as to go ashore and see so much beauty; but the bottom was shoal and I could not anchor except far from land and the wind was very good for going to this cape where I am anchored now, to which I gave the name Cabo Hermoso, because such it is. And so I did not anchor in that bight and also because I saw this cape from there, so green and so beautiful; and likewise are all the other things and lands of these islands, so that I do not know where to go first; nor do my eyes grow tired of seeing such beautiful verdure and so different from ours. And I even believe that there are among them many plants and many trees which in Spain are valued for dyes and for medicinal spices; but I am not acquainted with them, which gives me much sorrow. And when I arrived here at this cape the smell of the flowers or trees that came from land was so good and soft that it was the sweetest thing in the world. . . .

Sunday 21 October 1492

. . . Here there are some big lakes and over and around them the groves are marvelous. And here and in all of the island the groves are all green and the verdure like that in April in Andalusia [the south of Spain]. And the singing of the small birds [is so marvelous] that it seems that a man would never want to leave this place. And [there are] flocks of parrots that obscure the sun; and birds of so many kinds and sizes, and so different from ours, that it is a marvel. And also there are trees of a thousand kinds and all [with] their own kinds of fruit and all smell so that it is a marvel. I am the most sorrowful man in the world, not being acquainted with them. Because I am quite certain that all of them are things of value; and I am bringing samples of them, and likewise of the plants. . . .

SOURCE The Diario of Christopher Columbus's First Voyage to America 1492–1493, abstr. Fray Bartolomé de Las Casas, trans. Oliver Dunn and J. E. Kelley, Jr. (Norman: University of Oklahoma Press, 1989), pp. 99–111, passim. Footnotes removed. Reprinted by permission.

I should like to leave today for the island of Cuba, which I believe must be Cipango [Japan] according to the indications that these people give of its size and wealth, and I will not delay here any longer nor . . . around this island in order to go to the town, as I had decided [to do], in order to talk to this king or lord. [This] is so as not to delay much, since I see that here there is no gold mine, and that to go around these islands there is need of many kinds of wind, and the wind does not blow just as men would wish. And since one should go where there is large-scale commerce, I say that there is no reason to delay but [reason] to go forward and investigate much territory until we encounter a very profitable land; although my understanding is that this land may be very profitable in spices. But that I do not recognize them burdens me with the greatest sorrow in the world; for I see a thousand kinds of trees, each of which has its own kind of fruit, and they are green now as in Spain in the months of May and June; and there are a thousand kinds of plants, and the same with flowers and of everything. Nothing was recognized except this aloe, of which today I also ordered a lot brought to the ship to take to Your Highnesses. . . .

Searching for Gold

Europe faced a constant drain of its precious metals through the luxury trade with Asia, via a host of middlemen. Rulers did what they could to keep a supply on hand for internal trade, but the draw of eastern goods was too great. As economies slowly recovered during the fifteenth century, the pressure grew to find new sources of the metals. The silver mines of Central Europe flourished from 1470–1540, while some gold was drawn by panning rivers. Portuguese voyages to West Africa managed to get directly into coastal contact with the caravan trade to the Bambus, the gold-mining center of the Sudan. Silver circulates in a slow-moving economy; gold is the currency for an expanding economy. As population increased and trade expanded, Europe experienced a gold famine.

> *"who has gold has a treasure with which he gets what he wants"*

Columbus had to justify his expeditions by locating valuable goods, in particular gold. A theory of the day postulated a relationship between the closeness of the sun and the location of deposits. This fixed idea drove Columbus ever southward toward the equator on his voyages. In 1492 he could not locate the enormous mines he was sure were close at hand, or at least on the next island. Beginning with his second voyage in 1493, he set islanders to panning grains of gold from their rivers. Every three months, each native fourteen years or older had to bring to the forts a small bell filled with gold dust. In exchange, they had hung around their necks a copper token, stamped with the date. Anyone caught without an updated token had his or her hands cut off as punishment.

In the first selection, a letter discussing his fourth voyage (1502–1504), an aged and exhausted Columbus rambles in a deluded way that the mines of Veragua (today's Panama) are those of the biblical King Solomon. His reference to bringing souls to paradise refers to Catholic doctrine, which claims that the charitable purchase of a certificate of indulgence shortens the time a tormented soul is delayed in purgatory, an unpleasant stopping point before entering heaven.

The author of the second selection, José de Acosta, was a Spanish Jesuit missionary who saw the gold mines of Mexico and the mountain of silver at Potosí, Bolivia, which is still being worked. His discussion exemplifies the fanciful view of the day concerning where precious metals were to be found, along with a reasonable description of how the extraction process worked. Imbedded in the writing is his sense of the deep fascination gold had, and has, for Europeans.

Amerindians were confused about this passion for gold as an object of desire in itself, since it was not their medium of exchange. An Aztec sneered: "as if they were monkeys, the Spanish lifted up the gold banners and gold necklaces. . . . Like hungry pigs they craved that gold, swinging the banners of gold from side to side."

Columbus's Letter About the Fourth Voyage, 1502–1504

When I discovered the Indies, I said they were the world's wealthiest realm. I spoke of gold, pearls, precious stones, spices and of the markets and fairs. But, because not everything turned up at once, I was vilified. . . .

The Genoese, the Venetians and everyone who has pearls, precious stones and other things of value, they all carry them to the ends of the earth to barter and convert into gold. O, most excellent gold! Who has gold has a treasure with which he gets what he wants, imposes his will on the world, and even helps souls to paradise. When the lords of these lands in the region of Veragua [Panama] die, they bury their gold with the corpse, so they say.

SOURCE Columbus's *Lettera Rarissima* to the Sovereigns, 7 July 1503 in *Journals and Other Documents on the Life and Voyages of Christopher Columbus*, trans. and ed. S. E. Morison (New York: The Heritage Press, 1963), pp. 382–383, passim. Reprinted by permission.

On one voyage 674 quintals [one quintal = 101.42 lbs] of gold were brought to Solomon, besides what the merchants and mariners took, and what was paid in Arabia. From this gold he made 200 lances and 300 shields, and he made the canopy which was to be above them of gold plates embellished by precious stones. He made many other objects out of gold, and many huge vessels richly embellished with precious stones. Josephus [ancient Jewish author] mentions this in his history, *de Antiquitatibus.* The matter is also described in Chronicles and in the Book of Kings [Bible]. Josephus says that this gold was obtained in Aurea [in East Africa]. If so, I declare that those mines of the Aurea are but a part of these in Veragua, which extend westward 20 days' journey and are at the same distance from the pole and the equator. Solomon bought all that gold, precious stones and silver; and you can give orders to collect it if you see fit.

Acosta

Gold, silver, and metals grow naturally in land that is barren and unfruitful. And we see, that in lands of good temperature, the which are fertile with grass and fruits, there are seldom found any mines; for that Nature is contented to give them vigor to bring forth fruits more necessary for the preservation and maintenance of the life of beasts and men. And contrariwise to lands that are very rough, dry, and barren (as in the highest mountains and inaccessible rocks of a rough temper) they find mines of silver, of quick-silver, and of gold; and all those riches (which come into Spain since the West Indies were discovered) have been drawn out of such places which are rough and full, bare and fruitless: yet the taste of this money makes these places pleasing and agreeable, well inhabited with numbers of people. . . .

We find not that the Indians in former times used gold, silver, or any other metal for money, and for the price of things, but only for ornament, . . . whereof there was great quantity in their temples, palaces, and tombs, with a thousand kinds of vessels of gold and silver, which they had. They used no gold nor silver to traffic or buy but did change and sell one thing for another, as Homer and Pliny report of the Ancients. They had some other things of greater esteem which went current amongst them for price, and instead of coins; and unto this day this custom continues amongst the Indians, as in the Provinces of Mexico, instead of money they use cacao, which is a small fruit, and therewith buy what they will. In Peru they use coca to the same end, the which is a leaf the Indians esteem much, as in Paraguay, they have stamps of iron for coin, and cotton woven in Santa Cruz de la Sierra. Finally, the manner of the Indians traffic, and their buying and selling, was to

SOURCE José de Acosta, *The Natural and Moral History of the Indies* [1590], trans. Edward Grimston (London, 1604). Book IV, Chs. 3–4. English modernized.

exchange, and give things for things: and although there were great marts and famous fairs, yet had they no need of money, nor of brokers, for that every one had learned what he was to give in exchange for every kind of merchandise. . . .

Gold amongst other metals has been always held the most excellent, and with reason, being the most durable and incorruptible of all others; for fire which consumes and diminishes the rest amends it, and brings it to perfection. Gold which has often passed through the fire, keeps his color, and is most fine and pure. . . . And although his substance and body be firm and solid, yet does it yield and bow wonderfully; the beaters and drawers of gold know well the force it has to be drawn out without breaking. All which things well considered, with other excellent properties, will give men of Judgment to understand, wherefor the Holy Scripture do compare Charity to

TAKING REVENGE *This woodcut illustrates a book of travels to the New World by an Italian adventurer. In one passage of his history, he gleefully recounts how a group of mainland natives, driven to distraction by the pressure on them to find gold for the Spanish, wreaked vengeance on their tormentors by pouring molten gold down their throats. The story is probably too fine an example of poetic justice to be true. The illustration is of ethnographic interest, however, because it accurately shows an aspect of male costume.*

gold. To conclude, there is little need to relate the excellencies thereof to make it more desirable. For the greatest excellency it has, is to be known, as it is, amongst men, for the supreme power and greatness of the world.

Coming therefore to our subject; at the Indies there is great abundance of this metal, and it is well known by approved histories that the Incas of Peru did not content themselves with great and small vessels of gold, as pots, cups, goblets, and flagons; with bowls or great vessels, but they had chairs also and litters of massive gold, and in their temples they had set up many Images of pure gold, whereof they find some yet at Mexico, but not such store as when the first Conquerors came into the one and the other kingdom, who found great treasure, and without doubt there was much more hidden in the earth by the Indians. It would seem ridiculous to report that they have made their horse shoes of silver for want of iron, and that they have paid three hundred crowns for a bottle of wine, and other strange things; and yet in truth this has come to pass, yes and greater matters. They draw gold in those parts after three sorts, or at the least, I have seen all three used. For either they find gold in grains, in powder, or in stone. They do call gold in grains, small morsels of gold, which they find whole, without mixture of any other metal, which hath no need of melting or refining in the fire: and they call them pippins, for that commonly they are like pippins, or seeds of melons. . . . There is another kind which the Indians call *papas* [potatoes] and sometimes they find pieces very fine and pure, like to small round roots, the which is rare in that metal, but usual in gold. They find little of this gold in pippin, in respect of the other kinds. Gold in stone is a vein of gold that grows or ingendereth within the stone or flint, as I have seen in the mines of Saruma, within the government of Salinas [Ecuador], very great stones pierced and intermixed with gold; others that were half gold, and half stone. The gold which grow in this manner is found in pits or mines, which have veins like silver mines, but it is very hard to draw it forth . . . .

The most famous gold is that of Carabaya in Peru, and of Valdivia in Chile, for that it rise with his alloy and perfection, which is twenty-three carats and a half, and sometimes more. They make account likewise of the gold of Veragua [Panama] to be very fine. They bring much gold to Mexico from the Philippines, and China, but commonly it is weak, and of base alloy. Gold is commonly found mixed with silver or with copper, but that which is mixed with silver is commonly of fewer carats than that which is mixed with copper. If there be a fifth part of silver . . . it is then properly called Electrum, which has the property to shine more at the light of the fire than fine gold or fine silver. That which is incorporated with copper, is commonly of a higher value. They refine powdered gold in basins, washing it in many waters until the sand falls from it, and the gold, as most heavy, remains in the bottom. They refine it likewise with quick-silver and strong water, for . . . this water has the virtue to separate gold from dross, or from other metals. After it is purified and molten, they make bricks or small bars to carry it to Spain for being in powder they cannot transport it from the Indies, for they can neither custom it, mark it, nor take assay, until it is melted down. . . .

Today the great treasure of Spain comes from the Indies, because God has appointed the one realm to serve the other by giving up its wealth so as to be under good governance, thus mutually enjoying one another's goods and privileges.

Questions

1. What roles did spices play in the lives of Europeans during the Medieval and Renaissance eras?
2. What made spices so expensive by the time they reached the user?
3. How many unlabeled spices can you recognize out of their containers?
4. Columbus seemed to be confused by the vegetation he found on the islands. What could he have expected to see if he were really in Asia?
5. Why were Europeans so anxious to find gold?
6. In what type of terrain did sixteenth-century explorers expect to find precious metals?
7. Why, according to Acosta, does Spain have the right and the duty to take all the gold and silver from the New World?
8. Where, according to Columbus, did the biblical King Solomon get his gold?

The Short Route to Asia

The Search for Japan

The Polos were an important merchant dynasty in Venice, where commerce was compatible with aristocratic status, unlike the rest of Europe. Marco's father Niccolò, and uncle Maffeo, left him home while they traveled to the court of the Mongol emperor of Cathay (China). After returning with a letter from the great Khan to the pope asking that holy men be sent to teach the Mongols about Christianity, they set out again during 1271 in the company of friars. Marco, who was fifteen at the time, would not be able to return for twenty-three years. Shortly after his homecoming, Marco was caught in the crossfire of a war between Venice and Genoa. While in a Genoese jail for three years, he met a literary man to whom he dictated from memory an accurate account of his astonishing travels, which are excerpted in the first selection.

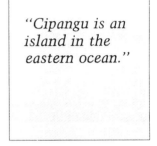

"Cipangu is an island in the eastern ocean."

The Mongol dominions, formed shortly before the Polos set out, stretched from the China Sea to the Crimea. This made it possible for merchants to travel long distances safely. Although Marco never visited Cipangu, it loomed large when he was at the imperial court, because Kublai, the emperor, made two attempts to conquer it. *Cipangu* or *Zipangu* were European adaptations of the Chinese *Jin-pen-kwé*, derived in turn from the islanders' *Nippon* ("land of the rising sun"). Possibly *Japan* is our variant of the Malay form, *Japún*.

By the time Columbus read the *Travels* in one of the first printed copies, the Mongol empire had long since disintegrated. This was not known to him or to anyone else in Europe. His trust in the book as a guide was rather like consulting the original Bell telephone directory to look up someone in Los Angeles.

Paolo Toscanelli was at the center of a group of Florentine humanist scholars deeply interested in geographic investigation. They commissioned maps, on which they speculated that far to the west of Ireland lay uncharted islands, which they denominated the Antilles, after a classical reference. Toscanelli accepted Marco Polo's estimate that the Asian mainland extended much farther east than previously thought, and that Japan lay another 1,500 miles out to sea. At that time, the circumference of the globe was believed to be 25,000 miles. By deciding that the globe's circumference was approximately 20,000 miles (a less accurate figure) Toscanelli concluded that only 2,500 miles of Atlantic sailing would take a ship from Spain to Japan.

Much is known about Toscanelli, but every aspect of his presumed corre-spondence with Columbus, reprinted in its entirety as the second selection, has been called into question. One view is that Columbus wrote to the old scholar, who was willing to help him but did not bother to draw up a fresh letter, and so sent along a copy of an earlier one he had prepared for Fernam Martins to transmit to the king of Portugal. Both Columbus and Toscanelli were knowledgeable about the spice trade, the former as an associate of Genoese groups, and the latter as a member of his family's firm. A second possibility is that Columbus found the detailed letter, and perhaps a sea chart, in the king's files, made a copy to further his ambitions in Castile, and concocted the rest of the correspondence to explain how he came into pos-session of the information. The third possibility is that all the material was forged by an unknown person for unclear reasons.

This is the sort of fascinating problem that may never be solved, but every biographer feels an urge to try it. If the letters are not fabrications, the material they incorporate from Marco Polo, their encouragement to sail west, and the chart showing islands in the Ocean Sea (possibly the one mentioned in his logbook, Document 15) help to explain Columbus's ability to sway influential persons whom he took into his confidence.

When news of the first voyage reached Italy, knowledgeable observers in Florence and Genoa decided Columbus had done little more than reach mid-Atlantic islands. Columbus had no doubt, however, that he was in eastern waters, a delusion that can be noted in the third selection, which is drawn from entries in his logbook.

Marco Polo

Cipangu [Japan] is an island in the eastern ocean . . . of considerable size; its inhabitants have fair complexions, are well made, and are civilized in their manners. Their religion is the worship of idols. They are independent of every foreign power, and governed only by their own kings. They have gold in the greatest abundance, its sources being inexhaustible, but as the king does not allow of its being exported, few merchants visit the country, nor is it frequented by much shipping from other parts. To this circumstance we are to attribute the extraordinary rich-ness of the sovereign's palace, according to what we are told by those who have access to the place. The entire roof is covered with a plating of gold, in the same manner as we cover houses, or more properly churches, with lead. The ceilings of the halls are of the same precious metal; many of the apart-ments have small tables of pure gold, of considerable thickness; and the windows also have golden ornaments. So vast, indeed, are the riches of the palace, that it is impossible to convey an idea of them. In this island there

SOURCE *The Travels of Marco Polo the Venetian*, ed. Thomas Wright (London: Henry G. Bohn, 1854), pp. 350–353, passim.

are pearls also, in large quantities, of a red (pink) colour, round in shape, and of great size, equal in value to, or even exceeding that of the white pearls. . . .

The reader should, however, be informed that the idolatrous inhabitants of these islands, when they seize the person of an enemy, who has not the means of effecting his ransom for money, invite to their house all their relations and friends, and putting their prisoner to death, dress and eat the body, in a convivial manner, asserting that human flesh surpasses every other in the excellence of its flavour. . . .

It is to be understood that the sea in which the island of Cipangu is situated is called the Sea of Chin [China Sea], and so extensive is this eastern sea, that according to the report of experienced pilots and mariners who frequent it, and to whom the truth must be known, it contains no fewer than seven thousand four hundred and forty islands, mostly inhabited. It is said that of the trees which grow in them, there are none that do not yield a fragrant smell. They produce many spices and drugs, particularly lignum-aloes and pepper, in great abundance, both white and black. It is impossible to estimate the value of the gold and other articles found in the islands; but their distance from the continent is so great, and the navigation attended with so much trouble and inconvenience, that the vessels engaged in the trade, from the ports of Zaiton and Quinsay, do not reap large profits, being obliged to consume a whole year in their voyage, sailing in the winter and returning in the summer. For in these regions only two winds prevail; one of them during the winter, and the other during the summer season; so that they must avail themselves of the one for the outward, and of the other for the homeward-bound voyage. These countries are far remote from the continent of India. In terming this sea the Sea of Chin, we must understand it, nevertheless, to be a part of the ocean; for as we speak of the English Sea, or of the Aegean Sea, so do the eastern people of the Sea of Chin and of the Indian Sea; whilst all of them are comprehended under the general term of the ocean. We shall here cease to treat further of these countries and islands, as well on account of their lying so far out of the way, as of my not having visited them personally, and of their not being under the dominion of the Grand Khan. . . .

The Toscanelli Letters

T o Christopher Columbus, [from] Paul, the physician, health:

I notice the splendid and lofty desire thou hast to journey whither grow the spices, and as answer to thy letter I send thee a copy of another letter I wrote some time back to a friend and servant of the Most Serene King of Portugal, before the wars of Castile, in reply to another which

SOURCE Spanish version in Las Casas, *História de las Indias*, vol. I, book 1, ch. 12, pp. 92–93; trans. Henry Vignaud, in *Toscanelli and Columbus* (London: Sands & Co., 1902), pp. 305–321, passim.

by command of H.H. [His Highness], he wrote me on the said matter, and I send thee another such chart for navigating as is the one I sent him, by which thou shalt be satisfied of thy request; which copy is the one following.

To Fernam Martins, Canon of Lisbon, Paul the physician sends greetings.

I have had pleasure in learning of the favour and condescension which you enjoy from your most liberal and most magnificent King, and though I have other ofttimes spoken of the very short route which there is hence to the Indies where the spices grow—a shorter sea-route than that which you take for Guinea [Africa]—you tell me that His Highness now demands of me a statement and ocular demonstration in order that the said route be understood and taken; and though I, for my part, know that I can show it him in the form of a globe (such as the world is), I have resolved—it being a simpler task and of easier comprehension—to show the said route on a map such as those made for navigating, and thus I send it to H.M. [Alfonso V] made and drawn by my hand: whereon is given all the extremity of the west, starting from Ireland southwards to the end of Guinea, with all the islands that are on this route, opposite which [islands] due west is the beginning of the Indies with the islands and places whither you can deviate by the equinoctial line, and for what distance—that is to say, in how many leagues you can reach those places most rich in all manner of spice, and of jewels, and of precious stones; and be not amazed if I call west [the place] where the spice grows, for it is commonly said that it grows in the east, yet who so steers west will always find the said parts in the west, and who so goes east overland will find the same parts in the east. . . .

The straight lines which are lengthwise on the said map show the distance that there is from west to east; the others which are crosswise show the distance from north to south. I have also given on the said map many places in the extent of India, whither one might go should there befall some mischance of storm or of head winds or any other hap that betided unforeseen, and also in order that all these parts may be well known, whereof you should much delight.

Know likewise that in all those islands there live and traffic none but merchants, bearing in mind that there is there as great an assemblage of vessels, sailors, merchants, and merchandise as in all the rest of the world, and in particular at a most superb port named Zaiton, where 100 huge vessels of pepper load and unload yearly, besides the other numerous vessels carrying the other spices.

This land is very populous, and in it are many provinces and many kingdoms and cities out of number beneath the sway of a Prince called [the] Great Khan [Mongol ruler of China], which name, in our vernacular, means King of Kings; whose abode is for the most time in the province of Cathay [China]. His predecessors wished greatly to hold intercourse and converse with Christians, and some two hundred years ago they sent to the Holy Father [praying] that he would send them many wise men and doctors who might teach them our faith, but those whom he sent returned on the road, because of obstacle[s]; and likewise to Pope Eugenius came an ambassador who related unto him the great friendship that they bear to Christians, and I have talked much with him of many things . . . .

And from the city of Lisbon, straight to the west, in the said map are 26 spaces, and in each one of them there are 250 miles as far as the most superb and mighty city of Quinsay, which has a circumference of 100 miles, which are 25 leagues, wherein are ten bridges of marble. The name of which city in our vernacular means City of Heaven; whereof are related marvels manifold concerning the dimensions of its manufactures and revenues (this space is almost the third part of the globe), which city is in the province of Mango, close to the city of Cathay, wherein the King mostly dwells, and from the island of Antilia—that which you call Seven Cities—whereof we have information, to the most superb city of Cipango [Japan], there are ten spaces, which are 2500 miles, that is to say 625 leagues, which island is exceeding rich in gold and pearls and precious stones.

Know that they cover the temples and royal dwellings with pure gold; thus the route being unknown, all these things are hidden, and one may go thither very safely. Many other things might be said, but as I have already spoken to you by word of mouth and you are of excellent thoughtfulness, I know that there is naught left for you to understand, and in so much I expatiate no more. And may this satisfy your demands so far as the shortness of time and my pursuits allow; and thus I remain most ready to satisfy and serve His Highness to such extent as he may command.

Done in the city of Florence on the 25 of June of the year 1474.

Columbus's Logbook, 1492

Sunday 21 October

. . . And afterwards I will leave for another very large island that I believe must be Cipango [Japan] according to the indications that these Indians that I have give me, and which they call Colba. In it they say there are many and very large ships and many traders. And from this island [I will go to] another which they call Bohío, which also they say is very big. And the others which are in between I will also see on the way; and, depending on whether I find a quantity of gold or spices, I will decide what I am to do. But I have already decided to go to the mainland and to the city of Quinsay [in Asia] and to give Your Highnesses' letters to the Grand Khan [Mongol ruler of China] and to ask for, and to come with, a reply.

Source *The Diario of Christopher Columbus's First Voyage to America 1492–1493,* abstr. Fray Bartolomé de Las Casas, trans. Oliver Dunn and J. E. Kelley, Jr. (Norman: University of Oklahoma Press, 1989), pp. 109–129, passim. Footnotes removed. Reprinted by permission.

Wednesday 24 October

Tonight at midnight I weighed anchors from the island of Isabela [Fortunate/ Crooked Islands], from the Cabo del Isleo, which is in the northern part, where I was staying, to go to the island of Cuba, which I heard from these people was very large and of great commerce and that there were there gold and spices and great ships and merchants; and they showed me that [sailing] to the west-southwest I would go to it. And I believe so, because I believe that it is so according to the signs that all the Indians of these islands and those that I have with me make (because I do not understand them through speech) [and] that it is the island of Cipango of which marvelous things are told. And in the spheres that I saw and in world maps it is in this region.

Friday 26 October

He went from the southern part of the said islands five or six leagues. It was all shoal. He anchored there. The Indians that he brought said that from the islands to Cuba was a journey of a day and a half in their dugouts, which are small vessels made of a single timber which do not carry sails. These are canoes. He left from there for Cuba, because from the signs that the Indians gave him of its size and of its gold and pearls he thought it must be it, that is, Cipango.

Sunday 28 October

While he was going toward land with the ships, two dugouts or canoes came out. And when they saw that the sailors were getting into the launch and were rowing to go look at the depth of the river in order to know where they should anchor, the canoes fled. The Indians said that in that island there were gold mines and pearls, and the Admiral saw a likely place for pearls and clams, which are a sign of them. And the Admiral understood that large ships from the Grand Khan came there and that from there to *tierra firme* [the mainland] was a journey of ten days. The Admiral named that river and harbor San Salvador.

Tuesday 30 October

He went out of the Rio de Mares to the northwest and, after he had gone 15 leagues, saw a cape full of palms and named it Cabo de Palmas. The Indians in the caravel *Pinta* said that behind that cape there was a river and that from the river to Cuba was a four-day journey. And the captain of the *Pinta* said that he understood that this Cuba was a city and that that land was a very big landmass that went far to the north, and that the king of that land was at war with the Grand Khan, whom they call *cami*, and his land or city, Faba, and many other names. The Admiral decided to go to that river and to send a present to the king of the land and to send him the letter of the sovereigns. And for this purpose he had a sailor who had gone on the same kind of mission in Guinea, and certain Indians from Guanahaní wished to go with him so that afterward they would be returned to their own land. In the opinion of the Admiral he was distant from the equinoctial line 42 degrees toward the northern side (if the text from which I took this is not corrupt). And he says that he must strive to go to the Grand Khan, whom he thought was somewhere around there, or to the city of Cathay [China], which belongs to the Grand Khan. For he says that it is very large, according to what he was told before he left Spain. All this land, he says, is low and beautiful, and the sea deep.

Thursday 1 November

. . . They all speak the same language and all are friends and I believe that all of these islanders are friends and that they wage war with the Grand Khan, whom they call *cavila* and the province, Basan. And they also go naked like the others. The Admiral [Columbus] says this. The river, he says, is very deep; and in the mouth, ships can be laid alongside the shore. Fresh water is short a league of reaching the mouth, and it is very fresh. And it is certain, the Admiral says, that this is *tierra firme* and that I am, he says, off Zayto [Zaiton, an Asian city] and Quinsay a hundred leagues more or less from the one and from the other; and well this is shown by the sea, which comes in a way other than the way it has until now. And yesterday when I was going to the northwest I found that it was cold.

Land Beyond Ireland

Pierre d'Ailly (Petrus Ailliacus), Cardinal of Cambrai, France, who wrote the *Imago Mundi (The Picture of the World)* in about 1414, intended his book to be a careful review of the academic geography known in his day. This is a very difficult selection to read because it refers to so many ancient authors, all tumbled together. He incorporated into his book an updated version of Ptolemy's *Geographia*, translated from the ancient Greek by the Arabs and thence into Latin. Ptolemy, writing about 130 A.D., had rejected the excellent estimate for the circumference of the globe made earlier, deciding instead upon a size about one-sixth too small. Further, he stretched China out far beyond its eastern limit.

> "the east and the west are near by, since a small sea separates them."

Reading the *Imago Mundi* encouraged Columbus to calculate the space from the Canary Islands to Japan at one-quarter the actual distance. Columbus's personal copy is heavily annotated, although scholars are uncertain if most of the notes date from before the first voyage, or after, when he was anxious to find information to bolster his belief that he had actually reached the Orient.

Columbus did not spend all his time in libraries looking for literary verification that the world was small and the distance to the Indies short. He spent time at wharves in Lisbon, and on the docks of Madeira and the Azores. The Portuguese sailors went far out into the sea to catch favorable winds for sailing to the coast of Africa, and to fish. They were familiar with the Sargasso Sea and its mid-Atlantic area of doldrums. Bold English fishermen were already working the vast schools near Newfoundland.

In the sixteenth century, when the Spanish crown was engaged in a lengthy lawsuit contesting the inheritance of the Admiral's family, a story useful to the crown's advocates surfaced about an unknown pilot who was blown off course, discovered the New World, and told Columbus about it just before he died. Ferdinand Columbus was anxious to discredit this story. In the biography he wrote, excerpted for the second selection, he presented his father's memories of hearing sailors' personal accounts and some secondhand stories told in taverns.

Imago Mundi

T he investigation into the quantity of the habitable earth demands that we should consider "habitability" from two angles. One has respect to the heaven; that is, how much of it can be inhabited on account of the Sun, and how much cannot. On this sufficient was said previously in a general way. From another angle it must be considered with respect to the water, i.e., how far the water is in the way. To this we now turn, and on it there are various opinions among the wise men. Ptolemy in his book *The Arrangement of the Sphere (Dispositione Spere)* would have almost a sixth part of the earth habitable because of the water. So also his *Algamestus*, in Book II, says that there is no known habitation except on one fourth of the earth, i.e., where we live; and that it extends lengthwise from east to west, the equator being in the middle. Its breadth is from the equator to the pole; and it is a fourth of the colurus [sphere]. Aristotle, however, in the close of his book on *The Heaven and the Earth* would have it that more than a fourth is inhabited. Averroes confirms this. Aristotle says that a small sea lies between the confines of Spain on the western side and the beginnings of India on the eastern side. He is not speaking of Hither Spain *(certeriori)* which in these times is commonly known as Spain, but of Farther Spain *(ulteriori)* which is now called Africa. On this topic certain authors have spoken, such as Pliny, Orosius, and Isidore. Moreover Seneca in the fifth book of the *Naturalium* holds that the sea is navigable in a few days if the wind is favorable. Pliny in the *Naturalibus* Book II informs us

SOURCE Petrus Ailliacus, *Imago Mundi*, trans. E. F. Keever (Wilmington, N.C., 1948).

that it has been navigated from the Arabian Sea to the Pillars of Hercules in rather a short time. From these and many other reckonings, on which I shall expand when I speak of the ocean, some apparently conclude that the sea is not so great that it can cover three quarters of the earth. Add to this the judgment of Esdras in his IV Book [Bible] where he says that six parts of the earth are inhabited and the seventh is covered with water. The authority of this book the Saints have held in reverence and by it have established sacred truths. . . .

There ought to be an abundance of water toward the poles of the earth because those regions are cold on account of their distance from the sun; and the cold accumulates moisture. Therefore the water runs down from one pole toward the other into the body of the sea and spreads out between the confines of Spain and the beginning of India, of no great width, in such a way that the beginning of India can be beyond the middle of the equinoctial circle and approach beneath the earth quite close to the coast of Spain. Likewise Aristotle and his commentator in the *Libro Coeli et Mundi* came to the same conclusion because there are so many elephants in those regions. Says Pliny: "Around Mt. Atlas elephants abound." So also in India and even in ulterior Spain there are great herds of elephants. But, reasons Aristotle, the elephants in both those places ought to show similar characteristics; if widely separated they would not have the same characteristics. Therefore he concludes those countries are close neighbors and that a small sea intervenes; and moreover that the sea covers three-quarters of the earth; that the beginnings of the east and the west are near by, since a small sea separates them.

Old Sailors' Tales

The Admiral [Columbus] . . . was impressed by the many fables and stories which he heard from various persons and sailors who traded to the western islands and seas of the Azores and Madeira. Since these stories served his design, he was careful to file them away in his memory. I shall tell them here in order to satisfy those who take delight in such curiosities.

A pilot of the Portuguese King, Martín Vicente by name, told him that on one occasion, finding himself four hundred and fifty leagues west of Cape St. Vincent, he fished out of the sea a piece of wood ingeniously carved, but not with iron. For this reason and because for many days the winds had blown from the west, he concluded this wood came from some islands to the west.

SOURCE From *The Life of the Admiral Christopher Columbus by His Son Ferdinand.* trans. and annotated by Benjamin Keen, 1959, pp. 24–27, passim. Reprinted by permission of the translator.

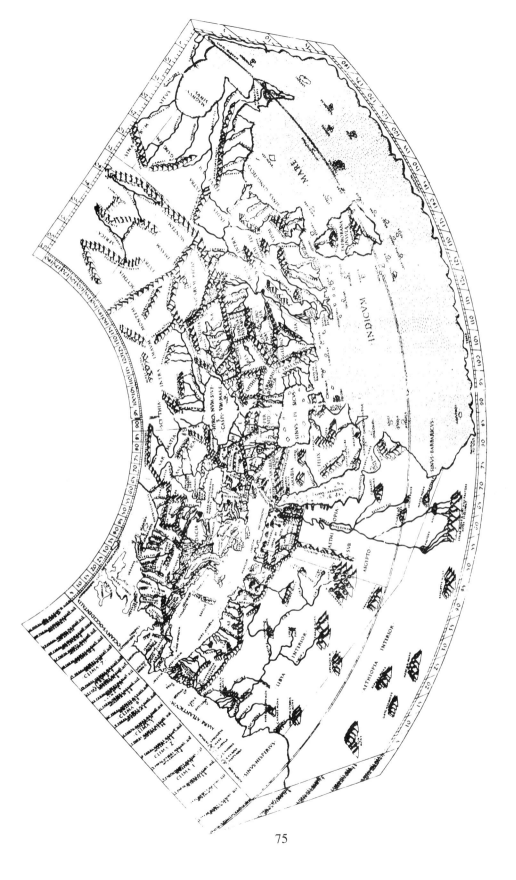

Pedro Correa, who was married to a sister of the Admiral's wife, told him that on the island of Pôrto Santo he had seen another piece of wood brought by the same wind, carved as well as the aforementioned one, and that canes had also drifted in, so thick that one joint held nine decanters of wine. He said that in conversation with the Portuguese King he had told him the same thing and had shown him the canes. Since such canes do not grow anywhere in our lands, he was sure that the wind had blown them from some neighboring islands or perhaps from India. Ptolemy [ancient Greek writer] in the first book of his *Geography*, Chapter 17, writes that such canes are found in the eastern parts of the Indies. Some persons in the Azores also told him that after the wind had blown for a long time from the west, the sea cast on the shores of those islands (especially of Graciosa and Fayal) pine trees that do not grow on those islands or anywhere in that region. On the island of Flores, which is one of the Azores, the sea flung ashore two dead bodies with broad faces and different in appearance from the Christians.

The Admiral also tells that in 1484 an inhabitant of the island of Madeira came to Portugal to ask the King for a caravel in order to discover some land which he swore he saw every year and always in the same situation; his story agreed with that of others who claimed to have seen it from an island of the Azores. On the basis of such stories, the charts and maps of ancient days showed certain islands in that region. . . .

One Diogo de Teive also went in search of that island. His pilot, Pedro de Velasco by name, a native of Palos de Moguer, told the Admiral in Santa María de la Rábida that they had departed from Fayal and sailed more than one hundred and fifty leagues to the southwest. On their return they discovered the island of Flores, to which they were guided by the many birds they saw flying in that direction; as they knew them to be land and not marine birds, they decided they must be flying to some resting place. Then they steered northeast until they reached Cape Clear at the western end of Ireland. Although they encountered very high westerly winds in this region, the sea remained calm. They decided this must be due to the fact that the sea was sheltered by some land on the west; but since it was already August and they feared the onset of winter, they gave up the search for that island. This happened forty years before the discovery of our Indies.

PTOLEMY, MAP OF KNOWN WORLD (1478) *Columbus owned and carefully studied this map (p. 75) originally created by a Greek scholar who lived in the second century* A.D. *It uses an innovative grid pattern to locate the inhabited area known to the ancient world. Even today the Earth is measured, as on this map, in 360° of longitude. This second printed version of the map did not take into account Portuguese voyages that proved the Indian Sea was not landlocked. East India is small, whereas the island of "Taprobana" (probably Sri Lanka) is very large. Indochina is roughly sketched, with China extending eastward beyond a "Great Gulf." Columbus was encouraged by this distortion to believe that Asia occupied vastly more of the globe than, in fact, it does.*

This story was confirmed to the Admiral by a one-eyed sailor in the port of Santa María, who told him that on a voyage he had made to Ireland he saw that land, which at the time he supposed to be a part of Tartary; that it turned westward (it must have been what is now called the Land of Cod); and that foul weather prevented them from approaching it. The Admiral says that this account agrees with one given him by Pedro de Velasco, a Galician, who told him in the city of Murcia in Castile that on a voyage to Ireland they sailed so far northwest that they saw land to the west of Ireland; this land, the Admiral thought, was the same that a certain Fernão Dulmo tried to discover. I relate this just as I found it told in my father's writings, that it may be known how from small matters some draw substance for great deeds.

QUESTIONS

1. What would make the island of Cipangu (Japan) worth visiting?
2. In what ways does the account of the kingdom of Cipangu fit the description offered by Prester John (Document 9) of his dominions?
3. What similarities are there between the account of customs in Cipangu and the description of "Lamory" by Sir John Mandeville (Document 6)?
4. How would Toscanelli's correspondence have enlightened Columbus?
5. How much knowledge of Marco Polo's book does Toscanelli demonstrate?
6. How did reading *Imago Mundi* encourage Columbus that by sailing west, he would reach Asia?
7. According to the ancient experts cited in the cardinal's book, what percentage of the earth might Columbus expect to be covered with water?
8. Analyze the common points in stories Columbus heard from sailors he met while in Portugal and its possessions.

Contact in
Meso-America

Premonitions

The Western Hemisphere was populated by a vast assortment of peoples with social organizations ranging from the rudimentary to the highly sophisticated. Few reasonable generalizations can be made for such a diverse group. Although several peoples are grouped together in this and the next reading to bring out similarities in the way they approached the coming of the Europeans, it is best to recall that they are vastly different in every other respect.

> *"everything shall become a desert because other men are coming to the earth."*

The Taínos of the island of Hispaniola, whose views are presented in the first selection, are discussed in the introductions to Documents 22 and 23. The people of Michoacán, later designated by the name Tarascan, spoke a language unrelated to their neighbors in Mesoamerica. These Tarascans, featured in the second selection, lived in Western Mexico around Lake Pátzcuaro. They were in independent kingdoms during pre-Hispanic times, until they were brought into a union during the fifteenth century by a line of aggressive leaders who fought off the Aztecs.

The background of the Aztecs is discussed in the introduction to Document 25. They believed that a legendary god, the Toltec chieftain Quetzal-cóatl, would return from out of the east to reclaim his dominion during a One-Reed year, which recurred every fifty-second year in the sacred calendar. The Aztec story is presented in the third selection. By a remarkable coincidence, the Spanish adventurer Cortés arrived on the coast in 1519, a One-Reed year. He thus may have had the preliminary advantage of cautious treatment by the Great Speaker Moctezuma.

Humans have lived in Peru since at least 8,000 B.C. Advanced cultures developed in different parts, but they were not unified until the Incas set out from Cuzco on a path of conquest, which in fifty years brought under their control the area of present-day Peru, Bolivia, northern Argentina, Chile, and Ecuador. The population was heavily concentrated in the high valleys between the mountain ranges and at a few locations on the Pacific coastal plains, near mountain streams. The prediction in the final selection, made by the last Inca who led an undivided realm, was as influential in its own way as the one in the Aztec reading.

Many Amerindian groups have in common these melancholy presentiments about the coming of the white man, but it is, of course, open to question if such defeatist sentiments came before or after the fact. Predictions created to suit events are a way to fit new phenomena into old patterns. If all was foretold, then the blow of the unexpected is softened and ancient ways rejustified.

The Taínos of Hispaniola

The natives of Hispaniola were much impressed by the arrival of the Spaniards. Formerly two *caciques* [chiefs], of whom one was the father of Guarionex, fasted for fifteen days in order to consult the *cemes* [images] about the future. This fast having disposed the *cemes* in their favour, they answered that within a few years a race of men wearing clothes would land in the island and would overthrow their religious rites and ceremonies, massacre their children, and make them slaves. This prophecy had been taken by the younger generation to apply to the cannibals; and thus whenever it became known that the cannibals had landed anywhere, the people took flight without even attempting any resistance. But when the Spaniards landed, the islanders then referred the prophecy to them, as being the people whose coming was announced. And in this they were not wrong, for they are all under the dominion of the Christians, and those who resisted have been killed. . . .

The Tarascan of Mexico

These people say that during the four years before the Spaniards came to the land, their temples were burned from top to bottom, that they closed them and they would be burned again, and that the rock walls fell as their temples were made of flagstones. They did not know the cause of this except that they held it to be an augury. Likewise, they saw two large comets in the sky and thought that their gods were to conquer or destroy a village and that they were to do it for them. These people imitate parts of their dreams and do as much of what they dreamed as they can. They report their dreams to the chief priest, who in turn conveys the information to the Cazonci [Chief Tzíntzícha Tangaxoan]. They say that the poor who bring in wood and sacrifice their ears dream about their gods who are reported as having told them that they would be given food and that they should marry such and such Christian girls. If this were a kind of omen they dared not tell it to the Cazonci.

SOURCE *De Orbe Novo. The Eight Decades of Peter Martyr D'Anghera*, trans. F. A. MacNutt (New York: G. P. Putnam's Sons, 1912), p. 176.

SOURCE *The Chronicles of Michoacán*, pp. 53–57, trans. and ed. by Eugene R. Craine and Reginald C. Reindorp. Copyright © 1970 by the University of Oklahoma Press.

A priest related that, before the Spaniards came, he had dreamed that people would come bringing strange animals which turned out to be the horses which he had not known. In this dream these people entered the houses of the chief priests and slept there with their horses. They also brought many chickens that soiled the temples. He said he dreamed this two or three times in considerable fear for he did not know what it was until the Spaniards came to this province. When the Spaniards reached the city, they lodged in the houses of the chief priests with their horses where they held their prayer and kept their vigil. Before the Spaniards arrived they [the Spaniards] all had smallpox and measles, from which large numbers of people died, along with many lords and high families. All the Spaniards of the time are unanimous in that this disease was general throughout New Spain, for which reason it is to be given credence. The people are in accord in that measles and smallpox were unknown until the Spaniards brought them to the land.

The priest also indicated that the priests of the mother of Cueraváperi [goddess of agriculture and fertility], who were in a village called Cinape-cuaro, had come to the father of the dead Cazonci and reported the following dream or revelation prophesying the destruction of the house of their gods, an event which actually happened in Ucareo: the lord of the village of Ucareo, whose name was Vigen [Vigel], had a concubine among his other women, and the Goddess Cueraváperi, mother of all the earthly gods, came and took that woman from her own house. These people say that all their gods frequently enter their houses and take people to be sacrificed to them. The goddess, without leaving the village, took the woman first a little way toward the road to Mexico City and then directed her to go out of the village on the road to Araro. Then putting the woman down the goddess untied a gourd dish shaped like a bowl, which was tied to her skirt, and after washing it in water, prepared a beverage made of water and something like a white seed. She gave this beverage to the woman who, upon drinking it, grew faint, and the goddess told her to walk on alone, saying: "I am not to take you; there is one, all dressed up, who is to take you; I shall neither harm you nor sacrifice you, nor will he who is to take you. You will be taken where there is a council and you will hear all that is said in that council. Then you shall report it all to the King Zangua [Zuangua], who is over all of us."

The woman walked along the road and soon met a white eagle, whistling and bristling his feathers, and with a great wart over large eyes which indicated that he was the God Curicaveri. The eagle greeted her, telling her that she was welcome, and she returned the greeting, saying, "Lord, may you have good fortune." The eagle replied, "Climb up on my wings and do not be afraid of falling." As soon as the woman was seated, the eagle, whistling, rose with her and took her through a forest where there was a spring heated by brimstone and as dawn was breaking placed her on the top of a very high mountain called Xanoatajacanzio [Xanoato Huacío]. . . .

To the woman it seemed that they were all in a very large house and the eagle told her to be seated and she would hear everything that was said.

By this time the sun had risen and the God Curitacaheri was washing his head with soap. He had removed his braid, but he usually wore a wreath of colors on his head, some wooden ear ornaments, miniature earthen jugs around his neck and was covered with a thin blanket. His brother, called Tiripanienquarencha, was with him and they looked very handsome. All the other gods greeted them and extended a welcome to which Curitacaheri replied: "Well, you have all arrived, be sure that no one has been forgotten or was not called." They replied that they were all present and they began asking among themselves, "Have the Gods of the Left Hand arrived too?" The answer was that all were present, and again Curitacaheri urged them to be sure that they had not forgotten to call someone. Once more they assured him that everyone was there. Then he said, "Let my brother tell you what has to be said, and I do not want to go into the house." Then spoke Tiripanienquarencha, saying: "Come close, you Gods of the Left Hand and of the Right. My brother has told me what to tell you. . . .

'You First-born Gods and you, Gods of the Left Hand, gird yourselves for suffering and let it be as it was determined by the gods. How can we contradict what has been established? We do not know what this is about. In fact, was it not decided and ordered in the beginning, that no two of us gods should be together before the light came so that we should not kill ourselves nor lose our deity? It was ordered then that the earth should become calm at once and make two revolutions; that they were to be thus forever, and this which all we gods had agreed upon was not to change before the light came.' Now, we do not know what these words are. The gods tried to contradict this change but under no circumstances were they allowed to speak. Let it be as the gods will it. You First-born Gods and you Gods of the Left Hand, go all of you to your houses and do not bring back that wine you have.

"Break all those jugs for it shall not be from here on as it has been up to now when we were very prosperous. Break all the wine tubs everywhere, leave off the sacrifice of men and bring no more offerings with you because from now on it is not to be that way. No more kettledrums are to be sounded, split them all asunder. There will be no more temples or fireplaces, nor will any more smoke rise, everything shall become a desert because other men are coming to the earth. They will spare no end of the earth, to the Left Hand and to the Right, and everywhere all the way to the edge of the sea and beyond. The singing will be all one for there will not be as many songs as we had but only one throughout the land. And you, woman, who are here pretending not to hear us, publish this and make it known to Zuangua the King, who is in charge of all of us." All the gods of the council replied, saying it would be so and began to wipe the tears from their eyes. The council broke up and that vision was seen no more.

The Aztec of Mexico

 hen night came and everyone was asleep the king [Moctezuma] went to a terrace on the roof. Having watched there until midnight

SOURCE Diego de Durán, *The Aztecs: The History of the Indies of New Spain*, trans. Doris Heyden and Fernanda Horcasitas (New York: Orion Press, 1964), pp. 247–271, passim. Footnotes eliminated.

he saw the comet appear with its brilliant tail, whereupon he was astonished. Then he remembered what Nezahualpilli had said, and he was so filled with fear that he thought his death would arrive within the hour.

The next day Moctezuma called in the priests, sorcerers, soothsayers, diviners and astrologers and consulted them, but they claimed that they had not seen any signs in the sky, for which the king had them jailed.

Then Moctezuma asked the king of Texcoco to tell him what it meant. "O lord," responded Nezahualpilli, "your vassals, the astrologers, soothsayers and diviners, have been careless! That sign in the heavens has been there for some time and yet you describe it to me now as if it were a new thing. I thought that you had already discovered it and that your astrologers had explained it to you. Since you now tell me you have seen it I will answer you that that brilliant star appeared in the heavens many days ago. It is an ill omen for our kingdoms; terrible, frightful things will come upon them. In all our lands and provinces there will be great calamities and misfortunes, not a thing will be left standing. Death will dominate the land! All our dominions will be lost and all of this will be done with the permission of the Lord of the Heights, of the Day and the Night and of the Wind. You will be witness to these things since it will all happen in your time. For as soon as I depart from the city of Mexico I go to die. You will never behold me again; this is the last visit in which we will see each other in this life. I long to hide, to flee from the labor and afflictions which await you. Do not be faint, do not feel anguish or despair! Make your heart wide, strengthen your spirit and manly chest against these predestined troubles!"

Moctezuma then wept bitterly, saying, "O Lord of All Created Things! O mighty gods who give life or death! Why have you decreed that many kings shall have reigned proudly but that my fate is to witness the unhappy destruction of Mexico? Why should I be the one to see the death of my wives and children and the loss of my powerful kingdoms and dominions and of all that the Aztecs have conquered with their mighty arms and strength of their chests? What shall I do? Where shall I hide? Where shall I conceal myself? Alas, if only I could turn into stone, wood, or some other earthly matter rather than suffer that which I so dread! But what can I do, O powerful monarch, but await that which you have predicted? For this reason I kiss your hands and thank you. Alas, I cannot at this moment become a bird in order to fly into the woods and hide in their depths." With these words, says the *Chronicle*, the two kings said farewell to each other with great sadness. . . .

Moctezuma was so disturbed that he was half desirous that the events which had been predicted take place immediately. In the midst of his preoccupation he called the chieftains of the wards, asking them if they had dreamed anything regarding the arrival of the strangers whose coming he so feared. He told them to reveal these dreams even though they might be contrary to his desires, since he wished to know the truth in this much-talked-of matter.

The heads of the wards told him that they had dreamed nothing nor had they seen or heard anything about this affair. He answered, "Then I beg you, my friends, to tell all the old men and women of the wards to inform me of whatever dreams they may have had, be they in my favor or against me. Also, tell the priests to reveal any visions they may see, such as ghosts or other phantoms that appear at night in the woods and dark places. Let them ask these apparitions about things to come. It will also be good to give this advice to those who wander about in the late hours; if they encounter the woman who roams the streets weeping and moaning, let them ask her why she weeps and moans."

Soon Moctezuma was notified that certain old people had dreamed strange things and they were brought before him. Said one old man, "Powerful lord, we do not wish to offend your ears or fill your heart with anxiety to make you ill. However, we are forced to obey you and we will describe our dreams to you. Know then, that these last nights the Lords of Sleep have shown us the temple of Huitzilopochtli [patron god of war] burning with frightful flames, the stones falling one by one until it was totally destroyed. We also saw Huitzilopochtli himself fallen, cast down upon the floor! This is what we have dreamed!"

Moctezuma then asked the old women and received the following answer, "My son, do not be troubled in your heart for what we are about to tell you, although it has frightened us much. In our dreams we, your mothers, saw a mighty river enter the doors of your royal palace, smashing the walls in its fury. It ripped up the walls from their foundation, carrying beams and stones with it until nothing was left standing. We saw it reach the temple and this too was demolished. We saw the great chieftains and lords filled with fright, abandoning the city and fleeing toward the hills. This is what we have dreamed!"

Moctezuma listened attentively to what the old men and women had described. When he saw that it was not in his favor but that it confirmed the earlier ill omens he ordered that the dreamers be cast in jail. There they were to be given food in small measures until they starved to death. After this no one wished to tell his dreams to Moctezuma. . . .

Moctezuma became even more worried and attempted to discover what kind of people had come to his land, their place of origin, lineage and, above all, whether they planned to return. For this reason he called Teoctlamacazqui and conversed with him in private. He said that he wanted to know more about those who had just departed and that he wished to have a painting made of them. He wished the picture to be drawn in his presence but said that it must be done secretly.

Teoctlamacazqui answered that he was willing to have this picture made, whereupon he ordered that the best artist of Mexico, an old man, be brought. Moctezuma told this man that he should not reveal anything that might happen, under pain of death. The painter was cowed, exclaiming that he was not a man to uncover secrets of such a great and mighty lord. His paints were brought to him and Teoctlamacazqui began to tell him what he should depict. The artist drew a picture of the ship in the way it had been seen, showing the Spaniards with their long beards and white faces. He painted their clothing in different colors, their hats upon their heads and their swords in their belts. When Moctezuma saw this he marveled and gazed upon the painting for a long time. Having looked, he said to Teoctlamacazqui, "Were these things as they have been painted here?" The answer was, "Yes, O lord, they are exactly so; I have not lied or added anything!"

Moctezuma paid the artist for his work, saying, "Brother, I beg you to answer me this question: by any chance do you know anything about what you have painted? Did your ancestors leave you a drawing or description of these men who were to arrive in this land?" The painter answered, "Powerful lord, I will not lie to you or deceive you—you are the image of the god. Therefore I will tell you that I and my ancestors never were occupied with any arts save those of painting pictures and other symbols. My ancestors were merely the artists of past kings and they depicted what they were ordered. Therefore, I know nothing of that which you ask me; if I tried to answer your question my answer would be a lie."

Moctezuma then ordered him to question the other artisans of his profession, asking if they possessed some picture coming down from their ancestors regarding those who might come to this land and possess it. The artist agreed to do so and for several days he inquired. But the painter was unable to find out anything certain and therefore returned to Moctezuma and told him that he had discovered nothing exact regarding these things. . . .

Moctezuma was about to call the painters of books from Xochimilco, but the noble Tlillancalqui Teoctlamacazqui said to him, "Powerful lord, do not tire yourself or waste time in questioning so many men. None of them will be able to tell you what you desire to know as clearly as an ancient man from Xochimilco whom I know well. His name is Quilaztli and he is well informed in all matters which concern ancient history and painted books. If you wish I will bring him to you; I will tell him what you wish to know and he will produce his antique paintings." The king thanked him, commanding him to bring the old man immediately. When the latter appeared he brought with him his painted manuscripts. He appeared before Moctezuma, Angry Lord, who received him well because he was a venerable old man and of fine appearance.

Said Quilaztli to the sovereign, "O mighty lord, if because I tell you the truth I am to die, nevertheless I am here in your presence and you may do what you wish to me!" Before showing him the papers, he narrated that mounted men would come to this land in a great wooden house. This structure was to lodge many men, serving them as a home; within it they would eat and sleep. On the surface of this house they would cook their food, walk and play as if they were on firm land. They were to be white, bearded men, dressed in different colors and on their heads they would wear round coverings. Other human beings were to arrive with them, mounted on beasts similar to deer and others on eagles which would fly like the wind. These men were to possess the country, settle in all its cities, multiply in great numbers and be owners of gold, silver and precious stones.

"So that you may see," continued Quilaztli, "that what I say is the truth, behold it drawn here! This painting was bequeathed to me by my ancestors." He then took out an ancient picture on which were depicted the ship and the men dressed in the same manner as those which the king already knew through his painting. There he also saw other men mounted on horses or on flying eagles, all of them dressed in different colors, wearing their hats and swords.

Moctezuma, seeing the similarity between what the old man described and what appeared upon his painting, almost lost his senses and began to weep and to show anguish. Uncovering his chest to the elder, he cried out, "O brother Quilaztli, I now see that your ancestors were verily wise and well informed. Only a few days ago the men that you have shown me on your painting arrived in this land from the east. They came in the wooden house that you have described, dressed in the same colors and manner that appear in your drawing. I will show you how I ordered that they be painted: behold them here! However, one thing consoles me; I have sent them a present and begged them to go away in peace. They have obeyed me, departed, and I doubt if they will return."

"It is possible, O mighty prince," exclaimed Quilaztli, "that they came and went away again! Listen to the words I will say to you, and if I lie I am willing to have you annihilate me, my children and my descendants! Behold, before two years have passed, or at the most three, the strangers will return to these lands. Their coming was meant only to find a convenient way to return. Even though they said to you that they were returning to their native country, do not believe them! They will not go that far but will turn back when they have gone half way!"

Three years later, when Moctezuma had almost forgotten these things, news came from the sea that a hill was moving to and fro upon the waters again.

The Incas of Peru

One day, as Huaina Capac [twelfth sovereign of Peru, 1493–1527] was coming out of a lake in which he had just bathed, near Quito, he was suddenly seized with a sensation of chill, which was followed by one of intense heat. His condition [smallpox from Europeans?] grew

SOURCE *The Incas. The Royal Commentaries of the Inca Garcilaso de la Vega, 1539–1616,* trans. Maria Jolas from French ed. by Alain Gheerbrant, intro. by Alain Gheerbrant (New York: The Orion Press, 1961), pp. 287–288.

worse and worse and, after a few days, he realized that the predictions concerning his death were about to come true.

Further signs had appeared in the sky, amongst which was a huge green comet; lightning had struck in his own house; and the *amautas* [philosophers] had for several years agreed with the soothsayers in predicting his approaching end which, according to what they said, would constitute the prelude to an avalanche of calamities from which neither the Empire nor the royal line of the Incas would be able to recover. And Huaina Capac knew all that, although these sinister predictions continued to be hidden from the people, out of fear lest the entire nation should pine away of despair.

The king, therefore, summoned his sons, his relatives, and all the governors and captains who could reach the palace in time, and he spoke to them as follows:

"Know ye," he said, "that the moment has come when I must go and rest beside our father the Sun. Already, a long time ago, he made it known to me that he would call me from a lake or from a river. The indisposition with which I was seized upon leaving the water is therefore a sign which I cannot mistake. When I am dead, cut my body open; take my heart and my entrails and bury them in the city of Quito that I have so dearly cherished; then take my body to Cuzco, to lie beside those of my forefathers. I commend to you my beloved son, Atahualpa. May he reign in my stead over the kingdom of Quito and over all the lands that he succeeds in conquering; and you, captains of my army, you shall serve him with the love and loyalty that you owe to your king; obey him in all things, because all that he will ask of you, it is I who shall have revealed it to him, on orders from our father the Sun."

These were the last words that Huaina Capac addressed to his sons and relatives. He then had all his other captains and *curacas* [officials] summoned, all those who were not of royal blood. After making the same recommendations to them, he concluded as follows:

"Our father the Sun disclosed to us a long time ago that we should be twelve Incas, his own sons, to reign on this earth; and that then, new, hitherto unknown people would arrive; that they would obtain victory and subject all of our kingdoms to their Empire, as well as many other lands. I think that the people who came recently by sea to our own shores are the ones referred to. They are strong, powerful men, who will outstrip you in everything. The reign of the twelve Incas ends with me. I can therefore certify to you that these people will return shortly after I shall have left you, and that they will accomplish what our father the Sun predicted they would: they will conquer our Empire, and they will become its only lords. I order you to obey and serve them, as one should serve those who are superior in every way; because their law will be better than ours, and their weapons will be more powerful and invincible than yours. Dwell in peace; my father the Sun is calling me, I shall go to rest at his side."

Initial Impressions

Unfortunately, no record survives telling what the Caribbean natives thought of Columbus and his men. No doubt it was something like later records of European contact with the New World. Aztec accounts of the fall of their empire were written as early as 1528, only seven years after the collapse. The shock and surprise expressed in the first selection may have given the invaders an initial advantage, although that did not last long. European technical superiority was not clear-cut because Cortés's men had few swords, pikes, or knives. His firearms numbered a mere thirteen muskets, four light cannon, and ten bronze cannon. Besides, the powder for these arms was damp most of the time. The Spanish did not lack adaptability, however; when their impressive iron suits proved a liability in the climate, they abandoned them in favor of the local quilted cotton armor.

> "they were very different from us, in face and costume, . . ."

The Aztec lords had made religion almost a private cult, excluding commoners. The high born were godlike, according to their rites, so it is not surprising that the same status was at first granted the Spanish. Since the principal Aztec deities were nourished by blood-letting ceremonies, it was logical for the emissaries to pour that sacred fluid over gift offerings of food, should the Spanish actually have turned out to be gods.

The Tarascan account in the second selection was compiled by a Franciscan about 1540, on the basis of earlier narratives. It gives an accurate sense of the complexity of the impressions made on the inhabitants of western Mexico by the Spanish. The text also demonstrates the natives' effort to locate parallels within their own lives that would help them make sense of the behavior of the newcomers.

The third selection presents the views of the Incas of Peru about the outsiders. It again points out the initial response by a native group that the white men might be gods. A fourteenth-century ruler had been encouraged in the major victory of Inca expansion by the god Viracochas, in whose name he then developed a cult. The Inca rulers were themselves treated as gods—children of the sun—so it was not unreasonable to think the foreigners, although obviously in the form of men, could in some sense be divine. They too were called Viracochas.

An Aztec Account

Seventh Chapter, in which is related the account by which the messengers who had gone to see the boats reported to Moctezuma.

And when this was done, they thereupon reported to Moctezuma; so they told him how they had gone marveling, and they showed him what [the Spaniards'] food was like.

And when he had so heard what the messengers reported, he was terrified, he was astounded. And much did he marvel at their food.

Especially did it cause him to faint away when he heard how the gun, at [the Spaniards'] command, discharged [the shot]; how it resounded as if it thundered when it went off. It indeed bereft one of strength; it shut off one's ears. And when it discharged, something like a round pebble came forth from within. Fire went showering forth; sparks went blazing forth. And its smoke smelled very foul; it had a fetid odor which verily wounded the head. And when [the shot] struck a mountain, it was as if it were destroyed, dissolved. And a tree was pulverized; it was as if it vanished; it was as if someone blew it away.

All iron was their war array. In iron they clothed themselves. With iron they covered their heads. Iron were their swords. Iron were their crossbows. Iron were their shields. Iron were their lances.

And those which bore them upon their backs, their deer [horses], were as tall as roof terraces.

And their bodies were everywhere covered; only their faces appeared. They were very white; they had chalky faces; they had yellow hair, though the hair of some was black. Long were their beards; they also were yellow. They were yellow-bearded. [The Negroes' hair] was kinky, it was curly.

And their food was like fasting food [ordinary human food]—very large, white; not heavy like [tortillas]; like maize stalks, good-tasting as if of maize stalk flour; a little sweet, a little honeyed. It was honeyed to eat; it was sweet to eat.

And their dogs were very large. They had ears folded over; great dragging jowls. They had fiery eyes—blazing eyes; they had yellow eyes—fiery yellow eyes. They had thin flanks—flanks with ribs showing. They had gaunt stomachs. They were very tall. They were nervous; they went about panting, with tongues hanging. They were spotted like ocelots; they were varicolored.

And when Moctezuma so heard, he was much terrified. It was as if he fainted away. His heart saddened; his heart failed him. . . .

Then at that time Moctezuma sent emissaries. He sent all evil men— soothsayers, magicians. And he sent the elders, the hardy [warriors], the brave [warriors] to secure [for the Spaniards] all the food they would need: turkey hens, eggs, white tortillas, and what they might desire. And in order that their hearts might be well satisfied, they were to look to them well. He sent captives so that they might be prepared: perchance [the Spaniards] would drink their blood. And thus did the messengers do.

But when [the Spaniards] beheld this, much were they nauseated. They spat; they closed their eyes tight, they shut their eyes; they shook their heads. And [the emissaries] had soaked the food in blood, they had covered it

Source Bernardino de Sahagún, *Florentine Codex: General History of the Things of New Spain,* trans. A. J. O. Anderson and C. E. Dibble (Salt Lake City: School of American Research and University of Utah, 1950–1982), *Book XIII: The Conquest of Mexico,* Chaps. XVI, XVII, XXIII, pp. 44–66. Reprinted by permission.

with blood. Much did it revolt them; it nauseated them. For strongly did it reek of blood.

And Moctezuma had acted thus because he thought them gods, he took them to be gods, he worshipped them as gods. They were called, they were named "gods come from heaven." . . .

A Tarascan Account

W hen the Indians first saw the Spaniards, they marveled at such strange people who did not eat the same kind of food or get drunk as the Indians did. They called the Spanish *Tucupacha*, which means gods, and *Teparacha*, which means big men and is also used to mean gods, and *Acacecha*, meaning people who wear caps and hats. As time passed they began to call them Christians and to believe that they had come from heaven. They were sure that the Spaniards' clothes were the skins of men such as the Indians themselves used on feast occasions. Some called the horses deer, others *tuycen*, which were something like horses which the Indians made from pigweed bread for use in the feast of *Cuingo* and to which they fastened manes of false hair. The Indians who first saw the horses told the *Cazonci* [Chief Tzíntzícha Tangaxoan] that the horses talked, that when the Spaniards were on horseback they told the horses where they were to go as they pulled on the reins. They also said that Mother Cueravaperi [goddess of agriculture and fertility] had given them the wheat, seeds, and wine they brought when they came to the land. When they saw the religious so poorly dressed, wearing their crowns and not wanting either gold or silver, they were astonished. Since the priests had no women, the Indians thought they were priests of a god who had come to the land and called them *Curitiecha* as they did their own priests who wore fiber wreaths on their heads and some false temples. They were amazed that the priests did not dress as the other Spaniards, and they said how fortunate are these who want nothing.

As time went by some of their priests and witches made the Indians believe that the religious were dead men, that the habits they wore were shrouds, that, in their houses at night they shed their forms, become skeletons, go to the Inferno where they have their women, and return by morning. This tale lasted a long time, until they began to understand more. The witches also said that the Spaniards did not die, that they were immortal, that the baptismal water which was sprinkled on their heads was blood, and that the Spaniards split open the heads of their children. For these reasons they dared not baptize their children for they did not want them to die. The Indians called the crosses Holy Mary, because they did not know the doctrine and they thought the crosses were gods like those they had.

When they were told that they were to go to heaven, they did not believe it, saying that they had never seen anyone go. They would not believe anything the religious told them nor did they trust them. They said the

SOURCE *The Chronicles of Michoacán*, pp. 87–89, trans. and ed. by Eugene R. Craine and Reginald C. Reindorp. Copyright © 1970 by the University of Oklahoma Press.

Spaniards were all as one and they were sure that the Monks had been born with their habits on and had never been children. These beliefs also were long lived and even now they still do not believe that the Monks had mothers. When the religious said mass, the Indians thought that they could see the present and the future by looking in the holy water. They did not trust those witches [Catholic priests] and would not tell the truth in confession for fear they would be killed. Should an Indian go to confession, all the others would spy on him to see how he did it, and the more so if it were a woman. Afterward they wanted to know what the priest had asked and said, and they told everyone all about it.

The Castilian women were called *Cuchahecha* which means ladies and goddesses. They thought that the letters which they were sent to deliver could talk so they dared not lie at any time. They marveled at every new thing they saw, for they are greatly interested in novelties. They called horseshoes "coats of mail" and "iron shoes" for horses. In Taxcala [Tlaxcala] they brought rations of chickens for the horses as well as for the Spaniards. They were astonished to hear what the priests preached to them and called them witches who knew everything they did at home, or they knew it because somebody told on them, or because they had confessed to them.

An Inca Account

They said they had seen beings quite different from us landing in their country, different as much by their conduct as by their clothing. They resembled the Viracochas [one of two chief deities], that name by which we referred, in times gone by, to the Creator of all things. Thus they named them, first because they were very different from us, in face and costume, second because they saw them riding on the backs of huge animals with silver feet (this from the sparks struck out by the iron shoes). Another reason was that they saw the strange beings converse with one another, silently, by means of pieces of white cloth, just as easily as one man speaks to another by word of mouth (this from their reading of letters and books). Then again, they called them Viracochas, because of their remarkable appearance. There were great differences of feature between them; some had black beards, some red. They saw them eat from silver plates. Furthermore, they possessed *Yllapas*, the name we give to thunderbolts (this was because of their armament, which they thought to be bolts from heaven).

SOURCE Titu Cusi Yupangui (Diego de Castro), *Relación de la Conquista del Perú y Hechos del Inca Manco II* [1570], *Colección de libros y documentos referentes a la Historia del Perú*, 1st series, vol. II, Lima, 1916, pp. 8–9, in Nathan Wachtel, *The Vision of the Vanquished. The Spanish Conquest of Peru Through Indian Eyes, 1530–1570* (New York: The Harvester Press, 1977), p. 45.

1. Locate the common themes in the various Amerindian premonitions or prophesies about the coming of the white man.
2. What were the principal signs, in atmospheric disturbances and in dreams, that something tragic was about to happen?
3. What in Aztec myths or about their history predisposed the Aztec leader Moctezuma to think the arrival of the strangers on the coast was expected?
4. How much would the old gods in the various societies help in dealing with anticipated threats to the survival of their peoples?
5. What did Amerindians find most astonishing about the technology, appearance, or way of life of the Spanish?
6. What was hateful or distasteful to native groups about the white man? What was worthy of admiration?

Díaz

Bernal Díaz del Castillo, born in 1492, died on his estates in Guatemala at age eighty-nine, the last of the survivors of the subjugation of Mexico. He had joined Cortés on the march to the capital city of the Aztecs with no misgivings about the rightness of his cause or the severity of the penalties his comrades inflicted on those pagans "who sat in darkness," indulging in human sacrifice on a massive scale.

> *"they could not distinguish him from an Indian, . . ."*

The old warrior wrote his history to ensure that his heirs secured the financial recognition from the crown he believed they deserved for his contribution to the expansion of the empire. He was goaded into recording the heroic activities of the captains and soldiers because they were neglected by Cortés, who seldom mentioned anybody but himself (Document 25); by historians with whom he took issue; and by Las Casas, who condemned the conquerors for their cruelty and brutality. Díaz was no scholar, but he wrote in a blunt style that has stood the test of time longer than his rivals because it remains vivid.

During the exploration of the Yucatan coast under Francisco Hernandez de Córdoba, Díaz first learned that some shipwrecked Castilians had fallen into the hands of native chiefs. At the time he did not make much of this, but two years later, in 1519 under Cortés's prompting, an effort was made to locate them. One captive left but the other stayed behind. The issue of the pull of a different way of life on some Europeans is brought to life by this episode. Strangers were often incorporated into the tribes in kinship ceremonies, when they were given full rights. The attractiveness of marriage to native women could be strong, as is indicated by Document 49. Cortés was right to be disturbed that the second Castilian refused to return, for he eventually was to lead his new people in battle against his old people.

n his diligence, Cortés sent for me [Bernal Días] and a Basque called Martin Ramos, to ask us what we thought about the Campeche Indians' cries of *"castilan, castilan!"* that I mentioned in my account of our expedition under Francisco Hernandez de Cordóba. When we had carefully described the incident once more, Cortés said that he had often thought about it, and wondered whether there might not be some Spaniards living in that country. "I think it would be a good thing," he said, "to ask these chiefs of Cozumel if they know anything about them."

So through Melchior (the man from Cape Catoche, who now understood a little Spanish and knew the language of Cozumel very well), all the chiefs were questioned, and each one of them answered that they knew of certain Spaniards, whom they described. They said that some *caciques* [chiefs] who lived two days' journey inland held them as slaves, and that here in Cozumel were some Indian traders who had spoken to them only two days before. We were all delighted with this news, and Cortés told the chiefs that letters—which in their language they call *amales*—must be sent to them at once to summon them to the island. He gave beads to the chiefs and to the Indians who carried the letters, and spoke kindly to them, telling them that when they returned he would give them some more beads. The *cacique* advised Cortés to send a ransom to their owners, so that they might let them come; and this Cortés did, giving the messengers various sorts of beads. Then he ordered the two smallest ships to be got ready. These he sent to the coast near Cape Catoche, where the larger ship was to wait for eight days, which allowed enough time for the letters to be taken and for a reply to arrive; and when it did so the smaller vessel was to bring Cortés immediate news. Cape Catoche is only twelve miles from Cozumel, and within sight of it.

In his letter Cortés said: "Gentlemen and brothers, here in Cozumel I have heard that you are captives in the hands of a *cacique*. I beg you to come to this place at once, and for this purpose have sent a ship with soldiers, in case you need them, also a ransom to be given to those Indians with whom you are living. The ship will wait for you eight days. Come as quickly as you can, and you will be welcomed and looked after by me. I am staying at this island with five hundred soldiers, and eleven ships in which I am going, please God, to a town called Tabasco or Champoton."

The two vessels were soon dispatched with the two Indian traders of Cozumel, who carried the letter on board, and in three hours they had crossed the straits. The messengers were then landed with their letters and the ransom, and in two days these were delivered to a Spaniard called Jeronimo de Aguilar. For this we discovered to be his name, and I shall call him by it henceforth. When he had read the letter and received the ransom, he carried the beads delightedly to his master the *cacique* and begged leave to depart. The *cacique* gave him permission to go wherever he wished, and Aguilar set out for the place some fifteen miles away where his comrade,

Source *The Conquest of New Spain*, pp. 59–65, passim, by Bernal Díaz, translated by J. M. Cohen (Penguin Classics, 1963), copyright © J. M. Cohen, 1963. Reproduced by permission of Penguin Books Ltd.

Gonzalo Guerrero, was living. But on hearing the contents of the letter Gonzalo answered: "Brother Aguilar, I am married and have three children, and they look on me as a *cacique* here, and a captain in time of war. Go, and God's blessing be with you. But my face is tattooed and my ears are pierced. What would the Spaniards say if they saw me like this? And look how handsome these children of mine are! Please give me some of those beads you have brought, and I will tell them that my brothers have sent them from my own country." And Gonzalo's Indian wife spoke to Aguilar very angrily in her own language: "Why has this slave come here to call my husband away? Go off with you, and let us have no more of your talk."

Then Aguilar spoke to Gonzalo again, reminding him that he was a Christian and should not destroy his soul for the sake of an Indian woman. Besides, if he did not wish to desert his wife and children, he could take them with him. But neither words nor warnings could persuade Gonzalo to come. I believe he was a sailor and hailed from Palos.

When Jeronimo de Aguilar saw that Gonzalo would not come, he at once went with the two Indian messengers to the place where their ship had been waiting for him. But when he arrived he could see no ship. For the eight days that Ordaz had been ordered to stay had expired; and after giving him one more day, he had returned to Cozumel without news of the Spanish captives. On finding no ship, Aguilar returned sadly to his master in the town where he had been living. . . .

When the Spaniard Aguilar learnt that we had returned to Cozumel with the ships, he was very joyful and gave thanks to God. He then came in all haste with the two Indians who had carried the letters and the ransom, and embarked in a canoe. Since he could pay well with the green beads we had sent him, he had soon hired one with six Indian oarsmen, who rowed so hard that, meeting no head wind, they quickly crossed the twelve-mile strait between the island and the mainland.

When they reached the coast of Cozumel and were disembarking, some soldiers who had gone out hunting—for there were wild pigs on the island—reported to Cortés that a large canoe had come from the direction of Cape Catoche and had beached near the town. Cortés sent Andres de Tapia and two other soldiers to see what was happening, since it was something new for Indians to come fearlessly into our neighbourhood in large canoes. So they set out. As soon as the Indians who had brought Aguilar saw the Spaniards, they took fright, and wanted to get back in their canoe and put out to sea. But Aguilar told them in their own language not to be afraid, for these men were his brothers. When Andres de Tapia saw that they were Indians—for Aguilar looked exactly like one—he immediately sent to tell Cortés that there were seven Cozumel Indians in the canoe. As he leapt ashore, however, Aguilar exclaimed in inarticulate and clumsy Spanish: "God and the blessed Mary of Seville!" Then Tapia went to embrace him, and the soldier who was beside him, seeing that he was a Spaniard, ran hurriedly to Cortes to beg a reward for being the first with the news. We were all delighted when we heard it.

Tapia quickly brought the Spaniard to the place where Cortés was, but before they got there some soldiers asked Tapia: "Where is this Spaniard?"

Although they were close beside him, they could not distinguish him from an Indian, for he was naturally dark, and had his hair untidily cut like an Indian slave. He carried a paddle on his shoulder and had an old sandal on one foot, the other sandal being tied to his belt. He wore a very ragged old cloak, and a tattered loincloth to cover his private parts; and in his cloak was tied an object which proved to be a very old prayer-book.

When Cortés saw him in this condition he was as much deceived as the others, and asked Tapia where this Spaniard was. When Aguilar heard his question, he squatted down in Indian fashion and answered: "I am he." Cortés at once ordered him to be given a shirt and doublet and breeches, a cloak and some sandals, for he had no other clothes. Cortés asked him his name and history and when he had come to that country. The man answered, pronouncing with difficulty, that his name was Jeronimo de Aguilar, that he came from Ecija and was in holy orders. He said that eight years ago he had been wrecked with fifteen other men and two women on a voyage from Darien to the island of Santo Domingo, where he had some differences at law with a certain Enciso y Valdivia. They were carrying with them ten thousand gold pesos and the documents of the case, when the ship in which they were travelling struck the Alacranes and could not be floated off. He, his companions, and the two women had then got into the ship's boat, thinking strong that they were thrown ashore in this country, where the *calachiones* [chiefs] of the district had divided them up, sacrificing many of his companions to their idols. Some too had died of disease, and the two women only recently of overwork, for they had been made to grind corn. The Indians had intended to sacrifice him, but one night he had escaped and fled to that *cacique* with whom he had been living ever since. Now, he said, the only survivors were himself and a certain Gonzalo Guerrero, whom he had gone to summon but who had refused to come.

Aguilar thanked God for his deliverance, and Cortés promised that he would be well looked after and compensated. He then asked him about the country and the towns. Aguilar answered that, having been a slave, he only knew about hewing wood and drawing water and working in the maize-fields, and that he had only once made a journey of some twelve miles when he was sent with a load, under which he had collapsed, for it was heavier than he could carry. He understood, however, that there were many towns. When questioned about Gonzalo Guerrero, he said that he was married and had three children, that he was tattooed, and that his ears and lower lip were pierced, that he was a seaman and a native of Palos, and that the Indians considered him very brave. Aguilar also related how a little more than a year ago, when a captain and three ships arrived at Cape Catoche—this must have been our expedition under Francisco Hernandez de Cordóba—it had been at Guerrero's suggestion that the Indians had attacked them, and that he had been there himself in the company of that *cacique* of a great town, about whom I spoke when describing that expedition. When Cortés heard this he exclaimed: "I wish I could get my hands on him. For it will never do to leave him here."

1. Why was it difficult for the first Europeans in the New World to see the Amerindians clearly, with an innocent eye?
2. In what ways did the Judeo-Christian tradition and the enthusiasm for classical antiquity eventually assist European intellectuals to incorporate the New World discoveries into their mental framework?
3. Why did Gonzalo Guerrero decide to stay with his captors, whereas Jeronimo de Aguilar struggled to return to his people?
4. What attractions did native society offer Guerrero?
5. Why was Cortés upset that he had to leave a Spaniard behind with the natives?

The Virgin of Guadalupe

The Virgin of Guadalupe has served for centuries as an important symbol to Mexican-Americans, who place her in sculptures on home altars, paint her image on the sides of buildings, and even etch her figure on the windows of low-rider, custom automobiles. Her image serves many different functions for Mexican-American culture. She is, first of all, a symbol of *la neuva raza,* the new race of people that emerged from the intermarriage of Spanish colonizers and Native Americans. "La Morena," or the Dark Virgin, who appeared on Mount Tepeyac, an ancient place of worship of Tonantzin, the Aztec Earth Mother goddess, identifies herself as one of Juan Diego's people and has dark skin like an Indian's. The Virgin also symbolizes Mexican nationalism, in contrast to the figure of "Our Lady of the Conquest," the Spanish mother-saint, and Anglo-American freedom symbols. The victory of the Mexicans at Monterrey during the Mexican War was credited to the Virgin, and the Treaty of Guadalupe Hidalgo that ended that conflict (bringing most of the far West into the United States) was signed at Guadalupe. Finally, the Virgin of Guadalupe symbolizes to Mexican-Americans the values of the Catholic Church, women, and the family.

History of the Miraculous Apparition of the Virgin of Guadalupe in 1531[1]

Herein is told, in all truth, how by a great miracle the illustrious Virgin, Blessed Mary, Mother of God, Our Lady, appeared anew, in the place known as Tepeyacac.

She appeared first to an Indian named Juan Diego; and later her divine Image appeared in the presence of the first Bishop of Mexico, Don Fray Juan de Zumárraga; also there are told various miracles which have been done. It was ten years

---

[1] The original version of this text was published in Náhuatl, the language of the Aztecs, by Bachiller Luis Lazo de Vega, Chaplain of the Sanctuary of Our Lady of Guadalupe, in 1649, over a century after the event. The text is believed to be the work of Antonio Valeriano, a contemporary of Juan Diego and Bishop Zumárraga. The story of the Virgin's appearance is essentially an oral tradition, however, and to this day it is maintained as such among Mexican-Americans.

after the beginning of bringing water from the mountain of Mexico, when the arrow and the shield had been put away, when in all parts of the country there was tranquillity which was beginning to show its light, and faith and knowledge of Him was being taught through Whose favor we have our being, Who is the only true God.

In the year 1531, early in the month of December, it happened that an humble Indian, called Juan Diego, whose dwelling, it is said, was in Quahutítlan, although for divine worship he pertained to Tlatilolco, one Saturday very early in the morning, while he was on his way to divine worship according to his custom, when he had arrived near the top of the hill called Tepeyacac, as it was near dawn, he heard above the hill a singing like that when many choice birds sing together, their voices resounding as if echoing throughout the hills; he was greatly rejoiced; their song gave him rapture exceeding that of the bell-bird and other rare birds of song.

Juan Diego stopped to wonder and said to himself: *Is it I who have this good fortune to hear what I hear? Or am I perhaps only dreaming? Where am I? Perhaps this is the place the ancients, our forefathers, used to tell about—our grandfathers— the flowery land, the fruitful land? Is it perchance the earthly paradise?*

And while he was looking towards the hilltop, facing the east, from which came the celestial song, suddenly the singing stopped and he heard someone calling as if from the top of the hill, saying: *Juan.* Juan Diego did not dare to go there where he was being called; he did not move, perhaps in some way marvelling; yet he was filled with great joy and delight, and then, presently, he began to climb to the summit where he was called.

And, when he was nearing it, on the top of the peak he saw a lady who was standing there who had called him from a distance, and, having come into her presence, he was struck with wonder at the radiance of her exceeding great beauty, her garments shining like the sun; and the stones of the hill, and the caves, reflecting the brightness of her light were like precious gold; and he saw how the rainbow clothed the land so that the cactus and other things that grew there seemed like celestial plants, their leaves and thorns shining like gold in her presence. He made obeisance and heard her voice, her words, which rejoiced him utterly when she asked, very tenderly, as if she loved him:

Listen, xocoyote[2] mio, Juan, where are you going?

And he replied: *My Holy One, my Lady, my Damsel, I am on my way to your house at Mexico-Tlatilulco; I go in pursuit of the holy things which our priests teach us.*

Whereupon She told him, and made him aware of her divine will, saying: *You must know, and be very certain in your heart, my son, that I am truly the eternal Virgin, holy Mother of the True God, through Whose favor we live, the Creator, Lord of Heaven, and the Lord of the Earth. I very much desire that they build me a church here, so that in it I may show and may make known and give all my love, my mercy and my help and my protection—I am in truth your merciful mother—to you and to all the other people dear to me who call upon me, who search for me, who confide in me; here I will hear their sorrow, their words, so that I may make perfect and cure their illnesses, their labors, and their calamities. And so that my intention may be made known, and my mercy, go now to the episcopal palace of the Bishop of Mexico*

[2] *Xocoyote*: This Náhuatl word is variously translated into Spanish as if it were "my little son" or "my dear son." *Xocoyota* is the form for "daughter."

and tell him that I send you to tell him how much I desire to have a church built here, and tell him very well all that you have seen and all that you have heard; and be sure in your heart that I will pay you with glory and you will deserve much that I will repay you for your weariness, your work, which you will bear diligently doing what I send you to do. Now hear my words, my dear son, and go and do everything carefully and quickly.

Then he humbled himself before her and said: *My Holy One, my Lady, I will go now and fulfill your commandment.*

And straightway he went down to accomplish that with which he was charged, and took the road that leads straight to Mexico.

And when he had arrived within the city, he went at once to the episcopal palace of the Lord Bishop, who was the first [Bishop] to come, whose name was Don Fray Juan de Zumárraga, a religious of St. Francis. And having arrived there, he made haste to ask to see the Lord Bishop, asking his servants to give notice of him. After a good while they came to call him, and the Bishop advised them that he should come in; and when he had come into his presence, he knelt and made obeisance, and then after this he related the words of the Queen of Heaven, and told besides all that he had seen and all that he had heard. And [the Bishop] having heard all his words and the commandment as if he were not perfectly persuaded, said in response:

My son, come again another time when we can be more leisurely; and I will hear more from you about the origin of this; I will look into this about which you have come, your will, your desire.

And he departed with much sorrow because he had not been able to convince him of the truth of his mission.

Thereupon he returned that same day and went straightway to the hill where he had seen the Queen of Heaven, who was even then standing there where he had first seen Her, waiting for him, and he, having seen Her, made obeisance, kneeling upon the ground, and said:

My Holy One, most noble of persons, My Lady, my Xocoyota, my Damsel, I went there where You sent me; although it was most difficult to enter the house of the Lord Bishop, I saw him at last, and in his presence I gave him your message in the way You instructed me; he received me very courteously, and listened with attention; but he answered as if he could not be certain and did not believe; he told me: Come again another time when we can be at leisure, and I will hear you from beginning to end; I will look into that about which you come, what it is you want and ask me for. He seemed to me, when he answered, to be thinking perhaps that the church You desire to have made here was perchance not Your will, but a fancy of mine. I pray You, my Holy One, my Lady, my Daughter, that any one of the noble lords who are well known, reverenced and respected be the one to undertake this so that Your words will be believed. For it is true that I am only a poor man; I am not worthy of being there where You send me; pardon me, my Xocoyota, I do not wish to make your noble heart sad; I do not want to fall into your displeasure.

Then the always noble Virgin answered him, saying: *Hear me, my son, it is true that I do not lack for servants or ambassadors to whom I could entrust my message so that my will could be verified, but it is important that you speak for me in this matter, weary as you are; in your hands you have the means of verifying, of making plain my desire, my will; I pray you, my xocoyote, and advise you with much care, that you go again tomorrow to see the Bishop and represent me; give him an understanding of my desire, my will, that he build the church that I ask; and tell him once again that it is the eternal Virgin, Holy Mary, the Mother of God, who sends you to him.*

And Juan Diego answered her, saying: *Queen of Heaven, my Holy One, my Damsel, do not trouble your heart, for I will go with all my heart and make plain Your voice, Your words. It is not because I did not want to go, or because the road is stony, but only because perhaps I would not be heard, and if I were heard I would not be believed. I will go and do your bidding and tomorrow in the afternoon about sunset I will return to give the answer to your words the Lord Bishop will make; and now I leave You, my Xocoyota, my Damsel, my Lady; meanwhile, rest You.*

With this, he went to his house to rest. The next day being Sunday, he left his house in the morning and went straightway to Tlatilulco, to attend Mass and the sermon. Then, being determined to see the Bishop, when Mass and the sermon were finished, at ten o'clock, with all the other Indians he came out of the church; but Juan Diego left them and went to the palace of the Lord Bishop. And having arrived there, he spared no effort in order to see him and when, after great difficulty, he did see him again, he fell to his knees and implored him to the point of weeping, much moved, in an effort to make plain the words of the Queen of Heaven, and that the message and the will of the most resplendent Virgin would be believed; that the church be built as She asked, where She wished it.

But the Lord Bishop asked Juan Diego many things, to know for certain what had taken place, questioning him: Where did he see Her? What did the Lady look like whom he saw? And he told the Lord Bishop all that he had seen. But although he told him everything exactly, so that it seemed in all likelihood that She was the Immaculate Virgin, Mary most pure, the beloved Mother of Our Lord Jesus Christ, the Bishop said he could not be certain. He said: It is not only with her words that we have to do, but also to obtain that for which she asks. It is very necessary to have some sign by which we may believe that it is really the Queen of Heaven who sends you.

And Juan Diego, having heard him, said to the Lord Bishop: *My Lord, wait for whatever sign it is that you ask for, and I will go at once to ask the Queen of Heaven, who sent me.* And the Lord Bishop, seeing that he had agreed, and so that he should not be confused or worried, in any way, urged him to go; and then, calling some of his servants in whom he had much confidence, he asked them to follow and to watch where he went and see whomsoever it was that he went to see, and with whom he might speak. And this was done accordingly, and when Juan Diego reached the place where a bridge over the river, near the hill, met the royal highway, they lost him, and although they searched for him everywhere they could not find him in any part of that land. And so they returned, and not only were they weary, but extremely annoyed with him, and upon their return they abused him much with the Lord Bishop, over all that had happened, for they did not believe in him; they said that he had been deceiving him, and had imagined all that he had come to relate to him, or perhaps he had dreamed it, and they agreed and said that if he should come again they would seize him and chastise him severely so that he would not lie another time.

The next day, Monday, when Juan Diego was to bring some sign by which he might be believed, he did not return, since, when he arrived at his house, an uncle of his who was staying there, named Juan Bernardino, was very ill of a burning fever; Juan Diego went at once to bring a doctor and then he procured medicine; but there still was no time because the man was very ill. Early in the morning his uncle begged him to go out to bring one of the priests from Tlatilulco so that he might be confessed, for he was very certain that his time had come to die, now that he was too weak to rise, and could not get well.

And on Tuesday, very early in the morning, Juan Diego left his house to go to Tlatilulco to call a priest, and as he was nearing the hill on the road which lies at the foot of the hill towards the west, which was his usual way, he said to himself: *If I go straight on, without doubt I will see Our Lady and She will persuade me to take the sign to the Lord Bishop; let us first do our duty; I will go first to call the priest for my poor uncle; will he not be waiting for him?*

With this he turned to another road at the foot of the slope and was coming down the other side towards the east to take a short cut to Mexico; he thought that by turning that way the Queen of Heaven would not see him, but She was watching for him, and he saw Her on the hilltop where he had always seen Her before, coming down that side of the slope, by the shortest way, and She said to him:

Xocoyote mio, where are you going? What road is this you are taking?

And he was frightened; it is not known whether he was disgusted with himself, or was ashamed, or perhaps he was struck with wonder; he prostrated himself before Her and greeted her, saying: *My Daughter, my Xocoyota, God keep You, Lady. How did You waken? And is your most pure body well, perchance? My Holy One, I will bring pain to your heart—for I must tell You, my Virgin, that an uncle of mine, who is Your servant, is very sick, with an illness so strong that without doubt he will die of it; I am hastening to Your house in Mexico to call one of Our Lord's dear ones, our priests, to come to confess him, and when I have done that, then I will come back to carry out Your commandment. My Virgin, my Lady, forgive me, be patient with me until I do my duty, and then tomorrow I will come back to You.*

And having heard Juan Diego's explanation, the most holy and immaculate Virgin replied to him:

Listen, and be sure, my dear son, that I will protect you; do not be frightened or grieve, or let your heart be dismayed; however great the illness may be that you speak of, am I not here, I who am your mother, and is not my help a refuge? Am I not of your kind?[3] *Do not be concerned about your uncle's illness, for he is not now going to die; be assured that he is now already well. Is there anything else needful?* (And in that same hour his uncle was healed, as later he learned.)

And Juan Diego, having heard the words of the Queen of Heaven, greatly rejoiced and was convinced, and besought Her that She would send him again to see the Lord Bishop, to carry him some sign by which he could believe, as he had asked.

Whereupon the Queen of Heaven commanded him to climb up to the top of the hill where he had always seen her, saying: *Climb up to the top of the hill, my xocoyote, where you have seen me stand, and there you will find many flowers; pluck them and gather them together, and then bring them down here in my presence.*

Then Juan Diego climbed up the hill and when he had reached the top he marvelled to see blooming there many kinds of beautiful flowers of Castile, for it

---

[3] The Virgin identifies herself as an Indian.

was then very cold, and he marvelled at their fragrance and odor. Then he began to pluck them, and gathered them together carefully, and wrapped them in his mantle, and when he had finished he descended and carried to the Queen of Heaven all the flowers he had plucked. She, when she had seen them, took them into her immaculate hands, gathered them together again, and laid them in his cloak once more and said to him:

My xocoyote, all these flowers are the sign that you must take to the Bishop; in my name tell him that with this he will see and recognize my will and that he must do what I ask; and you who are my ambassador worthy of confidence, I counsel you to take every care that you open your mantle only in the presence of the Bishop, and you must make it known to him what is is that you carry, and tell him how I asked you to climb to the top of the hill to gather the flowers. Tell him also all that you have seen, so that you will persuade the Lord Bishop and he will see that the church is built for which I ask.

And the Queen of Heaven having acquainted him with this, he departed, following the royal highway which leads directly to Mexico; he traveled content, because he was persuaded that now he would succeed; he walked carefully, taking great pains not to injure what he was carrying in his mantle; he went glorying in the fragrance of the beautiful flowers. When he arrived at the Bishop's palace, he encountered his majordomo and other servants and asked them to tell the Bishop that he would like to see him; but none of them would, perhaps because it was still very early in the morning or, perhaps recognizing him, they were vexed or, because they knew how others of their household had lost him on the road when they were following him. They kept him waiting there a long time; he waited very humbly to see if they would call him, and when it was getting very late, they came to him to see what it was he was carrying as a proof of what he had related. And Juan Diego, seeing that he could not hide from them what he was carrying, when they had tormented him and jostled him and knocked him about, let them glimpse that he had roses, to deliver himself from them; and they, when they saw that they were roses of Castile, very fragrant and fresh, and not at all in their season, marvelled and wanted to take some of them. Three times they made bold to take them, but they could not because, when they tried to take them, they were not roses that they touched, but were as if painted or embroidered. Upon this, they went to the Lord Bishop to tell him what they had seen, and that the Indian who was there often before had come again and wanted to see him, and that they had kept him waiting there a long time.

The Lord Bishop, having heard this, knew that now this was the sign that should persuade him whether what the Indian had told him was true. He straightway asked that he be brought in to see him.

Having come into his presence, Juan Diego fell to his knees (as he had always done) and again related fully all that he had seen, and full of satisfaction and wonder he said: *My Lord, I have done that which you asked me; I went to tell my Holy One, the Queen of Heaven, the beloved Virgin Mary, Mother of God, how you asked me for some sign that you might believe that it was She who desired you to build Her the church for which She asked. And also I told Her how I had given my word that I would bring you some sign so that you could believe in what She had put in my care, and She heard with pleasure your suggestion and found it good, and just now, early this morning, She told me to come again to see you and I asked Her for the sign that I had asked Her to give me, and then She sent me to the hilltop where I have always seen Her, to pluck the flowers that I should see there. And when I had plucked them, I took them to the foot of the mountain where She had remained, and She gathered them into her immaculate hands and then put them again into my mantle for me to bring them to you. Although I knew very well that the hilltop was not a place for flowers, since it is a place of thorns, cactuses, caves and mezquites, I was not confused and did not doubt Her. When I reached the summit I saw there was a garden there of flowers with quantities of the fragrant flowers which are found in Castile; I took them and carried them to the Queen of Heaven and She told me that I must bring them to you, and now I have done it, so that you may see the sign that you ask for in order to do Her bidding, and so that you will see that my word is true. And here they are.*

Whereupon he opened his white cloak, in which he was carrying the flowers, and as the roses of Castile dropped out to the floor, suddenly there appeared the most pure image of the most noble Virgin Mary, Mother of God, just exactly as it is, even now, in Her holy house, in Her church which is named Guadalupe;[4] and the Lord Bishop, having seen this, and all those who were with him, knelt down and gazed with wonder; and then they grew sad, and were sorrowful, and were aghast, and the Lord Bishop with tenderness and weeping begged Her forgiveness for not having done Her bidding at once. And when he had finished, he untied from Juan Diego's neck the cloak on which was printed the figure of the Queen of Heaven. And then he carried it into his chapel; and Juan Diego remained all that day in the house of the Bishop, who did not want him to go. And the following day the Bishop said to him: *Come, show us where it is the Queen of Heaven wishes us to build Her church.* And when he had shown them where it was, he told them that he wanted to go to his house to see his uncle Juan Bernardino who had been very ill and he had set out for Tlatilulco to get a priest to confess him, but the Queen of Heaven had told him that he was already cured.

They did not let him go alone, but went with him to his house, and when they arrived there, they saw that his uncle was well and that nothing was now the matter with him; and the uncle wondered much when he saw such a company with his nephew, and all treating him with great courtesy, and he asked him: *How is it they treat you this way? And why do they reverence you so much?*

And Juan Diego told him that when he had gone from the house to call a confessor for him, he saw the Queen of Heaven on the hill called Tepeyacac and She had sent him to Mexico to see the Lord Bishop to have a church built for Her. And that She had also told him not to worry about his uncle, that he was now well.

Whereupon his uncle showed great joy and told him that it was true that at that very hour he had been healed, and that he himself had seen exactly that same Person, and that She had told him how She had sent him to Mexico to see the

---

[4] The original significance of this word is unclear. It is probably a Hispanic form of a compound derived from the Náhuatl (Aztec) word for "snake," *coatl,* and the Spanish word for "crush, trample," *llope.* Thus, *coatl-llope,* "she crushes the serpent." Interestingly, the image described here is clearly modelled on traditional Catholic figures of Immaculate Mary, Queen of Heaven, statues of whom (based on Genesis 3:15) feature the Virgin standing on a half-moon, crushing with her foot the Devil, represented as a snake. In addition, the Aztec culture hero is Quetzalcoatl, the Plumed Serpent, and the Virgin is requesting that her Cathedral be built over the site of an Aztec place of worship, which, in fact, it was.

Bishop, and also that when he saw him again, to tell him all that he had seen also, and how, miraculously, he had been restored to health, and that the most holy Image of the Immaculate Virgin should be called Santa María de Guadalupe.

And after this they brought Juan Bernardino into the Lord Bishop's presence so that he might tell him under oath all that he had just related; and the Bishop kept the two men (that is, Juan Diego and Juan Bernardino) as his guests in his own house several days until the church for the Queen of Heaven was built where Juan Diego had shown them. And the Lord Bishop moved the sacred Image of the Queen of Heaven, which he had in his chapel, to the cathedral so that all the people could see it.

All the city was in a turmoil upon seeing Her most holy portrait; they saw that it had appeared miraculously, that no one in the world had painted it on Juan Diego's mantle; for this, on which the miraculous Image of the Queen of Heaven appeared, was *ayate,* a coarse fabric made of cactus fibre, rather like homespun, and well woven, for at that time all the Indian people covered themselves with *ayate,* except the nobles, the gentlemen and the captains of war, who dressed themselves in cloaks of cotton, or in cloaks made of wool.

The esteemed *ayate* upon which the Immaculate Virgin, Our Sovereign Queen, appeared unexpectedly is made of two pieces sewn together with threads of cotton; the height of Her sacred Image from the sole of Her foot to the top of Her head measures six hands, and one woman's hand. Her sacred face is very beautiful, grave, and somewhat dark; her precious body, according to this, is small; her hands are held at her breast; the girdle at her waist is violet; her right foot only shows, a very little, and her slipper is earthen in color; her robe is rose-colored; in the shadows it appears deeper red, and it is embroidered with various flowers outlined in gold; pendant at her throat is a little gold circlet which is outlined with a black line around it; in the middle it has a cross; and one discovers glimpses of another, inner vestment of white cotton, daintily gathered at her wrists. The outer mantle which covers her from her head almost to her feet is of heavenly blue; half-way down its fullness hangs in folds, and it is bordered with gold, a rather wide band of gold thread, and all over it there are golden stars which are in number forty-six. Her most holy head is turned towards the right and is bending down; and on her head above her mantle she wears a shining gold crown, and at her feet there is the new moon with its horns pointed upward; and exactly in the middle of it the Immaculate Virgin is standing, and, it would seem also, in the middle of the sun, since its rays surround her everywhere. These rays number a hundred; some are large and others are small; those on each side of her sacred face and those above her head number twelve, in all they number fifty on each side. And outside the edges of this and her robes She is encircled with white clouds. This divine Image as it is described stands above an angel, half of whose body only appears, since he is in the midst of clouds. The angel's outstretched arms hold the edges of her outer robes as they hang in folds near her sacred feet. His garment is of rosy color with a gold ornament at his neck; his wings are made or composed of various sizes of feathers, and it seems as if he were very happy to be accompanying the Queen of Heaven.

1649

Two Worlds Discover
Each Other

Five centuries have passed since Christopher Columbus's first voyage across the At-
lantic and since the revelation to both hemispheres of unknown lands and peoples.
European statesmen, merchants, and scholars, spurred on by the Renaissance quest
for knowledge and aided by the newly invented printing press, eagerly sought infor-
mation about the newfound lands across the sea. Travelers to America were urged
by their friends and sponsors to write about what they saw. Thus we have accounts
left by people from all walks of life, from common seafarers to highly trained schol-
ars, as they all tried to fit America and its diverse peoples into a framework that
made sense. All humanity must be descended from Noah, according to the Bible.
Therefore the ancestors of the Indians must have been known to the ancient world.
Many writers concluded that the Americans were the descendents of the Ten Lost
Tribes of Israel.

As Christians, they believed that God had chosen their time to reveal the West-
ern Hemisphere and had given them the task of converting the Indians. As they
wrote about Native Americans' religion, marriage customs, law, inheritance, and
food, partly with a view to gauging how ripe they were for conversion, the Europe-
ans invented a kind of ethnology, a new science of humankind. Their writings give
many hints that the Indians themselves were analyzing the newcomers, attempting
to fit them into a framework from their own experience. Each side misunderstood
much about the other.

No European involved in the encounter ever wrote from a purely scholarly or
religious perspective. All the accounts are practical in focus, because expeditions were
financed by merchants. Thus all reveal a constant preoccupation with the kinds of
rich products to be found in America. No one believed that the land would be ap-
preciated merely for its own sake; voyages were enormously expensive, and only the
discovery of valuable commodities would make constant contact worthwhile for Eu-
ropean backers. On their side, the Americans were interested in acquiring articles,
particularly equipment and weapons of metal, that the newcomers offered in ex-
change for their furs and precious metals. Trade quickly became the chief medium
of cultural exchange.

Jacques Cartier, who explored the St. Lawrence River for France in the mid-1530s, found the large city of Hochelaga at the future site of Montreal. His account, reprinted in the first selection, contains a very early description of Indian life, including the practice of smoking tobacco.

Indian interpretations of events were gathered by European reporters. The legend of Maushop and his alienation, the subject of the second document, was one that appeared in many forms. Thomas Harriot collected Indian reactions to the colonists and the dramatic change the newcomers brought. The account in the third selection by Harriot, an Oxford-educated scholar, can be compared to that in the final document of shipmaster Arthur Barlowe, who describes the same people. Both men were sent by Sir Walter Raleigh to Roanoke in the 1580s.

Jacques Cartier Observes the St. Lawrence and Its People, 1635–1636

... And we sailed on in as fine weather as one could wish until [Saturday] October 2, when we arrived at Hochelaga, which is about forty-five leagues from the spot where we had left our bark. During this interval we came across on the way many of the people of the country, who brought us fish and other provisions, at the same time dancing and showing great joy at our coming. And in order to win and keep their friendship, the Captain made them a present of some knives, beads and other small trifles, whereat they were greatly pleased. And on reaching Hochelaga, there came to meet us more than a thousand persons, both men, women and children, who gave us as good a welcome as ever father gave to his son, making great signs of joy; for the men danced in one ring, the women in another and the children also apart by themselves. After this they brought us quantities of fish, and of their bread, which is made of Indian corn, throwing so much of it into our long-boats that it seemed to rain bread. Seeing this the Captain, accompanied by several of his men, went on shore; and no sooner had he landed than they all crowded about him and about the others, giving them a wonderful reception. And the women brought their babies in their arms to have the Captain and his companions touch them, while all held a merry-making which lasted more than half an hour. Seeing their generosity and friendliness, the Captain had the women all sit down in a row and gave them some tin beads and other trifles; and to some of the men he gave knives. Then he returned on board the long-boats to sup and pass the night, throughout which the Indians remained on the bank of the river, as near the long-boats as they could get, keeping many fires burning all night, and dancing and calling out every moment aguyase which is their term of salutation and joy.

How the Captain and the Gentlemen, accompanied by twenty-five
well-armed and marshalled sailors, went to visit the village of Hochelaga;
and of the situation of the place.

At daybreak the next day, the Captain, having put on his armour, had his men marshalled for the purpose of paying a visit to the village and home of these people, and to a mountain which lies near the town. The Captain was accompanied by the gentlemen and by twenty sailors, the remainder having been left behind to guard the long-boats. And he took three Indians of the village as guides to conduct them thither. When we had got under way, we discovered that the path was as well-trodden as it is possible to see, and that the country was the finest and most excellent one could find anywhere, being everywhere full of oaks, as beautiful as in any forest in France, underneath which the ground lay covered with acorns. And after marching about a league and a half, we met on the trail one of the headmen of the village of Hochelaga, accompanied by several Indians, who made signs to us that we should rest at that spot near a fire they had lighted on the path; which we did. Thereupon this headman began to make a speech and to harangue us, which, as before mentioned, is their way of showing joy and friendliness, welcoming in this way the Captain and his company. The Captain presented him with a couple of hatchets and a couple of knives, as well as with a cross and a crucifix, which he made him kiss and then hung it about his neck. For these the headman thanked the Captain. When this was done we marched on, and about half a league thence, found that the land began to be cultivated. It was fine land with large fields covered with the corn of the country, which resembles Brazil millet, and is about as large or larger than a pea. They live on this as we do on wheat. And in the middle of these fields is situated and stands the village of Hochelaga, near and adjacent to a mountain, the slopes of which are fertile and are cultivated, and from the top of which one can see for a long distance. We named this mountain "Mount Royal" [Mont Royal]. The village is circular and is completely enclosed by a wooden palisade in three tiers like a pyramid. The top one is built crosswise, the middle one perpendicular and the lowest one of strips of wood placed lengthwise. The whole is well joined and lashed after their manner, and is some two lances in height. There is only one gate and entrance to this village, and that can be barred up. Over this gate and in many places about the enclosure are species of galleries with ladders for mounting to them, which galleries are provided with rocks and stones for the defence and protection of the place. There are some fifty houses in this village, each about fifty or more paces in length, and twelve or fifteen in width, built completely of wood and covered in and bordered up with large pieces of the bark and rind of trees, as broad as a table, which are well and cunningly lashed after their manner. . . . This whole tribe gives itself to manual labor and to fishing merely to obtain the necessities of life; for they place no value upon the goods of this world, both because they are unacquainted with them, and because they do not move from home and are not nomads like those of Canada and of the Saguenay, notwithstanding that the Canadians and some eight or nine other tribes along this river are subjects of theirs. . . .

... They are by no means a laborious people and work the soil with short bits of wood about half a sword in length. With these they hoe their corn which they call ozisy, in size as large as a pea. Corn of a similar kind grows in considerable quantities in Brazil. They have also a considerable quantity of melons, cucumbers, pumpkins, pease and beans of various colours and unlike our own. Furthermore they have a plant, of which a large supply is collected in summer for the winter's consumption. They hold it in high esteem, though the men alone make use of it in the following manner. After drying it in the sun, they carry it about their necks in a small skin pouch in lieu of a bag, together with a hollow bit of stone or wood. Then at frequent intervals they crumble this plant into powder, which they place in one of the openings of the hollow instrument, and laying a live coal on top, such at the other end to such an extent, that they fill their bodies so full of smoke, that it streams out of their mouths and nostrils as from a chimney. They say it keeps them warm and in good health, and never go about without these things. We made a trial of this smoke. When it is in one's mouth, one would think one had taken powdered pepper, it is so hot. The women of this country work beyond comparison more than the men, both at fishing, which is much followed, as well as at tilling the ground and other tasks. Both the men, women and children are more indifferent to the cold than beasts; for in the coldest weather we experienced, and it was extraordinary severe, they would come to our ships every day across the ice and snow, the majority of them almost stark naked, which seems incredible unless one has seen them. While the ice and snow last, they catch a great number of wild animals such as fawns, stags and bears, hares, martens, foxes, otters and others. Of these they brought us very few; for they are heavy eaters and are niggardly with their provisions. They eat their meat quite raw, merely smoking it, and the same with their fish. From what we have seen and been able to learn of these people, I am of opinion that they could easily be moulded in the way one would wish. May God in His holy mercy turn His countenance towards them. Amen.

Maushop Leaves New England:
An Indian Legend About Colonization

On the west end of Martha's Vineyard, are high cliffs of variegated coloured earths, known by the name of *Gayhead*. On the top of the hill is a large cavity, which has the appearance of the crater of an extinguished volcano, and there are evident marks of former subterraneous fires. The Indians who live about this spot have a tradition that a certain deity resided there before the Europeans came into America, that his name was *Maushop*; that he used to step out on a ledge of rocks which ran into the sea, and take up a whale, which he broiled for his own eating on the coals of the aforesaid volcano, and often invited the Indians to dine with him, or gave them the relicks of his meal. That once to shew their gratitude to *Maushop* for his very great kindness to them, they made an offering to him of all the tobacco which grew upon the island in one season. This was scarcely sufficient to fill his great pipe, but he received the present very graciously, smoked his pipe, and turned out the ashes of it into the sea, which formed the island of Nantucket. Upon the coming of the Europeans into America, *Maushop* retired in disgust, and has never since been seen.

Thomas Harriot Forecasts
Indian-Colonist Relationships, 1588*

Of the Nature and Manners of the People

It resteth I speak a word or two of the natural inhabitants, their natures and manners, ... as that you may know, how that they in respect of troubling our inhabiting and planting, are not to be feared, but that they shall have cause both to fear and love us, that shall inhabit with them.

They are a people clothed with loose mantles made of Deer skins, & aprons of the same round about their middles; all else naked; of such a difference of statures only as we in England, having no edge tools or weapons of iron or steel to offend us withal, neither know they how to make any: those weapons that they have, are only bows made of Witch hazel, & arrows of reeds, flat edged truncheons also of wood about a yard long, neither have they anything to defend themselves but targets made of barks, and some armours made of sticks wickered together with thread. . . .

Their manner of wars amongst themselves is either by sudden surprising one another most commonly about the dawning of the day, or moonlight, or else by ambushes, or some subtle devices. Set battles are very rare, except it fall out where there are many trees, where either part may have some hope of defence, after the delivery of every arrow, in leaping behind some or other.

---

*Some of the spelling in this document has been modernized.

If there fall out any wars between us & them, what their fight is likely to be, we having advantages against them so many manner of ways, as by our discipline, our strange weapons and devices else, especially by ordinance great and small, it may be easily imagined; by the experience we have had in some places, the turning up of their heels against us in running away was their best defence. In respect of us they are a people poor, and for want of skill and judgment in the knowledge and use of our things, do esteem our trifles before things of greater value: Notwithstanding in their proper manner considering the want of such means as we have, they seem very ingenious; For although they have no such tools, nor any such crafts, sciences and arts as we; yet in those things they do, they show excellence of wit. And by how much they upon due consideration shall find our manner of knowledges and crafts to exceed theirs in perfection, and speed for doing or execution, by so much the more is it probable that they should desire our friendships & love, and have the greater respect for pleasing and obeying us. Whereby may be hoped if means of good government be used, that they may in short time be brought to civility and the embracing of true religion.

Some religion they have already, which although it be far from the truth, yet being as it is, there is hope it may be the easier and sooner reformed.

They believe that there are many Gods which they call *Montóac,* but of different sorts and degrees; one only chief and great God, which hath been from all eternity. Who as they affirm when he purposed to make the world, made first other gods of a principal order to be as means and instruments to be used in the creation and government to follow; and after the Sun, Moon, and Stars as petty gods, and the instruments of the other order more principal. First they say were made waters, out of which by the gods was made all diversity of creatures that are visible or invisible.

For mankind they say a woman was made first, which by the working of one of the gods, conceived and brought forth children: And in such sort they say they had their beginning. But how many years or ages have passed since, they say they can make no relation, having no letters nor other such means as we to keep records of the particularities of times past, but only tradition from father to son. . . .

They believe also the immortality of the soul, that after this life as soon as the soul is departed from the body, according to the works it hath done, it is either carried to heaven the habitacle of gods, there to enjoy perpetual bliss and happiness, or else to a great pit or hole, which they think to be in the furthest parts of their part of the world toward the sunset, there to burn continually: the place they call *Popogusso.* . . .

Most things they saw with us, as Mathematical instruments, sea compasses, the virtue of the lodestone in drawing iron, a perspective glass whereby was showed many strange sights, burning glasses, wildfire works, guns, books, writing and reading, spring clocks that seem to go of themselves, and many other things that we had, were so strange unto them, and so far exceeded their capacities to comprehend the reason and means how they should be made and done, that they thought they were rather the works of gods than of men, or at the leastwise they had been given and taught us of the gods. Which made many of them to have such opinion of us, as that if they knew not the truth of god and religion already, it was rather to be had from us, whom God so specially loved than from a people that were so simple, as they found themselves to be in comparison of us. Whereupon greater credit was given unto that we spoke of concerning such matters.

Many times and in every town where I came, according as I was able, I made declaration of the contents of the Bible; that therein was set forth the true and only GOD, and his mighty works, that therein was contained the true doctrine of salvation through Christ, with many particularities of Miracles and chief points of religion, as I was able then to utter, and thought fit for the time. And although I told them the book materially & of itself was not of any such virtue, as I thought they did conceive, but only the doctrine therein contained; yet would many be glad to touch it, to embrace it, to kiss it, to hold it to their breasts and heads, and stroke over all their body with it; to show their hungry desire of that knowledge which was spoken of.

The *Wiroans* with whom we dwelt called *Wingina,* and many of his people would be glad many times to be with us at our prayers, and many times call upon us both in his own town, as also in others whither he sometimes accompanied us, to pray and sing Psalms; hoping thereby to be partaker of the same effects which we by that means also expected.

Twice this *Wiroans* was so grievously sick that he was like to die, and as he lay languishing, doubting of any help by his own priests, and thinking he was in such danger for offending us and thereby our god, sent for some of us to pray and be a means to our God that it would please him either that he might live, or after death dwell with him in bliss, so likewise were the requests of many others in the like case.

On a time also when their corn began to wither by reason of a drought which happened extraordinarily, fearing that it had come to pass by reason that in something they had displeased us, many would come to us & desire us to pray to our God of England, that he would preserve their corn, promising that when it was ripe we also should be partakers of the fruit.

There could at no time happen any strange sickness, losses, hurts, or any other cross unto them, but that they would impute to us the cause or means thereof for offending or not pleasing us.

One other rare and strange accident, leaving others, will I mention before I end, which moved the whole country that either knew or heard of us, to have us in wonderful admiration.

There was no town where we had any subtle device practiced against us, we leaving it unpunished or not revenged (because we sought by all means possible to win them by gentleness) but that within a few days after our departure from every such town, the people began to die very fast, and many in short space; in some towns about twenty, in some forty, in some sixty, & in one six score, which in truth was very many in respect of their numbers. This happened in no place that we could learn but where we had been where they used some practice against us, and after such time; The disease also was so strange, that they neither knew what it was, nor how to cure it; the like by report of the oldest men in the country never happened before, time out of mind. A thing specially observed by us, as also by the natural inhabitants themselves.

Insomuch that when some of the inhabitants which were our friends & especially the *Wiroans Wingina* had observed such effects in four or five towns to follow their wicked practices, they were persuaded that it was the work of our God through our means, and that we by him might kill and slay whom we would without weapons and not come near them.

And thereupon when it had happened that they had understanding that any of their enemies had abused us in our journeys, hearing that we had wrought no revenge with our weapons, & fearing upon some cause the matter should so rest: did come and entreat us that we would be a means to our God that they as others that had dealt ill with us might in like sort die; alleging how much it would be for our credit and profit as also theirs; and hoping furthermore that we would do so much at their requests in respect of the friendship we profess them.

Whose entreaties although we showed that they were ungodly, affirming that our God would not subject himself to any such prayers and requests of men: that indeed all things have been and were to be done according to his good pleasure as he had ordained: and that we to show ourselves his true servants ought rather to make petition for the contrary, that they with them might live together with us, be made partakers of his truth & serve him in righteousness; but notwithstanding in such sort, that we refer that as all other things, to be done according to his divine will & pleasure, and as by his wisdom he had ordained to be best.

Yet because the effect fell out so suddenly and shortly after according to their desires, they thought nevertheless it came to pass by our means, and that we in using such speeches unto them did but dissemble the matter, and therefore came unto us to give us thanks in their manner that although we satisfied them not in promise, yet in deeds and effect we had fulfilled their desires.

This marvelous accident in all the country wrought so strange opinions of us, that some people could not tell whether to think us gods or men, and the rather because that all the space of their sickness, there was no man of ours known to die, or that was especially sick: they noted also that we had no women among us, neither that we did care for any of theirs.

Some therefore were of opinion that we were not born of women, and therefore not mortal, but that we were men of an old generation many years past then risen again to immortality. . . .

Arthur Barlowe Sees America
as the Garden of Eden, 1584

The next day there came unto us divers boats, and in one of them the King's brother, accompanied with forty or fifty men, very handsome and goodly people, and in their behavior as mannerly and civil as any of Europe. His name was Granganimeo, and the king is called Wingina, the country Wingandacoa, and now by Her Majesty Virginia. The manner of his coming was in this sort: he left his boats altogether as the first man did a little from the ships by the shore, and came along to the place over against the ships, followed with forty men. When he came to the place, his servants spread a long mat upon the ground, on which he sat down, and at the other end of the mat four others of his company did the like, the rest of his men stood round about him, somewhat afar off: when we came to the shore to him with our weapons, he never moved from his place, nor any of the other four, nor never mistrusted any harm to be offered from us, but sitting still he beckoned us to come and sit by him, which we performed: and being set he made all signs of joy and welcome, striking on his head and his breast and afterwards on ours, to show we were all one, smiling and making show the best he could of all love, and familiarity. After he had made a long speech unto us, we presented him with divers things, which he received very joyfully, and thankfully. None of the company durst speak one word all the time: only the four which were at the other end, spake one in the other's ear very softly. . . .

. . . A day or two after this, we fell to trading with them, exchanging some things that we had, for Chamois, Buff, and Deer skins: when we showed him all our packet of merchandise, of all things that he saw, a bright tin dish most pleased him, which he presently took up and clapped it before his breast, and after made a hole in the brim thereof and hung it about his neck, making signs that it would defend him against his enemies' arrows: for those people maintain a deadly and terrible war, with the people and King adjoining. We exchanged our tin dish for twenty skins, worth twenty Crowns, or twenty Nobles: and a copper kettle for fifty skins worth fifty Crowns. They offered us good exchange for our hatchets, and axes, and for knives, and would have given any thing for swords: but we would not depart with any. After two or three days the King's brother came aboard the ships, and drank wine, and eat of our meat and of our bread, and liked exceedingly thereof: and after a few days overpassed, he brought his wife with him to the ships, his daughter and two or three children: his wife was very well favoured, of mean stature, and very bashful: she had on her back a long cloak of leather, with the fur side next to her body, and before her a piece of the same: about her forehead she had a band of white Coral, and so had her husband many times: in her ears she had bracelets of pearls hanging down to her middle, (whereof we delivered your worship a little bracelet) and those were of the bigness of good peas. The rest of her women of the better sort had pendants of copper hanging in

---

Some of the spelling in this document has been modernized.

either ear, and some of the children of the king's brother and other noble men, have five or six in either ear: he himself had upon his head a broad plate of gold, or copper, for being unpolished we knew not what metal it should be, neither would he by any means suffer us to take it off his head, but feeling it, it would bow very easily. His apparel was as his wife's, only the women wear their hair long on both sides, and the men but on one. They are of colour yellowish, and their hair black for the most part, and yet we saw children that had very fine auburn, and chestnut coloured hair. . . .

. . . And we both noted there, and you have understood since by these men, which we brought home, that no people in the world carry more respect to their King, Nobility, and Governours, then these do. . . .

The King's brother had great liking of our armour, a sword, and divers other things which we had: and offered to lay a great box of pearl in gage [pawn] for them: but we refused it for this time, because we would not make them know, that we esteemed thereof, until we had understood in what places of the country the pearl grew: which now your Worship doth very well understand.

He was very just of his promise: for many times we delivered him merchandise upon his word, but ever he came within the day and performed his promise. He sent us every day a brace or two of fat Bucks, Conies [rabbits], Hares, Fish the best of the world. He sent us divers kinds of fruits, Melons, Walnuts, Cucumbers, Gourds, Peas, and divers roots, and fruits very excellent good, and of their Country corn, which is very white, fair and well tasted, and groweth three times in five months: in May they sow, in July they reap, in June they sow, in August they reap: in July they sow, in September they reap: only they cast the corn into the ground, breaking a little of the soft turf with a wooden mattock, or pickaxe: our selves proved the soil, and put some of our Peas in the ground, and in ten days they were of fourteen inches high: they have also Beans very fair of divers colours and wonderful plenty: some growing naturally, and some in their gardens, and so have they both wheat and oats. . . .

. . . We were entertained with all love, and kindness, and with as much bounty, after their manner, as they could possibly devise. We found the people most gentle, loving, and faithful, void of all guile, and treason, and such as lived after the manner of the golden age. The earth bringeth forth all things in abundance, as in the first creation, without toil or labour. The people only care to defend themselves from the cold, in their short winter, and to feed themselves with such meat as the soil affordeth: . . .

The European colonization of America was undertaken by nations and supported by religious organizations. These sponsors had large goals, arguing that colonization would benefit Europeans and Americans equally. Europe would gain the goods of the newly discovered continents. In return the Americans would receive the unparalleled gift of Christianity by which to enrich their spiritual lives, and European manufactured goods with which to enhance their material lives.

This vision rested on a series of partial misperceptions. Early writers overestimated the easy wealth to be gained in America. Europe would become rich from American products, but these would require great labor and organization to produce. The welcome given early expeditions by Native Americans also misled reporters, who eagerly sought any indication that the Indians willingly and easily would relinquish their own culture and traditions for a European style of life. In reality the natives were interested in choosing from European culture the elements that would make their traditional lives fuller or more efficient. They had no desire to give up a satisfying way of life and, if pushed too hard, would resist in ways that Europeans interpreted as treachery. Disappointment at all levels fed conflict.

A further misperception concerned tribal organization. Europeans tended to see complex hierarchical structures headed by powerful leaders, where modern scholars more typically see decentralized organization, with village- or band-level leaders operating on a consensual basis. It is as misleading to speak of "the Indians" as it is to refer to "the Spanish" or "the English." Neither side was unified. Within the European empires, religious leaders argued with military officers about the paths to follow. Native Americans, with often long-standing rivalries, fought each other and vied for power in the changed situation. At the most fundamental level individuals formed friendships and families across ethnic lines and ultimately faced painful choices.

❧ D O C U M E N T S

Spanish explorer Francisco Vásquez de Coronado, lured by reports of golden cities to the north, led a two-year expedition (described in the first document by Pedro de Castañeda) through the American Southwest as far as central Kansas. Fray Alonso de Benavides, convinced of prospects for many conversions among the Pueblo and Apache Indians, in the second selection urges the Spanish authorities to concentrate efforts on the New Mexico territory. The Pueblo Revolt of 1680 so shocked the Spanish authorities that they collected testimony about its extent and causes. The reports excerpted in the third document include Indians' affirmations that proscription of their own religion drove them to rebel, as well as statements by missionaries about their suffering.

England arrived late on the colonization scene, and English promoters feared that Spain, which had grown wealthy and powerful on riches from America, would take over both continents entirely. Men such as Richard Hakluyt, whose *Discourse of Western Planting* is excerpted in the fourth document, tried to persuade Queen Elizabeth and English merchants and gentry to invest in colonization, lest England lose out in the race for international status. In the final document Ralph Lane, governor of Roanoke, the colony founded as a result of this campaign, reveals the ways in which the colonists, despite their swaggering attitude toward the Carolina Algonquians, were unprepared for the American environment and completely dependent on their Indian neighbors for food.

An Account of Coronado's Exploration
of the Southwest, 1540–1542

Cibola* is seven villages. The largest is called Maçaque. The houses are ordinarily three or four stories high, but in Maçaque there are houses with four and seven stories. These people are very intelligent. They cover their privy parts and all the immodest parts with cloths made like a sort of table napkin, with fringed edges and a tassel at each corner, which they tie over the hips. They wear long robes of feathers and of the skins of hares, and cotton blankets. The women wear blankets, which they tie or knot over the left shoulder, leaving the right arm out. These serve to cover the body. They wear a neat well-shaped outer garment of skin. They gather their hair over the two ears, making a frame which looks like an old-fashioned headdress.

This country is a valley between rocky mountains. They cultivate corn, which does not grow very high. The ears start at the very foot, and each large fat stalk bears about 800 grains, something not seen before in these parts. There are large numbers of bears in this province, and lions, wild-cats, deer, and otter. There are very fine turquoises, although not so many as was reported. They collect the pine nuts each year, and store them up in advance. A man does not have more than one wife. There are estufas or hot rooms in the villages, which are the courtyards or places where they gather for consultation. They do not have chiefs as in New Spain, but are ruled by a council of the oldest men. They have priests who preach to them, whom they call papas. These are the elders. They go up on the highest roof of the village and preach to the village from there, like public criers, in the morning while the sun is rising, the whole village being silent and sitting in the galleries to listen. They tell them how they are to live, and I believe that they give certain commandments for them to keep, for there is no drunkenness among them nor sodomy nor sacrifices, neither do they eat human flesh nor steal, but they are usually at work. The estufas belong to the whole village. It is a sacrilege for the women to go into the estufas to sleep. They make the cross as a sign of peace. They burn their dead, and throw the implements used in their work into the fire with the bodies. . . .

Tiguex is a province with twelve villages on the banks of a large, mighty river; some villages on one side and some on the other. . . .

. . . [The villages] are governed by the opinions of the elders. They all work together to build the villages, the women being engaged in making the mixture and the walls, while the men bring the wood and put it in place. They have no lime, but they make a mixture of ashes, coals, and dirt which is almost as good as mortar, for when the house is to have four stories, they do not make the walls more than half a yard thick. They gather a great pile of twigs of thyme and sedge grass and set it afire, and when it is half coals and ashes they throw a quantity of dirt and water on it and mix it all together. They make round balls of this, which they use instead of stones after they are dry, fixing them with the same mixture, which comes to be like a stiff

---

*Coronado's Cibola is Háwikuh Pueblo.

clay. Before they are married the young men serve the whole village in general, and fetch the wood that is needed for use, putting it in a pile in the courtyard of the villages, from which the women take it to carry to their houses.

The young men live in the estufas, which are in the yards of the village. . . . When any man wishes to marry, it has to be arranged by those who govern. The man has to spin and weave a blanket and place it before the woman, who covers herself with it and becomes his wife. The houses belong to the women, the estufas to the men. If a man repudiates his woman, he has to go to the estufa. It is forbidden for women to sleep in the estufas, or to enter these for any purpose except to give their husbands or sons something to eat. The men spin and weave. The women bring up the children and prepare the food. The country is so fertile that they do not have to break up the ground the year round, but only have to sow the seed, which is presently covered by the fall of snow, and the ears come up under the snow. In one year they gather enough for seven. A very large number of cranes and wild geese and crows and starlings live on what is sown, and for all this, when they come to sow for another year, the fields are covered with corn which they have not been able to finish gathering. . . .

. . . They keep the separate houses where they prepare the food for eating and where they grind the meal, very clean. This is a separate room or closet, where they have a trough with three stones fixed in stiff clay. Three women go in here, each one having a stone, with which one of them breaks the corn, the next grinds it, and the third grinds it again. They take off their shoes, do up their hair, shake their clothes, and cover their heads before they enter the door. A man sits at the door playing on a fife while they grind, moving the stones to the music and singing together. They grind a large quantity at one time, because they make all their bread of meal soaked in warm water, like wafers. They gather a great quantity of brushwood and dry it to use for cooking all through the year. There are no fruits good to eat in the country, except the pine nuts. They have their preachers. . . .

Cicuye[*] is a village of nearly five hundred warriors, who are feared throughout that country. It is square, situated on a rock, with a large court or yard in the middle, containing the estufas. The houses are all alike, four stories high. One can go over the top of the whole village without there being a street to hinder. There are corridors going all around it at the first two stories, by which one can go around the whole village. These are like outside balconies, and they are able to protect themselves under these. The houses do not have doors below, but they use ladders, which can be lifted up like a drawbridge, and so go up to the corridors which are on the inside of the village. As the doors of the houses open on the corridor of that story, the corridor serves as a street. The houses that open on the plain are right back of those that open on the court, and in time of war they go through those behind them. The village is inclosed by a low wall of stone. There is a spring of water inside which they are able to divert. The people of this village boast that no one has been able to conquer them and

---

[*]Cicuye is modern Pecos Indians.

that they conquer whatever villages they wish. The people and their customs are like those of the other villages. . . .

Fray Alonso de Benavides Reports New Mexico Indians Eager for Conversion, 1634

On February 27 of the same year, 1632, Father Fray Martín de Arvide, who had spent many years in preaching the divine word in New Mexico [suffered martyrdom]. The great pueblo of Picuries had fallen to his lot. Here he converted more than two hundred Indians, suffering great hardships and personal dangers, as these people are the most indomitable of that kingdom. He founded a church and convent large enough to minister to all the baptized. Among the newly converted, there was a young man, a son of one of the principal sorcerers. On a certain occasion, the latter undertook to pervert his son and dissuade him from what the padre taught. When the father was informed of it, he left the convent with a crucifix in his hands and, filled with apostolic spirit, he went to the place where the infernal minister was perverting that soul and began to remonstrate with him, saying, "Is it not sufficient that you yourself want to go to hell without desiring to take your son also?" Addressing the young man, he said, "Son, I am more your father and I love you more than he, for he wants to take you with him to the suffering of hell, while I wish you to enjoy the blessings of being a Christian." With divine zeal, he advanced these and other arguments. The old sorcerer arose, grasped a large club near by, and struck the blessed father such a blow on the head that he felled him and then he and others dragged him around the plaza and ill-treated him cruelly. Miraculously he escaped from their hands; although very eager to offer his life to its Giver, God preserved him for a later occasion.

As a result of this the Indians rebelled, so that for several years that pueblo refused to receive a friar who might preach our holy Catholic faith to them. This situation continued until the year 1628 when I stationed there Father Andrés de Zea, who converted many people. . . .

. . . All the Indians are now converted, baptized, and very well ministered to, with thirty-three convents and churches in the principal pueblos and more than one hundred and fifty churches throughout the other pueblos; here, where scarcely thirty years earlier all was idolatry and worship of the devil, without any vestige of civilization, today they all worship our true God and Lord. The whole land is dotted with churches, convents, and crosses along the roads. The people are so well taught that they now live like perfect Christians. They are skilled in all the refinements of life, especially in the singing of organ chants, with which they enhance the solemnity of the divine service.

All these nations settled in this most northerly region in order to escape the intolerable cold and to find there a milder climate, but they met with opposition and resistance from the native inhabitants of this whole land, that is, from the huge Apache nation. In fact, the Apaches surround the above-mentioned nations on all sides and have continuous wars with them.

Thus, since we had converted all these nations, we endeavored to convert the Apaches, who alone are more numerous than all the others together, and even more numerous than the people of New Spain. These Indians are very spirited and belligerent. They are a people of a clearer and more subtle understanding, and as such they laugh at the other nations because they worship idols of wood and stone. The Apaches worship only the sun and the moon. They wear clothing, and although their chief sustenance is derived from hunting, they also plant much corn. Their houses are modest, but adequate for protection against the cold spells of that region. In this nation only, the husband often has as many wives as he can support. This also depends on rank, for it is a mark of prestige to have numerous wives. They cut off the nose and ears of the woman taken in adultery. They pride themselves on never lying but on always speaking the truth. The people of this nation are countless, for they occupy the whole of New Mexico. Thus, armies of more than thirty thousand have been seen on the way to war against each other, the fields swarming with them. They have no one king who governs them, in general, but in each district or province they allow themselves to be ruled by one who is famous for some brave deed. The neighboring provinces, however, always heed and have respect for someone from a larger province. . . .

Starting, then, with that portion of this nation nearest to the Pira [Piro] nation, which is the first we meet on reaching New Mexico, there is, on the opposite bank of the Rio del Norte to the west, the province and tribe of the Xila Apaches. It is fourteen leagues from the pueblo of San Antonio Senecú, where their chief captain, called Sanaba, oftentimes comes to gamble. After he had heard me preach to the Piros several times, he became inclined to our holy Catholic faith and confided his thoughts to me; and when I had satisfied him in regard to certain difficulties that he had encountered, he determined to become a Christian and said that he wanted to go and tell his people in order that they too should become Christians. This he did, and within a few days he returned to see me, with some of his people already converted by what he had told them. Confirming them in their good intentions, I persuaded them, since they were the chief lords, that, as a good beginning to their Christianity, they should at once erect a cross in the center of the plaza of their pueblo so that I could find and worship it when I came to visit them. They promised me to do this and departed very happy. And, although I, because of the demands of my office and the lack of friars, could not go there that year, withal I learned that Captain Sanaba was an apostolic preacher and desired that all of his tribe should be converted, and he had already prepared them for it.

After the lapse of a few days, I returned there to ascertain the state of that conversion. When Captain Sanaba heard that I had arrived at San Antonio Senecú, he came those fourteen leagues to see me, accompanied by many of his people. After I had welcomed him with honor in the presence of all, he presented me with a folded chamois, which is a dressed deerskin. It is customary among these people, when going to visit someone, to bring a gift. I accepted it to gratify him, although I told him that I did not want anything from him except that he and all his people should become Christians. He asked me to unfold the chamois and see what was painted on it. This I did and saw that it had been decorated with the sun and the moon, and above each a cross, and although the symbolism was apparent to me, I asked him about it. He responded in these formal words: "Father, until now we have not known any benefactors as great as the sun and the moon, because the sun lights us by day, warms us, and makes our plants grow; the moon lights us by night. Thus we worship them as our gods. But, now that you have taught us who God, the creator of all things is, and that the sun and the moon are His creatures, in order that you might know that we now worship only God, I had these crosses, which are the emblem of God, painted above the sun and the moon. We have also erected one in the plaza, as you commanded."

Only one who has worked in these conversions can appreciate the joy that such happenings bring to a friar when he sees the results of his preaching. Recognizing this gift as the fruit of the divine word, I took the chamois and placed it on the high altar as a banner won from the enemy and as evidence of the high intelligence of this nation, for I do not know what more any of the ancient philosophers could have done. With this I bade farewell to him and his people, who were very happy. Within a few days he came more than sixty leagues to see me, rejoicing that all of his people had decided to become Christians. In his own name and in behalf of all of them he rendered obedience to me in the name of our holy mother, the church. With this good start, I founded that conversion in their pueblo of Xila, placing it in charge of Father Fray Martín del Espíritu Santo, who administered it with great courage during the year 1628.

New Mexico's Indians Rebel Against Suppression of Their Native Religion, 1680: Four Accounts

Alonso García to Fray Francisco de Ayeta

The señor governor tells me to advise your reverence of the state in which he finds himself, which must certainly arouse great pity in every one, at seeing so many children and women on foot, naked, and dying of hunger, according to reports that have reached us, they not having been able to escape with even a shirt.

The señor governor informs me that all the rest are coming in the same plight. Let your reverence reflect upon the afflictions that the señor governor and all those of us who are present will have experienced. I am going out to meet the señor governor and to ascertain his lordship's decision, leaving all the families in this place, guarded by most of the men.

It is said that nothing remains of the temples and sacred vestments—that they have burned everything. From your reverence's report and from the necessary slowness of the señor governor, I judge that he will arrive here at about the same time as the wagons with the supplies. That which the señor governor urges me most strongly is to advise your reverence as quickly as possible, for the relief of such great suffering.

118

Meanwhile, may our Lord keep your reverence for the protection of so many poor people, who desire to see you with the spiritual increase which your reverence merits. In this place of Fray Cristóbal, to-day, September 4, 1680. Your reverence's humblest servant, who kisses your feet.

Alonso García

Fray Antonio de Sierra to Fray Francisco de Ayeta

... My escape from [La Isleta] was a divine dispensation, through circumstances which I will tell personally, or of which your reverence will learn from many persons. All the rest have perished. The Indians who have done the greatest harm are those who have been most favored by the religious and who are most intelligent. Many of them have already paid with their lives in the fighting in the villa, where the entire battery was, as well as a large number of Indians. The latter, terrified by the conflict, gave the Spaniards an opportunity to retire from the villa with small loss, although that of Sargento Mayor Andrés Gómez Parra and other soldiers was a great one. According to reports, few were wounded, among them the señor governor. . . .

Statement of One of the Rebellious Christian Indians

... Having been asked his name and of what place he is a native, his condition, and age, he said that his name is Don Pedro Nanboa, that he is a native of the pueblo of Alameda, a widower, and somewhat more than eighty years of age. Asked for what reason the Indians of this kingdom have rebelled, forsaking their obedience to his Majesty and failing in their obligation as Christians, he said that for a long time, because the Spaniards punished sorcerers and idolaters, the nations of the Teguas, Taos, Pecuríes, Pecos, and Jemez had been plotting to rebel and kill the Spaniards and the religious, and that they had been planning constantly to carry it out, down to the present occasion. Asked what he learned, saw and heard in the juntas and parleys that the Indians have held, what they have plotted among themselves, and why the Indians have burned the church and profaned the images of the pueblo of Sandia, he said that he has not taken part in any junta, nor has he harmed any one; that what he has heard is that the Indians do not want religious or Spaniards. Because he is so old, he was in the cornfield when he learned from the Indian rebels who came from the sierra that they had killed the Spaniards of the jurisdiction and robbed all their haciendas, sacking their houses. Asked whether he knows about the Spaniards and religious who were gathered in the pueblo of La Isleta, he said that it is true that some days ago there assembled in the said pueblo of La Isleta the religious of Sandia, Jemez, and Zia, and that they set out to leave the kingdom with those of the said pueblo of La Isleta and the Spaniards—not one of whom remained—taking along their property. The Indians did not fight with them because all the men had gone with the other nations to fight at the villa and destroy the governor and captain-general and all the people who were with him. He declared that the resentment which all the Indians have in their hearts has been so strong, from the time this kingdom was discovered, because the religious and the Spaniards took away their idols and forbade their sorceries and idolatries; that they have inherited successively from their old men the things pertaining to their ancient customs; and that he has heard this resentment spoken of since he was of an age to understand. What he has said is the truth and what he knows, under the oath taken, and he signs and ratifies it, it being read and explained to him in his language through the interpretation of Captain Sebastián Montaño, who signed it with his lordship, as the said Indian does not know how, before me, the present secretary.

Antonio de Otermín

Statement of Pedro García

... [T]here appeared before his lordship an Indian named Pedro García, a sworn witness in these *autos,* and he stated under oath that he remembers distinctly that the captains of the Tagnos told him before the revolt that they had desired and discussed it in these parts for more than twelve years; that the said Indians wished to rebel because they resented it greatly that the religious and the Spaniards should deprive them of their idols, their dances, and their superstitions. . . .

A brief Collection of certain reasons to induce her Majesty and the state to take in hand the western voyage and the planting there.

1. The soil yieldeth and may be made to yield all the several commodities of Europe, and of all kingdoms, dominions and Territories that England tradeth with, that by trade of merchandize cometh into this Realm.

2. The passage thither and home is neither too long nor too short, but easy and to be made twice in the year.

3. The passage cutteth not near the trade of any Prince, nor near any of their countries or Territories and is a safe passage, and not easy to be annoyed by Prince or potentate whatsoever.

4. The passage is to be performed at all times of the year. . . .

5. And where England now for certain hundred years last past by the peculiar commodities of wools, and of later years by clothing of the same, hath raised itself from meaner state to greater wealth and much higher honor, might and power than before, to the equalling of the princes of the same to the greatest potentates of this part of the world. It cometh now so to pass that by the great endeavor of the increase of the trade of wools in Spain and in the West Indies now daily more and more multiplying, That the wools of England and the cloth made of the same, will become base, and every day more base than other, which prudently weighed, it behoveth this Realm if it mean not to return to former old meanness and baseness, but to stand in present and late former honor glory and force, and not negligently and sleepingly to slide into beggary, to foresee and to plant at Norumbega [New England] or some like place. . . .

6. This enterprise may stay the Spanish king from flowing over all the face of that waste firm [mainland] of America, if we seat and plant there in time, in time I say, and we by planting shall let him from making more short and more safe returns out of the noble ports of the purposed places of our planting. . . . How easy a matter may it be to this Realm swarming at this day with valiant youths rusting and hurtful by lack of employment, and having good makers of cable and of all sorts of cordage, and the best and most cunning shipwrights of the world to be Lords of all those Seas, and to spoil Philip's [King Philip II of Spain] Indian navy, and to deprive him of yearly passage of his Treasure into Europe, and consequently to abate the pride of Spain and of the supporter of the great Antichrist of Rome, and to pull him down in equality to his neighbor princes, and consequently to cut off the common mischiefs that comes to all Europe by the peculiar abundance of his Indian Treasure, and this without difficulty.

7. . . . [T]his Realm shall have by that mean ships of great burden and of great strength for the defence of this Realm.

8. This new navy of mighty new strong ships so in trade to that Norumbega and to the coasts there, shall never be subject to arrest of any prince or potentate, as the navy of this Realm from time to time hath been in the ports of the empire.

9. The great mass of wealth of the Realm embarked in the merchants' ships

---

Some of the spelling in this document has been modernized.

carried out in this new course, shall not lightly in so far distant a course from the coast of Europe be driven by winds and Tempests into ports of any foreign prince. . . .

10. No foreign commodity that comes into England comes without payment of custom once, twice, or thrice before it come into the Realm, and so all foreign commodities become dearer [more expensive] to the subjects of this Realm, and by this course to Norumbega foreign prince's customs are avoided, and the foreign commodities cheaply purchased, they become cheap to the subjects of England to the common benefit of the people, and to the saving of great Treasure in the Realm, whereas now the Realm becometh poor by the purchasing of foreign commodities in so great a mass at so excessive prices.

11. At the first traffic [trade] with the people of those parts, the subjects of this Realm for many years shall change many cheap commodities of these parts, for things of high valor [value] there not esteemed, and this to the great enriching of the Realm, if common use fail not.

12. By the great plenty of those Regions the merchants and their factors shall lie there cheap, buy and repair their ships cheap, and shall return at pleasure without stay or restraint of foreign Prince . . . and so he shall be rich and not subject to many hazards, but shall be able to afford the commodities for cheap prices to all subjects of the Realm.

13. . . . [B]y thousands of things there to be done, infinite numbers of the English nation may be set on work to the unburdening of the Realm with many that now live chargeable to the state at home.

14. If the sea coast serve for making of salt, and the inland for wine, oils, oranges, lemons, figs, etc., and for making of iron, all which with much more is hoped, without sword drawn, we shall cut the comb of the French, of the Spanish, of the Portuguese, and of enemies, and of doubtful friends to the abating of their wealth and force, and to the greater saving of the wealth of the Realm.

15. . . . [W]e may out of those parts receive the mass of wrought wares that now we receive out of France, Flanders, Germany, etc. and so we may daunt the pride of some enemies of this Realm, or at the least in part purchase those wares, that now we buy dearly of the French and Fleming, better cheap, and in the end for the part that this Realm was wont to receive drive them out of trade to idleness for the setting of our people on work.

16. We shall by planting there enlarge the glory of the gospel and from England plant sincere religion, and provide a safe and a sure place to receive people from all parts of the world that are forced to flee for the truth of God's word.

17. If frontier wars there chance to arise, and if thereupon we shall fortify, it will occasion the training up of our youth in the discipline of war, and make a number fit for the service of the wars and for the defence of our people there and at home.

18. The Spaniards govern in the Indies with all pride and tyranny; and like as when people of contrary nature at the sea enter into Gallies, where men are tied as slaves, all yell and cry with one voice *liberta, liberta,* as desirous of liberty and freedom, so no doubt whensoever the Queen of England, a prince of such clemency, shall seat upon that firm of America, and shall be reported throughout all that tract to use the natural people there with all humanity, courtesy, and freedom, they will yield themselves to her government and revolt clean from the Spaniard.

... [A]nd if it be high policy to maintain the poor people of this Realm in work, I dare affirm that if the poor people of England were five times so many as they be, yet all might be set on work in and by working linen and such other things of merchandise as the trade in the Indies doth require.

19. The present short trades causeth the mariner to be cast off, and oft to be idle and so by poverty to fall to piracy. But this course to Norumbega being longer and a continuance of the employment of the mariner doth keep the mariner from idleness and from necessity, and so it cutteth off the principal actions of piracy, and the rather because no rich prey for them to take cometh directly in their course or any thing near their course.

20. Many men of excellent wits of divers singular gifts overthrown ... by some folly of youth, that are not able to live in England may there be raised again, and do their Country good service. . . .

21. Many soldiers and servitors in the end of the wars that might be hurtful to this Realm, may there be unladen, to the common profit and quiet of this Realm, and to our foreign benefit there as they may be employed.

22. The fry [children] of the wandering beggars of England that grow up idly and hurtful and burdenous to this Realm, may there be unladen, better bred up, and may people waste Countries to the home and foreign benefit, and to their own more happy state.

23. If England cry out and affirm that there is so many in all trades that one cannot live for another as in all places they do, This Norumbega (if it be thought so good) offereth the remedy.

Governor Ralph Lane Describes the Roanoke Colony's Attack on the Roanoke Indians, 1586

The King was advised and of himself disposed, as a ready mean to have assuredly brought us to ruin in the month of March 1586. himself also with all his Savages to have run away from us, and to have left his ground in the Island unsowed: which if he had done, there had been no possibility in common reason, (but by the immediate hand of God) that we could have been preserved from starving out of hand. For at that time we had no weirs for fish, neither could our men skill of the making of them, neither had we one grain of Corn for seed to put into the ground. . . .

... The manner of their enterprise was this.

Tarraquine and Andacon two principal men about Pemisapan, and very lusty fellows, with twenty more appointed to them had the charge of my person to see an order taken for the same, which they meant should in this sort have been executed. In the dead time of the night they would have beset my house, and put fire in the reeds that the same was covered with: meaning (as it was likely) that myself would have come running out of a sudden amazed in my shirt without arms, upon the instant whereof they would have knocked out my brains.

Some of the spelling in this document has been modernized.

The same order was given to certain of his fellows, for M. Heriots [Harriot's]: so for all the rest of our better sort, all our houses at one instant being set on fire as afore is said, and that as well for them of the fort, as for us at the town. Now to the end that we might be the fewer in number together, and so be the more easily dealt withal (for indeed ten of us with our arms prepared, were a terrour to a hundred of the best sort of them,) they agreed and did immediately put it in practise, that they should not for any copper sell us any victuals whatsoever: besides that in the night they should send to have our weirs robbed, and also to cause them to be broken, and once being broken never to be repaired again by them. By this means the King stood assured, that I must be enforced for lack of sustenance there, to disband my company into sundry places to live upon shellfish, for so the Savages themselves do, going to Hatorask, Croatoan, and other places, fishing and hunting, while their grounds be in sowing, and their corn growing: which failed not his expectation. For the famine grew so extreme among us, or weirs failing us of fish, that I was enforced to send Captaine Stafford with 20 with him to Croatoan my Lord Admiral's Island to serve two turns in one, that is to say, to feed himself and his company, and also to keep watch if any shipping came upon the coast to warn us of the same. . . .

These mischiefs being all instantly upon me and my company to be put in execution, it stood me in hand to study how to prevent them, and also to save all others, which were at that time as aforesaid so far from me: where-upon I sent to Pemisapan to put suspicion out of his head, that I meant presently to go to Croatoan, for that I had heard of the arrival of our fleet, (though I in truth had neither heard nor hoped for so good adventure,) and that I meant to come by him, to borrow of his men to fish for my company, & to hunt for me at Croatoan, as also to buy some four days' provision to serve for my voyage.

He sent me word that he would himself come over to Roanoak, but from day to day he deferred, only to bring the Weopomeioks with him & the Mandoags, whose time appointed was within eight days after. It was the last of May 1586 when all his own Savages began to make their assembly at Roanoak, at his commandment sent abroad unto them, and I resolved not to stay longer upon his coming over, since he meant to come with so good company, but thought good to go and visit him with such as I had, which I resolved to do the next day: but that night I meant by the way to give them in the Island a canvisado [a sudden attack], and at the instant to seize upon all the canoes about the Island, to keep him from advertisements. . . .

. . . The next morning with the light horseman & one Canoe taking 25 with the Colonel of the Chesepians, and the Sergeant major, I went to Dasamonquepeio: and being landed, sent Pemisapan word by one of his own Savages that met me at the shore, that I was going to Croatoan, and meant to take him in the way. . . . Here upon the king did abide my coming to him, and finding myself amidst seven or eight of his principal Weroances and followers, (not regarding any of the common sort) I gave the watch-word agreed upon, (which was, Christ our victory) and immediately those his chief men and himself had by the mercy of God for our deliverance, that which they had purposed for us. The king himself being shot through by the Colonel with a pistol, lying on the ground for dead, & I looking as watchfully for the saving of Manteo's friends, as others were busy that none of the rest should escape, suddenly he started up, and ran away as though he had not been touched, insomuch as he overran all the company, being by the way shot thwart the buttocks by mine Irish boy with my petronel. In the end an Irish man serving me, one Nugent, and the deputy provost, undertook him; and following him in the woods, overtook him: and I in some doubt lest we had lost both the king & my man by our own negligence to have been intercepted by the Savages, we met him returning out of the woods with Pemisapan's head in his hand. . . .

A Gentleman of Elvas fl. 1537–1557

The text that follows is an account of the Hernando de Soto expedition of 1539–43, which explored from Florida to Oklahoma, rediscovering the Mississippi River (which had been first explored by Alonso Alvarez de Piñeda), where de Soto died of fever. The text, taken directly from a translation by Richard Hakluyt, has not been modernized. Hakluyt anglicized all Spanish first names.

This selection about Juan Ortiz from the account given by a "Gentleman from Elvas" shows the possibility of peaceable relations between the Spanish and the native populations.

PRIMARY WORKS

The Discovery and Conquest of Terra Florida, trans. Richard Hakluyt, 1611 (First printing, 1609); rpt. Burt Franklin, n. d. (First published in Evora, Portugal, in 1557.)

from The Discovery and Conquest of Terra Florida

Chapter VIII
Of some inrodes that were made into the countrie; and how there was a Christian found, which had bin long time in the power of an Indian Lord.

From the towne of Ucita, the Governour sent the alcalde mayor, Baltasar de Gallegos, with 40 horsemen and 80 footemen, into the countrie, to see if they could take any Indians; and the captaine, John Rodriguez Lobillo, another way with 50 footemen; the most of them were swordmen and target-tours, and the rest were shot and crossebowmen. They passed through a countrie full of bogges, where horses could not travell. Halfe a league from the campe, they lighted upon certaine cabins of Indians neere a river; the people that were in them leaped into the river; yet they

---

[12] Basques from northern Spain.

tooke foure Indian women; and twentie Indians charged us, and so distressed us, that wee were forced to retire to our campe, being, as they are, exceeding readie with their weapons. It is a people so warlike and so nimble, that they care not a whit for any footemen. For if their enemies charge them, they runne away, and if they turne their backs, they are presently upon them. And the thing that they most flee, is the shot of an arrow. They never stand still, but are alwaies running and traversing from one place to another; by reason whereof neither crossebow nor arcubuse can aime at them; and before one crossebowman can make one shot, an Indian will discharge three or foure arrowes; and he seldome misseth what hee shooteth at. An arrow, where it findeth no armour, pierceth as deepely as a crossebow. Their bowes are very long, and their arrowes are made of certain canes like reedes, very heavie, and so strong, that a sharpe cane passeth thorow a target; some they arme in the point with a sharpe bone of a fish like a chisel, and in others they fasten certaine stones like points of diamants. For the most part, when they light upon an armour, they breake in the place where they are bound together. Those of cane do split and pierce a coate of maile, and are more hurtfull then the other. John Rodriguez Lobillo returned to the campe with six men wounded, whereof one died, and brought the foure Indian women, which Baltasar Gallegos had taken in the cabins or cotages. Two leagues from the towne, comming into the plaine field, he espied ten or eleven Indians, among whom was a Christian, which was naked, and scorched with the sunne, and had his armes razed after the manner of the Indians, and differed nothing at all from them. And as soone as the horsemen saw them, they ran toward them. The Indians fled, and some of them hid themselves in a wood, and they overtooke two or three of them, which were wounded; and the Christian, seeing an horseman runne upon him with his lance, began to crie out, Sirs, I am a Christian, slay me not, nor these Indians, for they have saved my life. And straight-way he called them, and put them out of feare, and they came foorth of the wood unto them. The horsemen tooke both the Christian and the Indians up behind them; and toward night came into the campe with much joy; which thing being knowne by the Governour, and them that remained in the campe, they were received with the like.

Chapter IX
How this Christian came to the land of Florida, and who he was; and what conference he had with the Governour.

This Christian's name was John Ortiz, and he was borne in Sivil,[1] in worshipful parentage. He was twelve yeeres in the hands of the Indians. He came into this countrie with Pamphilo de Narvaez,[2] and returned in the ships to the Island of Cuba, where the wife of the Governour, Pamphilo de Narvaez, was: and by his commandement, with twenty or thirty other, in a brigandine, returned backe againe to Florida; and comming to the port in the sight of the towne, on the shore they saw

---

[1] Seville in southern Spain.
[2] Pánfilo de Narváez, the leader of Cabeza de
Vaca's ill-fated expedition in 1528.

a cane sticking in the ground, and riven at the top, and a letter in it: and they beleeved that the Governour had left it there to give advertisement of himselfe, when he resolved to goe up into the land; and they demanded it of foure or five Indians, which walked along the sea shore; and they bad them, by signes, to come on shore for it, which, against the will of the rest, John Ortiz and another did. And as soone as they were on land, from the houses of the towne issued a great number of Indians, which compassed them about, and tooke them in a place where they could not flee; and the other, which sought to defend himselfe, they presentlie killed upon the place, and tooke John Ortiz alive, and carried him to Ucita their lord. And those of the brigandine sought not to land, but put themselves to sea, and returned to the island of Cuba. Ucita commanded to bind John Ortiz hand and foote upon foure stakes aloft upon a raft, and to make a fire under him, that there he might bee burned. But a daughter of his desired him that he would not put him to death, alleaging that one only Christian could do him neither hurt nor good, telling him, that it was more for his honour to keepe him as a captive. And Ucita granted her request, and commanded him to be cured of his wounds; and as soone as he was whole, he gave him the charge of the keeping of the temple, because that by night the wolves did cary away the dead corpses out of the same; who commended himselfe to God, and tooke upon him the charge of his temple. One night the wolves gate from him the corpes of a little child, the sonne of a principal Indian; and going after them, he threw a darte at one of the wolves, and strooke him that carried away the corps, who, feeling himselfe wounded, left it, and fell downe dead neere the place; and hee not woting[3] what he had done, because it was night, went backe againe to the temple; the morning being come, and finding not the bodie of the child, he was very sad. As soone as Ucita knew thereof, he resolved to put him to death; and sent by the tract, which he said the wolves went, and found the bodie of the child, and the wolfe dead a little beyond: whereat Ucita was much contented with the Christian, and with the watch which hee kept in the temple, and from thence forward esteemed him much. Three yeeres after hee fell into his hands, there came another lord, called Mocoço, who dwelleth two daies journy from the port, and burned his towne. Ucita fled to another towne that he had in another sea port. Thus John Ortiz lost his office and favour that he had with him. These people being worshippers of the divell, are wont to offer up unto him the lives and blood of their Indians, or of any other people they can come by; and they report, that when he will have them doe that sacrifice unto him, he speaketh with them, and telleth them that he is athirst, and willeth them to sacrifice unto him. John Ortiz had notice by the damsell that had delivered him from the fire, how her father was determined to sacrifice him the day following, who willed him to flee to Mocoço, for shee knew that he would use him well; for she heard say, that he had asked for him, and said he would be glad to see him; and because he knew not the way, she went with him halfe a league out of the towne by night, and set him in the way, and returned, because she would not be discovered. John Ortiz travailed all that night, and by the morning came unto a river, which is in the territorie of Mocoço; and there he saw two Indians fishing; and because they were in war with the people of Ucita, and their languages were different, and hee knew not the language of Mocoço, he was afraid (because he could not tell them who hee was, nor how hee came thither, nor

[3] Knowing.

127

was able to answer any thing for himselfe) that they would kill him, taking him for one of the Indians of Ucita; and before they espied him, he came to the place where they had laid their weapons; and as soone as they saw him, they fled toward the towne; and although he willed them to stay, because he meant to do them no hurt, yet they understood him not, and ran away as fast as ever they could. And as soone as they came to the towne with great outcries, many Indians came forth against him, and began to compasse him to shoote at him: John Ortiz seeing himselfe in so great danger, shielded himselfe with certaine trees, and began to shreeke out, and crie very loud, and to tell them that he was a Christian, and that he was fled from Ucita, and was come to see and serve Mococo his lord. It pleased God, that at that very instant there came thither an Indian that could speake the language and understood him, and pacified the rest, who told them what hee said. Then ran from thence three or foure Indians to beare the newes to their lord, who came foorth a quarter of a league from the towne to receive him, and was very glad of him. He caused him presently to sweare according to the custome of the Christians, that he would not run away from him to any other lord, and promised him to entreate him very well; and that if at any time there came any Christians into that countrie, he would freely let him goe, and give him leave to goe to them; and likewise tooke his oth to performe the same, according to the Indian custome.

About three yeares after, certaine Indians, which were fishing at sea two leagues from the towne, brought newes to Mococo that they had seene ships; and hee called John Ortiz, and gave him leave to go his way; who, taking his leave of him, with all the haste he could, came to the sea, and finding no ships, he thought it to be some deceit, and that the cacique had done the same to learne his mind; so he dwelt with Mococo nine yeeres, with small hope of seeing any Christians. As soone as our Governor arrived in Florida, it was knowne to Mococo, and straightway he signified to John Ortiz that Christians were lodged in the towne of Ucita: and he thought he had jested with him, as hee had done before, and told him, that by this time he had forgotten the Christians, and thought of nothing else but to serve him. But he assured him that it was so, and gave him licence to goe unto them; saying unto him, that if hee would not doe it, and if the Christians should goe their way, he should not blame him, for he had fulfilled that which hee had promised him. The joy of John Ortiz was so great, that hee could not beleeve that it was true; notwithstanding, he gave him thankes, and tooke his leave of him; and Mococo gave him tenne or eleven principall Indians to beare him companie; and as they went to the port where the Governour was, they met with Baltasar de Gallêgos, as I have declared before.

As soone as he was come to the campe, the Governour commanded to give him a sute of apparrell, and very good armour, and a faire horse, and enquired of him, whether hee had notice of any countrie, where there was any gold or silver? He answered, No, because he never went ten leagues compasse from the place where he dwelt; but that thirty leagues from thence dwelt an Indian lord, which was called Parocossi, to whom Mococo and Ucita, with al the rest of that coast, paied tribute, and that hee peradventure[4] might have notice of some good countrie; and that his land was better then that of the sea coast, and more fruitfull and plentifull of maiz; whereof the Governour received great contentment; and said, that he desired no

---

[4] Perhaps.

more then to finde victuals, that hee might goe into the maine land, for the land of Florida was so large that in one place or other there could not chuse but bee some rich countrie. The cacique Mococo came to the port to visit the Governor, and made this speech following:

Right hie and mightie Lord, I being lesser in mine owne conceit for to obey you, then any of those which you have under your command; and greater in desire to doe you greater services, doe appeare before your Lordship with so much confidence of receiving favour, as if in effect this my good will were manifested unto you in workes: not for the small service I did unto you, touching the Christian which I had in my power, in giving him freely his libertie (for I was bound to doe it to preserve mine honour, and that which I had promised him), but because it is the part of great men to use great magnificences: and I am perswaded, that as in bodily perfections, and commanding of good people, you doe exceede all men in the world, so likewise you doe in the parts of the minde, in which you may boast of the bountie of nature. The favour which I hope for of your Lordship is, that you would hold mee for yours, and bethinke your selfe to command me any thing, wherein I may doe you service.

The Governour answered him, that although in freeing and sending him the Christian, he had preserved his honour and promise, yet he thanked him, and held it in such esteeme, as it had no comparison; and that hee would alwaies hold him as his brother, and would favour him in all things to the utmost of his power. Then he commanded a shirt to be given him, and other things, wherewith the cacique being verie well contented, tooke his leave of him, and departed to his owne towne.

1557

René Goulaine de Laudonnière   fl. 1562–1582

With Jean Ribault, René Goulaine de Laudonnière, a French Huguenot (Protestant), attempted to make two French settlements in Florida—the first at Port Royal in 1562, and the second at Fort Cardine in 1564. The French settlements, marred by shortages in supplies and the mutinous behavior of unhappy participants, could not withstand the greater naval and supply strength of the Spanish forces led by Pedro Menéndez de Avilés, who wrested Fort Cardine from Ribault and Laudonnière in 1566.

The text that follows is a translation made by Richard Hakluyt, slightly modernized.

PRIMARY WORKS

A Notable History Containing Four Voyages Made By Certain French Captains unto Florida, trans. Richard Hakluyt, 1587; rpt. by H. Stevens, Sons and Stiles, 1964.

from A Notable Historie Containing Foure Voyages Made by Certaine French Captaines unto Florida

The good cheere being done, and the discourses ended, my men embarked themselves againe with intention to bring me those good newes unto the fort *Caroline.* But after they had sayled a very long whyle downe the river, and were come within three leagues of us, the tide was so strong against them, that they were constrayned to goe on land, and to retire themselves because of the night unto the dwelling of a certain *Paracoussy* named *Molona,* which shewed himselfe very glad of their arrival: for he desired to know some newes of *Thimogoua,* and thought that the French men went thither for none other occasion but for to invade them. Which captain *Vasseur* perceiving dissembled so wel, that he made him beleeve that he went to *Thimogoua,* with none other intention, but to subdue them, and to destroy them with the edge of the sword without mercy, but that their purpose had not such successe as they desired, because that the people of *Thimogoua* being advertised of this enterprise, retired into the woods, and saved themselves by flight: yet neverthelesse they had taken some as they were flying away which carried to newes thereof unto their fellowes. The *Paracoussy* was so glad of this relation, that he enterrupted him, and asked *Vasseur* of the beginning and maner of his execution, and praied him that he would shew him by signes how all things passed. Immediatly *Frauncis la Caille* the seargeant of my band took his sword in his hand, saying that with the point thereof he had thrust through two Indians which ran into the woods, and that his companions had done no lesse for their parts. And that if fortune had so favoured them, that they had not bin discovered by the men of *Thimogoua,* they had had a victorie most glorious and worthy of eternall memory. Hereupon the *Paracoussy* shewed himselfe so wel satisfied, that he could not devise how to gratifie our men, which he caused to come into his house to feast them more honorably: and having made captaine *Vasseur* to sit next him, and in his own chaire (which the Indians esteeme for the chiefest honour) and then underneath him two of his sonnes, goodly and might fellowes, he commanded al the rest to place themselves as they thought good. This done, the Indians came according to their good custom, to present their drink *Cassine* to the *Paracoussy,* and then to certaine of his chiefest friends, and the Frenchmen. Then he which brought it set the cup aside, and drew out a little dagger which hung stucke up in the roofe of the house, and like a mad man he lift his head aloft, and ran apace, and went and smote an Indian which sate alone in one of the corners of the hall, crying with a loud voyce, *Hyou,* the poore Indian stirring not at al for the blow, which he seemed to endure paciently. He which held the dagger went quickly to put the same in his former place, and began again to give us drink, as he did before: but he had not long continued, and had scarcely given 3. or 4. thereof, but he left his bowle againe, tooke the dagger in his hand, and quickly returned unto him which he had stroken before, to whom he gave a very sore blow on the side, crying *Hyou,* as he had done before: then he went to put the dagger in his place, and set him self down among the rest. A little while after, he that had bin stroken fel down backwards, stretching out his armes and legs as if he had bin ready to yeld up the latter gaspe. And then the younger soone of the *Paracoussy* apparrelled in a long white skin, fel down at the feet of him that was fallen backward, weeping bitterly halfe a quarter of an houre: after two other of his brethren clad in like apparel, came about him that was so stricken, and began to sigh pitifully. Their mother bearing a little infant in her arms came from another part, and going to the place where her sonnes were, at the first she used infinit numbers of outcries, then one while lifting up her eies to heaven, an other while falling down unto the ground, she cried so dolefully, that her lamentable mournings would have moved the most hard and stonie heart in the world with pity. Yet this sufficed not, for there came in a company of young gyrles which did never lyn weeping for a long while in the place where the Indian was fallen down, whom afterward they took, and with the saddest gestures they could devise, caried him away into another house a little way of from the great hal of the *Paracoussy,* and continued their weepings and mournings by the space of two long houres: in which meane while the Indians ceassed not to drink Cassine, but with such silence that one word was not heard in the parler. *Vasseur* beeing grieved that hee understood not these ceremonies, demaunded of the *Paracoussy* what these thinges meant: which answered him slowly, *Thimogoua, Thimogoua,* with out saying any more. Beeing more displeased then he was before with so slight an answeare, he turned unto another Indian the *Paracoussyes* brother, who was a *Paracoussy* as well as his brother, called *Malica,* which made him a like answere as he did at the first, praying him to aske no more of these matters, and to have patience for that time. The subtile old *Paracoussy* praied him within a while after to shew him his sword, which he would not deny him, thinking that hee would have behelde the fashion of his weapons: but he soone perceived that it was to another end: for the old man holding it in his hand, beheld it a long while on every place to see if he could find any blood upon it which might shew that any of their enemies had bin killed: (for the Indians are woont to bring their weapons wherwith their enemies have bin defeated with some blood upon them, for a token of their victories.) But seeing no signe thereof upon it, he was upon the point to say unto him, that he had killed none of the men of *Thimogoua,* when as *Vasseur* preventing that which he might object, declared and shewed to him by signes the maner of his enterprise, adding that by reason of the 2. Indians which he had slaine, his sword was so bloudy, that he was inforced to wash and make it cleane a long while in the river: which the old man beleeved to be like to be true, and made no maner of reply thereunto. *Vasseur, la Caille,* and their other companions went out of the hall to go into the roome whither they had carried the Indian: there they found the *Paracoussy* sitting upon tapistries made of smal reeds, which was at meat after the Indian fashion, and the Indian that was smitten hard by him, lying upon the selfsame tapistry, about whom stood the wife of the *Paracoussy,* with all the young damsels which before bewailed him in the hall: which did nothing els but warme a great deale of mosse in steede of napkins to rub the Indians side. Hereupon our men asked the *Paracoussy* again, for what occasion the Indian was so persecuted in his presence: he answered, that this was nothing els but a kind of ceremony wherby they would cal to mind the death and persecutions of the *Paracoussies* their ancestors executed by their enemy *Thimogoua:* alledging moreover, that as often as he himself, or any of his friends and alies returned from the countrey, without they brought the heads of their enimies, or without bringing home some prisoner, he used for a perpetual memory of al his predecessors, to beate the best beloved of all his children, with the selfsame weapons, wherewith they had bin killed in times past: to the ende that by renewing of the wounde their death should be lamented afresh.

1587

Pedro Menéndez de Avilés 1519–1574

Pedro Menéndez de Avilés, a Spanish privateer and adventurer of noble descent, became a captain-general under Philip II and with his own ships set out to establish the Florida territory under Spanish dominion. His group attained Fort Caroline on the May River in 1566, thus ending French Huguenot colonial incursion (led by Jean Ribault and René Goulaine de Laudonnière) in that area. Menéndez de Avilés is the founder of the oldest permanent city in the U.S., St. Augustine, 1565.

PRIMARY WORKS

The Settlement of Florida, ed. Charles E. Bennett, 1968. The letters were translated by Jeannette Thurber Connor.

from Letter to Philip II (October 15, 1565)

I wrote to your Majesty by the galleon San Salvador on the tenth of September, the day on which she left from this port; the duplicate of the letter goes with this one; and immediately after, within that very hour, I being on the bar in a shallop, with two boats laden with artillery and munitions, the four French galleons we had pursued came upon us, with two other pinnaces at the poop, to prevent our disembarking here, and to take from us our artillery and supplies; and although the time was unfavorable for crossing the bar, I preferred to fight, at the risk of drowning myself there with one hundred and fifty persons who were with me, and with the bronze artillery and demi-culverins, rather than see myself in their power and thus strengthen them. It was Our Lord's will to save us miraculously, for the tide was low and there was but a scant fathom and a half of water on the bar, while the ship needed a full fathom and a half; and they, seeing I had escaped them, came to talk with me, saying I should surrender and have no fear, and then went off to search for the galleon, for let it be understood that they held she could not escape from them. Within two days a hurricane and very great storm came upon them, and as it seemed to me that they could not have returned to their fort, that they were in danger of shipwreck, and that to come to look for me as they had, they must have brought with them the greater part of the best forces they had; that their fort would remain weakened, and that now was the opportunity to go and attack it. I discussed with the captains the fine undertaking we might carry through, and it appeared so

to them likewise; I at once had five hundred men equipped—three hundred ar-
quebusiers, the others with pikes and bucklers, although there were few of these
last—and we made up our knapsacks, wherein each man put six pounds of biscuit
which he carried on his back; also his wine bottle, containing from three quarts to
a gallon of wine, and his arms; for each captain and solider, and I first to set the
example, carried this food and the arms on his back. As we did not know the way,
we thought we should arrive in two days, and that there would be but six or eight
leagues to march, for so two Indians who came with us had told us by signs. Setting
out from this Fort of St. Augustine in this order and with this determination, on the
eighteenth of September we met with rivers so swollen by the great rainfall, that by
the evening of the nineteenth we had walked at least fifteen leagues, when we
encamped one league from the fort more or less; more than fifteen leagues, in order
to avoid the rivers, all through swamps and wilderness, through a region never
before trod. On the twentieth, the eve of the day of the blessed apostle and evangelist San Mateo, at dawn when the day was breaking, we prayed to Our Lord and His
Blessed Mother, beseeching them to give us victory over those Lutherans,[1] as we
had already agreed to attack openly with twenty ladders which we were carrying;
and His Divine Majesty granted us such favor, and guided events in such a manner,
that we took the fortress and all that it contained without the slaughter of a single
man of ours, and with the wounding of but one, who has already recovered. One
hundred and thirty-two men were killed, and next day ten more, who were captured in the woods, and among them many gentlemen; and he who was governor
and alcalde, who called himself Monsieur Laudonnière, a relative of the Admiral of
France, and who had been his majordomo, fled to the woods; a soldier pursued him
and dealt him a blow with his pike; we can not find out what has become of him.
About fifty or sixty persons escaped either to the woods, or by swimming, or in two
boats of the three ships which they had in front of the fort. I sent at once to their
ships a trumpeter to make them surrender, and give up their arms and vessels, but
they would not. We sent one of the ships to the bottom with artillery which was
there in the fort, and the other rescued the people and went down stream, where
one league away, there were two other ships with many supplies, which were among
the seven that had come from France, and had not yet been unloaded.

As it appeared to me that I ought not to lose this prize, I set out for this Fort of
Saint Augustine to prepare three boats that were here, with which to go in search of
them, but they were warned by the Indians; and since the French were few in
number, they took the two best ships of the three they had, and sank the other;
within three days they fled, and being advised of this, I gave up my journey. My men
wrote me from the fort that after those ships had departed, there appeared in the
woods about twenty Frenchmen, who go about in their shirts, many of them
wounded, and it is thought that among them may be Monsieur Laudonnière. I have
dispatched orders that they shall try to capture them by every means possible, and
work justice upon them. There were found, counting women, girls, and boys under
fifteen years, about fifty persons, and very great is my anxiety at seeing them in the
company of my people, because of their evil sect, and I feared Our Lord would
punish me if I used cruelty towards them, for eight or ten of the boys were born

---

[1] The French referred to were actually Huguenots,
followers of Calvin, not Luther.

here. These Frenchmen had many friends among the Indians, who have shown much sorrow for their loss, especially for that of two or three teachers of their wicked doctrine who taught the caciques and Indians, who followed around after them as the apostles followed Our Lord, for it is a marvelous thing to see how the Lutherans have bewitched this poor savage people. I shall try everything possible to gain the good will of these Indians who were friends of these Frenchmen, and to have no occasion to break with them; for if one does not resist them by action, they are such great traitors and thieves and so envious, that one cannot well live with them. The caciques and Indians who are their enemies all show me friendship, which I keep and shall keep with them, even if it be not to their liking, for their malicious disposition shall play no part in making me do anything else.

On the twenty-eighth of September the Indians came to inform me that many Frenchmen were six leagues from here by the seashore, who had lost their ships, and had escaped by swimming and in the boats. I took fifty soldiers and arrived with them at break of day; and keeping my people in ambush, I went forth with one companion along a river, as they were on the other side and I on this. I spoke with them and told them I was Spanish, and they told me they were French; they asked me, either with or without my companion, to swim the river to where they were, as it was narrow. I replied that we did not know how to swim; that one of them should cross over, upon assurance of safety. They agreed to do it, and sent over a man of good understanding, a shipmaster.

He related to me in detail that they had sailed from their fort with four galleons and eight pinnaces which each carried twenty-four oars, with four hundred picked soldiers and two hundred sailors; Juan Ribao (Jean Ribault)[2] as General, Monsieur La Grange who was General of the infantry, and other good captains and soldiers and gentlemen, with the intention of seeking and engaging me at sea; and, in case I had landed, of landing their forces in those pinnaces and attacking me. He said that if they had wished to land, they could well have done so, but they had not dared; and that desiring to return to their fort, a hurricane and storm overtook them, so that from twenty to twenty-five leagues from here three of their galleons were destroyed; and they carried about four hundred persons, of whom one hundred and forty only were there alive; as to the rest, some had been drowned, others killed by the Indians, and about fifty of them the Indians had captured and carried away; that Jean Ribault with his flagship was five leagues from them, anchored in three fathoms, aground on some shoals, without any masts, for he had had them cut down, and that there were on board the ship about two hundred people, little less; that they believe he is lost; and that all the bronze artillery, whereof there were many and very good pieces, with the ammunition, were lost in those three vessels; that part of them were on the ship of Jean Ribault, and they considered that he was certainly lost. And he told me that his companions, those captains and soldiers who were safe, prayed that I should give them safe conduct to go to their fort, since they were not at war with Spaniards. I answered him that we had taken their fort and killed

---

[2] Ribault was the leader of the failed attempt to establish a French Huguenot settlement at Port Royal, South Carolina. Having gone back to France, Ribault returned to America, intending to attempt yet another fortification (Fort Caroline) in 1565, when he was met by Menéndez de Avilés.

those in it, because they had erected it there without Your Majesty's permission, and because they were implanting their evil Lutheran sect in these Your Majesty's provinces; and that I, as Governor and Captain-General of these provinces, would wage a war of fire and blood against all those who should come to people these lands and implant the wicked Lutheran sect; seeing that I had come by Your Majesty's command to spread the Gospel in these parts, to enlighten the natives as to what the Holy Mother Church of Rome says and believes, so that they may save their souls; and that therefore I would not give them safe conduct; rather would I follow them on land and sea, until I had taken their lives. He begged me to let him return with this message, and he promised that he would swim back at night; he asked also that I should grant him his life. I did it because I saw he was dealing truthfully with me, and he could make clear to me many things; and immediately after he had returned to his companions, there came a gentleman to tempt me, Monsieur Laudonnière's lieutenant, who was very crafty in these matters; and having conferred with me, he offered that they should lay down their arms, and give themselves up, provided I spared their lives. I replied to him that they could give up their arms, and place themselves at my mercy, for me to do with them that which Our Lord should command me; and from this he could not move me, nor will he, unless God Our Lord inspire me otherwise. And thus he went back with this answer, and they came over and laid down their arms, and I had their hands tied behind them, and had them put to the knife.

Only sixteen were left, of whom twelve were Breton sailors whom they had kidnapped, the other four being carpenters and calkers, people of whom I had need. It appeared to me that to chastise them in this manner would be serving God Our Lord and Your Majesty, so that henceforth this wicked sect shall leave us more free to implant the Gospel in these parts, enlighten the natives, and bring them to allegiance to Your Majesty; and forasmuch as this land is very large, there will be much to do these fifty years, but good beginnings give hope of good endings, and so I hope in Our Lord that He will give me success in everything, that I and my descendants may give these kingdoms to Your Majesty free and unobstructed, and that the people thereof may become Christians; for this is what particularly interests me, as I have written to Your Majesty; and we shall gain much reputation with the Indians, and shall be feared by them, even though we make them gifts.

Meditating on what Jean Ribault had done, I concluded that within ten leagues of where he was anchored with his ship, the three other ships of his company had been lost; that whether he should be wrecked or whether he abandoned his ship, he would land his forces and entrench himself, landing what provisions he could from his ship, and would occupy himself in getting out what bronze guns he could from the three ships; that if his vessel were not lost he would repair damages as best he could from the masts and rigging of the other three ships, and would come back to the fort, thinking it still his; but that if the ship were lost, getting together all the forces he could, he would march along the shore. If he does this, I am waiting for him, so that, with God's help, he will be destroyed; yet he may go inland to a cacique who is friendly to him and very powerful, who is about thirty leagues distant from him; and if this is the case I shall go there to seek him, for it is not fitting that he or his companions remain alive; and if he comes with his ship to the fort, I have provided at the bar two cannon and two demi-culverins wherewith to send him to the bottom after he shall have entered; a brigantine is kept in readiness to capture the men, and I shall do everything possible to prevent him from escaping.

The articles found in the fort were only four bronze pieces, of from ten to fifteen quintals, because as they had brought their cannons from France dismounted and as ballast, they took all the others, and all the rest of the munitions, on the galleons when they went in search of me. There were found, besides, twenty-five bronze muskets weighing two quintals; about twenty quintals of powder, and all the ammunition for these pieces; one hundred and seventy casks of flour, three to a ton; about twenty pipes of wine, as they had not unloaded the greater part of the supplies. . . . I supplicate Your Majesty that for love of Our Lord, you command that what is due me be delivered to me with great promptness, and that those supplies be provided which are for Your Majesty's account; likewise the men's pay, and the pay to be given over there to the two hundred soldiers, so that all may be here during April, and by the beginning of May I may go to Santa Elena and to the Bay of Santa María, which is the outpost and frontier that Your Majesty must hold to be master of these parts; for unless this be done, we shall have done nothing, and if the French set foot there, much money will be spent, and much time must elapse, before they can be driven out from there; and it is not well to treat this matter lightly. . . .

And because they are Lutherans, and in order that such an evil sect may not survive in these parts, I shall so strive for my part, and induce the Indians my friends to do so on theirs, that within five or six months very few, if any, will remain alive; and of the thousand French who had landed when I arrived in these provinces, with their fleet of twelve sails, two ships only have escaped, badly damaged, with forty or fifty people on board. As they are ill-provided and equipped, they may not reach France; and if these should arrive, they would not bring news of the death of Jean Ribault and the destruction of his armada; the later they come to know of this in France, the better it will be, because their minds are at rest, thinking they have strong forces here. And now it is more necessary than ever that everything I ask for be provided with great diligence and secrecy, so that it may be here during April, and the coming summer I can gain control of this coast of Florida, and thus Your Majesty will soon be master thereof, without opposition or anxiety; and being master of Florida, you will secure the Indies and the navigation thereto. And I assure Your Majesty that henceforth you can sustain Florida at very little cost, and it will yield Your Majesty much money, and will be worth more to Spain than New Spain, or even Peru. It can be said that this land is a suburb of Spain; for in truth, it took me no more than forty days of sailing to come to it, and ordinarily as many more are necessary to return to those kingdoms. Owing to the burning of the fort, we endure very great hunger, as the flour was burned, and the biscuit that I brought here is becoming stale and giving out. If we are not succored soon, we shall suffer, and many will pass away from this world from starvation; but trusting that Your Majesty is sure that I am serving you with fidelity and love, and that in everything I am dealing truthfully and shall continue to do so, I say no more, except that I shall advise Your Majesty, in every way I can, of all that may occur. May Our Lord keep and cause to prosper the royal Catholic person of Your Majesty, with the extension of greater kingdoms and dominions, as Christianity has need thereof, and we, Your

Majesty's servants, desire. From these provinces of Florida, on the beach of San Pelayo and Fort of St. Augustine, on the fifteenth of October in the year 1565.

Your Majesty's humble servant, who kisses your royal hands.

P. Menéndez

1968

To a Jesuit Friend[1] (October 15, 1566)

Through letters from Pedro del Castillo I have heard of the many favors done me in all those kingdoms, by the Order of the Society of Jesus: and by means of their prayers, Our Lord has granted me many mercies, and does each day, giving me victory and success in all the things to which we have set our hand, I and the Spaniards who are with me, since we arrived in these provinces. And although we have suffered the greatest hunger, hardships, and perils, and there have been some who could not endure them, and who, like weak men, became discouraged; yet others never felt them, and I among them, although the greatest sinner of them all, for I was certain I was undergoing them for Our Lord, and his reward would not fail me; and I went about more hale and hearty, contented, and cheerful than ever I had been, even in the period of greatest need, when each week the Indians came two or three times, killing two or three of our men and wounding others, and we had nothing to eat; nor had those of us in one fort known for two months whether those in the other were dead or alive. On the eve of St. Peter's Day, (on that same day I sailed from Spain with the Armada, bound for this land), seventeen ships appeared off this harbor of St. Augustine, and all entered safely. They brought fifteen hundred soldiers and five hundred sailors, much artillery and munitions, and were all laden with supplies; whereupon everyone received great pleasure and con-solation, and those who were in this fort would meet one another, weeping for joy, their eyes and hands raised to heaven, praising Our Lord.

At that time I was not in this fort. I came within eight days: and when I did, I saw all the goods and succor that His Majesty the King Don Philip was sending us, and that Our Lord had brought them in safety.

On the one hand, I received the greatest satisfaction at seeing how well the King Our Lord had aided us; but on the other, I felt distressed and lost, on seeing that no one from the Society had come, nor indeed any learned religious; for on account of the many caciques we have for friends, the good judgment and under-standing of the natives of these provinces, and the great desire they have to become Christians and know the Law of Jesus Christ, six such religious could accomplish more in one month than many thousands of men such as we could in many years; we even need them for our own instruction. And it is wasted time to think that the

[1] The Jesuits were a religious society founded by St. Ignatius Loyola in 1534. The Jesuits, and later the Franciscans, supported by Avilés, established missions as far north as Virginia, one mission in the area of the later Jamestown settlement.

137

Holy Gospel can be established in this land with the army alone. Your worship may be certain, if I am not mistaken, that the Word of Our Lord will spread in these parts; for the ceremonies of these people consist in great measure in adoring the sun and moon, and dead deer and other animals they hold as idols; and each year they have three or four festivals for their devotions, during which they worship the sun, and remain three days without eating, drinking, or sleeping; these are their fast days. And he who is weak, and cannot endure this, is considered a bad Indian, and therefore looked upon with contempt by their noble caste; and he who comes through these hardships the best is held to be one of the most important men, and treated with utmost courtesy.

They are a people of such strength; very agile and swift, and great swimmers; they carry on many wars against one another, and no powerful cacique is known among them. I have not wanted to be friends with any cacique in order to make war on his enemy, even though he were also mine, because I tell them that Our Lord is in heaven, and is the Cacique of all the caciques of the earth, and of all that which is created; and He is angry with them because they make war and kill one another like beasts. And thus a few have allowed me to make them friends, and have left their idols and asked me to give them crosses before which they may worship; I have already given them some, and they worship them, and I have given them some youths and soldiers to teach them the Christian Doctrine.

They have begged me to let them become Christians like us, and I have replied to them that I am expecting your worships, in order that you may make vocabularies and soon learn their language; and that then you will tell them how to become Christians, and undeceive them as to how, not being so, they serve and hold for their Master the most wicked creature in the world, who is the devil, and that he misleads them; but once they are Christians, they will be undeceived and serve Our Lord, who is the Cacique of heaven and earth; and then, happy and joyful, they will be our brothers in truth and we will give them of what we may have.

And as I had told them that with this expected succor, these religious would come, who would soon be able to talk to them and teach them to be Christians; and they did not come—the Indians held me to be a liar, and some of them have become irritated, saying that I am deceiving them; and the caciques, my enemies, laugh at them and at me.

It has done the greatest harm, that none of your worships, nor any other learned religious, have come to instruct these people; for as they are great traitors and liars, if, with time and labor, peace with them is not confirmed, so as to open the door to the preaching of the Holy Gospel, the caciques confirming what the religious say, later we shall accomplish nothing, they thinking that we deceive them. May Our Lord inspire that good Society of Jesus to send to these parts as many as six of its members—may they be such—for they will certainly reap the greatest reward.

On the fourteenth of September, 1566, with a contrary wind, there arrived a vessel near this harbor of St. Augustine, about two leagues therefrom; and as it appeared to me that she did not recognize the harbor, I sent a boat, equipped as a skiff with many oars, to get her inside; but there was a heavy sea, and the tide was contrary, and the boat could not go out, and within two days a tempest arose. Fifteen days afterwards a boat was found, anchored, with six Flemings aboard, and no supplies of any kind, in the river of Fort San Mateo, near the sea; and two of the men were wounded to death with arrows. There was likewise a Spaniard among them.

They said that the day before, one league from there, Indians, our enemies, had killed Father Martínez, of the Society, and three other men; and that the ship which had passed by here was the hooker on board in which he came, and she did not recognize the harbor; and it was fifteen days since the pilot of the hooker had landed them in the boat, to try to reconnoiter where they were; and as a storm came up, they could not return to the hooker; and that all these days they had met with many Indians who said they were my friends and brothers; that they had received and entertained them very well, and one league from the Fort of San Mateo this misfortune had happened to them; that Father Martínez brought all the messages from the Holy Father, and these and all the rest he brought were lost. Blessed be Our Lord in all things. And since the Divine Majesty permits and wills it so to be, let us give infinite thanks for it all: since those of us who are here deserve so little that Our Lord desired to give us this calamity by removing from our company such a blessing as was Father Martínez, of whom we Spaniards who are in this land, stood in such need, as well as the natives thereof.

I have believed that the hooker has not been lost, and that she has arrived at the island of Puerto Rico, or Santo Domingo, or Cuba. I am dispatching a boat to go to these islands and aboard her a servant of mine; and wherever that hooker may wish to go, I have ordered her pilot to sail to Havana; and he is to carry with him and take care of the two Fathers of the Society who are coming on her; and they shall busy themselves until the end of February, when the winter shall be passed, in preparing vocabularies and learning the language of the land of Carlos, a cacique who is a great friend. And there in Havana there are people who know the language very well; and at the beginning of March they shall go in two days to that cacique, for the sailing is very good; and then to these forts, without again embarking, and through a land which is thickly settled; for most of the villages through which they have to pass are our friends; they have crosses that I have given them, and youths and soldiers who are teaching them the doctrine.

We have not gone inland, because of fortifying ourselves on the coast and trying to make friends with its caciques, so that we can feel secure behind our backs; and therefore we have not seen any large towns, although there are many Indians and boys. There is news that inland there are many people, and a great report of a Salt River which goes to China; wherefore it is expedient that the religious who may come to these parts be truly religious; otherwise, it were better that they should not come. And since your worship understands this better than I can write it, this is enough so that the Society may provide what is fitting in the matter.

I shall be in those kingdoms some time in May, at the latest; and, it may be, many days before; and it would not suit me to remain in those kingdoms later than July, that I may return to this coast in good weather, and bring over in the greatest safety the persons who may come with me, because then the weather and the navigation are good for coming to these provinces.

And I shall bring and serve and entertain those members of the Society, and any other religious who may wish to come, as if they were the King himself; and I shall give orders in these parts, as long as I live, that they be respected as Our Lord's Ministers, trusting that he who may not deserve this treatment shall be brought to deserve it by his companions; and in case they were unable to do this, they should send him back to those kingdoms; because in this new land it is needful that all this should be. And it is a thing with which God Our Lord will be most pleased because it is from the religious that all good teaching and example must come, and for this reason he must be respected and revered.

Many times I kiss the hands of all those gentlemen of the Society; may they have the reward of Our Lord for the many favors they do me in entreating Our Lord to help and protect me in all things. And I therefore beg them as a mercy, as much as I can, to continue to do so. And if this should reach your worship in Cadiz, tell Pedro del Castillo that I kiss his hands, and he is to consider this letter as his.

May Our Lord keep and increase your worship's most magnificent person and estate, as I desire. From Florida, from this Fort of St. Augustine, on the fifteenth of October, of the year 1566.

Your worship's servant,
Pero Menéndez
1968

British Colonies in the Seventeenth and Eighteenth Centuries

The Chesapeake: England's First Successful Colonization

English colonization differed from the successful Spanish example in that it was fostered by private enterprise. The royal government issued their charters, but overseas ventures were entirely planned and financed by joint-stock companies, corporations created for the purpose. Some of these companies were very small groups of wealthy men, but the Virginia Company, sponsor of the first successful American colony, hit on the idea of setting the price of each share relatively low and opening membership to a wide variety of investors across the country.

Such innovation was necessary because founding a colony was immensely expensive. Stocking a venture with settlers and supplying them over the years until they built an infrastructure and could feed themselves meant constant outlay. And backers expected much more than mere self-sufficiency from the settlers. They had hazarded their money in the expectation of receiving a return on that investment; thus settlers were under overwhelming pressure to find or develop a product of value. Otherwise the colonists feared abandonment by the company.

The earliest returns from America came in the form of furs and fish, but neither enterprise required an expensive colony to support it. Settlers and backers quickly realized that no gold or other easy wealth existed; if colonies were to succeed, they must develop a true commodity, to be produced by their own labor. After a decade of hardship, Virginia colonists began to cultivate tobacco in earnest, and this crop became the Chesapeake's gold. Then they most needed labor to till the region's abundant land. This labor was provided by adapting an English institution, temporary servitude. In England most young men and women spent their adolescence in a series of annual contracts as servants before marrying and setting up on their own in their mid-twenties. In America they served a term of several years to pay for their overseas passage. The payoff was a grant of land of their own when the term expired—something that most could never attain in England, where inflation and population explosion squeezed opportunities.

In the course of the later seventeenth century, the temporary servitude of English men and women who were destined to become landowners and full members of society was largely replaced by permanent servitude (slavery) of African men and women who were forever excluded from membership in Chesapeake society. Historians continue to debate how and why this transition came about.

Captain John Smith is one of the most famous names associated with early colonization. During Jamestown's first year (1607–1608) he explored Chesapeake Bay, in the course of which he was captured and brought before the region's overlord, Powhatan. The famous episode in which the chief's young daughter Pocahontas saved Smith's life was probably a symbolic death and rebirth as an Indian. It was followed by his adoption as a subchief, or werowance, under Powhatan. Smith, who wrote about himself in the third person, used his capacity to communicate by writing and examples of European technology to dazzle his captors. In the excerpts reprinted in the first document, Smith describes his accomplishments as president of the colony, especially in forcing the unwilling settlers to work and feed themselves. He comments incidentally on the introduction of destructive rats and on the colonists' learning from the Indians how to cope with the new environment. Finally he describes the terrible starving time that befell the settlers after he had been forced out of the colony.

In 1620 the Virginia Company, with tobacco established and the offer of a headright (guaranteed land), published a new call for investment and emigration, which is reprinted as the second document. In the third selection historian Walter Woodward offers up satire on this campaign, presenting it as a modern condominium offering. Richard Frethorne, who went to Virginia as a servant, wrote his parents in 1623 of the realities of his experience and his desire to return home. Frethorne penned his letter, which is excerpted in document four, in the aftermath of the concerted Indian attack of 1622. The Chesapeake encompassed the colonies of Virginia and Maryland. *A Relation of Maryland* (1635) published a blank indenture form (see the fifth document) providing for a servant to serve "according to the custom of the country"; illiterate recruits, of whom there were many, could not read what they signed. In the sixth selection, written later in the century, promoter George Alsop answers the charge that servitude in the Chesapeake was more like slavery. In the final document planter-historian Robert Beverley describes the completed transition to African slavery by the early eighteenth century, and the benefits that accrued to English servants.

Captain John Smith on Early Jamestown (1607–1610)

And now the winter approaching, the rivers became so covered with swans, geese, ducks, and cranes, that we daily feasted with good bread, Virginia peas, pumpkins, and putchamins [persimmons], fish, fowl, and diverse sorts of wild beasts as fat as we could eat them: so that none of our Tuftaffaty humorists desired to go for *England.*

But our *Comedies* never endured long without a *Tragedy*; some idle exceptions being muttered against Captain *Smith,* for not discovering the head of *Chickahamania* river, and [being] taxed by the Council, to be too slow in

---

Some of the spelling in this document has been modernized.

so worthy an attempt. The next voyage he proceeded so far that with much labour by cutting of trees insunder he made his passage; but when his Barge could pass no farther, he left her in a broad bay out of danger of shot, commanding none should go ashore til his return: himself with two English and two Savages went up higher in a Canoe; but he was not long absent, but his men went ashore, whose want of government gave both occasion and opportunity to the Savages to surprise one *George Cassen,* whom they slew, and much failed not to have cut of[f] the boat and all the rest. . . .

Six or seven weeks those Barbarians kept him prisoner, many strange triumphs and conjurations they made of him, yet he so demeaned himself amongst them, as he not only diverted them from surprising the Fort, but procured his own liberty, and got himself and his company such estimation amongst them, that those Savages admired him more than their own Quiyouckosucks. . . .

He demanding for their Captain, they showed him *Opechankanough,* King of *Pamavnkee,* to whom he gave a round Ivory double compass Dial. Much they marveled at the playing of the Fly and Needle, which they could see so plainly, and yet not touch it, because of the glass that covered them. But when he demonstrated by that Globe-like Jewel the roundness of the earth, and skies, the sphere of the Sun, Moon, and Stars, and how the Sun did chase the night round about the world continually; the greatness of the Land and Sea, the diversity of Nations, variety of complexions, and how we were to them *Antipodes,* and many other such like matters, they all stood as amazed with admiration.

Notwithstanding, within an hour after they tied him to a tree, and as many as could stand about him prepared to shoot him: but the King holding up the Compass in his hand, they all laid down their Bows and Arrows, and in a triumphant manner led him to *Orapaks,* where he was after their manner kindly feasted, and well used.

Their order in conducting him was thus; Drawing themselves all in file, the King in the middle had all their Pieces and Swords born before him. Captain *Smith* was led after him by three great Savages, holding him fast by each arm: and on each side six went in file with their Arrows nocked. But arriving at the Town [*Orapaks*] (which was but only thirty or forty hunting houses made of Mats, which they remove as they please, as we our tents) all the women and children staring to behold him, the soldiers first all in file . . . and on each flank, officers as Sergeants to see them keep their orders. A good time they continued this exercise, and then cast themselves in a ring, dancing in such several Postures, and singing and yelling out such hellish notes and screeches; being strangely painted, every one his quiver of Arrows, and at his back a club; on his arm a Fox or an Otter's skin, or some such matter for his vambrace [armor for forearm]; their heads and shoulders painted red, . . . which Scarlet-like colour made an exceeding handsome show; his Bow in his hand, and the skin of a Bird with her wings abroad dried, tied on his head, a piece of copper, a white shell, a long feather, with a small rattle growing at the tails of their snak[e]s tied to it, or some such like toy. All this while *Smith* and the King stood in the middest guarded, as before is said: and after three dances they all departed. *Smith* they conducted to a long house, where thirty or forty tall fellows did guard him; and ere long more bread and venison was brought him than would have served twenty men. I think his stomach at that time was not very good; what he left they put in baskets and tied over his head. About midnight they set the meat again before him, all this time not one of them would eat a bit with him, till the next morning they brought him as much more; and then did they eat all the old, and reserved the new as they had done the other, which made him think they would fat him to eat him. Yet in this desperate estate to defend him from the cold, one *Maocassater* brought him his gown, in requital of some beads and toys *Smith* had given him at his first arrival in *Virginia*. . . .

. . . [His captors] made all the preparations they could to assault *James* town, craving his advice; and for recompence he should have life, liberty, land, and women. In part of a Table book [tablet] he wrote his mind to them at the Fort, what was intended, how they should follow that direction to affright the messengers, and without fail send him such things as he wrote for. And an Inventory with them. The difficultie and danger, he told the Savages, of the Mines, great guns, and other Engines exceedingly affrighted them, yet according to his request they went to *James* town, in as bitter weather as could be of frost and snow, and within three days returned with an answer.

But when they came to *Jame[s]* town, seeing men sally out as he had told them they would, they fled; yet in the night they came again to the same place where he had told them they should receive an answer, and such things as he had promised them: which they found accordingly, and with which they returned with no small expedition, to the wonder of them all that heard it, that he could either divine, or the paper could speak. . . .

After this they brought him a bag of gunpowder, which they carefully preserved till the next spring, to plant as they did their corn; because they would be acquainted with the nature of that seed. . . .

At last they brought him to *Werowocomoco* where was *Powhatan* their Emperor. Here more than two hundred of those grim Courtiers stood wondering at him, as he had been a monster; till *Powhatan* and his train had put themselves in their greatest braveries. Before a fire upon a seat like a bedstead, he sat covered with a great robe, made of *Rarowcun* [raccoon] skins, and all the tails hanging by. On either hand did sit a young wench of 16 or 18 years, and along on each side the house, two rows of men, and behind them as many women, with all their heads and shoulders painted red: many of their heads bedecked with the white down of Birds; but every one with something: and a great chain of white beads about their necks.

At his entrance before the King, all the people gave a great shout. The Queen of *Appamatuck* was appointed to bring him water to wash his hands, and another brought him a bunch of feathers, instead of a Towel to dry them: having feasted him after their best barbarous manner they could, a long consultation was held, but the conclusion was, two great stones were brought before *Powhatan*: then as many as could laid hands on him, dragged him to them, and thereon laid his head, and being ready with their clubs, to beat out his brains, *Pocahontas* the King's dearest daughter, when no entreaty could prevail, got his head in her arms, and laid her own upon his to save him from death: whereat the Emperour was contented he should live to make him hatchets, and her bells, beads, and copper; for they thought him aswell of all occupations as themselves. For the King himself will make his own robes, shoes, bows, arrows, pots; plant, hunt, or do anything so well as the rest....

Two days after [7 *Jan.* 1608], *Powhatan* having disguised himself in the most fearfulest manner he could, caused Captain *Smith* to be brought forth to a great house in the woods, and there upon a mat by the fire to be left alone. Not long after from behind a mat that divided the house, was made the most dolefulest noise he ever heard; then Powhatan more like a devil than a man, with some two hundred more as black as himself, came unto him and told him now they were friends, and presently he should go to *James* town, to send him two great guns, and a grindstone, for which he would give him the Country of *Capahowosick,* and forever esteem him as his son *Nantaquoud....*

Now ever once in four or five days, *Pocahontas* with her attendants, brought him so much provision, that saved many of their lives, that else for all this had starved with hunger....

His relation of the plenty he had seen, especially at *Werawocomoco,* and of the state and bounty of *Powhatan,* (which till that time was unknown) so revived their dead spirits (especially the love of *Pocahontas*) as all men's fear was abandoned....

What was done in three months having Victuals.
The Store devoured by Rats, how we lived
three months of such natural fruits
as the Country afforded.

Now we so quietly followed our business, that in three months we made three or four Last of Tar, Pitch, and Soap ashes; produced a trial of Glass; made a Well in the Fort of excellent sweet water, which till then was wanting; built some twenty houses; re-covered our Church: provided Nets and Weirs for fishing; and to stop the disorders of our disorderly thieves, and the Savages, built a Blockhouse in the neck of our Isle, kept by a Garrison to entertain the Savages' trade, and none to pass nor repass Savage nor Christian without the president's order. Thirty or forty Acres of ground we digged and planted. Of three sows in eighteen months, increased 60 and odd Pigs. And near 500 chickens brought up themselves without having any meat given them: but the Hogs were transported to Hog Isle: where also we built a blockhouse with a garrison to give us notice of any shipping, and for their exercise they made Clapboard and wainscot, and cut down trees.

We built also a fort for a retreat near a convenient River upon a high commanding hill, very hard to be assaulted and easy to be defended; but ere it was finished this defect caused a stay.

In searching our casked corn, we found it half rotten, and the rest so consumed with so many thousands of Rats that increased so fast, but their original was from the ships, as we knew not how to keep that little we had.

This did drive us all to our wits end, for there was nothing in the country but what nature afforded.

Until this time *Kemps* and *Tassore* were fettered prisoners, and did double task and taught us how to order and plant our fields: whom now for want of victual we set at liberty, but so well they liked our company they did not desire to go from us. . . .

And to express their loves, for 16 days continuance, the Country people brought us (when least) 100 a day, of Squirrels, Turkeys, Deer and other wild beasts.

But this want of corn occasioned the end of all our works, it being work sufficient to provide victual. . . .

Till this present, by the hazard and endeavors of some thirty or forty, this whole Colony had ever been fed. We had more Sturgeon, than could be devoured by Dog and Man, of which the industrious by drying and pounding, mingled with Caviar, Sorél and other wholesome herbs would make bread and good meat: others would gather as much *Tockwhogh* roots in a day as would make them bread a week, so that of those wild fruits, and what we caught, we lived very well in regard of such a diet.

But such was the strange condition of some 150, that had they not beene forced *nolens, volens,* perforce to gather and prepare their victual they would all have starved or have eaten one another. Of those wild fruits the Savages often brought us, and for that the president would not fulfill the unreasonable desire of those distracted Gluttonous Loiterers, to sell not only our kettles, hoes, tools, and iron, nayswords, pieces, and the very Ordnance and houses, might they have prevailed to have been but Idle: for those Savage fruits, they would have had imparted all to the Savages, especially for one basket of Corn they heard of to be at *Powhatans*, fifty miles from our Fort. . . .

. . . [H]e argued the case in this manner.

Fellow soldiers, I did little think any so false to report, or so many to be so simple to be persuaded, that I either intend to starve you, or that *Powhatan* at this present hath corn for himself, much less for you; or that I would not have it, if I knew where it were to be had. Neither did I think any so malicious as now I see a great many; yet it shall not so passionate me, but I will do my best for my most maligner. But dream no longer of this vain hope from *Powhatan*, nor that I will longer forbear to force you from your Idleness, and punish you if you rail. But if I find any more runners for Newfoundland with the Pinnace, let him assuredly look to arrive at the Gallows. You cannot deny but that by the hazard of my life many a time I have saved yours, when (might your own wills have prevailed) you would have starved; and will do still whether I will or not; But I protest by that God that made me, since necessity hath not power to force you to gather for yourselves those fruits the earth doth yield, you shall not only gather for yourselves, but those that are sick. As yet I never had more from the store than the worst of you: and all my English extraordinary provision that I have, you shall see me divide it amongst the sick.

And this Savage trash you so scornfully repine at; being put in your mouths your stomachs can digest: if you would have better, you should have brought it; and therefore I will take a course you shall provide what is to be had. The sick shall not starve, but equally share of all our labors; and he that gathereth not

146

every day as much as I do, the next day shall be set beyond the river, and be banished from the Fort as a drone, till he amend his conditions or starve....

Now we all found the loss of Captain *Smith,* yea his greatest maligners could now curse his loss: as for corn provision and contribution from the Savages, we had nothing but mortal wounds, with clubs and arrows; as for our Hogs, Hens, Goats, Sheep, Horse, or what lived, our commanders, officers and Savages daily consumed them, some small proportions sometimes we tasted, till all was devoured; then swords, arms, pieces, or any thing, we traded with the Savages, whose cruel fingers were so oft imbrewed in our blood, that what by their cruelty, our Governours indiscretion, and the loss of our ships, of five hundred within six months after Captain *Smith's* departure, there remained not past sixty men, women and children, most miserable and poor creatures; and those were preserved for the most part, by roots, herbs, acorns, walnuts, berries, now and then a little fish: they that had starch in these extremities, made no small use of it; yea, even the very skins of our horses.

Nay, so great was our famine, that a Savage we slew and buried, the poorer sort took him up again and eat him; and so did diverse one another boiled and stewed with roots and herbs: And one amongst the rest did kill his wife, powdered [*salted*] her, and had eaten part of her before it was known; for which he was executed, as he well deserved: now whether she was better roasted, boiled or carbonado'd [*grilled*], I know not; but of such a dish as powdered wife I never heard of.

This was that time, which still to this day we called the starving time; it were too vile to say, and scarce to be believed, what we endured: but the occasion was our own, for want of providence industry and government, and not the barrennesse and defect of the Country, as is generally supposed; ... Yet had we been even in Paradise itselfe with these Governours, it would not have been much better with us; yet there was amongst us, who had they had the government as Captain *Smith* appointed, but that they could not maintain it, would surely have kept us from those extremities of miseries. This in ten days more, would have supplanted us all with death....

The Virginia Company's Declaration on Virginia, 1620

After the many disasters, wherewith it pleased Almighty God to suffer the great Enemy of all good Actions and his Instruments, to encounter and interrupt, to oppress and keep weak, this noble Action for the planting of *Virginia,* with Christian Religion, and English people: It having pleased him now contrarily of his especial great grace, so to bless and prosper our late careful endevours, as well for the repairing of all former breaches, as for supplying of the present defects, wherewith the Colony was kept down, that it hath as it were on a sudden grown to double that height, strength, plenty, and prosperity, which it had in former times attained: We have thought it now the

---

Some of the spelling in this document has been modernized.

peculiar duty of our place, accordingly as it hath been also ordered by a general Court, to Summon as it were by a kind of loving invitement, the whole Body of the Noble and other worthy Adventurers, as well to the consurving and perfecting of this happy work, as to the reaping of the fruit of their great expenses and travails.

And first to remove that unworthy aspersion, wherewith ill disposed minds, guiding their Actions by corrupt ends have both by Letters from thence, and by rumours here at home, sought unjustly to stain and blemish that Country, as being barren and unprofitable; We have thought it necessary for the full satisfaction of all, to make it publicly known, that by diligent examination we have assuredly found, those Letters and Rumours to have been false and malicious; procured by practice, and suborned to evil purposes: and contrarily disavowed by the testimony upon Oath of the chief Inhabitants of all the Colony; by whom we are ascertained, that the Country is rich, spacious and well watered; temperate as for the Climate; very healthful after men are a little accustomed to it; abounding with all God's natural blessings: The Land replenished with the goodliest Woods in the world, and those full of *Deer,* and other Beasts for sustenance: The Seas and Rivers (whereof many are exceeding fair and navigable,) full of excellent Fish, and of all sorts desirable; both Water and Land yielding Fowl in very great store and variety: In Sum, a Country, too good for ill people; and we hope reserved by the providence of God, for such as shall apply themselves faithfully to his service, and be a strength and honour to our King and Nation. But touching those Commodities for which that Country is proper, and which have been lately set up for the Adventurers' benefit: we refer you to a true note of them, lately delivered in a great and general Court, and hereunto annexed for your better information. By which and other approved information brought unto us, We rest in great assurance, that this Country, as it is seated near the midst of the world, between the extremities of heat and cold; So it also participateth of the benefits of both, and is capable (being assisted with skill and industry) of the richest commodities of most parts of the Earth. The rich Furs, Caviar, and Cordage, which we draw from *Russia* with so great difficulty, are to be had in *Virginia,* and the parts adjoining, with ease and plenty. The Masts, Planks, and Boards, and Pitch and Tar, the Pot-ashes and Soap-ashes, the Hempe and Flax, (being the materials of Linen,) which now we fetch from *Norway, Denmark, Poland,* and *Germany,* are there to be had in abundance and great perfection. The *Iron,* which hath so wasted our *English* Woods, that itself in short time must decay together with them, is to be had in *Virginia,* (where wasting of Woods is a benefit) for all good conditions answerable to the best in the world. The Wines, Fruit, and Salt of *France* and *Spain;* The Silks of *Persia* and *Italy,* will be found also in *Virginia,* and in no kind of worth inferior. We omit here a multitude of other natural Commodities, dispersed up and down the divers parts of the world: of Woods, Roots, and Berries, for excellent Dyes: of Plants and other Drugs, for Physical service: of sweet Woods, Oils, and Gums, for pleasure and other use: of Cotton-wool, and Sugar Canes: all which may there also be had in abundance, with an infinity of other more: And will conclude with these three, Corn, Cattle and

Fish, which are the substance of the food of man. The Grains of our Country do prosper there very well: Of Wheat they have great plenty: But their *Maize,* being the natural Grain of that Country, doth far exceed in pleasantness, strength, and fertility. The Cattle which we have transported thither, (being now grown nearer to five hundred) become much bigger of Body, than the breed from which they came: The Horses also more beautiful, and fuller of courage. And such is the extraordinary fertility of that *Soil,* that the *Does* of their *Deer* yield two Fawns at a birth, and sometimes three. The Fishings at *Cape Cod,* being within those Limits, will in plenty of Fish be equal to those of *New-found-Land,* and in goodness and greatness much superiour. To conclude, it is a Country, which nothing but ignorance can think ill of, and which no man but of a corrupt mind and ill purpose can defame. . . .

JAMESTOWN ESTATES

For As Little As £10 12s. 6d., You, Too, Can Own A Share of Paradise.

From the moment the gentle, southern breezes waft your pinnace to the verdant, gardenlike shore, you'll know this is where you belong. Jamestown Estates, where only a few are living a life those in England can hardly imagine.

Jamestown Estates — another proud project of the Virginia Company — combines the best in colonial living with the excitement, adventure, and opportunity for which the Virginia Company is famous.

At Jamestown Estates, your every need is provided for in an environment that shows how caring people can live in symbiotic dominance of nature. And only Jamestown Estates offers an exclusive low cholesterol meal plan, the Sure-Fit™ exercise program, and a unique "Friends Together" living arrangement. In all details, Jamestown Estates is designed with your peace and well-being in mind. Each of our charming, thatch-roofed cottages — which you will share with congenial, adventuresome people just like yourself (specially designed to maximize both privacy and interpersonal contact) — has a spectacular river view. At Jamestown Estates, nature itself invites you to relax, reflect, converse with new-found friends, and share stories of your New World experiences, while becoming the sort of person you've always wanted to be. But it's not all play at Jamestown Estates — not by a long shot. For Jamestown Estates offers one of the most active labor markets in the New World. Whatever you do, you can do it better here.

Our employment office has many people anxious to welcome you to our growing work force.

No single ad can tell you all the remarkable things you'll want to know about Jamestown Estates. Consider, however, some of these exceptionally valuable Jamestown Pluses:
• 24-hour security, palisaded grounds.
• Hunting, fishing right on premises. Native guides teach you to hunt like a lord.
• The Sotweed Garden Center — learn how to plant like a pro. No experience necessary.
• Regularly scheduled "Trash For Treasure" excursions to the nearby Pamunkey Flea Market. Come & "Meet the Chief."
• And, as a special bonus to those who visit Jamestown Estates soon, we are introducing a new program called the Headright System* — your chance to receive 50 acres of land just for bringing yourself (or someone you know) to experience this new world of opportunity.
• Coming with a group? Ask about our Particular Plantations™ Program. Build your private world right here in our new one.

Finally, for those who appreciate the phenomenal profit potential of New World investment, there is the chance to secure shares in the Virginia Company itself, — a once in a lifetime time opportunity — starting at just £10 12s. 6d. To find out more, contact your nearest friendly, knowledgeable Virginia Company Representative.

---

* Headright™ and Headright System™ are registered trademarks of the Virginia Company. Offer void where prohibited.

Virginia   A WHOLE NEW WORLD

Walter Woodward, "Jamestown Estates," *William and Mary Quarterly*, 3d ser., XLVII (1991), 116–117. Reprinted by permission.

Richard Frethorne Writes to His Mother and Father, 1623

Loving and kind father and mother, my most humble duty remembered to you hoping in God of your good health, as I my self am at the making hereof, this is to let you understand that I your Child am in a most heavy Case by reason of the nature of the Country is such that it Causeth much sickness, as the scurvy and the bloody flux [dysentery], and divers other diseases, which maketh the body very poor, and Weak, and when we are sick there is nothing to Comfort us; for since I came out of the ship, I never ate any thing but peas and loblollie (that is water gruel) as for deer or venison I never saw any since I came into this land, there is indeed some fowl, but We are not allowed to go and get it, but must Work hard both early and late for a mess of water gruel, and a mouthful of bread, and beef, a mouthful of bread for a penny loaf must serve for 4 men which is most pitiful if you did know as much as I, when people cry out day, and night, Oh that they were in England without their limbs and would not care to lose any limb to be in England again, yea though they beg from door to door, for we live in fear of the Enemy every hour, yet we have had a Combat with them on the Sunday before Shrovetide, and we took two alive, and make slaves of them, but it was by policy, for we are in great danger, for our Plantation is very weak, by reason of the dearth, and sickness, of our Company, for we came but Twenty for the merchants, and they half dead Just; as we look every hour When two more should go, yet there came some for other men yet to live with us, of which there is but one alive, and our Lieutenant is dead, and his father, and his brother, and there was some 5 or 6 of the last year's 20 of which there is but 3 left, so that we are fain to get other men to plant with us, and yet we are but 32 to fight against 3000 if they should Come, and the nighest help that We have is ten miles of us, and when the rogues overcame this place last, they slew 80 persons. How then shall we doe for we lie even in their teeth, they may easily take us but that God is merciful, and can save with few as well as with many; as he showed to Gilead and like Gilead's soldiers if they lapped water, we drink water which is but Weak, and I have nothing to Comfort me, nor there is nothing to be gotten here but sickness, and death, except that one had money to lay out in some things for profit; But I have nothing at all, no not a shirt to my backe, but two Rags nor no Clothes, but one poor suit, nor but one pair of shoes, but one pair of stockings, but one Cap, but two bands, my Cloak is stolen by one of my own fellows, and to his dying hour would not tell me what he did with it but some of my fellows saw him have butter and beef out of a ship, which my Cloak I doubt [think] paid for, so that I have not a penny, nor a half penny Worth to help me to either spice, or sugar, or strong Waters, without the which one cannot live here, for as strong beer in England doth fatten and strengthen them so water here doth wash and weaken these here, only keep life and soul together. But I am not half a quarter so strong as I was in England, and all is for want

---

Some of the spelling in this document has been modernized.

of victuals, for I do protest unto you, that I have eaten more in a day at home than I have allowed me here for a Week. You have given more than my day's allowance to a beggar at the door; and if Mr. Jackson had not relieved me, I should be in a poor Case, but he like a father and she like a loving mother doth still help me, for when we go up to James Town that is 10 miles of us, there lie all the ships that Come to the land, and there they must deliver their goods, and when we went up to Town as it may be on Monday, at noon, and come there by night, then load the next day by noon, and go home in the afternoon, and unload, and then away again in the night, and be up about midnight, then if it rained, or blowed never so hard we must lie on the boat on the water, and have nothing but a little bread, for when we go into the boat we have a loaf allowed to two men, and it is all if we stayed there 2 days, which is hard, and must lie all that while in the boat, but that Goodman Jackson pitied me and made me a Cabin to lie in always when I come up, and he would give me some poor Jacks [fish] home with me which Comforted me more than peas, or water gruel. Of they be very godly folks, and love me very well, and will do any thing for me, and he much marveled that you would send me a servant to the Company. He sayeth I had been better knocked on the head, and Indeed so I find it now to my great grief and misery, and saith, that if you love me you will redeem me suddenly, for which I do entreat and beg, and if you cannot get the merchants to redeem me for some little money then for God's sake get a gathering or entreat some good folks to lay out some little sum of money, in meal, and Cheese and butter, and beef, any eating meat will yield great profit, oil and vinegar is very good, but father there is great loss in leaking, but for God's sake send beef and Cheese and butter or the more of one sort and none of another, but if you send Cheese it must be very old Cheese, and at the Cheesemonger's you may buy good Cheese for twopence farthing or half-penny that will be liked very well, but if you send Cheese you must have a Care how you pack it in barrels, and you must put Cooper's chips between every Cheese, or else the heat of the hold will rot them, and look whatsoever you send me be it never so much, look what I make of it. I will deal truly with you. I will send it over, and beg the profit to redeem me, and if I die before it Come I have entreated Goodman Jackson to send you the worth of it, who hath promised he will. If you send you must direct your letter to Goodman Jackson, at James Town, a Gunsmith. . . . Good Father do not forget me, but have mercy and pity my miserable Case. I know if you did but see me you would weep to see me, for I have but one suit, but it is a strange one, it is very well guarded, wherefore for God's sake pity me. I pray you to remember my love to all my friends, and kindred, I hope all my Brothers and sisters are in good health, and as for my part I have set down my res-olution that certainly Will be, that is, that the Answer of this letter will be life or death to me, there good Father send as soon as you can, and if you send me any thing let this be the mark.

ROT

RICHARD FRETHORNE
Martin's Hundred

The forme of binding a servant.

This Indenture *made the* day of
in the
yeere of our Soveraigne Lord King Charles, *&c.*
betweene *of the one*
party, and *on the*
other party, Witnesseth, *that the said*
doth hereby covenant promise, and
grant, to and with the said
his Executors and Assignes, to serve him from
the day of the date hereof, untill his first and
next arrivall in Maryland; *and after for and*
during the tearme of *yeeres, in such*
service and imployment, as he the said
or his assignes shall there im-
ploy him, according to the custome of the Countrey
in the like kind. In consideration whereof, the said
doth promise
and grant, to and with the said
to pay for his passing, and to
find him with Meat, Drinke, Apparell and Lodg-
ing, with other necessaries during the said terme;
and at the end of the said terme, to give him one
whole yeeres provision of Corne, and fifty acres of
Land, according to the order of the countrey. In
witnesse whereof, the said
hath hereunto put his hand and seale, the day and
yeere above written.
Sealed and delivered in
the presence of H

The usuall terme of binding a servant, is for
five yeers; but for any artificer, or one that shall
deserve more then ordinary, the Adventurer
shall doe well to shorten that time, and adde
encouragements of another nature (as he shall
see cause) rather then to want such usefull men.

George Alsop on the Benefits of Servitude, 1666

*The necessariness of Servitude proved, with the common usage
of Servants in Mary-Land, together with their Priviledges.*

... There is no truer Emblem of Confusion either in Monarchy or
Domestick Governments, then when either the Subject, or the Servant, strives
for the upper hand of his Prince, or Master, and to be equal with him, from
whom he receives his present subsistance: Why then, if Servitude be so necessary that no place can be governed in order, nor people live without it, this
may serve to tell those which prick up their ears and bray against it, That
they are none but Asses, and deserve the Bridle of a strict commanding power
to rein them in: For I'me certainly confident, that there are several Thousands
in most Kingdoms of Christendom, that could not at all live and subsist,
unless they had served some prefixed time, to learn either some Trade, Art,
or Science, and by either of them to extract their present livelihood.

Then methinks this may stop the mouths of those that will undiscreetly
compassionate them that dwell under necessary Servitudes; for let but Parents
of an indifferent capacity in Estates, when their Childrens age by computation
speak them seventeen or eighteen years old, turn them loose to the wide
world, without a seven years working Apprenticeship (being just brought up
to the bare formality of a little reading and writing) and you shall immediately
see how weak and shiftless they'le be towards the maintaining and supporting
of themselves; and (without either stealing or begging) their bodies like a
Sentinel must continually wait to see when their Souls will be frighted away
by the pale Ghost of a starving want.

Then let such, where Providence hath ordained to live as Servants, either
in England or beyond Sea, endure the pre-fixed yoak of their limited time
with patience, and then in a small computation of years, by an industrious
endeavour, they may become Masters and Mistresses of Families themselves.
And let this be spoke to the deserved praise of Mary-Land, That the four
years I served there were not to me so slavish, as a two years Servitude of
a Handicraft Apprenticeship was here in London.... Not that I write this to
seduce or delude any, or to draw them from their native soyle, but out of a
love to my Countrymen, whom in the general I wish well to, and that the
lowest of them may live in such a capacity of Estate, as that the bare interest
of their Livelihoods might not altogether depend upon persons of the greatest
extendments....

They whose abilities cannot extend to purchase their own transportation
over into Mary-Land, (and surely he that cannot command so small a sum
for so great a matter, his life must needs be mighty low and dejected) I say
they may for the debarment of a four years sordid liberty, go over into this
Province and there live plentiously well. And what's a four years Servitude
to advantage a man all the remainder of his dayes, making his predecessors
happy in his sufficient abilities, which he attained to partly by the restrainment
of so small a time?

Now those that commit themselves unto the care of the Merchant to carry them over, they need not trouble themselves with any inquisitive search touching their Voyage; for there is such an honest care and provision made for them all the time they remain aboard the Ship, and are sailing over, that they want for nothing that is necessary and convenient.

The Merchant commonly before they go aboard the Ship, or set themselves in any forwardness for their Voyage, has Conditions of Agreements drawn between him and those that by a voluntary consent become his Servants, to serve him, his Heirs or Assigns, according as they in their primitive acquaintance have made their bargain, some two, some three, some four years; and whatever the Master or Servant tyes himself up to here in England by Condition, the Laws of the Province will force a performance of when they come there: Yet here is this Priviledge in it when they arrive, If they dwell not with the Merchant they made their first agreement withall, they may choose whom they will serve their prefixed time with; and after their curiosity has pitcht on one whom they think fit for their turn, and that they may live well withall, the Merchant makes an Assignment of the Indenture over to him whom they of their free will have chosen to be their Master, in the same nature as we here in England (and no otherwise) turn over Covenant Servants or Apprentices from one Master to another. Then let those whose chaps are always breathing forth those filthy dregs of abusive exclamations, ... against this Country of Mary-Land, saying, That those which are transported over thither, are sold in open Market for Slaves, and draw in Carts like Horses; which is so damnable an untruth, that if they should search to the very Center of Hell, and enquire for a Lye of the most antient and damned stamp, I confidently believe they could not find one to parallel this: For know, That the Servants here in Mary-Land of all Colonies, distant or remote Plantations, have the least cause to complain, either for strictness of Servitude, want of Provisions, or need of Apparel: Five dayes and a half in the Summer weeks is the alotted time that they work in; and for two months, when the Sun predominates in the highest pitch of his heat, they claim an antient and customary Priviledge, to repose themselves three hours in the day within the house, and this is undeniably granted to them that work in the Fields.

In the Winter time, which lasteth three months (*viz.*) December, January, and February, they do little or no work or imployment, save cutting of wood to make good fires to sit by, unless their Ingenuity will prompt them to hunt the Deer, or Bear, or recreate themselves in Fowling, to slaughter the Swans, Geese, and Turkeys (which this Country affords in a most plentiful manner:) For every Servant has a Gun, Powder and Shot allowed him, to sport him withall on all Holidayes and leasurable times, if he be capable of using it, or be willing to learn. . . .

. . . He that lives in the nature of a Servant in this Province, must serve but four years by the Custom of the Country; and when the expiration of his time speaks him a Freeman, there's a Law in the Province, that enjoyns his Master whom he hath served to give him Fifty Acres of Land, Corn to serve him a whole year, three Sutes of Apparel, with things necessary to them, and Tools to work withall; so that they are no sooner free, but they are ready to set up for themselves, and when once entred, they live passingly well.

The Women that go over into this Province as Servants, have the best luck here as in any place of the world besides; for they are no sooner on shoar, but they are courted into a Copulative Matrimony, which some of them (for aught I know) had they not come to such a Market with their Virginity might have kept it by them until it had been mouldy.... Men have not altogether so good luck as Women in this kind, or natural preferment, without they be good Rhetoricians, and well vers'd in the Art of perswasion, then (probably) they may ryvet themselves in the time of their Servitude into the private and reserved favour of their Mistress, if Age speak their Master deficient.

In short, touching the Servants of this Province, they live well in the time of their Service, and by their restrainment in that time, they are made capable of living much better when they come to be free; which in several other parts of the world I have observed, That after some servants have brought their indented and limited time to a just and legal period by Servitude, they have been much more incapable of supporting themselves from sinking into the Gulf of a slavish, poor, fettered, and intangled life, then all the fastness of their pre-fixed time did involve them in before....

Robert Beverley on the Servants and Slaves in Virginia, 1705

Their Servants, they distinguish by the Names of Slaves for Life, and Servants for a time.

Slaves are the Negroes, and their Posterity, following the condition of the Mother, according to the Maxim, *partus sequitur ventrem* [status proceeds from the womb]. They are call'd Slaves, in respect of the time of their Servitude, because it is for Life.

Servants, are those which serve only for a few years, according to the time of their Indenture, or the Custom of the Country. The Custom of the Country takes place upon such as have no Indentures. The Law in this case is, that if such Servants be under Nineteen years of Age, they must be brought into Court, to have their Age adjudged; and from the Age they are judg'd to be of, they must serve until they reach four and twenty: But if they be adjudged upwards of Nineteen, they are then only to be Servants for the term of five Years.

The Male-Servants, and Slaves of both Sexes, are imployed together in Tilling and Manuring the Ground, in Sowing and Planting Tobacco, Corn, &c. Some Distinction indeed is made between them in their Cloaths, and Food; but the Work of both, is no other than what the Overseers, the Freemen, and the Planters themselves do.

Sufficient Distinction is also made between the Female-Servants, and Slaves; for a White Woman is rarely or never put to work in the Ground, if she be good for any thing else: And to Discourage all Planters from using any Women so, their Law imposes the heaviest Taxes upon Female-Servants working in the Ground, while it suffers all other white Women to be absolutely exempted: Whereas on the other hand, it is a common thing to work a Woman Slave out of Doors; nor does the Law make any distinction in her Taxes, whether her Work be Abroad, or at Home.

Because I have heard how strangely cruel, and severe, the Service of this Country is represented in some parts of *England;* I can't forbear affirming, that the work of their Servants, and Slaves, is no other than what every common Freeman do's. Neither is any Servant requir'd to do more in a Day, than his Overseer. And I can assure you with a great deal of Truth, that generally their Slaves are not worked near so hard, nor so many Hours in a Day, as the Husbandmen, and Day-Labourers in *England.* An Overseer is a Man, that having served his time, has acquired the Skill and Character of an experienced Planter, and is therefore intrusted with the Direction of the Servants and Slaves.

But to compleat this account of Servants, I shall give you a short Relation of the care their Laws take, that they be used as tenderly as possible.

By the Laws of their Country.

1. All Servants whatsoever, have their Complaints heard without Fee, or Reward; but if the Master be found Faulty, the charge of the Complaint is cast upon him, otherwise the business is done *ex Officio.*
2. Any Justice of Peace may receive the Complaint of a Servant, and order every thing relating thereto, till the next County-Court, where it will be finally determin'd.
3. All Masters are under the Correction, and Censure of the County-Courts, to provide for their Servants, good and wholsome Diet, Clothing, and Lodging.
4. They are always to appear, upon the first Notice given of the Complaint of their Servants, otherwise to forfeit the Service of them, until they do appear.
5. All Servants Complaints are to be receiv'd at any time in Court, without Process, and shall not be delay'd for want of Form; but the Merits of the Complaint must be immediately inquir'd into by the Justices; and if the Master cause any delay therein, the Court may remove such Servants, if they see Cause, until the Master will come to Tryal.
6. If a Master shall at any time disobey an Order of Court, made upon any Complaint of a Servant; the Court is impower'd to remove such Servant forthwith to another Master, who will be kinder; Giving to the former Master the produce only, (after Fees deducted) of what such Servants shall be sold for by Publick Outcry.
7. If a Master should be so cruel, as to use his Servant ill, that is faln Sick, or Lame in his Service, and thereby render'd unfit for Labour, he must be remov'd by the Church-Wardens out of the way of such Cruelty, and boarded in some good Planters House, till the time of his Freedom, the charge of which must be laid before the next County-Court, which has power to levy the same from time to time, upon the Goods and Chattels of the Master; After which, the charge of such Boarding is to come upon the Parish in General.
8. All hired Servants are intituled to these Priviledges.
9. No Master of a Servant, can make a new Bargain for Service, or other Matter with his Servant, without the privity and consent of a Justice of Peace, to prevent the Master's Over-reaching, or scareing such Servant into an unreasonable Complyance.

10. The property of all Money and Goods sent over thither to Servants, or carry'd in with them; is reserv'd to themselves, and remain intirely at their disposal.
11. Each Servant at his Freedom, receives of his Master fifteen Bushels of Corn, (which is sufficient for a whole year) and two new Suits of Cloaths, both Linnen and Woollen; and then becomes as free in all respects, and as much entituled to the Liberties, and Priviledges of the Country, as any other of the Inhabitants or Natives are.
12. Each Servant has then also a Right to take up fifty Acres of Land, where he can find any unpatented: But that is no great Privilege, for any one may have as good a right for a piece of Eight.

This is what the Laws prescribe in favour of Servants, by which you may find, that the Cruelties and Severities imputed to that Country, are an unjust Reflection. For no People more abhor the thoughts of such Usage, than the *Virginians,* nor take more precaution to prevent it.

New England: The Settlement of the Puritan Colonies

At first European colonizers had little interest in the area between Chesapeake Bay and the St. Lawrence River. One short-lived attempt to settle a colony in Maine at the same time as Jamestown (1607) had convinced investors that the region was both inhospitable and unlikely to yield products of value. Attention focused on the north—on Newfoundland and the great Canadian river—where the rich fishing grounds and abundance of fur-bearing animals had attracted hundreds of voyages every year since shortly after the time of the region's discovery. These expeditions came in the spring and left in the autumn. There seemed little reason to build expensive colonies on those cold, rocky shores.

New England, then called the North Part of Virginia, became attractive when a new kind of colony was planned—transfers of entire communities of English men and women who sought an environment in which they could thrive and worship God as they saw fit. Plymouth on Cape Cod was settled in 1620 by a small group of Puritan Separatists who viewed the Church of England as so corrupt that they had separated themselves entirely from it. Then in 1630 a huge exodus of Puritans founded Massachusetts Bay. These emigrants, in contrast to the Separatists, considered themselves still loyal members of the church, who merely wished to reform it by example. Thousands left England in the 1630s, partly because of the same economic distress that fed migration to the Chesapeake but also because Charles I and his archbishop of Canterbury, William Laud, increasingly were pushing the church in directions the Puritans abhorred, and requiring conformity.

The Puritans chose New England because its environment was conducive to small family farms rather than great plantations; its lack of rich crops would keep out those who might seek to pervert their godly experiment. They found the land depleted of its native population by a disastrous plague that had struck shortly before Plymouth's founding; a second wave of European disease devastated the Indians in the early 1630s. Some Puritans, whose providential outlook disposed them to look for God's will in all events, saw this as divine intervention on their behalf, clearing the land for their habitation.

The Pilgrims, whose backers had forced them to take a large number of skilled colonists who were not Puritans, quickly sent back reports to their friends in England, which were published in 1622. These excerpts, in the first document, describe the Mayflower Compact, by which they and the non-Puritan "strangers" agreed to live, and the first Thanksgiving, celebrated in an early spirit of peace with their Wampanoag Indian neighbors. William Bradford, Plymouth's governor, kept a journal of events. In the excerpt reprinted as the second document, Bradford describes the Pilgrims' increasingly tense relationship with their Indian neighbors and their growing suspicion of even their interpreters, Squanto and Hobbomock.

John Winthrop, governor of Massachusetts Bay, gave a famous sermon on board the *Arbella,* the ship carrying the first Puritan contingent. In the excerpts featured in the third selection, he outlines the distinctive characteristics of his colony, bound together as it was by a common purpose. Winthrop's images have been re-shaped many times in American history. In the fourth selection John Pond, a far humbler member of the *Arbella* fleet, writes to his father for help, as Richard Frethorne had done from Virginia (see Chapter 3), in facing the rigors of the new plantation. Both New England colonies experienced a high death rate in their first years. In the fifth document minister Thomas Welde writes to his former parishioners in England, certifying that after two years the colony was firmly established. "The Summons to New England," the sixth selection, is a ballad ridiculing the Puritans' claims of both the bounty of their land and the purity of their religious life; it affords insight into the opposition they faced. In the seventh selection William Wood offers up a "true, lively, and experimental description" of New England in which he views the colonists' Indian neighbors with sympathy and interest and analyzes the changes wrought in the native people's gender roles by the coming of the English. Miantonomo, chief of the Narragansetts, presents a much darker picture of the Indians' changed situation in the final selection.

Plymouth's Pilgrims on the Mayflower Compact and the First Thanksgiving, 1620, 1621

The Mayflower Compact, 1620

This day before we came to harbor, observing some not well affected to unity and concord, but gave some appearance of faction, it was thought good there should be an association and agreement, that we should combine together in one body, and to submit to such government and governors, as we should by common consent agree to make and choose, and set our hands to this that follows word for word.

In the name of God, Amen. We whose names are underwritten, the loyal Subjects of our dread sovereign Lord King James, by the grace of God of Great Britain, France, and Ireland King, Defender of the Faith, etc.

Having under-taken for the glory of God, and advancement of the Chris-

---

Some of the spelling in this document has been modernized.

tian Faith, and honor of our King and Country, a Voyage to plant the first Colony in the Northern parts of VIRGINIA, do by these presents solemnly and mutually in the presence of God and one of another, covenant, and combine our selves together into a civil body politic, for our better ordering and preservation, and furtherance of the ends aforesaid; and by virtue hereof to enact, constitute, and frame such just and equal Laws, Ordinances, acts, constitutions, offices from time to time, as shall be thought most meet and convenient for the general good of the Colony: unto which we promise all due submission and obedience. In witness whereof we have here-under subscribed our names. Cape Cod 11 of November, in the year of the reign of our sovereign Lord King James, of England, France, and Ireland 18 and of Scotland 54. Anno Domino 1620.

The First Thanksgiving, 1621

A Letter Sent from New-England to a friend in these parts . . .

Loving, and old Friend, although I received no Letter from you by this Ship, yet foreasmuch as I know you expect the performance of my promise, which was, to write unto you truly and faithfully of all things, I have therefore at this time sent unto you accordingly. Referring you for further satisfaction to our more large Relations. You shall understand, that in this little time, that a few of us have been here, we have built seven dwelling houses, and four for the use of the Plantation, and have made preparation for divers other. We set the last Spring some twentie Acres of Indian-Corne, and sowed some six Acres of Barley and Peas, and according to the manner of the Indian, we manured our ground with Herrings or rather Shads, which we have in great abundance, and take with great ease at our doors. Our Corne did prove well, and God be praised, we had a good increase of our Indian-Corne, and our Barley indifferent good, but our Peas not worth the gathering, for we feared they were too late sown. They came up very well, and blossomed, but the Sun parched them in the blossom. Our harvest being gotten in, our Governor sent four men on fowling, that so we might after a more special manner rejoice together, after we had gathered the fruit of our labors. They four in one day killed as much fowl, as with a little help beside, served the Company almost a week, at which time amongst other Recreations, we exercised our Arms, many of the Indians coming amongst us, and amongst the rest their greatest King Massasoit, with some ninety men, whom for three days we entertained and feasted, and they went out and killed five Deer, which they brought to the Plantation and bestowed on our Governor, and upon the Captain, and others. And although it be not always so plentiful, as it was at this time with us, yet by the goodness of God, we are so far from want, that we often wish you partakers of our planty. We have found the Indians very faithful in their Covenant of Peace with us; very loving and ready to pleasure us. We often go to them, and they come to us; some of us have been fifty miles by Land in the Country with them; the occasions and Relations whereof you shall understand by our general and more full Declaration of such things as are worth the noting. Yea it hath pleased God so to possess the Indians with a fear of us, and love unto us, that not only the greatest King amongst them called Massasoit, but also all the Princes and people round about us, have either made suit unto us, or been glad of any occasion to make peace with us, so that seven of them at once have sent their messengers to us to that end ... willingly to be under the protection, and subjects to our sovereign Lord King James, so that there is now great peace amongst the Indians themselves, which was not formerly, neither would have been but for us. And we for our parts walk as peaceably and safely in the wood, as in the highways in England, we entertain them familiarly in our houses, and they as friendly bestowing their Venison on us. They are a people without any Religion, or knowledge of any God, yet very trusty, quick of apprehension, ripe witted, just.

Governor William Bradford on the Plymouth Colonists' Relations with the Indians, Early 1620s

Anno. 1621

... But about the 16. *of March* a certain Indian came boldly amongst them, and spoke to them in broken English, which they could well understand, but marvelled at it. At length they understood by discourse with him, that he was not of these parts, but belonged to the eastern parts, where some English-ships came to fish, with whom he was acquainted, & could name sundry of them by their names, amongst whom he had got his language. He became profitable to them in acquainting them with many things concerning the state of the country in the east-parts where he lived, which was afterwards profitable unto them; as also of the people hear, of their names, number, & strength; of their situation & distance from this place, and who was chief amongst them. His name was *Samaset;* he tould them also of another Indian whose name was *Squanto,* a native of this place, who had been in England & could speak better English than himself. Being, after some time of entertainment & gifts, dismissed, a while after he came again, & 5 more with him, & they brought again all the tools that were stolen away before, and made way for the coming of their great Sachem, called *Massasoyt;* who, about 4 *or* 5 *days after,* came with the chief of his friends & other attendance, with the aforesaid *Squanto.* With whom, after friendly entertainment, & some gifts given him, they made a peace with him (which hath now continued this 24 years) in these terms.

1. That neither he nor any of his, should injure or do hurt to any of their people.
2. That if any of his did any hurt to any of theirs, he should send the offender, that they might punish him.
3. That if anything were taken away from any of theirs, he should cause it to be restored; and they should do the like to his.

Some of the spelling in this document has been modernized.

4. If any did unjustly war against him, they would aid him; if any did war against them, he should aid them.

5. He should send to his neighbours confederates, to certify them of this, that they might not wrong them, but might be likewise comprised in the conditions of peace.

6. That when their men came to them, they should leave their bows & arrows behind them.

After these things he returned to his place called *Sowams,* some 40 mile from this place, but *Squanto* continued with them, and was their interpreter, and was a special instrument sent of God for their good beyond their expectation. He directed them how to set their corn, where to take fish, and to procure other commodities, and was also their pilot to bring them to unknown places for their profit, and never left them till he died. He was a *native of this place,* & scarce any left alive besides himself. He was carried away with diverse others by one *Hunt,* a master of a ship, who thought to sell them for slaves in Spain; but he got away for England, and was entertained by a merchant in London, & employed to New-found-land & other parts, & lastly brought hither into these parts by one Mr. *Dermer,* a gentle-man employed by Sir Ferdinando Gorges & others, for discovery, & other designs in these parts. . . .

. . . Then the sickness began to fall sore amongst them, and the weather so bad as they could not make much sooner any dispatch. Againe, the Govr. & chief of them, seeing so many die, and fall down sick daily, thought it no wisdom to send away the ship, their condition considered, and the danger they stood in from the Indians, till they could procure some shelter; and therefore thought it better to draw some more charge upon themselves & friends, than hazard all. . . .

Afterwards they (as many as were able) began to plant their corn, in which service Squanto stood them in great stead, showing them both the manner how to set it, and after how to dress & tend it. Also he tould them except they got fish & set with it (in these old grounds) it would come to nothing, and he showed them that in the middle of April they should have store enough come up the brook, by which they began to build, and taught them how to take it, and where to get other provisions necessary for them; all which they found true by trial & experience. Some English seed they sow, as wheat & peas, but it came not to good, either by the badness of the seed, or lateness of the season, or both, or some other defect.

In this month of *April* whilst they were busy about their seed, their Govr. (Mr. John Carver) came out of the field very sick, it being a hot day; he complained greatly of his head, and lay down, and within a few hours his senses failed, so as he never spoke more till he died, which was within a few days after. Whose death was much lamented, and caused great heaviness amongst them, as there was cause. He was buried in the best manner they could, with some volleys of shot by all that bore arms; and his wife, being a weak woman, died within 5 or 6 weeks after him.

Shortly after William Bradford was chosen Govr. in his stead, and being not yet recovered of his illness, in which he had been near the point of death, Isaak Allerton was chosen to be an Assistant unto him, who, by renewed election every year, continued sundry years together, which I hear note once for all. . . .

Having in some sort ordered their business at home, it was thought meet to send some abroad to see their new friend Massasoyet, and to bestow upon him some gratuity to bind him the faster unto them; as also that hereby they might view the country, and see in what manner he lived, what strength he had about him, and how the ways were to his place, if at any time they should have occasion. So the 2 *of July* they sent Mr. Edward Winslow & Mr. Hopkins, with the foresaid Squanto for their guide, who gave him a suit of clothes, and a horseman's coat, with some other small things, which were kindly accepted; but they found but short comons [food rations], and came both weary & hungry home. For the Indians used then to have nothing so much corn as they have since the English have stored them with their hoes, and seen their industry in breaking up new grounds therewith. *They found his place to be* 40 *miles from hence,* the soil good, & the people not many, being dead & abundantly wasted in the late great mortality which fell in all these parts about *three years* before the coming of the English, wherein thousands of them died, they not being able to bury one another; their skulls and bones were found in many places lying still above ground, where their houses & dwellings had been; a very sad spectacle to behold. But they brought word that the Narighansets lived but on the other side of that great bay, & were a strong people, & many in number, living compact together, & had not been at all touched with this wasting plague. . . .

Thus their peace & acquaintance was pretty well established with the natives about them; and there was another Indian called *Hobamack* come to live amongst them, a proper lusty man, and a man of account for his valour & parts amongst the Indians, and continued very faithful and constant to the English till he died. . . .

After this, the 18 of September: they sent out their shallop [small boat] to the Massachusetts, with 10 men, and Squanto for their guide and interpreter, to discover and view that bay, and trade with the natives; the which they performed, and found kind entertainment. The people were much afraid of the Tarentins, a people to the eastward which used to come in harvest time and take away their corn, & many times kill their persons. They returned in safety, and brought home a good quantity of beaver, and made report of the place, wishing they had been there seated; (but it seems the Lord, who assigns to all men the bounds of their habitations, had appointed it for another use). And thus they found the Lord to be with them in all their ways, and to bless their outgoings & incomings, for which let his holy name have the praise forever, to all posterity.

They began now to gather in the small harvest they had, and to fit up their houses and dwellings against winter, being all well recovered in health & strength, and had all things in good plenty; for as some were thus employed in affairs abroad, others were exercised in fishing, about cod, & bass, & other fish, of which they took good store, of which every family had their portion.

All the summer there was no want. And now began to come in store of fowl, as winter approached, of which this place did abound when they came first (but afterward decreased by degrees). And besides water fowl, there was great store of wild Turkeys, of which they took many, besides venison, &c. Besides they had about a peck a meal a week to a person, or now since harvest, Indian corn to the proportion. Which made many afterwards write so largely of their plenty here to their friends in England, which were not fained, but true reports....

... [T]he great people of the Narigansets, in a braving manner, sent a messenger unto them with a bundle of arrows tied about with a great snake-skin; which their interpreters told them was a threatening & a challenge. Upon which the Govr., with the advice of others, sent them a round answer, that if they had rather have war than peace, they might begin when they would; they had done them no wrong, neither did they fear them, or should they find them unprovided. And by another messenger sent the snake-skin back with bullets in it; but they would not receive it, but sent it back again.... And it is like the reason was their own ambition, who, (since the death of so many of the Indians,) thought to dominate & lord it over the rest, & conceived the English would be a bar in their way, and saw that Massasoyt took shelter already under their wings.

But this made them the more carefully to look to themselves, so as they agreed to enclose their dwellings with a good strong pale, and make flankers in convenient places, with gates to shut, which were every night locked, and a watch kept, and when need required there was also warding in the daytime. And the company was by the Captain's and the Govr.'s advise, divided into 4 squadrons, and every one had their quarter appointed them, unto which they were to repair upon any sudden alarme. And if there should be any cry of fire, a company were appointed for a guard, with muskets, whilst others quenched the same, to prevent Indian treachery. This was accomplished very cheerfully, and the town impailed round by the beginning of March, in which every family had a pretty garden plot secured. And herewith I shall end this year....

Anno 1622

At the spring of the year they had appointed the Massachusetts to come again and trade with them, and began now to prepare for that voyage about the later end of March. But upon some rumors heard, Hobamak, their Indian, told them upon some jealousies he had, he feared they were joined with the Narighansets and might betray them if they were not careful. He intimated also some jealousy of Squanto, by what he gathered from some private whisperings between him and other Indians. But they resolved to proceed, and sent out their shallop with 10 of their chief men about the beginning of April, and both Squanto & Hobamake with them, in regard of the jealousy between them. But they had not been gone long, but an Indian belonging to Squanto's family came running in seeming great fear, and told them that many of the Narihgansets, with Corbytant, and he thought also Massasoyte, were coming against them; and he got away to tell them, not without danger. And being examined by the Govr., he made as if they were at hand, and would still be looking back, as if they were at his heels. At which the Govr. caused them to take arms & stand on their guard, and supposing the boat to be still within hearing (by reason it was calm) caused a warning piece or 2 to be shot of, the which they heard and came in. But no Indians appeared; watch was kept all night, but nothing was seen. Hobamak was confidente for Massasoyt, and thought all was false; yet the Govr. caused him to send his wife privately, to see what she could observe (pretending other occasions), but there was nothing found, but all was quiet. After this they proceeded on their voyage to the Massachusetts, and had good trade, and returned in safety, blessed be God.

But by the former passages, and other things of like nature, they began to see that Squanto sought his own ends, and played his own game, by putting the Indians in fear, and drawing gifts from them to enrich himself; making them believe he could stir up war against whom he would, & make peace for whom he would. Yea, he made them believe they kept the plague buried in the ground, and could send it among whom they would, which did much terrify the Indians, and made them depend more on him, and seek more to him than to Massasoyte, which procured him envy, and had like to have cost him his life. For after the discovery of his practices, Massasoyt sought it both privately and openly; which caused him to stick close to the English, & never durst go from them till he died. They also made good use of the emulation that grew between Hobamack and him, which made them carry more squarely. And the Govr. seemed to countenance the one, and the Captain the other, by which they had better intelligence, and made them both more diligent. . . .

. . . Squanto fell sick of an Indian fever, bleeding much at the nose (which the Indians take for a symptom of death), and within a few days died there; desiring the Govr. to pray for him, that he might go to the Englishmen's God in heaven, and bequeathed sundry of his things to sundry of his English friends, as remembrances of his love; of whom they had a great loss. . . .

Governor John Winthrop of Massachusetts Bay Gives a Model of Christian Charity, 1630

1. For the persons, we are a Company professing ourselves fellow members of Christ, In which respect only though we were absent from each other many miles, and had our employments as far distant, yet we ought to account ourselves knit together by this bond of love, and live in the exercise of it, if we would have comfort of our being in Christ. . . .

2. for the work we have in hand, it is by a mutual consent through a special overruling providence, and a more than an ordinary approbation of the Churches of Christ to seek out a place of Cohabitation and Consortship under a due form of Government both civil and ecclesiastical. In such cases as this the care of the public must oversway all private respects, by which not only conscience, but mere

---

Some of the spelling in this document has been modernized.

Civil policy doth bind us; for it is a true rule that particular estates cannot subsist in the ruin of the public.

3. The end is to improve our lives to do more service to the Lord the comfort and increase of the body of christ whereof we are members that ourselves and posterity may be the better preserved from the Common corruptions of this evil world to serve the Lord and work out our Salvation under the power and purity of his holy Ordinances.

4. for the means whereby this must be effected, they are 2fold, a Conformity with the work and end we aim at, these we see are extraordinary, therefore we must not content ourselves with usual ordinary means whatsoever we did or ought to have done when we lived in England, the same must we do and more also where we go: That which the most in their Churches maintain as a truth in profession only, we must bring into familiar and constant practice, as in this duty of love we must love brotherly without dissimulation, we must love one another with a pure heart fervently we must bear one another's burdens, we must not look only on our own things, but also on the things of our brethren, neither must we think that the lord will bear with such failings at our hands as he doth from those among whom we have lived. . . .

. . . Thus stands the cause between God and us, we are entered into Covenant with him for his worke, we have taken out a Commission, the Lord hath given us leave to draw our own Articles we have professed to enterprise these Actions upon these and these ends, we have hereupon besought him of favour and blessing: Now if the Lord shall please to hear us, and bring us in peace to the place we desire, then hath he ratified this Covenant and sealed our Commission, [and] will expect a strict performance of the Articles contained in it, but if we shall neglect the observation of these Articles which are the ends we have propounded, and dissembling with our God, shall fall to embrace this present world and prosecute our carnal intentions, seeking great things for ourselves and our posterity, the Lord will surely break out in wrath against us be revenged of such a perjured people and make us know the price of the breach of such a Covenant.

Now the only way to avoid this shipwreck and to provide for our posterity is to follow the Counsel of Micah, to do Justly, to love mercy, to walk humbly with our God, for this end, we must be knit together in this work as one man, we must entertain each other in brotherly Affection, we must be willing to abridge ourselves of our superfluities, for the supply of others' necessities, we must uphold a familiar Commerce together in all meekness, gentleness, patience and liberality, we must delight in each other, make others' Conditions our own, rejoice together, mourn together, labour, and suffer together, always having before our eyes our Commission and Community in the work, our Community as members of the same body, so shall we keep the unity of the spirit in the bond of peace, the Lord will be our God and delight to dwell among us, as his own people and will command a blessing upon us in all our ways, so that we shall see much more of his wisdom power goodness and truth than formerly we have been acquainted with, we shall find that the God of Israel is among us, when ten of us shall be able to resist a thousand of our enemies, when he shall make us a praise and glory, that men shall say of succeeding plantations: the lord make it like that of New England: for we must Consider that we shall be as a City upon a Hill, the eyes of all people are upon us; so that if we shall deal falsely with our god in this work we have undertaken and so cause him to withdraw his present help from us, we shall be made a story and a by-word through the world, we shall open the mouths of enemies to speak evil of the ways of god and all professors for God's sake; we shall shame the faces of many of gods worthy servants, and cause their prayers to be turned into Curses upon us till we be consumed out of the good land whether we are going. . . .

Colonist John Pond Writes to His Mother and Father for Help, 1631

Most loving and kind Father and Mother:

My humble duty remembered unto you, trusting in God you are in good health, and I pray, remember my love unto my brother Joseife, and thank him for his kindness that I found at his hand at London, which was not the value of a farthing. I know, loving Father, and do confess that I was an undutiful child unto you when I lived with you and by you, for the which I am much sorrowful and grieved for it, trusting in God that He will so guide me that I will never offend you so any more, and I trust in God that you will forgive me for it, and my writing unto you is to let you understand what a country this new' Eingland is where we live.

Here are but few eingeines [Indians], and a great sort of them died this winter. It was thought it was of the plague. They are a crafty people and they will cozen and cheat, and they are a subtle people, and whereas we did expect great store of beaver, here is little or none to be had, and their Sackemor John weigheth it, and many of us truck with them and it layeth us many times in eight shillings a pound. They are proper men and clean-jointed men, and many of them go naked with a skin about their loins, but some of them get eingellische menes [Englishmen's] parell [apparel].

And the country is very rocky and hilly and some champion [open] ground, and the soil is very fleet [shallow], and here is some good ground and marsh ground, but here is no Michaelmas [autumnal] spring. Cattle thrive well here, but they give small store of milk. The best cattle for profit is swines, and a good swine is here at five pounds price and a goat is worth three pounds, a gardene [garden?] goat. Here is timber good store and acorns good store, and here is good store of fish, if we had boats to go eight or ten leagues to sea to fish in. Here are good store of wild fowl, but they are hard to come by. It is harder to get a shot than it is in ould eingland. And people here are subject to disease, for here have died of the scurvy and of the burning fever two hundred and odd, besides many layeth lame, and all Sudberey men

John Pond, letter to his father and mother, March 15, 1631, in Everett Emerson, ed., *Letters from New England* (Amherst: University of Massachusetts Press, 1976), 64–66. Reprinted Courtesy of Massachusetts Historical Society.

are dead but three and the women and some children. And provisions are here at a wonderful rate. Wheat meal is fourteen shillings a bushel and peas ten shillings and malt ten shillings and eindey seid [Indian seed] wheat is fifteen shillings and their other wheat is ten shillings, butter twelve pence a pound, and cheese is eight pence a pound, and all kinds of spices very dear and almost none to be got, and if this ship had not come when it did, we had been put to a wonderful straight, but thanks be to God for sending of it in. I received from the ship a hogshead of meal, and the governor telleth me of a hundredweight of cheese, the which I have received part of it. I humbly thank you for it. I did expect two cows, the which I had none nor I do not earnestly desire that you should send me any because the country is not so as we did expect it. Therefore, loving Father, I would entreat you that you would send me a firkin of butter and a hogshead of malt unground, for we drink nothing but water, and a coarse cloth of four-pound price, so it be thick. And for the freight, if you of your love will send them, I will pay the freight, for here is nothing to be got without we had commodities to go into the east parts amongst the eingeines [Indians] to truck, for here where we live is no beaver, and here is no cloth to be had to make no apparel, and shoes are at five shillings a pair for me, and that cloth that is worth two shillings eight pence a yard is worth here five shillings. So I pray, father, send me four or five yards of cloth to make us some apparel, and, loving Father, though I be far distant from you, yet I pray you remember me as your child, and we do not know how long we may subsist, for we cannot live here without provisions from ould eingland. Therefore, I pray, do not put away your shopstuff, for I think that in the end if I live it must be my living, for we do not know how long this plantation will stand, for some of the merchants that did uphold it have turned off their men and have given it over. Besides, God hath taken away the chiefest stud in the land, Mr. Johnson and the lady Arabella his wife, which was the chiefest man of estate in the land and one that would have done most good.

Here came over twenty-five passengers and there come back again four score and odd persons and as many more would have come if they had where-withal to bring them home, for here are many that came over the last year, which was worth two hundred pounds afore they came out of ould eingland that between this and Michaelmas will be hardly worth thirty pounds, so here we may live if we have supplies every year from ould eingland; otherwise we cannot subsist. I may, as I will work hard, set an ackorne [acre] of eindey [Indian] wheat and if we do not set it with fish and that will cost twenty shillings, and if we set it without fish they shall have but a poor crop.

So, Father, I pray consider of my cause, for here will be but a very poor being and no being without, loving Father, your help with provisions from ould eingland. I had thought to have came home in this ship, for my provisions were almost all spent, but that I humbly thank you for your great love and kindness in sending me some provisions, or else I should and mine have been half famished, but now I will, if it please God that I have my health, I will plant what corn I can, and if provisions be no cheaper between this and Michaelmas and that I do not hear from you what I was best to do, I purpose to come home at Michaelmas.

My wife remembers her humble duty unto you and to my mother and my love to my brother Joseife and to Sarey myler. Thus I leave you to the protection of almighty God.

> from Walltur Toune [Watertown] in new eingland   [no signature]
> the 15 of March 1630[/1]

We were wonderful sick as we came at sea with the smallpox. No man thought that I and my little child would have lived, and my boy is lame and my girl too, and there died in the ship that I came in fourteen persons. To my loving father William Ponde at Etherston in Suffolcke give these.

The Reverend Thomas Welde Describes the Success of the Massachusetts Bay Colony, 1632

Most dear and well beloved in Tarling [Welde's former parish], even all that love the Lord Jesus Christ's gospel, and myself, rich and poor, weak and strong, young and old, male and female, I [write] unto you all in one letter, wanting time to mention you all in particular, you being all dear unto me, yea, most dear to my heart in Jesus Christ, for whom I bow the knee to the Father of lights, longing to hear of your great welfare and spiritual growth in his dear son. From your presence though I be placed and must see your faces no more, yet I shall after a few weary days ended and all tears wiped away, and though happily never on earth yet in the New Jerusalem. . . .

. . . Here I find three great blessings, peace, plenty, and health in a comfortable measure. The place well agreeth with our English bodies that they were never so healthy in their native country. Generally all here as never could be rid of the headache, toothache, cough, and the like are now better and freed here, and those that were weak are now well long since, and I can hear of but two weak in all the plantation. God's name be praised. And although there was wanting at the first that provision at the first glut of people that came over two years since, but blessed be God, here is plenty of corn that the poorest have enough. Corn is here at five shillings six pence a bushel. In truth you cannot imagine what comfortable diet the Indian corn doth make and what pleasant and wholesome food it makes. Our cattle of all do thrive and feed exceedingly. I suppose that such as are to come need bring no more or little or no provision except malt (but no more of these things). I would have none aim at outward matters in such an attempt as this, iest the Lord meet him in the way as he met Balaam with a drawn sword, but at things of an higher nature and more spiritual nature.

O how hath my heart been made glad with the comforts of His house and the spiritual days in the same wherein all things are done in the form and pattern showed in the mount, members provided, church officers elected and ordained, sacrament administered, scandals prevented, censured, fast days

Reprinted from *Letters from New England: The Massachusetts Bay Colony, 1629–1638,* Everett Emerson, ed., pp. 94–98 (Amherst: University of Massachusetts Press, 1976). Copyright © 1976 by The University of Massachusetts Press.

and holy feast days and all such things by authority commanded and performed according to the precise rule. Mine eyes, blessed be God, do see such administration of justice in civil government, all things so righteously, so religiously and impartially carried, I am already fully paid for my voyage who never had so much in the storms at sea as one repenting thought rested in my heart. Praised and thanked be God who moved my heart to come and made open the way to me. And I profess if I might have my wish in what part of the world to dwell I know no other place on the whole globe of the earth where I would be rather than here. We say to our friends that doubt this, Come and see and taste. Here the greater part are the better part....

"The Summons to New England," n. d.

Let all the Purisidian sect,
I mean the counterfeit elect,
All zealous bankroute Punke devout,
Preachers suspended, rabble rout,—
Let them sell all, and out of hand
Prepare to go to New England,
    To build New Babel strong and sure,
    Now called a church unspotted, pure.

There milk from springs like rivers flows,
And honey upon hawthorne grows;
Hemp, wools, & flax there grows on trees;
Their mould is fat, & cut like cheese;
All fruit & herbs springs in the fields;
Tobacco in great plenty yields;
    And there shall be a church most pure,
    Where you may find salvation sure.

There's venison, of all sorts, great store;
Both stag & buck, wild goat & boar;
And yet so tame, as you with ease
May eat your fill,—take what you please.
There's beavers plenty; yea, so many,
That you may have 2 skins a penny.
    Above all this, a church most pure:
    There to be saved you may be sure.

There's flights of fowls do cloud the light;
And turkeys, threescore pounds in weight,
And big as ostriches. Their geese
Are sold with thanks for pence a-piece.
Of duck & mallard, widgeon [a duck], teal,
Twenty, for 2 pence, make a meal.
    Yea, & a church unspotted, pure,
    Within whose bosom all are sure.

Some of the spelling in this document has been modernized.

Lo, there in shoals all sorts of fish,
Of salt sea & of water fresh,—
King cod, pore John, & habberdines [a kind of cod],—
Are taken with your hooks & lines:
A painful fisher on the shore
May take of each twenty in an hour.
     But, above all, a church most pure,
     Where you may live & die secure.

There, twice a year, all sorts of grain
Do down like hail from the heavens rain.
You never need to serve or plough:
There's plenty of all things inough.
Wine, sweet & wholesome, drops from trees,
As clear as crystal, without lees.
     Yea, & a church unspotted, pure,
     From dregs of Papistry secure.

No feasts, or festival set-days,
Are here observed. The Lord we praise,
Though not in churches rich & strong,
Yet where no mass was ever sung.
The bulls of Bason war not here;
Surplice & cap dare not appear.
     Old order all they will abjure:
     This church hath all things new & pure.

No discipline shall there be used:
The law of nature they have chused.
All that the spirit seems to move,
Each man may take, & that approve.
There's government without command;
There's unity without a band;
     A synagogue unspotted, pure,
     Where lust & pleasures dwell secure.

Lo, in this church all shall be free
T' enjoy all Christian liberty.
All things made common. To void strife,
Each man may have another's wife;
And keep a handmaid too, if need,
To multiply, increase, and breed.
     And is not this foundation sure
     To raise a church unspotted, pure?

The native people, though yet wild,
Are all by nature kind & mild,
And apt already (by report)
To live in this religious sort.
Soon to conversion they'll be brought,
When Warham's miracles are wrought;
     Who, being sanctified & pure,
     May, by the Spirit, them allure.

Let Amsterdam send forth her brats,
Her fugitives & runnigates;
Let Bedlam, Newgate, & the Clink
Disgorge themselves into the sink;
Let Brydewell & the Stewes be swept,—
And all sent thither to be kept:
    So may *our* church, cleans'd & made pure,
    Keep both itself & State secure.

William Wood on the Indians' Response to the English Presence, 1634

First of their [the Indians'] stature, most of them being between five or six foot high, straight bodied, strongly composed, smooth-skinned, merry countenanced, of complexion something more swarthy than Spaniards, black haired, high foreheaded, black eyed, out-nosed, broad shouldered, brawny armed, long and slender handed, out breasted, small waisted, lank bellied, well thighed, flat kneed, handsome grown legs, and small feet. In a word, take them when the blood brisks in their veins, when the flesh is on their backs and marrow in their bones, when they frolic in their antic deportments and Indian postures, and they are more amiable to behold (though only in Adam's livery) than many a compounded fantastic in the newest fashion.

It may puzzle belief to conceive how such lusty bodies should have their rise and daily supportment from so slender a fostering, their houses being mean, their lodging as homely, commons scant, their drink water, and nature their best clothing. In them the old proverb may well be verified: *Natura paucis contenta* ["Nature is satisfied with a few things"], for though this be their daily portion they still are healthful and lusty. I have been in many places, yet did I never see one that was born either in redundance or defect a monster, or any that sickness had deformed, or casualty made decrepit, saving one that had a bleared eye and another that had a wen on his cheek. The reason is rendered why they grow so proportionable and continue so long in their vigor (most of them being fifty before a wrinkled brow or gray hair bewray their age) is because they are not brought down with suppressing labor, vexed with annoying cares, or drowned in the excessive abuse of overflowing plenty, which oftentimes kills them more than want, as may appear in them. For when they change their bare Indian commons for the plenty of England's fuller diet, it is so contrary to their stomachs that death or a desperate sickness immediately accrues, which makes so few of them desirous to see England.

Their swarthiness is the sun's livery, for they are born fair. Their smooth skins proceed from the often annointing of their bodies with the oil of fishes and the fat of eagles, with the grease of raccoons, which they hold in summer the best antidote to keep their skin from blistering with the scorching sun, and it is their best armor against the mosquitoes, the surest expeller of the hairy excrement, and stops the pores of their bodies against the nipping winter's cold.

Their black hair is natural, yet it is brought to a more jetty color by oiling, dyeing, and daily dressing. Sometimes they wear it very long, hanging down in a loose, disheveled, womanish manner; otherwhile tied up hard and short like a horse tail, bound close with a fillet, which they say makes it grow the faster. They are not a little fantastical or custom-sick in this particular, their boys being not permitted to wear their hair long till sixteen years of age, and then they must come to it by degrees, some being cut with a long foretop, a long lock on the crown, one of each side of his head, the rest of his hair being cut even with the scalp. The young men and soldiers wear their hair long on the one side, the other side being cut short like a screw. Other cuts they have as their fancy befools them, which would torture the wits of a curious barber to imitate. But though they be thus wedded to the hair of their head, you cannot woo them to wear it on their chins, where it no sooner grows but it is stubbed up by the roots, for they count it as an unuseful, cumbersome, and opprobrious excrement, insomuch as they call him an Englishman's bastard that hath but the appearance of a beard, which some have growing in a staring fashion like the beard of a cat, which makes them the more out of love with them, choosing rather to have no beards than such as should make them ridiculous. . . .

To satisfy the curious eye of women readers, who otherwise might think their sex forgotten or not worthy a record, let them peruse these few lines wherein they may see their own happiness, if weighed in the woman's balance of these ruder Indians who scorn the tutorings of their wives or to admit them as their equals—though their qualities and industrious deservings may justly claim the preeminence and command better usage and more conjugal esteem, their persons and features being every way correspondent, their qualifications more excellent, being more loving, pitiful, and modest, mild, provident, and laborious than their lazy husbands.

Their employments be many: first their building of houses, whose frames are formed like our garden arbors, something more round, very strong and handsome, covered with close-wrought mats of their own weaving which deny entrance to any drop of rain, though it come both fierce and long, neither can the piercing north wind find a cranny through which he can convey his cooling breath. They be warmer than our English houses. At the top is a square hole for the smoke's evacuation, which in rainy weather is covered with a pluver [rain cover]. These be such smoky dwellings that when there is good fires they are not able to stand upright, but lie all along under the smoke, never using any stools or chairs, it being as rare to see an Indian sit on a stool at home as it is strange to see an Englishman sit on his heels abroad. Their houses are smaller in the summer when their families be dispersed by reason of heat and occasions. In winter they make some fifty or threescore foot long, forty or fifty men being inmates under one roof. And as is their husbands' occasion, these poor tectonists [builders or carpenters] are often troubled like snails to carry their houses on their backs, sometime to fishing places, other times to hunting places, after that to a planting place where it abides the longest.

Another work is their planting of corn, wherein they exceed our English husbandmen, keeping it so clear with their clamshell hoes as if it were a garden rather than a corn field, not suffering a choking weed to advance his audacious head above their infant corn or an undermining worm to spoil his spurns. Their corn being ripe they gather it, and drying it hard in the sun convey it to their barns, which be great holes digged in the ground in form of a brass pot, sealed with rinds of trees, wherein they put their corn, covering it from the inquisitive search of their gourmandizing husbands who would eat up both their allowed portion and reserved seed if they knew where to find it. But our hogs having found a way to unhinge their barn doors and rob their garners, they are glad to implore their husbands' help to roll the bodies of trees over their holes to prevent those pioneers whose thievery they as much hate as their flesh.

Another of their employments is their summer processions to get lobsters for their husbands, wherewith they bait their hooks when they go afishing for bass or codfish. This is an everyday's walk, be the weather cold or hot, the waters rough or calm. They must dive sometimes over head and ears for a lobster, which often shakes them by their hands with a churlish nip and bids them adieu. The tide being spent, they trudge home two or three miles with a hundredweight of lobsters at their backs, and if none, a hundred scowls meet them at home and a hungry belly for two days after. Their husbands having caught any fish, they bring it in their boats as far as they can by water and there leave it; as it was their care to catch it, so it must be their wives' pains to fetch it home, or fast. Which done, they must dress it and cook it, dish it, and present it, see it eaten over their shoulders; and their loggerships having filled their paunches, their sweet lullabies scramble for their scraps. In the summer these Indian women, when lobsters be in their plenty and prime, they dry them to keep for winter, erecting scaffolds in the hot sunshine, making fires likewise underneath them (by whose smoke the flies are expelled) till the substance remain hard and dry. In this manner they dry bass and other fishes without salt, cutting them very thin to dry suddenly before the flies spoil them or the rain moist them, having a special care to hang them in their smoky houses in the night and dankish weather.

In summer they gather flags [probably cattail], of which they make mats for houses, and hemp and rushes, with dyeing stuff of which they make curious baskets with intermixed colors and protractures [drawings or designs] of antic imagery. These baskets be of all sizes from a quart to a quarter [eight bushels], in which they carry their luggage. In winter they are their husbands' caterers, trudging to the clam banks for their belly timber, and their porters to lug home their venison which their laziness exposes to the wolves till they impose it upon their wives' shoulders. They likewise sew their husbands' shoes and weave coats of turkey feathers, besides all their ordinary household drudgery which daily lies upon them, so that a big belly hinders no business, nor a childbirth takes much time, but the young infant being greased and

175

sooted, wrapped in a beaver skin, bound to his good behavior with his feet up to his bum upon a board two foot long and one foot broad, his face exposed to all nipping weather, this little papoose travels about with his bare-footed mother to paddle in the icy clam banks after three or four days of age have sealed his passboard and his mother's recovery.

For their carriage it is very civil, smiles being the greatest grace of their mirth; their music is lullabies to quiet their children, who generally are as quiet as if they had neither spleen or lungs. To hear one of these Indians unseen, a good ear might easily mistake their untaught voice for the warbling of a well-tuned instrument, such command have they of their voices.

These women's modesty drives them to wear more clothes than their men, having always a coat of cloth or skins wrapped like a blanket about their loins, reaching down to their hams, which they never put off in company. If a husband have a mind to sell his wife's beaver petticoat, as sometimes he doth, she will not put it off until she have another to put on. Commendable is their mild carriage and obedience to their husbands, notwithstanding all this—their [husband's] customary churlishness and savage inhumanity—not seeming to delight in frowns or offering to word it with their lords, not presuming to proclaim their female superiority to the usurping of the least title of their husband's charter, but rest themselves content under their helpless condition, counting it the woman's portion.

Since the English arrival, comparison hath made them miserable, for seeing the kind usage of the English to their wives, they do as much condemn their husbands for unkindness and commend the English for their love, as their husbands—commending themselves for their wit in keeping their wives industrious—do condemn the English for their folly in spoiling good working creatures. These women resort often to the English houses, where *pares cum paribus congregatae* ["equals gathered with equals"], in sex I mean, they do somewhat ease their misery by complaining and seldom part without a relief. If her husband come to seek for his squaw and begin to bluster, the English woman betakes her to her arms, which are the warlike ladle and the scalding liquors, threatening blistering to the naked runaway, who is soon expelled by such liquid comminations.

In a word, to conclude this woman's history, their love to the English hath deserved no small esteem, ever presenting them something that is either rare or desired, as strawberries, hurtleberries, raspberries, gooseberries, cherries, plums, fish, and other such gifts as their poor treasury yields them. But now it may be that this relation of the churlish and inhumane behavior of these ruder Indians towards their patient wives may confirm some in the belief of an aspersion which I have often heard men cast upon the English there, as if they should learn of the Indians to use their wives in the like manner and to bring them to the same subjection—as to sit on the lower hand and to carry water and the like drudgery. But if my own experience may out-balance an ill-grounded scandalous rumor, I do assure you, upon my credit and reputation, that there is no such matter, but the women find there as much love, respect, and ease as here in old England. I will not deny but that some poor people may carry their own water. And do not the poorer sort in England do the same, witness your London tankard bearers and your country cottagers? But this may well be known to be nothing but the rancorous venom of some that bear no good will to the plantation. For what need they carry water, seeing everyone hath a spring at his door or the sea by his house?

Thus much for the satisfaction of women, touching this entrenchment upon their prerogative, as also concerning the relation of these Indian squaws.

Miantonomo's Call for Indian Unity, 1642

A while after this came Miantenomie from Block-Island to Mantacut with a troop of men . . . ; and instead of receiving presents, which they used to do in their progress, he gave them gifts, calling them brethren and friends, for so are we all Indians as the English are, and say brother to one another; so must we be one as they are, otherwise we shall be all gone shortly, for you know our fathers had plenty of deer and skins, our plains were full of deer, as also our woods, and of turkies, and our coves full of fish and fowl. But these English having gotten our land, they with scythes cut down the grass, and with axes fell the trees; their cows and horses eat the grass, and their hogs spoil our clam banks, and we shall all be starved; therefore it is best for you to do as we, for we are all the Sachems from east to west, both Moquakues and Mohauks joining with us, and we are all resolved to fall upon them all, at one appointed day; and therefore I am come to you privately first, because you can persuade the Indians and Sachem to what you will, and I will send over fifty Indians to Block-Island, and thirty to you from thence, and take an hundred of Southampton Indians with an hundred of your own here; and when you see the three fires that will be made forty days hence, in a clear night, then do as we, and the next day fall on and kill men, women, and children, but no cows, for they will serve to eat till our deer be increased again. . . .

Colonial Women

The first residents of the first permanent English colony in mainland North America were males. Jamestown, Virginia, founded in 1607, had no white female residents for more than a decade, because Virginia was planned to be solely a trading and military outpost. Even so, the early settlers rapidly realized that the future of their colony lay in agriculture, specifically in the cultivation of tobacco, a crop native to the Americas. As the great tobacco boom began, the first English women finally arrived in Virginia (1619). But because of the traditional English sexual division of labor—which identified men as the most appropriate cultivators of crops—tobacco planters seeking indentured servants to work in their fields imported large numbers of male laborers but relatively few females. Accordingly, women long remained a minority of the population in Virginia, and also in Maryland, the second colony founded in the Chesapeake region (1634).

Farther north, in the Pilgrim and Puritan settlements in New England around Cape Cod and the great bay of Massachusetts, women came with their menfolk on the first ships in the 1620s. There the settlers intended from the beginning to establish farms and re-create, if possible, the social and economic structure they had left behind in England. The New Englanders were able to come close to accomplishing that goal because of their nearly balanced numbers of men and women, and because they quickly began subsistence farming rather than relying on the production and sale of a staple crop like tobacco.

The dramatic differences between the Chesapeake and New England colonies in the seventeenth century have attracted the attention of many historians. How, they have asked, did the migration from England affect the status of women? Were they better off in the Chesapeake, where they made up only a small proportion of the population, or in New England, where they were nearly half the settlers? And what was the impact of Puritan ideology and theology on women's lives? Were Puritan women more oppressed, or less so, than Anglicans, Catholics, or Quakers?

These important questions have proved difficult to answer because of a lack of readily accessible source material. Few of the Chesapeake settlers—men or women —could read and write, so most of the evidence for that region comes from public records. In New England, because Puritans believed that each person should be able to read the Bible, more people acquired literacy skills. Therefore, the residents of the northern colonies also produced sermons, letters, and diaries, most of them written by men. The nature of these sources has had a major impact on historians' discussions of the experiences of seventeenth-century white women.

Anne Bradstreet (1612–1672) was the best-known woman writer in colonial America; the four poems that compose the first document, written after she moved to New England in 1630, express her views on women and writing, and on her family life. Bradstreet's ideas on women's intellectual activity stand in sharp contrast to those revealed in the second selection by John Winthrop, the governor of Massachusetts Bay; in his 1645 account, he comments on the insanity of the wife of another New England political leader. The third document, a selection from the famous sermon by Cotton Mather, *Ornaments for the Daughters of Zion* (1698), shows that Puritan men carefully defined female virtue; it included modesty, piety, and humility. In the fourth selection, written in 1666, George Alsop, a former indentured servant in Maryland, described the lives that men and women could expect to lead in that Chesapeake colony, and their prospects for advancement. For men, Alsop predicted success in farming or trade, for women success in finding a suitable husband. The remaining selections—all from the court records of Maryland—suggest the variety of circumstances women actually encountered there, and the treatment of women by the law. The fifth document is the prenuptial agreement arranged in 1654 by the widow Jane Moore and her fiancé Peter Godson. The sixth is the 1668 disposition of the estate of Richard Pinner, whose widow had remarried without a prenuptial settlement. The last selection is the official record of the 1661 bastardy trial of Elesabeth Lockett and Thomas Bright.

Four Poems by Anne Bradstreet, 1643–1669

The Prologue.

1.

To sing of Wars, of Captains, and of Kings,
Of Cities founded, Common-wealths begun,
For my mean pen are too superiour things:
Or how they all, or each their dates have run
Let Poets and Historians set these forth,
My obscure Lines shall not so dim their worth.

.   .   .

5.

I am obnoxious to each carping tongue
Who says my hand a needle better fits,
A Poets pen all scorn I should thus wrong,
For such despite they cast on Female wits:
If what I do prove well, it won't advance,
They'l say it's stoln, or else it was by chance.

But sure the Antique Greeks were far more mild
Else of our Sexe, why feigned they those Nine
And poesy made, *Calliope's* own Child;
So 'mongst the rest they placed the Arts Divine,
But this weak knot, they will full soon untie,
The Greeks did nought, but play the fools & lye.

7.

Let Greeks be Greeks, and women what they are
Men have precedency and still excell,
It is but vain unjustly to wage warre;
Men can do best, and women know it well
Preheminence in all and each is yours;
Yet grant some small acknowledgement of ours.

An EPITAPH
On my dear and ever honoured Mother
Mrs. Dorothy Dudley,
who deceased **Decemb. 27. 1643.** *and of her age,* **61:**

Here lyes,
A Worthy Matron of unspotted life,
A loving Mother and obedient wife,
A friendly Neighbor, pitiful to poor,
Whom oft she fed, and clothed with her store;
To Servants wisely aweful, but yet kind,
And as they did, so they reward did find:
A true Instructer of her Family,
The which she ordered with dexterity.
The publick meetings ever did frequent,
And in her Closet constant hours she spent;
Religious in all her words and wayes,
Preparing still for death, till end of dayes:
Of all her Children, Children, liv'd to see,
Then dying, left a blessed memory.

To my Dear and loving Husband.

If ever two were one, then surely we.
If ever man were lov'd by wife, then thee;
If ever wife was happy in a man,
Compare with me ye women if you can.
I prize thy love more then whole Mines of gold,
Or all the riches that the East doth hold.
My love is such that Rivers cannot quench,
Nor ought but love from thee, give recompence.
Thy love is such I can no way repay,
The heavens reward thee manifold I pray.
Then while we live, in love lets so persever,
That when we live no more, we may live ever.

In memory of my dear grand-child
Anne Bradstreet.
*Who deceased June 20. 1669. being three years and
seven Moneths old.*

With troubled heart & trembling hand I write,
The Heavens have chang'd to sorrow my delight.
How oft with disappointment have I met,
When I on fading things my hopes have set?
Experience might 'fore this have made me wise,
To value things according to their price:
Was ever stable joy yet found below?
Or perfect bliss without mixture of woe.
I knew she was but as a withering flour,
That's here to day, perhaps gone in an hour;
Like as a bubble, or the brittle glass,
Or like a shadow turning as it was.
More fool then I to look on that was lent,
As if mine own, when thus impermanent.
Farewel dear child, thou ne're shall come to me,
But yet a while, and I shall go to thee;
Mean time my throbbing heart's chear'd up with this
Thou with thy Saviour art in endless bliss.

John Winthrop on Mistress Hopkins's Madness, 1645

Mr. Hopkins, the governor of Hartford upon Connecticut, came to Boston, and brought his wife with him, (a godly young woman, and of special parts,) who was fallen into a sad infirmity, the loss of her understanding and reason, which had been growing upon her divers years, by occasion of her giving herself wholly to reading and writing, and had written many books. Her husband, being very loving and tender of her, was loath to grieve her; but he saw his error, when it was too late. For if she had attended her household affairs, and such things as belong to women, and not gone out of her way and calling to meddle in such things as are proper for men, whose minds are stronger, etc., she had kept her wits, and might have improved them usefully and honorably in the place God had set her. He brought her to Boston, and left her with her brother, one Mr. Yale, a merchant, to try what means might be had here for her. But no help could be had.

Cotton Mather on the Virtuous Woman, 1698

The virtuous Woman counts the best Female favour to be deceitful, the best Female Beauty to be vain. By favour is meant, a comely Presence, an handsome carriage, a decent gesture, a ready wit agreeably expressing itself, with all other graceful motions, and what soever procures favour for a woman among her neighbors. The virtuous Woman is willing to have this favour so far as is consistent with virtue; she counts it a favour of God for one to be graced with it; But still she looks upon it as a deceitful thing. She is careful that she do not hereby deceive herself, or be contemptuous towards others. Careful she likewise is, lest hereby she deceive unwary men, into those Amours which bewitching looks and smiles so often betray the children of Men. . . .

By Beauty is meant, a good Proportion and Symmetry of the parts, and a skin well varnished, or that which Chrysostem calls, a good mixture of Blood and flegm spining through a good skin; with all the harmonious Air of the Countenance, which recommends itself, as a Beauty to the Eye of the Spectator. The virtuous woman is not unthankful for this Beauty, when the God of Nature has bestowed any of it on her; and yet she counts it no virtue for her to be very sensible of her being illustrated with such a Beauty. But still she looks upon it as a vain thing. She reckons it so vain, that she has no assurance for the continuance of it . . . for a thousand casualties may soon destroy that idol of the Amorites. And upon these thoughts, a virtuous woman takes heed of becoming so deceitful and vain, as many women are tempted by their Favour and Beauty to become. . . .

The Fear of God is that which the heart of a virtuous woman is under the power of. The Female sex is naturally the fearful sex; but the Fear of God is that which exceeds (and sometimes extinguishes) other fears in the virtuous woman. To state this matter aright, we are to know that the Fear of God is an Old Testament Expression, as the Love of God is a New Testament one. It may then be said of a virtuous woman, that she is a religious woman; that [she] has bound herself to that God, whom she had by the sin and the fall of her first mother [Eve] departed from; she has a love which does not cast out the fear that is no fault, but confirm and settle her in that Fear of God; that all kind of Piety and Charity is prevailing in her disposition; that sobriety and Righteousness and Godliness are visible in her whole Behaviour; and, that she does Justice, loves Mercy, and walks Humbly with her God.

George Alsop on the Lives of Servants in Maryland, 1666

They whose abilities cannot extend to purchase their own transportation over into Mary-Land, (and surely he that cannot command so small a sum for so great a matter, his life must needs be mighty low and dejected) I say they may for the debarment of a four years sordid liberty, go over into this Province and there live plentiously well. And what's a four years Servitude to advantage a man all the remainder of his dayes, making his predecessors happy in his sufficient abilities, which he attained to partly by the restrainment of so small a time?

Now those that commit themselves unto the care of the Merchant to carry them over, they need not trouble themselves with any inquisitive search touching their Voyage; for there is such an honest care and provision made for them all the time they remain aboard the Ship, and are sailing over, that they want for nothing that is necessary and convenient.

The Merchant commonly before they go aboard the Ship, or set themselves in any forwardness for their Voyage, has Conditions of Agreements drawn between him and those that by a voluntary consent become his Servants, to serve him, his Heirs or Assigns, according as they in their primitive acquaintance have made their bargain, some two, some three, some four years; and whatever the Master or Servant tyes himself up to here in England by Condition, the Laws of the Province will force a performance of when they come there: Yet here is this Priviledge in it when they arrive, If they dwell not with the Merchant they made their first agreement withall, they may choose whom they will serve their prefixed time with; and after their curiosity has pitcht on one whom they think fit for their turn, and that they may live well withall, the Merchant makes an Assignment of the Indenture over to him whom they of their free will have chosen to be their Master, in the same nature as we here in England (and no otherwise) turn over Covenant Servants or Apprentices from one Master to another. . . .

The Servants here in Mary-Land of all Colonies, distant or remote Plantations, have the least cause to complain, either for strictness of Servitude, want of Provisions, or need of Apparel: Five dayes and a half in the Summer weeks is the alotted time that they work in; and for two months, when the Sun predominates in the highest pitch of his heat, they claim an antient and customary Priviledge, to repose themselves three hours in the day within the house, and this is undeniably granted to them that work in the Fields.

In the Winter time, which lasteth three months (*viz.*) December, January, and February, they do little or no work or imployment, save cutting of wood to make good fires to sit by, unless their Ingenuity will prompt them to hunt the Deer, or Bear, or recreate themselves in Fowling, to slaughter the Swans, Geese, and Turkeys (which this Country affords in a most plentiful manner): For every Servant has a Gun, Powder and Shot allowed him, to sport him withall on all Holidayes and leasurable times, if he be capable of using it, or be willing to learn.

Now those Servants which come over into this Province, being Artificers, they never (during their Servitude) work in the Fields, or do any other imployment save that which their Handicraft and Mechanick endeavours are capable of putting them upon, and are esteem'd as well by their Masters, as those that imploy them, above measure. He that's a Tradesman here in Mary-Land (though a Servant), lives as well as most common Handicrafts do in London, though they may want something of that Liberty which Freemen have, to go and come at their pleasure; yet if it were rightly understood and considered, what most of the Liberties of the several poor Tradesmen are taken up about, and what a care and trouble attends that thing they call Liberty, which according to the common translation is but Idleness, and (if weighed in the Ballance of a just Reason) will be found to be much heavier and cloggy then the four years restrainment of a Mary-Land Servitude. He that lives in the nature of a Servant in this Province, must serve but four years by the Custom of the Country; and when the expiration of his time speaks him a Freeman, there's a Law in the Province, that enjoyns his Master whom he hath served to give him Fifty Acres of Land, Corn to serve him a whole year, three Sutes of Apparel, with things necessary to them, and

Tools to work withall; so that they are no sooner free, but they are ready to set up for themselves, and when once entred, they live passingly well.

The Women that go over into this Province as Servants, have the best luck here as in any place of the world besides; for they are no sooner on shoar, but they are courted into a Copulative Matrimony, which some of them (for aught I know) had they not come to such a Market with their Virginity, might have kept it by them untill it had been mouldy, unless they had let it out by a yearly rent to some of the Inhabitants of Lewknors-lane, or made a Deed of Gift of it to Mother Coney, having only a poor stipend out of it, untill the Gallows or Hospital called them away. Men have not altogether so good luck as Women in this kind, or natural preferment, without they be good Rhetoricians, and well vers'd in the Art of perswasion, then (probably) they may ryvet themselves in the time of their Servitude into the private and reserved favour of their Mistress, if Age speak their Master deficient.

In short, touching the Servants of this Province, they live well in the time of their Service, and by their restrainment in that time, they are made capable of living much better when they come to be free.

Prenuptial Agreement of Jane Moore and Peter Godson, 1654

Know all men by these presents that Whereas my Husband Richard Moore being Sick and weake upon his death bed did Call to his wife Jane Moore and desired her to bring him the will which he had formerly made and he perused it, and after that he Cancelled it and Caused it to be burnt and made his wife whole and Sole Executor to Sett and dispose of amongst her Children as She will, Richard Manship and Elizabeth Manship his wife being present at the Same time

Know all men by these presents that I Jane Moore the wife of Richard Moore deceased doe bind over the four hundred Acres of Land which we now live upon to be Equally Divided betwixt my three Sons, Viz. Richard Moore Roger Moore and Timothy Moore, and they to be of age when they are Come to Eighteen, and the Maids at fifteen, and fourteen head of female Cattell for Seven Children for their use with all the Increase, the Males being taken out of them and as they Come to age or Marry their Shares to be taken out proportionably, and if any of these Children Should dye the Cattell to goe amongst the rest, and for the Land She is to Enjoy it So Long as She the Said Jane doth Live, and then to Come to the Children
Teste Richard Recklesse   The marke of Jane O Moore
the marke of George W White

Know all men by these presents That Whereas I Peter Godson Chirurgeon intending to Intermarry with Jane Moore of Calvert County in the Province of Maryland widdow, have agreed and doe hereby Consent and agree (in Case the Said Marriage take Effect) not to lay any Clayme to or

Intermeddle with all or any part of the Estate late of Richard Moore deceased late husband of the Said Jane Moore mentioned in the within written Deed or Conveyance to be by the Said Jane disposed of to her Childrens use, but will Leave the Same to the Said Children accordingly   Wittness my hand this Sixt day of July 1654
Test Tho: Hatton   the Marke of Peter G Godson

Proceedings on the Estate of Richard Pinner, 1668

Whereas Ann Pinner alias Attkins the relict [widow] of Richd Pinner late dec^d had Administration Committed to her of the Goods & Chattles of the said Richard Pinner who dyed (as the Office was then inform'd) intestate since which there doth appear a will of the said Richard Pinners Wherefore upon information given the Court that Georg Attkins since marrying the said Relict and doth dayly imbezill & wast the Estate of the said Richard Pinners dec^d whereby in time the said Pinners Orphants will be totally depriv'd of theire right thereto, It is Ordred that Administration be Committed to the said Ann Pinner alias Attkins wth the said will annexed upon the Estate of the said Richard Pinner deceased she being named Executrix in the said Will, and that her now husband George Attkins is not to have any Intrest in or to meddle with any part or parcell of the said Estate which shall be duely brought in and Administred upon by Vertue of the aforegoing Administration, neither is the said George Attkins to bee burdened withall or molested wth any of the debts that shall ensue thereon or which properly doth or which hereafter shall be accompted due from the Estate of the said Richard Pinner dec^d

The Trial of Elesabeth Lockett and Thomas Bright, 1661

Robert Martine Junior sworne in the behalfe of Elesabeth Lockett
    Saith that he Cannot Remmember that thare wase any Munye broken betwext thomas Bright and the said Elesabeth to the best of his knowledg and farther saith not
Teste Me   Tobye wells Clk   the marke of Robert ℛ Martine

    The Examination of Fransis Nash sworne and examined in Court
    Saith that about the midell of summer thes deponant wase goinge with Robert martine and Thomas Bright towards goodman Martins house thes deponant heard the said Bright say th^t theare wase a peace of Munye Broke betwext hime and Elesabeth lockett and further saith not
Jurat quorum Me   the mark of Fransis ИF Nash
    Will: Coursey

    Ann Doob Ann Hill & Catheren Gammer sworne in Court saith
    That Elesabeth Lockett begunn hur Laboure on teusday night and so Remained tell wensday night and about Cooke Crowing she wase Delivered

and all that ever she Confest wase that it wase thomas Brights Child and you^r Deponants asked hur w^t hur master Dide to hure in the husks in the tobaco house and she answered so well as she could that hur master Did butt tickell hur and we Cauld hur into the sheed wheare Mistres blunt and Ann Doob Examiened hure agayne and bade hure speak the Trewth and kathern Gammer heard us and all that Ever she Confest wase that she never knew any other mane in three quarters of a yeare and that she never knew hur Master but by his face and Hands and that the Child wase goote when hur Master wase att Severen wheare that night thomas Bright would not goe to beed butt lay upon the forme and when the sarvants wase aslepe he came to the beed to hur and that night the Child wase goote and when the Childs heed wase in the Birth Mrs Blunt tooke the booke and swore hure & all that she said it wase thomas Brights Child and further saith not

signum

Ann ✝ Doobe

Catheren ♂ Gammer

Ann ᘔ Hill

Sarah Tourson sworne in Court

Saith That she cann Remmember nothing but that she still cried oute on thomas Bright and further saith not

the marke of Sarah **SED** Tourson

Elesabeth Lockett sworne in Court saith that Thomas Bright wase the father of hure Child and no other mane but himself and that theare wase a peace of Munny brooken betwext theme and that he promised hur Mariege before the Child wase gott and further saith not

the marke of Elesabeth *ᴡ* Lockett

Wheraras Elesabeth Lookett and thomas Bright hath binn plainly Convicted for basterdy the Court passinge Judgment that the said Elesabeth should have twenty lashes on hur backe well layd on she hath Craved the bennefett of the Act of Indemnity which the Court doth grant and doth order that Thomas Bright shall pay the Chargges that did Inshue by thayre unlawfull doinge and Cost of seut only the charge that Mrs. Conner hath benn at for keepinge of the child that the said Elesabeth shall pay or make sattisfaiction for

Enslavement of Africans

The institution of slavery evolved slowly until the late seventeenth century. Georgia was a holdout in the trend toward slavery. But as the series of documents in the first selection encompassing the period 1735 to 1750 reveals, sentiment for slave labor quickly mounted in the colony, culminating in the repeal of the act prohibiting slavery there. In the half-century from 1700 to 1750, the southern colonies increasingly formalized master-slave relationships and restricted the liberties of slaves, as the second document, from South Carolina, reflects. These regulations emerged alongside the sharp upsurge in slave importations, as well as rising fears over slaves' growing numbers. The South Carolina statute was a direct response to a brief, but bloody, slave revolt in 1739 in the Stono River district, 20 miles outside of Charleston. Slaves worked out their own accommodation to the restrictions, including leaving their masters for extended periods of time. The last excerpt, from Colonel Landon Carter's diary, demonstrates both the exasperation of a leading Virginia planter and the support runaways received from the larger slave community.

The Debate over Slavery in Georgia, 1735–1750

Minutes of the Georgia Privy Council, 1735

April 3, 1735.

An Act for rendering the Colony of Georgia more Defencible by Prohibiting the Importation and use of Black Slaves or Negroes into the same.

Whereas Experience hath Shewn that the manner of Settling Colonys and Plantations with Black Slaves or Negroes hath obstructed the Increase of English and Christian Inhabitants therein who alone can in case of a War be relyed on for the Defence and Security of the same, and hath Exposed the Colonys so settled to the Insurrections Tumults and Rebellions of such Slaves and Negroes and in Case of a Rupture with any Foreign State who should Encourage and Support such Rebellions might Occasion the utter Ruin and loss of such Colonys, For the preventing therefore of so great inconveniences in the said Colony of Georgia. We the Trustees for Establishing the Colony of Georgia in America humbly beseech Your Majesty That it may be Enacted And be it Enacted that from and after the four and twentieth day of June which shall be in the Year of Our Lord One Thousand Seven hundred and thirty five if any Person or Persons whatsoever shall import or bring or shall cause to be imported or brought or shall sell or Barter or use in any manner or way whatsoever in the said Province or in any Part or Place therein any Black or Blacks Negroe or Negroes such Person or Persons for every such Black or Blacks Negroe or Negroes so imported or brought or caused to be imported or brought or sold Bartered or used within the said Province Contrary to the intent and meaning of this Act shall forfeit and lose the Sum of fifty pounds Sterling Money of Great Britain. . . .

Diary of the Earl of Egmont, 1735–1738

Wednesday, 3 [September 1735]. The Scots settled at Joseph's Town having applied for the liberty of making use of negro slaves, we acquainted one of their number, who came over to solicit this and other requests made by them to us, that it could not be allowed, the King having passed an Act against it, of which we read part to him. . . .

Monday, 17 [November 1735]. A letter was read from Mr. Samuel Eveleigh that he had quitted his purpose of settling in Georgia, and was returned to Carolina, because we allow not the use of negro slaves, without which he pretends our Colony will never prove considerable by reason the heat of the climate will not permit white men to labour as the negroes do, especially in raising rice, nor can they endure the wet season when rice is to be gathered in. . . .

Thursday, 24 [November 1737]. . . . That Mr. ——— Mackay had without leave on his own head settled on ——— Wilmington Island and employed negroes. N. B. Smart care must be taken of this, for many are disposed to follow his example.

Remonstrance of the Inhabitants of Savannah, 1738

SAVANNAH, 9th December, 1738.

To the Honorable the Trustees for Establishing the Colony of Georgia in America.

May it please your Honors: We whose names are underwritten, being all settlers, freeholders and inhabitants in the province of Georgia, and being sensible of the great pains and care exerted by you in endeavoring to settle this colony, since it has been under your protection and management, do unanimously join to lay before you, with the utmost regret, the following particulars. . . . Timber is the only thing we have here which we might export, and notwithstanding we are obliged to fall it in planting our land, yet we cannot manufacture it for a foreign market but at double the expense of other colonies; as for instance, the river of May, which is but twenty miles from us, with the allowance of negroes, load vessels with that commodity at one half of the price that we can do; and what should induce persons to bring ships here, when they can be loaded with one half of the expense so near us; therefore the timber on the land is only a continual charge to the possessors of it, though of very great advantage in all the northern colonies, where negroes are allowed, and consequently, labor cheap. We do not in the least doubt but that in time, silk and wine may be produced here, especially the former; but since the cultivation of the land with white servants only, cannot raise provisions for our families as before mentioned, therefore it is likewise impossible to carry on these manufactures according to the present constitution. It is very well known, that Carolina can raise every thing that this colony can, and they having their labor so much cheaper will always ruin our market, unless we are in some measure on a footing with them. . . . Your honors, we imagine, are not insensible of the numbers that have left this province, not being able to support themselves and families any longer. . . .

The want of the use of negroes, with proper limitation; which, if granted, would both occasion great numbers of white people to come here, and also render us capable to subsist ourselves, by raising provisions upon our lands, until we could make some produce fit for export, in some measure to balance our importation. We are very sensible of the inconveniences and mischiefs that have already, and do daily arise from an unlimited use of negroes; but we are as sensible that these may be prevented by a due limitation, such as so many to each white man, or so many to such a quantity of land, or in any other manner which your Honors shall think most proper.

Diary of the Earl of Egmont, 1739

Wednesday, 17 Jany. 1738/9. I. Col. Oglethorpe wrote again to the Trustees, to shew further inconveniences arrising from the allowing the use of Negroes, *viz.* 1. That it is against the principles by which the Trustees associated together, which was to releive the distressed, whereas we should occasion the misery of thousands in Africa, by setting Men upon using arts to buy and bring into perpetual slavery the poor people, who now live free there. 2. Instead of strengthning, we should weaken the Frontiers of America. 3. Give away to the Owners of slaves that land which was design'd as a Refuge to persecuted Protestants. 4. Prevent all improvements of silk and wine. 5. And glut the Markets with more of the American Comodities, which do already but too much interfere with the English produce.

James Oglethorpe to the Trustees of Georgia, 1739

SAVANNAH 12th March 1738/9.

Gentlemen, . . . Mr. Williams is very angry, and hath got the poor People of Savannah, many of whom are deeply in Debt to him, to sign the Petition for Negroes, which affirms that white men cannot work in this Province. This Assertion I can disprove by hundreds of Witnesses, all the Saltzburghers, the people at Darien, many at Frederica, and Savannah, and all the Industrious in the Province. The idle ones are indeed for Negroes. If the Petition is countenanced the Province is ruined. Mr. Williams and Doctor Talfeur will buy most of the Lands at Savannah with Debts due to them, and the Inhabitants must go off and be succeeded by Negroes. Yet the very debtors have been weak enough to sign their Desire of Leave to sell.

Diary of the Earl of Egmont, 1739–1740

[Tuesday], 13 March 1738/9. The Saltsburgers at Ebenezer wrote and sign'd a Counter-representation to that sent by the Inhabitants of Savannah, earnestly desiring of Genl. Oglethorpe that Negroes and change of Tenure may not be allow'd of in the Province. In it they express their happy

condition, and desire the encouragement they had might be given to others to joyn them.

The Reverend John Martin Bolzius to the
Reverend George Whitefield, 1745

EBENEZER Dec. 24th 1745.

Revd. and Dear Sir, Besides the Blessings, the Lord was pleased to impart to my Soul in your and Mrs. Whitefield's Conversation, I felt many Griefs and troubles in my heart Since my Return from Bethesda and Savannah, arising from the unhappy News, I heard at Savannah and from your Self, that you are induced to petition the Honble. Trustees for giving their Consent to the Introduction of Negroes into this our Colony, for which you think to be Under Necessity with Respect to the Maintainance of the Orphan House. Dont be amazed, Sir at my Boldness to write to you in this Secular Affair, in which I would not meddle at all, if not the Love to your Worthy person, to my Congregation and to this Colony Oblidged me to it. For the Introduction of Negroes inconsistent with the prayseworthy Scheme of the Honble. Trustees our Lawful and Bountiful Superiours, will be very Mischievous to the happy Settling of this Colony, and Especially to the poor white Labouring people in many Respects, and the Sighs of them would be unprofitable for you or any other, who joins with the principles and aims of the Wishers for Negroe Overseer. A Common white Labourer white Man of the meaner Sort can get his and his Family's Livelyhood honestly in Carolina, except he embraces the Sorry Imploy of a Negroe Overseers. A Common white Labourer in Charles-Town (I am told) has no more Wages, than a Negroe for his work *Viz.* 7 *s.* Cur. or 12 *d.* Sterl. a Day, for which it is in my Opinion impossible to find Victuals, Lodging and washing, much less Cloaths. In case he would Settle and Cultivate a plantation, is not all good and Convenient Ground at the Sea Coasts and Banks of the Rivers taken up in Large Quantities by the Merchants and Other Gentlemen? Consequently the poor white Inhabitants are forced to possess Lands, remote from the Conveniencys of Rivers and from Town to their great Disappointment to Sell their produce. Being not inclined to give their Produce of their Plantations or Other Sort of Work for Such a Low price, as Negroes can afford, they find no market, then they are discouraged and Obliged to Seek their Livelihood in the Garrisons, Forts, Scout-Boats, Trading Boats or to be imploy'd amongst the Negroes upon a Gentleman's Plantation, or they are forced to take Negroes upon Credit, of which they will find in Process of time the Sad Consequences on Account of their Debts. I hear the Negroes in Carolina learn all Sorts of trade, which takes away the bread of a poor white trades' man Like wise.

I have Considered the Strength of your Arguments by which you seem to be induced to promote the Introduction of Negroes, as far as it lyes in your power.

First you think the Providence of God has Appointed this Colony rather for the work of black Slaves than for Europians, because of the hot Climate, to which the Negroes are better used than white people.

But, Dear Sir, give me Leave to say, that every honest Labourer amongst us will testify the Contrary and that in some parts of Germany in the Middle of the Summer being the Only Season there to make Hay, and to bring in their Crop, is as hot as here. And if it be so, that in the 3 Months of the Summer it is too hot for white people to work with the hoe in the field, is it so with the plow Can they not Chuse the Morning and Afternoon Hours for Labouring in the Field? Have they not 9 Months in the Year time Enough to prepare the Ground for Europian and Countrey Grain? Which preference they enjoy not in the Northern Parts, by Reason of the Deep Snow and the Exceeding Cold Weather. . . .

II. Your Second Argument for the Introduction of Negroes was, that the Trustees have laid out about 250,000 Pounds Sterl. for Establishing this Colony, and almost to no purpose. . . . There are so many Thousands of Protestants in Germany, who would embrace eagerly an Invitation to this Colony, if they could meet with Encouragement, as they will in time, and it is a Thousand pity, that you will help to make this Retirement and Refuge for poor persecuted or Necessitous Protestants, a Harbour of Black Slaves, and deprive them of the benefit to be Settled here. . . .

III. Your third Argument was, that you have laid out great Sums of Money for Building and Maintaining the Orphan House, which you could not continue without Negroes, and this be the Case of Other Gentlemen in the Colony.

But let me intreat you, Sir, not to have regard for a Single Orphan House, and to Contribute Some thing Mischievous to the Overthrow of the prayseworthy Scheme of the Trustees with Respect to the whole Colony.

IV. Your Last Argument for Negroes was, as I remember, that you intended to bring them to the Knowledge of Christ.

But, Sir, my Heart wishes, that first the White people in the Colony and Neighbourhood may be brought to the Saving and Experimental Knowledge of Christ. As long as they are for this World, and take Advantage of the poor black Slaves, they will increase the Sins of the Land to a great Heighth. If a Minister had a Call to imploy his Strength and time to Convert Negroes, he has in Carolina a Large Field. Dont believe, Sir, the Language of those persons, who wish the Introduction of Negroes under pretence of promoting their Spiritual Happiness, as well as in a Limited Number and under some Restrictions. I am sure, that if the Trustees allow'd to one thousand White Settlers so many Negroes, in a few Years you would meet in the Streets, So as in Carolina, with many Malattoes, and many Negroe Children, which in process of time will fill the Colony. The Assembly in Carolina have made good Laws and Restrictions in favour of the White people, but how many are, who pay regard and Obedience to them? not better would fare the Restrictions and Good Laws of the Trustees. I will not mention the great Danger, to which we are exposed by the Introduction of Negroes with Respect to the Spaniards, and it is a Groundless thing, to say, that one of the Articles of Peace with Spain must be not to give Shelter to the Negroes at Augustine, who would run away.

Repeal of the Act Excluding Negroes, 1750

May it please Your Majesty,

The Trustees for establishing the Colony of Georgia in America in pursuance of the Powers and in Obedience to the Directions to them given by Your Majesty's most Gracious Charter humbly lay before Your Majesty the following Law Statute and Ordinance which they being for that purpose assembled have prepared as fit and necessary for the Government of the said Colony and which They most humbly present under their Common Seal to Your most Sacred Majesty in Council for your Majesty's most Gracious Approbation and Allowance.

An Act for repealing an Act Intituled (An Act for rendering the Colony of Georgia more defensible by prohibiting the Importation and Use of Black Slaves or Negroes into the same) and for permitting the Importation and Use of them in the Colony under proper Restrictions and Regulations, and for other Purposes therein mentioned.

Whereas an Act was passed by his Majesty in Council in the Eighth Year of his Reign Intituled (an Act for rendering the Colony of Georgia more defensible by prohibiting the Importation and Use of Black Slaves or Negroes into the same) by which Act the Importation and Use of Black Slaves or Negroes in the said Colony was absolutely prohibited and forbid under the Penalty therein mentioned and whereas at the time of passing the said Act the said Colony of Georgia being in its Infancy the Introduction of Black Slaves or Negroes would have been of dangerous Consequence but at present it may be a Benefit to the said Colony and a Convenience and Encouragement to the Inhabitants thereof to permit the Importation and Use of them into the said Colony under proper Restrictions and Regulations without Danger to the said Colony as the late War hath been happily concluded and a General Peace established. Therefore we the Trustees for establishing the Colony of Georgia in America humbly beseech Your Majesty that it may be Enacted And be it enacted That the said Act and every Clause and Article therein contained be from henceforth repealed and made void and of none Effect and be it Further Enacted that from and after the first day of January in the Year of Our Lord One thousand seven hundred and fifty it shall and may be lawful to import or bring Black Slaves or Negroes into the Province of Georgia in America and to keep and use the same therein under the Restrictions and Regulations hereinafter mentioned and directed to be observed concerning the same And for that purpose be it Further Enacted that from and after the said first day of January in the Year of Our Lord One thousand seven hundred and fifty it shall and may be lawful for every Person inhabiting and holding and cultivating Lands within the said Province of Georgia and having and constantly keeping one white Man Servant on his own Lands capable of bearing Arms and aged between sixteen and sixty five Years to have and keep four Male Negroes or Blacks upon his Plantation there and so in Proportion to the Number of such white Men Servants capable of bearing Arms and of such Age as aforesaid as shall be kept by every Person within the said Province.

South Carolina Restricts the Liberties of Slaves, 1740

I. *And be it enacted,* . . . That all negroes and Indians, (free Indians in amity with this government, and negroes, mulattoes and mustizoes, who are now free, excepted,) mulattoes or mustizoes who now are, or shall hereafter be, in this Province, and all their issue and offspring, born or to be born, shall be, and they are hereby declared to be, and remain forever hereafter, absolute slaves. . . .

XXIII. *And be it further enacted* by the authority aforesaid, That it shall not be lawful for any slave, unless in the presence of some white person, to carry or make use of fire arms, or any offensive weapons whatsoever, unless such negro or slave shall have a ticket or license, in writing, from his master, mistress or overseer, to hunt and kill game, cattle, or mischievous birds, or beasts of prey, and that such license be renewed once every month, or unless there be some white person of the age of sixteen years or upwards, in the company of such slave, when he is hunting or shooting, or that such slave be actually carrying his master's arms to or from his master's plantation, by a special ticket for that purpose, or unless such slave be found in the day time actually keeping off rice birds, or other birds, within the plantation to which such slave belongs, lodging the same gun at night within the dwelling house of his master, mistress or white overseer. . . .

XXXII. *And be it further enacted* by the authority aforesaid, That if any keeper of a tavern or punch house, or retailer of strong liquors, shall give, sell, utter or deliver to any slave, any beer, ale, cider, wine, rum, brandy, or other spirituous liquors, or strong liquor whatsoever, without the license or consent of the owner, or such other person who shall have the care or government of such slave, every person so offending shall forfeit the sum of five pounds, current money, for the first offence. . . .

XXXIV. And *whereas,* several owners of slaves have permitted them to keep canoes, and to breed and raise horses, neat cattle and hogs, and to traffic and barter in several parts of this Province, for the particular and peculiar benefit of such slaves, by which means they have not only an opportunity of receiving and concealing stolen goods, but to plot and confederate together, and form conspiracies dangerous to the peace and safety of the whole Province; *Be it therefore enacted* by the authority aforesaid, That it shall not be lawful for any slave so to buy, sell, trade, traffic, deal or barter for any goods or commodities, (except as before excepted,) nor shall any slave be permitted to keep any boat, perriauger or canoe, or to raise and breed, for the use and benefit of such slave, any horses, mares, neat cattle, sheep or hogs, under pain of forfeiting all the goods and commodities which shall be so bought, sold, traded, trafficked, dealt or bartered for, by any slave, and of all the boats, perriaugers or canoes, cattle, sheep or hogs, which any slave shall keep, raise or breed for the peculiar use, benefit and profit of such slave. . . .

XXXVII. And *whereas,* cruelty is not only highly unbecoming those who profess themselves christians, but is odious in the eyes of all men who have any sense of virtue or humanity; therefore, to refrain and prevent barbarity being exercised towards slaves, *Be it enacted* by the authority aforesaid, That if any person or persons whosoever, shall wilfully murder his own slave, or the slave of any other person, every such person shall, upon conviction thereof, forfeit and pay the sum of seven hundred pounds, current money, and shall be rendered, and is hereby declared altogether and forever incapable of holding, exercising, enjoying or receiving the profits of any office, place or employment, civil or military, within this Province. . . .

XXXVIII. *And be it further enacted* by the authority aforesaid, That in case any person in this Province, who shall be owner, or shall have the care, government or charge of any slave or slaves, shall deny, neglect or refuse to allow such slave or slaves, under his or her charge, sufficient cloathing, covering or food, it shall and may be lawful for any person or persons, on behalf of such slave or slaves, to make complaint to the next neighboring justice, in the parish where such slave or slaves live or are usually employed. . . .

XLIII. And *whereas,* it may be attended with ill consequences to permit a great number of slaves to travel together in the high roads without some white person in company with them; *Be it therefore enacted* by the authority aforesaid, That no men slaves exceeding seven in number, shall hereafter be permitted to travel together in any high road in this Province, without some white person with them. . . .

XLV. And *whereas,* the having of slaves taught to write, or suffering them to be employed in writing, may be attended with great inconveniences; *Be it therefore enacted* by the authority aforesaid, That all and every person and persons whatsoever, who shall hereafter teach, or cause any slave or slaves to be taught, to write, or shall use or employ any slave as a scribe in any manner of writing whatsoever, hereafter taught to write, every such person and persons, shall, for every such offence, forfeit the sum of one hundred pounds current money.

XLVI. And *whereas,* plantations settled with slaves without any white person thereon, may be harbours for runaways and fugitive slaves; *Be it therefore enacted* by the authority aforesaid, That no person or persons hereafter shall keep any slaves on any plantation or settlement, without having a white person on such plantation or settlement.

Landon Carter on the Problem of Runaway Slaves, 1766

12. [March] *Wednesday.*

At night found that my ox carter, Simon, was run away and examined Billy the foreman who said he complained of the belly ake and went away, The Overseer being an [illegible] ordnance at Court.

24. *Thursday*.

Simon, one of the Outlaws, came home. He run away the 12th of March and by being out and doing mischief was outlawed in all the Churches 2 several Sundays and on the 10th of this month having a great suspicion that he was entertained at my home quarter where his Aunt and Sisterinlaw lives, Mr. Carter's favourite maid; I had him R[illegible] watched by Talbot and Tom with Guns loaded with small shot and Toney withdrew. Just at dark according to my suspicion they came along my lane; over the Lucern field talking loudly as if secure they should be concealed When Talbot commanding them to stand, upon their running, shot Simon in the right leg foot and ham. He got away and Simon has stayed out ever since then so that he has been now shot to this day 14 days. . . .

. . . It seems that Simon the runaway was shot at only about 11 days agoe. And he did not come in himself; for Mangorike Will seeing a smoke yesterday amongst Some Cedars by the side of the corn field when he was working; at night went to see what it was, and was long hunting for it as smoke is but rarely seen in the night. At last he got to some burnt Coals and saw no one there, but creeping through the Cedars he came to a fire burning and Simon lying by it; Who instantly started up to run away, but Billy was too swift and after a small struggle made him surrender and brought him in to Tom and Nassau who concealed this from me, in order to make as if the fellow came in himself. Willy says he was not lame last night, although he has now strummed it on account of his leg being shot. I shall punish him accordingly. . . .

25. *Friday*.

. . . My man Bart came in this day, he has been gone ever since New year's day. His reason is only that I had ordered him a whipping for saying he then brought in two load of wood when he was coming with his first load only. This he still insists on was truth. Although the whole plantation asserts the contrary, and the boy with him. He is the most incorrigeable villain I beleive alive, and has deserved hanging; which I will get done if his mate in roguery can be tempted to turn evidence against him.

Bart broke open the house in which he was tyed and locked up; he got out before 2 o'clock but not discovered till night. Talbot is a rogue. He was put in charge of him. I do imagine the gardiner's boy Sam, a rogue I have suspected to have maintained Bart and Simon all the while they have been out. And I sent this boy with a letter to the Island ferry at breakfast, but he never returned although he was seen coming back about 12 and was seen at night by Hart George at night pretending to be looking for his Cattle. I kept this fellow up two nights about these fellows before And have given Rit the Miller a light whipping as having fed them by the hands of Gardiner Sam. . . .

27. *Sunday*.

Yesterday my son brought a story from Lansdown old Tom, that Johnny my gardiner had harboured Bart and Simon all the while they were out,

Sometimes in his inner room and sometimes in my Kitchen Vault. Tom had this from Adam his wife's grandson That they were placed in the Vault in particular the day my Militia were hunting for them.

This Simon owned, and the boy Adam repeated it to me; but Tom of Landsdown said that George belonging to Capn. Beale saw them in my quarter when he came from setting my Weir. It seemed to me so plausible that I sent Johnny [to] Goal and locked his son in Law Postilion Tom up. Note: every body denyed they had ever seen them and in Particular Mrs. Carter's wench Betty, wife to Sawney, brother of Simon, denyed that she had ever seen them; as she did to me with great impudence some days agoe. However Capn. Beale's George this day came to me and before Mrs. Carter told the story and in Simon's hearing That coming from the Weir he went into Frank's room and then into Sawney's room, when Simon came in to them. So that favourites and all are liars and villains.

These rogues could not have been so entertained without some advantage to those who harboured them; from whence I may conclude the making away of my wool, wheat etc., and the death of my horses.

The Origins of
American Foreign Policy

Americans were once proud members of the British Empire. For over 150 years that membership brought good profit at low cost and protection against the French in North America. But in the 1760s, after victory in the French and Indian War, the mother country began to impose new taxes and regulations that shattered the relationship. In 1776 the American colonials chose independence through revolution. They selected that dangerous course not only because of perceived British perfidy, but also because of their own New World sense of themselves as different from—indeed, superior to—the Old World of monarchy, relentless international rivalry, and corrupted institutions.

Geographical isolation from Europe helped spawn such notions of exceptionalism, as did the American doctrine of mission and God-favored destiny the Puritans had etched on American memory. Colonials from New England to Georgia had also become accustomed to making their own decisions, governing themselves at the local level in what one historian has tagged "island communities," and expanding their landholdings and commerce without much interference from the British Crown and Parliament. Yet when the founding fathers declared independence and then worked to gain and preserve it in a doubting and hostile world, they felt compelled to appeal for help from Europe, particularly France. They became conspicuously uneasy about calling upon the decadent Old World to save their fresh New World experiment, because the linkage so violated what some scholars have labeled American "isolationism." At the same time, however, American leaders saw in their new treaties and nationhood the opportunity to reform traditional world politics to ensure the country's safety and prosperity.

As children of empire, early national leaders naturally dreamed of a new and ever-expanding American empire. They recognized the obstacles to expansion: Native Americans, European powers, and their own sectional and political differences. In fact, many of the nation's founders thought that internal squabbling and the absence of a strong central government threatened not just expansionism but independence itself. A persuasive argument for the Constitution, rat-

197

ified in 1789, was that it would permit the new United States to devise a coherent and respected foreign policy.

Historians have debated the relative importance of isolationism, expansionism, imperialism, and idealism as characteristics of early American foreign policy. And they have wondered to what extent American leaders understood and exercised power in eighteenth-century world affairs. But they have agreed that Americans ardently claimed that their upstart republic held a unique international position that would transform the world community. Why Americans came to think so is explained by the documents and essays in this chapter.

✳ D O C U M E N T S

John Winthrop, the first governor of Massachusetts Bay, defined the Puritan mission in a lay sermon of June 1630, aboard ship off the New England coast. The second document, from John Adams' diary of late 1775, recounts this founding father's case for alliance with France, but cautions against entanglement in Europe's wars. Thomas Paine, who had moved from England to Philadelphia just two years before independence was declared, invigorated the revolutionary spirit with his popular 1776 tract *Common Sense,* wherein he demanded severance from the British Empire. The Declaration of Independence of July 4, 1776, outlined American grievances against the mother country. The two treaties with France provided not only for alliance, but also for principles that would govern foreign commerce. The seventh document is a celebratory statement by Ezra Stiles, president of Yale College. Delivered as a Connecticut election sermon in May 1783, the message reveals the American penchant for seeing the new United States as the best hope for mankind. America's birth certificate, in preliminary form, was signed by British and American emissaries on November 30, 1782. The final Treaty of Peace was signed in Paris on September 3, 1783, and ratifications were exchanged on May 12, 1784. The last document presents the parts of the United States Constitution of 1789 that cover foreign policy.

John Winthrop's City Upon a Hill, 1630

Now the onely way to avoyde this shipwracke and to provide for our posterity is to followe the Counsell of Micah, to doe Justly, to love mercy, to walke humbly with our God, for this end, wee must be knitt together in this worke as one man, wee must entertaine each other in brotherly Affeccion, wee must be willing to abridge our selves of our superfluities, for the supply of others necessities, wee must uphold a familiar Commerce together in all meekenes, gentlenes, patience and liberallity, wee must delight in eache other, make others Condicions our owne rejoyce together, mourne together, labour, and suffer together, allwayes haveing before our eyes our Commission and Community in the worke, our Community as members of the same body, soe shall wee keepe the unitie of the spirit in the bond of peace, the Lord will be our God and delight to dwell among us, as his owne people and will commaund a blessing upon us in all our wayes, soe that wee shall see much more of his wisdome power goodnes and truthe then formerly wee have beene acquainted with, wee shall finde that the God of Israell is among us, when tenn of us shall be able to resist a thousand of our enemies, when hee shall make us a prayse and glory, that men shall say of succeeding plantacions: the lord make it like that of New England: for wee must Consider that wee shall be as a Citty upon a Hill, the eies of all people are uppon us; soe that if wee shall deale falsely with our god in this worke wee have undertaken and soe cause him to withdrawe his present help from us, wee shall be made a story and a by-word through the world, wee shall open the mouthes of enemies to speake evill of the wayes of god and all professours for Gods sake; wee shall shame the faces of many of gods worthy servants, and cause theire prayers to be turned into Cursses upon us till wee be consumed out of the good land whether wee are going: And to shutt upp this discourse with that exhortacion of Moses that faithfull servant of the Lord in his last farewell to Israell Deut. 30. Beloved there is now sett before us life, and good, deathe and evill in that wee are Commaunded this day to love the Lord our God, and to love one another to walke in his wayes and to keepe his Commaundements and his Ordinance, and his lawes, and the Articles of our Covenant with him that wee may live and be multiplyed, and that the Lord our God may blesse us in the land whether wee goe to possesse it: But if our heartes shall turne away soe that wee will not obey, but shall be seduced and worshipp other Gods our pleasures, and proffitts, and serve them, it is propounded unto us this day, wee shall surely perishe out of the good Land whether wee passe over this vast Sea to possesse it;

> Therefore lett us choose life,
> that wee, and our Seede,
> may live; by obeyeing his
> voyce, and cleaveing to him,
> for hee is our life, and
> our prosperity.

John Adams on Connection with France, 1775

Some Gentlemen doubted of the Sentiments of France, thought She would frown upon Us as Rebells and be afraid to countenance the Example. I replied to these Gentlemen, that I apprehended they had not attended to the relative Situation of France and England. That it was the unquestionable Interest of France that the British continental Colonies should be independent. That Britain by the Conquest of Canada and their naval Tryumphs during the last War, and by her vast Possessions in America and the East Indies, was exalted to a height of Power and Preeminence that France must envy and could not endure. But there was much more than pride and Jealousy in the Case. Her Rank, her Consideration in Europe, and even her Safety and Independence was at stake. The Navy of Great Britain was now Mistress of the Seas all over the Globe. The Navy of France almost annihilated. Its Inferiority was so great and obvious, that all the Dominions of France in the West Indies and in the East Indies lay at the Mercy of Great Britain, and must remain so as long as North America belonged to Great Britain, and afforded them so many harbours abounding with Naval Stores and Resources of all kinds and so many Men and Seamen ready to assist them and Man their Ships. That Interest could not lie, that the Interest of France was so obvious, and her Motives so cogent, that nothing but a judicial Infatuation of her Councils could restrain her from embracing Us. That our Negotiations with France ought however, to be conducted with great caution and with all the foresight We could possibly obtain. That We ought not to enter into any Alliance with her, which should entangle Us in any future Wars in Europe, that We ought to lay it down as a first principle and a Maxim never to be forgotten, to maintain an entire Neutrality in all future European Wars. That it never could be our Interest to unite with France, in the destruction of England, or in any measures to break her Spirit or reduce her to a situation in which she could not support her Independence. On the other hand it could never be our Duty to unite with Britain in too great a humiliation of France. That our real if not our nominal Independence would consist in our Neutrality. If We united with either Nation, in any future War, We must become too subordinate and dependent on that nation, and should be involved in all European Wars as We had been hitherto. That foreign Powers would find means to corrupt our People to influence our Councils, and in fine We should be little better than Puppetts danced on the Wires of the Cabinetts of Europe. We should be the Sport of European Intrigues and Politicks. That therefore in preparing Treaties to be proposed to foreign Powers and in the Instructions to be given to our Ministers, We ought to confine ourselves strictly to a Treaty of Commerce. That such a Treaty would be an ample Compensation to France, for all the Aid We should want from her. The Opening of American Trade, to her would be a vast resource for her Commerce and Naval Power, and a great Assistance to her in protecting her East and West India Possessions as well as her Fisheries: but that the bare dismemberment of the British Empire, would be to her an incalculable Security and Benefit, worth more than all the Exertions We should require of her even if it should draw her into another Eight or ten Years War.

Thomas Paine's "Common Sense," 1776

I have heard it asserted by some, that as America has flourished under her former connection with Great Britain, the same connection is necessary towards her future happiness, and will always have the same effect. Nothing can be more fallacious than this kind of argument. We may as well assert that because a child has thrived upon milk, that it is never to have meat, or that the first twenty years of our lives is to become a precedent for the next twenty. But even this is admitting more than is true; for I answer roundly, that America would have flourished as much, and probably much more, had no European power taken any notice of her. The commerce by which she hath enriched herself are the necessaries of life, and will always have a market while eating is the custom of Europe.

But she has protected us, say some. That she hath engrossed us is true, and defended the continent at our expense as well as her own, is admitted; and she would have defended Turkey from the same motive, *viz.* for the sake of trade and dominion.

Alas! we have been long led away by ancient prejudices and made large sacrifices to superstition. We have boasted the protection of Great Britain, without considering, that her motive was *interest* not *attachment;* and that she did not protect us from *our enemies on our account;* but from *her enemies* on *her own account,* from those who had no quarrel with us on any *other account,* and who will always be our enemies on the *same account.* Let Britain waive her pretensions to the continent, or the continent throw off the dependance, and we should be at peace with France and Spain, were they at war with Britain. The miseries of Hanover's last war ought to warn us against connections. . . .

But Britain is the parent country, say some. Then the more shame upon her conduct. Even brutes do not devour their young, nor savages make war upon their families; wherefore, the assertion, if true, turns to her reproach; but it happens not to be true, or only partly so, and the phrase *parent* or *mother country* hath been jesuitically adopted by the king and his parasites, with a low papistical design of gaining an unfair bias on the credulous weakness of our minds. Europe, and not England, is the parent country of America. This new world hath been the asylum for the persecuted lovers of civil and religious liberty from *every part* of Europe. Hither have they fled, not from the tender embraces of the mother, but from the cruelty of the monster; and it is so far true of England, that the same tyranny which drove the first emigrants from home, pursues their descendants still.

In this extensive quarter of the globe, we forget the narrow limits of three hundred and sixty miles (the extent of England) and carry our friendship on a larger scale; we claim brotherhood with every European Christian, and triumph in the generosity of the sentiment. . . .

Much hath been said of the united strength of Britain and the colonies, that in conjunction they might bid defiance to the world. But this is mere presumption; the fate of war is uncertain, neither do the expressions mean any thing; for this continent would never suffer itself to be drained of inhabitants, to support the British arms in either Asia, Africa or Europe.

Besides, what have we to do with setting the world at defiance? Our plan is commerce, and that, well attended to, will secure us the peace and friendship of all Europe; because it is the interest of all Europe to have America a free port. Her trade will always be a protection, and her barrenness of gold and silver secure her from invaders. . . .

Europe is too thickly planted with kingdoms to be long at peace, and whenever a war breaks out between England and any foreign power, the trade of America goes to ruin, *because of her connection with Britain.* The next war may not turn out like the last, and should it not, the advocates for reconciliation now will be wishing for separation then, because neutrality in that case would be a safer convoy than a man of war. Every thing that is right or reasonable pleads for separation. The blood of the slain, the weeping voice of nature cries, 'TIS TIME TO PART. Even the distance at which the Almighty hath placed England and America is a strong and natural proof that the authority of the one over the other, was never the design of heaven. . . .

Small islands not capable of protecting themselves are the proper objects for government to take under their care; but there is something absurd, in supposing a Continent to be perpetually governed by an island. In no instance hath nature made the satellite larger than its primary planet; and as England and America, with respect to each other, reverse the common order of nature, it is evident that they belong to different systems. England to Europe: America to itself. . . .

O! ye that love mankind! Ye that dare oppose not only the tyranny but the tyrant, stand forth! Every spot of the old world is overrun with oppression. Freedom hath been hunted round the globe. Asia and Africa have long expelled her. Europe regards her like a stranger, and England hath given her warning to depart. O! receive the fugitive, and prepare in time an asylum for mankind. . . .

In almost every article of defence we abound. Hemp flourishes even to rankness, so that we need not want cordage. Our iron is superior to that of other countries. Our small arms equal to any in the world. Cannon we can cast at pleasure. Saltpeter and gunpowder we are every day producing. Our knowledge is hourly improving. Resolution is our inherent character, and courage has never yet forsaken us. Wherefore, what is it that we want? Why is it that we hesitate? From Britain we can expect nothing but ruin. If she is once admitted to the government of America again, this continent will not be worth living in. Jealousies will be always arising; insurrections will be constantly happening; and who will go forth to quell them? Who will venture his life to reduce his own countrymen to a foreign obedience? The difference between Pennsylvania and Connecticut, respecting some unlocated lands, shows the insignificance of a British government, and fully proves that nothing but continental authority can regulate continental matters. . . .

I shall conclude these remarks, with the following timely and well-intended hints. We ought to reflect, that there are three different ways by which an independency may hereafter be effected; and that *one* of those *three,* will, one day or other, be the fate of America, viz. By the legal voice of the people in Congress; by a military power; or by a mob: It may not always happen that our soldiers are citizens, and the multitude a body of reasonable men; virtue, as I have already remarked, is not hereditary, neither is it perpetual. Should an independency be brought about by the first of those means, we have every opportunity and every encouragement before us, to form the noblest, purest constitution on the face of the earth. We have it in our power to begin the world over again. A situation, similar to the present, hath not happened since the days of Noah until now. The birthday of a new world is at hand, and a race of men, perhaps as numerous as all Europe contains, are to receive their portion of freedom from the events of a few months. The reflection is awful, and in this point of view, how trifling, how ridiculous, do the little paltry cavilings of a few weak or interested men appear, when weighed against the business of a world. . . .

The Declaration of Independence, 1776

When, in the course of human events, it becomes necessary for one people to dissolve the political bonds which have connected them with another, and to assume, among the powers of the earth, the separate and equal station to which the laws of nature and of nature's God entitle them, a decent respect to the opinions of mankind requires that they should declare the causes which impel them to the separation.

We hold these truths to be self-evident: That all men are created equal; that they are endowed by their Creator with certain unalienable rights; that among these are life, liberty, and the pursuit of happiness; that, to secure these rights, governments are instituted among men, deriving their just powers from the consent of the governed; that whenever any form of government becomes destructive of these ends, it is the right of the people to alter or to abolish it, and to institute new government, laying its foundation on such principles, and organizing its powers in such form, as to them shall seem most likely to effect their safety and happiness. Prudence, indeed, will dictate that governments long established should not be changed for light and transient causes; and accordingly all experience hath shown that mankind are more disposed to suffer, while evils are sufferable, than to right themselves by abolishing the forms to which they are accustomed. But when a long train of abuses and usurpations, pursuing invariably the same object, evinces a design to reduce them under absolute despotism, it is their right, it is their duty, to throw off such government, and to provide new guards for their future security. Such has been the patient sufferance of these colonies; and such is now the necessity which constrains them to alter their former systems of government. The history of the present King of Great Britain is a history of repeated injuries and usurpations, all having in direct object the establishment of an absolute tyranny over these states. To prove this, let facts be submitted to a candid world.

He has refused his assent to laws, the most wholesome and necessary for the public good.

He has forbidden his governors to pass laws of immediate and pressing importance, unless suspended in their operation till his assent should be obtained; and, when so suspended, he has utterly neglected to attend to them.

He has refused to pass other laws for the accommodation of large districts of people, unless those people would relinquish the right of representation in the legislature, a right inestimable to them, and formidable to tyrants only.

He has called together legislative bodies at places unusual, uncomfortable, and distant from the depository of their public records, for the sole purpose of fatiguing them into compliance with his measures.

He has dissolved representative houses repeatedly, for opposing, with manly firmness, his invasions on the rights of people.

He has refused for a long time, after such dissolutions, to cause others to be elected; whereby the legislative powers, incapable of annihilation, have returned to the people at large for their exercise; the state remaining, in the mean time, exposed to all the dangers of invasions from without and convulsions within.

He has endeavored to prevent the population of these states; for that purpose obstructing the laws for naturalization of foreigners; refusing to pass others to encourage their migration hither, and raising the conditions of new appropriations of lands.

He has obstructed the administration of justice, by refusing his assent to laws for establishing judiciary powers.

He has made judges dependent on his will alone, for the tenure of their offices, and the amount and payment of their salaries.

He has erected a multitude of new offices, and sent hither swarms of officers to harass our people and eat out their substance.

He has kept among us, in times of peace, standing armies, without the consent of our legislatures.

He has affected to render the military independent of, and superior to, the civil power.

He has combined with others to subject us to a jurisdiction foreign to our constitution, and unacknowledged by our laws, giving his assent to their acts of pretended legislation:

For quartering large bodies of armed troops among us;

For protecting them, by a mock trial, from punishment for any murders which they should commit on the inhabitants of these states;

For cutting off our trade with all parts of the world;

For imposing taxes on us without our consent;

For depriving us, in many cases, of the benefits of trial by jury;

For transporting us beyond seas, to be tried for pretended offenses;

For abolishing the free system of English laws in a neighboring province, establishing therein an arbitrary government, and enlarging its boundaries, so as to render it at once an example and fit instrument for introducing the same absolute rule into these colonies;

For taking away our charters, abolishing our most valuable laws, and altering fundamentally the forms of our governments;

For suspending our own legislatures, and declaring themselves invested with power to legislate for us in all cases whatsoever.

He has abdicated government here, by declaring us out of his protection and waging war against us.

He has plundered our seas, ravaged our coasts, burned our towns, and destroyed the lives of our people.

He is at this time transporting large armies of foreign mercenaries to complete the works of death, desolation, and tyranny already begun with circumstances of cruelty and perfidy scarcely paralleled in the most barbarous ages, and totally unworthy the head of a civilized nation.

He has constrained our fellow-citizens, taken captive on the high seas, to bear arms against their country, to become the executioners of their friends and brethren, or to fall themselves by their hands.

He has excited domestic insurrection among us, and has endeavored to bring on the inhabitants of our frontiers the merciless Indian savages, whose known rule of warfare is an undistinguished destruction of all ages, sexes, and conditions.

In every stage of these oppressions we have petitioned for redress in the most humble terms; our repeated petitions have been answered only by repeated injury. A prince, whose character is thus marked by every act which may define a tyrant, is unfit to be the ruler of a free people.

Nor have we been wanting in our attentions to our British brethren. We have warned them, from time to time, of attempts by their legislature to extend an unwarrantable jurisdiction over us. We have reminded them of the circumstances of our emigration and settlement here. We have appealed to their native justice and magnanimity; and we have conjured them, by the ties of our common kindred, to disavow these usurpations, which would inevitably interrupt our connections and correspondence. They, too, have been deaf to the voice of justice and of consanguinity. We must, therefore, acquiesce in the necessity which denounces our separation, and hold them, as we hold the rest of mankind, enemies in war, in peace friends.

We, therefore, the representatives of the United States of America, in General Congress assembled, appealing to the Supreme Judge of the world for the rectitude of our intentions, do, in the name and by the authority of the good people of these colonies, solemnly publish and declare, that these United Colonies are, and of right ought to be, FREE AND INDEPENDENT STATES; that they are absolved from all allegiance to the British crown, and that all political connection between them and the state of Great Britain is, and ought to be, totally dissolved; and that, as free and independent states, they have full power to levy war, conclude peace, contract alliances, establish commerce, and do all other acts and things which independent states may of right do. And for the support of this declaration, with a firm reliance on the protection of Divine Providence, we mutually pledge to each other our lives, our fortunes, and our sacred honor.

Treaty of Amity and Commerce with France, 1778

Article 2.   The most Christian King, and the United States engage mutually not to grant any particular Favour to other Nations in respect of Commerce and Navigation, which shall not immediately become common to the other Party, who shall enjoy the same Favour, freely, if the Concession was freely made, or on allowing the same Compensation, if the Consession was Conditional. . . .

Article 19.   It shall be lawful for the Ships of War of either Party &

Privateers freely to carry whithersoever they please the Ships and Goods taken from their Enemies, without being obliged to pay any Duty to the Officers of the Admiralty or any other Judges; nor shall such Prizes be arrested or seized, when they come to and enter the Ports of either Party; nor shall the Searchers or other Officers of those Places search the same or make examination concerning the Lawfulness of such Prizes, but they may hoist Sail at any time and depart and carry their Prizes to the Places express'd in their Commissions, which the Commanders of such Ships of War shall be obliged to shew: On the contrary no Shelter or Refuge shall be given in their Ports to such as shall have made Prize of the Subjects, People or Property of either of the Parties; but if such shall come in, being forced by Stress of Weather or the Danger of the Sea, all proper means shall be vigorously used that they go out and retire from thence as soon as possible. . . .

Article 25.   . . . And it is hereby stipulated that free Ships shall also give a freedom to Goods, and that every thing shall be deemed to be free and exempt, which shall be found on board the Ships belonging to the Subjects of either of the Confederates, although the whole lading or any Part thereof should appertain to the Enemies of either, contraband Goods being always excepted. It is also agreed in like manner that the same Liberty be extended to Persons, who are on board a free Ship, with this Effect, that although they be Enemies to both or either Party, they are not to be taken out of that free Ship, unless they are Soldiers and in actual Service of the Enemies.

Article 26.   This Liberty of Navigation and Commerce shall extend to all kinds of Merchandizes, excepting those only which are distinguished by the name of contraband; And under this Name of Contraband or prohibited Goods shall be comprehended, Arms, great Guns, Bombs with the fuzes, and other things belonging to them, Cannon Ball, Gun powder, Match, Pikes, Swords, Lances, Spears, halberds, Mortars, Petards, Granades Salt Petre, Muskets, Musket Ball, Bucklers, Helmets, breast Plates, Coats of Mail and the like kinds of Arms proper for arming Soldiers, Musket rests, belts, Horses with their Furniture, and all other Warlike Instruments whatever. These Merchandizes which follow shall not be reckoned among Contraband or prohibited Goods, that is to say, all sorts of Cloths, and all other Manufacturers woven of any wool, Flax, Silk, Cotton or any other Materials whatever; all kinds of wearing Apparel together with the Species, whereof they are used to be made; gold & Silver as well coined as uncoin'd, Tin, Iron, Latten, Copper, Brass Coals, as also Wheat and Barley and any other kind of Corn and pulse; Tobacco and likewise all manner of Spices; salted and smoked Flesh, salted Fish, Cheese and Butter, Beer, Oils, Wines, Sugars and all sorts of Salts; & in general all Provisions, which serve for the nourishment of Mankind and the sustenence of Life; furthermore all kinds of Cotton, hemp, Flax, Tar, Pitch, Ropes, Cables, Sails, Sail Cloths, Anchors and any Parts of Anchors; also Ships Masts, Planks, Boards and Beams of what Trees soever; and all other Things proper either for building or repairing Ships, and all other Goods whatever, which have not been worked into the form of any Instrument or thing prepared for War by Land or by Sea, shall not be reputed Contraband, much less such as have been already wrought and made up for any other Use; all which shall be wholly reckoned among free Goods: as likewise all other Merchandizes and things, which are not comprehended and particularly mentioned in the foregoing enumeration of contraband Goods: so that they may be transported and carried in the freest manner by the Subjects of both Confederates even to Places belonging to an Enemy such Towns or Places being only excepted as are at that time beseiged, blocked up or invested. . . .

Treaty of Alliance with France, 1778

Article 1.   If War should break out betwan france and Great Britain, during the continuence of the present War betwan the United States and England, his Majesty and the said united States, shall make it a common cause, and aid each other mutually with their good Offices, their Counsels, and their forces, according to the exigence of Conjunctures as becomes good & faithful Allies.

Article 2.   The essential and direct End of the present defensive alliance is to maintain effectually the liberty, Sovereignty, and independance absolute and unlimited of the said united States, as well in Matters of Gouvernement as of commerce. . . .

Article 5.   If the united States should think fit to attempt the Reduction of the British Power remaining in the Northern Parts of America, or the Islands of Bermudas, those Contries or Islands in case of Success, shall be confederated with or dependant upon the said united States.

Article 6.   The Most Christian King renounces for ever the possession of the Islands of Bermudas as well as of any part of the continent of North america which before the treaty of Paris in 1763. or in virtue of that Treaty, were acknowledged to belong to the Crown of Great Britain, or to the united States heretofore called British Colonies, or which are at this Time or have lately been under the Power of The King and Crown of Great Britain.

Article 7.   If his Most Christian Majesty shall think proper to attack any of the Islands situated in the Gulph of Mexico, or near that Gulph, which are at present under the power of Great Britain, all the said Isles, in case of success, shall appertain to the Crown of france.

Article 8.   Neither of the two Parties shall conclude either Truce or Peace with Great Britain, without the formal consent of the other first obtain'd; and they mutually engage not to lay down their arms, until the Independence of the united states shall have been formally or tacitly assured by the Treaty or Treaties that shall terminate the War. . . .

Article 11.   The two Parties guarantee mutually from the present time and forever, against all other powers, to wit, the united states to his most Christian Majesty the present Possessions of the Crown of france in America as well as those which it may acquire by the future Treaty of peace: and his most Christian Majesty guarantees on his part to the united states, their liberty, Sovereignty, and Independence absolute, and unlimited, as well in Matters of Government as commerce and also thair Possessions, and the additions or conquests that their Confederation may obtain during the war, from any of the Dominions now or heretofore possessed by Great Britain in North America, conformable to the 5th & 6th articles above written, the whole as their Possessions shall be fixed and assured to the said States at the moment of the cessation of their present War with England. . . .

Ezra Stiles's "The United States Elevated to Glory and Honour," 1783

Already does the new constellation of the United States begin to realize this glory. It has already risen to an acknowledged sovereignty among the republicks and kingdoms of the world. And we have reason to hope, and I believe to expect, that God has still greater blessings in store for this vine which his own right hand hath planted, to make us "high among the nations in praise, and in name, and in honour." The reasons are very numerous, weighty, and conclusive.

In our civil constitutions, those impediments are removed which obstruct the progress of society towards perfection: Such, for instance, as respect the tenure of estates, and arbitrary government. The vassalage of dependent tenures, the tokens of ancient conquests by Goths and Tartars, still remain all over Asia and Europe. In this respect, as well as others, the world begins to open its eyes. One grand experiment in particular has lately been made. The present Empress of Russia, by granting lands in freehold in her vast wilderness of Volkouskile, together with religious liberty, has allured and already draughted from Poland and Germany a colonization of six hundred thousand souls in six years only, from 1762 to 1768.

Liberty, civil and religious, has sweet and attractive charms. The enjoyment of this, with property, has filled the English settlers in America with a most amazing spirit, which has operated, and still will operate, with great energy. Never before has the experiment been so effectually tried, of every man's reaping the fruits of his labour and feeling his share in the aggregate system of power. The ancient republicks did not stand on the people at large; and therefore no example or precedent can be taken from them. Even men of arbitrary principles will be obliged, if they would figure in these states, to assume the patriot so long that they will at length become charmed with the sweets of liberty.

Our degree of population is such as to give us reason to expect that this will become a great people. It is probable that within a century from our independence the sun will shine on fifty million of inhabitants in the United States. This will be a great, a very great nation, nearly equal to half Europe. Already has our colonization extended down the Ohio and to Koskaseah on the Mississippi. And if the present ratio of increase should be rather diminished in some of the elder settlements, yet an accelerated multiplication will attend our general propagation and overspread the whole territory westward for ages. So that before the Millennium, the English settlements in America may become more numerous millions than that greatest dominion on earth, the Chinese empire. Should this prove a future fact, how applicable would be the text, when the Lord shall have made his American Israel "high above all nations which he hath made," in numbers, "and in praise, and in name, and in honour!"

I am sensible some will consider these as visionary Utopian ideas. And so they would have judged had they lived in the apostolick age and been told that by the time of Constantine the empire would have become christian. As visionary that the twenty thousand souls which first settled New-England should be multiplied to near a million in a century and a half. As visionary that the Ottoman empire must fall by the Russian. As visionary to the Catholicks is the certain downfall of the Pontificate. As Utopian would it have been to the loyalists, at the battle of Lexington, that in less than eight years the independence and sovereignty of the United States should be acknowledged by four European sovereignties, one of which should be Britain herself. How wonderful the revolutions, the events of Providence! We live in an Age of Wonders. We have lived an age in a few years. We have seen more wonders accomplished in eight years than are usually unfolded in a century. . . .

This great American revolution, this recent political phenomenon of a new sovereignty arising among the sovereign powers of the earth, will be attended to and contemplated by all nations. Navigation will carry the American flag around the globe itself and display the Thirteen Stripes and New Constellation at Bengal and Canton on the Indus and Ganges, on the Whang-ho and the Yang-tse-kiang; and with commerce will import the wisdom and literature of the east. That prophecy of Daniel is now literally fulfilling—there shall be an universal travelling "too and fro, and knowledge shall be increased." This knowledge will be brought home and treasured up in America: and being here digested and carried to the highest perfection, may reblaze back from America to Europe, Asia and Africa, and illumine the world with TRUTH and LIBERTY. . . .

Little would Civilians have thought ages ago that the world should ever look to America for models of government and polity. Little did they think of finding this most perfect polity among the poor outcasts, the contemptible people of New-England, and particularly in the long despised civil polity of Connecticut; a polity conceived by the sagacity and wisdom of a Winthrop, a Wyllys, a Ludlow, Haynes, Hopkins, Hooker, and the other first settlers of Hartford, in 1636. And while Europe and Asia may hereafter learn that the most liberal principles of law and civil polity are to be found on this side of the Atlantick, they may also find the true religion here depurated from the rust and corruption of ages, and learn from us to reform and restore the church to its primitive purity. It will be long before the ecclesiastical pride of the splendid European hierarchies can submit to learn wisdom from those whom they have been inured to look upon with sovereign contempt. But candid and liberal disquisition will sooner or later have a great effect. Removed from the embarrassments of corrupt systems, and the dignities and blinding opulence connected with them, the unfettered mind can think with a noble enlargement, and with an unbounded freedom go wherever the light of truth directs. Here will be no bloody tribunals, no cardinals inquisitors-general, to bend the human mind, forcibly to control the understanding, and put out the light of reason, the candle of the Lord, in man; to force an innocent Galileo to renounce truths demonstrable as the light of day. Religion may here receive its last, most liberal, and impartial examination. Religious liberty is peculiarly friendly to fair and generous disquisition. Here deism will have its full chance; nor need libertines more to complain of being overcome by any weapons but the gentle, the powerful ones of argument and truth. Revelation will be found to stand the test to the ten thousandth examination.

There are three coetaneous events to take place whose fruition is certain from prophecy, the annihilation of the Pontificate, the reassembling of the Jews, and the fulness of the Gentiles. That liberal and candid disquisition of Christianity, which will most assuredly take place in America, will prepare Europe for the first event, with which the other will be connected, when especially on the return of the twelve tribes to the Holy Land, there will burst forth a degree of evidence hitherto unperceived and of efficacy to convert a world. More than three quarters of mankind yet remain heathen. Heaven put a stop to the propagation of Christianity when the church became corrupted with the adoration of numerous deities and images, because this would have been only exchanging an old for a new idolatry. Nor is Christendom now larger than it was nine centuries ago. The promising prospects of the *Propaganda fide* at Rome are coming to nothing: and it may be of the divine destiny that all other attempts for gospelizing the nations of the earth shall prove fruitless, until the present Christendom itself be recovered to the primitive purity and simplicity. At which time, instead of the Babel confusion of contradicting missionaries, all will harmoniously concur in speaking one language, one holy faith, one apostolick religion to an unconverted world. At this period, and in effecting this great event, we have reason to think that the United States may be of no small influence and consideration. It was of the Lord to send Joseph into Egypt, to save much people, and to shew forth his praise. It is of the Lord that "a woman clothed with the sun, and the moon under her feet," and upon "her head a crown of twelve stars," (not to say thirteen) should "flee into the wilderness, where she hath a place prepared of God" (Rev. xii. 1 & 6), and where she might be the repository of Wisdom, and "keep the commandments of God, and have the testimony of Jesus." It may have been of the Lord that Christianity is to be found in such great purity in this church exiled into the wilderness of America; and that its purest body should be evidently advancing forward, by an augmented natural increase and spiritual edification, into a singular superiority—with the ultimate subserviency to the glory of God, in converting the world.

Treaty of Peace, 1783

Article 1st. His Britannic Majesty acknowledges the said United States, viz. New-Hampshire Massachusetts Bay, Rhode-Island & Providence Plantations, Connecticut, New York, New Jersey, Pennsylvania, Delaware, Maryland, Virginia, North Carolina, South Carolina & Georgia, to be free sovereign & Independent States; that he treats with them as such, and for himself his Heirs & Successors, relinquishes all Claims to the Government Propriety & Territorial Rights of the same & every Part thereof.

Article 2d. [boundaries]

Article 3d. It is agreed that the People of the United States shall continue to enjoy unmolested the Right to take Fish of every kind on the Grand Bank and on all the other Banks of New-foundland, also in the Gulph of St. Lawrence, and at all other Places in the Sea where the Inhabitants of both Countries used at any time heretofore to fish. And also that the Inhabitants of the United States shall have Liberty to take Fish of every Kind on such Part of the Coast of New-foundland as British Fishermen shall use, (but not to dry or cure the same on that Island) And also on the Coasts Bays & Creeks of all other of his Britannic Majesty's Dominions in America, and that the American Fishermen shall have Liberty to dry and cure Fish in any of the unsettled Bays Harbours and Creeks of Nova Scotia, Magdalen Islands, and Labrador, so long as the same shall remain unsettled but so soon as the same or either of them shall be settled, it shall not be lawful for the said Fishermen to dry or cure Fish at such Settlement, without a previous Agreement for that purpose with the Inhabitants, Proprietors or Possessors of the Ground.

Article 4th. It is agreed that Creditors on either Side shall meet with no lawful Impediment to the Recovery of the full Value in Sterling Money of all bona fide Debts heretofore contracted.

Article 5th. It is agreed that the Congress shall earnestly recommend it to the Legislatures of the respective States to provide for the Restitution of all Estates, Rights and Properties which have been confiscated belonging to real British Subjects. . . . And that Persons of any other Description shall have free Liberty to go to any Part or Parts of any of the thirteen United States and therein to remain twelve Months unmolested in their

Endeavours to obtain the Restitution of such of their Estates Rights & Properties as may have been confiscated. . . .

And it is agreed that all Persons who have any Interest in confiscated Lands, either by Debts, Marriage Settlements, or otherwise, shall meet with no lawful Impediment in the Prosecution of their just Rights.

Article 6th. That there shall be no future Confiscations made nor any Prosecutions commenc'd against any Person or Persons for or by Reason of the Part, which he or they may have taken in the present War, and that no Person shall on that Account suffer any future Loss or Damage, either in his Person Liberty or Property; and that those who may be in Confinement on such Charges at the Time of the Ratification of the Treaty in America shall be immediately set at Liberty, and the Prosecutions so commenced be discontinued.

Article 7th. There shall be a firm and perpetual Peace between his Britannic Majesty and the said States and between the Subjects of the one, and the Citizens of the other, wherefore all Hostilities both by Sea and Land shall from henceforth cease: All Prisoners on both Sides shall be set at Liberty, and his Britannic Majesty shall with all convenient speed, and without causing any Destruction, or carrying away any Negroes or other Property of the American Inhabitants, withdraw all his Armies, Garrisons & Fleets from the said United States, and from every Port, Place and Harbour within the same; leaving in all Fortifications the American Artillery that may be therein: And shall also Order & cause all Archives, Records, Deeds & Papers belonging to any of the said States, or their Citizens, which in the Course of the War may have fallen into the Hands of his Officers, to be forthwith restored and deliver'd to the proper States and Persons to whom they belong.

Foreign Policy Powers in the Constitution, 1789

Article I. *Section 8.* The Congress shall have power

To lay and collect taxes, duties, imposts, and excises, to pay the debts and provide for the common defense and general welfare of the United States; but all duties, imposts and excises shall be uniform throughout the United States;

To borrow money on the credit of the United States;

To regulate commerce with foreign nations, and among the several States, and with the Indian tribes;

To establish an uniform rule of naturalization, and uniform laws on the subject of bankruptcies throughout the United States;

To coin money, regulate the value thereof, and of foreign coin, and fix the standard of weights and measures; . . .

To define and punish piracies and felonies committed on the high seas and offenses against the law of nations;

To declare war, grant letters of marque and reprisal, and make rules concerning captures on land and water;

To raise and support armies, but no appropriation of money to that use shall be for a longer term than two years;

To provide and maintain a navy;

To make rules for the government and regulation of the land and naval forces;

To provide for calling forth the militia to execute the laws of the Union, suppress insurrections, and repel invasions;

To provide for organizing, arming, and disciplining the militia, and for governing such part of them as may be employed in the service of the United States, reserving to the States respectively the appointment of the officers, and the authority of training the militia according to the discipline prescribed by Congress;

To exercise exclusive legislation in all cases whatsoever, over such district (not exceeding ten miles square) as may, by cession of particular States, and the acceptance of Congress, become the seat of government of the United States, and to exercise like authority over all places purchased by the consent of the legislature of the State, in which the same shall be, for erection of forts, magazines, arsenals, dock-yards, and other needful buildings;—and

To make all laws which shall be necessary and proper for carrying into execution the foregoing powers, and all other powers vested by this Constitution in the government of the United States, or in any department or officer thereof. . . .

Section 10. No State shall enter into any treaty, alliance, or confederation; grant letters of marque and reprisal; coin money; emit bills of credit; make anything but gold and silver coin a tender in payment of debts; pass any bill of attainder, ex post facto law, or law impairing the obligation of contracts, or grant any title of nobility.

No State shall, without the consent of Congress, lay any imposts or duties on imports or exports, except what may be absolutely necessary for executing its inspection laws: and the net produce of all duties and imposts, laid by any State on imports or exports, shall be for the use of the treasury of the United States; and all such laws shall be subject to the revision and control of the Congress.

No State shall, without the consent of Congress, lay any duty of tonnage, keep troops or ships of war in time of peace, enter into any agreement or compact with another State, or with a foreign power, or engage in war, unless actually invaded, or in such imminent danger as will not admit of delay. . . .

Article II. *Section 2.* The President shall be commander in chief of the army and navy of the United States, and of the militia of the several States, when called into the actual service of the United States; he may require the opinion, in writing, of the principal officer in each of the executive departments, upon any subject relating to the duties of their respective offices, and he shall have power to grant reprieves and pardons for offenses against the United States, except in cases of impeachment.

He shall have power, by and with the advice and consent of the Senate, to make treaties, provided two-thirds of the Senators present concur; and he shall nominate, and by and with the advice and consent of the Senate, shall appoint ambassadors, other public ministers and consuls, . . .

Article III. *Section 1.* The judicial power of the United States shall be vested in one Supreme Court, and in such inferior courts as the Congress may from time to time ordain and establish. . . .

Section 2. The judicial power shall extend to all cases, in law and equity, arising under this Constitution, the laws of the United States, and treaties made, or which shall be made, under their authority;—to all cases affecting ambassadors, other public ministers and consuls;—to all cases of admiralty and maritime jurisdiction;—to controversies to which the United States shall be a party;—to controversies between two or more States;—*between a State and citizens of another State;*—between citizens of different States;—between citizens of the same State claiming lands under grants of different States, and between a State, or the citizens thereof, and foreign states, citizens or subjects.

In all cases affecting ambassadors, other public ministers and consuls, and those in which a State shall be party, the Supreme Court shall have original jurisdiction. . . .

Article IV. Section 3. The Congress shall have power to dispose of and make all needful rules and regulations respecting the territory or other property belonging to the United States; and nothing in this Constitution shall be so construed as to prejudice any claims of the United States, or of any particular State. . . .

Article VI. This Constitution, and the laws of the United States which shall be made in pursuance thereof; and all treaties made, or which shall be made, under the authority of the United States, shall be the supreme law of the land; and the judges in every State shall be bound thereby, anything in the Constitution or laws of any State to the contrary notwithstanding. . . .

The New Nation

The Creation of the Constitution of 1787

The United States Constitution of 1787 is the oldest operating written constitution in the world. It has been so often and so genuinely celebrated, and for so many generations, that it possesses the stature of a sacred text. In American civic culture, reverence for the Constitution is a fundamental dogma that sustains the document's vitality. For unlike a king or a military dictator, the Constitution commands no armies; it compels obedience to its doctrines only through the force of public allegiance.

Veneration for the men who created the Constitution is a corollary of this positive preconditioning and is expressed in our designation of them as the founding fathers. As with the document itself, it has been difficult to achieve a realistic and balanced assessment of these political leaders. During much of the twentieth century, ever since the publication in 1913 of Charles A. Beard's Economic Interpretation of the Constitution, historians and textbooks have debated the heroic myth and an unheroic antimyth. In the Beardian or Progressive interpretation, as in its neo-Progressive successors, the Constitution has been described as the creation of practical, even selfish, politicians, men bent on forming a government to defend a system of wealth and privilege in which they shared. Although this debate has subsided in the past two decades, it has taught us to recognize—as did the delegates to the convention—that interests, especially those concerning money and power, were ever present forces in politics, then as now. In addition, we have learned that acknowledging the play of interests in the formation of the Constitution does not deny the reality of public spirit and commitment to ideals of liberty. The mingling of interests and idealism was critical to the Constitution's success.

Moreover, we have come to recognize that the design of the Constitution was a contingent event. Not only was it not designed in heaven or by a band of demigods; it was not even the preconceived plan of any one delegate or set of delegates. The Constitution that the framers sent on to Congress in September 1787 resulted from a three-month negotiation and debate in which possibilities were tested, rejected, and then revised and adjusted according to the changing perspectives of various delegates. No one who signed the Constitution saw it as *perfect, but all hoped that it would be good enough to serve the material and political interests of their own state and region, as well as the United States.*

✴ *D O C U M E N T S*

James Madison was the most important individual in shaping the collective achievement known as the Constitution of 1787. The thirty-six-year-old Virginia delegate made an influential analysis of the defects of the Confederation and its interaction with the state governments in a private memorandum that he circulated among his colleagues and that appears below as the first document. Titling the essay "Vices of the Political System of the United States," Madison offered a view of the problem that supplied the starting point for the Virginia Plan. This plan, which is reproduced here as the second document, was presented to the convention by the more senior John Randolph, the Virginia governor. The plan became the foundation on which, with alterations, the delegates constructed the Constitution.

The Virginia Plan, which called for a national government that linked population and power, was challenged directly by the New Jersey Plan, the third selection. This plan offered a more limited revision of the Articles, one that retained the principle of equality among the states. The delegates debated these two plans (see the fourth document) for a few days before laying aside the New Jersey Plan. Thereafter, they debated a wide range of topics. The selections comprising the fifth document treat democracy and the legislature, sectional interests and legislative apportionment, the qualifications for voters, and slavery and slave imports, and they provide only a sample of what went on. The fact that the debates were closed to the public—secret in fact—enabled the delegates to speak freely on controversial subjects. The final document, the Constitution, is the product of all of the delegates.

James Madison on the Vices of the Political System of the United States, 1787

1. Failure of the States to Comply with the Constitutional Requisitions

This evil has been so fully experienced both during the war and since the peace, results so naturally from the number and independent authority of the States and has been so uniformly examplified in every similar Confederacy, that it may be considered as not less radically and permanently inherent in, than it is fatal to the object of, the present System.

2. Encroachments by the States on the Federal Authority

Examples of this are numerous and repetitions may be foreseen in almost every case where any favorite object of a State shall present a temptation. Among these examples are the wars and Treaties of Georgia with the Indians—The unlicensed compacts between Virginia and Maryland, and between Pena. & N. Jersey—the troops raised and to be kept up by Massts.

3. Violations of the Law of Nations and of Treaties

From the number of Legislatures, the sphere of life from which most of their members are taken, and the circumstances under which their legislative business is carried on, irregularities of this kind must frequently happen. Accordingly not a year has passed without instances of them in some one or other of the States. The Treaty of peace—the treaty with France—the treaty with Holland have each been violated. The causes of these irregularities must necessarily produce frequent violations of the law of nations in other respects. . . .

4. Trespasses of the States on the Rights of Each Other

These are alarming symptoms, and may be daily apprehended as we are admonished by daily experience. See the law of Virginia restricting foreign vessels to certain ports—of Maryland in favor of vessels belonging to her own citizens—of N. York in favor of the same.

Paper money, instalments of debts, occlusion of Courts, making property a legal tender, may likewise be deemed aggressions on the rights of other States. As the Citizens of every State aggregately taken stand more or less in the relation of Creditors or debtors, to the Citizens of every other States, Acts of the debtor State in favor of debtors, affect the Creditor State, in the same manner, as they do its own citizens who are relatively creditors towards other citizens. . . .

The practice of many States in restricting the commercial intercourse with other States, and putting their productions and manufactures on the same footing with those of foreign nations, though not contrary to the federal articles, is certainly adverse to the spirit of the Union, and tends to beget retaliating regulations, not less expensive & vexatious in themselves, than they are destructive of the general harmony.

5. Want of Concert in Matters Where Common Interest Requires It

This defect is strongly illustrated in the state of our commercial affairs. How much has the national dignity, interest, and revenue suffered from this cause? Instances of inferior moment are the want of uniformity in the laws concerning naturalization & literary property; of provision for national seminaries, for grants of incorporation for national purposes, for canals and other works of general utility, wch. may at present be defeated by the perverseness of particular States whose concurrence is necessary.

6. Want of Guaranty to the States of Their Constitutions and Laws Against Internal Violence

The confederation is silent on this point and therefore by the second article the hands of the federal authority are tied. According to Republican Theory, Right and power being both vested in the majority, are held to be synonimous. According to fact and experience a minority may in an appeal to force, be an overmatch for the majority. 1. If the minority happen to include all such as possess the skill and habits of military life, & such as possess the great pecuniary resources, one third only may conquer the remaining two thirds. 2. One third of those who participate in the choice of the rulers, may be rendered a majority by the accession of those whose poverty excludes them from a right of suffrage, and who for obvious reasons will be more likely to join the standard of sedition than that of the established Government. 3. Where slavery exists the republican Theory becomes still more fallacious.

7. Want of Sanction to the Laws, and of Coercion in the Government of the Confederacy

A sanction is essential to the idea of law, as coercion is to that of Government. The federal system being destitute of both, wants the great vital principles of a Political Cons[ti]tution. Under the form of such a Constitution, it is in fact nothing more than a treaty of amity of commerce and of alliance, between so many independent and Sovereign States. . . . It is no longer doubted that a unanimous and punctual obedience of 13 independent bodies, to the acts of the federal Government, ought not be calculated on. Even during the war, when external danger supplied in some degree the defect of legal & coercive sanctions, how imperfectly did the States fulfil their obligations to the Union? In time of peace, we see already what is to be expected. . . .

8. Want of Ratification by the People of the Articles of Confederation

In some of the States the Confederation is recognized by, and forms a part of the constitution. In others however it has received no other sanction than that of the Legislative authority. From this defect two evils result: 1. Whenever a law of a State happens to be repugnant to an act of Congress, particularly when the latter is of posterior date to the former, it will be at least questionable whether the latter must not prevail; and as the question must be decided by the Tribunals of the State, they will be most likely to lean on the side of the State.

2. As far as the Union of the States is to be regarded as a league of sovereign powers, and not as a political Constitution by virtue of which they are become one sovereign power, so far it seems to follow from the doctrine of compacts, that a breach of any of the articles of the confederation by any of the parties to it, absolves the other parties from their respective obligations, and gives them a right if they chuse to exert it, of dissolving the Union altogether.

9. Multiplicity of Laws in the Several States

In developing the evils which viciate the political system of the U.S. it is proper to include those which are found within the States individually, as well as those which directly affect the States collectively, since the former class have an indirect influence on the general malady and must not be overlooked in forming a compleat remedy. Among the evils then of our situation may well be ranked the multiplicity of laws from which no State is exempt. As far as laws are necessary, to mark with precision the duties of those who are to obey them, and to take from those who are to administer them a discretion, which might be abused, their number is the price of liberty. As far as the laws exceed this limit, they are a nusance: a nusance of the most pestilent kind. Try the Codes of the several States by this test, and what a luxuriancy of legislation do they present. The short period of independency has filled as many pages as the century which preceded it. . . .

10. Mutability of the Laws of the States

This evil is intimately connected with the former yet deserves a distinct notice as it emphatically denotes a vicious legislation. We daily see laws repealed or superseded, before any trial can have been made of their merits; and even before a knowledge of them can have reached the remoter districts within which they were to operate. In the regulations of trade this instability becomes a snare not only to our citizens but to foreigners also.

11. Injustice of the Laws of States

If the multiplicity and mutability of laws prove a want of wisdom, their injustice betrays a defect still more alarming: more alarming not merely because it is a greater evil in itself, but because it brings more into question the fundamental principle of republican Government, that the majority who rule in such Governments, are the safest Guardians both of public Good and of private rights. To what causes is this evil to be ascribed?

These causes lie

1. in the Representative bodies.
2. in the people themselves.

1. Representative appointments are sought from three motives. 1. ambition, 2. personal interest, 3. public good. Unhappily the two first are proved by experience to be most prevalent. Hence the candidates who feel them, particularly, the second, are most industrious, and most successful in pursuing their object: and forming often a majority in the legislative Councils, with interested views, contrary to the interest, and views, of their Constituents, join in a perfidious sacrifice of the latter to the former. A succeeding election it might be supposed, would displace the offenders, and repair the mischief. But how easily are base and selfish measures, masked by pretexts of public good and apparent expediency? How frequently will a repetition of the same arts and industry which succeeded in the first instance, again prevail on the unwary to misplace their confidence?

How frequently too will the honest but unenligh[t]ened representative be the dupe of a favorite leader, veiling his selfish views under the professions of public good, and varnishing his sophistical arguments with the glowing colours of popular eloquence?

2. A still more fatal if not more frequent cause lies among the people themselves. All civilized societies are divided into different interests and factions, as they happen to be creditors or debtors—Rich or poor—husbandmen, merchants or manufacturers—members of different religious sects—followers of different political leaders—inhabitants of different districts—owners of different kinds of property &c &c. In republican Government the majority however composed, ultimately give the law. Whenever therefore an apparent interest or common passion unites a majority what is to restrain them from unjust violations of the rights and interests of the minority, or of individuals? Three motives only 1. a prudent regard to their own good as involved in the general and permanent good of the Community. This consideration although of decisive weight in itself, is found by experience to be too often unheeded. It is too often forgotten, by nations as well as by individuals that honesty is the best policy. 2dly. respect for character. However strong this motive may be in individuals, it is considered as very insufficient to restrain them from injustice. In a multitude its efficacy is diminished in proportion to the number which is to share the praise or the blame. Besides, as it has reference to public opinion, which within a particular Society, is the opinion of the majority, the standard is fixed by those whose conduct is to be measured by it. The public opinion without the Society, will be little respected by the people at large of any Country. Individuals of extended views, and of national pride, may bring the public proceedings to this standard, but the example will never be followed by the multitude. Is it to be imagined that an ordinary citizen or even an assemblyman of R. Island in estimating the policy of paper money, ever considered or cared in what light the measure would be viewed in France or Holland; or even in Massts or Connect.? It was a sufficient temptation to both that it was for their interest: it was a sufficient sanction to the latter that it was popular in the State; to the former that it was so in the neighbourhood. 3dly. will Religion the only remaining motive be a sufficient restraint? It is not pretended to be such on men individually considered. Will its effect be greater on them considered in an aggregate view? quite the reverse. The conduct of every popular assembly acting on oath, the strongest of religious Ties, proves that individuals join without remorse in acts, against which their consciences would revolt if proposed to them under the like sanction, separately in their closets. When indeed Religion is kindled into enthusiasm, its force like that of other passions, is increased by the sympathy of a multitude. But enthusiasm is only a temporary state of religion, and while it lasts will hardly be seen with pleasure at the helm of Government. Besides as religion in its coolest state, is not infallible, it may become a motive to oppression as well as a restraint from injustice. Place three individuals in a situation wherein the interest of each depends on the voice of the others, and give to two of them an interest opposed to the rights of the third? Will the latter be secure? The prudence of every man would shun the danger. The rules & forms of justice suppose & guard against it. Will two thousand

in a like situation be less likely to encroach on the rights of one thousand? The contrary is witnessed by the notorious factions & oppressions which take place in corporate towns limited as the opportunities are, and in little republics when uncontrouled by apprehensions of external danger. If an enlargement of the sphere is found to lessen the insecurity of private rights, it is not because the impulse of a common interest or passion is less predominant in this case with the majority; but because a common interest or passion is less apt to be felt and the requisite combinations less easy to be formed by a great than by a small number. The Society becomes broken into a greater variety of interests, of pursuits, of passions, which check each other, whilst those who may feel a common sentiment have less opportunity of communication and concert. It may be inferred that the inconveniences of popular States contrary to the prevailing Theory, are in proportion not to the extent, but to the narrowness of their limits.

The great desideratum in Government is such a modification of the Sovereignty as will render it sufficiently neutral between the different interests and factions, to controul one part of the Society from invading the rights of another, and at the same time sufficiently controuled itself, from setting up an interest adverse to that of the whole Society. In absolute Monarchies, the prince is sufficiently neutral towards his subjects, but frequently sacrifices their happiness to his ambition or his avarice. In small Republics, the sovereign will is sufficiently controuled from such a Sacrifice of the entire Society, but is not sufficiently neutral towards the parts composing it. As a limited Monarchy tempers the evils of an absolute one; so an extensive Republic meliorates the administration of a small Republic.

An auxiliary desideratum for the melioration of the Republican form is such a process of elections as will most certainly extract from the mass of the Society the purest and noblest characters which it contains; such as will at once feel most strongly the proper motives to pursue the end of their appointment, and be most capable to devise the proper means of attaining it.

12. Impotence of the Laws of the States

[Madison's memorandum ends here.]

John Randolph Presents the Virginia Plan, 1787*

Mr. Randolph then opened the main business. He expressed his regret, that it should fall to him, rather than those, who were of longer standing in life and political experience, to open the great subject of their mission. But, as the convention had originated from Virginia, and his colleagues supposed that some proposition was expected from them, they had imposed this task on him.

---

* From James Madison's notes.

He then commented on the difficulty of the crisis, and the necessity of preventing the fulfilment of the prophecies of the American downfall.

He observed that in revising the fœderal system we ought to inquire (1) into the properties which such a government ought to possess, (2) the defects of the Confederation, (3) the danger of our situation, and (4) the remedy.

1. The character of such a government ought to secure (1) against foreign invasion; (2) against dissentions between members of the Union, or seditions in particular States; (3) to procure to the several States various blessings, of which an isolated situation was incapable; (4) to be able to defend itself against incroachment; and (5) to be paramount to the State Constitutions.

2. In speaking of the defects of the Confederation he professed a high respect for its authors, and considered them as having done all that patriots could do, in the then infancy of the science of constitutions and of confederacies—when the inefficiency of requisitions was unknown—no commercial discord had arisen among any States—no rebellion had appeared as in Massachusetts—foreign debts had not become urgent—the havoc of paper money had not been foreseen—treaties had not been violated—and perhaps nothing better could be obtained from the jealousy of the States with regard to their sovereignty.

He then proceeded to enumerate the defects: (1) that the Confederation produced no security against foreign invasion; Congress not being permitted to prevent a war nor to support it by their own authority. . . . (2) That the fœderal government could not check the quarrels between States, nor a rebellion in any, not having constitutional power nor means to interpose according to the exigency. (3) That there were many advantages which the United States might acquire, which were not attainable under the Confederation—such as a productive impost, counteraction of the commercial regulations of other nations, pushing of commerce ad libitum, etc., etc. (4) That the fœderal government could not defend itself against incroachments from the States. (5) That it was not even paramount to the State Constitutions, ratified, as it was in many of the States.

3. He next reviewed the danger of our situation, and appealed to the sense of the best friends of the United States—the prospect of anarchy from the laxity of government everywhere; and to other considerations.

4. He then proceeded to the remedy; the basis of which he said must be the republican principle.

He proposed as conformable to his ideas the following resolutions, which he explained one by one.

[Virginia Plan]

1. Resolved, that the Articles of Confederation ought to be so corrected and enlarged as to accomplish the objects proposed by their institution; namely, "common defence, security of liberty and general welfare."

2. Resolved therefore, that the rights of suffrage in the National Legislature ought to be proportioned to the quotas of contribution, or to the

number of free inhabitants, as the one or the other rule may seem best in different cases.

3. Resolved, that the National Legislature ought to consist of two branches.

4. Resolved, that the members of the first branch of the National Legislature ought to be elected by the people of the several States every [blank] for the term of [blank]; to be of the age of [blank] years at least, to receive liberal stipends by which they may be compensated for the devotion of their time to the public service; to be ineligible to any office established by a particular State, or under the authority of the United States, except those peculiarly belonging to the functions of the first branch, during the term of service, and for the space of [blank] after its expiration; to be incapable of re-election for the space of [blank] after the expiration of their term of service, and to be subject to recall.

5. Resolved, that the members of the second branch of the National Legislature ought to be elected by those of the first, out of a proper number of persons nominated by the individual Legislatures, to be of the age of [blank] years at least; to hold their offices for a term sufficient to ensure their independence; to receive liberal stipends, by which they may be compensated for the devotion of their time to the public service; and to be ineligible to any office established by a particular State, or under the authority of the United States, except those peculiarly belonging to the functions of the second branch, during the term of service, and for the space of [blank] after the expiration thereof.

6. Resolved, that each branch ought to possess the right of originating Acts; that the National Legislature ought to be impowered to enjoy the legislative rights vested in Congress by the Confederation, and moreover to legislate in all cases to which the separate States are incompetent, or in which the harmony of the United States may be interrupted by the exercise of individual legislation; to negative all laws passed by the several States, contravening, in the opinion of the National Legislature the articles of Union; and to call forth the force of the Union against any member of the Union failing to fulfil its duty under the articles thereof.

7. Resolved, that a National Executive be instituted; to be chosen by the National Legislature for the term of [blank] years, to receive punctually at stated times, a fixed compensation for the services rendered, in which no increase nor diminution shall be made so as to affect the magistracy, existing at the time of increase or diminution, and to be ineligible a second time; and that besides a general authority to execute the national laws, it ought to enjoy the executive rights vested in Congress by the Confederation.

8. Resolved, that the Executive and a convenient number of the National Judiciary, ought to compose a Council of Revision with authority to examine every Act of the National Legislature before it shall operate, and every Act of a particular Legislature before a negative thereon shall be final; and that the dissent of the said Council shall amount to a rejection, unless the Act of the National Legislature be again passed, or that of a particular Legislature be again negatived by [blank] of the members of each branch.

9. Resolved, that a National Judiciary be established to consist of one or more supreme tribunals, and of inferior tribunals to be chosen by the National Legislature, to hold their offices during good behaviour; and to receive punctually at stated times fixed compensation for their services, in which no increase or diminution shall be made so as to affect the persons actually in office at the time of such increase or diminution. That the jurisdiction of the inferior tribunals shall be to hear and determine in the first instance, and of the supreme tribunal to hear and determine in the dernier resort, all piracies and felonies on the high seas, captures from an enemy, cases in which foreigners or citizens of other States applying to such jurisdictions may be interested, or which respect the collection of the national revenue; impeachments of any National officers, and questions which may involve the national peace and harmony.

10. Resolved, that provision ought to be made for the admission of States lawfully arising within the limits of the United States, whether from a voluntary junction of government and territory or otherwise, with the consent of a number of voices in the National Legislature less than the whole.

11. Resolved, that a republican government and the territory of each State, except in the instance of a voluntary junction of Government and territory, ought to be guarantied by the United States to each State.

12. Resolved, that provision ought to be made for the continuance of Congress and their authorities and privileges, until a given day after the reform of the articles of Union shall be adopted, and for the completion of all their engagements.

13. Resolved, that provision ought to be made for the amendment of the Articles of Union whensoever it shall seem necessary, and that the assent of the National Legislature ought not to be required thereto.

14. Resolved, that the legislative, executive and judiciary powers within the several States ought to be bound by oath to support the articles of Union.

15. Resolved, that the amendments which shall be offered to the Confederation by the Convention, ought at a proper time or times, after the approbation of Congress, to be submitted to an assembly or assemblies of representatives recommended by the several Legislatures to be expressly chosen by the people, to consider and decide thereon.

William Patterson Proposes the New Jersey Plan, 1787

Mr. Patterson, laid before the Convention the plan which he said several of the deputations wished to be substituted in place of that proposed by Mr. Randolph. . . :

1. Resolved, that the articles of Confederation ought to be so revised, corrected & enlarged, as to render the federal Constitution adequate to the exigencies of Government, & the preservation of the Union.

2. Resolved, that in addition to the powers vested in the U. States in Congress, by the present existing articles of Confederation, they be authorized to pass acts for raising a revenue, by levying a duty or duties on

all goods or merchandizes of foreign growth or manufacture, imported into any part of the U. States, by Stamps on paper, vellum or parchment, and by a postage on all letters or packages passing through the general post-office, to be applied to such federal purposes as they shall deem proper & expedient; to make rules & regulations for the collection thereof; and the same from time to time, to alter & amend in such manner as they shall think proper: to pass Acts for the regulation of trade & commerce as well with foreign nations as with each other: provided that all punishments, fines, forfeitures & penalties to be incurred for contravening such acts rules and regulations shall be adjudged by the Common law Judiciaries of the State in which any offence contrary to the true intent & meaning of such Acts rules & regulations shall have been committed or perpetrated, . . . subject nevertheless, for the correction of all errors, both in law & fact in rendering Judgment, to an appeal to the Judiciary of the U. States.

3. Resolved, that whenever requisitions shall be necessary, instead of the rule for making requisitions mentioned in the articles of Confederation, the United States in Congress be authorized to make such requisitions in proportion to the whole number of white & other free citizens & inhabitants of every age sex and condition including those bound to servitude for a term of years & three fifths of all other persons not comprehended in the foregoing description, except Indians not paying taxes; that if such requisitions be not complied with, in the time specified therein, to direct the collection thereof in the non complying States & for that purpose to devise and pass acts directing & authorizing the same; provided that none of the powers hereby vested in the U. States in Congress shall be exercised without the consent of at least [blank] States, and in that proportion if the number of Confederated States should hereafter be increased or diminished.

4. Resolved, that the U. States in Congress be authorized to elect a federal Executive to consist of [blank] persons, to continue in office for the term of [blank] years, to receive punctually at stated times a fixed compensation for their services, in which no increase or diminution shall be made so as to affect the persons composing the Executive at the time of such increase or diminution, to be paid out of the federal treasury; to be incapable of holding any other office or appointment during their time of service and for [blank] years thereafter; to be ineligible a second time, & removeable by Congress on application by a majority of the Executives of the several States; that the Executives besides their general authority to execute the federal acts ought to appoint all federal officers not otherwise provided for, & to direct all military operations; provided that none of the persons composing the federal Executive shall on any occasion take command of any troops, so as personally to conduct any military enterprise as General or in other capacity.

5. Resolved, that a federal Judiciary be established to consist of a supreme Tribunal the Judges of which to be appointed by the Executive, & to hold their offices during good behaviour, to receive punctually at stated times a fixed compensation for their services in which no increase or diminution shall be made, so as to affect the persons actually in office at the

time of such increase or diminution; that the Judiciary so established shall have authority to hear & determine in the first instance on all impeachments of federal officers, & by way of appeal in the dernier resort in all cases touching the rights of Ambassadors, in all cases of captures from an enemy, in all cases of piracies & felonies on the high Seas, in all cases in which foreigners may be interested, in the construction of any treaty or treaties, or which may arise on any of the Acts for regulation of trade, or the collection of the federal Revenue: that none of the Judiciary shall during the time they remain in office be capable of receiving or holding any other office or appointment during their time of service, or for [blank] thereafter.

6. Resolved, that all Acts of the U. States in Congress made by virtue & in pursuance of the powers hereby & by the articles of Confederation vested in them, and all Treaties made & ratified under the authority of the U. States shall be the supreme law of the respective States so far forth as those Acts or Treaties shall relate to the said States or their Citizens, and that the Judiciary of the several States shall be bound thereby in their decisions, any thing in the respective laws of the Individual States to the contrary notwithstanding; and that if any State, or any body of men in any State shall oppose or prevent the carrying into execution such acts or treaties, the federal Executive shall be authorized to call forth the power of the Confederated States, or so much thereof as may be necessary to enforce and compel an obedience to such Acts, or an observance of such Treaties.

7. Resolved, that provision be made for the admission of new States into the Union.

8. Resolved, the rule for naturalization ought to be the same in every State.

9. Resolved, that a Citizen of one State committing an offense in another State of the Union, shall be deemed guilty of the same offense as if it had been committed by a Citizen of the State in which the offense was committed.

Congress Debates the New Jersey and Virginia Plans, 1787

Mr. Lansing called for the reading of the 1st resolution of each plan, which he considered as involving principles directly in contrast; that of Mr. Patterson says he sustains the sovereignty of the respective States, that of Mr. Randolph distroys it: the latter requires a negative on all the laws of the particular States; the former, only certain general powers for the general good. The plan of Mr. R. in short absorbs all power except what may be exercised in the little local matters of the States which are not objects worthy of the supreme cognizance. He grounded his preference of Mr. P.'s plan, chiefly on two objections against that of Mr. R. 1. want of power in the Convention to discuss & propose it. 2. the improbability of its being adopted. 1. He was decidedly of opinion that the power of the Convention was restrained to amendments of a federal nature, and having for their basis the Confederacy in being. The Act of Congress The tenor of the Acts of the States, the Commissions produced by the several deputations all proved this. And this limitation of the power to an amendment of the Confederacy, marked the opinion of the States, that it was unnecessary & improper to go farther. He was sure that this was the case with his State. N. York would never have concurred in sending deputies to the convention, if she had supposed the deliberations were to turn on a consolidation of the States, and a National Government.

2. was it probable that the States would adopt & ratify a scheme, which they had never authorized us to propose? and which so far exceeded what they regarded as sufficient? . . . The States will never feel a sufficient confidence in a general Government to give it a negative on their laws. The Scheme is itself totally novel. There is no parallel to it to be found. The authority of Congress is familiar to the people, and an augmentation of the powers of Congress will be readily approved by them.

Mr. Patterson, said as he had on a former occasion given his sentiments on the plan proposed by Mr. R. he would now avoiding repetition as much as possible give his reasons in favor of that proposed by himself. He preferred it because it accorded 1. with the powers of the Convention, 2. with the sentiments of the people. If the confederacy was radically wrong, let us return to our States, and obtain larger powers, not assume them of ourselves. . . . Our object is not such a Government as may be best in itself, but such a one as our Constituents have authorized us to prepare, and as they will approve. If we argue the matter on the supposition that no Confederacy at present exists, it can not be denied that all the States stand on the footing of equal sovereignty. All therefore must concur before any can be bound. If a proportional representation be right, why do we not vote so here? If we argue on the fact that a federal compact actually exists, and consult the articles of it we still find an equal Sovereignty to be the basis of it. He reads the 5th art: of the Confederation giving each State a vote—& the 13th declaring that no alteration shall be made without unanimous consent. This is the nature of all treaties. . . . It is urged that two branches in the Legislature are necessary. Why? for the purpose of a check. But the reason for the precaution is not applicable to this case. Within a particular State, where party heats prevail, such a check may be necessary. In such a body as Congress it is less necessary, and besides, the delegations of the different States are checks on each other. Do the people at large complain of Congress? No, what they wish is that Congress may have more power. If the power now proposed be not eno', the people hereafter will make additions to it. With proper powers Congress will act with more energy & wisdom than the proposed National Legislature; being fewer in number, and more secreted & refined by the mode of election. The plan of Mr. R will also be enormously expensive. Allowing Georgia & Delaware two representatives each in the popular branch the aggregate number of that branch will be 180. Add to it half as many for the other branch and you have 270. members coming once at least a year from the most distant as well as the most central parts of the republic. In the present deranged state of our finances can so expensive a system be seriously thought of? By enlarging the powers of Congress the greatest part of this expence will be saved, and all purposes will be answered. At least a trial ought to be made.

Mr. [James] Wilson [Pennsylvania] entered into a contrast of the principal points of the two plans so far he said as there had been time to examine the one last proposed. These points were 1. in the Virginia plan there are 2 & in some degree 3 branches in the Legislature: in the plan from N.J. there is to be a single legislature only—2. Representation of the people at large is the basis of the one:—the State Legislatures, the pillars of the other—3. proportional representation prevails in one:—equality of suffrage in the other—4. A single Executive Magistrate is at the head of the one:—a plurality is held out in the other.—5. in the one the majority of the people of the U. S. must prevail:—in the other a minority may prevail. 6. the National Legislature is to make laws in all cases to which the separate States are incompetent &–:—in place of this Congress are to have additional power in a few cases only—7. A negative on the laws of the States:—in place of this coertion to be substituted—8. The Executive to be removeable on impeachment & conviction;—in one plan: in the other to be removeable at the instance of a majority of the Executives of the States—9. Revision of the laws provided for in one:—no such check in the other—10. inferior national tribunals in one:—none such in the other. 11. In the one jurisdiction of National tribunals to extend &c—; an appellate jurisdiction only allowed in the other. 12. Here the jurisdiction is to extend to all cases affecting the National peace & harmony: there, a few cases only are marked out. 13. finally the ratification is in this to be by the people themselves:—in that by the legislative authorities according to the 13 art: of the Confederation.

With regard to the power of the Convention, he conceived himself authorized to conclude nothing, but to be at liberty to propose any thing. In this particular he felt himself perfectly indifferent to the two plans.

With regard to the sentiments of the people, he conceived it difficult to know precisely what they are. Those of the particular circle in which one moved, were commonly mistaken for the general voice. He could not persuade himself that the State Governments & Sovereignties were so much the idols of the people, nor a National Government so obnoxious to them, as some supposed. . . . Where do the people look at present for relief from the evils of which they complain? Is it from an internal reform of their Governments? no, Sir. It is from the National Councils that relief is expected. For these reasons he did not fear, that the people would not follow us into a national Government and it will be a further recommendation of Mr. R.'s plan that it is to be submitted to them, and not to the Legislatures, for ratification.

Proceeding now to the 1st point on which he had contrasted the two plans, he observed that anxious as he was for some augmentation of the federal powers, it would be with extreme reluctance indeed that he could ever consent to give powers to Congress he had two reasons either of which was sufficient. 1. Congress as a Legislative body does not stand on the people. 2. it is a single body. 1. He would not repeat the remarks he had formerly made on the principles of Representation. he would only say that an inequality in it, has ever been a poison contaminating every branch of Government. . . . The Impost, so anxiously wished for by the public was defeated not by any of the larger States in the Union. 2. Congress is a single Legislature. Despotism comes on Mankind in different Shapes, sometimes in an Executive, sometimes in a Military, one. Is there no danger of a Legislative despotism? Theory & practice both proclaim it. If the Legislative authority be not restrained, there can be neither liberty nor stability; and it can only be restrained by dividing it within itself, into distinct and independent branches. In a single House there is no check, but the inadequate one, of the virtue & good sense of those who compose it.

On another great point, the contrast was equally favorable to the plan reported by the Committee of the whole. It vested the Executive powers in a single Magistrate. The plan of N. Jersey, vested them in a plurality. In order to controul the Legislative authority, you must divide it. In order to controul the Executive you must unite it. One man will be more responsible than three. Three will contend among themselves till one becomes the master of his colleagues. In the triumvirates of Rome first Caesar, then Augustus, are witnesses of this truth. The Kings of Sparta, & the Consuls of Rome prove also the factious consequences of dividing the Executive Magistracy. . . .

Mr. [Charles] PINKNEY [South Carolina], the whole comes to this, as he conceived. Give N. Jersey an equal vote, and she will dismiss her scruples, and concur in the National system. He thought the Convention authorized to go any length in recommending, which they found necessary to remedy the evils which produced this Convention. . . .

Congress Debates the Issues, 1787

Democracy and the Lower House*

In committee of the whole on Mr. Randolph's propositions.

The 3d Resolution "that the National Legislature ought to consist of two branches" was agreed to without debate or dissent, except that of Pennsylvania, given probably from complaisance to Doctor Franklin, who was understood to be partial to a single House of legislation.

Resolution 4, first clause "that the members of the first branch of the National Legislature ought to be elected by the people of the several States" being taken up,

Mr. Sherman [Conn.] opposed the election by the people, insisting that it ought to be by the State Legislatures. The people, he said, immediately should have as little to do as may be about the government. They want information, and are constantly liable to be misled.

Mr. Gerry [Mass.]. The evils we experience flow from the excess of democracy. The people do not want virtue, but are the dupes of pretended patriots. In Massachusetts it had been fully confirmed by experience that they are daily misled into the most baneful measures and opinions by the false reports circulated by designing men, and which no one on the spot can refute. One principal evil arises from the want of due provision for those

---

* Madison's notes for May 31, 1787.

employed in the administration of government. It would seem to be a maxim of democracy to starve the public servants. He mentioned the popular clamour in Massachusetts for the reduction of salaries and the attack made on that of the Governor, though secured by the spirit of the Constitution itself. He had he said been too republican heretofore: he was still however republican, but had been taught by experience the danger of the levilling spirit.

Mr. Mason [Va.] argued strongly for an election of the larger branch by the people. It was to be the grand depository of the democratic principle of the Government. It was, so to speak, to be our House of Commons. It ought to know and sympathise with every part of the community; and ought therefore to be taken not only from different parts of the whole republic, but also from different districts of the larger members of it, which had in several instances, particularly in Virginia, different interests and views arising from difference of produce, of habits, etc., etc. He admitted that we had been too democratic, but was afraid we should incautiously run into the opposite extreme. We ought to attend to the rights of every class of the people. He had often wondered at the indifference of the superior classes of society to this dictate of humanity and policy; considering that however affluent their circumstances, or elevated their situations might be, the course of a few years not only might but certainly would distribute their posterity throughout the lowest classes of society. Every selfish motive, therefore, every family attachment, ought to recommend such a system of policy as would provide no less carefully for the rights and happiness of the lowest than of the highest orders of citizens.

Mr. Wilson [Penn.] contended strenuously for drawing the most numerous branch of the Legislature immediately from the people. He was for raising the federal pyramid to a considerable altitude, and for that reason wished to give it as broad a basis as possible. No government could long subsist without the confidence of the people. In a republican government this confidence was peculiarly essential. . . .

Mr. Madison considered the popular election of one branch of the National Legislature as essential to every plan of free government. He observed that in some of the States one branch of the Legislature was composed of men already removed from the people by an intervening body of electors. That if the first branch of the general legislature should be elected by the State Legislatures, the second branch elected by the first, the Executive by the second together with the first; and other appointments again made for subordinate purposes by the Executive, the people would be lost sight of altogether; and the necessary sympathy between them and their rulers and officers, too little felt. He was an advocate for the policy of refining the popular appointments by successive filtrations, but thought it might be pushed too far. . . .

Mr. Gerry did not like the election by the people. . . . Experience he said had shewn that the State legislatures drawn immediately from the people did not always possess their confidence. . . . He seemed to think the people might nominate a certain number out of which the State legislatures should be bound to choose.

Mr. Butler [S. C.] thought an election by the people an impracticable mode.

On the question for an election of the first branch of the National Legislature by the people:

Mass. ay. Conn. div. N.Y. ay. N.J. no. Penn. ay. Del. div. Va. ay. N.C. ay. S.C. no. Geo. ay.

Sectional Interests and Legislative Apportionment*

Mr. Randolph's motion requiring the Legislature to take a periodical census for the purpose of redressing inequalities in the representation, was resumed.

Mr. Sherman [Conn.] was against shackling the Legislature too much. We ought to choose wise and good men, and then confide in them.

Mr. Mason [Va.] The greater the difficulty we find in fixing a proper rule of representation, the more unwilling ought we to be, to throw the task from ourselves, on the General Legislature. He did not object to the conjectural ratio which was to prevail in the outset; but considered a revision from time to time according to some permanent and precise standard as essential to the fair representation required in the first branch. According to the present population of America, the northern part of it had a right to preponderate, and he could not deny it. But he wished it not to preponderate hereafter when the reason no longer continued. From the nature of man we may be sure that those who have power in their hands will not give it up while they can retain it. On the contrary we know they will always when they can rather increase it. If the southern States therefore should have three-quarters of the people of America within their limits, the Northern will hold fast the majority of representatives. One quarter will govern the three-quarters. The southern States will complain: but they may complain from generation to generation without redress. Unless some principle therefore which will do justice to them hereafter shall be inserted in the Constitution, disagreeable as the declaration was to him, he must declare he could neither vote for the system here, nor support it in his State. . . . He urged that numbers of inhabitants, though not always a precise standard of wealth, was sufficiently so for every substantial purpose.

Mr. Williamson [N.C.] was for making it the duty of the Legislature to do what was right and not leaving it at liberty to do or not do it. He moved that Mr. Randolph's proposition be postponed in order to consider the following: "that in order to ascertain the alterations that may happen in the population and wealth of the several States, a census shall be taken of the free white inhabitants and three-fifths of those of other descriptions on the first year after this Government shall have been adopted, and every [blank] year thereafter; and that the representation be regulated accordingly."

Mr. Randolph agreed that Mr. Williamson's proposition should stand in the place of his. . . .

Mr. Butler [S.C.] and General [C. C.] Pinckney [S.C.] insisted that

---

* Madison's notes for July 11, 1787.

blacks be included in the rule of representation, equally with the whites: and for that purpose moved that the words "three-fifths" be struck out.

Mr. Gerry [Mass.] thought that three-fifths of them was to say the least the full proportion that could be admitted.

Mr. Gorham. [Mass.] This ratio was fixed by Congress as a rule of taxation. Then it was urged by the delegates representing the States having slaves that the blacks were still more inferior to freemen. At present when the ratio of representation is to be established, we are assured that they are equal to freemen. The arguments on the former occasion had convinced him that three-fifths was pretty near the just proportion, and he should vote according to the same opinion now.

Mr. Butler insisted that the labour of a slave in South Carolina was as productive and valuable as that of a freeman in Massachusetts, that as wealth was the great means of defence and utility to the nation they were equally valuable to it with freemen; and that consequently an equal representation ought to be allowed for them in a government which was instituted principally for the protection of property, and was itself to be supported by property.

Mr. Mason could not agree to the motion, notwithstanding it was favorable to Virginia, because he thought it unjust. It was certain that the slaves were valuable, as they raised the value of land, increased the exports and imports, and of course the revenue; would supply the means of feeding and supporting an army, and might in cases of emergency become themselves soldiers. As in these important respects they were useful to the community at large, they ought not to be excluded from the estimate of representation. He could not, however, regard them as equal to freemen, and could not vote for them as such. He added as worthy of remark, that the southern States have this peculiar species of property, over and above the other species of property common to all the States.

Mr. Williamson reminded Mr. Gorham that if the southern States contended for the inferiority of blacks to whites when taxation was in view, the eastern States on the same occasion contended for their equality. He did not, however, either then or now, concur in either extreme, but approved of the ratio of three-fifths.

On Mr. Butler's motion for considering blacks as equal to whites in the apportionment of representation.

Mass. no. Conn. no. [N.Y. not on floor.] N.J. no. Pa. no. Del. ay. Md. no. Va. no. N.C. no. S.C. ay. Geo. ay . . .

Mr. Rutledge contended for the admission of wealth in the estimate by which representation should be regulated. The western States will not be able to contribute in proportion to their numbers; they should not therefore be represented in that proportion. The Atlantic States will not concur in such a plan. He moved that "at the end of [blank] years after the first meeting of the Legislature, and of every [blank] years thereafter, the Legislature shall proportion the Representation according to the principles of wealth and population." . . .

Mr. Gouverneur Morris. . . . He could not persuade himself that numbers would be a just rule at any time. The remarks of [Mr. Mason] relative to the western country had not changed his opinion on that head. Among other objections, it must be apparent they would not be able to furnish men equally enlightened, to share in the administration of our common interests. The busy haunts of men, not the remote wilderness, was the proper school of political talents. If the western people get the power into their hands, they will ruin the Atlantic interests. The back members are always most averse to the best measures. He mentioned the case of Pennsylvania formerly. The lower part of the State had the power in the first instance. They kept it in their own hands, and the country was the better for it. Another objection with him against admitting the blacks into the census, was that the people of Pennsylvania would revolt at the idea of being put on a footing with slaves. They would reject any plan that was to have such an effect. . . .

Mr. Madison [Va.]. . . . To reconcile the gentleman with himself, it must be imagined that he determined the human character by the points of the compass. The truth was that all men having power ought to be distrusted to a certain degree. The case of Pennsylvania had been mentioned, where it was admitted that those who were possessed of the power in the original settlement, never admitted the new settlements to a due share of it. England was a still more striking example. The power there had long been in the hands of the boroughs, of the minority; who had opposed and defeated every reform which had been attempted. Virginia was in a less degree another example. With regard to the western States, he was clear and firm in opinion that no unfavorable distinctions were admissible either in point of justice or policy. He thought also that the hope of contributions to the Treasury from them had been much underrated. . . . He could not agree that any substantial objection lay against fixing numbers for the perpetual standard of Representation. It was said that Representation and taxation were to go together; that taxation and wealth ought to go together, that population and wealth were not measures of each other. He admitted that in different climates, under different forms of Government, and in different stages of civilization, the inference was perfectly just. He would admit that in no situation numbers of inhabitants were an accurate measure of wealth. He contended however that in the United States it was sufficiently so for the object in contemplation. Altho' their climate varied considerably, yet as the governments, the laws, and the manners of all were nearly the same, and the intercourse between different parts perfectly free, population, industry, arts, and the value of labour, would constantly tend to equalize themselves. . . .

On the question on the first clause of Mr. Williamson's motion as to taking a census of the free inhabitants, it passed in the affirmative. Mass. ay. Cont. ay. N.J. ay. Pa. ay. Del. no. Md. no. Va. ay. N.C. ay. S.C. no. Geo. no.

The next clause as to three-fifths of the negroes being considered,

Mr. King [Mass.], being much opposed to fixing numbers as the rule of representation, was particularly so on account of the blacks. He thought the admission of them along with whites at all, would excite great discontents among the States having no slaves. . . .

Mr. Wilson did not well see on what principle the admission of blacks in the proportion of three-fifths could be explained. Are they admitted as citizens? then why are they not admitted on an equality with white citizens?

233

are they admitted as property? then why is not other property admitted into the computation? These were difficulties however which he thought must be overruled by the necessity of compromise. He had some apprehensions also from the tendency of the blending of the blacks with the whites, to give disgust to the people of Pennsylvania as had been intimated by his colleague. But he differed from him in thinking numbers of inhabitants so incorrect a measure of wealth. He had seen the western settlements of Pennsylvania, and on a comparison of them with the city of Philadelphia could discover little other difference, than that property was more unequally divided among individuals here than there. Taking the same number in the aggregate in the two situations he believed there would be little difference in their wealth and ability to contribute to the public wants.

Mr. Gouverneur Morris was compelled to declare himself reduced to the dilemma of doing injustice to the southern States or to human nature, and he must therefore do it to the former. For he could never agree to give such encouragement to the slave trade as would be given by allowing them a representation for their negroes, and he did not believe those States would ever confederate on terms that would deprive them of that trade.

On the question for agreeing to include three-fifths of the blacks:

Mass. no. Cont. ay. N.J. no. Pa. no. Del. no. Md. no. Va. ay. N.C. ay. S.C. no. Geo. ay.*

Qualifications for Voters[†]

Mr. Gouverneur Morris [Pa.] moved to . . . restrain the right of suffrage to freeholders.

Mr. Fitzsimons [Penn.] seconded the motion.

Mr. Williamson [N.C.] was opposed to it.

Mr. Wilson [Pa.] . . . It was difficult to form any uniform rule of qualifications for all the States. Unnecessary innovations he thought too should be avoided. It would be very hard and disagreeable for the same persons at the same time to vote for Representatives in the State Legislature and to be excluded from a vote for those in the National Legislature.

Mr. Gouverneur Morris. Such a hardship would be neither great nor novel. The people are accustomed to it and not dissatisfied with it in several of the States. In some the qualifications are different for the choice of the Governor and of the Representatives; in others for different houses of the Legislature. . . .

Mr. Ellsworth [Conn.] thought the qualifications of the electors stood on the most proper footing. The right of suffrage was a tender point, and strongly guarded by most of the State Constitutions. The people will not readily subscribe to the National Constitution if it should subject them to be disfranchised. The States are the best judges of the circumstances and temper of their own people.

Col. Mason [Va.]. The force of habit is certainly not attended to by those gentlemen who wish for innovations on this point. Eight or nine States

---

* Later this provision was passed.
† Madison's notes for August 7, 1787.

have extended the right of suffrage beyond the freeholders; what will the people there say if they should be disfranchised? A power to alter the qualifications would be a dangerous power in the hands of the Legislature.

Mr. Butler [S.C.]. There is no right of which the people are more jealous than that of suffrage. Abridgments of it tend to the same revolution as in Holland where they have at length thrown all power into the hands of the Senates, who fill up vacancies themselves, and form a rank aristocracy.

Mr. Dickinson [Pa.] had a very different idea of the tendency of vesting the right of suffrage in the freeholders of the country. He considered them as the best guardians of liberty; and the restriction of the right to them as a necessary defence against the dangerous influence of those multitudes without property and without principle with which our country like all others, will in time abound. As to the unpopularity of the innovation, it was in his opinion chimerical. The great mass of our citizens is composed at this time of freeholders, and will be pleased with it.

Mr. Ellsworth. How shall the freehold be defined? Ought not every man who pays a tax, to vote for the representative who is to levy and dispose of his money? Shall the wealthy merchants and manufacturers, who will bear a full share of the public burdens, be not allowed a voice in the imposition of them? Taxation and representation ought to go together.

Mr. Gouverneur Morris. He had long learned not to be the dupe of words. The sound of aristocracy, therefore, had no effect on him. It was the thing, not the name, to which he was opposed, and one of his principal objections to the Constitution as it is now before us, is that it threatens this country with an aristocracy. The aristocracy will grow out of the House of Representatives. Give the votes to people who have no property, and they will sell them to the rich who will be able to buy them. We should not confine our attention to the present moment. The time is not distant when this country will abound with mechanics and manufacturers who will receive their bread from their employers. Will such men be the secure and faithful guardians of liberty? Will they be the impregnable barrier against aristocracy? He was as little duped by the association of the words "taxation and representation." The man who does not give his vote freely is not represented. It is the man who dictates the vote. Children do not vote. Why? because they want prudence, because they have no will of their own. The ignorant and the dependent can be as little trusted with the public interest. He did not conceive the difficulty of defining "freeholders" to be insuperable. Still less, that the restriction could be unpopular. Nine-tenths of the people are at present freeholders, and these will certainly be pleased with it. As to merchants, etc., if they have wealth and value the right, they can acquire it. If not, they don't deserve it.

Col. Mason. We all feel too strongly the remains of antient prejudices, and view things too much through a British medium. A freehold is the qualification in England, and hence it is imagined to be the only proper one. The true idea in his opinion was that every man having evidence of attachment to and permanent common interest with the society ought to share in all its rights and privileges. Was this qualification restrained to freeholders? Does no other kind of property but land evidence a common interest in the proprietor? Does nothing besides property mark a permanent attachment? Ought the merchant, the monied man, the parent of a number of children whose fortunes are to be pursued in his own country, to be viewed as suspicious characters, and unworthy to be trusted with the common rights of their fellow citizens?

Mr. Madison [Va.] The right of suffrage is certainly one of the fundamental articles of republican government, and ought not to be left to be regulated by the Legislature. A gradual abridgment of this right has been the mode in which aristocracies have been built on the ruins of popular forms. Whether the Constitutional qualification ought to be a freehold, would with him depend much on the probable reception such a change would meet with in States where the right was now exercised by every description of people. In several of the States a freehold was now the qualification. Viewing the subject in its merits alone, the freeholders of the country would be the safest depositories of Republican liberty. In future times a great majority of the people will not only be without landed, but any other sort of, property. These will either combine under the influence of their common situation; in which case, the rights of property and the public liberty will not be secure in their hands: or what is more probable, they will become the tools of opulence and ambition, in which case there will be equal danger on another side. . . .

Dr. Franklin [Pa.] It is of great consequence that we should not depress the virtue and public spirit of our common people; of which they displayed a great deal during the war, and which contributed principally to the favorable issue of it. . . . He did not think that the elected had any right in any case to narrow the privileges of the electors. . . . He was persuaded also that such a restriction as was proposed would give great uneasiness in the populous States. The sons of a substantial farmer, not being themselves freeholders, would not be pleased at being disfranchised, and there are a great many persons of that description.

Mr. Mercer [Md.] The Constitution is objectionable in many points, but in none more than the present. He objected to the footing on which the qualification was put, but particularly to the mode of election by the people. The people can not know and judge of the characters of candidates. The worst possible choice will be made. . . .

Mr. Rutledge [Va.] thought the idea of restraining the right of suffrage to the freeholders a very unadvised one. It would create division among the people and make enemies of all those who should be excluded.

Slavery and the Importation of Slaves*

Mr. Sherman [Conn.] . . . disapproved of the slave trade; yet as the States were now possessed of the right to import slaves, as the public good did not require it to be taken from them, and as it was expedient to have as few objections as possible to the proposed scheme of government, he thought it best to leave the matter as we find it. He observed that the abolition of slavery seemed to be going on in the United States, and that the good sense

---

* Madison's notes for August 22, 25, 1787.

of the several States would probably by degrees compleat it. He urged on the Convention the necessity of despatching its business.

Col. Mason [Va.] This infernal trafic originated in the avarice of British merchants. The British Government constantly checked the attempts of Virginia to put a stop to it. The present question concerns not the importing States alone but the whole Union. The evil of having slaves was experienced during the late war. Had slaves been treated as they might have been by the enemy, they would have proved dangerous instruments in their hands. . . . Maryland and Virginia he said had already prohibited the importation of slaves expressly. North Carolina had done the same in substance. All this would be in vain if South Carolina and Georgia be at liberty to import. The western people are already calling out for slaves for their new lands, and will fill that country with slaves if they can be got thro' South Carolina and Georgia. Slavery discourages arts and manufactures. The poor despise labor when performed by slaves. They prevent the immigration of whites, who really enrich and strengthen a country. They produce the most pernicious effect on manners. Every master of slaves is born a petty tyrant. They bring the judgment of Heaven on a country. As nations cannot be rewarded or punished in the next world, they must be in this. By an inevitable chain of causes and effects, Providence punishes national sins, by national calamities. He lamented that some of our eastern brethren had from a lust of gain embarked in this nefarious traffic. As to the States being in possession of the right to import, this was the case with many other rights, now to be properly given up. He held it essential in every point of view that the General Government should have power to prevent the increase of slavery.

Mr. Ellsworth [Conn.] As he had never owned a slave could not judge of the effects of slavery on character: he said, however, that if it was to be considered in a moral light we ought to go farther and free those already in the country. As slaves also multiply so fast in Virginia and Maryland that it is cheaper to raise than import them, whilst in the sickly rice swamps foreign supplies are necessary; if we go no farther than is urged, we shall be unjust towards South Carolina and Georgia. Let us not intermeddle. As population increases, poor laborers will be so plenty as to render slaves useless. Slavery in time will not be a speck in our country. Provision is already made in Connecticut for abolishing it, and the abolition has already taken place in Massachussets. As to the danger of insurrections from foreign influence, that will become a motive to kind treatment of the slaves.

Mr. Pinckney [S.C.] If slavery be wrong, it is justified by the example of all the world. He cited the case of Greece, Rome, and other antient States; the sanction given by France, England, Holland, and other modern States. In all ages one half of mankind have been slaves. If the southern States were let alone they will probably of themselves stop importations. He would himself as a citizen of South Carolina vote for it. An attempt to take away the right as proposed will produce serious objections to the Constitution, which he wished to see adopted.

General Pinckney [S.C.] declared it to be his firm opinion that if himself and all his colleagues were to sign the Constitution and use their personal influence, it would be of no avail towards obtaining the assent of their constituents. South Carolina and Georgia cannot do without slaves. As to Virginia, she will gain by stopping the importations. Her slaves will rise in value, and she has more than she wants. It would be unequal to require South Carolina and Georgia to confederate on such unequal terms. He said the royal assent before the Revolution had never been refused to South Carolina as to Virginia. He contended that the importation of slaves would be for the interest of the whole Union. The more slaves, the more produce to employ the carrying trade, the more consumption also; and the more of this, the more of revenue for the common treasury. . . .

Mr. Dickinson [Pa.] considered it as inadmissible on every principle of honor and safety that the importation of slaves should be authorised to the States by the Constitution. The true question was whether the national happiness would be promoted or impeded by the importation, and this question ought to be left to the National Government, not to the States particularly interested. . . .

Mr. Rutledge [Va.]. If the Convention thinks that North Carolina, South Carolina, and Georgia will ever agree to the plan, unless their right to import slaves be untouched, the expectation is vain. The people of those States will never be such fools as to give up so important an interest. . . .

Mr. Gouverneur Morris wished the whole subject to be committed, including the clauses relating to taxes on exports and to a navigation act. These things may form a bargain among the northern and southern States. . . .

General Pinckney moved to strike out the words "the year eighteen hundred" as the year limiting the importation of slaves, and to insert the words "the year eighteen hundred and eight".

Mr. Gorham seconded the motion.

Mr. Madison. Twenty years will produce all the mischief that can be apprehended from the liberty to import slaves. So long a term will be more dishonorable to the national character, than to say nothing about it in the Constitution.

On the motion; which passed in the affirmative.

N.H. ay. Mass. ay. Conn. ay. N.J. no. Pa. no. Del. no. Md. ay. Va. no. N.C. ay. S.C. ay. Geo. ay. . . .

The first part of the report was then agreed to, amended as follows,

The migration or importation of such persons as the several States now existing shall think proper to admit, shall not be prohibited by the Legislature prior to the year 1808.

N.H. Mass. Conn. Md. N.C. S.C. Geo.: ay
N.J. Pa. Del. Va.   .   .   .   .   no

The Constitution of the United States of America, 1787

We, the people of the United States, in order to form a more perfect union, establish justice, insure domestic tranquillity, provide for the common defense, promote the general welfare, and secure the blessings of liberty to ourselves and our posterity, do ordain and establish this Constitution for the United States of America.

Article One

Section 1. All legislative powers herein granted shall be vested in a Congress of the United States, which shall consist of a Senate and House of Representatives.

Section 2. The House of Representatives shall be composed of members chosen every second year by the people of the several States, and the electors in each State shall have the qualifications requisite for electors of the most numerous branch of the State legislature.

No person shall be a Representative who shall not have attained to the age of twenty five years, and been seven years a citizen of the United States, and who shall not, when elected, be an inhabitant of that State in which he shall be chosen.

Representatives and direct taxes shall be apportioned among the several States which may be included within this Union, according to their respective numbers, which shall be determined by adding to the whole number of free persons, including those bound to service for a term of years, and excluding Indians not taxed, three-fifths of all other persons. The actual enumeration shall be made within three years after the first meeting of the Congress of the United States, and within every subsequent term of ten years, in such manner as they shall by law direct. The number of Representatives shall not exceed one for every thirty thousand, but each State shall have at least one Representative; and until such enumeration shall be made, the State of New Hampshire shall be entitled to choose three, Massachusetts eight, Rhode Island and Providence Plantations one, Connecticut five, New York six, New Jersey four, Pennsylvania eight, Delaware one, Maryland six, Virginia ten, North Carolina five, South Carolina five, and Georgia three.

When vacancies happen in the representation from any State, the executive authority thereof shall issue writs of election to fill such vacancies.

The House of Representatives shall choose their Speaker and other officers, and shall have the sole power of impeachment.

Section 3. The Senate of the United States shall be composed of two Senators from each State, chosen by the legislature thereof, for six years; and each Senator shall have one vote.

Immediately after they shall be assembled in consequence of the first election, they shall be divided as equally as may be into three classes. The seats of the Senators of the first class shall be vacated at the expiration of the second year; of the second class, at the expiration of the fourth year, and of the third class, at the expiration of the sixth year, so that one-third may be chosen every second year; and if vacancies happen by resignation or otherwise during the recess of the legislature of any State, the executive thereof may make temporary appointments until the next meeting of the legislature, which shall then fill such vacancies.

No person shall be a Senator who shall not have attained to the age of thirty years, and been nine years a citizen of the United States, and who shall not, when elected, be an inhabitant of that State for which he shall be chosen.

The Vice-President of the United States shall be President of the Senate, but shall have no vote, unless they be equally divided.

The Senate shall choose their other officers, and also a President pro tempore in the absence of the Vice-President, or when he shall exercise the office of President of the United States.

The Senate shall have the sole power to try all impeachments. When sitting for that purpose, they shall be on oath or affirmation. When the President of the United States is tried, the Chief Justice shall preside: and no person shall be convicted without the concurrence of two-thirds of the members present.

Judgment in cases of impeachment shall not extend further than to removal from office, and disqualification to hold and enjoy any office of honor, trust, or profit under the United States; but the party convicted shall, nevertheless, be liable and subject to indictment, trial, judgment, and punishment, according to law.

Section 4. The times, places, and manner of holding elections for Senators and Representatives shall be prescribed in each State by the legislature thereof; but the Congress may at any time by law make or alter such regulations, except as to the places of choosing Senators.

The Congress shall assemble at least once in every year, and such meeting shall be on the first Monday in December, unless they shall by law appoint a different day.

Section 5. Each house shall be the judge of the elections, returns, and qualifications of its own members, and a majority of each shall constitute a quorum to do business; but a smaller number may adjourn from day to day, and may be authorized to compel the attendance of absent members, in such manner, and under such penalties, as each house may provide.

Each house may determine the rules of its proceedings, punish its members for disorderly behavior, and, with the concurrence of two-thirds, expel a member.

Each house shall keep a journal of its proceedings, and from time to time publish the same, excepting such parts as may in their judgment require secrecy, and the yeas and nays of the members of either house on any question shall, at the desire of one-fifth of those present, be entered on the journal.

Neither house, during the session of Congress, shall, without the consent of the other, adjourn for more than three days, nor to any other place than that in which the two houses shall be sitting.

Section 6. The Senators and Representatives shall receive a compensation for their services, to be ascertained by law and paid out of the Treasury of the United States. They shall, in all cases except treason, felony, and breach of the peace, be privileged from arrest during their attendance at the session of their respective houses, and in going to and returning from the same; and for any speech or debate in either house they shall not be questioned in any other place.

No Senator or Representative shall, during the time for which he was elected, be appointed to any civil office under the authority of the United States, which shall have been created, or the emoluments whereof shall have been increased during such time; and no person holding any office under the United States shall be a member of either house during his continuance in office.

Section 7. All bills for raising revenue shall originate in the House of Representatives; but the Senate may propose or concur with amendments as on other bills.

Every bill which shall have passed the House of Representatives and the Senate shall, before it becomes a law, be presented to the President of the United States; if he approve he shall sign it, but if not he shall return it, with his objections, to that house in which it shall have originated, who shall enter the objections at large on their journal and proceed to reconsider it. If after such reconsideration two-thirds of that house shall agree to pass the bill, it shall be sent, together with the objections, to the other house, by which it shall likewise be reconsidered, and if approved by two-thirds of that house it shall become a law. But in all such cases the votes of both houses shall be determined by yeas and nays, and the names of the persons voting for and against the bill shall be entered on the journal of each house respectively. If any bill shall not be returned by the President within ten days (Sundays excepted) after it shall have been presented to him, the same shall be a law, in like manner as if he had signed it, unless the Congress by their adjournment prevent its return, in which case it shall not be a law.

Every order, resolution, or vote to which the concurrence of the Senate and House of Representatives may be necessary (except on a question of adjournment) shall be presented to the President of the United States; and before the same shall take effect, shall be approved by him, or being disapproved by him, shall be repassed by two-thirds of the Senate and House of Representatives, according to the rules and limitations prescribed in the case of a bill.

Section 8. The Congress shall have power to lay and collect taxes, duties, imposts, and excises, to pay the debts and provide for the common defense and general welfare of the United States; but all duties, imposts, and excises shall be uniform throughout the United States;

To borrow money on the credit of the United States;

To regulate commerce with foreign nations and among the several States, and with the Indian tribes;

To establish an uniform rule of naturalization, and uniform laws on the subject of bankruptcies throughout the United States;

To coin money, regulate the value thereof, and of foreign coin, and fix the standard of weights and measures;

To provide for the punishment of counterfeiting the securities and current coin of the United States;

To establish post-offices and post-roads;

To promote the progress of science and useful arts by securing for limited times to authors and inventors the exclusive right to their respective writings and discoveries;

To constitute tribunals inferior to the Supreme Court;

To define and punish piracies and felonies committed on the high seas and offenses against the law of nations;

To declare war, grant letters of marque and reprisal, and make rules concerning captures on land and water;

To raise and support armies, but no appropriation of money to that use shall be for a longer term than two years;

To provide and maintain a navy;

To make rules for the government and regulation of the land and naval forces;

To provide for calling forth the militia to execute the laws of the Union, suppress insurrections, and repel invasions;

To provide for organizing, arming, and disciplining the militia, and for governing such part of them as may be employed in the service of the United States, reserving to the States respectively the appointment of the officers, and the authority of training the militia according to the discipline prescribed by Congress;

To exercise exclusive legislation in all cases whatsoever over such district (not exceeding ten miles square) as may, by cession of particular States and the acceptance of Congress, become the seat of the Government of the United States, and to exercise like authority over all places purchased by the consent of the legislature of the State in which the same shall be, for the erection of forts, magazines, arsenals, dockyards, and other needful buildings; and

To make all laws which shall be necessary and proper for carrying into execution the foregoing powers, and all other powers vested by this Constitution in the Government of the United States, or in any department or officer thereof.

Section 9. The migration or importation of such persons as any of the States now existing shall think proper to admit shall not be prohibited by the Congress prior to the year one thousand eight hundred and eight, but a tax or duty may be imposed on such importation, not exceeding ten dollars for each person.

The privilege of the writ of habeas corpus shall not be suspended, unless when in cases of rebellion or invasion the public safety may require it.

No bill of attainder or ex post facto law shall be passed.

No capitation or other direct tax shall be laid, unless in proportion to the census or enumeration hereinbefore directed to be taken.

No tax or duty shall be laid on articles exported from any State.

No preference shall be given by any regulation of commerce or revenue to the ports of one State over those of another; nor shall vessels bound to or from one State be obliged to enter, clear, or pay duties in another.

No money shall be drawn from the Treasury but in consequence of appropriations made by law; and a regular statement and account of the receipts and expenditures of all public money shall be published from time to time.

No title of nobility shall be granted by the United States; and no person holding any office of profit or trust under them shall, without the consent of the Congress, accept of any present, emolument, office, or title, of any kind whatever, from any king, prince, or foreign State.

Section 10. No State shall enter into any treaty, alliance, or confederation; grant letters of marque and reprisal; coin money; emit bills of credit; make anything but gold and silver coin a tender in payment of debts; pass any bill of attainder, ex post facto law, or law impairing the obligation of contracts, or grant any title of nobility.

No State shall, without the consent of Congress, lay any imposts or duties on imports or exports, except what may be absolutely necessary for executing its inspection laws; and the net produce of all duties and imposts, laid by any State on imports or exports, shall be for the use of the Treasury of the United States; and all such laws shall be subject to the revision and control of the Congress.

No State shall, without the consent of Congress, lay any duty of tonnage, keep troops or ships of war in time of peace, enter into any agreement or compact with another State or with a foreign power, or engage in war, unless actually invaded or in such imminent danger as will not admit of delay.

Article Two

Section 1. The executive power shall be vested in a President of the United States of America. He shall hold his office during the term of four years, and together with the Vice-President, chosen for the same term, be elected as follows:

Each State shall appoint, in such manner as the legislature thereof may direct, a number of electors, equal to the whole number of Senators and Representatives to which the State may be entitled in the Congress; but no Senator or Representative, or person holding an office of trust or profit under the United States, shall be appointed an elector.

[The electors shall meet in their respective States and vote by ballot for two persons, of whom one at least shall not be an inhabitant of the same State with themselves. And they shall make a list of all the persons voted for, and of the number of votes for each; which list they shall sign and certify, and transmit sealed to the seat of the government of the United States, directed to the President of the Senate. The President of the Senate shall, in the presence of the Senate and House of Representatives, open all the certificates, and the votes shall then be counted. The person having the greatest number of votes shall be the President, if such number be a majority of the whole number of electors appointed; and if there be more than one who have such majority, and have an equal number of votes, then the House of Representatives shall immediately choose by ballot one of them for President; and if no person have a majority, then from the five highest on the list the said House shall in like manner choose the President. But in choosing the President the votes shall be taken by States, the representation from each State having one vote; a quorum for this purpose shall consist of a member or members from two-thirds of the States, and a majority of all the States shall be necessary to a choice. In every case, after the choice of the President, the person having the greatest number of votes of the electors shall be the Vice-President. But if there should remain two or more who have equal votes, the Senate shall choose from them by ballot the Vice-President.*

The Congress may determine the time of choosing the electors and the day on which they shall give their votes, which day shall be the same throughout the United States.

No person except a natural-born citizen, or a citizen of the United States at the time of the adoption of this Constitution, shall be eligible to the office of President; neither shall any person be eligible to that office who shall not have attained to the age of thirty-five years, and been fourteen years a resident within the United States.

In case of the removal of the President from office, or of his death, resignation, or inability to discharge the powers and duties of the said office, the same shall devolve on the Vice-President, and the Congress may by law provide for the case of removal, death, resignation, or inability, both of the President and Vice-President, declaring what officer shall then act as President, and such officer shall act accordingly until the disability be removed or a President shall be elected.

The President shall, at stated times, receive for his services a compensation, which shall neither be increased nor diminished during the period for which he shall have been elected, and he shall not receive within that period any other emolument from the United States or any of them.

Before he enter on the execution of his office he shall take the following oath or affirmation:

"I do solemnly swear (or affirm) that I will faithfully execute the office of President of the United States, and will to the best of my ability preserve, protect, and defend the Constitution of the United States."

Section 2. The President shall be Commander-in-chief of the Army and Navy of the United States, and of the militia of the several States when called into the actual service of the United States; he may require the opinion, in writing, of the principal officer in each of the executive departments, upon any subject relating to the duties of their respective offices, and he shall have power to grant reprieves and pardons for offenses against the United States, except in cases of impeachment.

He shall have power, by and with the advice and consent of the Senate, to make treaties, provided two-thirds of the Senators present concur; and he shall nominate, and, by and with the advice and consent of the Senate, shall appoint ambassadors, other public ministers and consuls, judges of the Supreme Court, and all other officers of the United States, whose appointments are not herein otherwise provided for, and which shall be established

---

* This procedure was changed by the Twelfth Amendment.

by law; but the Congress may by law vest the appointment of such inferior officers, as they think proper, in the President alone, in the courts of law, or in the heads of departments.

The President shall have power to fill up all vacancies that may happen during the recess of the Senate, by granting commissions which shall expire at the end of their next session.

Section 3. He shall from time to time give to the Congress information of the state of the Union, and recommend to their consideration such measures as he shall judge necessary and expedient; he may, on extraordinary occasions, convene both houses, or either of them, and in case of disagreement between them with respect to the time of adjournment, he may adjourn them to such time as he shall think proper; he shall receive ambassadors and other public ministers; he shall take care that the laws be faithfully executed, and shall commission all the officers of the United States.

Section 4. The President, Vice-President, and all civil officers of the United States shall be removed from office on impeachment for and conviction of treason, bribery, or other high crimes and misdemeanors.

Article Three

Section 1. The judicial power of the United States shall be vested in one Supreme Court, and in such inferior courts as the Congress may from time to time ordain and establish. The judges, both of the supreme and inferior courts, shall hold their offices during good behavior, and shall, at stated times, receive for their services a compensation which shall not be diminished during their continuance in office.

Section 2. The judicial power shall extend to all cases, in law and equity, arising under this Constitution, the laws of the United States, and treaties made, or which shall be made, under their authority; to all cases affecting ambassadors, other public ministers, and consuls; to all cases of admiralty and maritime jurisdiction; to controversies to which the United States shall be a party; to controversies between two or more States; between a State and citizens of another State; between citizens of different States; between citizens of the same State claiming lands under grants of different States, and between a State, or the citizens thereof, and foreign States, citizens, or subjects.

In all cases affecting ambassadors, other public ministers and consuls, and those in which a State shall be a party, the Supreme Court shall have original jurisdiction. In all the other cases before mentioned the Supreme Court shall have appellate jurisdiction, both as to law and fact, with such exceptions and under such regulations as the Congress shall make.

The trial of all crimes, except in cases of impeachment, shall be by jury; and such trial shall be held in the State where the said crimes shall have been committed; but when not committed within any State, the trial shall be at such place or places as the Congress may by law have directed.

Section 3. Treason against the United States shall consist only in levying war against them, or in adhering to their enemies, giving them aid and comfort. No person shall be convicted of treason unless on the testimony of two witnesses to the same overt act, or on confession in open court.

The Congress shall have power to declare the punishment of treason, but no attainder of treason shall work corruption of blood or forfeiture except during the life of the person attainted.

Article Four

Section 1. Full faith and credit shall be given in each State to the public acts, records, and judicial proceedings of every other State. And the Congress may by general laws prescribe the manner in which such acts, records, and proceedings shall be proved, and the effect thereof.

Section 2. The citizens of each State shall be entitled to all privileges and immunities of citizens in the several States.

A person charged in any State with treason, felony, or other crime, who shall flee from justice, and be found in another State, shall, on demand of the executive authority of the State from which he fled, be delivered up, to be removed to the State having jurisdiction of the crime.

No person held to service or labor in one State, under the laws thereof, escaping into another, shall, in consequence of any law or regulation therein, be discharged from such service or labor, but shall be delivered up on claim of the party to whom such service or labor may be due.

Section 3. New States may be admitted by the Congress into this Union; but no new State shall be formed or erected within the jurisdiction of any other State; nor any State be formed by the junction of two or more States or parts of States, without the consent of the legislatures of the States concerned as well as of the Congress.

The Congress shall have power to dispose of and make all needful rules and regulations respecting the territory or other property belonging to the United States; and nothing in this Constitution shall be so construed as to prejudice any claims of the United States or of any particular State.

Section 4. The United States shall guarantee to every State in this Union a republican form of government, and shall protect each of them against invasion, and on application of the legislature, or of the executive (when the legislature cannot be convened), against domestic violence.

Article Five

The Congress, whenever two-thirds of both houses shall deem it necessary, shall propose amendments to this Constitution, or, on the application of the Legislatures of two-thirds of the several States, shall call a convention for proposing amendments, which, in either case, shall be valid to all intents and purposes, as part of this Constitution, when ratified by the Legislatures of three-fourths of the several States, or by conventions in three-fourths thereof, as the one or the other mode of ratification may be proposed by the Congress; provided that no amendment which may be made prior to the Year One thousand eight hundred and eight shall in any manner affect the first and fourth Clauses in the Ninth Section of the first Article; and that no State, without its consent, shall be deprived of its equal suffrage in the Senate.

Article Six

All debts contracted and engagements entered into, before the adoption of this Constitution, shall be as valid against the United States under this Constitution, as under the Confederation.

This Constitution and the laws of the United States which shall be made in pursuance thereof and all treaties made, or which shall be made, under the authority of the United States, shall be the supreme law of the land; and the judges in every State shall be bound thereby, anything in the Constitution or laws of any State to the contrary notwithstanding.

The Senators and Representatives before mentioned, and the members of the several State Legislatures, and all executive and judicial officers, both of the United States and of the several States, shall be bound by oath or affirmation, to support this Constitution; but no religious test shall ever be required as a qualification to any office or public trust under the United States.

Article Seven

The ratification of the Conventions of nine States shall be sufficient for the establishment of this Constitution between the States so ratifying the same.

Done in convention by the unanimous consent of the States present the seventeenth day of September in the year of our Lord one thousand seven hundred and eighty-seven and of the independence of the United States of America the twelfth, in witness whereof we have hereunto subscribed our names.

G. WASHINGTON—President
and deputy from Virginia

Women's Views of the New Nation

In many ways the American Revolution changed the course of history for the residents of what had been Britain's mainland North American colonies. In 1774 the Americans were colonials, subjects of a monarchy based thousands of miles away across the Atlantic Ocean and participants in a traditional political system. Less than a decade later they were successful revolutionaries, the founders of an independent republic—the first colonists in history to win their freedom and establish a nation of their own.

Such dramatic events, it could be argued, impinged primarily on men, not women. After all, men alone fought in the armies, voted in the new republic's elections, drafted state and national constitutions, and served in legislative bodies. Women traditionally did not take part in politics; their domain was the domestic sphere, whereas the public world was defined exclusively as men's arena. Did the Revolution, then, affect women? If so, what was its impact? Or can the Revolution be safely ignored by historians of women because it held so little meaning for their subjects?

✢ D O C U M E N T S

In March 1776, recognizing that the United States, which had already been at war with Great Britain for nearly a year, would soon declare independence, Abigail Adams wrote to her congressman husband John in Philadelphia, reminding him to "remember the ladies" in the nation's "new code of laws." She thus initiated the first-known exchange in American history on the subject of women's rights; the first document consists of the Adamses' comments to each other on the matter. Drawing on revolutionary ideas of women's equality with men, in 1779 Susanna Wright wrote a poem in praise of her friend, Elizabeth Norris, reprinted here as the second selection. The following year, after the Americans had suffered one of their worst defeats of the war when Charleston, South Carolina, fell to the British forces, a broadside entitled "The Sentiments of an American Woman" (the third document) proposed a nationwide Ladies Association to contribute to the welfare of the troops. Many years after the Revolution, Sarah Osborn, who had traveled with her husband and the American army, recalled her experiences, reprinted as the final selection, when she applied for a government pension in 1837.

Abigail and John Adams's
"Remember the Ladies" Letters, 1776

Abigail Adams to John Adams:

Braintree March 31 1776

I long to hear that you have declared an independancy—and by the way in the new Code of Laws which I suppose it will be necessary for you to make I desire you would Remember the Ladies, and be more generous and favourable to them than your ancestors. Do not put such unlimited power into the hands of the Husbands. Remember all Men would be tyrants if they could. If perticuliar care and attention is not paid to the Laidies we are determined to foment a Rebelion, and will not hold ourselves bound by any Laws in which we have no voice, or Representation.

That your Sex are Naturally Tyrannical is a Truth so thoroughly established as to admit of no dispute, but such of you as wish to be happy willingly give up the harsh title of Master for the more tender and endearing one of Friend. Why then, not put it out of the power of the vicious and the Lawless to use us with cruelty and indignity with impunity. Men of Sense in all Ages abhor those customs which treat us only as the vassals of your Sex. Regard us then as Beings placed by providence under your protection and in immitation of the Supreem Being make use of that power only for our happiness.

John to Abigail:

Ap. 14. 1776

As to Declarations of Independency, be patient. Read our Privateering Laws, and our Commercial Laws. What signifies a Word.

As to your extraordinary Code of Laws, I cannot but laugh. We have been told that our Struggle has loosened the bands of Government every where. That Children and Apprentices were disobedient—that schools and Colledges were grown turbulent—that Indians slighted their Guardians and Negroes grew insolent to their Masters. But your Letter was the first Intimation that another Tribe more numerous and powerfull than all the rest were grown discontented.—This is rather too coarse a Compliment but you are so saucy, I wont blot it out.

Depend upon it, We know better than to repeal our Masculine systems. Altho they are in full Force, you know they are little more than Theory. We dare not exert our Power in its full Latitude. We are obliged to go fair, and softly, and in Practice you know We are the subjects. We have only the Name of Masters, and rather than give up this, which would compleatly subject Us to the Despotism of the Peticoat, I hope General Washington, and all our brave Heroes would fight. I am sure every good Politician would plot, as long as he would against Despotism, Empire, Monarchy, Aristocracy, Oligarchy, or Ochlocracy,—A fine Story indeed. I begin to think the Ministry as deep as they are wicked. After stirring up Tories, Landjobbers, Trimmers, Bigots, Canadians, Indians, Negroes, Hanoverians, Hessians, Russians, Irish Roman Catholicks, Scotch Renegadoes, at last they have stimulated the   to demand new Priviledges and threaten to rebell.

Abigail to John:

B[raintre]e May 7 1776

I can not say that I think you very generous to the Ladies, for whilst you are proclaiming peace and good will to Men, Emancipating all Nations, you insist upon retaining an absolute power over Wives. But you must remember that Arbitrary power is like most other things which are very hard, very liable to be broken—and notwithstanding all your wise Laws and Maxims we have it in our power not only to free our selves but to subdue our Masters, and without violence throw both your natural and legal authority at our feet—

"Charm by accepting, by submitting sway
Yet have our Humour most when we obey."

Susanna Wright's "To Eliza Norris—at Fairhill," c. 1779

Since Adam, by our first fair Mother won
To share her fate, to taste, & be undone,
And that great law, whence no appeal must lie,
Pronounc'd a doom, that he should rule & die,
The partial race, rejoicing to fulfill
This pleasing dictate of almighty will
(With no superior virtue in their mind),
Assert their right to govern womankind.
But womankind call reason to their aid,
And question when or where that law was made,
That law divine (a plausible pretence)
Oft urg'd with none, & oft with little sense,
From wisdom's source no origin could draw,
That form'd the man to keep the sex in awe;

Extract from poem by Susanna Wright, "To Eliza Norris—at Fairhill," in Pattie Cowell, ed., *Signs*, VI (1980–81), 799–800. Reprinted by permission of The University of Chicago Press.

Say Reason governs all the mighty frame,
And Reason rules in every one the same,
No right has man his equal to control,
Since, all agree, there is no sex in soul;
Weak woman, thus in agreement grown strong,
Shakes off the yoke her parents wore too long;
But he, who arguments in vain had tried,
Hopes still for conquest from the yielding side,
Soft soothing flattery & persuasion tries,
And by a feign'd submission seeks to rise,
Steals, unperceiv'd, to the unguarded heart,
    And there reigns tyrant.

. . .

Indulge man in his darling vice of sway,
He only rules those who of choice obey;
When strip'd of power, & plac'd in equal light,
Angels shall judge who had the better right,
All you can do is but to let him see
That woman still shall sure his equal be,
By your example shake his ancient law,
And shine yourself, the finish'd piece you draw.

The Sentiments of an American Woman, 1780

On the commencement of actual war, the Women of America manifested a firm resolution to contribute as much as could depend on them, to the deliverance of their country. Animated by the purest patriotism, they are sensible of sorrow at this day, in not offering more than barren wishes for the success of so glorious a Revolution. They aspire to render themselves more really useful ; and this sentiment is universal from the north to the south of the Thirteen United States. Our ambition is kindled by the fame of those heroines of antiquity, who have rendered their sex illustrious, and have proved to the universe, that, if the weakness of our Constitution, if opinion and manners did not forbid us to march to glory by the same paths as the Men, we should at least equal, and sometimes surpass them in our love for the public good. I glory in all that which my sex has done great and commendable. I call to mind with enthusiasm and with admiration, all those acts of courage, of constancy and patriotism, which history has transmitted to us : The people favoured by Heaven, preserved from destruction by the virtues, the zeal and the revolution of Deborah, of Judith, of Esther ! The fortitude of the mother of the Macchabees, in giving up her sons to die before her eyes : Rome saved from the fury of a victorious enemy by the efforts of Volumnia, and other Roman Ladies : So many famous sieges where the Women have been seen forgeting the weakness of their sex, building new walls, digging trenches with their feeble hands, furnishing arms to their defenders, they themselves darting the missile weapons on the enemy, resigning the ornaments of their apparel, and their fortune, to fill the public treasury, and to hasten the deliverance of their country ; burying themselves under its ruins ; throwing themselves into the flames rather than submit to the disgrace of humiliation before a proud enemy.

Born for liberty, disdaining to bear the irons of a tyrannic Government, we associate ourselves to the grandeur of those Sovereigns, cherished and revered, who have held with so much splendour the scepter of the greatest States, The Batildas, the Elizabeths, the Maries, the Catharines, who have extended the empire of liberty, and contented to reign by sweetness and justice, have broken the chains of slavery, forged by tyrants in the times of ignorance and barbarity. The Spanish Women, do they not make, at this moment, the most patriotic sacrifices, to encrease the means of victory in the hands of their Sovereign. He is a friend to the French Nation. They are our allies. We call to mind, doubly interested, that it was a French Maid who kindled up amongst her fellow-citizens, the flame of patriotism buried under long misfortunes : It was the Maid of Orleans who drove from the kingdom of France the ancestors of those same British, whose odious yoke we have just shaken off ; and whom it is necessary that we drive from this Continent.

But I must limit myself to the recollection of this small number of atchievements. Who knows if persons disposed to censure, and sometimes too severely with regard to us, may not disapprove our appearing acquainted even with the actions of which our sex boasts ? We are at least certain, that he cannot be a good citizen who will not applaud our efforts for the relief of the armies which defend our lives, our possessions, our liberty ? The situation of our soldiery has been represented to me; the evils inseparable from war, and the firm and generous spirit which has enabled them to support these. But it has been said, that they may apprehend, that, in the course of a long war, the view of their distresses may be lost, and their services be forgotten. Forgotten ! never ; I can answer in the name of all my sex. Brave Americans, your disinterestedness, your courage, and your constancy will always be dear to America, as long as she shall preserve her virtue.

We know that at a distance from the theatre of war, if we enjoy any tranquility, it is the fruit of your watchings, your labours, your dangers. If I live happy in the midst of my family ; if my husband cultivates his field, and reaps his harvest in peace ; if, surrounded with my children, I myself nourish the youngest, and press it to my bosom, without being affraid of seeing myself separated from it, by a ferocious enemy ; if the house in which we dwell ; if our barns, our orchards are safe at the present time from the hands of those incendiaries, it is to you that we owe it. And shall we hesitate to evidence to you our gratitude ? Shall we hesitate to wear a cloathing more simple ; hair dressed less elegant, while at the price of this small privation, we shall deserve your benedictions. Who, amongst us, will not renounce with the highest pleasure, those vain ornaments, when she shall consider that the valiant defenders of America will be able to draw some advantage from the money which she may have laid out in these ; that they will be better defended from the rigours of the seasons, that after their painful toils, they will receive some extraordinary and unexpected relief ; that these presents will perhaps be valued by them at a greater price, when they will have it in their power to say : *This is the offering of the Ladies.* The time is arrived to display the same sentiments which animated us at the beginning of the Revolution, when we renounced the use of teas, however agreeable to our taste, rather than receive them from our persecutors ; when we made it appear to them that we placed former necessaries in the rank of superfluities, when our liberty was interested ; when our republican and laborious hands spun the flax, prepared the linen intended for the use of our soldiers ; when exiles and fugitives we supported with courage all the evils which are the concomitants of war. Let us not lose a moment ; let us be engaged to offer the homage of our gratitude at the altar of military valour, and you, our brave deliverers, while mercenary slaves combat to cause you to share with them, the irons with which they are loaded, receive with a free hand our offering, the purest which can be presented to your virtue,

By an AMERICAN WOMAN
[Esther DeBerdt Reed]

Sarah Osborn's Narrative, 1837

That she was married to Aaron Osborn, who was a soldier during the Revolutionary War. That her first aquaintance with said Osborn commenced in Albany, in the state of New York, during the hard winter of 1780. That deponent then resided at the house of one John Willis, a blacksmith in said city. That said Osborn came down there from Fort Stanwix and went to work at the business of blacksmithing for said Willis and continued working at intervals for a period of perhaps two months. Said Osborn then informed deponent that he had first enlisted at Goshen in Orange County, New York. That he had been in the service for three years, deponent thinks, about one year of that time at Fort Stanwix, and that his time was out. And, under an assurance that he would go to Goshen with her, she married him at the house of said Willis during the time he was there as above mentioned, to wit, in January 1780. . . .

That after deponent had married said Osborn, he informed her that he was returned during the war, and that he desired deponent to go with him. Deponent declined until she was informed by Captain Gregg that her husband should be put on the commissary guard, and that she should have the means of conveyance either in a wagon or on horseback. That deponent then in the same winter season in sleighs accompanied her husband and the forces under command of Captain Gregg on the east side of the Hudson river to Fishkill, then crossed the river and went down to West Point. . . .

Deponent further says that she and her husband remained at West Point till the departure of the army for the South, a term of perhaps one year and a

Sarah Osborn, Narrative, 1837, in John Dann, ed., *The Revolution Remembered,* 1980, 241–246, The University of Chicago Press.

half, but she cannot be positive as to the length of time. While at West Point, deponent lived at Lieutenant Foot's, who kept a boardinghouse. Deponent was employed in washing and sewing for the soldiers. Her said husband was employed about the camp. . . .

When the army were about to leave West Point and go south, they crossed over the river to Robinson's Farms and remained there for a length of time to induce the belief, as deponent understood, that they were going to take up quarters there, whereas they recrossed the river in the nighttime into the Jerseys and traveled all night in a direct course for Philadelphia. Deponent was part of the time on horseback and part of the time in a wagon. Deponent's said husband was still serving as one of the commissary's guard. . . .

They continued their march to Philadelphia, deponent on horseback through the streets, and arrived at a place towards the Schuylkill where the British had burnt some houses, where they encamped for the afternoon and night. Being out of bread, deponent was employed in baking the afternoon and evening. Deponent recollects no females but Sergeant Lamberson's and Lieutenant Forman's wives and a colored woman by the name of Letta. The Quaker ladies who came round urged deponent to stay, but her said husband said, "No, he could not leave her behind." Accordingly, next day they continued their march from day to day till they arrived at Baltimore, where deponent and her said husband and the forces under command of General Clinton, Captain Gregg, and several other officers, all of whom she does not recollect, embarked on board a vessel and sailed down the Chesapeake. There were several vessels along, and deponent was in the foremost. . . . They continued sail until they had got up the St. James River as far as the tide would carry them, about twelve miles from the mouth, and then landed, and the tide being spent, they had a fine time catching sea lobsters, which they ate.

They, however, marched immediately for a place called Williamsburg, as she thinks, deponent alternately on horseback and on foot. There arrived, they remained two days till the army all came in by land and then marched for Yorktown, or Little York as it was then called. The York troops were posted at the right, the Connecticut troops next, and the French to the left. In about one day or less than a day, they reached the place of encampment about one mile from Yorktown. Deponent was on foot and the other females above named and her said husband still on the commissary's guard. Deponent's attention was arrested by the appearance of a large plain between them and Yorktown and an entrenchment thrown up. She also saw a number of dead Negroes lying round their encampment, whom she understood the British had driven out of the town and left to starve, or were first starved and then thrown out. Deponent took her stand just back of the American tents, say about a mile from the town, and busied herself washing, mending, and cooking for the soldiers, in which she was assisted by the other females; some men washed their own clothing. She heard the roar of the artillery for a number of days, and the last night the Americans threw up entrenchments, it was a misty, foggy night, rather wet but not rainy. Every soldier threw up for himself, as she understood, and she afterwards saw and went into the entrenchments. Deponent's said husband was there throwing up entrenchments, and deponent cooked and carried in beef, and bread, and coffee (in a gallon pot) to the soldiers in the entrenchment.

On one occasion when deponent was thus employed carrying in provisions, she met General Washington, who asked her if she "was not afraid of the cannonballs?"

She replied, "No, the bullets would not cheat the gallows," that "It would not do for the men to fight and starve too."

They dug entrenchments nearer and nearer to Yorktown every night or two till the last. While digging that, the enemy fired very heavy till about nine o'clock next morning, then stopped, and the drums from the enemy beat excessively. . . .

All at once the officers hurrahed and swung their hats, and deponent asked them, "What is the matter now?"

One of them replied, "Are not you soldier enough to know what it means?"

Deponent replied, "No."

They then replied, "The British have surrendered."

Deponent, having provisions ready, carried the same down to the entrenchments that morning, and four of the soldiers whom she was in the habit of cooking for ate their breakfasts.

Deponent stood on one side of the road and the American officers upon the other side when the British officers came out of the town and rode up to the American officers and delivered up [their swords, which the deponent] thinks were returned again, and the British officers rode right on before the army, who marched out beating and playing a melancholy tune, their drums covered with black handkerchiefs and their fifes with black ribbands tied around them, into an old field and there grounded their arms and then returned into town again to await their destiny. . . .

On going into town, she noticed two dead Negroes lying by the market house. She had the curiosity to go into a large building that stood nearby, and there she noticed the cupboards smashed to pieces and china dishes and other ware strewed around upon the floor, and among the rest a pewter cover to a hot basin that had a handle on it. She picked it up, supposing it to belong to the British, but the governor came in and claimed it as his, but said he would have the name of giving it away as it was the last one out of twelve that he could see, and accordingly presented it to deponent, and she afterwards brought it home with her to Orange County and sold it for old pewter, which she has a hundred times regretted.

African Americans in the Revolutionary Age

Prince Hall 1735?–1807

If Prince Hall had not actually lived, he most certainly would have been invented— which is to say that the pioneering socialization he achieved for and among early black Americans would have been realized sooner or later by some colonial black American. Whether in seemingly passive enslavement or as modestly protesting free persons, blacks were clearly too vital, too fundamentally hardy, to have long been excluded from dignified social groupings, and, thereafter, from variously finding their own American way.

Hall organized some fourteen free black Bostonians in 1775 into a society that eventually became an official, degree-granting Masonic order, "African Lodge No. 459" (later No. 370) on May 6, 1787. As Master of this first lodge, Hall continued his work and brought together an association of black Masonic Grand Lodges that would proliferate into what is today a flourishing, worldwide fraternal society. (In 1977 there were more than 500,000 members of such lodges.) Hall is also remembered as one of the more prolific writers of early black America.

Born sometime between 1735 and 1738 at a place still unknown, Hall seems to have been a slave or indentured servant in the Boston household of leather-dresser William Hall from 1749 until 1770, when he was freed. Thereafter he made a decent living as a leather-dresser, caterer, and perhaps as a shop owner. From the year 1762, Hall was a member of the Reverend Andrew Crosswell's Congregational church on School Street, and "in full communication therewith, for a number of years," he may well have functioned as an unordained preacher to fellow Masons and other interested blacks on the premises of the School Street church, which was abandoned in 1764, when an epidemic of small pox struck Boston.

In his own home for most of 1789, Hall housed the Reverend John Marrant (1755–1791), then enroute back to his chosen home in London from a lengthy preaching tour of Eastern Canada. In London in 1785, Marrant had become the first black American ordained minister. Hall also made Marrant a chaplain for his Lodge; for the Lodge Marrant preached at Fanueil Hall an inspirational sermon published later that year.

From 1777 until four months before his death in December, 1807, Prince Hall composed and published a group of writings, including letters to London Masonic officials, the Countess of Huntingdon, Boston newspapers, and prominent blacks in Providence and Philadelphia, but most notably he published a series of petitions on behalf of his Masons and free blacks in general. He solicited the abolition of Massachusetts slavery (1777). He petitioned for the proffered but rejected military assistance of some 700 blacks for use by Governor James Bowdoin (who was trying to put down Shays's Rebellion in the western part of the state, 1786). In January of 1787, with 73 other blacks, Hall petitioned the General Court for financial or other assistance in support of plans for blacks to emigrate to Africa. In October of that year, he petitioned, unsuccessfully, for public education for children of taxpaying Boston blacks. Hall himself is on record in the "Taxing Books" as having paid both real estate and poll taxes from 1780 onwards. He also petitioned, this time successfully, on behalf of three Boston blacks who were kidnapped into slavery but quickly released (1788). In 1792, he published a racially stimulating Charge to fellow Lodge members; in 1797 he published another such Charge. On May 6, 1806, Hall and a white man, John Vinal of Boston, once a member of Hall's School Street church, gave a deposition acknowledging joint receipt of three thousand dollars for the sale of the church property. Finally, on August 31, 1807, Hall signed another deposition, in effect a testimony of Vinal's character; both of these depositions remain in manuscript.

Prince Hall was much concerned with the organization and dignifying of his fellow Masons, to be sure, but he was just as concerned with the future of the enslaved black American: because black slavery was primarily a white American issue, he was necessarily concerned with the future of America and Americans.

William H. Robinson
Brown University

SECONDARY WORKS

Sidney Kaplan, "Prince Hall: Organizer," in *The Black Presence in the Era of The American Revolution 1770–1800,* 1973; Charles H. Wesley, *Prince Hall: Life and Legacy,* 1977; Joseph A. Walker, *Black Squares & Compass/200 Years of Prince Hall/Freemasonry,* 1979.

To the Honorable Council & House of Representatives for the State of Massachusetts-Bay in General Court assembled January 13th 1777.[1]

The Petition of a great number of Negroes who are detained in a state of Slavery in the Bowels of a free & Christian Country Humbly Shewing

That your Petitioners apprehend that they have, in common with all other Men, a natural & unalienable right to that freedom, which the great Parent of the Universe hath bestowed equally on all Mankind, & which they have never forfeited by any compact or agreement whatever—But they were unjustly dragged, by the cruel hand of Power, from their dearest friends, & some of them even torn from the embraces of their tender Parents. From a populous, pleasant and plentiful Country—& in Violation of the Laws of Nature & of Nation & in defiance of all the tender feelings of humanity, brought hither to be sold like Beasts of Burden, & like them condemned to slavery for Life—Among a People professing the mild Religion of Jesus—A People not insensible of the sweets of rational freedom—Nor without spirit to resent the unjust endeavours of others to reduce them to a State of Bondage & Subjection—Your Honors need not to be informed that a Life of Slavery, like that of your petitioners, deprived of every social privilege, of every thing requisite to render Life even tolerable, is far worse than Non-Existence—In imitation of the laudable example of the good People of these States, your Petitioners have long & patiently waited the event of Petition after Petition by them presented to the legislative Body of this State, & can not but with grief reflect that their success has been but too similar—They can not but express their astonishment, that it has never been considered, that every principle from which America has acted in the course of her unhappy difficulties with Great-Britain, pleads stronger than a thousand arguments in favor of your Petitioners. They therefore humbly beseech your Honors, to give this Petition its due weight & consideration, & cause an Act of the Legislature to be passed, whereby they may be restored to the enjoyment of that freedom which is the natural right of all Men—& their Children (who were born in this Land of Liberty) may not be held as Slaves after they arrive at the age of twenty one years—So may the Inhabitants of this State (no longer chargeable with the inconsistency of acting, themselves, the part which they condemn & oppose in others) be prospered in their present glorious struggles for Liberty; & have those blessings secured to them by Heaven, of which benevolent minds can not wish to deprive their fellow Men.

[1] This is from a typescript of an "improved" version, on file at the Massachusetts Archives, volume 212, p. 132; an original, semi-complete version was published by Jeremy Belknap in the *Massachusetts Historical Collections. Fifth Series, No. 3* (Boston, 1788).

And your Petitioners, as in Duty Bound shall ever pray.

Lancaster Hill
Peter Bess
Brister Slenten
Prince Hall
Jack Purpont *his mark*

Nero Suneto *his mark*

Newport Symner *his mark*

Job Lock

Negroes Petition to the Honble
Gen¹Assembly—Mass.
March 18
Judge Sargeant
M. Balton
M. Appleton
Coll. Brooks
M. Stony
W. Lowell
Matter Atlege
W. Davis

1788

Gustavus Vassa (Olaudah Equiano) 1745–1797

Olaudah Equiano and his sister were kidnapped in Africa, in what is present-day Nigeria. The eleven-year-old Equiano was later separated from his sister and placed aboard a slave ship headed for the West Indies. After experiencing the horrors of the Middle Passage, Equiano arrived in Barbados and was soon transported to Virginia, where he was purchased by a British captain for service aboard his ship; thus Equiano was spared the harsh plantation life most slaves were sentenced to upon their arrival in the New World.

Eventually, Equiano was given the name of Gustavus Vassa, which was, ironically, the name of a Swedish freedom fighter. Equiano remained a slave for almost ten years, serving on various vessels engaged in commerce and sometimes in naval warfare along the coast of Europe and in the Mediterranean. He crossed the Atlantic many times on voyages to the American colonies and the Caribbean islands. All the while, the young slave worked on his own at profit-making ventures, in order to accumulate enough money to buy his freedom—which he was able to do despite many troubles and false hopes. Equiano became a free man on July 10, 1766. He continued his life at sea for many years, sailing on exploratory expeditions to the Arctic and to Central America and on numerous seagoing business enterprises, including the transporting of slaves. During this time, Equiano witnessed the deepest cruelties of slavery and its dire effects on men and women in several areas of the world. He became a kind of Gulliver, traveling to distant places and observing the strange and awful practices of people in many lands.

Equiano's friends in England and on the sailing vessels taught him to read and write and introduced him to Christianity. In his later years, Equiano settled in England, where his Christian faith deepened and where he furthered his education. Equiano was involved in the controversial and disastrous undertaking in 1787 to send poor blacks to Sierra Leone. His objections to the mismanagement of the project caused his dismissal from his commissary role and drew criticism from many quarters. He recovered from this debacle, however, and later, when the abolition of the slave trade became a fiery issue in Parliament, Equiano dedicated himself to the anti-slavery cause by visiting abolitionist leaders and writing letters to newspapers and important officials, including a lengthy letter to Queen Charlotte. His most important contribution was the publication in England and the United States of his well-written and fascinating two-volume autobiography, *The Interesting Narrative of Olaudah Equiano,* subscribed to by many of the key men and women in the abolitionist crusade. The work was widely read, translated into several languages, and published well into the nineteenth century on both sides of the Atlantic. Several editions were printed, some of them including poems by Phillis Wheatley. The Methodist founder, John Wesley, had high regard for Equiano's work: on his deathbed, Wesley requested that Equiano's autobiography be read to him. In 1792, a news item appeared in the *Gentleman's Magazine* announcing the marriage of Englishwoman Susanna Cullen and Olaudah Equiano. Two daughters were born to the couple in the next few years. Equiano died on March 31, 1797.

Equiano's autobiography was the prototype of the slave narratives of the nineteenth century. It set the pattern for the countless narratives—both nonfictional and fictional—that have influenced American literature down to the present day. Equiano followed the spiritual autobiographical tradition of his day derived from Augustine and Bunyan and adapted by Puritans and later by his Quaker contemporaries. Yet Equiano added to the genre a new dimension—that of social protest. In addition, his use of irony in the depiction of himself as an enterprising character places his work in the secular autobiographical tradition established by Benjamin Franklin.

Angelo Costanzo
Shippensburg University of Pennsylvania

PRIMARY WORKS

The Interesting Narrative of the Life of Olaudah Equiano, or Gustavus Vassa, the African, 1789.

SECONDARY WORKS

Paul Edwards, *The Life of Olaudah Equiano,* 1969; Angelo Costanzo, *Surprizing Narrative: Olaudah Equiano and the Beginnings of Black Autobiography,* 1987.

from The Interesting Narrative of the Life of Olaudah Equiano, or Gustavus Vassa, the African. Written by Himself.

Chapter 2

I hope the reader will not think I have trespassed on his patience in introducing myself to him, with some account of the manners and customs of my country. They had been implanted in me with great care, and made an impression on my mind, which time could not erase, and which all the adversity and variety of fortune I have since experienced, served only to rivet and record: for, whether the love of one's country be real or imaginary, or a lesson of reason, or an instinct of nature, I still look back with pleasure on the first scenes of my life, though that pleasure has been for the most part mingled with sorrow.

I have already acquainted the reader with the time and place of my birth. My father, besides many slaves, had a numerous family, of which seven lived to grow up, including myself and sister, who was the only daughter. As I was the youngest of the sons, I became, of course, the greatest favorite with my mother, and was always with her; and she used to take particular pains to form my mind. I was trained up from my earliest years in the art of war: my daily exercise was shooting and throwing javelins, and my mother adorned me with emblems, after the manner of our greatest warriors. In this way I grew up till I had turned the age of eleven, when an end was put to my happiness in the following manner: Generally, when the grown people in the neighborhood were gone far in the fields to labor, the children assembled together in some of the neighboring premises to play; and commonly some of us used to get up a tree to look out for any assailant, or kidnapper, that might come upon us—for they sometimes took those opportunities of our parents' absence, to attack and carry off as many as they could seize. One day as I was watching at the top of a tree in our yard, I saw one of those people come into the yard of our next neighbor but one, to kidnap, there being many stout young people in it. Immediately on this I gave the alarm of the rogue, and he was surrounded by the stoutest of them, who entangled him with cords, so that he could not escape, till some of the grown people came and secured him. But, alas! ere long it was my fate to be thus attacked, and to be carried off, when none of the grown people were nigh. One day, when all our people were gone out to their works as usual, and only I and my dear sister were left to mind the house, two men and a woman got over our walls, and in a moment seized us both, and, without giving us time to cry out, or make resistance, they stopped our mouths, and ran off with us into the nearest wood. Here they tied our hands, and continued to carry us as far as they could, till night came on, when we reached a small house, where the robbers halted for refreshment, and spent the night. We were then unbound, but were unable to take any food; and, being quite overpowered by fatigue and grief, our only relief was some sleep, which allayed our misfortune for a short time. The next morning we left the house, and continued travelling all the day. For a long time we had kept the woods, but at last we came into a road which I believed I knew. I had now some hopes of being delivered; for we had advanced but a little way before I discovered some people at a distance, on which I began to cry out for their assistance; but my cries had no other effect than to make them tie me faster and stop my mouth, and then they put me into a large sack. They also stopped my sister's mouth, and tied her hands; and in this manner we proceeded till we were out of sight of these people. When we went to rest the following night, they offered us some victuals, but we refused it and the only comfort we had was in being in one another's arms all that night, and bathing each other with our tears. But alas we were soon deprived of even the small comfort of weeping together. The next day proved a day of greater sorrow than I had yet experienced; for my sister and I were then separated, while we lay clasped in each other's arms. It was in vain that we had sought them not to part us; she was torn from me, and immediately carried away, while I was left in a state of distraction not to be described. I cried and grieved continually; and for several days did not eat anything but what they forced into my mouth. At length, after many days' travelling, during which I had often changed masters, I got into the hands of a chieftain, in a very pleasant country. This man had two wives and some children, and they all used me extremely well, and did all they could do to comfort me; particularly the first wife, who was something like my mother. Although I was a great many days' journey from my father's house, yet these people spoke exactly the same language with us. This first master of mine, as I may call him, was a smith, and my principal employment was working his bellows, which were the same kind as I had seen in my vicinity. They were in some respects not unlike the stoves here in gentlemen's kitchens, and were covered over with leather; and in the middle of that leather a stick was fixed, and a person stood up, and worked it in the same manner as is done to pump water out of a cask with a hand pump. I believe it was gold he worked, for it was of a lovely bright yellow color, and was worn by the women on their wrists and ankles. I was there I suppose about a month, and they at last used to trust me some little distance from the house. This liberty I used in embracing every opportunity to inquire the way to my own home; and I also sometimes, for the same purpose, went with the maidens, in the cool of the evenings, to bring pitchers of water from the springs for the use of the house. I had also remarked where the sun rose in the morning, and set in the evening, as I had travelled along; and I had observed that my father's house was towards the rising of the sun. I therefore determined to seize the first opportunity of making my escape, and to shape my course for that quarter; for I was quite oppressed and weighed down by grief after my mother and friends; and my love of liberty, ever great, was strengthened by the mortifying circumstance of not daring to eat with the free-born children, although I was mostly their companion. While I was projecting my escape one day, an unlucky event happened, which quite disconcerted my plan, and put an end to my hopes. I used to be sometimes employed in assisting an elderly slave to cook and take care of the poultry; and one morning, while I was feeding some chickens, I happened to toss a small pebble at one of them, which hit it on the middle, and directly killed it. The old slave, having soon after missed the chicken, inquired after it; and on my relating the accident (for I told her the truth, for my mother would never suffer me to tell a lie), she flew into a violent passion, and threatened that I should suffer for it; and, my master being out, she immediately went and told her mistress what I had done. This alarmed me very much, and I expected an instant flogging, which to me was uncommonly dreadful, for I had seldom been beaten at home. I therefore resolved to fly; and accordingly I ran into a thicket that was hard by, and hid myself in the bushes. Soon afterwards my mistress and the slave returned, and, not seeing me, they searched all the house, but not finding me, and I not making answer when they called to me, they thought I had run away, and the whole neighborhood was raised in the pursuit of me. In that part of the country, as in ours, the houses and villages were skirted with woods, or shrubberies, and the bushes were so thick that a man could readily conceal himself in them, so as to elude the strictest search. The neighbors continued the whole day looking for me, and several times many of them came within a few yards of the place where I lay hid. I expected every moment, when I heard a rustling among the trees, to be found out, and punished by my master; but they never discovered me, though they were often so near that I even heard their conjectures as they were looking about for me; and I now learned from them that any attempts to return home would be hopeless. Most of them supposed I had fled towards home; but the distance was so great, and the way so intricate, that they thought I could never reach it, and that I should be lost in the woods. When I heard this I was seized with a violent panic, and abandoned myself to despair. Night, too, began to approach, and aggravated all my fears. I had before entertained hopes of getting home, and had determined when it should be dark to make the attempt; but I was now convinced it was fruitless, and began to consider that, if possibly I could escape all other animals, I could not those of the human kind; and that, not knowing the way, I must perish in the woods. Thus was I like the hunted deer—

——Every leaf and every whisp'ring breath,
Convey'd a foe, and every foe a death.

I heard frequent rustlings among the leaves, and being pretty sure they were snakes, I expected every instant to be stung by them. This increased my anguish, and the horror of my situation became now quite insupportable. I at length quitted the thicket, very faint and hungry, for I had not eaten or drank anything all the day, and crept to my master's kitchen, from whence I set out at first, which was an open shed, and laid myself down in the ashes with an anxious wish for death, to relieve me from all my pains. I was scarcely awake in the morning, when the old woman slave, who was the first up, came to light the fire, and saw me in the fireplace. She was very much surprised to see me, and could scarcely believe her own eyes. She now promised to intercede for me, and went for her master, who soon after came, and, having slightly reprimanded me, ordered me to be taken care of, and not ill treated.

Soon after this, my master's only daughter, and child by his first wife, sickened and died, which affected him so much that for sometime he was almost frantic, and really would have killed himself, had he not been watched and prevented. However, in a short time afterwards he recovered, and I was again sold. I was now carried to the left of the sun's rising, through many dreary wastes and dismal woods, amidst the hideous roarings of wild beasts. The people I was sold to used to carry me very often, when I was tired, either on their shoulders or on their backs. I saw many convenient well-built sheds along the road, at proper distances, to accommodate the merchants and travellers, who lay in those buildings along with their wives, who often accompany them; and they always go well armed.

From the time I left my own nation, I always found somebody that understood me till I came to the sea coast. The languages of different nations did not totally differ, nor were they so copious as those of the Europeans, particularly the English. They were therefore, easily learned; and, while I was journeying thus through Africa, I acquired two or three different tongues. In this manner I had been travelling for a considerable time, when, one evening, to my great surprise, whom should I see brought to the house where I was but my dear sister! As soon as she saw me, she gave a loud shriek, and ran into my arms—I was quite overpowered; neither of us could speak, but, for a considerable time, clung to each other in mutual embraces, unable to do anything but weep. Our meeting affected all who saw us; and, indeed, I must acknowledge, in honor of those sable destroyers of human rights, that I never met with any ill treatment, or saw any offered to their slaves, except tying them, when necessary, to keep them from running away. When these people knew we were brother and sister, they indulged us to be together; and the man, to whom I supposed we belonged, lay with us, he in the middle, while she and I held one another by the hands across his breast all night; and thus for a while we forgot our misfortunes, in the joy of being together; but even this small comfort was soon to have an end; for scarcely had the fatal morning appeared when she was again torn from me forever! I was now more miserable, if possible, than before. The small relief which her presence gave me from pain, was gone, and the wretchedness of my situation was redoubled by my anxiety after her fate, and my apprehensions lest her sufferings should be greater than mine, when I could not be with her to alleviate them. Yes, thou dear partner of all my childish sports! thou sharer of my joys and sorrows! happy should I have ever esteemed myself to encounter every misery for you and to procure your freedom by the sacrifice of my own. Though you were early forced from my arms, your image has been always riveted in my heart, from which neither time nor fortune have been able to remove it; so that, while the thoughts of your sufferings have damped my prosperity, they have mingled with adversity and increased its bitterness. To that Heaven which protects the weak from the strong, I commit the care of your innocence and virtues, if they have not already received their full reward, and if your youth and delicacy have not long since fallen victims to the violence of the African trader, the pestilential stench of a Guinea ship, the seasoning in the European colonies or the lash and lust of a brutal and unrelenting overseer.

I did not long remain after my sister. I was again sold, and carried through a number of places, till after travelling a considerable time, I came to a town called Tinmah, in the most beautiful country I had yet seen in Africa. It was extremely rich, and there were many rivulets which flowed through it, and supplied a large pond in the centre of the town, where the people washed. Here I first saw and tasted cocoanuts, which I thought superior to any nuts I had ever tasted before; and the trees, which were loaded, were also interspersed among the houses, which had commodious shades adjoining, and were in the same manner as ours, the insides being neatly plastered and whitewashed. Here I also saw and tasted for the first time, sugar-cane. Their money consisted of little white shells, the size of the finger nail. I was sold here for one hundred and seventy-two of them, by a merchant who lived and brought me there. I had been about two or three days at his house, when a wealthy widow, a neighbor of his, came there one evening, and brought with her an only son, a young gentleman about my own age and size. Here they saw me; and, having taken a fancy to me, I was bought of the merchant, and went home with them. Her house and premises were situated close to one of those rivulets I have mentioned, and were the finest I ever saw in Africa: they were very extensive, and she had a number of slaves to attend her. The next day I was washed and perfumed, and when meal time came, I was led into the presence of my mistress, and ate and drank before her with her son. This filled me with astonishment; and I could scarce help expressing my surprise that the young gentleman should suffer me, who was bound, to eat with him who was free; and not only so, but that he would not at any time either eat or drink till I had taken first, because I was the eldest, which was agreeable to our custom. Indeed, every thing here, and all their treatment of me, made me forget that I was a slave. The language of these people resembled ours so nearly, that we understood each other perfectly. They had also the very same customs as we. There were likewise slaves daily to attend us, while my young master and I, with other boys, sported with our darts and bows and arrows, as I had been used to do at home. In this resemblance to my former happy state, I passed about two months; and I now began to think I was to be adopted into the family, and was beginning to be reconciled to my situation, and to forget by degrees my misfortunes, when all at once the delusion vanished; for, without the least previous knowledge, one morning early, while my dear master and companion was still asleep, I was awakened out of my reverie to fresh sorrow, and hurried away even amongst the uncircumcised.

Thus, at the very moment I dreamed of the greatest happiness, I found myself most miserable; and it seemed as if fortune wished to give me this taste of joy only to render the reverse more poignant. The change I now experienced was as painful as it was sudden and unexpected. It was a change indeed, from a state of bliss to a scene which is inexpressible by me, as it discovered to me an element I had never before beheld, and till then had no idea of, and wherein such instances of hardship and cruelty continually occurred, as I can never reflect on but with horror.

All the nations and people I had hitherto passed through, resembled our own in their manners, customs, and language; but I came at length to a country, the inhabitants of which differed from us in all those particulars. I was very much struck with this difference, especially when I came among a people who did not circumcise, and ate without washing their hands. They cooked also in iron pots, and had European cutlasses and cross bows, which were unknown to us, and fought with their fists among themselves. Their women were not so modest as ours, for they ate, and drank, and slept with their men. But above all, I was amazed to see no sacrifices or offerings among them. In some of those places the people ornamented themselves with scars, and likewise filed their teeth very sharp. They wanted sometimes to ornament me in the same manner, but I would not suffer them; hoping that I might some time be among a people who did not thus disfigure themselves, as I thought they did. At last I came to the banks of a large river which was covered with canoes, in which the people appeared to live with their household utensils and provisions of all kinds. I was beyond measure astonished at this, as I had never before seen any water larger than a pond or a rivulet; and my surprise was mingled with no small fear when I was put into one of these canoes, and we began to paddle and move along the river. We continued going on thus till night, and when we came to land, and made fires on the banks, each family by themselves; some dragged their canoes on shore, others stayed and cooked in theirs, and laid in them all night. Those on the land had mats, of which they made tents, some in the shape of little houses; in these we slept; and after the morning meal, we embarked again and proceeded as before. I was often very much astonished to see some of the women, as well as the men, jump into the water, dive to the bottom, come up again, and swim about. Thus I continued to travel, sometimes by land, sometimes by water, through different countries and various nations, till the end of six or seven months after I had been kidnapped, I arrived at the sea coast. It would be tedious and uninteresting to relate all the incidents which befell me during this journey, and which I have not yet forgotten; of the various hands I passed through, and the manners and customs of all the different people among whom I lived—I shall therefore only observe, that in all the places where I was, the soil was exceedingly rich; the pumpkins, eadas, plantains, yams, &c. &c., were in great abundance, and of incredible size. There were also vast quantities of different gums, though not used for any purpose, and everywhere a great deal of tobacco. The cotton even grew quite wild, and there was plenty of red-wood. I saw no mechanics whatever in all the way, except such as I have mentioned. The chief employment in all these countries was agriculture, and both the males and females, as with us, were brought up to it, and trained in the arts of war.

The first object which saluted my eyes when I arrived on the coast, was the sea, and a slave ship, which was then riding at anchor, and waiting for its cargo. These filled me with astonishment, which was soon converted into terror, when I was carried on board. I was immediately handled, and tossed up to see if I were sound, by some of the crew; and I was now persuaded that I had gotten into a world of bad spirits, and that they were going to kill me. Their complexions, too, differing so much from ours, their long hair, and the language they spoke (which was very different from any I had ever heard), united to confirm me in this belief. Indeed, such were the horrors of my views and fears at the moment, that, if ten thousand worlds had been my own, I would have freely parted with them all to have exchanged my condition with that of the meanest slave in my own country. When I looked round the ship too, and saw a large furnace of copper boiling, and a multitude of black people of every description chained together, every one of their countenances expressing dejection and sorrow, I no longer doubted of my fate; and, quite overpowered with horror and anguish, I fell motionless on the deck and fainted. When I recovered a little, I found some black people about me, who I believed were some of those who had brought me on board, and had been receiving their pay; they talked to me in order to cheer me, but all in vain. I asked them if we were not to be eaten by those white men with horrible looks, red faces, and long hair. They told me I was not, and one of the crew brought me a small portion of spirituous liquor in a wine glass; but, being afraid of him, I would not take it out of his hand. One of the blacks, therefore, took it from him and gave it to me, and I took a little down my palate, which, instead of reviving me, as they thought it would, threw me into the greatest consternation at the strange feeling it produced, having never tasted any such liquor before. Soon after this, the blacks who brought me on board went off, and left me abandoned to despair.

I now saw myself deprived of all chance of returning to my native country, or even the least glimpse of hope of gaining the shore, which I now considered as friendly; and I even wished for my former slavery in preference to my present situation, which was filled with horrors of every kind, still heightened by my ignorance of what I was to undergo. I was not long suffered to indulge my grief; I was soon put down under the decks, and there I received such a salutation in my nostrils as I had never experienced in my life: so that, with the loathsomeness of the stench, and crying together, I became so sick and low that I was not able to eat, nor had I the least desire to taste anything. I now wished for the last friend, death, to relieve me; but soon, to my grief, two of the white men offered me eatables; and, on my refusing to eat, one of them held me fast by the hands, and laid me across, I think, the windlass, and tied my feet, while the other flogged me severely. I had never experienced anything of this kind before, and, although not being used to the water, I naturally feared that element the first time I saw it, yet, nevertheless, could I have got over the nettings, I would have jumped over the side, but I could not; and besides, the crew used to watch us very closely who were not chained down to the decks, lest we should leap into the water; and I have seen some of these poor African prisoners most severely cut, for attempting to do so, and hourly whipped for not eating. This indeed was often the case with myself. In a little time after, amongst the poor chained men, I found some of my own nation, which in a small degree gave ease to my mind. I inquired of these what was to be done with us? They gave me to understand, we were to be carried to these white people's country to work for them. I then was a little revived, and thought, if it were no worse than working, my situation was not so desperate; but still I feared I should be put to death, the white people looked and acted, as I thought, in so savage a manner; for I had never seen among any people such instances of brutal cruelty; and this not only shown towards us blacks, but also to some of the whites themselves. One white man in particular I saw, when we were permitted to be on deck, flogged so unmercifully with a large rope near the foremast, that he died in consequence of it; and they tossed him over the side as they would have done a brute. This made me fear these people the more; and I expected nothing less than to be treated in the same manner. I could not help expressing my fears and apprehensions to some of my countrymen; I asked them if these people had no country, but lived in this hollow place (the ship)? They told me they did not, but came from a distant one. "Then," said I, "how comes it in all our country we never heard of them?" They told me because they lived so very far off. I then asked where were their women? had they any like themselves? I was told they had. "And why," said I, "do we not see them?" They answered, because they were left behind. I asked how the vessel could go? They told me they could not tell; but that there was cloth put upon the masts by the help of the ropes I saw, and then the vessel went on; and the white men had some spell or magic they put in the water when they liked, in order to stop the vessel. I·was exceedingly amazed at this account, and really thought they were spirits. I therefore wished much to be from amongst them, for I expected they would sacrifice me; but my wishes were vain—for we were so quartered that it was impossible for any of us to make our escape.

While we stayed on the coast I was mostly on deck; and one day, to my great astonishment, I saw one of these vessels coming in with the sails up. As soon as the whites saw it, they gave a great shout, at which we were amazed; and the more so, as the vessel appeared larger by approaching nearer. At last, she came to an anchor in my sight, and when the anchor was let go, I and my countrymen who saw it, were lost in astonishment to observe the vessel stop—and were now convinced it was done by magic. Soon after this the other ship got her boats out, and they came on board of us, and the people of both ships seemed very glad to see each other. Several of the strangers also shook hands with us black people, and made motions with their hands, signifying I suppose, we were to go to their country, but we did not understand them.

· At last when the ship we were in, had got in all her cargo, they made ready with many fearful noises, and we were all put under deck, so that we could not see how they managed the vessel. But this disappointment was the least of my sorrow. The stench of the hold while we were on the coast was so intolerably loathsome, that it was dangerous to remain there for any time, and some of us had been permitted to stay on the deck for the fresh air; but now that the whole ship's cargo were confined together, it became absolutely pestilential. The closeness of the place, and the heat of the climate, added to the number in the ship, which was so crowded that each had scarcely room to turn himself, almost suffocated us. This produced copious perspirations, so that the air soon became unfit for respiration, from a variety of loathsome smells, and brought on a sickness among the slaves, of which many died—thus falling victims to the improvident avarice, as I may call it, of their purchasers. This wretched situation was again aggravated by the galling of the chains, now became insupportable, and the filth of the necessary tubs, into which the children often fell, and were almost suffocated. The shrieks of the women, and the groans of the dying, rendered the whole a scene of horror almost inconceivable. Happily perhaps, for myself, I was soon reduced so low here that it was thought necessary to keep me almost always on deck; and from my extreme youth I was not put in fetters. In this situation I expected every hour to share the fate of my companions, some of whom were almost daily brought upon deck at the point of death, which I began to hope would soon put an end to my miseries. Often did I think many of the inhabitants of the deep much more happy than myself. I envied them the freedom they enjoyed, and as often wished I could change my condition for theirs. Every circumstance I met with, served only to render my state more painful, and heightened my apprehensions, and my opinion of the cruelty of the whites.

One day they had taken a number of fishes; and when they had killed and satisfied themselves with as many as they thought fit, to our astonishment who were on deck, rather than give any of them to us to eat, as we expected, they tossed the remaining fish into the sea again, although we begged and prayed for some as well as we could, but in vain; and some of my country men, being pressed by hunger, took an opportunity, when they thought no one saw them, of trying to get a little privately; but they were discovered, and the attempt procured them some very severe floggings. One day, when we had a smooth sea and moderate wind, two of my wearied countrymen who were chained together (I was near them at the time), preferring death to such a life of misery, somehow made through the nettings and jumped into the sea; immediately, another quite dejected fellow, who, on account of his illness, was suffered to be out of irons, also followed their example; and I believe many more would very soon have done the same, if they had not been prevented by the ship's crew, who were instantly alarmed. Those of us that were the most active, were in a moment put down under the deck; and there was such a noise and confusion amongst the people of the ship as I never heard before, to stop her, and get the boat out to go after the slaves. However, two of the wretches were drowned, but they got the other, and afterwards flogged him unmercifully, for thus attempting to prefer death to slavery. In this manner we continued to undergo more hardships than I can now relate, hardships which are inseparable from this accursed trade. Many a time we were near suffocation from the want of fresh air, which we were often without for whole days together. This, and the stench of the necessary tubs, carried off many.

During our passage, I first saw flying fishes, which surprised me very much; they used frequently to fly across the ship, and many of them fell on the deck. I also now first saw the use of the quadrant; I had often with astonishment seen the mariners make observations with it, and I could not think what it meant. They at last took notice of my surprise; and one of them, willing to increase it, as well as to gratify my curiosity, made me one day look through it. The clouds appeared to me to be land, which disappeared as they passed along. This heightened my wonder; and I was now more persuaded than ever, that I was in another world, and that every thing about me was magic. At last, we came in sight of the island of Barbadoes, at which the whites on board gave a great shout, and made many signs of joy to us. We did not know what to think of this; but as the vessel drew nearer, we plainly saw the harbor, and other ships of different kinds and sizes, and we soon anchored amongst them, off Bridgetown. Many merchants and planters now came on board, though it was in the evening. They put us in separate parcels, and examined us attentively. They also made us jump, and pointed to the land, signifying we were to go there. We thought by this, we should be eaten by these ugly men, as they appeared to us; and, when soon after we were all put down under the deck again, there was much dread and trembling among us, and nothing but bitter cries to be heard all the night from these apprehensions, insomuch, that at last the white people got some old slaves from the land to pacify us. They told us we were not to be eaten, but to work, and were soon to go on land, where we should see many of our country people. This report eased us much. And sure enough, soon after we were landed, there came to us Africans of all languages.

We were conducted immediately to the merchant's yard, where we were all pent up together, like so many sheep in a fold, without regard to sex or age. As every object was new to me, everything I saw filled me with surprise. What struck me first, was, that the houses were built with bricks and stories, and in every other respect different from those I had seen in Africa; but I was still more astonished on seeing people on horseback. I did not know what this could mean; and, indeed, I thought these people were full of nothing but magical arts. While I was in this astonishment, one of my fellow prisoners spoke to a countryman of his, about the horses, who said they were the same kind they had in their country. I understood them, though they were from a distant part of Africa; and I thought it odd I had not seen any horses there; but afterwards, when I came to converse with different Africans, I found they had many horses amongst them, and much larger than those I then saw.

We were not many days in the merchant's custody, before we were sold after their usual manner, which is this: On a signal given (as the beat of a drum), the buyers rush at once into the yard where the slaves are confined, and make choice of that parcel they like best. The noise and clamor with which this is attended and the eagerness visible in the countenances of the buyers, serve not a little to increase the apprehension of terrified Africans, who may well be supposed to consider them as the ministers of the destruction to which they think themselves devoted. In this manner, without scruple, are relations and friends separated, most of them never to see each other again. I remember, in the vessel in which I was brought over, in the men's apartment, there were several brothers, who, in the sale, were sold in different lots; and it was very moving on this occasion, to see and hear their cries at parting. O, ye nominal Christians! might not an African ask you—Learned you this from your God, who says unto you, Do unto all men as you would men should do unto you? Is it not enough that we are torn from our country and friends, to toil for your luxury and lust of gain? Must every tender feeling be likewise sacrificed to your avarice? Are the dearest friends and relations, now rendered more dear by their separation from their kindred, still to be parted from each other, and thus prevented from cheering the gloom of slavery, with the small comfort of being together, and mingling their sufferings and sorrows? Why are parents to lose their children, brothers their sisters, or husbands their wives? Surely, this is a new refinement in cruelty, which, while it has no advantage to atone for it, thus aggravates distress, and adds fresh horrors even to the wretchedness of slavery.

Chapter 3

I now totally lost the small remains of comfort I had enjoyed in conversing with my countrymen; the women too, who used to wash and take care of me were all gone different ways, and I never saw one of them afterwards.

I stayed in this island for a few days, I believe it could not be above a fortnight, when I, and some few more slaves, that were not saleable amongst the rest, from very much fretting, were shipped off in a sloop for North America. On the passage we were better treated than when we were coming from Africa, and we had plenty of rice and fat pork. We were landed up a river a good way from the sea, about Virginia county, where we saw few or none of our native Africans, and not one soul who could talk to me. I was a few weeks weeding grass and gathering stones in a plantation; and at last all my companions were distributed different ways, and only myself was left. I was now exceedingly miserable, and thought myself worse off than any of the rest of my companions, for they could talk to each other, but I had no person to speak to that I could understand. In this state, I was constantly grieving and pining, and wishing for death rather than anything else. While I was in this plantation, the gentleman, to whom I suppose the estate belonged, being unwell, I was one day sent for to his dwelling-house to fan him; when I came into the room where he was I was very much affrighted at some things I saw, and the more so as I had seen a black woman slave as I came through the house, who was cooking the dinner, and the poor creature was cruelly loaded with various kinds of iron machines; she had one particularly on her head, which locked her mouth so fast that she could scarcely speak; and could not eat nor drink. I was much astonished and shocked at this contrivance, which I afterwards learned was called the iron muzzle. Soon after I had a fan put in my hand, to fan the gentleman while he slept; and so I did indeed with great fear. While he was fast asleep I indulged myself a great deal in looking about the room, which to me appeared very fine and curious. The first object that engaged my attention was a watch which hung on the chimney, and was going. I was quite surprised at the noise it made, and was afraid it would tell the gentleman anything I might do amiss; and when I immediately after observed a picture hanging in the room, which appeared constantly to look at me, I was still more affrighted, having never seen such things as these before. At one time I thought it was something relative to magic; and not seeing it move, I thought it might be some way the whites had to keep their great men when they died, and offer them libations as we used to do our friendly spirits. In this state of anxiety I remained till my master awoke, when I was dismissed out of the room, to my no small satisfaction and relief; for I thought that these people were all made up of wonders. In this place I was called Jacob; but on board the *African Snow,* I was called Michael. I had been some time in this miserable, forlorn, and much dejected state, without having anyone to talk to, which made my life a burden, when the kind and unknown hand of the Creator (who in very deed leads the blind in a way they know not) now began to appear, to my comfort; for one day the captain of a merchant ship, called the *Industrious Bee,* came on some business to my master's house. This gentleman, whose name was Michael Henry Pascal, was a lieutenant in the royal navy, but now commanded this trading ship, which was somewhere in the confines of the county many miles off. While he was at my master's house, it happened that he saw me, and liked me so well that he made a purchase of me. I think I have often heard him say he gave thirty or forty pounds sterling for me; but I do not remember which. However, he meant me for a present to some of his friends in England: and as I was sent accordingly from the house of my then master (one Mr. Campbell) to the place where the ship lay; I was conducted on horseback by an elderly black man (a mode of travelling which appeared very odd to me). When I arrived I was carried on board a fine large ship, loaded with tobacco, &c., and just ready to sail for England. I now thought my condition much mended; I had sails to lie on, and plenty of good victuals to eat; and everybody on board used me very kindly, quite contrary to what I had seen of any white people before; I therefore began to think that they were not all of the same disposition. A few days after I was on board we sailed for England. I was still at a loss to conjecture my destiny. By this time, however, I could smatter a little imperfect English; and I wanted to know as well as I could where we were going. Some of the people of the ship used to tell me they were going to carry me back to my own country, and this made me very happy. I was quite rejoiced at the idea of going back, and thought if I could get home what wonders I should have to tell. But I was reserved for another fate, and was soon undeceived when we came within sight of the English coast. While I was on board this ship, my captain and master named me *Gustavus Vassa*. I at that time began to understand him a little, and refused to be called so, and told him as well as I could that I would be called Jacob; but he said I should not, and still called me Gustavus: and when I refused to answer to my new name, which I at first did, it gained me many a cuff; so at length I submitted, and by which I have been known ever since. The ship had a very long passage; and on that account we had very short allowance of provisions. Towards the last, we had only one pound and a half of bread per week, and about the same quantity of meat, and one quart of water a day. We spoke with only one vessel the whole time we were at sea, and but once we caught a few fishes. In our extremities the captain and people told me in jest they would kill and eat me; but I thought them in earnest, and was depressed beyond measure, expecting every moment to be my last. While I was in this situation, one evening they caught, with a good deal of trouble, a large shark, and got it on board. This gladdened my poor heart exceedingly, as I thought it would serve the people to eat instead of their eating me; but very soon, to my astonishment, they cut off a small part of the tail, and tossed the rest over the side. This renewed my consternation; and I did not know what to think of these white people, though I very much feared they would kill and eat me. There was on board the ship a young lad who had never been at sea before, about four or five years older than myself: his name was Richard Baker. He was a native of America, had received an excellent education, and was of the most amiable temper. Soon after I went on board, he showed me a great deal of partiality and attention, and in return I grew extremely fond of him. We at length became inseparable; and, for the space of two years, he was of very great use to me, and was my constant companion and instructor. Although this dear youth had many slaves of his own, yet he and I have gone through many sufferings together on shipboard; and we have many nights lain in each other's bosoms when we were in great distress. Thus such a friendship was cemented between us as we cherished till his death, which, to my very great sorrow, happened in the year 1759, when he was up the Archipelago, on board his Majesty's ship the *Preston:* an event which I have never ceased to regret, as I lost at once a kind interpreter, an agreeable companion, and a faithful friend; who, at the age of fifteen, discovered a mind superior to prejudice; and who was not ashamed to notice, to associate with, and to be the friend and instructor of one who was ignorant, a stranger, of a different complexion, and a slave! My master had lodged in his mother's house in America; he respected him very much, and made him always eat with him in the cabin. He used often to tell him jocularly that he would kill and eat me. Sometimes he would say to me—the black people were not good to eat, and would ask me if we did not eat people in my country. I said, No; then he said he would kill Dick (as he always called him) first, and afterwards me. Though this hearing relieved my mind a little as to myself, I was alarmed for Dick, and whenever he was called I used to be very much afraid he was to be killed; and I would peep and watch to see if they were going to kill him; nor was I free from this consternation till we made the land. One night we lost a man overboard; and the cries and noise were so great and confused, in stopping the ship, that I, who did not know what was the matter, began, as usual, to be very much afraid, and to think they were going to make an offering with me, and perform some magic; which I still believed they dealt in. As the waves were very high, I thought the Ruler of the seas was angry, and I expected to be offered up to appease him. This filled my mind with agony, and I could not any more, that night, close my eyes again to rest. However, when daylight appeared, I was a little eased in my mind; but still, every time I was called, I used to think it was to be killed. Some time after this, we saw some very large fish, which I afterwards found were called grampusses. They looked to me exceedingly terrible, and made their appearance just at dusk, and were so near as to blow the water on the ship's deck. I believed them to be the rulers of the sea; and as the white people did not make any offerings at any time, I thought they were angry with them; and at last, what confirmed my belief was, the wind just then died away, and a calm ensued, and in consequence of it the ship stopped going. I supposed that the fish had performed this, and I hid myself in the fore part of the ship, through fear of being offered up to appease them, every minute peeping and quaking; but my good friend Dick came shortly towards me, and I took an opportunity to ask him, as well as I could, what these fish were. Not being able to talk much English, I could but just make him understand my question; and not at all, when I asked him if any offerings were to be made to them; however, he told me these fish would swallow anybody which sufficiently alarmed me. Here he was called away by the captain, who was leaning over the quarter-deck railing, and looking at the fish; and most of the people were busied in getting a barrel of pitch to light for them to play with. The captain now called me to him, having learned some of my apprehensions from Dick; and having diverted himself and others for some time with my fears, which appeared ludicrous enough in my crying and trembling, he dismissed me. The barrel of pitch was now lighted and put over the side into the water. By this time it was just dark, and the fish went after it; and to my great joy, I saw them no more.

However, all my alarms began to subside when we got sight of land; and at last the ship arrived at Falmouth, after a passage of thirteen weeks. Every heart on board seemed gladdened on our reaching the shore, and none more than mine. The captain immediately went on shore, and sent on board some fresh provisions, which we wanted very much. We made good use of them, and our famine was soon turned into feasting, almost without ending. It was about the beginning of the spring 1757, when I arrived in England and I was near twelve years of age at that time. I was very much struck with the buildings and the pavement of the streets in Falmouth; and, indeed, every object I saw, filled me with new surprise. One morning, when I got upon deck, I saw it covered all over with the snow that fell over night. As I had never seen anything of the kind before, I thought it was salt: so I immediately ran down to the mate, and desired him, as well as I could, to come and see how somebody in the night had thrown salt all over the deck. He, knowing what it was, desired me to bring some of it down to him. Accordingly I took up a handful of it, which I found very cold indeed; and when I brought it to him he desired me to taste it. I did so, and I was surprised beyond measure. I then asked him what it was; he told me it was snow, but I could not in anywise understand him. He asked me, if we had no such thing in my country; I told him, No. I then asked him the use of it, and who made it; he told me a great man in the heavens, called God. But here again I was to all intents and purposes at a loss to understand him; and the more so, when a little after I saw the air filled with it, in a heavy shower, which fell down on the same day. After this I went to church; and having never been at such a place before, I was again amazed at seeing and hearing the service. I asked all I could about it, and they gave me to understand it was worshipping God, who made us and all things. I was still at a great loss, and soon got into an endless field of inquiries, as well as I was able to speak and ask about things. However, my little friend Dick used to be my best interpreter; for I could make free with him, and he always instructed me with pleasure. And from what I could understand by him of this God, and in seeing these white people did not sell one another as we did, I was much pleased; and in this I thought they were much happier than we Africans. I was astonished at the wisdom of the white people in all things I saw; but was amazed at their not sacrificing, or making any offerings, and eating with unwashed hands, and touching the dead. I likewise could not help remarking the particular slenderness of their women, which I did not at first like; and I thought they were not so modest and shame-faced as the African women.

I had often seen my master and Dick employed in reading: and I had a great curiosity to talk to the books as I thought they did, and so to learn how all things had a beginning. For that purpose I have often taken up a book, and have talked to it, and then put my ears to it, when alone, in hopes it would answer me; and I have been very much concerned when I found it remained silent.

My master lodged at the house of a gentleman in Falmouth, who had a fine little daughter about six or seven years of age, and she grew prodigiously fond of me, insomuch that we used to eat together, and had servants to wait on us. I was so much caressed by this family that it often reminded me of the treatment I had received from my little noble African master. After I had been here a few days, I was sent on board of the ship; but the child cried so much after me that nothing could pacify her till I was sent for again. It is ludicrous enough, that I began to fear I should be betrothed to this young lady; and when my master asked me if I would stay there with her behind him, as he was going away with the ship, which had taken in the tobacco again, I cried immediately, and said I would not leave him. At last, by stealth, one night I was sent on board the ship again; and in a little time we sailed for Guernsey, where she was in part owned by a merchant, one Nicholas Doberry. As I was now amongst a people who had not their faces scarred, like some of the African nation where I had been, I was very glad I did not let them ornament me in that manner when I was with them. When we arrived at Guernsey, my master placed me to board and lodge with one of his mates, who had a wife and family there; and some months afterwards he went to England, and left me in care of this mate, together with my friend Dick. This mate had a little daughter, aged about five or six years, with whom I used to be much delighted. I had often observed that when her mother washed her face it looked very rosy, but when she washed mine it did not look so. I therefore tried oftentimes myself if I could not by washing make my face of the same color as my little play-mate, Mary, but it was all in vain; and I now began to be mortified at the difference in our complexions. This woman behaved to me with great kindness and attention, and taught me everything in the same manner as she did her own child, and, indeed, in every respect treated me as such. I remained here till the summer of the year 1757, when my master, being appointed first lieutenant of his Majesty's ship the *Roebuck,* sent for Dick and me, and his old mate. On this we all left Guernsey, and set out for England in a sloop, bound for London. As we were coming up towards the Nore, where the *Roebuck* lay, a man-of-war's boat came along side to press our people, on which each man run to hide himself. I was very much frightened at this, though I did not know what it meant, or what to think or do. However I went and hid myself also under a hencoop. Immediately afterwards, the press-gang came on board with their swords drawn, and searched all about, pulled the people out by force, and put them into the boat. At last I was found out also; the man that found me held me up by the heels while they all made their sport of me, I roaring and crying out all the time most lustily; but at last the mate, who was my conductor, seeing this, came to my assistance, and did all he could to pacify me; but all to very little purpose, till I had seen the boat go off. Soon afterwards we came to the Nore, where the *Roebuck* lay; and, to our great joy, my master came on board to us, and brought us to the ship. When I went on board this large ship, I was amazed indeed to see the quantity of men and the guns. However, my surprise began to diminish as my knowledge increased; and I ceased to feel those apprehensions and alarms which had taken such strong possession of me when I first came among the Europeans, and for some time after. I began now to pass to an opposite extreme; I was so far from being afraid of anything new which I saw, that after I had been some time in this ship, I even began to long for an engagement. My griefs, too, which in young minds are not perpetual, were now wearing away; and I soon enjoyed myself pretty well, and felt tolerably easy in my present situation. There was a number of boys on board, which still made it more agreeable; for we were always together, and a great part of our time was spent in play. I remained in this ship a considerable time, during which we made several cruises, and visited a variety of places; among others we were twice in Holland, and brought over several persons of distinction from it, whose names I do not now remember. On the passage, one day, for the diversion of those gentlemen, all the boys were called on the quarter-deck, and were paired proportionably, and then made to fight; after which the gentlemen gave the combatants from five to nine shillings each. This was the first time I ever fought with a white boy; and I never knew what it was to have a bloody nose before. This made me fight most desperately, I suppose considerably more than an hour; and at last, both of us being weary, we were parted. I had a great deal of this kind of sport afterwards, in which the captain and the ship's company used very much to encourage me. . . .

Chapter 7

Every day now brought me nearer my freedom, and I was impatient till we proceeded again to sea, that I might have an opportunity of getting a sum large enough to purchase it. I was not long ungratified; for, in the beginning of the year 1766, my master bought another sloop, named the *Nancy,* the largest I had ever seen. She was partly laden, and was to proceed to Philadelphia; our captain had his choice of three, and I was well pleased he chose this, which was the largest; for, from his having a large vessel, I had more room, and could carry a larger quantity of goods with me. Accordingly, when we had delivered our old vessel, the *Prudence,* and completed the lading of the *Nancy,* having made near three hundred per cent, by four barrels of pork I brought from Charleston, I laid in as large a cargo as I could, trusting to God's providence to prosper my undertaking. . . .

When we had unladen the vessel, and I had sold my venture, finding myself master of about forty-seven pounds—I consulted my true friend, the captain, how I should proceed in offering my master the money for my freedom. He told me to come on a certain morning, when he and my master would be at breakfast together. Accordingly, on that morning I went, and met the captain there, as he had appointed. When I went in I made my obeisance to my master, and with my money in my hand, and many fears in my heart, I prayed him to be as good as his offer to me, when he was pleased to promise me my freedom as soon as I could purchase it. This speech seemed to confound him, he began to recoil, and my heart that instant sunk within me. "What," said he, "give you your freedom? Why, where did you get the money? Have you got forty pounds sterling?" "Yes, sir," I answered. "How did you get it?" replied he. I told him, very honestly. The captain then said he knew I got the money honestly, and with much industry, and that I was particularly careful. On which my master replied, I got money much faster than he did; and said he would not have made me the promise he did if he had thought I should have got the money so soon. "Come, come," said my worthy captain, clapping my master on the back, "Come, Robert (which was his name), I think you must let him have his freedom; you have laid your money out very well; you have received a very good interest for it all this time, and here is now the principal at last. I know Gustavus has earned you more than a hundred a year, and he will save you money, as he will not leave you. Come, Robert, take the money." My master then said he would not be worse than his promise; and, taking the money, told me to go to the Secretary at the Register Office, and get my manumission drawn up. These words of my master were like a voice from heaven to me. In an instant all my trepidation was turned into unutterable bliss; and I most reverently bowed myself with gratitude, unable to express my feelings, but by the overflowing of my eyes, and a heart replete with thanks to God, while my true and worthy friend, the captain congratulated us both with a peculiar degree of heart-felt pleasure. As soon as the first transports of my joy were over, and that I had expressed my thanks to these my worthy friends, in the best manner I was able, I rose with a heart full of affection and reverence, and left the room, in order to obey my master's joyful mandate of going to the Register Office. As I was leaving the house I called to mind the words of the Psalmist, in the 126th Psalm, and like him, "I glorified God in my heart, in whom I trusted." These words had been impressed on my mind from the very day I was forced from Deptford to the present hour, and I now saw them, as I thought, fulfilled and verified. My imagination was all rapture as I flew to the Register Office; and, in this respect, like the apostle Peter[1] (whose deliverance from prison was so sudden and extraordinary that he thought he was in a vision), I could scarcely believe I was awake. Heavens! who could do justice to my feelings at this moment! Not conquering heroes themselves, in the midst of a triumph—Not the tender mother who has just regained her long lost infant, and presses it to her heart—Not the weary hungry mariner, at the sight of the desired friendly port—Not the lover, when he once more embraces his beloved mistress, after she has been ravished from his arms! All within my breast was tumult, wildness, and delirium! My feet scarcely touched the ground, for they were winged with joy; and, like Elijah, as he rose to Heaven, they "were with lightning sped as I went on." Everyone I met I told of my happiness, and blazed about the virtue of my amiable master and captain.

When I got to the office and acquainted the Register with my errand, he congratulated me on the occasion, and told me he would draw up my manumission for half price, which was a guinea. I thanked him for his kindness; and, having received it, and paid him, I hastened to my master to get him to sign it, that I might be fully released. Accordingly he signed the manumission that day; so that, before night, I, who had been a slave in the morning, trembling at the will of another, was become my own master, and completely free. I thought this was the happiest day I had ever experienced; and my joy was still heightened by the blessings and prayers of many of the sable race, particularly the aged, to whom my heart had ever been attached with reverence.

As the form of my manumission has something peculiar in it, and expresses the absolute power and dominion one man claims over his fellow, I shall beg leave to present it before my readers at full length.

> *Montserrat.*
>
> *To all men unto whom these presents shall come: I, Robert King, of the parish of St. Anthony, in the said island, merchant, send greeting. Know ye, that I, the aforesaid Robert King, for and in consideration of the sum of seventy pounds current money of the said island, to me in hand paid, and to the intent that a Negro man slave, named Gustavus Vassa, shall and may become free, having manumitted, emancipated, enfranchised, and set free, and by these presents do manumit, emancipate, enfranchise, and set free, the aforesaid Negro man slave, named Gustavus Vassa, for ever; hereby giving, granting and releasing unto him, the said Gustavus Vassa, all right, title, dominion, sovereignty, and property, which, as lord and master over the aforesaid Gustavus Vassa, I had, or now have, or by any means whatsoever I may or can hereafter possibly have over him, the aforesaid Negro, for ever. In witness whereof, I, the above said Robert King, have unto these presents set my hand and seal, this tenth day of July, in the year of our Lord one thousand seven hundred and sixty-six.*
>
> ROBERT KING

Signed, sealed, and delivered in the presence of Terry Legay, Montserrat.
Registered the within manumission at full length, this eleventh day of July 1766, in liber. D.

TERRY LEGAY, Register

---

[1] Acts 12:9.

In short, the fair as well as the black people immediately styled me by a new appellation, to me the most desirable in the world, which was freeman; and at the dances I gave, my Georgia superfine blue clothes made no indifferent appearance, as I thought. Some of the sable females, who formerly stood aloof, now began to relax and appear less coy; but my heart was still fixed on London, where I hoped to be ere long. So that my worthy captain and his owner, my late master, finding that the bent of my mind was towards London, said to me, "We hope you won't leave us, but that you will still be with the vessels." Here gratitude bowed me down; and none but the generous mind can judge of my feelings, struggling between inclination and duty. However, notwithstanding my wish to be in London, I obediently answered my benefactors, that I would go in the vessel, and not leave them; and from the day I was entered on board as an able-bodied sailor, at thirty-six shillings per month, besides what perquisites I could make. My intention was to make a voyage or two, entirely to please these my honored patrons; but I determined that the year following, if it pleased God, I would see old England once more, and surprise my old master, Captain Pascal, who was hourly in my mind; for I still loved him, notwithstanding his usage of me, and pleased myself with thinking what he would say, when he saw what the Lord had done for me in so short a time, instead of being, as he might perhaps suppose, under the cruel yoke of some planter. With these kind of reveries I used often to entertain myself, and shorten the time till my return; and now, being as in my original free African state, I embarked on board the *Nancy,* after having got all things ready for our voyage. In this state of serenity, we sailed for St. Eustatius; and having smooth seas and calm weather, we soon arrived there. After taking our cargo on board, we proceeded to Savannah, in Georgia, in August, 1766. While we were there, as usual, I used to go for the cargo up the rivers in boats; and on this business have been frequently beset by alligators, which were very numerous on that coast; and shot many of them when they have been near getting into our boats, which we have with great difficulty sometimes prevented, and have been very much frightened at them. I have seen a young one sold in Georgia alive for six pence. . . .

1789

Phillis Wheatley 1753–1784

Known best for her Christian verses reflecting orthodox piety, Phillis Wheatley (Peters) in fact wrote on a wide variety of topics. A kidnapped African slave child, aged about seven years old, she was sold from the South Market in Boston to well-to-do Susanna Wheatley. She was raised in a pious Christian household, and the precocious child evidently experienced special, much-indulged comfort and only token slavery. (Phillis Wheatley was manumitted by October 18, 1773.) Tutored by family members, she quickly learned English, Latin, and the Bible, and she began writing in 1765, four years after her landing in Boston harbor.

She wrote to Reverend Samson Occom, a converted Christian Mohican Indian minister, and she sent a poem to Reverend Joseph Sewall of Boston's Old South Church. Both this letter and poem are not extant, but a poem from this early period remains: in 1767, when she was about thirteen or fourteen years old, Phillis Wheatley published her first verses in a Newport, Rhode Island, newspaper. By 1772 she had composed enough poems that she could advertise twenty-eight of them in *The Boston Censor* for February 29, March 14, and April 11. She hoped to publish a volume of her poems that year in Boston.

The range of her topical concerns was already evident in these twenty-eight titles. Along with poems on morality and piety, the volume offered patriotic American pieces, an epithalamium, and a short, racially self-conscious poem, "Thoughts on Being Brought from Africa to America." Had enough subscribers for this volume come forward, it would have been printed. But advertisements brought no subscribers, for reasons in part racially motivated. Phillis was encouraged by her doting and undaunted mistress to revise her manuscripts, in preparation for a volume that Susanna Wheatley had arranged, with the prestigious cooperation of the Countess of Huntingdon, to have published in London in 1773, complete with an engraved likeness of the poet as a frontispiece. This was the first volume known to have been published by a black American, man or woman.

The array of poems included in the London-published volume indicates the breadth of the poet's accomplishment. It included not only Christian elegies, but also a highly original English translation from the Latin of Ovid, Biblical paraphrases, and poems about nature, imagination, and memory. Like any good poet who sought patrons, Wheatley also included flattering salutes to an English captain and the Earl of Dartmouth, two happy pieces on the good fortunes of two ladies, and even a playful rebus to James Bowdoin. She included as well her poem on being brought from Africa to America, a metrical salute to a local black Boston artist, and, in several poems, racially self-conscious tags, reminding readers that she was African. In more than thirty posthumously published letters and variants, and in several poems published after her 1773 volume, Phillis Wheatley would continue to register her racial awareness, but nowhere more bitingly than in her 1774 letter to Samson Occom.

In the fall of 1779, she ran (six times) proposals for a projected third volume, of thirty-three poems and thirteen letters. The work was to be dedicated to Benjamin Franklin. But again, as in 1772 and 1773, these 1779 proposals were rejected by Bostonians. In the *Boston Magazine* for September, 1784, there would be printed a final solicitation for subscribers to this third volume, but there would be no such book in print by the time Phillis Wheatley died three months later on December 5. She was buried obscurely on December 8, along with the body of the last of three infant children.

For historical as well as literary reasons, Phillis Wheatley's life is important. Despite her ability as a poet, she was not accepted by whites of her generation; thus, her life evidences the effects of racial injustice. Her first volume, the projected 1772 Boston publication, was advertised by printers, who although they knew better, claimed that they could not credit "ye performances to be by a Negro." It certainly was no secret that Wheatley was a black poet. In the half-dozen poems she published in America and London before and during the time she solicited Boston subscribers for her 1772 book, she was almost always identified as a black poet. While her second collection, published as *Poems,* went through at least four London printings for a run of about 1200 copies, in America the same volume fared poorly early on. Phillis received a second lot of 300 copies of her *Poems* from London in May of 1774, but as late as 1778 she could write to a friend in New Haven and ask for return to her of copies of her "books that remain unsold," announcing with unfounded bravado that she "could easily dispose of them here for 12/Lm°" (*i.e.,* twelve pounds Legal money). Her book was never reprinted in America during her lifetime; the first American reprinting appeared in Philadelphia in 1786, two years after she had died.

But if her early rejection seems peculiarly American, so too was her gradual acceptance and success. *Poems* was eventually reprinted more than two dozen times in America and Europe, and selections appear with regularity in American textbooks. An autographed copy of her book sells today for several thousands of dollars.

William H. Robinson
Brown University

PRIMARY WORKS

Poems, 1773; Anonymous, *Memoir and Poems of Phillis Wheatley, A Native African and a Slave,* 1834; Charles Deane, *Letters of Phillis Wheatley, the Negro Slave Poet of Boston,* 1864; Charles F. Heartman, *Phillis Wheatley (Phillis Peters). Poems and Letters. First Collected Edition,* 1915; Julian D. Mason, ed., *The Poems of Phillis Wheatley,* 1966.

SECONDARY WORKS

William H. Robinson, *Phillis Wheatley and Her Writings,* 1984.

On the Death of the Rev. Mr. George Whitefield 1770[1]

Hail, happy saint, on thine immortal throne,
Possest of glory, life, and bliss unknown;
We hear no more the music of thy tongue,
Thy wonted auditories cease to throng.
5 Thy sermons in unequall'd accents flow'd,
And ev'ry bosom with devotion glow'd;
Thou didst in strains of eloquence refin'd
Inflame the heart, and captivate the mind.
Unhappy we the setting sun deplore,
10 So glorious once, but ah! it shines no more.

Behold the prophet in his tow'ring flight!
He leaves the earth for heav'n's unmeasur'd height,

[1] From Phillis Wheatley, *Poems on Various Subjects, Religious and Moral,* (1773). Personal chaplain to Lady Huntingdon since 1749, the Reverend George Whitefield (1714–1770) was a fiery and enormously popular English evangelist who conducted frequent prayer visits to America, preaching in the Boston area at least six times between 1750 and 1770. His favorite American undertaking was the establishment of Bethesda, an orphanage outside of Savannah, Georgia, which he built in 1764 with rationalized slave labor. The text, above, is a revision of the poem which first appeared as a 62-line broadside in Boston in October, 1770, and was widely reprinted in Boston, Newport, New York, Philadelphia, and London. Another revised version, in 64 lines, was published in London in 1771. The poem established Phillis Wheatley's international reputation.

And worlds unknown receive him from our sight.
There *Whitefield* wings with rapid course his way,
15 And sails to *Zion* through vast seas of day.
Thy pray'rs, great saint, and thine incessant cries
Have pierc'd the bosom of thy native skies.
Thou moon hast seen, and all the stars of light,
How he has wrestled with his God by night.
20 He pray'd that grace in ev'ry heart might dwell,
He long'd to see *America* excel;
He charg'd its youth that ev'ry grace divine
Should with full lustre in their conduct shine;
That Saviour, which his soul did first receive,
25 The greatest gift that ev'n a God can give,
He freely offer'd to the num'rous throng,
That on his lips with list'ning pleasure hung.

"Take him, ye wretched, for your only good,
"Take him[,] ye starving sinners, for your food;
30 "Ye thirsty, come to this life-giving stream,
"Ye preachers, take him for your joyful theme;
"Take him[,] my dear *Americans,*["] he said,
"Be your complaints on his kind bosom laid:
"Take him, ye *Africans,* he longs for you,
35 "*Impartial Saviour* is his title due:
"Wash'd in the fountain of redeeming blood,
"You shall be son, and kings, and priests to God."

Great *Countess,*[2] we *Americans* revere
Thy name, and mingle in thy grief sincere;
40 *New England* deeply feels, the *Orphans* mourn,
Their more than father will no more return.

But, though arrested by the hand of death,
Whitefield no more exerts his lab'ring breath,
Yet let us view him in th'eternal skies,
45 Let ev'ry heart to this bright vision rise;
While the tomb safe retains its sacred trust,
Till life divine re-animates his dust.

1770

[2] The Countess of *Huntingdon,* to whom Mr.
Whitefield was Chaplain. [Wheatley's note]

On the Death of Dr. Samuel Marshall 1771[1]

Through thickest glooms look back, immortal shade,
On that confusion which thy death has made;
Or from *Olympus'* height look down and see
A *Town* involv'd in grief bereft of thee.
5 Thy *Lucy* sees thee mingle with the dead,
And rends the graceful tresses from her head,
Wild in her woe, with grief unknown opprest[,]
Sigh follows sigh[,] deep heaving from her breast.

Too quickly fled, ah! whither art thou gone?
10 Ah! lost for ever to thy wife and son!
The hapless child, thine only hope and heir,
Clings round his mother's neck, and weeps his sorrows there.
The loss of thee on *Tyler's* soul returns,
And *Boston* for her dear physician mourns.

15 When sickness call'd for *Marshall's* healing hand,
With what compassion did his soul expand?
In him we found the father and the friend:
In life how lov'd! how honour'd in his end!

And must not then our *Aesculapius*[2] stay
20 To bring his ling'ring infant into day?
The babe unborn in the dark womb is tost,
And seems in anguish for its father lost.

Gone is *Apollo* from his house of earth,
But leaves the sweet memorials of his worth:
25 The common parent, whom we all deplore,
From yonder world unseen must come no more,
Yet 'midst our woes immortal hopes attend
The spouse, the sire, the universal friend.

1773

[1] From Phillis Wheatley's *Poems* (1773), revised from the first appearance of the poem, also in 28 lines, in *The Boston Evening Post* (7 October, 1771), p. 3. Dr. Samuel Marshall (1735–1771) graduated from Harvard College in 1754, and prepared for a medical career in London hospitals, qualifying as an M.D. in 1761. He returned to Boston in 1765, married Lucy Tyler and purchased a newer home on Congress Street, not far from Phillis Wheatley's King Street (today's State Street) home. Marshall fathered one son, but died on September 29, 1771. Widely respected, he was described in his obituary in *The Boston Evening Post* (30 September) as "highly esteemed . . . a very skillful Physician, Surgeon and Man Midwife . . . ; his death therefore is to be lamented as a public loss to the community. . . . " A relative of Phillis's mistress, Marshall likely tended the poet in her chronic medical problems.

[2] Aesculapius, the son of Phoebus Apollo and the princess Coronis, was regarded as "the father of medicine."

To a Lady on the Death of her Husband[1]

Grim monarch! see, depriv'd of vital breath,
A young physician in the dust of death:
Dost thou go on incessant to destroy,
Our griefs to double, and lay waste our joy?
5 *Enough* thou never yet wast known to say,
Though millions die, the vassals of thy sway:
Nor youth, nor science, nor the ties of love,
Nor aught on earth thy flinty heart can move.
The friend, the spouse from his dire dart to save,
10 In vain we ask the sovereign of the grave.
Fair mourner, there see thy lov'd *Leonard*[2] laid,
And o'er him spread the deep impervious shade;
Clos'd are his eyes, and heavy fetters keep
His sense bound in never-waking sleep,
15 Till time shall cease, till many a starry world
Shall fall from heav'n, in dire confusion hurl'd,
Till nature in her final wreck shall lie,
And her last groan shall rend the azure sky:
Not, not till then his active soul shall claim
20 His body, a divine immortal frame.

But see the softly-stealing tears apace
Pursue each other down the mourner's face;
But cease thy tears, bid ev'ry sigh depart,
And cast the load of anguish from thine heart:
25 From the cold shell of his great soul arise,
And look beyond, thou native of the skies;
There fix thy view, where fleeter than the wind
Thy *Leonard* mounts, and leaves the earth behind.
Thyself prepare to pass the vale of night
30 To join for ever on the hills of light:
To thine embrace his joyful spirit moves
To thee, the partner of his earthly loves;
He welcomes thee to pleasures more refin'd,
And better suited to th'immortal mind.

1773

---

[1] From Phillis Wheatley's volume of *Poems,* 1773; this is a revision of the poem which first appeared in Boston as a broadside during the summer of 1771.

[2] Dr. Thomas Leonard (1744–1771) who married Thankfull Leonard (1744–1772), the "Lady" in the title. Phillis was especially fond of Thankfull (Hubbard) Leonard.

On Imagination

Thy various works, imperial queen, we see,
How bright their forms! how deck'd with pomp by thee!
Thy wond'rous acts in beauteous order stand,
And all attest how potent is thine hand.

5   From *Helicon's*[1] refulgent heights attend,
Ye sacred choir, and my attempts befriend:
To tell her glories with a faithful tongue,
Ye blooming graces, triumph in my song.

Now here, now there, the roving *Fancy* flies,
10 Till some lov'd object strikes her wand'ring eyes,
Whose silken fetters all the senses bind,
And soft captivity involves the mind.

Imagination! who can sing thy force?
Or who describe the swiftness of thy course?
15 Soaring through air to find the bright abode,

Th' empyreal palace of the thund'ring God,
We on thy pinions[2] can surpass the wind,
And leave the rolling universe behind:
From star to star the mental optics rove,
20 Measure the skies, and range the realms above.
There in one view we grasp the mighty whole,
Or with new worlds amaze th'unbounded soul.

Though *Winter* frowns to *Fancy's* raptur'd eyes
The fields may flourish, and gay scenes arise;
25 The frozen deeps may break their iron bands,
And bid their waters murmur o'er the sands.
Fair *Flora*[3] may resume her fragrant reign,
And with her flow'ry riches deck the plain;
Sylvanus[4] may diffuse his honours round,
30 And all the forest may with leaves be crown'd:
Show'rs may descend, and dews their gems disclose,
And nectar sparkle on the blooming rose.

[1] Helicon, one of several earthly mountain homes of the Greek muses.
[2] Pinions are "wings."
[3] Flora, Roman goddess of flowers.
[4] Sylvanus, in Greek mythology, helper of woodsmen.

Such is thy pow'r, nor are thine orders vain,
O thou the leader of the mental train:
35 In full perfection all thy works are wrought,
And thine the sceptre o'er the realms of thought.
Before thy throne the subject-passions bow,
Of subject-passions sov'reign ruler Thou;
At thy command joy rushes on the heart,
40 And through the glowing veins the spirits dart.

Fancy might now her silken pinions try
To rise from earth, and sweep th'expanse on high;
From *Tithon's*[5] bed now might *Aurora* rise,
Her cheeks all glowing with celestial dies,
45 While a pure stream of light o'erflows the skies.
The monarch of the day I might behold,
And all the mountains tipt with radiant gold,
But I reluctant leave the pleasing views,
Which *Fancy* dresses to delight the *Muse:*
50 *Winter* austere forbids me to aspire,
And northern tempests damp the rising fire;
They chill the tides of *Fancy's* flowing sea,
Cease then, my song, cease the unequal lay.

1773

[5] Tithon (*i.e.,* Tithonus), husband to Aurora, goddess of the dawn, father of her black Ethiopian
son, Memnon, whose death in battle is told in
The Iliad.

To the University of Cambridge, in New England[1]

While an intrinsic ardor prompts to write,
The muses promise to assist my pen;
'Twas not long since I left my native shore
The land of errors, and *Egyptian* gloom:
5 Father of mercy, 'twas thy gracious hand
Brought me in safety from those dark abodes.

Students, to you 'tis giv'n to scan the heights
Above, to traverse the ethereal space,
And mark the systems of revolving worlds.
10 Still more, ye sons of science ye receive
The blissful news by messengers from heav'n,
How *Jesus'* blood for your redemption flows.
See him with hands out-strecht upon the cross;
Immense compassion in his bosom glows;
15 He hears revilers, nor resents their scorn:
What matchless mercy in the Son of God!
When the whole human race by sin has fall'n,
He deign'd to die that they might rise again,
And share with him in the sublimest skies,
20 Life without death, and glory without end.

Improve your privileges while they stay,
Ye pupils, and each hour redeem, that bears
Or good or bad report of you to heav'n.
Let sin, that baneful evil to the soul,
25 By you be shunn'd, nor once remit your guard;
Suppress the deadly serpent in its egg.
Ye blooming plants of human race divine,
An *Ethiop*[2] tells you 'tis your greatest foe;
Its transient sweetness turns to endless pain,
30 And in immense perdition sinks the soul.

1773

---

[1] The University of Cambridge, in New England, *i.e.,* Harvard College in Cambridge, Massachusetts. The text is from Wheatley's *Poems* (1773).

[2] In several poems, both in her volume and in separately published pieces and variants, Phillis variously registered her racial self-consciousness.

Philis's[sic] Reply to the Answer in our Last by the Gentleman in the Navy.[1]

For one bright moment, heavenly goddess! shine,
Inspire my song and form the lays divine.
Rochford,[2] attend. Beloved of Phoebus! hear,
A truer sentence never reach'd thine ear;
5 Struck with thy song, each vain conceit resign'd
A soft affection seiz'd my grateful mind,
While I each golden sentiment admire;
In thee, the muse's bright celestial fire.
The generous plaudit 'tis not mine to claim,
10 A muse untutor'd, an unknown to fame.

The heavenly sisters[3] pour thy notes along
And crown their bard with every grace of song.
My pen, least favour'd by the tuneful nine,
Can never rival, never equal thine;
15 Then fix the humble Afric muse's seat
At British Homer's[4] and Sir Isaac's[5] feet.
Those bards whose fame in deathless strains arise
Creation's boast, and fav'rites of the skies.
In fair description are thy powers display'd
20 In artless grottos, and the sylvan shade;
Charm'd with thy painting,[6] how my bosom burns!
And pleasing Gambia on my soul returns,[7]
With native grace in spring's luxuriant reign,
Smiles the gay mead, and Eden blooms again,
25 The various bower, the tuneful flowing stream,

[1] This headnote was presumably written by Joseph Greenleaf, editor of *The Royal American Magazine,* in whose December, 1774, issue Phillis had published a poem, "To A Gentleman in the Navy"; in that same issue was also printed an anonymous poem, "The Answer," written by "the gentleman in the navy," a response to Phillis's poem. In the January, 1775, issue of *The Royal American Magazine,* Phillis published this poem.

[2] This name cannot be found among rosters of Royal Naval officers in Boston in 1774. Presumably, "Rochford" was a verse-writing Royal Naval officer who had served off the coast of Africa, and in 1774 was based in Boston, possibly billeted in the Wheatley household on King Street, where Phillis may still have been living. She may be referring to William Henry Zuyles-tein, fourth Earl of Rochford (1723–1781), who, although not in Boston, had much to do with royal fleet actions abroad.

[3] The Greek muses.

[4] John Milton (1608–1674), poet, author of "Paradise Lost."

[5] Sir Isaac Newton (1642–1727), English natural philosopher and mathematician.

[6] In the anonymous poem, "The Answer," the writer was complimentary to Africa, which he calls " . . . the guilded shore, the happy land,/ Where spring and autumn gentle hand in hand."

[7] Phillis may be remembering her African birthplace. Whether or not she is being autobiographical in her extended praises for things African (lines 21–34), she is the first black American poet to so rhapsodize about Africa.

The soft retreats, the lovers['] golden dream.
Her soil spontaneous, yields exhaustless stores;
For phoebus revels on her verdant shores.
Whose flowery births, a fragrant train appear,
30 And crown the youth throughout the smiling year.
There, as in Britain's favour'd isle, behold
The bending harvest ripen into gold!
Just are thy views of Afric's blissful plain,
On the warm limits of the land and main.
35   Pleas'd with the theme, see sportive fancy play,
In realms devoted to the God of day!
Europa's bard, who with great depth explor'd,
Of nature, and thro' boundless systems soar'd,
Thro' earth, thro' heaven, and hell's profound domain,
40 Where night eternal holds her awful reign.
But, lo! in him Britania's prophet dies,
And whence, ah! whence, shall other *Newtons* rise?
Muse, bid thy Rochford's matchless pen display
The charms of friendship in the sprightly lay:
45 Queen of his song, thro' all his numbers shine,
And plausive glories, goddess; shall be thine!
With partial grace thou mak'st his verse excel,
And *his* the glory to describe so well.
Cerulean bard![8] to thee these strains belong,
50 The Muse's darling and the prince of song.

December 5th, 1774

To His Excellency General Washington

SIR.

I Have taken the freedom to address your Excellency in the enclosed poem, and entreat your acceptance, though I am not insensible of its inaccuracies. Your being appointed by the Grand Continental Congress to be Generalissimo of the armies of North America, together with the fame of your virtues, excite sensations not easy to suppress. Your generosity, therefore, I presume, will pardon the attempt. Wishing your Excellency all possible success in the great cause you are so generously engaged in. I am,

Your Excellency's most obedient humble servant,
PHILLIS WHEATLEY.

---

[8] Rochford, whom Phillis is poetically thanking for his complimentary poem, "The Answer." Uniforms of the Royal Naval officers were "cerulean," or sky-blue.

Providence, Oct. 26, 1775.
His Excellency Gen. Washington.

Celestial choir! enthron'd in realms of light,
  Columbia's[1] scenes of glorious toils I write.
While freedom's cause her anxious breast alarms,
She flashes dreadful in refulgent arms.
5 See mother earth her offspring's fate bemoan,
And nations gaze at scenes before unknown!
See the bright beams of heaven's revolving light
Involved in sorrows and the veil of night!
  The goddess comes, she moves divinely fair,
10 Olive and laurel binds her golden hair:
Wherever shines this native of the skies,
Unnumber'd charms and recent graces rise.
  Muse! bow propitious while my pen relates
How pour her armies through a thousand gates,
15 As when Eolus[2] heaven's fair face deforms,
Enwrapp'd in tempest and a night of storms;
Astonish'd ocean feels the wild uproar,
The refluent surges beat the sounding shore;
Or thick as leaves in Autumn's golden reign,
20 Such, and so many, moves the warrior's train.
In bright array they seek the work of war,
Where high unfurl'd the ensign waves in air.
Shall I to Washington their praise recite?
Enough thou know'st them in the fields of fight.
25 Thee, first in peace and honours,—we demand
The grace and glory of thy martial band.
Fam'd for thy valour, for thy virtues more,
Hear every tongue thy guardian aid implore!
  One century scarce perform'd its destined round,
30 When Gallic powers Columbia's fury found;[3]
And so may you, whoever dares disgrace
The land of freedom's heaven-defended race!
Fix'd are the eyes of nations on the scales,
For in their hopes Columbia's arm prevails.
35 Anon Britannia droops the pensive head,
While round increase the rising hills of dead.
Ah! cruel blindness to Columbia's state!
Lament thy thirst of boundless power too late.
  Proceed, great chief, with virtue on thy side,
40 Thy ev'ry action let the goddess guide.

[1] America.
[2] God of the winds.
[3] A reference to the French and Indian War (or the Seven Years War) 1756–63, from which the "Americans" emerged triumphant over the French.

A crown, a mansion, and a throne that shine,
With gold unfading, WASHINGTON! be thine.

1776

Liberty and Peace,

A Poem by Phillis Peters[1]

___

Lo! Freedom comes. Th'prescient Muse foretold,
All Eyes th'accomplish'd Prophecy behold:
Her Port describ'd, *"She moves divinely fair,*
"Olive and Laurel bind her golden Hair."
5   She, the bright Progeny of Heaven, descends,
And every grace her sovereign Step attends;
For now kind Heaven, indulgent to our Prayer,
In smiling *Peace* resolves the Din of *War.*
Fix'd in *Columbia* her illustrious Line,
10 And bids in thee her future Councils shine.
To every Realm her Portals open'd wide,
Receives from each the full commercial Tide.
Each Art and Science now with rising Charms,
Th' expanding Heart with Emulation warms.
15 E'en great *Britannia* sees with dread Surprize,
And from the dazzling Splendors turns her Eyes!
Britain, whose Navies swept th'*Atlantic* o'er,
And Thunder sent to every distant Shore:
E'en thou, in Manners cruel as thou art,
20 The Sword resign'd, resume the friendly Part!
For *Galia*'s Power espous'd *Columbia*'s Cause,
And new-born *Rome* shall give *Britannia* Law,
Nor unremember'd in the grateful Strain,
Shall princely *Louis'* friendly Deeds remain;
25 The generous Prince[2] th'impending Vengeance eye's,
Sees the fierce Wrong, and to the rescue flies.
Perish that Thirst of boundless Power, that drew
On *Albion*'s Head the Curse to Tyrants due.
But thou appeas'd submit to Heaven's decree,

___

[1] Phillis married John Peters, a free, literate, and
ambitious black shopkeeper of Boston in April of
1778, the two of them becoming parents to three
children who all died in infancy.

[2] "The generous Prince": France joined the Americans as allies in June, 1778.

289

30 That bids this Realm of Freedom rival thee!
Now sheathe the Sword that bade the Brave attone
With guiltless Blood for Madness not their own.
Sent from th'Enjoyment of their native Shore
Ill-fated—never to behold her more!
35 From every Kingdom on *Europa*'s Coast
Throng'd various Troops, their Glory, Strength and Boast.
With heart-felt pity fair *Hibernia* saw
Columbia menac'd by the Tyrant's Law:
On hostile Fields fraternal Arms engage,
40 And mutual Deaths, all dealt with mutual Rage;
The Muse's Ear hears mother Earth deplore
Her ample Surface smoak with kindred Gore:
The hostile Field destroys the social Ties,
And ever-lasting Slumber seals their Eyes.
45 *Columbia* mourns, the haughty Foes deride,
Her Treasures plunder'd, and her Towns destroy'd:
Witness how *Charlestown's* curling Smoaks arise,
In sable Columns to the clouded Skies!
The ample Dome, high-wrought with curious Toil,
50 In one sad Hour³ the savage Troops despoil.
Descending *Peace* the Power of War confounds;
From every Tongue coelestial *Peace* resounds:
As from the East th'illustrious King of Day,
With rising Radiance drives the Shades away,
55 So Freedom comes array'd with Charms divine,
And in her Train Commerce and Plenty shine.
Britannia owns her Independent Reign,
Hibernia, Scotia, and the Realms of *Spain;*
And great *Germania*'s ample Coast admires
60 The generous Spirit that *Columbia* fires.
Auspicious Heaven shall fill with fav'ring Gales,
Where e'er *Columbia* spreads her swelling Sails:
To every Realm shall *Peace* her Charms display,
And Heavenly *Freedom* spreads her golden Ray.

1785

³ From three until four p.m. on June 17, 1776, the Battle of Bunker Hill, on the Charlestown peninsula, just across the bay from North Boston, was fought between outnumbered Americans and British troops, who finally achieved a costly victory, losing over 1000 of their own, while Americans suffered the losses of 450 men. Once ashore, the British troops vindictively burned down the town of Charlestown, then home for some 3000 persons, the flames burning all that afternoon and into that night, the rising smoke blackening the skies, or, as Phillis puts it, "The ample Dome" was "high wrought with curious Toil."

To the Rt. Hon'ble the Countess of Huntingdon[1]

Most noble Lady,

The occasion of my addressing your Ladiship will, I hope, apologize for this my boldness in doing it. it (sic) is to enclose a few lines on the decease of your worthy chaplain, the Rev'd Mr. Whitefield, in the loss of whom, I sincerely sympathize with your Ladiship: but your great loss which is his Greater gain, will, I hope, meet with infinite reparation, in the presence of God, the Divine Benefactor whose image you bear by filial imitation.

The Tongues of the learned are insufficient, much less the pen of an untutor'd African, to paint in lively characters, the excellencies of this Citizen of Zion! I beg an Interest in your Ladiship's Prayers, and am

With great humility
Your Ladiship's most Obedient
Humble Servant

Phillis Wheatley
Boston Oct. 25th 1770

To the Right Hon'ble/ The Earl of Dartmouth[1] per favour of/ Mr. Wooldridge[2]

My Lord,

The Joyful occasion which has given me this Confidence in addressing your Lordship in the enclose'd, will, I hope, sufficiently apologize for this freedom from an African, who with the (now) happy America, exults with equal trans-

[1] The Countess of Huntingdon, Selina Hastings (1702–1791), religious zealot, expended most of her considerable fortune for the support of her dissident form of English Methodism. It was the countess who acted as Phillis's English patron when she allowed Phillis to dedicate *Poems on Various Subjects, Religious and Moral* (London, 1773) to herself; and it was at the countess's insistence that Phillis's portrait was painted and then engraved as a frontispiece for the collection of poems, the first known published volume by a black American. The text of this letter is from one of two manuscript versions, both housed among the Countess's papers in the Cheshunt Foundation at Cambridge University in England.

[1] William Legge (1753–1801), third Earl of Dartmouth, appointed Secretary for the North Amer-

ican colonies in August, 1772, to the measured approval of some colonists who recognized Dartmouth's sympathetic ear for colonial grievances.

[2] Thomas Wooldridge (d. 1794), a minor English functionary traveling throughout the colonies in the employ of Lord Dartmouth. Wooldridge visited and interviewed Phillis in Boston, promising that he would deliver the above poem and its cover letter, and he did so, the manuscripts of both being located among the Earl of Dartmouth's papers in the County Record Office, Stafford, England. Also located there is Wooldridge's letter in manuscript, dated "New York Nov. 24th 1772," which describes his interview with Phillis.

port in the view of one of its greatest advocates Presiding, with the Special tenderness of a Fatherly heart, over the American department.

Nor can they, my Lord, be insensible of the Friendship so much exemplified in your endeavors in their behalf, during the late unhappy disturbances.[3] I sincerely wish your Lordship all Possible success, in your undertakings for the Interest of North America.

That the united Blessings of Heaven and Earth may attend you here, and the endless Felicity of the invisible state, in the presence of the Divine Benefactor may be your portion hereafter, is the hearty desire of, My Lord,

Your Lordship's most Ob[t]. & devoted Hum[e]. Serv[t].
Phillis Wheatley
Boston, N.E. Oct 10, 1772

The following is an extract of a letter from Phillis, a Negro girl of Mr. Wheatley's, of this town; to the Rev. Samson Occom, dated the 11th of February, 1774.[1]

Reverend and honoured Sir,

"I have this day received your obliging kind epistle, and am greatly satisfied with your reasons respecting the negroes, and think highly reasonable what you offer in vindication of their natural rights: Those that invade them cannot be insensible that the divine light is chasing away the thick darkness which broods over the land of Africa; and the chaos which has reigned so long, is converting into beautiful order, and reveals more and more clearly the glorious dispensation of civil and religious liberty, which are so inseparably united, that there is little or no enjoyment of one without the other: Otherwise, perhaps, the Israelites had been less solicitous for their freedom from Egyptian slavery; I do not say they would have been contented without it, by no means; for in every human breast God has implanted a principle, which we call love of freedom; it is impatient of oppression, and pants for deliverance; and by the leave of our modern Egyptians I will assert, that the same principle lives in us. God grant deliverance in his own way and time, and get him honour upon all those whose

---

[3] Phillis refers to several riotous reactions to various British financial and legal impositions on the colonies.

[1] First printed in the *Connecticut Gazette* for March 11, 1774, probably at the behest of the converted Mohegan Indian minister, the Reverend Samson Occom (1723–1792), Phillis's longtime friend, who lived near New London where the *Gazette* was printed. This Wheatley letter was widely reprinted in almost a dozen other New England newspapers, of both Whig and Tory persuasions. The text above is from the printing in the *Newport (R.I.) Mercury* for April 11. This is Phillis Wheatley's strongest anti-slavery statement in print.

avarice impels them to countenance and help forward the calamities of their fellow creatures. This I desire not for their hurt, but to convince them of the strange absurdity of their conduct, whose words and actions are so diametrically opposite. How well the cry for liberty, and the reverse disposition for the exercise of oppressive power over others agree—I humbly think it does not require the penetration of a philosopher to determine."—

1774

Movement West

The Treaty of Paris in 1783, and the Louisiana Purchase only twenty years later, in 1803, allowed the new United States of America to claim vast areas of land, first beyond the Appalachian Mountains and then beyond the Mississippi River. The second event can be considered the point at which the trans-Mississippi West entered United States history. Even as a U.S. delegation to Paris negotiated possible land purchases from France, President Thomas Jefferson initiated plans for an exploratory expedition to the Far West. Starting on May 14, 1804, Meriwether Lewis and William Clark led their "Corps of Discovery" up the Missouri River, across the Rocky Mountains, and down the Clearwater, Snake, and Columbia rivers to the Pacific. On September 23, 1806, they returned to St. Louis. The Lewis and Clark expedition launched a century of western explorations that received national attention and created new popular heroes like John Charles Frémont, Clarence King, and John Wesley Powell. These government-sponsored explorations also demonstrated that the trans-Mississippi would be a region regularly subject to the plans and policies of national officials typically located on the east coast in distant Washington, D.C.

In nineteenth-century exploration and national land policy, eastern expectations sometimes conflicted with western desires. Ultimately, the role of the federal government in the discovery, mapping, and sale of western lands gave way to a demand by many westerners that they control the development of the West. The seeds of today's controversies over who owns the West may be said to have begun with the Land Ordinance of 1785, the Northwest Ordinance of 1787, the Louisiana Purchase of 1803, and the Lewis and Clark expedition of 1804–1806.

Y *D O C U M E N T S*

The three documents reproduced here present different levels of expectation and perception in the act of exploration. The first selection, Thomas Jefferson's instructions to Meriwether Lewis in 1803, reflects nearly pure expectation. The president indicated in great detail what he hopes Lewis and Clark will record during their trek up the Missouri River and across the Rocky Mountains to the Pacific Ocean. In the second document, Meriwether Lewis's entry in the expedition's journals for June 13, 1805, the author describes his attempts to carry out

Jefferson's instructions. At the Great Falls of the Missouri River, near the present-day city of Great Falls, Montana, Lewis wrote of his frustration at trying to convey the beauty of nature through the written word and scientific measurement. Major Stephen H. Long of the government's Topographical Engineers led an expedition west in the summer of 1820. Following the Platte River across present-day Nebraska and then proceeding along the south branch of that river into present-day Colorado, Long's party eventually reached Pike's Peak in mid-July before turning back. His report, reproduced as the third document, appeared under the authorship of Edwin James, the expedition's physician. The map that accompanied this account labeled the area east of the Rocky Mountains as the Great American Desert. Long and James seemed most interested in the agricultural usefulness of the land they explored. Given their expectations, might they have presented the Great Falls of the Missouri very differently from Meriwether Lewis?

Thomas Jefferson's Instructions to Meriwether Lewis, 1803

To Meriwether Lewis, esquire, captain of the first regiment of infantry of the United States of America:

Your situation as secretary of the president of the United States, has made you acquainted with the objects of my confidential message of January 18, 1803, to the legislature; you have seen the act they passed, which, though expressed in general terms, was meant to sanction those objects, and you are appointed to carry them into execution.

Instruments for ascertaining, by celestial observations, the geography of the country through which you will pass, have been already provided. Light articles for barter and presents among the Indians, arms for your attendants, say for from ten to twelve men, boats, tents, and other travelling apparatus, with ammunition, medicine, surgical instruments, and provisions, you will have prepared, with such aids as the secretary at war can yield in his department; and from him also you will receive authority to engage among our troops, by voluntary agreement, the number of attendants above-mentioned; over whom you, as their commanding officer, are invested with all the powers the laws give in such a case.

As your movements, while within the limits of the United States, will be better directed by occasional communications, adapted to circumstances as they arise, they will not be noticed here. What follows will respect your proceedings after your departure from the United States.

Your mission has been communicated to the ministers here from France, Spain, and Great Britain, and through them to their governments; and such assurances given them as to its objects, as we trust will satisfy them. The country of Louisiana having been ceded by Spain to France, the passport you have from the minister of France, the representative of the present sovereign of the country, will be a protection with all its subjects; and that from the minister of England will entitle you to the friendly aid of any traders of that allegiance with whom you may happen to meet.

The object of your mission is to explore the Missouri river, and such principal streams of it, as, by its course and communication with the waters of the Pacific ocean, whether the Columbia, Oregan, Colorado, or any other river, may offer the most direct and practicable water-communication across the continent, for the purposes of commerce.

Beginning at the mouth of the Missouri, you will take observations of latitude and longitude, at all remarkable points on the river, and especially at the mouths of rivers, at rapids, at islands, and other places and objects distinguished by such natural marks and characters, of a durable kind, as that they may with certainty be recognised hereafter. The courses of the river between these points of observation may be supplied by the compass, the log-line, and by time, corrected by the observations themselves. The variations of the needle, too, in different places, should be noticed.

The interesting points of the portage between the heads of the Missouri, and of the water offering the best communication with the Pacific ocean, should also be fixed by observation; and the course of that water to the ocean, in the same manner as that of the Missouri.

Your observations are to be taken with great pains and accuracy; to be entered distinctly and intelligibly for others as well as yourself; to comprehend all the elements necessary, with the aid of the usual tables, to fix the latitude and longitude of the places at which they were taken; and are to be rendered to the war-office, for the purpose of having the calculations made concurrently by proper persons within the United States. Several copies of these, as well as of your other notes, should be made at leisure times, and put into the care of the most trust worthy of your attendants to guard, by multiplying them against the accidental losses to which they will be exposed. A further guard would be, that one of these copies be on the cuticular membranes of the paper-birch, as less liable to injury from damp than common paper.

The commerce which may be carried on with the people inhabiting the line you will pursue, renders a knowledge of those people important. You will therefore endeavour to make yourself acquainted, as far as a diligent pursuit of your journey shall admit, with the names of the nations and their numbers;

The extent and limits of their possessions;

Their relations with other tribes or nations;

Their language, traditions, monuments;

Their ordinary occupations in agriculture, fishing, hunting, war, arts, and the implements for these;

Their food, clothing, and domestic accommodations;

The diseases prevalent among them, and the remedies they use;

Moral and physical circumstances which distinguish them from the tribes we know;

Peculiarities in their laws, customs, and dispositions;

And articles of commerce they may need or furnish, and to what extent.

And, considering the interest which every nation has in extending and strengthening the authority of reason and justice among the people around them, it will be useful to acquire what knowledge you can of the state of morality, religion, and information among them; as it may better enable those who may endeavour to civilize and instruct them, to adapt their measures to the existing notions and practices of those on whom they are to operate.

Other objects worthy of notice will be—

The soil and face of the country, its growth and vegetable productions, especially those not of the United States;

The animals of the country generally, and especially those not known in the United States;

The remains and accounts of any which may be deemed rare or extinct;

The mineral productions of every kind, but more particularly metals, lime-stone, pit-coal, and saltpetre; salines and mineral waters, noting the temperature of the last, and such circumstances as may indicate their character;

Volcanic appearances;

Climate, as characterized by the thermometer, by the proportion of rainy, cloudy, and clear days; by lightning, hail, snow, ice; by the access and recess of frost; by the winds prevailing at different seasons; the dates at which particular plants put forth, or lose their flower or leaf; times of appearance of particular birds, reptiles or insects.

Although your route will be along the channel of the Missouri, yet you will endeavour to inform yourself, by inquiry, of the character and extent of the country watered by its branches, and especially on its southern side. The North river, or Rio Bravo, which runs into the gulf of Mexico, and the North river, or Rio Colorado, which runs into the gulf of California, are understood to be the principal streams heading opposite to the waters of the Missouri, and running southwardly. Whether the dividing grounds between the Missouri and them are mountains or flat lands, what are their distance from the Missouri, the character of the intermediate country, and the people inhabiting it, are worthy of particular inquiry. The northern waters of the Missouri are less to be inquired after, because they have been ascertained to a considerable degree, and are still in a course of ascertainment by English traders and travellers; but if you can learn any thing certain of the most northern source of the Missisipi, and of its position relatively to the Lake of the Woods, it will be interesting to us. Some account too of the path of the Canadian traders from the Missisipi, at the mouth of the Ouisconsing to where it strikes the Missouri, and of the soil and rivers in its course, is desirable.

In all your intercourse with the natives, treat them in the most friendly and conciliatory manner which their own conduct will admit; allay all jealousies as to the object of your journey; satisfy them of its innocence; make them acquainted with the position, extent, character, peaceable and commercial dispositions of the United States; of our wish to be neighbourly, friendly, and useful to them, and of our dispositions to a commercial intercourse with them; confer with them on the points most convenient as mutual emporiums, and the articles of most desirable interchange for them and us. If a few of their influential chiefs, within practicable distance, wish to visit

297

us, arrange such a visit with them, and furnish them with authority to call on our officers on their entering the United States, to have them conveyed to this place at the public expense. If any of them should wish to have some of their young people brought up with us, and taught such arts as may be useful to them, we will receive, instruct, and take care of them. Such a mission, whether of influential chiefs, or of young people, would give some security to your own party. Carry with you some matter of the kine-pox [cowpox]; inform those of them with whom you may be of its efficacy as a preservative from the small-pox, and instruct and encourage them in the use of it. This may be especially done wherever you winter.

As it is impossible for us to foresee in what manner you will be received by those people, whether with hospitality or hostility, so is it impossible to prescribe the exact degree of perseverance with which you are to pursue your journey. We value too much the lives of citizens to offer them to probable destruction. Your numbers will be sufficient to secure you against the unauthorized opposition of individuals, or of small parties; but if a superior force, authorized, or not authorized, by a nation, should be arrayed against your further passage, and inflexibly determined to arrest it, you must decline its further pursuit and return. In the loss of yourselves we should lose also the information you will have acquired. By returning safely with that, you may enable us to renew the essay with better calculated means. To your own discretion, therefore, must be left the degree of danger you may risk, and the point at which you should decline, only saying, we wish you to err on the side of your safety, and to bring back your party safe, even if it be with less information.

As far up the Missouri as the white settlements extend, an intercourse will probably be found to exist between them and the Spanish posts of St. Louis opposite Cahokia, or St. Genevieve opposite Kaskaskia. From still further up the river the traders may furnish a conveyance for letters. Beyond that you may perhaps be able to engage Indians to bring letters for the government to Cahokia, or Kaskaskia, on promising that they shall there receive such special compensation as you shall have stipulated with them. Avail yourself of these means to communicate to us, at seasonable intervals, a copy of your journal, notes and observations of every kind, putting into cypher whatever might do injury if betrayed.

Should you reach the Pacific ocean, inform yourself of the circumstances which may decide whether the furs of those parts may not be collected as advantageously at the head of the Missouri (convenient as is supposed to the waters of the Colorado and Oregan or Columbia) as at Nootka Sound, or any other point of that coast; and that trade be consequently conducted through the Missouri and United States more beneficially than by the circumnavigation now practised.

On your arrival on that coast, endeavour to learn if there be any port within your reach frequented by the sea vessels of any nation, and to send two of your trusty people back by sea, in such way as shall appear practicable, with a copy of your notes; and should you be of opinion that the return of your party by the way they went will be imminently dangerous, then ship the whole, and return by sea, by the way either of Cape Horn, or the Cape of Good Hope, as you shall be able. As you will be without money, clothes, or provisions, you must endeavour to use the credit of the United States to obtain them; for which purpose open letters of credit shall be furnished you, authorizing you to draw on the executive of the United States, or any of its officers, in any part of the world, on which draughts can be disposed of, and to apply with our recommendations to the consuls, agents, merchants, or citizens of any nation with which we have intercourse, assuring them, in our name, that any aids they may furnish you shall be honourably repaid, and on demand. Our consuls, Thomas Hewes, at Batavia, in Java, William Buchanan, in the Isles of France and Bourbon, and John Elmslie, at the Cape of Good Hope, will be able to supply your necessities, by draughts on us.

Should you find it safe to return by the way you go, after sending two of your party round by sea, or with your whole party, if no conveyance by sea can be found, do so; making such observations on your return as may serve to supply, correct, or confirm those made on your outward journey.

On reentering the United States and reaching a place of safety, discharge any of your attendants who may desire and deserve it, procuring for them immediate payment of all arrears of pay and clothing which may have incurred since their departure, and assure them that they shall be recommended to the liberality of the legislature for the grant of a soldier's portion of land each, as proposed in my message to congress, and repair yourself, with your papers, to the seat of government.

To provide, on the accident of your death, against anarchy, dispersion, and the consequent danger to your party, and total failure of the enterprise, you are hereby authorized, by any instrument signed and written in your own hand, to name the person among them who shall succeed to the command on your decease, and by like instruments to change the nomination, from time to time, as further experience of the characters accompanying you shall point out superior fitness; and all the powers and authorities given to yourself are, in the event of your death, transferred to, and vested in the successor so named, with further power to him and his successors, in like manner to name each his successor, who, on the death of his predecessor, shall be invested with all the powers and authorities given to yourself. Given under my hand at the city of Washington, this twentieth day of June, 1803.

THOMAS JEFFERSON,
President of the United States of America.

Meriwether Lewis at the Great Falls of the Missouri, 1805

Thursday June 13th 1805.

This morning we set out about sunrise after taking breakfast off our venison and fish. we again ascended the hills of the river and gained the level country. the country through which we passed for the first six miles tho' more roling than that we had passed yesterday might still with propryety be deemed a level country; our course as yesterday was generally S W. the river from the place we left it appeared to make a considerable bend to the South. from the extremity of this roling country I overlooked a most beatifull and level plain of great extent or at least 50 or sixty miles; in this there were infinitely more buffaloe than I had ever before witnessed at a view. nearly in the direction I had been travling or S. W. two curious mountains presented themselves of square figures, the sides rising perpendicularly to the hight of 250 feet and appeared to be formed of yellow clay; their tops appeared to be level plains; these inaccessible hights appeared like the ramparts of immence fortifications; I have no doubt but with very little assistance from art they might be rendered impregnable. fearing that the river boar to the South and that I might pass the falls if they existed between this an the snowey mountains I altered my course nealy to the South leaving those insulated hills to my wright and proceeded through the plain; I sent Feels on my right and Drewyer and Gibson on my left with orders to kill some meat and join me at the river where I should halt for dinner. I had proceded on this course about two miles with Goodrich at some distance behind me whin my ears were saluted with the agreeable sound of a fall of water and advancing a little further I saw the spray arrise above the plain like a collumn of smoke which would frequently dispear again in an instant caused I presume by the wind which blew pretty hard from the S. W. I did not however loose my direction to this point which soon began to make a roaring too tremendious to be mistaken for any cause short of the great falls of the Missouri. here I arrived about 12 OClock having traveled by estimate about 15 Miles. I hurryed down the hill which was about 200 feet high and difficult of access, to gaze on this sublimely grand specticle. I took my position on the top of some rocks about 20 feet high opposite the center of the falls. this chain of rocks appear once to have formed a part of those over which the waters tumbled, but in the course of time has been seperated from it to the distance of 150 yards lying prarrallel to it and forming a butment against which the water after falling over the precipice beats with great fury; this barrier extends on the right to the perpendicular clift which forms that board [bound? border?] of the river but to the distance of 120 yards next to the clift it is but a few feet

Reprinted from *The Journals of the Lewis and Clark Expedition*, Volume 4, 283–87, edited by Gary E. Moulton, by permission of University of Nebraska Press.

above the level of the water, and here the water in very high tides appears to pass in a channel of 40 yds. next to the higher part of the ledg of rocks; on the left it extends within 80 or ninty yards of the lard. Clift which is also perpendicular; between this abrupt extremity of the ledge of rocks and the perpendicular bluff the whole body of water passes with incredible swiftness. immediately at the cascade the river is about 300 yds. wide; about ninty or a hundred yards of this next the Lard. bluff is a smoth even sheet of water falling over a precipice of at least eighty feet, the remaining part of about 200 yards on my right formes the grandest sight I ever beheld, the hight of the fall is the same of the other but the irregular and somewhat projecting rocks below receives the water in it's passage down and brakes it into a perfect white foam which assumes a thousand forms in a moment sometimes flying up in jets of sparkling foam to the hight of fifteen or twenty feet and are scarcely formed before large roling bodies of the same beaten and foaming water is thrown over and conceals them. in short the rocks seem to be most happily fixed to present a sheet of the whitest beaten froath for 200 yards in length and about 80 feet perpendicular. the water after decending strikes against the butment before mentioned or that on which I stand and seems to reverberate and being met by the more impetuous courant they role and swell into half formed billows of great hight which rise and again disappear in an instant. this butment of rock defends a handsom little bottom of about three acres which is deversified and agreeably shaded with some cottonwood trees; in the lower extremity of the bottom there is a very thick grove of the same kind of trees which are small, in this wood there are several Indian lodges formed of sticks. a few small cedar grow near the ledge of rocks where I rest. below the point of these rocks at a small distance the river is divided by a large rock which rises several feet above the water, and extends downwards with the stream for about 20 yards. about a mile before the water arrives at the pitch it decends very rappidly, and is confined on the Lard. side by a perpendicular clift of about 100 feet, on Stard. side it is also perpendicular for about three hundred yards above the pitch where it is then broken by the discharge of a small ravine, down which the buffaloe have a large beaten road to the water, for it is but in very few places that these anamals can obtain water near this place owing to the steep and inaccessible banks. I see several skelletons of the buffaloe lying in the edge of the water near the Stard. bluff which I presume have been swept down by the current and precipitated over this tremendious fall. about 300 yards below me there is another butment of solid rock with a perpendicular face and abot 60 feet high which projects from the Stard. side at right angles to the distance of 134 yds. and terminates the lower part nearly of the bottom before mentioned; there being a passage arround the end of this butment between it and the river of about 20 yardes; here the river again assumes it's usual width soon spreading to near 300 yards but still continues it's rappidity. from the reflection of the sun on the spray or mist which arrises from these falls there is a beatifull rainbow produced which adds not a little to the beauty of this majestically grand senery. after wrighting this imperfect discription

I again viewed the falls and was so much disgusted with the imperfect idea which it conveyed of the scene that I determined to draw my pen across it and begin agin, but then reflected that I could not perhaps succeed better than pening the first impressions of the mind; I wished for the pencil of Salvator Rosa or the pen of Thompson,* that I might be enabled to give to the enlightened world some just idea of this truly magnifficent and sublimely grand object, which has from the commencement of time been concealed from the view of civilized man; but this was fruitless and vain. I most sincerely regreted that I had not brought a crimee obscura** with me by the assistance of which even I could have hoped to have done better but alas this was also out of my reach; I therefore with the assistance of my pen only indeavoured to trace some of the stronger features of this seen by the assistance of which and my recollection aided by some able pencil I hope still to give to the world some faint idea of an object which at this moment fills me with such pleasure and astonishment, and which of it's kind I will venture to ascert is second to but one in the known world. I retired to the shade of a tree where I determined to fix my camp for the present and dispatch a man in the morning to inform Capt. C. and the party of my success in finding the falls and settle in their minds all further doubts as to the Missouri. the hunters now arrived loaded with excellent buffaloe meat and informed me that they had killed three very fat cows about ¾ of a mile hence. I directed them after they had refreshed themselves to go back and butcher them and bring another load of meat each to our camp determining to employ those who remained with me in drying meat for the party against their arrival. in about 2 hours or at 4 OClock P. M. they set out on this duty, and I walked down the river about three miles to discover if possible some place to which the canoes might arrive or at which they might be drawn on shore in order to be taken by land above the falls; but returned without effecting either of these objects; the river was one continued sene of rappids and cascades which I readily perceived could not be encountered with our canoes, and the Clifts still retained their perpendicular structure and were from 150 to 200 feet high; in short the river appears here to have woarn a channel in the process of time through a solid rock. on my return I found the party at camp; they had butchered the buffaloe and brought in some more meat as I had directed. Goodrich had caught half a douzen very fine trout and a number of both species of the white fish. these trout are from sixteen to twenty three inches in length, precisely resemble our mountain or speckled trout in form and the position of their fins, but the specks on these are of a deep black instead of the red or goald colour of those common to the U.' States. these are furnished long sharp

* Salvator Rosa, a seventeenth-century Italian landscape painter, generally painted wild, desolate scenes. James Thomson, an eighteenth-century Scottish poet, was a forerunner of the English Romantic movement; his best-known poem was "The Seasons."
** A camera obscura, basically a box with a lens mounted on one wall; light entering through the lens would project an image on the opposite wall of the dark box, which an artist could then trace, getting an almost photographic image.

teeth on the pallet and tongue and have generally a small dash of red on each side behind the front ventral fins; the flesh is of a pale yellowish red, or when in good order, of a rose red.—

I am induced to believe that the Brown, the white and the Grizly bear of this country are the same species only differing in colour from age or more probably from the same natural cause that many other anamals of the same family differ in colour. one of those which we killed yesterday was of a creemcoloured white while the other in company with it was of the common bey or rdish brown, which seems to be the most usual colour of them. the white one appeared from it's tallons and teath to be the youngest; it was smaller than the other, and although a monstrous beast we supposed that it had not yet attained it's growth and that it was a little upwards of two years old. the young cubs which we have killed have always been of a brownish white, but none of them as white as that we killed yesterday. one other that we killed sometime since which I mentioned sunk under some driftwood and was lost, had a white stripe or list of about eleven inches wide entirely arround his body just behind the shoalders, and was much darker than these bear usually are. the grizly bear we have never yet seen. I have seen their tallons in possession of the Indians and from their form I am perswaded if there is any difference between this species and the brown or white bear it is very inconsiderable. There is no such anamal as a black bear in this open country or of that species generally denominated the black bear

my fare is really sumptuous this evening; buffaloe's humps, tongues and marrowbones, fine trout parched meal pepper and salt, and a good appetite; the last is not considered the least of the luxuries.

The Stephen Long Expedition's Report of a Frontier Barrier, 1821

Of the country situated between the meridian of the Council Bluff and the Rocky Mountains

We next proceed to a description of the country westward of the assumed meridian, and extending to the Rocky Mountains, which are its western boundary. This section embraces an extent of about four hundred miles square, lying between 96 and 105 degrees of west longitude, and between 35 and 42 degrees of north latitude.

Proceeding westwardly across the meridian above specified, the hilly country gradually subsides, giving place to a region of vast extent, spreading towards the north and south, and presenting an undulating surface, with nothing to limit the view or variegate the prospect, but here and there a hill, knob, or insulated tract of table-land. At length the Rocky Mountains break upon the view, towering abruptly from the plains, and mingling their snow-capped summits with the clouds.

On approaching the mountains, no other change is observable in the general aspect of the country, except that the isolated knobs and table-lands above alluded to become more frequent and more distinctly marked, the bluffs by which the valleys of watercourses are bounded present a greater abundance of rocks, stones lie in greater profusion upon the surface, and the soil becomes more sandy and sterile. If, to the characteristics above intimated, we add that of an almost complete destitution of woodland (for not more than one thousandth part of the section can be said to possess a timber-growth) we shall have a pretty correct idea of the general aspect of the whole country. . . .

Immediately at the base of the mountains, and also at those of some of the insular table-lands, are situated many remarkable ridges, rising in the form of parapets, to the height of between fifty and one hundred and fifty feet. These appear to have been attached to the neighbouring heights, of which they once constituted a part, but have, at some remote period, been cleft asunder from them by some extraordinary convulsion of nature, which has prostrated them in their present condition.

The rocky stratifications, of which these ridges are principally composed, and which are exactly similar to those of the insulated table-lands, are variously inclined, having various dips, from forty-five to eighty degrees.

Throughout this section of country the surface is occasionally characterized by water-worn pebbles, and gravel of granite, gneiss, and quartz, but the predominant characteristic is sand, which in many instances prevails almost to the entire exclusion of vegetable mould. Large tracts are often to be met with, exhibiting scarcely a trace of vegetation. The whole region, as before hinted, is almost entirely destitute of a timber-growth of any description. In some few instances, however, sandy knobs and ridges make their appearance, thickly covered with red cedars of a dwarfish growth. There are also some few tracts clad in a growth of pitch pine and scrubby oaks; but, in general, nothing of vegetation appears upon the uplands but withered grass of a stinted growth, no more than two or three inches high, prickly pears profusely covering extensive tracts, and weeds of a few varieties, which, like the prickly pear, seem to thrive best in the most arid and sterile soil. . . .

In regard to this extensive section of country, I do not hesitate in giving the opinion, that it is almost wholly unfit for cultivation, and of course uninhabitable by a people depending upon agriculture for their subsistence. Although tracts of fertile land considerably extensive are occasionally to be met with, yet the scarcity of wood and water, almost uniformly prevalent, will prove an insuperable obstacle in the way of settling the country. This objection rests not only against the section immediately under consideration, but applies with equal propriety to a much larger portion of the country. Agreeably to the best intelligence that can be had, concerning the country both northward and southward of the section, and especially to the inferences deducible from the account given by Lewis and Clarke of the country situated between the Missouri and the Rocky Mountains above the river Platte, the vast region commencing near the sources of the Sabine, Trinity, Brases, and Colorado, and extending northwardly to the forty-ninth degree of north latitude, by which the United States' territory is limited in that direction, is throughout of a similar character. The whole of this region seems peculiarly adapted as a range for buffaloes, wild goats, and other wild game; incalculable multitudes of which find ample pasturage and subsistence upon it.

This region, however, viewed as a frontier, may prove of infinite importance to the United States, inasmuch as it is calculated to serve as a barrier to prevent too great an extension of our population westward, and secure us against the machinations or incursions of an enemy that might otherwise be disposed to annoy us in that part of our frontier.

*The assumption of white Anglo-Saxon cultural superiority infused many histori-
cal developments in the nineteenth-century United States. Was this assumption
the same as racism? In government policies toward American Indians and Mexicans, the possibility of racist motivations has been considered by several historians. Linked with this question is the commitment to national expansion that
nineteenth-century Americans often referred to as "Manifest Destiny." Did racism spur white Americans and their national government to remove the Indians
from the eastern United States to territories west of the Mississippi, and then to
pursue wars of land acquisition against the western Indians and the nation of
Mexico? When different cultures collide, are the aggressive acts of the victorious,
dominant society too readily considered "racist"? Can other motivations, even
good intentions, sometimes explain what happened?*

Y DOCUMENTS

The first four documents present justifications for and reactions to the policy of
Indian removal. In 1835, leaders of a small faction of the Cherokees, representing possibly one thousand of the sixteen thousand tribal members, signed the
Treaty of New Echota. Ratified by the U.S. Congress in 1836, this treaty forced
the ultimate removal of the Cherokees to the Indian Territory west of the Mississippi River. Not surprisingly, Congressman Charles Eaton Haynes of Georgia,
in whose state most of the Cherokee Nation was located, supported a bill to finance the removal mandated by the treaty. His remarks, reprinted as the first
document, summarize some of the history of the removal policy. Haynes argues
that the Indians need to be removed because of the presence of degrading white
neighbors who might overwhelm them. In the second selection, President Andrew Jackson's annual message of 1835, the chief executive communicates a
similar perspective. He maintains that the Indians can attain prosperity and progress only if they are separated from whites. Like Haynes, Jackson stresses the
benefits to be gained by the native Americans.

The third document is the statement by the Cherokees' National Council of
August 1, 1838—two months before the main body of the tribe left on its forced
march, the Trail of Tears. It is an eloquent rebuttal of the Treaty of New Echota
and of the removal policy. The Trail of Tears lasted from October 1838 to March
1839. At least two thousand of the sixteen thousand Cherokees died on this journey to the Indian Territory in what is now Oklahoma. In November 1838, Commissioner of Indian Affairs T. Harley Crawford did not know of this high rate of
mortality when he wrote about what he considered a humane and benevolent
policy of removal. Crawford's report on Indian relations appears as the fourth
selection.

The final four documents present opinions about and observations of Mexicans. In the fifth document, dating from early January 1848, Senator John C.
Calhoun of South Carolina, the great advocate of black slavery, argues before
Congress at the conclusion of the Mexican War that the conquered nation should
not be incorporated into the United States. He bases his view on a system of
racial hierarchy that placed some Indian tribes above the Mexicans. Later in the
same month, Senator John A. Dix of New York spoke to Congress of an inevitable expansion of the United States that he believed dictated the annexation of
some of Mexico and its peoples. Dix's prejudiced plea is reprinted as the sixth
selection. Both Calhoun and Dix had clear opinions of the undesirable results of
mixing the races.

In the seventh document, an excerpt from the 1845 *Emigrants' Guide to California and Oregon*, author Lansford W. Hastings displays a negative view of the Mexicans in Alta California and of their religion. In the final selection, published in 1848, Edwin Bryant, a visitor to California, expresses a more positive and far less judgmental attitude toward the Hispanic Californians than Hastings's. Still, each man reveals deeply felt personal beliefs about class distinctions and racial mixing.

Charles Eaton Haynes on Indian Removal, 1836

When [the Andrew Jackson] administration came into power, seven years ago, it found a partial system of Indian colonization west of the Mississippi in operation; partial, not in withholding its benefits from any tribe which might desire to enjoy them, but only inasmuch as it embraced but a portion of the tribes then residing east of the Mississippi. The principal of these were a portion of the Creeks and Cherokees, to which have been since added the Choctaws and Chickasaws, with numerous smaller bands, together with a treaty in 1832 contemplating the removal of the remaining and greater portion of the Creeks; and, lately, the treaty with the Cherokees, to provide for the fulfilment of which the present appropriation is asked at our hands. Within the last six or seven years, the policy of removing and colonizing the Indians in the States east of the Mississippi, to the westward of that river, in a region remote from the habitation of the white man, has been among the topics of universal and bitter discussion from one end of the Union to the other. Nor on any other subject has the course of General Jackson's administration been more violently or unjustly assailed. And here I take leave to say, that so far from Indian hostilities having been provoked, either by the negligence or injustice of that administration, they may, with much greater justice, be ascribed to the political philanthropy, so loudly and pharisaically displayed by its political opponents; and I will further say, that should war arise on the part of the Cherokees, the sin of it lies not at the door of this administration, or its supporters. It may not be amiss to inquire, briefly, into the history of Indian emigration west of the Mississippi. If I am not greatly mistaken, one of the motives which induced Mr. Jefferson to desire the annexation of Louisiana to the United States was the prospective removal of the eastern Indians to its remote and uninhabited regions.

Certain it is, that in January, 1809, when addressed by a Cherokee delegation on that subject, he encouraged their examination of the country high up on Arkansas and White rivers, and promised to aid them in their emigration to it, if they should desire to remove after having explored it. It is believed that a portion of the tribe did emigrate to that country not long afterwards. Within the first year of Mr. Monroe's administration, the year 1819, a treaty was made with the whole tribe, providing for the emigration of such portion as might wish to join their brethren west of the Mississippi; and if the terms of that treaty had not been materially changed by another entered into in the year 1819, there can be but little doubt that a much larger number would have done so. But it may be answered, that, so far, the Government had not entered upon any general system upon this subject; and that, in the partial emigrations which had then taken place, it rather followed, than attempted to lead, the inclination of the Indians. However this may have been, the whole aspect of the question was changed by the especial message communicated to Congress by Mr. [James] Monroe, on the 27th of January, 1825, in which he stated that it had long occupied the attention of the Government, and recommended a general plan of Indian emigration and colonization west of the Mississippi, accompanied by an elaborate report of the Secretary of War on the subject. But a short period of Mr. Monroe's term of service then remained unexpired; but he did not go out of office until he had communicated to the Senate the treaty of the Indian Spring, of February of the same year, which provided, among other things, for an exchange of territory, and the removal of such of the Creek Indians as might desire it, beyond the Mississippi, and the operation of which treaty was arrested by his successor, in the manner I have already stated.

In 1826, an arrangement was made by the then Chief Magistrate for the removal of a portion of the Creeks to the west of the Mississippi; and in 1828, a treaty with the Cherokees of the west, which looked to the same object. Thus it appears, that, although by the act of Congress passed in May, 1830, and the treaties concluded with the Choctaws in 1830, with the Creeks in 1832, the Seminoles in 1834, and more recently with the Cherokees, and within the same period with many smaller bands, the scheme of Indian emigration and colonization west of the States and Territories beyond the Mississippi has been enlarged and systematized, its germe has a much earlier date, and the whole was recommended by Mr. Monroe in 1825. . . . It might, therefore, on the score of time and the authority of high names, be considered worse than useless to explain or defend it. But as this is the last time that I propose ever to discuss this subject, I hope I may be permitted to present a few considerations, derived from experience and the nature of things, why this system is best, both for the whites and the Indians, and especially for the latter. The races are as separate and distinct as color, character, and general condition, could well make them; the one possessing the arts and knowledge of cultivated life—the other the rude, unpolished nature of the savage. The consequence might, therefore, be naturally expected, that it is impossible that they should constitute one community with any thing like practical equality between them. Nor has experience in the slightest degree disappointed the deductions which a sound logic would have derived from these considerations. I have been told, and am in no way disposed to doubt it, that for many years past the remnants of Indian tribes still lingering in most of the old States of this Union have been treated with kindness and humanity. But of what avail have been all the efforts of ages to elevate their character and improve their condition? Alas! that character has continued to descend to the lowest depths of degradation, and that condition to unmitigated misery. Thus has it always been with the Indians, when surrounded by a white population; and thus it must always be, until the laws of nature and society shall undergo such change as can only be produced by the impress of the Deity. Nor can there be difficulty in explaining it. The poor Indian, (and in such condition he is indeed poor,) of inferior and degraded cast, associates with none of the white race, but such as are qualified to sink him into still deeper degradation. What, then, should be done to save the remnant from the moral pestilence which would inevitably await them, if relief and salvation shall be delayed until these causes shall be bought to operate upon them? There is no remedy but to remove them beyond the reach of the contamination which will surely come over them, if permitted to remain until they shall be surrounded by the causes to which I have adverted.

Andrew Jackson on Indian Removal, 1835

The plan of removing the aboriginal people who yet remain within the settled portions of the United States to the country west of the Mississippi River approaches its consummation. It was adopted on the most mature consideration of the condition of this race, and ought to be persisted in till the object is accomplished, and prosecuted with as much vigor as a just regard to their circumstances will permit, and as fast as their consent can be obtained. All preceding experiments for the improvement of the Indians have failed. It seems now to be an established fact that they can not live in contact with a civilized community and prosper. Ages of fruitless endeavors have at length brought us to a knowledge of this principle of intercommunication with them. The past we can not recall, but the future we can provide for. Independently of the treaty stipulations into which we have entered with the various tribes for the usufructuary rights they have ceded to us, no one can doubt the moral duty of the Government of the United States to protect and if possible to preserve and perpetuate the scattered remnants of this race which are left within our borders. In the discharge of this duty an extensive region in the West has been assigned for their permanent residence. It has been divided into districts and allotted among them. Many have already removed and others are preparing to go, and with the exception of two small bands living in Ohio and Indiana, not exceeding 1,500 persons, and of the Cherokees, all the tribes on the east side of the Mississippi, and extending from Lake Michigan to Florida, have entered into engagements which will lead to their transplantation.

The plan for their removal and reestablishment is founded upon the knowledge we have gained of their character and habits, and has been dictated by a spirit of enlarged liberality. A territory exceeding in extent that relinquished has been granted to each tribe. Of its climate, fertility, and capacity to support an Indian population the representations are highly favorable. To these districts the Indians are removed at the expense of the United States, and with certain supplies of clothing, arms, ammunition, and other indispensable articles; they are also furnished gratuitously with provisions for the period of a year after their arrival at their new homes. In that time, from the nature of the country and of the products raised by them, they can subsist themselves by agricultural labor, if they choose to resort to that mode of life; if they do not they are upon the skirts of the great prairies, where countless herds of buffalo roam, and a short time suffices to adapt their own habits to the changes which a change of the animals destined for their food may require. Ample arrangements have also been made for the support of schools; in some instances council houses and churches are to be erected, dwellings constructed for the chiefs, and mills for common use. Funds have been set apart for the maintenance of the poor; the most necessary mechanical arts have been introduced, and blacksmiths, gunsmiths, wheelwrights, millwrights, etc., are supported among them. Steel and iron, and sometimes salt, are purchased for them, and plows and other farming utensils, domestic animals, looms, spinning wheels, cards, etc., are presented to them. And besides these beneficial arrangements, annuities are in all cases paid, amounting in some instances to more than $30 for each individual of the tribe, and in all cases sufficiently great, if justly divided and prudently expended, to enable them, in addition to their own exertions, to live comfortably. And as a stimulus for exertion, it is now provided by law that "in all cases of the appointment of interpreters or other persons employed for the benefit of the Indians a preference shall be given to persons of Indian descent, if such can be found who are properly qualified for the discharge of the duties."

Such are the arrangements for the physical comfort and for the moral improvement of the Indians. The necessary measures for their political advancement and for their separation from our citizens have not been neglected. The pledge of the United States has been given by Congress that the country destined for the residence of this people shall be forever "secured and guaranteed to them." A country west of Missouri and Arkansas has been assigned to them, into which the white settlements are not to be pushed. No political communities can be formed in that extensive region, except those which are established by the Indians themselves or by the United States for them and with their concurrence. A barrier has thus been raised for their protection against the encroachment of our citizens, and guarding the Indians as far as possible from those evils which have brought them to their present condition. Summary authority has been given by law to destroy all ardent spirits found in their country, without waiting the doubtful result and slow process of a legal seizure. I consider the absolute and unconditional interdiction of this article among these people as the first and great step in their melioration. Halfway measures will answer no purpose. These can not successfully contend against the cupidity of the seller and the overpowering appetite of the buyer. And the destructive effects of the traffic are marked in every page of the history of our Indian intercourse.

Some general legislation seems necessary for the regulation of the relations which will exist in this new state of things between the Government and people of the United States and these transplanted Indian tribes, and for the establishment among the latter, and with their own consent, of some principles of intercommunication which their juxtaposition will call for; that moral may be substituted for physical force, the authority of a few and simple laws for the tomahawk, and that an end may be put to those bloody wars whose prosecution seems to have made part of their social system.

After the further details of this arrangement are completed, with a very general supervision over them, they ought to be left to the progress of events. These, I indulge the hope, will secure their prosperity and improvement, and a large portion of the moral debt we owe them will then be paid.

Statement of the National Council of the Cherokees, 1838

AQUOHEE CAMP, *August* 1, 1838.

Whereas, the title of the Cherokee people to their lands, is the most ancient, pure, and absolute known to man; its date is beyond the reach of human record; its validity confirmed and illustrated by possession and enjoyment antecedent to all pretence of claim by any other portion of the human race:

And whereas, the free consent of the Cherokee people is indispensable to a valid transfer of the Cherokee title; and whereas, the said Cherokee people have neither by themselves, nor their representatives, given such consent; it follows that the original title and ownership of said lands still vest in the Cherokee nation unimpaired and absolute:

Resolved, therefore, By the national committee and council, and people of the Cherokee nation, in general council assembled, That the whole Cherokee territory, as described in the first article of the treaty of 1819, between the United States and the Cherokee nation, still remains the rightful and undoubted property of the said Cherokee nation. And that all damages and losses, direct or incidental, resulting from the enforcement of the alleged stipulations of the pretended treaty of New Echota, are in justice and equity chargeable to the account of the United States.

And whereas, the Cherokee people have existed as a distinct national community, in the possession and exercise of the appropriate and essential attributes of sovereignty, for a period extending into antiquity beyond the dates and records and memory of man:

And whereas, these attributes, with the rights and franchises which they involve, have never been relinquished by the Cherokee people, but are now in full force and virtue.

And whereas, the natural, political, and moral relations subsisting among the citizens of the Cherokee nation towards each other, and towards the body politic, cannot in reason and justice be dissolved by the expulsion of the nation from its own territory by the power of the United States' Government:

Resolved, therefore, By the national committee and council, and people of the Cherokee nation, in general council assembled, That the inherent sovereignty of the Cherokee nation, together with the constitution, laws, and usages of the same, is, and by the authority aforesaid, is hereby declared in full force and virtue, and shall continue so to be, in perpetuity, subject to such modifications as the general welfare may render expedient.

Resolved, further, That the Cherokee people, in consenting to an investigation of their individual claims, and receiving payment upon them, and for their improvements, do not intend that it shall be so construed as yielding or giving their sanction or approval to the pretended treaty of 1835: nor as compromitting, in any manner, their just claim against the United States hereafter, for a full and satisfactory indemnification for their country, and for all individual losses and injuries.

And be it further Resolved, That the principal chief be, and he is hereby authorized to select and appoint such persons as he may deem necessary and suitable for the purpose of collecting and registering all individual claims against the United States, with the proofs, and to report to him their proceedings as they progress.

RICHARD TAYLOR,

President National Council.

GOING SNAKE,

Speaker of Council.

STEPHEN FOREMAN, *Clerk Nat. Committee.*

Capt. Brown,	Richard Foreman,	Samuel Christee,
Toonowee,	William,	Kotaquaskee,
Katelah,	Howestee,	Yoh-natsee,
Ooyah Kee,	Beaver Carrier,	Samuel Foreman.

Signed by a Committee in behalf of the people.

T. Hartley Crawford's Report on Indian Affairs, 1838

WAR DEPARTMENT,
Office of Indian Affairs, November 25, 1838.

SIR: In compliance with your directions, the following report is made of the transactions of this office for the last year.

The most striking feature of the peculiar relations that the Indians bear to the United States is their removal to the west side of the Mississippi— a change of residence effected under treaties, and with the utmost regard to their comfort that the circumstances of each admitted. The advance of white settlements, and the consuming effect of their approach to the red man's home, had long been observed by the humane with pain, as leading to the speedy extinction of the weaker party. But it is not believed that any suggestion of the policy now in a course of execution was authoritatively made prior to the commencement of the present century. Since, it has repeatedly, and at various intervals, received the sanction of the Chief Magistrates of the United States, and of one or the other House of Congress; without, however, any definite action, previous to the law passed eight years ago. Treaty engagements had been previously made for their removal West with several of the tribes; but the act referred to was a formal and general recognition of the measure, as desirable in regard of all the Indians within any State or Territory east of the Mississippi. Whatever apprehensions might have been honestly entertained of the results of this scheme, the arguments in favor of its adoption, deduced from observation, and the destructive effects of a continuance in their old positions, are so far strengthened by the success attendant upon its execution as to have convinced all, it is thought, of the humane and benevolent tendency of the measure. Experience had shown that, however commendable the efforts to meliorate a savage surrounded by a white population, they were not compensated to any great extent by the gratification which is the best reward of doing good. A few individuals in a still smaller number of tribes have been educated, and profited by the opportunities afforded them to become civilized and highly respectable men; but the mass has retrograded, giving by the contrast greater prominency to their more wisely judging brethren. What can even the moral and educated Indian promise himself in a white settlement? Equality he does not and cannot possess, and the influence that is the just possession of his qualities in the ordinary social relations of life is denied him. Separated from deteriorating associations with white men, the reverse will be the fact. A fair and wide field will be open before him, in which he can cultivate the moral and intellectual virtues of the human beings around him, and aid in elevating them to the highest condition which they are capable of reaching. If these views are correct, the reflection is pleasant that is derived from the belief that a greater sacrifice of feeling is not made in their removal than falls to the lot of our fellow-citizens, in the numerous changes of residence that considerations of bettering their condition are daily producing. Indeed, it cannot be admitted to be so great; for, while the white man moves west or south, accompanied by his family only, the Indians go by tribes, carrying with them all the pleasures of ancient acquaintance, common habits, and common interests. It can scarcely be contended that they are more susceptible of suffering at the breaking up of local associations than we are; for, apart from their condition not favoring the indulgence of the finer feelings, fact proves that they sell a part of their possessions without reluctance, and leave their cabins, and burial-places, and the mounds and monuments which were the objects of their pride or affection, for a remote position in the same district. For whatever they have ceded to the United States they have been amply compensated. I speak not of former times, to which reference is not made, but of later days. The case of the Cherokees is a striking example of the liberality of the Government in all its branches. By the treaty, they had stipulated to remove west of the Mississippi within two years from its ratification, which took place on 23d May, 1836. The obligations of the United States, State rights, and acts by virtue of those rights, and in anticipation of Cherokee removal, made a compliance with this provision of the treaty indispensable at the time stipulated, or as soon thereafter as it was practicable without harshness. To ensure it, General [Winfield] Scott was despatched to their late country, and performed a delicate and difficult duty, embarrassed by circumstances over which there is no human control, with great judgment and humanity.

John C. Calhoun on Incorporating Mexico, 1848

Sir, we have heard how much glory our country has acquired in this war. I acknowledge it to the full amount, Mr. President, so far as military glory is concerned. The army has done nobly, chivalrously; they have conferred honor on the country, for which I sincerely thank them.

. . . Now, sir, much as I regard military glory; much as I rejoice to behold our people in possession of the indomitable energy and courage which surmount all difficulties, and which class them amongst the first military people of the age, I would be very sorry indeed that our Government should lose any reputation for wisdom, moderation, discretion, justice, and those other high qualities which have distinguished us in the early stages of our history.

. . . It is without example or precedent, either to hold Mexico as a province, or to incorporate her into our Union. No example of such a line of policy can be found. We have conquered many of the neighboring tribes of Indians, but we never thought of holding them in subjection—never of incorporating them into our Union. They have either been left as an independent people amongst us, or been driven into the forests.

I know further, sir, that we have never dreamt of incorporating into our Union any but the Caucasian race—the free white race. To incorporate Mexico, would be the very first instance of the kind of incorporating an Indian race; for more than half of the Mexicans are Indians, and the other is composed chiefly of mixed tribes. I protest against such a union as that! Ours, sir, is the Government of a white race. The greatest misfortunes of Spanish America are to be traced to the fatal error of placing these colored races on an equality with the white race. That error destroyed the social arrangement which formed the basis of society. The Portuguese and ourselves have escaped—the Portuguese at least to some extent—and we are the only people on this continent which have made revolutions without being followed by anarchy. And yet it is professed and talked about to erect these Mexicans into a Territorial Government, and place them on an equality with the people of the United States. I protest utterly against such a project.

Sir, it is a remarkable fact, that in the whole history of man, as far as my knowledge extends, there is no instance whatever of any civilized colored races being found equal to the establishment of free popular government, although by far the largest portion of the human family is composed of these races. And even in the savage state we scarcely find them anywhere with such government, except it be our noble savages—for noble I will call them. They, for the most part, had free institutions, but they are easily sustained amongst a savage people. Are we to overlook this fact? Are we to associate with ourselves as equals, companions, and fellow-citizens, the Indians and mixed race of Mexico? Sir, I should consider such a thing as fatal to our institutions. . . .

I come now to the proposition of incorporating her into our Union. Well, as far as law is concerned, that is easy. You can establish a Territorial Government for every State in Mexico, and there are some twenty of them. You can appoint governors, judges, and magistrates. You can give the people a subordinate government, allowing them to legislate for themselves, whilst you defray the cost. So far as law goes, the thing is done. There is no analogy between this and our Territorial Governments. Our Territories are only an offset of our own people, or foreigners from the same regions from which we came. They are small in number. They are incapable of forming a government. It would be inconvenient for them to sustain a government, if it were formed; and they are very much obliged to the United States for undertaking the trouble, knowing that, on the attainment of their majority—when they come to manhood—at twenty-one—they will be introduced to an equality with all the other members of the Union. It is entirely different with Mexico. You have no need of armies to keep your Territories in subjection. But when you incorporate Mexico, you must have powerful armies to keep them in subjection. You may call it annexation, but it is a forced annexation, which is a contradiction in terms, according to my conception. You will be involved, in one word, in all the evils which I attribute to holding Mexico as a province. In fact, it will be but a Provincial Government, under the name of a Territorial Government. How long will that last? How long will it be before Mexico will be capable of incorporation into our Union? Why, if we judge from the examples before us, it will be a very long time. Ireland has been held in subjection by England for seven or eight hundred years, and yet still remains hostile, although her people are of kindred race with the conquerors. A few French Canadians on this continent yet maintain the attitude of hostile people; and never will the time come, in my opinion, Mr. President, that these Mexicans will be heartily reconciled to your authority. They have Castilian blood in their veins—the old Gothic, quite equal to the Anglo-Saxon in many respects—in some respects superior. Of all nations of the earth they are the most pertinacious—have the highest sense of nationality—hold out longest, and often even with the least prospect of effecting their object. On this subject also I have conversed with officers of the army, and they all entertain the same opinion, that these people are now hostile, and will continue so.

But, Mr. President, suppose all these difficulties removed; suppose these people attached to our Union, and desirous of incorporating with us, ought we to bring them in? Are they fit to be connected with us? Are they fit for self-government and for governing you? Are you, any of you, willing that your States should be governed by these twenty-odd Mexican States, with a population of about only one million of your blood, and two or three millions of mixed blood, better informed, all the rest pure Indians, a mixed blood equally ignorant and unfit for liberty, impure races, not as good as the Cherokees or Choctaws?

We make a great mistake, sir, when we suppose that all people are capable of self-government. We are anxious to force free government on all; and I see that it has been urged in a very respectable quarter, that it is the mission of this country to spread civil and religious liberty over all the world, and especially over this continent. It is a great mistake. None but people advanced to a very high state of moral and intellectual improvement are capable, in a civilized state, of maintaining free government; and amongst those who are so purified, very few, indeed, have had the good fortune of forming a constitution capable of endurance.

John A. Dix on Expansion and Mexican Lands, 1848

Sir, no one who has paid a moderate degree of attention to the laws and elements of our increase, can doubt that our population is destined to spread itself across the American continent, filling up, with more or less completeness, according to attractions of soil and climate, the space that intervenes between the Atlantic and Pacific oceans. This eventual, and, perhaps, in the order of time, this not very distant extension of our settlements over a tract of country, with a diameter, as we go westward, greatly disproportioned to its length, becomes a subject of the highest interest to us. On the whole extent of our northern flank, from New Brunswick to the point where the northern boundary of Oregon touches the Pacific, we are in contact with British colonists, having, for the most part, the same common origin with ourselves, but controlled and moulded by political influences from the Eastern hemisphere, if not adverse, certainly not decidedly friendly to us. The strongest tie which can be relied on to bind us to mutual offices of friendship and good neighborhood, is that of commerce; and this, as we know, is apt to run into rivalry, and sometimes becomes a fruitful source of alienation.

From our northern boundary, we turn to our southern. What races are to border on us here, what is to be their social and political character, and what their means of annoyance? Are our two frontiers, only seven parallels of latitude apart when we pass Texas, to be flanked by settlements having no common bond of union with ours? Our whole southern line is conterminous, throughout its whole extent, with the territories of Mexico, a large portion of which is nearly unpopulated. The geographical area of Mexico is about 1,500,000 square miles, and her population about 7,000,000 souls. The whole northern and central portion, taking the twenty-sixth parallel of latitude as the dividing line, containing more than 1,000,000 square miles, has about 650,000 inhabitants—about two inhabitants to three square miles. The southern portion, with less than 500,000 square miles, has a population of nearly six and a half millions of souls, or thirteen inhabitants to one square mile. The aboriginal races, which occupy and overrun a portion of California and New Mexico, must there, as everywhere else, give way before the advancing wave of civilization, either to be overwhelmed by it, or to be driven upon perpetually contracting areas, where, from a diminution of their accustomed sources of subsistence, they must ultimately become extinct by force of an invincible law. We see the operation of this law in every portion of this continent. We have no power to control it, if we would. It is the behest of Providence that idleness, and ignorance, and barbarism, shall give place to industry, and knowledge, and civilization. The European and mixed races, which possess Mexico, are not likely, either from moral or physical energy, to become formidable rivals or enemies. The bold and courageous enterprise which overran and conquered Mexico, appears not to have descended to the present possessors of the soil. Either from the influence of climate or the admixture of races—the fusion of castes, to use the technical phrase—the conquerors have, in turn, become the conquered. The ancient Castilian energy is, in a great degree, subdued; and it has given place, with many other noble traits of the Spanish character, to a peculiarity which seems to have marked the race in that country, under whatever combinations it is found—a proneness to civil discord, and a suicidal waste of its own strength.

With such a territory and such a people on our southern border, what is to be the inevitable course of empire? It needs no powers of prophecy to foretell. Sir, I desire to speak plainly: why should we not, when we are discussing the operation of moral and physical laws, which are beyond our control? As our population moves westward on our own territory, portions will cross our southern boundary. Settlements will be formed within the unoccupied and sparsely-peopled territory of Mexico. Uncongenial habits and tastes, differences of political opinion and principle, and numberless other elements of diversity will lead to a separation of these newly-formed societies from the inefficient government of Mexico. They will not endure to be held in subjection to a system, which neither yields them protection nor offers any incentive to their proper development and growth. They will form independent States on the basis of constitutions identical in all their leading features with our own; and they will naturally seek to unite their fortunes to ours. The fate of California is already sealed: it can never be reunited to Mexico. The operation of the great causes, to which I have alluded, must, at no distant day, detach the whole of northern Mexico from the southern portion of that republic. It is for the very reason that she is incapable of defending her possessions against the elements of disorder within and the progress of better influences from without, that I desire to see the inevitable political change which is to be wrought in the condition of her northern departments, brought about without any improper interference on our part.

An Emigrants' Guide Describes
the Mexicans in California, 1845

The entire population of Upper California, including foreigners, Mexicans and Indians, may be estimated at about thirty-one thousand human souls, of whom, about one thousand are foreigners, ten thousand are Mexicans, and the residue are Indians. By the term foreigners, I include all those who are not native citizens of Mexico, whether they have become citizens by naturalization, or whether they remain in a state of alienage. They consist, chiefly, of Americans, Englishmen, Frenchmen, Germans and Spaniards, but there is a very large majority of the former. The foreigners are principally settled at the various towns, and upon the Sacramento; those of whom who, are located at the latter place, consist almost entirely of our own citizens. The foreigners of this country are, generally, very intelligent; many of them have received all the advantages of an education; and they all possess an unusual degree of industry and enterprise. . . .

The Mexicans differ, in every particular, from the foreigners; ignorance and its concomitant, superstition, together with suspicion and superciliousness, constitute the chief ingredients, of the Mexican character. More indomitable ignorance does not prevail, among any people who make the least pretentions to civilization; in truth, they are scarcely a visible grade, in the scale of intelligence, above the barbarous tribes by whom they are surrounded; but this is not surprising, especially when we consider the relation, which these people occupy to their barbarous neighbors, in other particulars. Many of the lower order of them, have intermarried with the various tribes, and have resided with them so long, and lived in a manner so entirely similar, that it has become almost impossible, to trace the least distinctions between them, either in reference to intelligence, or complexion. There is another class, which is, if possible, of a lower order still, than those just alluded to, and which consists of the aborigines themselves, who have been slightly civilized, or rather *domesticated*. These two classes constitute almost the entire Mexican population, of California, and among them almost every variety and shade of complexion may be found, from the African black, to the tawny brown of our southern Indians. Although there is a great variety, and dissimilarity among them, in reference to their complexions, yet in their beastly habits and an entire want of all moral principle, as well as a perfect destitution of all intelligence, there appears to be a perfect similarity. A more full description of these classes, will be found, in what is said, in reference to the Indians, for as most of the lower order of Mexicans, are Indians in fact, whatever is said in reference to the one, will also be applicable to the other. The higher order of the Mexicans, in point of intelligence, are perhaps about equal, to the lower order of our citizens, throughout our western states; but among these even, are very few, who are, to any extent, learned or even intelligent. Learning and intelligence appear to be confined, almost entirely, to the priests, who are, generally, both learned and intelligent. The priests are not only the sole proprietors, of the learning and intelligence, but also, of the liberty and happiness of the people, all of which they parcel out to their blind votaries, with a very sparing hand; and thus it is, that all the Mexican people are kept, in this state of degrading ignorance, and humiliating vassalage. The priests here, not only have the possession of the keys of the understanding, and the door of liberty, but they also, have both the present and ultimate happiness, of these ignorant people, entirely at their disposal. Such at least, is the belief of the people, and such are the doctrines there taught by the priests. At times, I sympathize with these unfortunate beings, but again, I frequently think, that, perhaps, it is fortunate for the residue of mankind, that these semi-barbarians, are thus *ridden* and restrained, and if they are to be thus priest ridden, it is, no doubt, preferable, that they should retain their present *riders*.

Edwin Bryant's View of Hispanic Californians, 1848

The permanent population of that portion of Upper California situated between the Sierra Nevada and the Pacific, I estimate at 25,000. Of this number, 8,000 are Hispano-Americans, 5,000 foreigners, chiefly from the United States, and 12,000 christianized Indians. There are considerable numbers of wild or Gentile Indians inhabiting the valley of the San Joaquin, and the gorges of the Sierra, not included in this estimate. They are probably as numerous as the Christian Indians. The Indian population inhabiting the region of the Great Salt Lake, Mary's river, the oases of the Great Desert Basin, and the country bordering the Rio Colorado and its tributaries, being spread over a vast extent of territory, are scarcely seen, although the aggregate number is considerable.

The Californians do not differ materially from the Mexicans, from whom they are descended, in other provinces of that country. Physically and intellectually, the men, probably, are superior to the same race farther south, and inhabiting the countries contiguous to the city of Mexico. The intermixture of blood with the Indian and negro races has been less, although it is very perceptible.

The men, as a general fact, are well made, with pleasing, sprightly countenances, and possessing much grace and ease of manners, and vivacity of conversation. But hitherto they have had little knowledge of the world and of events, beyond what they have heard through Mexico, and derived from the super-cargoes of merchant-ships and whalemen touching upon the coast. There are no public schools in the country—at least I never heard of one. There are but few books. General Valléjo has a library with many valuable books, and this is the only one I saw, although there are others; but they are rare, and confined to a few families.

The men are almost constantly on horseback, and as horsemen excel any I have seen in other parts of the world. From the nature of their pursuits and amusements, they have brought horsemanship to a perfection challenging admiration and exciting astonishment. They are trained to the horse and the use of the lasso, (*riata,* as it is here called,) from their infancy. The first act of a child, when he is able to stand alone, is to throw his toy-lasso around the neck of a kitten; his next feat is performed on the dog; his next upon a goat or calf; and so on, until he mounts the horse, and demonstrates his skill upon horses and cattle. The crowning feat of dexterity with the *riata,* and of horsemanship, combined with daring courage, is the lassoing of the grisly bear. This feat is performed frequently upon this large and ferocious animal, but it is sometimes fatal to the performer and his horse. Well drilled, with experienced military leaders, such as would inspire them with confidence in their skill and prowess, the Californians ought to be the finest cavalry in the world. The Californian saddle is, I venture to assert, the best that has been invented, for the horse and the rider. Seated in one of these, it is scarcely possible to be unseated by any ordinary casualty. The bridle-bit is clumsily made, but so constructed that the horse is compelled to obey the rider upon the slightest intimation. The spurs are of immense size, but they answer to an experienced horseman the double purpose of exciting the horse, and of maintaining the rider in his seat under difficult circumstances.

For the pleasures of the table they care but little. With his horse and trappings, his sarape and blanket, a piece of beef and a *tortilla,* the Californian is content, so far as his personal comforts are concerned. But he is ardent in his pursuit of amusement and pleasure, and those consist chiefly in the fandango, the game of monte, horse-racing, and bull and bear baiting. They gamble freely and desperately, but pay their losses with the most strict punctuality, at any and every sacrifice, and manifest but little concern about them. They are obedient to their magistrates; and in all disputed cases decided by them, acquiesce without uttering a word of complaint. They have been accused of treachery and insincerity. Whatever may have been the grounds for these accusations in particular instances, I know not; but judging from my own observation and experience, they are as free from these qualities as our own people.

While the men are employed in attending to the herds of cattle and horses, and engaged in their other amusements, the women (I speak of the middle classes on the ranchos) superintend and perform most of the drudgery appertaining to housekeeping, and the cultivation of the gardens, from whence are drawn such vegetables as are consumed at the table. These are few, consisting of *frijoles,* potatoes, onions, and *chiles.* The assistants in these labors are the Indian men and women, legally reduced to servitude.

Antebellum Reform
and Reformers

The Democratic and Whig parties were not the only important vehicles for popular idealism after 1828. Far from the corridors of power, numerous short-lived political organizations—the Anti-Masons, the Working Men's parties, and various nativist groups—pressed their own grievances, often to see them adopted by the Whigs and Democrats. Other movements arose outside of politics, some of which opposed the entire idea of institutionalized party competition. Many of these reform efforts had roots in religious life, especially in the evangelical explosion known as the Second Great Awakening. (As suggested in the last chapter, the Awakening's moral imperatives also had a decisive effect among the Whigs.) Other movements drew on wholly different philosophical sources, ranging from British freethought and German metaphysics to the homespun democratic ideals of 1776. Collectively they spoke to the widespread anxieties of the era, as well as to the exhilarating hope that, with human effort and institutional reform, the world might be perfected.

It seems trite to ascribe this sudden pandemonium of reform to some vague notion about a ferment of freedom or a breakthrough of American individualism. Many Americans at the time, and today, would seek a more purely divine explanation. Current social and cultural historians have explored other possible origins, touching on group psychology, class conflicts, changing gender relations, and other developments. How satisfactory are these explanations? How else might we interpret the cross-cutting currents of reform? Why did some Americans support one or another kind of reformism while others did not? The sectional differences are striking: although southerners, black and white, experienced their own versions of the Second Great Awakening and knew something of benevolent reformism, many of the most popular northern movements made little headway or assumed very different shapes in the South. By the 1850s leading southern spokesmen would be likening the North, with its noisy reformers of every kind, to a kennel of squealing pups. Why? And is it even possible to speak, as some do, of an American reform impulse, considering that so many movements of the time conflicted with each other, either implicitly or openly?

No single chapter can cover all the important reform movements of the late 1820s and after. These documents sample materials from a few of the most interesting of them, moving across a wide intellectual and social spectrum.

Charles Grandison Finney was the outstanding northern proponent of the evangelical new measures associated with the Second Great Awakening, and he was a superb revival preacher. A selection from one of his sermons (the first document) explains some of his key theological tenets—important in their own right, as well as clues to understanding the religiously inspired moral reform movements. Lyman Beecher, the father of Harriet Beecher Stowe, Catharine Beecher, and Henry Ward Beecher, was an influential New England minister who initially distrusted Finney, only to join forces with him in the 1830s. By then Beecher had gained considerable notice for his work in temperance reform (see the second document), which eventually became one of the most powerful and controversial of the new movements. In document three, a cartoon by an impious, self-styled "Fanny Wright Mechanic" illustrates the resentments such religious reformers could provoke, particularly among those people most drawn to the Democratic party.

The "Fanny Wright" who inspired the antievangelical cartoon was Frances Wright, a British emigrée freethinker and feminist and one of the most electrifying radical speakers in America. Along with Thomas Skidmore (see Chapter 7), Wright was active in the dissenting circles in and around the original New York Working Men's movement. Before that, she and her associate, Robert Dale Owen (son of the British socialist Robert Owen) had lived in Tennessee, where they established a notorious community, Nashoba, for ex-slaves and white sympathizers. Wright and Owen's antislavery views and communitarian experiments were not the only sources of public disapproval: their ideas on free love and absolute racial and sexual equality (as explained by Wright in her defense of Nashoba, the fourth selection) scandalized even liberal opinion. With Wright, we run into a current of moral reform that clashed fiercely with evangelicalism and the cult of domesticity described earlier. A rather different, though related sort of feminism emerged with the birth of the woman suffrage movement in the 1840s, also documented in the fourth selection, in the famous Declaration of Sentiments issued by the Seneca Falls women's rights convention in 1848.

Not every reform movement was so radical; some were conservative, even reactionary. Nativist reform, the subject of the fifth two-part selection, had links to evangelicalism, the cultural restrictiveness of the Whigs, and the militant popular republicanism of the Jacksonians. All these currents joined in an outburst of despair and intolerance at the growing presence of Catholic immigrants. Samuel F. B. Morse, the painter and inventor, was a leading nativist writer and activist in the 1830s. Morse opposed violence, but his polemic against Catholic immigrants greatly emboldened the nativist cause. Nativism's ugliest side was revealed in the mob uprising that burned a Charlestown, Massachusetts, convent to the ground in 1834. (The antinativist cartoon from Boston featured at the end of the fifth selection denounced and ridiculed the rioters.)

Alongside the various social movements, some reformers tried to use public or semipublic institutions to help ameliorate American life—designing new forms of public schooling, reforming prisons, improving the condition of the poor, building mental asylums, and so forth. These efforts raised powerful philosophical claims about humanity, social uplift, and the state that defined their urge to do good. The reports of the Massachusetts school reformer Horace Mann, an excerpt from which is featured in the sixth selection, were among the strongest statements of these reformist purposes.

Labor reform is the focus of the seventh selection. In the 1830s such reform concentrated on trade-union efforts, which aimed at halting a steady deterioration of conditions and real wages. A mounting strike wave at mid-decade met, in turn, with stout resistance from employers, who used the courts to try and crush the unions. In 1836 the successful prosecution of a group of New York journeymen tailors for conspiracy led to an angry mass demonstration attended by upwards of thirty thousand protesters. Philip Hone's diary notes captured elite apprehensions at the impending unionist show of force; a transcript of the handbill that so alarmed Hone announced the depth of the unionists' fury. In the end, the demonstration was peaceful and the union movement survived, only to be destroyed, temporarily, by the calamitous impact of the financial panic in 1837.

Charles Grandison Finney on Sin and Redemption, 1835

Ezek. xviii, 31: Make you a new heart and a new spirit, for why will ye die?

. . . A change of heart . . . consists in changing the controlling preference of the mind in regard to the *end* of pursuit. The selfish heart is a preference of self-interest to the glory of God and the interests of his kingdom. A new heart consists in a preference of the glory of God and the interests of his kingdom to one's own happiness. In other words, it is a change from selfishness to benevolence, from having a supreme regard to one's own interest to an absorbing and controlling choice of the happiness and glory of God and his kingdom.

It is a change in the choice of a *Supreme Ruler*. The conduct of impenitent sinners demonstrates that they prefer Satan as the ruler of the world, they obey his laws, electioneer for him, and are zealous for his interests, even to martyrdom. They carry their attachment to him and his government so far as to sacrifice both body and soul to promote his interest and establish his dominion. A new heart is the choice of JEHOVAH as the supreme ruler; a deep-seated and abiding preference of his laws, and government, and character, and person, as the supreme Legislator and Governor of the universe.

Thus the world is divided into two great political parties; the difference between them is, that one party choose Satan as the god of this world, yield obedience to his laws, and are devoted to his interest. Selfishness is the law of Satan's empire, and all impenitent sinners yield it a willing obedience. The other party choose Jehovah for their governor, and consecrate themselves, with all their interests, to his service and glory. Nor does this change imply a constitutional alteration of the powers of body or mind, any more than a change of mind in regard to the form or administration of a human government. . . .

God has established a government, and proposed by the exhibition of his own character, to produce the greatest practicable amount of happiness in the universe. He has enacted laws wisely calculated to promote this object, to which he conforms all his own conduct, and to which he requires all his subjects perfectly and undeviatingly to conform theirs. After a season of obedience, Adam changed his heart, and set up for himself. So with every sinner, although he *does not first obey, as Adam did;* yet his wicked heart consists in setting up his own interest in opposition to the interest and government of God. In aiming to promote his own private happiness, in a way that is opposed to the general good. Self-gratification becomes the law to which he conforms his conduct. It is that minding of the flesh, which is enmity against God. A change of heart, therefore, is to prefer a different *end.* To prefer supremely the glory of God and the public good, to the promotion of his own interest; and whenever this preference is changed, we see of course a corresponding change of conduct. If a man change sides in politics, you will see him meeting with those that entertain the same views and feelings with himself; devising plans and using his influence to elect the candidate which he has now chosen. He has new political friends on the one side, and new political enemies on the other. So with a sinner; if his heart is changed, you will see that Christians become his friends—Christ his candidate. He aims at honoring him and promoting his interest in all his ways. Before, the language of his conduct was, "Let Satan govern the world." Now, the language of his heart and of his life is, "Let Christ rule King of nations, as he is King of saints." Before, his conduct said, "O Satan, let thy kingdom come, and let thy will be done." Now, his heart, his life, his lips cry out, "O Jesus, let thy kingdom come, let thy will be done on earth as it is in heaven." . . .

As God requires men to make to themselves a new heart, on pain of eternal death, it is the strongest possible evidence that they are able to do it. To say that he has commanded them to do it, without telling them they are able, is consummate trifling. Their ability is implied as strongly as it can be, in the command itself. . . .

The strivings of the Spirit of God with men, is not a physical scuffling, but a debate; a strife not of body with body, but of mind with mind; and that in the action and reaction of vehement argumentation. From these remarks, it is easy to answer the question sometimes put by individuals who seem to be entirely in the dark upon this subject, whether in converting the soul the Spirit acts directly on the mind, or on the truth. This is the same nonsense as if you should ask, whether an earthly advocate who had gained his cause, did it by acting directly and physically on the jury, or on his argument. . . .

You see from this subject that a sinner, under the influence of the Spirit of God, is just as free as a jury under the arguments of an advocate.

Here also you may see the importance of right views on this point. Suppose a lawyer, in addressing a jury, should not expect to change their minds by any thing he could say, but should wait for an invisible, and physical agency, to be exerted by the Holy Ghost upon them. And suppose, on the other hand, that the jury thought that in making up their verdict, they must be passive, and wait for a direct physical agency to be exerted upon them. In vain might the lawyer plead, and in vain might the jury hear, for until he pressed his arguments as if he was determined to bow their hearts, and until they make up their minds, and decide the question, and thus act like rational beings, both his pleading, and their hearing is in vain. So if a minister goes into a desk to preach to sinners, believing that they have no power to obey the truth, and under the impression that a direct physical influence must be exerted upon them before they *can* believe, and if his audience be of the same opinion, in vain does he preach, and in vain do they hear, "for they are yet in their sins;" they sit and quietly wait for some invisible hand to be stretched down from heaven, and perform some surgical operation, infuse some new principle, or implant some constitutional taste; *after* which they suppose they shall be *able* to obey God. Ministers should labor with sinners, as a lawyer does with a jury, and upon the same principles of mental philosophy; and the sinner should weigh his arguments, and make up his mind as upon oath and for his life, and give a verdict upon the spot, according to law and evidence. . . .

Sinner! instead of waiting and praying for God to change your heart, you should at once summon up your powers, put forth the effort, and change the governing preference of your mind. . . .

Sinner! your obligation to love God is equal to the excellence of his character, and your guilt in not obeying him is of course equal to your obligation. You cannot therefore for an hour or a moment defer obedience to the commandment in the text, without deserving eternal damnation. . . .

And now, sinner, while the subject is before you, will you yield? To keep yourself away from under the motives of the gospel, by neglecting church, and neglecting your Bible, will prove fatal to your soul. And to be careless when you do attend, or to hear with attention and refuse to make up your mind and yield, will be equally fatal. And now, "I beseech you, by the mercies of God, that you at *this time* render your body and soul, a living sacrifice to God, which is your reasonable service." Let the truth take hold upon your conscience—throw down your rebellious weapons—give up your refuges of lies—fix your mind steadfastly upon the world of consid- erations that should instantly decide you to close in with the offer of rec- onciliation while it now lies before you. Another moment's delay, and it may be too late forever. The Spirit of God may depart from you—the offer of life may be made no more, and this one more slighted offer of mercy may close up your account, and seal you over to all the horrors of eternal death. Hear, then, O sinner, I beseech you, and obey the word of the Lord—"Make you a new heart and a new spirit, for why will ye die?"

Lyman Beecher on the Temperance Crusade, 1826

No sin has fewer apologies than intemperance. The suffrage of the world is against it; and yet there is no sin so naked in its character, and whose commencement and progress is indicated by so many signs, concerning which there is among mankind such profound ignorance. All reprobate drunkenness; and yet, not one of the thousands who fall into it, dreams of danger when he enters the way that leads to it.

The soldier, approaching the deadly breach, and seeing rank after rank of those who preceded him swept away, hesitates sometimes and recoils from certain death. But men behold the effects upon others . . . they see them begin, advance, and end, in confirmed intemperance, and unappalled rush heedlessly upon the same ruin.

A part of this heedlessness arises from the undefined nature of the crime in its early stages, and the ignorance of men, concerning what may be termed the experimental [empirical] indications of its approach. Theft and falsehood are definite actions. But intemperance is a state of internal sensation, and the indications may exist long, and multiply, and the subject of them not be aware that they are the signs of intemperance. It is not unfrequent, that men become irreclaimable in their habits, without suspicion of danger. . . .

Intemperance is the sin of our land, and, with our boundless prosperity, is coming in upon us like a flood; and if anything shall defeat the hopes of the world, which hang upon our experiment of civil liberty, it is that river of fire, which is rolling through the land, destroying the vital air, and extending around an atmosphere of death. . . .

Ardent spirits, given as a matter of hospitality, is not unfrequently the occasion of intemperance. In this case the temptation is a stated inmate of the family. The utensils are present, and the occasions for their use are not unfrequent. And when there is no guest, the sight of the liquor, the state of the health, or even lassitude of spirits, may indicate the propriety of the "prudent use," until the prudent use becomes, by repetition, habitual use— and habitual use becomes irreclaimable intemperance. In this manner, doubtless, has many a father, and mother, and son, and daughter, been ruined forever.

In the commencement of this evil habit, there are many who drink to excess only on particular days, such as days for military exhibition, the anniversary of our independence, the birth-day of Washington, Christmas, New Year's day, election, and others of the like nature. When any of these holidays arrive, and they come as often almost as saints' days in the calendar, they bring with them, to many, the insatiable desire of drinking, as well as a dispensation from the sin, as efficacious and quieting to the conscience, as papal indulgences. . . .

There are others who feel the desire of drinking stirred up within them by the associations of place. They could go from end to end of a day's journey without ardent spirits, were there no taverns on the road. But the very sight of these receptacles of pilgrims awakens the desire "just to step in and take something." And so powerful does this association become, that many will no more pass the tavern than they would pass a fortified place with all the engines of death directed against them. There are in every city, town, and village, places of resort, which in like manner, as soon as the eye falls upon them, create the thirst of drinking. . . .

There is no remedy for intemperance but the cessation of it. Nature must be released from the unnatural war which is made upon her, and be allowed to rest, and then nutrition, and sleep, and exercise, will perform the work of restoration. Gradually the spring of life will recover tone, appetite will return, digestion become efficient, sleep sweet, and the muscular system vigorous, until the elastic heart with every beat shall send health through the system, and joy through the soul. . . .

In every city and town the poor-tax, created chiefly by intemperance, is augmenting. . . . [T]he frequency of going upon the town [relying on public welfare] has taken away the reluctance of pride, and destroyed the motives to providence which the fear of poverty and suffering once supplied. The prospect of a destitute old age, or of a suffering family, no longer troubles the vicious portion of our community. They drink up their daily earnings, and bless God for the poor-house, and begin to look upon it as, of right, the drunkard's home, and contrive to arrive thither as early as idleness and excess will give them a passport to this sinecure of vice. Thus is the insatiable destroyer of industry marching through the land, rearing poor-houses, and augmenting taxation: night and day, with sleepless activity, squandering property, cutting the sinews of industry, undermining vigor, engendering disease. . . .

Add the loss sustained by the subtraction of labor, and the shortened date of life, to the expense of sustaining the poor, created by intemperance; and the nation is now taxed annually more than the expense which would be requisite for the maintenance of government, and for the support of all our schools and colleges, and all the religious instruction of the nation. Already a portion of the entire capital of the nation is mortgaged for the support of drunkards. . . .

Every intemperate and idle man, whom you behold tottering about the streets and steeping himself at the stores, regards your houses and lands as pledged to take care of him,—puts his hands deep, annually, into your pockets, and eats his bread in the sweat of your brows, instead of his own; and with marvellous good nature you bear it. If a robber should break loose on the highway, to levy taxation, an armed force would be raised to hunt him from society. But the tippler may do it fearlessly, in open day, and not a voice is raised, not a finger is lifted.

Intemperance in our land is not accidental; it is rolling in upon us by the violation of some great laws of human nature. In our views, and in our practice as a nation, there is something fundamentally wrong; and the remedy, like the evil, must be found in the correct application of general principles. It must be a universal and national remedy.

What then is this universal, natural, and national remedy for intemperance?

IT IS THE BANISHMENT OF ARDENT SPIRITS FROM THE LIST OF LAWFUL ARTICLES OF COMMERCE, BY A CORRECT AND EFFICIENT PUBLIC SENTIMENT; SUCH AS HAS TURNED SLAVERY OUT OF HALF OUR LAND, AND WILL YET EXPEL IT FROM THE WORLD. . . .

We are not therefore to come down in wrath upon the distillers, and importers, and venders of ardent spirits. None of us are enough without sin to cast the first stone. For who would have imported, or distilled, or vended, if all the nominally temperate in the land had refused to drink? It is the buyers who have created the demand for ardent spirits, and made distillation and importation a gainful traffic. And it is the custom of the temperate too, which inundates the land with the occasion of so much and such unmanageable temptation. Let the temperate cease to buy—and the demand for ardent spirits will fall in the market three fourths, and ultimately will fail wholly, as the generation of drunkards shall hasten out of time.

To insist that men, whose capital is embarked in the production, or vending of ardent spirits, shall manifest the entire magnanimity and self-denial, which is needful to save the land, though the example would be glorious to them, is more than we have a right to expect or demand. Let the consumer do his duty, and the capitalist, finding his employment unproductive, will quickly discover other channels of useful enterprise. . . .

A Counterattack on Religious Reform, 1831

ADVERTISEMENT.

WANTED, for the use of the Bible, Tract, and Missionary Society, a number of JACKASSES of the real Tappaan breed: they must be in first-rate order.—A number of JENNIES are also wanted, but they must be of pious breed, and warranted not to run after the Jacks.

The plate above, represents a Jackass, well fed, and in fine order, laying golden eggs, which a Priest receives in his hand, wh-t with he other he lifts up his tail. He says to his colleague, who stands by the head of the ass, "We must administer a gentle dose of physic; he dont seem to give very freely." The ass, (who like Balaam's ass has the power of speech,) says, " I understand you, Mr. Parson; I know you are never satisfied until you have all; but I'll take care you dont reduce me to a skeleton. like my poor neighbour. whom your colleague is now kicking away.

An antievangelical cartoon by a self-styled "Fanny Wright Mechanic," from *The Magdalen Report Burlesqued*, 1831.

Feminist Declarations, 1828, 1848

Free Love and Racial Equality: Frances Wright Defends Nashoba, 1827

One nation, and, as yet, one nation only, has declared all men "born free and equal," and conquered the political freedom and equality of its citizens—with the lamentable exception, indeed, of its citizens of color. But is there not a liberty yet more precious than what is termed *national*, and an equality more precious than what is termed *political*? Before we are citizens, are we not human beings, and ère we can exercise equal rights, must we not possess equal advantages, equal means of improvement and of enjoyment?

Political liberty may be said to exist in the United States of America, and (without adverting to the yet unsettled, though we may fondly trust secured republics of America's southern continent) *only there*. Moral liberty exists *no where*.

By political liberty we may understand the liberty of speech and of action without incurring the violence of authority or the penalties of law. By moral liberty may we not understand the *free exercise of the liberty of speech and of action,* without incurring the intolerance of popular prejudice and ignorant public opinion? To secure the latter where the former liberty exists, what is necessary "but to will it." Far truer is the assertion as here applied to moral liberty than as heretofore applied to political liberty. To free ourselves of thrones, aristocracies and hierarchies, of fleets and armies, and all the arrayed panoply of organized despotism, it is *not* sufficient to will it. We must fight for it, and fight for it too with all the odds of wealth, and power, and position against us. . . . It is much to have *declared* men free and equal, but it shall be more when they are rendered so; when means shall be sought and found, and employed to develope all the intellectual and physical powers of all human beings, without regard to sex or condition, class, race, nation or color; and when men shall learn to view each other as members of one great family, with equal claims to enjoyment and equal capacities for labor and instruction, admitting always the sole differences arising out of the varieties exhibited in individual organization.

It were superfluous to elucidate, by argument, the baleful effects arising out of the division of labor as now existing, and which condemns the large half of mankind to an existence purely physical, and the remaining portion to pernicious idleness, and occasionally to exertions painfully, because solely, intellectual. He who lives in the single exercise of his mental faculties, however usefully or curiously directed, is equally an imperfect animal with the man who knows only the exercise of his muscles.

Let us consider the actual condition of our species. Where shall we find even a single individual, male or female, whose mental and physical powers have been fairly cultivated and developed? How then is it with the great family of human kind? We have addressed our ingenuity to improve the nature and beautify the forms of all the tribe of animals domesticated by our care, but man has still neglected man; ourselves, our own species, our own nature are deemed unworthy, even unbecoming, objects of experiment. Why should we refuse to the human animal care at least equal to that bestowed on the horse or the dog? His forms are surely not less susceptible of beauty, and his faculties, more numerous and exalted, may challenge, at the least, equal development. . . .

In the moral, intellectual and physical cultivation of both sexes should we seek, as we can only find, the source and security of human happiness and human virtue. Prejudice and fear are weak barriers against passions, which, inherent in our nature and demanding only judicious training to form the ornament, and supply the best joys of our existence, are maddened into violence by pernicious example and pernicious restraint, varied with as pernicious indulgence. Let us correct our views of right and wrong, correct our moral lessons, and so correct the practice of rising generations! Let us not teach that virtue consists in the crucifying of the affections and appetites, but in their judicious government. Let us not attach ideas of purity to monastic chastity, impossible to man or woman without consequences fraught with evil, nor ideas of vice to connections formed under the auspices of kind feelings. Let us enquire, not if a mother be a wife, or a father a husband, but if parents can supply to the creatures they have brought into being, all things requisite to render existence a blessing! Let the force of public opinion be brought against the thoughtless ignorance, or cruel selfishness, which, either with or without the sanction of a legal or religious permit, so frequently multiplies offspring beyond the resources of the parents. Let us check the force of passions, as well as their precocity, not by the idle terror of imaginary crime in the desire itself, but by the just and benevolent apprehension of bringing into existence, unhappy or imperfect beings. Let us teach the young mind to reason, and the young heart to feel, and instead of shrouding our bodies, wants, desires, senses, affections and faculties in mystery, let us court enquiry, and show that acquaintance with our own nature can alone guide us to judicious practice, and that in the consequence of human actions, exists the only true test of their virtue or their vice. . . .

The tyranny usurped by the matrimonial law over the most sacred of the human affections, can perhaps only be equalled by that of the unjust public opinion, which so frequently stamps with infamy, or condemns to martyrdom the best-grounded and most generous attachments, which ever did honor to the human heart, simply because unlegalized by human ceremonies, equally idle and offensive in the form and mischievous in the tendency.

This tyranny, as now exercised over the strongest and at the same time, if refined by mental cultivation, the noblest of the human passions, had probably its source in religious prejudice, or priestly rapacity, while it has found its plausible and more philosophical apology in the apparent dependence of children on the union of the parents. To this plea it might, perhaps, be replied, that the end, how important soever, is not secured by the means. That the forcible union of unsuitable and unsuited parents can little promote the happiness of the offspring; and, supposing the protection of children to be the real source and object of our code of morals and of our matrimonial laws, what shall we say of the effects of these humane provisions on the fate and fortunes of one large family of helpless innocents, born into the world in spite of all prohibitions and persecutions, and whom a cruel law, and yet more cruel opinion, disown and stigmatize. But how wide a field does this topic embrace? How much cruelty—how much oppression of the weak and the helpless does it not involve! The children denominated illegitimate, or *natural*, (as if in contradiction of others who should be *out of nature*, because *under law*) may be multiplied to any number by an unprincipled father, easily exonerated by law and custom from the duties of paternity, while these duties, and their accompanying shame, are left to a mother but too often rendered desperate by misfortune! And should we follow out our review of the law of civilized countries, we shall find the offspring termed legitimate, with whom honor and power and possession are associated, adjudged, in case of matrimonial dissensions to the father, who by means of this legal claim, has, not unfrequently, bowed to servitude the spirit of a fond mother, and held ber, as a galley slave, to the oar. . . .

Let us look into our streets, our hospitals, our asylums; let us look into the secret thoughts of the anxious parent trembling for the minds and bodies of sons starting into life, or mourning over the dying health of daughters condemned to the unnatural repression of feelings and desires inherent in their very organization and necessary alike to their moral and physical well-being. Or let us look to the victims—not of pleasure, not of love, nor yet of their own depravity, but of those ignorant laws, ignorant prejudices, ignorant code of morals, which condemn one portion of the female sex to vicious excess, another to as vicious restraint, and all to defenceless help-lessness and slavery, and generally the whole of the male sex to debasing licentiousness, if not to loathsome brutality. . . .

The strength of the prejudice of color as existing in the United States and in the European colonies can in general be little conceived and less understood in the old continent. Yet however whimsical it may there appear, is it in fact more ridiculous than the European prejudice of birth? The superior excellence which the one supposes in a peculiar descent or merely in a peculiar name, the other imagines in a peculiar complexion or set of features. And perhaps it is only by considering man in many countries and observing all his varying and contradictory prejudices that we can discover the equal absurdity of all.

Those to whom the American institutions and American character are familiar, and who have considered the question of American negro slavery in all its bearings, will probably be disposed to pronounce with the writer of this address that the emancipation of the colored population cannot be *progressive thro' the laws*. It must and can only be *progressive through the feelings;* and, through that medium, be finally complete and entire, involving at once political equality and the amalgamation of the races.

And has nature (as slave apologists would tell us) drawn a Rubicon between the human varieties of physiognomy and complexion, or must we enter into details to prove that no natural antipathy blinds the white Louis-ianian to the charms of the graceful quadroon—however the force of prej-udice or the fear of public censure makes of her his mistress, and of the white-skinned, but often not more accomplished or more attractive female, his wife? Or must we point to the intercourse in its most degraded forms where the child is the marketable slave of its father? Idle indeed is the assertion that the mixture of the races is not in nature. If not in nature, it could not happen; and, being in nature, since it *does* happen, the only question is whether it shall take place in good taste and good feeling and be made at once the means of sealing the tranquillity, and perfecting the liberty of the country, and of peopling it with a race more suited to its southern climate than the pure European,—or whether it shall proceed, as it now does, viciously and degradingly, mingling hatred and fear with the ties of blood—denied indeed, but stamped by nature herself upon the skin.

The education of the race of color would doubtless make the amalgamation more rapid as well as more creditable; and so far from considering the physical amalgamation of the two colors, when accompanied by a moral approximation, as an evil, it must surely be viewed as a good equally desirable for both. In this belief the more especial object of the founder of Nashoba is to raise the man of color to the level of the white. Where fitted by habits of industry and suitable dispositions to receive him as a brother and equal, and, after due trial, as proprietor trustee of the property; to educate his children with white children, and thus approaching their minds, tastes and occupations, to leave the affections of future generations to the dictates of free choice.

The Seneca Falls Convention
on the Equality of Men and Women, 1848

When, in the course of human events, it becomes necessary for one portion of the family of man to assume among the people of the earth a position different from that which they have hitherto occupied, but one to which the laws of nature and of nature's God entitle them, a decent respect to the opinions of mankind requires that they should declare the causes that impel them to such a course.

We hold these truths to be self-evident: that all men and women are created equal; that they are endowed by their Creator with certain inalienable rights; that among these are life, liberty, and the pursuit of happiness; that to secure these rights governments are instituted, deriving their just powers from the consent of the governed. Whenever any form of government becomes destructive of these ends, it is the right of those who suffer from it to refuse allegiance to it, and to insist upon the institution of a new government, laying its foundation on such principles, and organizing its powers in such form, as to them shall seem most likely to effect their safety and happiness. Prudence, indeed, will dictate that governments long established should not be changed for light and transient causes; and accordingly all experience hath shown that mankind are more disposed to suffer, while evils are sufferable, than to right themselves by abolishing the forms to which they were accustomed. But when a long train of abuses and usurpations, pursuing invariably the same object, evinces a design to reduce them under absolute despotism, it is their duty to throw off such government, and to provide new guards for their future security. Such has been the patient sufferance of the women under this government, and such is now the necessity which constrains them to demand the equal station to which they are entitled.

The history of mankind is a history of repeated injuries and usurpations on the part of man toward woman, having in direct object the establishment of an absolute tyranny over her. To prove this, let facts be submitted to a candid world.

He has never permitted her to exercise her inalienable right to the elective franchise.

He has compelled her to submit to laws, in the formation of which she had no voice.

He has withheld from her rights which are given to the most ignorant and degraded men—both natives and foreigners.

Having deprived her of this first right of a citizen, the elective franchise, thereby leaving her without representation in the halls of legislation, he has oppressed her on all sides.

He has made her, if married, in the eye of the law, civilly dead.

He has taken from her all right in property, even to the wages she earns.

He has made her, morally, an irresponsible being, as she can commit many crimes with impunity, provided they be done in the presence of her husband. In the covenant of marriage, she is compelled to promise obedience to her husband, he becoming to all intents and purposes, her master—the law giving him power to deprive her of her liberty, and to administer chastisement.

He has so framed the laws of divorce, as to what shall be the proper causes, and in case of separation, to whom the guardianship of the children shall be given, as to be wholly regardless of the happiness of women—the law, in all cases, going upon a false supposition of the supremacy of man, and giving all power into his hands.

After depriving her of all rights as a married woman, if single, and the owner of property, he has taxed her to support a government which recognizes her only when her property can be made profitable to it.

He has monopolized nearly all the profitable employments, and from those she is permitted to follow, she receives but a scanty remuneration. He closes against her all the avenues to wealth and distinction which he considers most honorable to himself. As a teacher of theology, medicine, or law, she is not known.

He has denied her the facilities for obtaining a thorough education, all colleges being closed against her.

He allows her in Church, as well as State, but a subordinate position, claiming Apostolic authority for her exclusion from the ministry, and, with some exceptions, from any public participation in the affairs of the Church.

He has created a false public sentiment by giving to the world a different code of morals for men and women, by which moral delinquencies which exclude women from society, are not only tolerated, but deemed of little account in man.

He has usurped the prerogative of Jehovah himself, claiming it as his right to assign for her a sphere of action, when that belongs to her conscience and to her God.

He has endeavored, in every way that he could, to destroy her confidence in her own powers, to lessen her self-respect, and to make her willing to lead a dependent and abject life.

Now, in view of this entire disfranchisement of one-half the people of this country, their social and religious degradation—in view of the unjust laws above mentioned, and because women do feel themselves aggrieved, oppressed, and fraudulently deprived of their most sacred rights, we insist that they have immediate admission to all the rights and privileges which belong to them as citizens of the United States.

In entering upon the great work before us, we anticipate no small amount of misconception, misrepresentation, and ridicule; but we shall use every instrumentality within our power to effect our object. We shall employ agents, circulate tracts, petition the State and National legislatures, and endeavor to enlist the pulpit and the press in our behalf. We hope this Convention will be followed by a series of Conventions embracing every part of the country.

Resolutions

Whereas, The great precept of nature is conceded to be, that "man shall pursue his own true and substantial happiness." Blackstone in his Commentaries remarks, that this law of Nature being coeval with mankind, and dictated by God himself, is of course superior in obligation to any other. It is binding over all the globe, in all countries and at all times; no human laws are of any validity if contrary to this, and such of them as are valid, derive all their force, and all their validity, and all their authority, mediately and immediately, from this original; therefore,

Resolved, That such laws as conflict, in any way, with the true and substantial happiness of woman, are contrary to the great precept of nature and of no validity, for this is "superior in obligation to any other."

Resolved, That all laws which prevent woman from occupying such a station in society as her conscience shall dictate, or which place her in a position inferior to that of man, are contrary to the great precept of nature, and therefore of no force or authority.

Resolved, That woman is man's equal—was intended to be so by the Creator, and the highest good of the race demands that she should be recognized as such.

Resolved, That the women of this country ought to be enlightened in regard to the laws under which they live, that they may no longer publish their degradation by declaring themselves satisfied with their present position, nor their ignorance, by asserting that they have all the rights they want.

Resolved, That inasmuch as man, while claiming for himself intellectual superiority, does accord to woman moral superiority, it is pre-eminently his duty to encourage her to speak and teach, as she has an opportunity, in all religious assemblies.

Resolved, That the same amount of virtue, delicacy, and refinement of behavior that is required of woman in the social state, should also be required of man, and the same transgressions should be visited with equal severity on both man and woman.

Resolved, That the objection of indelicacy and impropriety, which is so often brought against woman when she addresses a public audience, comes with a very ill-grace from those who encourage, by their attendance, her appearance on the stage, in the concert, or in feats of the circus.

Resolved, That woman has too long rested satisfied in the circumscribed limits which corrupt customs and a perverted application of the Scriptures have marked out for her, and that it is time she should move in the enlarged sphere which her great Creator has assigned her.

Resolved, That it is the duty of the women of this country to secure to themselves their sacred right to the elective franchise.

Resolved, That the equality of human rights results necessarily from the fact of the identity of the race in capabilities and responsibilities.

Resolved, therefore, That, being invested by the Creator with the same capabilities, and the same consciousness of responsibility for their exercise, it is demonstrably the right and duty of woman, equally with man, to promote every righteous cause by every righteous means; and especially in regard to the great subjects of morals and religion, it is self-evidently her right to participate with her brother in teaching them, both in private and in public, by writing and by speaking, by any instrumentalities proper to be used, and in any assemblies proper to be held; and this being a self-evident truth growing out of the divinely implanted principles of human nature, any custom or authority adverse to it, whether modern or wearing the hoary sanction of antiquity, is to be regarded as a self-evident falsehood, and at war with mankind.

[At the last session Lucretia Mott offered the following resolution.]

Resolved, That the speedy success of our cause depends upon the zealous and untiring efforts of both men and women, for the overthrow of the monopoly of the pulpit, and for the securing to woman an equal participation with men in the various trades, professions, and commerce.

Contemporary Views of Nativism, 1834, 1835

Nativism Attacked, 1834

"Defenders of the True Faith," cartoon, Boston, 1834, published following a violent attack on a Catholic convent in Charlestown, Massachusetts.

Samuel F. B. Morse on the Popish Plot, 1835

. . . I deem it a duty to warn the Christian community against the temptation to which they were exposed, in guarding against the political dangers arising from Popery, of leaving their proper sphere of action, and degrading themselves to a common political interest. This is a snare into which they might easily fall, and into which, if Popery could invite or force them, it might keep a jubilee, for its triumph would be sure. The propensity to resist by unlawful means the encroachments of an enemy, because that enemy uses such means against us, belongs to human nature. We are very apt to think, in the irritation of being attacked, that we may lawfully hurl back the darts of a foe, whatever may be their character; that we may "fight the Devil with fire," instead of the milder, yet more effective weapon of "the Lord rebuke thee." The same spirit of Christianity which forbids us to return railing for railing, and persecution for persecution, forbids the use of unlawful or even of doubtful means of defence, merely because an enemy uses them to attack us. If Popery, (as is unblushingly the case,) organizes itself at our elections, if it interferes politically and sells itself to this or that political demagogue or party, it should be remembered, that this is notoriously the true character of Popery. It is its nature. It cannot act otherwise. Intrigue is its appropriate business. But all this is foreign to Christianity. Christianity must not enter the political arena with Popery, nor be mailed in Popish armor. The weapons and stratagems of Popery suit not with the simplicity and frankness of Christianity. . . .

But whilst deprecating a *union of religious sects* to act politically against Popery, I must not be misunderstood as recommending no political opposition to Popery by the American community. I have endeavored to rouse Protestants to a renewed and more vigorous use of their religious weapons in their *moral* war with Popery, but I am not unmindful of another duty, the *political* duty, which the double character of Popery makes it necessary to urge upon American citizens, with equal force,—the imperious duty of defending the distinctive principles of our civil government. It must be sufficiently manifest to every republican citizen that the civil polity of Popery is in direct opposition to all which he deems sacred in government. He must perceive that Popery cannot from its very nature tolerate any of those civil rights which are the peculiar boast of Americans. Should Popery increase but for a little time longer in this country with the alarming rapidity with which, as authentic statistics testify, it is advancing at the present time, (and it must not be forgotten that despotism in Europe, in its desperate struggles for existence, is lending its powerful aid to the enterprise,) we may even in this generation learn by sad experience what common sagacity and ordinary research might now teach, in time to arrest the evil, that Popery cannot tolerate our form of government in any of its essential principles.

Popery does not acknowledge *the right of the people to govern;* but claims for itself the supreme right to govern all people and all rulers by divine right.

It does not tolerate *the Liberty of the Press;* it takes advantage indeed of our liberty of the press to use its own press against our liberty; but it proclaims in the thunders of the Vatican, and with a voice which it pronounces *infallible and unchangeable,* that it is a liberty *"never sufficiently to be execrated and detested."*

It does not tolerate *liberty of conscience* nor *liberty of opinion.* The one is denounced by the Sovereign Pontiff as *"a most pestilential error,"* and the other, *"a pest of all others most to be dreaded in a state."*

It is not responsible to the people in its financial matters. *It taxes at will, and is accountable to none but itself.*

Now these are *political* tenets held by Papists in close union with their religious belief, yet these are not *religious* but *civil* tenets; they belong to despotic government. Conscience cannot be pleaded against our dealing politically with them. They are separable from religious belief; and if Papists will separate them, and repudiate these noxious principles, and teach and act accordingly, the political duty of exposing and opposing Papists, on the ground of the enmity of their political tenets to our republican government, will cease. But can they do it? If they can, it behoves them to do it without delay. If they cannot, or will not, let them not complain of *religious* persecution, or of *religious* intolerance, if this republican people, when it shall wake to a sense of the danger that threatens its blood-bought institutions, shall rally to their defence with some show of indignation. Let them not whine about *religious* oppression, if the democracy turns its searching eye upon this secret treason to the state, and shall in future scrutinize with something of suspicion, the professions of those *foreign friends,* who are so ready to rush to a fraternal embrace. Let them not raise the cry of *religious* proscription, if American republicans shall stamp an indelible brand upon the *liveried slaves of a foreign* despot, . . . who now sheltered behind the shield of our religious liberty, dream of security, while sapping the foundations of our civil government. . . . America may for a time, sleep soundly, as innocence is wont to sleep, unsuspicious of hostile attack; but if any foreign power, jealous of the increasing strength of the embryo giant, sends its serpents to lurk within his cradle, let such presumption be assured that the waking energies of the infant are not to be despised, that once having grasped his foes, he will neither be tempted from his hold by admiration of their painted and gilded covering, nor by fear of the fatal embrace of their treacherous folds.

Horace Mann on the Philosophy of Public Schooling, 1846

. . . In the district-school-meeting, in the town-meeting, in legislative halls, everywhere, the advocates for a more generous education could carry their respective audiences with them in behalf of increased privileges for our children, were it not instinctively foreseen that increased privileges must be followed by increased taxation. Against this obstacle, argument falls dead. The rich man who has no children declares that the exaction of a contribution from him to educate the children of his neighbor is an invasion of his rights of property. The man who has reared and educated a family of children denounces it as a double tax when he is called upon to assist in educating the children of others also; or, if he has reared his own children without educating them, he thinks it peculiarly oppressive to be obliged to do for others what he refrained from doing even for himself. Another, having children, but disdaining to educate them with the common mass, withdraws them from the public school, puts them under what he calls "selecter influences," and then thinks it a grievance to be obliged to support a school which he [regards with contempt]. . . .

It seems not irrelevant, therefore . . . to inquire into the nature of a man's right to the property he possesses; and to satisfy ourselves respecting the question, whether any man has such an indefeasible title to his estates, or such an absolute ownership of them, as renders it unjust in the government to assess upon him his share of the expenses of educating the children of the community up to such a point as the nature of the institutions under which he lives, and the well-being of society, require.

I believe in the existence of a great, immortal, immutable principle of natural law, or natural ethics,—a principle antecedent to all human institutions, and incapable of being abrogated by any ordinance of man,—a principle of divine origin, which proves the *absolute right* to an education of every human being that comes into the world; and which, of course, proves the correlative duty of every government to see that the means of that education are provided for all.

In regard to the application of this principle of natural law,—that is, in regard to the extent of the education to be provided for all at the public expense,—some differences of opinion may fairly exist under different political organizations; but, under our republican government, it seems clear that the minimum of this education can never be less than such as is sufficient to qualify each citizen for the civil and social duties he will be called to discharge. . . .

The claim of a child, then, to a portion of pre-existent property, begins with the first breath he draws. The new-born infant must have sustenance and shelter and care. If the natural parents are removed, or parental ability fails; in a word, if parents either cannot or will not supply the infant's wants,—then society at large—the government having assumed to itself the ultimate control of all property—is bound to step in and fill the parent's place. To deny this to any child would be equivalent to a sentence of death, a capital execution of the innocent,—at which every soul shudders. It would be a more cruel form of infanticide than any which is practised in China or in Africa. . . .

The three following propositions, then, describe the broad and ever-during [enduring] foundation on which the common-school system of Massachusetts reposes:—

The successive generations of men, taken collectively, constitute one great commonwealth.

The property of this commonwealth is pledged for the education of all its youth, up to such a point as will save them from poverty and vice, and prepare them for the adequate performance of their social and civil duties.

The successive holders of this property are trustees, bound to the faithful execution of their trust by the most sacred obligations; and embezzlement and pillage from children and descendants have not less of criminality, and have more of meanness, than the same offences when perpetrated against contemporaries. . . .

Massachusetts is *parental* in her government. More and more, as year after year rolls by, she seeks to substitute prevention for remedy, and rewards for penalties. She strives to make industry the antidote to poverty, and to counterwork the progress of vice and crime by the diffusion of knowledge and the culture of virtuous principles. She seeks not only to mitigate those great physical and mental calamities of which mankind are the sad inheritors, but also to avert those infinitely greater moral calamities which form the disastrous heritage of depraved passions. Hence it has long been her policy to endow or to aid asylums for the cure of disease. She succors and maintains all the poor within her borders, whatever may have been the land of their nativity. She founds and supports hospitals for restoring reason to the insane;

and, even for those violators of the law whom she is obliged to sequestrate from society, she provides daily instruction and the ministrations of the gospel at the public charge. To those who, in the order of Nature and Providence, have been bereft of the noble faculties of hearing and of speech, she teaches a new language, and opens their imprisoned minds and hearts to conversation with men and to communion with God; and it hardly transcends the literal truth to say that she gives sight to the blind. . . . The public highway is not more open and free for every man in the community than is the public schoolhouse for every child; and each parent feels that a free education is as secure a part of the birthright of his offspring as Heaven's bounties of light and air. . . .

Labor Reform Considered, 1836

Philip Hone on the Labor Movement, 1836

June 6 [1836].—In corroboration of the remarks which I have occasionally made of late, on the spirit of faction and contempt of the laws which pervades the community at this time, is the conduct of the journeymen tailors, instigated by a set of vile foreigners (principally English), who, unable to endure the restraints of wholesome law, well administered in their own country, take refuge here, establish tradesunions, and vilify Yankee judges and juries. Twenty odd of these were convicted at the Oyer and Terminer of a conspiracy to raise their wages and to prevent any of the craft from working at prices less than those for which they struck. Judge Edwards gave notice that he would proceed to sentence them this day; but, in consequence of the continuance of Robinson's trial, the Court postponed the sentence until Friday.

This, however, being the day on which it was expected, crowds of people have been collected in the park, ready for any mischief to which they may have been instigated, and a most diabolical and inflammatory hand-bill was circulated yesterday, headed by a coffin. The Board of Aldermen held an informal meeting this evening, at which a resolution was adopted authorizing the Mayor to offer a reward for the discovery of the author, printer, publisher, or distributor of this incendiary publication. . . .

The Coffin Handbill, 1836

Journeymen tailors. A placard was seen in various parts of the city on Sunday, which contained within the representation of a coffin, the following words:

"The Rich against the Poor! Judge Edwards, the tool of the Aristocracy, against the People! Mechanics and workingmen! a deadly blow has been struck at your Liberty! The prize for which your fathers fought has been robbed from you! The Freemen of the North are now on a level with the slaves of the South! with no other privileges than laboring that drones may fatten on your life-blood! Twenty of your brethren have been found guilty for presuming to resist a reduction of their wages! and Judge Edwards has charged an American jury, and agreeably to that charge, they have established the precedent, that workingmen have no right to regulate the price of labor! or, in other words, the Rich are the only judges of the wants of the Poor Man! On Monday, June 6, 1836, these Freemen are to receive their sentence, to gratify the hellish appetites of the Aristocracy! On Monday, the Liberty of the Workingmen will be interred! Judge Edwards is to chant the Requiem! Go! Go! Go! every Freeman, every Workingman, and hear the hollow and the melancholy sound of the earth on the Coffin of Equality! Let the Court-room, the City-hall—yea, the whole Park, be filled with Mourners! But, remember, offer no violence to Judge Edwards! Bend meekly, and receive the chains wherewith you are to be bound! Keep the peace! Above all things keep the peace! . . ."

Ralph Waldo Emerson is often positioned as the "father" of American literature. As a poet, preacher, orator, and essayist, he articulated the new nation's prospects and needs and became a weighty exemplum of the American artist. Throughout the 19th century, Emerson's portrait gazed down from schoolhouse and library walls, where he was enshrined as one of America's great poets. His daughter Ellen, accompanying her father on one of his frequent lecture tours, reported the fun of "seeing all the world burn incense to Father." His calls for a scholar and a poet who would exploit the untapped materials of the nation served as literary credos for subsequent generations of writers, from Rebecca Harding Davis, Walt Whitman, and Frederick Douglass, to Hart Crane, Robert Frost, and A.R. Ammons. He was known for his critique of conventional values of property and ambition, yet his formulation of the self-reliant American was used to authorize the *laissez-faire* individualism of Horatio Alger and Andrew Carnegie. He was one of the first American writers to be recognized by the British and European literary establishments, read enthusiastically by Carlyle and Nietzche. To Matthew Arnold, he is the "voice oracular" who challenges the "bitter knowledge" of his "monstrous, dead, unprofitable world." To Irving Howe, Emerson is the dominant spirit of his age, the proponent of "the American newness." In F.O. Matthiessen's formulation of the "American Renaissance," Emerson is the initiating force "on which Thoreau built, to which Whitman gave extension, and to which Hawthorne and Melville were indebted by being forced to react against its philosophical assumptions." To Whitman and, subsequently, to Alfred Kazin, Emerson is the "founder" of the "procession of American literature."

The eminence of his public position made Emerson's approval a valued commodity, as Whitman showed when he printed a congratulatory letter from Emerson with the second edition of *Leaves of Grass*. It also made him a formidable predecessor with whom younger writers had to contend. Writers as diverse as Thoreau, Louisa May Alcott, and Elizabeth Stuart Phelps describe their emergence onto the literary scene in relationship to Emerson, to his influence as a teacher or writer, a speaker or austere presence. Yet even such acknowledgments as Whitman's famous remark—"I was simmering, simmering, simmering, and Emerson brought me to a boil"—position Emerson primarily as a precursor, important for his influence on others, rather than for his own work. As Joel Porte has argued, "Emerson's fate, somewhat like Shakespeare's, was that he came to be treated as an almost purely allegorical personage whose real character and work got submerged in his function as a touchstone of critical opinion." He becomes the founder of "Transcendentalism" or the spokesman for "Nature," the "optimist" who does not understand the world's evil or pain. He is thus removed from the march of time, idealized as a "primordial" figure whose vision isolates him from the political and social struggles of his age.

But Emerson was never simply a distant patriarchal figure sheltered from the material problems of his age. He constructed his "optative" exuberance despite the early deaths of his father, two of his brothers, his beloved young wife, and his first son, and despite his own serious bouts with lung disease and eye strain. He was a child both of privilege and penury, of family position and dependence. As he wrote early on in his journal: "It is my own humor to despise pedigree. I was educated to prize it." His father, the minister William Emerson, died when he was eight, and his mother, Ruth Haskins Emerson, supported the five children (three others died young) by taking in boarders and by periodically living with relatives in Concord. Emerson's education vacillated between Boston Latin school and private tutoring by his aunt Mary Moody Emerson. At Harvard, which he attended on scholarship, Emerson struggled with the academic curriculum and with his expected future as either a teacher or minister. But he also conducted a more satisfying private education of reading and journal-writing that would prepare him to be a writer, an American scholar and poet. Those aims had to wait, however, while Emerson helped support his family by teaching school. In 1825, he entered Harvard Divinity School, following nine generations of his family into the ministry. Yet six years after his ordination, he resigned the ministry, concerned that the "dogmatic theology" of "formal Christianity" looked only to past traditions and the words of the dead. "My business is with the living," he wrote in his journal. "I have sometimes thought that in order to be a good minister it was necessary to leave the ministry."

These years were full of personal tumult as well. In 1829, Emerson married Ellen Tucker, only to lose her sixteen months later to the tuberculosis that also threatened him. The pain of her death and his own sense of vulnerability may have hastened Emerson's decision to leave the ministry. With the substantial inheritance she left him, he had the means to make such a change, to travel on the continent, to buy books, and to write them. The inheritance, with the earnings he received from his lecture tours and his publications and with a lifetime of frugality and fiscal planning, made him financially secure. He supported an extended family, caring for his retarded brother for twenty years. In 1835, he married Lidian Jackson, and moved to Concord, where they had four children—Waldo, Ellen, Edith, and Edward Waldo, who later edited his father's works and journals. The death from scarlet fever of five-year-old Waldo was a blow to Emerson's faith in compensation. In his 1844 essay "Experience," he wrote from this loss, and from his urgent desire to regain the "practical power" that could persist despite personal and public griefs. "Life is not intellectual or critical, but sturdy," he argued. His subsequent career and personal life reflect a determined affirmation to be "an active soul." "I am *Defeated* all the time," he acknowledged, "yet to Victory I am born." Emerson continued his work into his seventies, relying on his daughter Ellen to help organize his last lectures and essays. He died in 1882, from pneumonia, and was buried in Concord, near Thoreau and Hawthorne.

Emerson's long career, and his financial and social security, allowed him to intervene decisively in the formation of American culture and letters. Although he generally resisted the call to public advocacy, he was sought after to support various social causes: he was urged to join the experimental commune of Brook Farm, prodded to take a leading role in the abolitionist movement and in the lobbying for women's rights. He spoke in defense of John Brown, in opposition to the Fugitive Slave Law. But, as Thoreau claimed in 1845, it was Emerson's "personal influence upon young persons [that was] greater than any man's." A follower praised "his magnanimous recognition of the work of others," adding that "no one ever came into personal contact with him without a new or renewed confidence in his own possibilities." Emerson's efforts on behalf of his fellow writers were of material importance, addressing the social impediments to publication and reputation. Through financial support, personal connections, or editorial efforts, he made possible publication of work by Thoreau and Bronson Alcott, Margaret Fuller and Jones Very. He loaned Thoreau the house at Walden Pond for his celebrated retreat and raised money to support the impoverished Alcott family, despite his own belief that a philosopher should earn his keep. He oversaw American printings of Carlyle's books and wrote prefaces for translations of Persian poets and of Plutarch. With Margaret Fuller, he edited *The Dial,* a short-lived but influential periodical. Young friends mined his eclectic library for books on "Oriental topics" or the latest translation of Goethe. Americans traveling abroad carried introductions from Emerson, and foreign travelers met their American counterparts at his Concord house. Unlike many authors of his day, Emerson insisted on some control over his books' physical production, on their proofreading and revision, their reprinting and marketing. He was active in contemporary struggles to attain an international copyright, to secure better publishing contracts and royalties, and to curtail unsupervised reprints and piracies of books.

Emerson's initial fame came from his critique of the literary, religious, and educational establishments of his day. He was known as an experimenter who urged Americans to reject their deference to old modes and values, to continental traditions. His chiding lectures about Harvard's religious and literary training, and his resignation from the clergy, made him a spokesman· for reformist positions, although it also aroused harsh criticism of him as a religious infidel, "a sort of mad dog," and a "dangerous man." At the first meeting of the Transcendental Club, Emerson decried the "tame" genius of the times that did not match the grandeur of "this Titanic continent," and he transformed Harvard's traditional Phi Beta Kappa oration on "The American Scholar" into a critique of the "meek young men" and "sluggard intellect of this continent" and a call for a new age when "we will walk on our own feet; we will work with our own hands; we will speak our own minds."

Emerson's work is characterized by a combination of homely metaphors and grandiose goals, by his insistence on the present and his expectations for the future. His outpouring of "private" writings reflects a practical economy of writing, in which journals serve as a "Savings Bank" for "deposit" of "earnings" to be reworked into lectures and essays. They demonstrate his incredible energy and discipline (he kept 182 journals and notebooks over his career, which he carefully reread, indexed, and cross-referenced for use in preparing his more "public" work); and they reflect an astounding ambition, evident in the titles of his college journals, "The Wide World" and "The Universe," and in such notebooks as "XO" ("Inexorable; Reality and Illusion").

Emerson's literary practices have always been provocative. A critic of his first book, *Nature,* was offended by language that is sometimes "coarse and blunt." He also protested that "the effort of perusal is often painful, the thoughts excited are frequently bewildering, and the results to which they lead us, uncertain and obscure. The reader feels as in a disturbed dream." Although modern readers are unlikely to be upset by Emerson's diction or references to sex and madness, he remains disturbing, seen as a "difficult" writer requiring vast annotation and philosophic glossing. Emerson was indeed an allusive writer, but his use of cultural materials provokes with a purpose. The context he constructs is adamantly untraditional, mixing quotations from classics and British poetry with oriental literature and Welsh bards. One metaphor will emerge from his interest in scientific or engineering experiments, another from local politics, and yet another from what his son Waldo said that morning. The problem in reading Emerson—as well as the pleasure—is in seeing how such eclecticism undermines conventions of authority and reference and challenges established modes of reading. His first book was hailed as wondrous, as the thunderous "original writings of an angel," and as the "forerunner of a new class of books, the harbinger of a new Literature." His essays propose conventional wisdom only to turn it inside out, to question and challenge it. They develop as conversations or as self-reflexive inquiries, refining and testing assumptions. Although the essays are often mined for their aphorisms, these "laws" have a dubious position in Emerson's work, serving less as universal truths than as cultural positions to be examined. His claims about his age and place, about the American poet, scholar, or preacher, are challenges to his fellow citizens and to himself. They suggest a practice, as Emily Dickinson would write, of dwelling in possibility, not in prose.

For himself, and for the American public, he advocated "creative reading as well as creative writing," rejecting traditional oppositions between thinking and acting, between the scholar and the worker, between the speculative and the practical. "Words are also actions," he wrote, "and actions are a kind of words." For despite the hopeful tone of much of the writing, Emerson's brand of self-reliance and his exuberant nationalism were an aspiration, to be achieved only through constant work, constant critique. He rejects poets who "are contented with a civil and conformed manner of living" and who "write poems from the fancy, at a safe distance from their own experience." To Emerson, the poet has a public role to fulfill, a "necessity to be published" so he "apprises us not of his wealth, but of the commonwealth." Although Emerson has been lionized as a man of learning and privilege, his ambition was to "write something which all can read, like *Robinson Crusoe*. And when I have written a paper or a book, I see with regret that it is not solid, with a right materialistic treatment, which delights everybody." He argued that writers must constantly scrutinize their own work, that they must refashion themselves in response to changing circumstances and audiences: "he is no master who cannot vary his forms and carry his own end triumphantly through the most difficult." The poet explores "the science of the real"; he "turns the world to glass, and shows us all things in their right series and procession." Emerson's aim as a writer was less to originate a tradition than to produce active readers, who would then refashion themselves and their culture: "Let me remind the reader that I am only an experimenter. Do not set the least value on what I do, or the least discredit on what I do not, as if I pretended to settle anything as true or false. I unsettle all things. No facts are to me sacred; none are profane; I simply experiment, an endless seeker, with no Past at my back."

Jean Ferguson Carr
University of Pittsburgh

PRIMARY WORKS

Ralph L. Rusk, ed., *The Letters of Ralph Waldo Emerson,* 1939; Joseph Slater, ed., *The Correspondence of Emerson and Carlyle,* 1964; Arthur C. McGiffert, Jr., *Young Emerson Speaks* [sermons]; Ralph H. Orth et al, eds., *The Poetry Notebooks of Ralph Waldo Emerson,* 1986; *The Journals of Ralph Waldo Emerson,* ed. Edward W. Emerson and Waldo Emerson Forbes, 10 vols., 1909–1914; William Gilman, Alfred R. Ferguson, Ralph H. Orth, et al, *The Journals and Miscellaneous Notebooks of R.W. Emerson,* 16 vols., 1960–86; Joel Porte, *Emerson in his Journals,* 1982; Stephen Whicher, Robert Spiller, and Wallace Williams, *The Early Lectures of R.W. Emerson,* 3 vols., 1959–71; *Emerson's Complete Works,* ed. J.E. Cabot, 12 vols., 1883–1893; *The Complete Works of Ralph Waldo Emerson,* ed. Edward W. Emerson, 12 vols., 1903–1904; Alfred R. Ferguson, Jean Ferguson Carr, Douglas E. Wilson, textual editors, *The Collected Works of R.W. Emerson,* 1971–

SECONDARY WORKS

Ralph L. Rusk, *The Life of Ralph Waldo Emerson,* 1949; Sherman Paul, *Emerson's Angle of Vision: Man and Nature in American Experience,* 1952; Hyatt H. Waggoner, *Emerson as Poet,* 1974; David T. Porter, *Emerson and Literary Change,* 1978; Gay Wilson Allen, *Waldo Emerson: A Biography,* 1981; Joel Porte, *Emerson, Prospect and Retrospect,* 1982; Donald Yannella, *Ralph Waldo Emerson,* 1982; Robert E. Burkholder and Joel Myerson, eds., *Critical Essays on Ralph Waldo Emerson,* 1983; Julie Ellison, *Emerson's Romantic Style,* 1984; Harold Bloom, ed., *Ralph Waldo Emerson,* 1985.

The American Scholar[1]

An Oration delivered before the Phi Beta Kappa Society, at Cambridge, August 31, 1837

Mr. President and Gentlemen,

I greet you on the re-commencement of our literary year. Our anniversary is one of hope, and, perhaps, not enough of labor. We do not meet for games of strength or skill, for the recitation of histories, tragedies, and odes, like the ancient Greeks; for parliaments of love and poesy, like the Troubadours; nor for the advancement of science, like our contemporaries in the British and European capitals. Thus far, our holiday has been simply a friendly sign of the survival of the love of letters amongst a people too busy to give to letters any more. As such, it is precious as the sign of an indestructible instinct. Perhaps the time is already come, when it ought to be, and will be, something else; when the sluggard intellect of this continent will look from under its iron lids, and fill the postponed expectation of the world with something better than the exertions of mechanical skill. Our day of dependence, our long apprenticeship to the learning of other lands, draws to a close. The millions, that around us are rushing into life, cannot always be fed on the sere remains of foreign harvests. Events, actions arise, that must be sung, that will sing themselves. Who can doubt, that poetry will revive and lead in a new age, as the star in the constellation Harp, which now flames in our zenith, astronomers announce, shall one day be the pole-star for a thousand years?

In this hope, I accept the topic which not only usage, but the nature of our association, seem to prescribe to this day,—the AMERICAN SCHOLAR. Year by year, we come up hither to read one more chapter of his biography. Let us inquire what light new days and events have thrown on his character, and his hopes.

It is one of those fables,[2] which, out of an unknown antiquity, convey an unlooked-for wisdom, that the gods, in the beginning, divided Man into men, that he might be more helpful to himself; just as the hand was divided into fingers, the better to answer its end.

[1] The original title for the address and 1837 pamphlet was "An Oration Delivered before the Phi Beta Kappa Society, at Cambridge, August 31, 1937." The 1849 title is the assigned topic of the annual Phi Beta Kappa lectures.

[2] A version of this fable appears in Plato and in Plutarch.

The old fable covers a doctrine ever new and sublime; that there is One Man,—present to all particular men only partially, or through one faculty; and that you must take the whole society to find the whole man. Man is not a farmer, or a professor, or an engineer, but he is all. Man is priest, and scholar, and statesman, and producer, and soldier. In the *divided* or social state, these functions are parcelled out to individuals, each of whom aims to do his stint of the joint work, whilst each other performs his. The fable implies, that the individual, to possess himself, must sometimes return from his own labor to embrace all the other laborers. But unfortunately, this original unit, this fountain of power, has been so distributed to multitudes, has been so minutely subdivided and peddled out, that it is spilled into drops, and cannot be gathered. The state of society is one in which the members have suffered amputation from the trunk, and strut about so many walking monsters,—a good finger, a neck, a stomach, an elbow, but never a man.

Man is thus metamorphosed into a thing, into many things. The planter, who is Man sent out into the field to gather food, is seldom cheered by any idea of the true dignity of his ministry. He sees his bushel and his cart, and nothing beyond, and sinks into the farmer, instead of Man on the farm. The tradesman scarcely ever gives an ideal worth to his work, but is ridden by the routine of his craft, and the soul is subject to dollars. The priest becomes a form; the attorney, a statutebook; the mechanic, a machine; the sailor, a rope of a ship.

In this distribution of functions, the scholar is the delegated intellect. In the right state, he is, *Man Thinking*. In the degenerate state, when the victim of society, he tends to become a mere thinker, or, still worse, the parrot of other men's thinking.

In this view of him, as Man Thinking, the theory of his office is contained. Him nature solicits with all her placid, all her monitory pictures; him the past instructs; him the future invites. Is not, indeed, every man a student, and do not all things exist for the student's behoof? And, finally, is not the true scholar the only true master? But the old oracle[3] said, 'All things have two handles: beware of the wrong one.' In life, too often, the scholar errs with mankind and forfeits his privilege. Let us see him in his school, and consider him in reference to the main influences he receives.

I. The first in time and the first in importance of the influences upon the mind is that of nature. Every day, the sun; and, after sunset, night and her stars. Ever the winds blow; ever the grass grows. Every day, men and women, conversing, beholding and beholden. The scholar is he of all men whom this spectacle most engages. He must settle its value in his mind. What is nature to him? There is never a beginning, there is never an end, to the inexplicable continuity of this web of God, but always circular power returning into itself. Therein it resembles his own spirit, whose beginning, whose ending, he never can find,—so entire, so boundless. Far, too, as her splendors shine, system on system shooting like rays, upward, downward, without centre, without circumference,—in the mass and in the particle, nature hastens to render account of herself to the mind. Classification begins. To the young mind, every thing is individual, stands by itself. By and by, it finds how to join two things, and see in them one nature; then three, then three thousand; and so, tyrannized over by its own unifying instinct, it goes on tying things together,

---

[3] The passage is from the Stoic philosopher Epictetus (1st–2nd cent. A.D.).

diminishing anomalies, discovering roots running under ground, whereby contrary and remote things cohere, and flower out from one stem. It presently learns, that, since the dawn of history, there has been a constant accumulation and classifying of facts. But what is classification but the perceiving that these objects are not chaotic, and are not foreign, but have a law which is also a law of the human mind? The astronomer discovers that geometry, a pure abstraction of the human mind, is the measure of planetary motion. The chemist finds proportions and intelligible method throughout matter; and science is nothing but the finding of analogy, identity, in the most remote parts. The ambitious soul sits down before each refractory fact; one after another, reduces all strange constitutions, all new powers, to their class and their law, and goes on for ever to animate the last fibre of organization, the outskirts of nature, by insight.

Thus to him, to this school-boy under the bending dome of day, is suggested, that he and it proceed from one root; one is leaf and one is flower; relation, sympathy, stirring in every vein. And what is that Root? Is not that the soul of his soul?— A thought too bold,—a dream too wild. Yet when this spiritual light shall have revealed the law of more earthly natures,—when he has learned to worship the soul, and to see that the natural philosophy that now is, is only the first gropings of its gigantic hand, he shall look forward to an ever expanding knowledge as to a becoming creator. He shall see, that nature is the opposite of the soul, answering to it part for part. One is seal, and one is print. Its beauty is the beauty of his own mind. Its laws are the laws of his own mind. Nature then becomes to him the measure of his attainments. So much of nature as he is ignorant of, so much of his own mind does he not yet possess. And, in fine, the ancient precept, "Know thyself," and the modern precept, "Study nature," become at last one maxim.

II. The next great influence into the spirit of the scholar, is, the mind of the Past,—in whatever form, whether of literature, of art, of institutions, that mind is inscribed. Books are the best type of the influence of the past, and perhaps we shall get at the truth,—learn the amount of this influence more conveniently,—by considering their value alone.

The theory of books is noble. The scholar of the first age received into him the world around; brooded thereon; gave it the new arrangement of his own mind, and uttered it again. It came into him, life; it went out from him, truth. It came to him, short-lived actions; it went out from him, immortal thoughts. It came to him, business; it went from him, poetry. It was dead fact; now, it is quick thought. It can stand, and it can go. It now endures, it now flies, it now inspires. Precisely in proportion to the depth of mind from which it issued, so high does it soar, so long does it sing.

Or, I might say, it depends on how far the process had gone, of transmuting life into truth. In proportion to the completeness of the distillation, so will the purity and imperishableness of the product be. But none is quite perfect. As no air-pump can by any means make a perfect vacuum, so neither can any artist entirely exclude the conventional, the local, the perishable from his book, or write a book of pure thought, that shall be as efficient, in all respects, to a remote posterity, as to cotemporaries, or rather to the second age. Each age, it is found, must write its own books; or rather, each generation for the next succeeding. The books of an older period will not fit this.

Yet hence arises a grave mischief. The sacredness which attaches to the act of creation,—the act of thought,—is transferred to the record. The poet chanting, was felt to be a divine man: henceforth the chant is divine also. The writer was a just and wise spirit: henceforward it is settled, the book is perfect; as love of the hero corrupts into worship of his statue. Instantly, the book becomes noxious: the guide is a tyrant. The sluggish and perverted mind of the multitude, slow to open to the incursions of Reason, having once so opened, having once received this book, stands upon it, and makes an outcry, if it is disparaged. Colleges are built on it. Books are written on it by thinkers, not by Man Thinking; by men of talent, that is, who start wrong, who set out from accepted dogmas, not from their own sight of principles. Meek young men grow up in libraries, believing it their duty to accept the views, which Cicero, which Locke, which Bacon, have given, forgetful that Cicero, Locke, and Bacon[4] were only young men in libraries, when they wrote these books.

Hence, instead of Man Thinking, we have the bookworm. Hence, the book-learned class, who value books, as such; not as related to nature and the human constitution, but as making a sort of Third Estate[5] with the world and the soul. Hence, the restorers of readings, the emendators, the bibliomaniacs of all degrees.

Books are the best of things, well used; abused, among the worst. What is the right use? What is the one end, which all means go to effect? They are for nothing but to inspire. I had better never see a book, than to be warped by its attraction clean out of my own orbit, and made a satellite instead of a system. The one thing in the world, of value, is the active soul. This every man is entitled to; this every man contains within him, although, in almost all men, obstructed, and as yet unborn. The soul active sees absolute truth; and utters truth, or creates. In this action, it is genius; not the privilege of here and there a favorite, but the sound estate of every man. In its essence, it is progressive. The book, the college, the school of art, the institution of any kind, stop with some past utterance of genius. This is good, say they,—let us hold by this. They pin me down. They look backward and not forward. But genius looks forward: the eyes of man are set in his forehead, not in his hindhead: man hopes: genius creates. Whatever talents may be, if the man create not, the pure efflux of the Diety is not his;—cinders and smoke there may be, but not yet flame. There are creative manners, there are creative actions, and creative words; manners, actions, words, that is, indicative of no custom or authority, but springing spontaneous from the mind's own sense of good and fair.

On the other part, instead of being its own seer, let it receive from another mind its truth, though it were in torrents of light, without periods of solitude, inquest, and self-recovery, and a fatal disservice is done. Genius is always sufficiently the enemy of genius by over influence. The literature of every nation bear me witness. The English dramatic poets have Shakspearized now for two hundred years.

Undoubtedly there is a right way of reading, so it be sternly subordinated. Man Thinking must not be subdued by his instruments. Books are for the scholar's idle times. When he can read God directly, the hour is too precious to be wasted in other men's transcripts of their readings. But when the intervals of darkness come, as come they must,—when the sun is hid, and the stars withdraw their shining,—we repair to the lamps which were kindled by their ray, to guide our steps to the

[4]Emerson lists "young men" who, as adults, altered Western intellectual practice: the Roman orator Cicero (106–43 B.C.), 17th-century British philosopher John Locke, and 17th-century essayist Francis Bacon.

[5]Term used in pre-revolutionary France and in England to define the political class of commoners.

East again, where the dawn is. We hear, that we may speak. The Arabian proverb says, "A fig tree, looking on a fig tree, becometh fruitful."

It is remarkable, the character of the pleasure we derive from the best books. They impress us with the conviction, that one nature wrote and the same reads. We read the verses of one of the great English poets, of Chaucer, of Marvell, of Dryden, with the most modern joy,—with a pleasure, I mean, which is in great part caused by the abstraction of all *time* from their verses. There is some awe mixed with the joy of our surprise, when this poet, who lived in some past world, two or three hundred years ago, says that which lies close to my own soul, that which I also had wellnigh thought and said. But for the evidence thence afforded to the philosophical doctrine of the identity of all minds, we should suppose some preëstablished harmony, some foresight of souls that were to be, and some preparation of stores for their future wants, like the fact observed in insects, who lay up food before death for the young grub they shall never see.

I would not be hurried by any love of system, by any exaggeration of instincts, to underrate the Book. We all know, that, as the human body can be nourished on any food, though it were boiled grass and the broth of shoes, so the human mind can be fed by any knowledge. And great and heroic men have existed, who had almost no other information than by the printed page. I only would say, that it needs a strong head to bear that diet. One must be an inventor to read well. As the proverb says, "He that would bring home the wealth of the Indies, must carry out the wealth of the Indies." There is then creative reading as well as creative writing. When the mind is braced by labor and invention, the page of whatever book we read becomes luminous with manifold allusion. Every sentence is doubly significant, and the sense of our author is as broad as the world. We then see, what is always true, that, as the seer's hour of vision is short and rare among heavy days and months, so is its record, perchance, the least part of his volume. The discerning will read, in his Plato or Shakspeare, only that least part,—only the authentic utterances of the oracle;—all the rest he rejects, were it never so many times Plato's and Shakspeare's.

Of course, there is a portion of reading quite indispensable to a wise man. History and exact science he must learn by laborious reading. Colleges, in like manner, have their indispensable office,—to teach elements. But they can only highly serve us, when they aim not to drill, but to create; when they gather from far every ray of various genius to their hospitable halls, and, by the concentrated fires, set the hearts of their youth on flame. Thought and knowledge are natures in which apparatus and pretension avail nothing. Gowns, and pecuniary foundations, though of towns of gold, can never countervail the least sentence or syllable of wit. Forget this, and our American colleges will recede in their public importance, whilst they grow richer every year.

III. There goes in the world a notion, that the scholar should be a recluse, a valetudinarian,—as unfit for any handiwork or public labor, as a penknife for an axe. The so-called 'practical men' sneer at speculative men, as if, because they speculate or *see,* they could do nothing. I have heard it said that the clergy,—who are always, more universally than any other class, the scholars of their day,—are addressed as women; that the rough, spontaneous conversation of men they do not hear, but only a mincing and diluted speech. They are often virtually disfranchised; and, indeed, there are advocates for their celibacy. As far as this is true of the studious classes, it is not just and wise. Action is with the scholar subordinate, but it is essential. Without it, he is not yet man. Without it, thought can never ripen into truth. Whilst the world hangs before the eye as a cloud of beauty, we cannot even see its beauty. Inaction is cowardice, but there can be no scholar without the heroic mind. The preamble of thought, the transition through which it passes from the unconscious to the conscious, is action. Only so much do I know, as I have lived. Instantly we know whose words are loaded with life, and whose not.

The world,—this shadow of the soul, or *other me,* lies wide around. Its attractions are the keys which unlock my thoughts and make me acquainted with myself. I run eagerly into this resounding tumult. I grasp the hands of those next me, and take my place in the ring to suffer and to work, taught by an instinct, that so shall the dumb abyss be vocal with speech. I pierce its order; I dissipate its fear; I dispose of it within the circuit of my expanding life. So much only of life as I know by experience, so much of the wilderness have I vanquished and planted, or so far have I extended my being, my dominion. I do not see how any man can afford, for the sake of his nerves and his nap, to spare any action in which he can partake. It is pearls and rubies to his discourse. Drudgery, calamity, exasperation, want, are instructors in eloquence and wisdom. The true scholar grudges every opportunity of action past by, as a loss of power.

It is the raw material out of which the intellect moulds her splendid products. A strange process too, this, by which experience is converted into thought, as a mulberry leaf is converted into satin. The manufacture goes forward at all hours.

The actions and events of our childhood and youth, are now matters of calmest observation. They lie like fair pictures in the air. Not so with our recent actions,—with the business which we now have in hand. On this we are quite unable to speculate. Our affections as yet circulate through it. We no more feel or know it, than we feel the feet, or the hand, or the brain of our body. The new deed is yet a part of life,—remains for a time immersed in our unconscious life. In some contemplative hour, it detaches itself from the life like a ripe fruit, to become a thought of the mind. Instantly, it is raised, transfigured; the corruptible has put on incorruption. Henceforth it is an object of beauty, however base its origin and neighborhood. Observe, too, the impossibility of antedating this act. In its grub state, it cannot fly, it cannot shine, it is a dull grub. But suddenly, without observation, the selfsame thing unfurls beautiful wings, and is an angel of wisdom. So is there no fact, no event, in our private history, which shall not, sooner or later, lose its adhesive, inert form, and astonish us by soaring from our body into the empyrean. Cradle and infancy, school and playground, the fear of boys, and dogs, and ferules, the love of little maids and berries, and many another fact that once filled the whole sky, are gone already; friend and relative, profession and party, town and country, nation and world, must also soar and sing.

Of course, he who has put forth his total strength in fit actions, has the richest return of wisdom. I will not shut myself out of this globe of action, and transplant an oak into a flower-pot, there to hunger and pine; nor trust the revenue of some single faculty, and exhaust one vein of thought, much like those Savoyards,[6] who, getting their livelihood by carving shepherds, shepherdesses, and smoking Dutchmen, for all Europe, went out one day to the mountain to find stock, and discovered that they had whittled up the last of their pinetrees. Authors we have, in numbers, who have written out their vein, and who, moved by a commendable prudence, sail for Greece or Palestine, follow the trapper into the prairie, or ramble round Algiers, to replenish their merchantable stock.

If it were only for a vocabulary, the scholar would be covetous of action. Life is our dictionary. Years are well spent in country labors; in town,—in the insight into trades and manufactures; in frank intercourse with many men and women; in science; in art; to the one end of mastering in all their facts a language by which to illustrate and embody our perceptions. I learn immediately from any speaker how much he has already lived, through the poverty or the splendor of his speech. Life lies behind us as the quarry from whence we get tiles and copestones for the masonry of to-day. This is the way to learn grammar. Colleges and books only copy the language which the field and the work-yard made.

But the final value of action, like that of books, and better than books, is, that it is a resource. That great principle of Undulation in nature, that shows itself in the inspiring and expiring of the breath; in desire and satiety; in the ebb and flow of the sea; in day and night; in heat and cold; and as yet more deeply ingrained in every atom and every fluid, is known to us under the name of Polarity,—these "fits of easy transmission and reflection," as Newton called them, are the law of nature because they are the law of spirit.

The mind now thinks; now acts; and each fit reproduces the other. When the artist has exhausted his materials, when the fancy no longer paints, when thoughts are no longer apprehended, and books are a weariness,—he has always the resource *to live.* Character is higher than intellect. Thinking is the function. Living is the functionary. The stream retreats to its source. A great soul will be strong to live, as well as strong to think. Does he lack organ or medium to impart his truths? He can still fall back on this elemental force of living them. This is a total act. Thinking is a partial act. Let the grandeur of justice shine in his affairs. Let the beauty of affection cheer his lowly roof. Those 'far from fame,' who dwell and act with him, will feel the force of his constitution in the doings and passages of the day better than it can be measured by any public and designed display. Time shall teach him, that the scholar loses no hour which the man lives. Herein he unfolds the sacred germ of his instinct, screened from influence. What is lost in seemliness is gained in strength. Not out of those, on whom systems of education have exhausted their culture, comes the helpful giant to destroy the old or to build the new, but out of unhandselled[7] savage nature, out of terrible Druids and Berserkirs, come at last Alfred and Shakspeare.[8]

I hear therefore with joy whatever is beginning to be said of the dignity and necessity of labor to every citizen. There is virtue yet in the hoe and the spade, for learned as well as for unlearned hands. And labor is everywhere welcome; always

[6] Natives of Savoy, region in the French Alps.
[7] Untamed, untouched by hand, inauspicious.
[8] Ancient Celtic priests and Norse warriors contrast with examples of British civilization, Shakespeare and Alfred, the 9th-century king who founded schools and instituted laws.

we are invited to work; only be this limitation observed, that a man shall not for the sake of wider activity sacrifice any opinion to the popular judgments and modes of action.

I have now spoken of the education of the scholar by nature, by books, and by action. It remains to say somewhat of his duties.

They are such as become Man Thinking. They may all be comprised in self-trust. The office of the scholar is to cheer, to raise, and to guide men by showing them facts amidst appearances. He plies the slow, unhonored, and unpaid task of observation. Flamsteed and Herschel,[9] in their glazed observatories, may catalogue the stars with the praise of all men, and, the results being splendid and useful, honor is sure. But he, in his private observatory, cataloguing obscure and nebulous stars of the human mind, which as yet no man has thought of as such,—watching days and months, sometimes, for a few facts; correcting still his old records;—must relinquish display and immediate fame. In the long period of his preparation, he must betray often an ignorance and shiftlessness in popular arts, incurring the disdain of the able who shoulder him aside. Long he must stammer in his speech; often forego the living for the dead. Worse yet, he must accept,—how often! poverty and solitude. For the ease and pleasure of treading the old road, accepting the fashions, the education, the religion of society, he takes the cross of making his own, and, of course, the self-accusation, the faint heart, the frequent uncertainty and loss of time, which are the nettles and tangling vines in the way of the self-relying and self-directed; and the state of virtual hostility in which he seems to stand to society, and especially to educated society. For all this loss and scorn, what offset? He is to find consolation in exercising the highest functions of human nature. He is one, who raises himself from private considerations, and breathes and lives on public and illustrious thoughts. He is the world's eye. He is the world's heart. He is to resist the vulgar prosperity that retrogrades ever to barbarism, by preserving and communicating heroic sentiments, noble biographies, melodious verse, and the conclusions of history. Whatsoever oracles the human heart, in all emergencies, in all solemn hours, has uttered as its commentary on the world of actions,—these he shall receive and impart. And whatsoever new verdict Reason from her inviolable seat pronounces on the passing men and events of to-day,—this he shall hear and promulgate.

These being his functions, it becomes him to feel all confidence in himself, and to defer never to the popular cry. He and he only knows the world. The world of any moment is the merest appearance. Some great decorum, some fetish of a government, some ephemeral trade, or war, or man, is cried up by half mankind and cried down by the other half, as if all depended on this particular up or down. The odds are that the whole question is not worth the poorest thought which the scholar has lost in listening to the controversy. Let him not quit his belief that a popgun is a popgun, though the ancient and honorable of the earth affirm it to be the crack of doom. In silence, in steadiness, in severe abstraction, let him hold by himself; add observation to observation, patient of neglect, patient of reproach; and bide his own time,—happy enough, if he can satisfy himself alone, that this day he has seen

[9] Seventeenth and 18th-century English astronomers.

something truly. Success treads on every right step. For the instinct is sure, that prompts him to tell his brother what he thinks. He then learns, that in going down into the secrets of his own mind, he has descended into the secrets of all minds. He learns that he who has mastered any law in his private thoughts, is master to that extent of all men whose language he speaks, and of all into whose language his own can be translated. The poet, in utter solitude remembering his spontaneous thoughts and recording them, is found to have recorded that, which men in crowded cities find true for them also. The orator distrusts at first the fitness of his frank confessions,—his want of knowledge of the persons he addresses,—until he finds that he is the complement of his hearers;—that they drink his words because he fulfills for them their own nature; the deeper he dives into his privatest, secretest presentiment, to his wonder he finds, this is the most acceptable, most public, and universally true. The people delight in it; the better part of every man feels, This is my music; this is myself.

In self-trust; all the virtues are comprehended. Free should the scholar be,— free and brave. Free even to the definition of freedom, "without any hindrance that does not arise out of his own constitution." Brave; for fear is a thing, which a scholar by his very function puts behind him. Fear always springs from ignorance. It is a shame to him if his tranquility, amid dangerous times, arise from the presumption, that, like children and women, his is a protected class; or if he seek a temporary peace by the diversion of his thoughts from politics or vexed questions, hiding his head like an ostrich in the flowering bushes, peeping into microscopes, and turning rhymes, as a boy whistles to keep his courage up. So is the danger a danger still; so is the fear worse. Manlike let him turn and face it. Let him look into its eye and search its nature, inspect its origin,—see the whelping of this lion,—which lies no great way back; he will then find in himself a perfect comprehension of its nature and extent; he will have made his hands meet on the other side, and can henceforth defy it, and pass on superior. The world is his, who can see through its pretension. What deafness, what stone-blind custom, what overgrown error you behold, is there only by sufferance,—by your sufferance. See it to be a lie, and you have already dealt it its mortal blow.

Yes, we are the cowed,—we the trustless. It is a mischievous notion that we are come late into nature; that the world was finished a long time ago. As the world was plastic and fluid in the hands of God, so it is ever to so much of his attributes as we bring to it. To ignorance and sin, it is flint. They adapt themselves to it as they may; but in proportion as a man has any thing in him divine, the firmament flows before him and takes his signet and form. Not he is great who can alter matter, but he who can alter my state of mind. They are the kings of the world who give the color of their present thought to all nature and all art, and persuade men by the cheerful serenity of their carrying the matter, that this thing which they do, is the apple which the ages have desired to pluck, now at last ripe, and inviting nations to the harvest. The great man makes the great thing. Wherever Macdonald sits, there is the head of the table. Linnæus makes botany the most alluring of studies, and wins it from the farmer and the herb-woman; Davy, chemistry; and Cuvier, fossils.[10] The

---

[10] Emerson extends the contemporary saying about a Scottish clan leader's authority to three influential scientists.

day is always his, who works in it with serenity and great aims. The unstable esti-mates of men crowd to him whose mind is filled with a truth, as the heaped waves of the Atlantic follow the moon.

For this self-trust, the reason is deeper than can be fathomed,—darker than can be enlightened. I might not carry with me the feeling of my audience in stating my own belief. But I have already shown the ground of my hope, in adverting to the doctrine that man is one. I believe man has been wronged; he has wronged himself. He has almost lost the light, that can lead him back to his prerogatives. Men are become of no account. Men in history, men in the world of to-day are bugs, are spawn, and are called 'the mass' and 'the herd.' In a century, in a millennium, one or two men; that is to say,—one or two approximations to the right state of every man. All the rest behold in the hero or the poet their own green and crude being,— ripened; yes, and are content to be less, so *that* may attain to its full stature. What a testimony,—full of grandeur, full of pity, is borne to the demands of his own nature, by the poor clansman, the poor partisan, who rejoices in the glory of his chief. The poor and the low find some amends to their immense moral capacity, for their acquiescence in a political and social inferiority. They are content to be brushed like flies from the path of a great person, so that justice shall be done by him to that common nature which it is the dearest desire of all to see enlarged and glorified. They sun themselves in the great man's light, and feel it to be their own element. They cast the dignity of man from their downtrod selves upon the shoul-ders of a hero, and will perish to add one drop of blood to make that great heart beat, those giant sinews combat and conquer. He lives for us, and we live in him.

Men such as they are, very naturally seek money or power; and power because it is as good as money,—the "spoils," so called, "of office." And why not? for they aspire to the highest, and this, in their sleep-walking, they dream is highest. Wake them, and they shall quit the false good, and leap to the true, and leave governments to clerks and desks. This revolution is to be wrought by the gradual domestication of the idea of Culture. The main enterprise of the world for splendor, for extent, is the upbuilding of a man. Here are the materials strown along the ground. The private life of one man shall be a more illustrious monarchy,—more formidable to its enemy, more sweet and serene in its influence to its friend, than any kingdom in history. For a man, rightly viewed, comprehendeth the particular natures of all men. Each philosopher, each bard, each actor, has only done for me, as by a delegate, what one day I can do for myself. The books which once we valued more than the apple of the eye, we have quite exhausted. What is that but saying, that we have come up with the point of view which the universal mind took through the eyes of one scribe; we have been that man, and have passed on. First, one; then, another; we drain all cisterns, and, waxing greater by all these supplies, we crave a better and more abundant food. The man has never lived that can feed us ever. The human mind cannot be enshrined in a person, who shall set a barrier on any one side to this unbounded, unboundable empire. It is one central fire, which, flaming now out of the lips of Etna, lightens the capes of Sicily; and, now out of the throat of Vesuvius, illuminates the towers and vineyards of Naples. It is one light which beams out of a thousand stars. It is one soul which animates all men.

But I have dwelt perhaps tediously upon this abstraction of the Scholar. I ought not to delay longer to add what I have to say, of nearer reference to the time and to this country.

Historically, there is thought to be a difference in the ideas which predominate over successive epochs, and there are data for marking the genius of the Classic, of the Romantic, and now of the Reflective or Philosophical age. With the views I have intimated of the oneness or the identity of the mind through all individuals, I do not much dwell on these differences. In fact, I believe each individual passes through all three. The boy is a Greek; the youth, romantic; the adult, reflective. I deny not, however, that a revolution in the leading idea may be distinctly enough traced.

Our age is bewailed as the age of Introversion. Must that needs be evil? We, it seems, are critical; we are embarrassed with second thoughts; we cannot enjoy any thing for hankering to know whereof the pleasure consists; we are lined with eyes; we see with our feet; the time is infected with Hamlet's unhappiness,—

"Sicklied o'er with the pale cast of thought."[11]

Is it so bad then? Sight is the last thing to be pitied. Would we be blind? Do we fear lest we should outsee nature and God, and drink truth dry? I look upon the discontent of the literary class, as a mere announcement of the fact, that they find themselves not in the state of mind of their fathers, and regret the coming state as untried; as a boy dreads the water before he has learned that he can swim. If there is any period one would desire to be born in,—is it not the age of Revolution; when the old and the new stand side by side, and admit of being compared; when the energies of all men are searched by fear and by hope; when the historic glories of the old, can be compensated by the rich possibilities of the new era? This time, like all times, is a very good one, if we but know what to do with it.

I read with joy some of the auspicious signs of the coming days, as they glimmer already through poetry and art, through philosophy and science, through church and state.

One of these signs is the fact, that the same movement which effected the elevation of what was called the lowest class in the state, assumed in literature a very marked and as benign an aspect. Instead of the sublime and beautiful; the near, the low, the common, was explored and poetized. That, which had been negligently trodden under foot by those who were harnessing and provisioning themselves for long journeys into far countries, is suddenly found to be richer than all foreign parts. The literature of the poor, the feelings of the child, the philosophy of the street, the meaning of household life, are the topics of the time. It is a great stride. It is a sign,—is it not? of new vigor, when the extremities are made active, when currents of warm life run into the hands and the feet. I ask not for the great, the remote, the romantic; what is doing in Italy or Arabia; what is Greek art, or Provençal minstrelsy; I embrace the common, I explore and sit at the feet of the familiar, the low. Give me insight into to-day, and you may have the antique and future worlds. What would we really know the meaning of? The meal in the firkin;[12] the milk in the pan; the ballad in the street; the news of the boat; the glance of the eye; the form and the gait of the body;—show me the ultimate reason of these matters; show me the sublime presence of the highest spiritual cause lurking, as always it does lurk, in these suburbs and extremities of nature; let me see every trifle bristling

---

[11] *Hamlet,* III, i: 85.
[12] Small wooden bowl.

with the polarity that ranges it instantly on an eternal law; and the shop, the plough, and the leger, referred to the like cause by which light undulates and poets sing;—and the world lies no longer a dull miscellany and lumber-room, but has form and order; there is no trifle; there is no puzzle; but one design unites and animates the farthest pinnacle and the lowest trench.

This idea has inspired the genius of Goldsmith, Burns, Cowper, and, in a newer time, of Goethe, Wordsworth, and Carlyle. This idea they have differently followed and with various success. In contrast with their writing, the style of Pope, of Johnson, of Gibbon, looks cold and pedantic. This writing is blood-warm. Man is surprised to find that things near are not less beautiful and wondrous than things remote. The near explains the far. The drop is a small ocean. A man is related to all nature. This perception of the worth of the vulgar is fruitful in discoveries. Goethe, in this very thing the most modern of the moderns, has shown us, as none ever did, the genius of the ancients.

There is one man of genius, who has done much for this philosophy of life, whose literary value has never yet been rightly estimated;—I mean Emanuel Swedenborg. The most imaginative of men, yet writing with the precision of a mathematician, he endeavored to engraft a purely philosophical Ethics on the popular Christianity of his time. Such an attempt, of course, must have difficulty, which no genius could surmount. But he saw and showed the connection between nature and the affections of the soul. He pierced the emblematic or spiritual character of the visible, audible, tangible world. Especially did his shade-loving muse hover over and interpret the lower parts of nature; he showed the mysterious bond that allies moral evil to the foul material forms, and has given in epical parables a theory of insanity, of beasts, of unclean and fearful things.

Another sign of our times, also marked by an analogous political movement, is, the new importance given to the single person. Every thing that tends to insulate the individual,—to surround him with barriers of natural respect, so that each man shall feel the world is his, and man shall treat with man as a sovereign state with a sovereign state;—tends to true union as well as greatness. "I learned," said the melancholy Pestalozzi,[13] "that no man in God's wide earth is either willing or able to help any other man." Help must come from the bosom alone. The scholar is that man who must take up into himself all the ability of the time, all the contributions of the past, all the hopes of the future. He must be an university of knowledges. If there be one lesson more than another, which should pierce his ear, it is, The world is nothing, the man is all; in yourself is the law of all nature, and you know not yet how a globule of sap ascends; in yourself slumbers the whole of Reason; it is for you to know all, it is for you to dare all. Mr. President and Gentlemen, this confidence in the unsearched might of man belongs, by all motives, by all prophecy, by all preparation, to the American Scholar. We have listened too long to the courtly muses of Europe. The spirit of the American freeman is already suspected to be timid, imitative, tame. Public and private avarice make the air we breathe thick and fat. The scholar is decent, indolent, complaisant. See already the tragic consequence. The mind of this country, taught to aim at low objects, eats upon itself.

[13] Swiss educator and theorist (1746–1827) who
influenced Bronson Alcott.

There is no work for any but the decorous and the complaisant. Young men of the fairest promise, who begin life upon our shores, inflated by the mountain winds, shined upon by all the stars of God, find the earth below not in unison with these,—but are hindered from action by the disgust which the principles on which business is managed inspire, and turn drudges, or die of disgust,—some of them suicides. What is the remedy? They did not yet see, and thousands of young men as hopeful now crowding to the barriers for the career, do not yet see, that, if the single man plant himself indomitably on his instincts, and there abide, the huge world will come round to him. Patience,—patience;—with the shades of all the good and great for company; and for solace, the perspective of your own infinite life; and for work, the study and the communication of principles, the making those instincts prevalent, the conversion of the world. Is it not the chief disgrace in the world, not to be an unit;—not to be reckoned one character;—not to yield that peculiar fruit which each man was created to bear, but to be reckoned in the gross, in the hundred, or the thousand, of the party, the section, to which we belong; and our opinion predicted geographically, as the north, or the south? Not so, brothers and friends,—please God, ours shall not be so. We will walk on our own feet; we will work with our own hands; we will speak our own minds. The study of letters shall be no longer a name for pity, for doubt, and for sensual indulgence. The dread of man and the love of man shall be a wall of defence and a wreath of joy around all. A nation of men will for the first time exist, because each believes himself inspired by the Divine Soul which also inspires all men.

1837/49

In 1830 no American reform movement seemed farther from its goals than antislavery. The movement's mainstream favored gradual emancipation, followed by colonization of the freed slaves—a plan that appeared to be heading nowhere. Meanwhile, radical freethinkers and artisans submerged their antislavery convictions in various antievangelical and labor insurgencies. Antislavery activities by free blacks had produced some forceful statements and would create an impressive movement but made little progress outside of the black community.

A fresh jolt came when the Bostonian William Lloyd Garrison broke with gradualism and in 1831 established The Liberator, *which advocated immediate abolition. Thereafter the immediatist cause enlisted tens of thousands of supporters, building partly on the passions and the organizational expertise of the northern evangelical reform empire. Never before in U.S. history had so many worked so hard toward forever ending American bondage—breaking the conspiracy of silence that had surrounded the issue for years. Still, only a tiny part of the white population acquired much sympathy for abolitionism. In the North as well as the South, abolitionists and their friends faced public scorn and mob violence. In politics, the managers of both major parties stayed determined to keep slavery discussions out of national affairs. And at the end of the 1830s, the abolitionists themselves divided sharply over strategy and tactics, between radical Garrisonians and more moderate, politically minded organizers.*

Under the circumstances, what is surprising is not that the abolitionists failed to gain greater success but that they succeeded as much as they did. What drove some Americans—but not others—to support them? How much did the emergence of immediatism reflect broader social and intellectual trends? What about the antiabolitionists? For obvious reasons, there has been a tendency to write these people off as hidebound conservatives who were flying in the face of history. Yet they certainly came closer than the abolitionists did to the majority American viewpoint in the 1830s. Just as much as their foes, they believed they were upholding Christian morality and the republic's well-being. Some claimed, with the utmost sincerity, that they were serving the best interests of black people. So, for that matter, did those Americans (mostly but not exclusively southerners) who replied to the abolitionists with increasingly vehement defenses of slavery as a way of life. Purely on the grounds of intellectual consistency—a matter distinct from the rights and wrongs of the issue—some proslavery conservatives more than held their own. What did all of these arguments say about the multiplying social and ideological divisions connected to slavery?

⊞ *D O C U M E N T S*

David Walker, a free black born in North Carolina who later moved to Boston, became active in the Massachusetts Colored Association and in 1829 published his famous incendiary abolitionist appeal, directed to "the colored citizens of the world" (excerpted in the first document). Several radical abolitionists (including William Lloyd Garrison) later said that Walker's shocking pamphlet helped goad them to greater militance despite their misgivings about its hints toward violent insurrection. Southern legislatures responded by outlawing the pamphlet's circulation and cracking down on blacks' education. Subsequent black abolitionists, foremost among them the ex-slave Frederick Douglass, would build upon Walker's themes.

David Walker died in mysterious circumstances in 1830. By then Garrison and others had begun to gravitate to the doctrine of immediatism. In the first issue of *The Liberator*, an excerpt of which is reprinted as the second document, Garrison proclaimed his uncompromising position and elaborated some of his other ideas about labor and justice. Two years later, the New-England Anti-Slavery Society offered a definition of immediatism (document three).

Angelina Grimké and her sister Sarah, after moving from their native South Carolina to New England, were especially active and articulate; their work would eventually force a rift within abolitionism over the question of women's rights. Angelina Grimké's appeal to Christian women of the South is excerpted in the fourth document.

African-American Abolitionism: David Walker Appeals to the Colored Citizens of the World, 1829

. . . [W]e, (coloured people of these United States of America) are the *most wretched, degraded* and *abject* set of beings that *ever lived* since the world began, and that the white Americans having reduced us to the wretched state of *slavery*, treat us in that condition *more cruel* (they being an enlighted and Christian people,) than any heathen nation did any people whom it had reduced to our condition. These affirmations are so well confirmed in the minds of all unprejudiced men, who have taken the trouble to read histories, that they need no elucidation from me. . . . [T]hose enemies who have for hundreds of years stolen our *rights,* and kept us ignorant of Him and His divine worship, he will remove. Millions of whom, are this day, so ignorant and avaricious, that they cannot conceive how God can have an attribute of justice, and show mercy to us because it pleased Him to make us black — which colour, Mr. Jefferson calls unfortunate!!!!!! As though we are not as thankful to our God, for having made us as it pleased himself, as they (the whites,) are for having made them white. They think because they hold us in their infernal chains of slavery, that we wish to be white, or of their color — but they are dreadfully deceived — we wish to be just as it pleased our Creator to have made us, and no avaricious and unmerciful wretches, have any business to make slaves of, or hold us in slavery. How would they like for us to make slaves of, and hold them in cruel slavery, and murder them as they do us? — But is Mr. Jefferson's assertions true? viz. "that it is unfortunate for us that our Creator has been pleased to make us *black.*" We will not take his say so, for the fact. The world will have an opportunity to see whether it is unfortunate for us, that our Creator *has made us* darker than the *whites.*

Fear not the number and education of our *enemies,* against whom we shall have to contend for our lawful right; guaranteed to us by our Maker; for why should we be afraid, when God is, and will continue, (if we continue humble) to be on our side?

The man who would not fight under our Lord and Master Jesus Christ, in the glorious and heavenly cause of freedom and of God — to be delivered from the most wretched, abject and servile slavery, that ever a people was afflicted with since the foundation of the world, to the present day — ought to be kept with all of his children or family, in slavery, or in chains, to be butchered by his *cruel enemies.* . . .

Here let me ask Mr. Jefferson, (but he is gone to answer at the bar of God, for the deeds done in his body while living,) I therefore ask the whole American people, had I not rather die, or be put to death, than to be a slave to any tyrant, who takes not only my own, but my wife and children's lives by the inches? Yea, would I meet death with avidity far! far!! in preference to such *servile submission* to the murderous hands of tyrants. Mr. Jefferson's very severe remarks on us have been so extensively argued upon by men whose attainments in literature, I shall never be able to reach, that I would not have meddled with it, were it not to solicit each of my brethren, who has the spirit of a man, to buy a copy of Mr. Jefferson's "Notes on Virginia," and put it in the hand of his son. For let no one of us suppose that the refutations which have been written by our white friends are enough—they are *whites*—we are *blacks*.

We, and the world wish to see the charges of Mr. Jefferson refuted by the blacks *themselves,* according to their chance; for we must remember that what the whites have written respecting this subject, is other men's labours, and did not emanate from the blacks. I know well, that there are some talents and learning among the coloured people of this country, which we have not a chance to develop, in consequence of oppression; but our oppression ought not to hinder us from acquiring all we can. For we will have a chance to develop them by and by. God will not suffer us, always to be oppressed. Our sufferings will come to an *end,* in spite of all the Americans this side of *eternity*. Then we will want all the learning and talents among ourselves, and perhaps more, to govern ourselves.—"Every dog must have its day," the American's is coming to an end. . . .

[A]t the close of the first Revolution in this country, with Great Britain, there were but thirteen States in the Union, now there are twenty-four, most of which are slave-holding States, and the whites are dragging us around in chains and in handcuffs, to their new States and Territories to work their mines and farms, to enrich them and their children—and millions of them believing firmly that we being a little darker than they, were made by our Creator to be an inheritance to them and their children for ever—the same as a parcel of *brutes*.

Are we MEN!!—I ask you, O my brethren! are we MEN? Did our Creator make us to be slaves to dust and ashes like ourselves? Are they not dying worms as well as we? Have they not to make their appearance before the tribunal of Heaven, to answer for the deeds done in the body, as well as we? Have we any other Master but Jesus Christ alone? Is he not their Master as well as ours?—What right then, have we to obey and call any other Master, but Himself? How we could be so *submissive* to a gang of men, whom we cannot tell whether they are *as good* as ourselves or not, I never could conceive. However, this is shut up with the Lord, and we cannot precisely tell—but I declare, we judge men by their works. . . .

Americans! notwithstanding you have and do continue to treat us more cruel than any heathen nation ever did a people it had subjected to the same condition that you have us. Now let us reason—I mean you of the United States, whom I believe God designs to save from destruction, if you will hear. For I declare to you, whether you believe it or not, that there are some on the continent of America, who will never be able to repent. God will surely destroy them, to show you his disapprobation of the murders they and you have inflicted on us. I say, let us reason; had you not better take our body, while you have it in your power, and while we are yet ignorant and wretched, not knowing but a little, give us education, and teach us the pure religion of our Lord and Master, which is calculated to make the lion lay down in peace with the lamb, and which millions of you have beaten us nearly to death for trying to obtain since we have been among you, and thus at once, gain our affection while we are ignorant? Remember Americans, that we must and shall be free and enlightened as you are, will you wait until we shall, under God, obtain our liberty by the crushing arm of power? Will it not be dreadful for you? I speak Americans for your good. We must and shall be free I say, in spite of you. You may do your best to keep us in wretchedness and misery, to enrich you and your children, but God will deliver us from under you. And wo, wo, will be to you if we have to obtain our freedom by fighting. Throw away your fears and prejudices then, and enlighten us and treat us like men, and we will like you more than we do now hate you, and tell us now no more about colonization, for America is as much our country, as it is yours.—

Treat us like men, and there is no danger but we will all live in peace and happiness together. For we are not like you, hard hearted, unmerciful, and unforgiving. What a happy country this will be, if the whites will listen. What nation under heaven, will be able to do any thing with us, unless God gives us up into its hand? But Americans, I declare to you, while you keep us and our children in bondage, and treat us like brutes, to make us support you and your families, we cannot be your friends. You do not look for it, do you? Treat us then like men, and we will be your friends. And there is not a doubt in my mind, but that the whole of the past will be sunk into oblivion, and we yet, under God, will become a united and happy people. The whites may say it is impossible, but remember that nothing is impossible with God. . . .

If any are anxious to ascertain who I am, know the world, that I am one of the oppressed, degraded and wretched sons of Africa, rendered so by the avaricious and unmerciful, among the whites.—If any wish to plunge me into the wretched incapacity of a slave, or murder me for the truth, know ye, that I am in the hand of God, and at your disposal. I count my life not dear unto me, but I am ready to be offered at any moment. For what is the use of living, when in fact I am dead. But remember, Americans, that as miserable, wretched, degraded and abject as you have made us in preceding, and in this generation, to support you and your families, that some of you, (whites) on the continent of America, will yet curse the day that you ever were born. You want slaves, and want us for your slaves!!! My colour will yet, root some of you out of the very face of the earth!!!!!! . . .

See your Declaration Americans!!! Do you understand your own language? Hear your language, proclaimed to the world, July 4th, 1776—

We hold these truths to be self evident—that ALL men are created EQUAL!! that they *are endowed by their creator with certain unalienable rights;* that among these are life, *liberty,* and the pursuit of happiness!!

Compare your own language above, extracted from your Declaration of Independence, with your cruelties and murders inflicted by your cruel and unmerciful fathers and yourselves on our fathers and on us—men who have never given your fathers or you the least provocation!!!!!!

Hear your language further!

> But when a long train of abuses and usurpation, pursuing invariably the same object, evinces a design to reduce them under absolute despotism, it is their *right*, it is their *duty,* to throw off such government, and to provide new guards for their future security.

Now, Americans! I ask you candidly, was your sufferings under Great Britain, one hundredth part as cruel and tyrannical as you have rendered ours under you? Some of you, no doubt, believe that we will never throw off your murderous government and "provide new guards for our future security." If Satan has made you believe it, will he not deceive you?* Do the whites say, I being a black man, ought to be humble, which I readily admit? I ask them, ought they not to be as humble as I? or do they think that they can measure arms with Jehovah? Will not the Lord yet humble them? or will not these very coloured people whom they now treat worse than brutes, yet under God, humble them low down enough? Some of the whites are ignorant enough to tell us, that we ought to be submissive to them that they may keep their feet on our throats. And if we do not submit to be beaten to death by them, we are bad creatures and of course must be damned, &c.

If any man wishes to hear this doctrine openly preached to us by the American preachers, let him go into the Southern and Western sections of this country—I do not speak from hear say—what I have written, is what I have seen and heard myself. No man may think that my book is made up of conjecture—I have travelled and observed nearly the whole of those things myself, and what little I did not get by my own observation, I received from those among the whites and blacks, in whom the greatest confidence may be placed.

The Americans may be as vigilant as they please, but they cannot be vigilant enough for the Lord, neither can they hide themselves, where he will not find and bring them out. . . .

William Lloyd Garrison Urges Immediate Abolition, 1831

To the Public

During my recent tour for the purpose of exciting the minds of the people by a series of discourses on the subject of slavery, every place that I visited gave fresh evidence of the fact, that a greater revolution in public sentiment

---

* The Lord has not taught the Americans that we will not some day or other throw off their chains and hand-cuffs from our hands and feet, and their devilish lashes (which some of them shall have enough of yet) from off our backs.

was to be effected in the free States—*and particularly in New-England*—than at the South. I found contempt more bitter, opposition more active, detraction more relentless, prejudice more stubborn, and apathy more frozen, than among slave-owners themselves. Of course, there were individual exceptions to the contrary. This state of things afflicted, but did not dishearten me. I determined, at every hazard, to lift up the standard of emancipation in the eyes of the nation, *within sight of Bunker Hill and in the birthplace of liberty*. That standard is now unfurled; and long may it float, unhurt by the spoliations of time or the missiles of a desperate foe—yea, till every chain be broken, and every bondman set free! Let Southern oppressors tremble—let their secret abettors tremble—let their Northern apologists tremble—let all the enemies of the persecuted blacks tremble. . . .

In defending the great cause of human rights, I wish to derive the assistance of all religions and of all parties.

Assenting to the "self-evident truth" maintained in the American Declaration of Independence, "that all men are created equal, and endowed by their Creator with certain inalienable rights—among which are life, liberty and the pursuit of happiness," I shall strenuously contend for the immediate enfranchisement of our slave population. In Park-Street Church, on the Fourth of July, 1829, in an address on slavery, I unreflectingly assented to the popular but pernicious doctrine of *gradual* abolition. I seize this opportunity to make a full and unequivocal recantation, and thus publicly to ask pardon of my God, of my country, and of my brethren the poor slaves, for having uttered a sentiment so full of timidity, injustice, and absurdity. A similar recantation, from my pen, was published in the *Genius of Universal Emancipation* at Baltimore, in September, 1829. My conscience is now satisfied.

I am aware that many object to the severity of my language; but is there not cause for severity? I *will be* as harsh as truth, and as uncompromising as justice. On this subject, I do not wish to think, or speak, or write, with moderation. No! no! Tell a man whose house is on fire to give a moderate alarm; tell him to moderately rescue his wife from the hands of the ravisher; tell the mother to gradually extricate her babe from the fire into which it has fallen;—but urge me not to use moderation in a cause like the present. I am in earnest—I will not equivocate—I will not excuse—I will not retreat a single inch—AND I WILL BE HEARD. The apathy of the people is enough to make every statue leap from its pedestal, and to hasten the resurrection of the dead.

It is pretended, that I am retarding the cause of emancipation by the coarseness of my invective and the precipitancy of my measures. *The charge is not true.* On this question my influence,—humble as it is,—is felt at this moment to a considerable extent, and shall be felt in coming years—not perniciously, but beneficially—not as a curse, but as a blessing; and posterity will bear testimony that I was right. I desire to thank God, that he enables me to disregard "the fear of man which bringeth a snare," and to speak his truth in its simplicity and power. . . .

Working Men

An attempt has been made—it is still making—we regret to say, with considerable success—to inflame the minds of our working classes against the more opulent, and to persuade men that they are contemned and oppressed by a wealthy aristocracy. That public grievances exist, is unquestionably true; but they are not confined to any one class of society. Every profession is interested in their removal—the rich as well as the poor. It is in the highest degree criminal, therefore, to exasperate our mechanics to deeds of violence, or to array them under a party banner; for it is not true, that, at any time, they have been the objects of reproach. Labor is not dishonorable. The industrious artisan, in a government like ours, will always be held in better estimation than the wealthy idler.

Our limits will not allow us to enlarge on this subject: we may return to it another time. We are the friends of reform; but that is not reform, which, in curing one evil, threatens to inflict a thousand others. . . .

Walker's Pamphlet

The Legislature of North Carolina has lately been sitting with closed doors, in consequence of a message from the Governor relative to the above pamphlet. The south may reasonably be alarmed at the circulation of Mr Walker's Appeal; for a better promoter of insurrection was never sent forth to an oppressed people. In a future number, we propose to examine it, as also various editorial comments thereon—it being one of the most remarkable productions of the age. We have already publicly deprecated its spirit.

The New-England Anti-Slavery Society on Immediatism, 1833

The New-England Anti-Slavery Society maintains that the slaves ought instantly to be emancipated from their fetters. It acknowledges no claims upon their persons by their masters. It regards the holders of slaves as guilty of a heinous sin. . . . It says to every individual—"Let the principle be clearly and firmly established in your mind that there is, and can be, no such thing as *property in man,* and you cannot, as a patriot, a philanthropist, or a disciple of Christ, oppose the immediate liberation of the slaves—you cannot but demand that liberation—you cannot be satisfied with any thing short of an immediate liberation." It is not for men of Christian integrity to calculate how far it is expedient to do wrong. . . .

The Board of Managers are satisfied that the doctrine of immediate abolition is opposed by many, not because they really mean to justify crime, but simply through ignorance or a misapprehension of its nature. It is associated in their minds with something undefinable, yet dreadful—they see, in imagination, cities and villages in flames, and blood flowing in torrents, and hear the roll of drums, the shouts of blood-thirsty savages, and the shrieks of the dying—and thus bringing upon themselves a strong delusion, they naturally stand aghast at the proposition. All this ruffling of mind is indeed ridiculous; but as it originates unwittingly in error, it merits a charitable allowance rather than satire.

What, then, is meant by IMMEDIATE ABOLITION?

It means, in the first place, that all title of property in the slaves shall instantly cease, because their Creator has never relinquished his claim of ownership, and because none have a right to sell their own bodies or buy those of their own species as cattle. Is there any thing terrific in this arrangement?

It means, secondly, that every husband shall have his own wife, and every wife her own husband, both being united in wedlock according to its proper forms, and placed under the protection of law. Is this unreasonable?

It means, thirdly, that parents shall have the control and government of their own children, and that the children shall belong to their parents. What is there sanguinary in this concession?

It means, fourthly, that all trade in human beings shall be regarded as felony, and entitled to the highest punishment. Can this be productive of evil?

It means, fifthly, that the tremendous power which is now vested in every slaveholder to punish his slaves without trial, and to a savage extent, shall be at once taken away. Is this undesirable?

It means, sixthly, that all those laws which not probit the instruction of the slaves, shall instantly be repealed, and others enacted, providing schools and instruction for their intellectual illumination. Would this prove a calamity?

It means, seventhly, that the planters shall employ their slaves as free laborers, and pay them just wages. Would this recompense infuriate them?

It means, eighthly, that the slaves, instead of being forced to labor for the exclusive benefit of others by cruel drivers, and the application of the lash upon their bodies, shall be encouraged to toil for the mutual profit of themselves and their employers, by the infusion of new motives into their hearts, growing out of their recognition and reward as men. Is this diabolical?

It means, finally, that right shall take the supremacy over wrong, principle over brute force, humanity over cruelty, honesty over theft, purity over lust, honor over baseness, love over hatred, and religion over heathenism. Is this wrong?

This is our meaning of Immediate Abolition. . . .

It will remove the cause of bloodshed and insurrection. No patrols at night, no standing army, will be longer needed to keep the slaves in awe. The planters may dismiss their fears, and sleep soundly; for, by one act, they will have transformed their enemies into grateful friends and servants.

Angelina Grimké Appeals to the
Christian Women of the South, 1836

. . . There is no difference in *principle*, in *Christian ethics*, between the despised slavedealer and the *Christian* who buys slaves from, or sells slaves to him; indeed, if slaves were not wanted by the respectable, the wealthy, and the religious in a community, there would be no slaves in that community, and of course no *slavedealers*. It is then the *Christians* and the *honorable men* and *women* of the South, who are the *main pillars* of this grand temple built to Mammon and to Moloch. It is the *most enlightened* in every country who are *most* to blame when any public sin is supported by public opinion. . . .

But it may be asked, why are *they* most culpable? I will tell you, my friends. It is because sin is imputed to us just in proportion to the spiritual light we receive. . . .

But perhaps you will be ready to query, why appeal to *women* on this subject? *We* do not make the laws which perpetuate slavery. *No* legislative power is vested in *us; we* can do nothing to overthrow the system, even if we wished to do so. To this I reply, I know you do not make the laws, but I also know that *you are the wives and mothers, the sisters and daughters of those who do;* and if you really suppose *you* can do nothing to overthrow slavery, you are greatly mistaken. You can do much in every way: four things I will name. 1st. You can read on this subject. 2d. You can pray over this subject. 3d. You can speak on this subject. 4th. You can *act* on this subject. I have not placed reading before praying because I regard it more important, but because, in order to pray aright, we must understand what we are praying for; it is only then we can "pray with the understanding and the spirit also." . . .

But you may say we are *women,* how can *our* hearts endure persecution? And why not? Have not *women* arisen in all the dignity and strength of moral courage to be the leaders of the people, and to bear a faithful testimony for the truth whenever the providence of God has called them to do so? Are there no *women* in that noble army of martyrs who are now singing the song of Moses and the Lamb? Who led out the women of Israel from the house of bondage, striking the timbrel, and singing the song of deliverance on the banks of that sea whose waters stood up like walls of crystal to open a passage for their escape? It was a *woman;* Miriam, the prophetess, the sister of Moses and Aaron. Who went up with Barak to Kadesh to fight against Jabin, King of Canaan, into whose hand Israel had been sold because of their iniquities? It was a *woman!* Deborah the wife of Lapidoth, the judge, as well as the prophetess of that backsliding people; Judges iv, 9. . . . What human voice first proclaimed to Mary that she should be the mother of our Lord? It was a *woman!* Elizabeth, the wife of Zacharias; Luke i, 42, 43. . . .

And what, I would ask in conclusion, have *women* done for the great and glorious cause of Emancipation? Who wrote that pamphlet which moved the heart of Wilberforce to pray over the wrongs, and his tongue to plead the cause of the oppressed African? It was a *woman,* Elizabeth Heyrick. Who labored assiduously to keep the sufferings of the slave continually before the British public? They were *women*. And how did they do it? By their needles, paint brushes and pens, by speaking the truth, and petitioning Parliament for the abolition of slavery. And what was the effect of their labors? Read it in the Emancipation bill of Great Britain. Read it, in the present state of her West India Colonies. Read it, in the impulse which has been given to the cause of freedom, in the United States of America. Have English women then done so much for the negro, and shall American women do nothing? Oh no! Already are there sixty female Anti-Slavery Societies in operation. These are doing just what the English women did, telling the story of the colored man's wrongs, praying for his deliverance, and presenting his kneeling image constantly before the public eye on bags and needle-books, card-racks, pen-wipers, pin-cushions, &c. Even the children of the north are inscribing on their handy work, "May the points of our needles prick the slaveholder's conscience." Some of the reports of these Societies exhibit not only considerable talent, but a deep sense of religious duty, and a determination to persevere through evil as well as good report, until every scourge, and every shackle, is buried under the feet of the manumitted slave.

The Ladies' Anti-Slavery Society of Boston was called last fall, to a severe trial of their faith and constancy. They were mobbed by "the gentle-men of property and standing," in that city at their anniversary meeting, and their lives were jeoparded by an infuriated crowd; but their conduct on that occasion did credit to our sex, and affords a full assurance that they will *never* abandon the cause of the slave. The pamphlet, Right and Wrong in Boston, issued by them in which a particular account is given of that "mob of broad cloth in broad day," does equal credit to the head and the heart of her who wrote it. I wish my Southern sisters could read it; they would then understand that the women of the North have engaged in this work from a sense of *religious duty,* and that nothing will ever induce them to take their hands from it until it is fully accomplished. They feel no hostility to you, no bitterness or wrath; they rather sympathize in your trials and difficulties; but they well know that the first thing to be done to help you, is to pour in the light of truth on your minds, to urge you to reflect on, and pray over the subject. This is all *they* can do for you, *you* must work out your own deliverance with fear and trembling, and with the direction and blessing of God, *you can do it.* Northern women may labor to produce a correct public opinion at the North, but if Southern women sit down in listless indifference and criminal idleness, public opinion cannot be rectified and purified at the South. It is manifest to every reflecting mind, that slavery must be abolished; the era in which we live, and the light which is over-spreading the whole world on this subject, clearly show that the time cannot be distant when it will be done. Now there are only two ways in which it can be effected, by moral power or physical force, and it is for *you* to choose which of these you prefer. Slavery always has, and always will produce insurrections wherever it exists, because it is a violation of the natural order of things, and no human power can much longer perpetuate it. The opposers of abolitionists fully believe this; one of them remarked to me not long since, there is no doubt there will be a most terrible overturning at the South in a few years, such cruelty and wrong, must be visited with Divine vengeance soon. Abolitionists believe, too, that this must inevitably be the case if you do not repent, and they are not willing to leave you to perish without entreating you, to save yourselves from destruction; well may they say with the apostle, "am I then your enemy because I tell you the truth," and warn you to flee from impending judgments. . . .

The *women of the South can overthrow* this horrible system of oppression and cruelty, licentiousness and wrong. Such appeals to your legislatures would be irresistible, for there is something in the heart of man which *will bend under moral suasion.* There is a swift witness for truth in his bosom, which *will respond to truth* when it is uttered with calmness and dignity. If you could obtain but six signatures to such a petition in only one state, I would say, send up that petition, and be not in the least discouraged by the scoffs and jeers of the heartless, or the resolution of the house to lay it on the table. It will be a great thing if the subject can be introduced into your legislatures in any way, even by *women,* and *they* will be the most likely to introduce it there in the best possible manner, as a matter of *morals* and *religion,* not of expediency or politics. You may petition, too, the different ecclesiastical bodies of the slave states. Slavery must be attacked with the whole power of truth and the sword of the spirit. You must take it up on *Christian* ground, and fight against it with Christian weapons, whilst your feet are shod with the preparation of the gospel of peace. And *you are now* loudly called upon by the cries of the widow and the orphan, to arise and gird yourselves for this great moral conflict, "with the whole armour of righteousness on the right hand and on the left."

The Industrial Revolution
in the
United States

The Rise of Northern Capitalism

Through the War of 1812, the conventional wisdom held that the United States would long be primarily a rural nation of small-scale producers. The Jeffersonians, in particular, foresaw an expansive democratic republic populated mainly by independent farmers, craftsmen, and their households. By the end of the nineteenth century, however, such prophecies would prove false; in fact, as early as the 1840s, interlocking developments in the North presaged the rise of a very different social order than the Jeffersonians had predicted.

After 1815, for example, the construction of numerous internal improvement projects shortened what had once seemed vast distances, and facilitated commerce. In the countryside, a combination of demographic pressures and revamped opportunities hastened the regional shift toward commercial production and reliance on merchant middlemen that had begun in the eighteenth century. Manufacturing enterprises ranging from steam-powered factories to tiny sweatshop garrets proliferated in the established seaboard cities and in new urban centers carved out of the wilderness. These cities, in turn, became a prominent feature of the northern landscape. Especially after 1840, a rising proportion of the new urban working class consisted of recent immigrants who brought customs and religious views to Yankee America that seemed exotic and (to some) threatening. Along with these changes came disorienting transformations in social relations, affecting everything from the most intimate aspects of domestic life to the most conspicuous displays of wealth and status.

Some historians have stressed the material benefits that accrued from this economic development, and have left a picture of spectacular progress and invention. Others have pointed to the social injuries that accompanied economic growth—the miseries of urban poverty, the widening of social and economic inequality, and the growing sense of dependence and powerlessness associated with wage labor. Today these disputes show up in arguments over the sources of what some scholars have called the market revolution. Did these changes arise from the unleashing of a preexisting American capitalism? Or did they mark a new departure, undertaken by some Americans at the direct expense of others? In a sense, scholars have returned to the same issues that divided the people whom they have studied. Did the rise of northern capitalism represent a triumph for basic American principles, a modification of those principles, or perhaps an outright denial?

The economic and social transformation of the northern countryside involved an uneven but ultimately irresistible shift away from established forms of general farming and local exchange (with only limited involvement in commercial markets) toward commercial production. What were the sources of this shift, and what were its consequences with regard to household and family life, rural class relations, and the wider regional economy? Certain clues appear in the first document, including excerpts from the letters of Mary Graham, the wife of a farmer and petty craftsman in western Massachusetts, and a brief statement from a didactic magazine for farmers. In the second selection, a biography of the New York merchant and political leader Gideon Lee maps a different road out of the countryside and couples it with a real-life celebration of a self-made man; Aléxis de Tocqueville's reflections on the American pursuit of wealth, from his *Democracy in America,* are more somber. Closely related to the rise of the new northern businessman was the elaboration of a distinctive code of female domestic duties, which quickly spread to northern middle-class families generally. In the third selection, two samplings illustrate some of the tensions between ideals and realities—one from a popular advice book, the other from the family correspondence of Abigail May Alcott, the reformer, wife of Bronson Alcott, and mother of Louisa May Alcott.

Women, many of them daughters of the countryside, also formed the bulk of the early labor force in some of the leading manufacturing sectors, especially the New England textile industry. The fourth selection includes a series of impressions of Lowell, Massachusetts, the most famous of the new factory towns. A different pattern of industrial growth, based on labor-intensive methods, unfolded in the major seaports, including New York. In the fifth document, a British immigrant cabinetmaker recalls his own New York experiences from a decade earlier; and a short report from the reform-minded *New York Tribune* provides another angle on conditions in the trade.

Two starkly opposed views of capitalist growth complete this documentary section. Thomas Skidmore, a Connecticut-born machinist, emerged as the leading spokesman of New York's Working Men's movement in 1829. His book of that same year, *The Rights of Man to Property!,* angrily indicted some of the fundamentals of the emerging order and offered a new social blueprint—one based on a peaceful, democratic, electoral revolution, a general division of property holdings, and an end to inheritance. A decade later, Alonzo Potter, an Episcopalian clergyman, delivered a stalwart defense of capitalist justice and wage labor.

Views on the Commercialization of the Countryside

Mary Graham Describes Life on a Massachusetts Farm, 1835–1844

Buckland, April 6th 1835

Near and very dear friends,

I believe I shant wait in silence any longer for a letter. We have traveled too and from the Post Office for weeks, in vain. I now sit down to inquire the cause—is it sickness of death, or have you removed to the far west, to seek the goodly land, or did you during the extreme cold weather last winter freeze up and have not yet thawed out. If this be the cause do write and let us know and we will try to render you some assistance. . . . Will tell you somthing about our own family. Here we are all in comfortable health. L and myself have had to work as hard as we have been able, and a good deal harder than we wanted to. We are very much confined at home. I have not visited an afternoon in the town of B[uckland] for more than a year except at N's twice or three times. I have shoes a plenty to bind, from six to eight and twelve pairs in a week—and with all the rest have got four as dirty, noisy, ragged children to take care of as any other woman, they look as though they would do to put out in the cornfields in about six or eight weeks to keep away the crows. . . .

Buckland Feb. 5, 1837

Dear Friends at Northamption . . .

Hardly know what to say about ourselves, but will say this we have plenty of hard work and poor keeping and money at interest, and are always like to have. I can hardly feel reconciled to not visiting you this winter, but so much to do and so much money at interest that we cant get enough to bear our expences down there back again. Of course we must stay at home. . . .

Buckland Feb. 12, 1839

Dear Brother and Sister . . .

I now seat myself to acknowledge the reception of a few lines from you some weeks since. Probably you have expected an answer before this, which I allow to be reasonable, but by way of apology will just say that I work in the shop most of the time. We have been unusually [crowded?] with work, have been obliged to be in the shop early and late. Of course not much time to write. . . . We received a letter from Clark and Caroline a few weeks since, they were in Indianna, New Albany, Floyd County. She has had a son and lost it. They were in comfortable health when they wrote. . . . We have had a terrible freshet and from accounts think it did considerable damage in your region. The bridge at the Falls barely escaped, one shop was washed away and several dwelling houses were in danger. Cousin G's was among the number. . . .
PS Perhaps you may wonder what I do in the shop so much. I do the pegging, hammer the leather and considerable of the fitting. . . .

Buckland March 3, 1844

Dear Brother and Sister,

I suppose I must answer your letter whether I want to or not. To tell the truth, I don't want to, for I don't feel like writing to anyone. You wanted all the news. I have some that is not very pleasant to me. In the first place, Lucius has sold us out of house and home with the [privilege] of staying here until the first of June. If he can rake and scrape enough after paying his debts to set his family down in Wisconsin he is determined to go. So you wonder that I feel sad. Nothing but poor health and poverty to begin with in a new country looks dark to me. But I can't help it, go we must I suppose if the means can be raised. Don't know as I shall be permitted to visit you, expect he will think that every dollar must be saved to go to the far West. Do come and see us *once more* for I can't endure that I shall never see you again. . . .

The New England Farmer *on the Rules of Commercial Production, 1849*

Industry, well directed, will give a man a competency in a few years. The greatest industry misapplied is useless . . .

[T]here is my friend, Nat Notional, the busiest and most industrious mortal in existence; as the old saying goes "he has too many irons in the fire," and with all his industry, he goes behindhand.

A few years ago, he concluded to give up the dairy business, in consequence of the low price of butter and cheese; sold his cows at a low figure, and purchased sheep at a high rate, for wool then demanded a high price. By the time he got fairly into the raising of wool, down went the price of wool, and up went the price of butter and cheese. He then sold his sheep, and purchased cows again, for cheese was up and wool was down. And finally, he changed his business so often, because he wasn't contented to thrive, little by little, as Seth Steady did, that he got completely used up, and is now only fit for California, or some other wool-gathering project. . . .

Perspectives on the Self-Made Man

A Sketch of the Life of Gideon Lee, 1843

Among the many distinguished sons of New England, she has none worthier to present to the rising generation, as a model of imitation, than he whose name furnishes the subject of this biographical notice—. . . .

GIDEON LEE was born in the town of Amherst, in the state of Massachusetts, on the 27th of April, 1778. He lost his father when quite a child, and was left to the care of his mother, of whom he always spoke in terms of the warmest affection. While yet in infancy, he went to reside with an uncle, a farmer, in whose service he discharged the humble duties of looking after the cattle, and was employed in such other occupations as were suitable to his strength and age. . . .

After remaining some time under the care, and in the employment of his uncle, he was apprenticed to the tanning and shoemaking—it being the practice then to conduct both branches by the same person—. . . . His genius, however, seemed better adapted to the tanning, for which department of the business he always retained a strong partiality. Up to this period his opportunities for acquiring knowledge were extremely limited: a few weeks schooling during the winter, and such books as accidentally fell in his way, were all the means vouchsafed to him. After learning his trade, or trades, he commenced business on his own account, in the town of Worthington, Mass., and by his industry and strict attention to it, soon won the regard and confidence of his neighbors. He was enabled to obtain credit for the purchase of leather, which he manufactured into shoes, always paying promptly for it at the period he had agreed. The first hundred dollars he earned, and that could honestly be called his own, he appropriated to educating himself at the *Westfield Academy;* and when that sum was exhausted, he again betook himself to his labor. His diligence and application were remarkable, usually working sixteen hours out of the twenty four. . . .

The great points in Mr. Lee's character developed themselves early. They were a strong love for, and veneration of, *truth*—a high sense of honor, an independent and laborious mind as well as body, a heart that embraced in its charities the physical and moral welfare of his fellows, punctuality in the discharge of *all* his duties, a love of order and of system, and an indomitable perseverence in accomplishing whatever measure he undertook. . . .

After prosecuting his business for some time in the manner detailed, he formed a partnership with a Mr. Hubbard; subsequently they were burned out, and he lost what little property he had accumulated. He then dissolved with his partner, and removed to the city of New York. But before establishing himself there, he made a voyage to St. Marys, Georgia, taking with him some small ventures of leather, and accompanying a party who went out for the purpose of cutting live-oak timber for the United States navy. . . .

He suffered much on this . . . journey; and before reaching New York, his money, the little that he had, was exhausted. . . .

In the year 1807, Mr. Lee married the daughter of Major Samuel Buffington, of Worthington, Mass., a distinguished soldier of the Revolution, and shortly after established himself in the city of New York, in the business in which he ultimately became so successful and eminent. He commenced in a little wooden shantee, in Ferry st., still standing, which he called "Fort Lee;" where, as he expressed it, he "entrenched himself." The custom among leather dealers at that day was, to sell on book account, and have annual settlements; he adopted a different plan, and instead of selling on account, he sold at lower prices, and took notes payable in bank. This was an innovation on an ancient custom, that was looked on with disfavor by his neighbors—a revolution that they stoutly resisted. But, aided by being appointed agent for an extensive tanning establishment, styled the "Hampshire Leather Manufactory," he overcame all opposition, and laid the foundation, in the city of New York, for a branch of domestic industry which speedily rivalled the other Atlantic cities. His punctuality in his payments, and the industry and fidelity with which he discharged the duties of the agency, won the confidence of the gentlemen who were the managers of the company, and contributed to give him a credit and standing which otherwise might

374

have taken years to obtain. His prudence and economy enabled him to accumulate means for enlarging his business; and, but for feeble health, the future to him was a bright path of success. . . . [His business secure, Lee entered politics in the 1820s and eventually was elected mayor of the city of New York.]

In his dying charge to his sons, he enjoined them always to "fill up the measure of time." "Be," said he, "always employed profitably in doing good, in building up; aim to promote the good of yourselves and of society; no one can do much good without doing some harm, but you will do less harm by striving to do good; be industrious, be honest." These were the last intelligible words he uttered, and were as characteristic as they were worthy of him. . . .

Aléxis de Tocqueville on the Pursuit of Wealth, 1835

In America I saw the freest and most enlightened men, placed in the happiest circumstances which the world affords; it seemed to me as if a cloud habitually hung upon their brow, and I thought them serious and almost sad even in their pleasures. . . .

It is strange to see with what feverish ardor the Americans pursue their own welfare; and to watch the vague dread that constantly torments them lest they should not have chosen the shortest path which may lead to it.

A native of the United States clings to this world's goods as if he were certain never to die; and he is so hasty in grasping at all within his reach, that one would suppose he was constantly afraid of not living long enough to enjoy them. He clutches everything, he holds nothing fast, but soon loosens his grasp to pursue fresh gratifications.

In the United States a man builds a house to spend his latter years in it, and he sells it before the roof is on; he plants a garden, and lets it [rents] just as the trees are coming into bearing; he brings a field into tillage, and leaves other men to gather the crops; he embraces a profession, and gives it up; he settles in a place, which he soon afterward leaves, to carry his changeable longings elsewhere. If his private affairs leave him any leisure, he instantly plunges into the vortex of politics; and if at the end of a year of unremitting labor he finds he has a few days' vacation, his eager curiosity whirls him over the vast extent of the United States, and he will travel fifteen hundred miles in a few days, to shake off his happiness. Death at length overtakes him, but it is before he is weary of his bootless chase of that complete felicity which is for ever on the wing.

At first sight there is something surprising in this strange unrest of so many happy men, restless in the midst of abundance. The spectacle itself is however as old as the world; the novelty is to see a whole people furnish an exemplification of it.

. . . He who has set his heart exclusively upon the pursuit of worldly welfare is always in a hurry, for he has but a limited time at his disposal to reach it, to grasp it, and to enjoy. The recollection of the brevity of life is a constant spur to him. Besides the good things which he possesses, he every instant fancies a thousand others which death will prevent him from trying if he does not try them soon. This thought fills him with anxiety, fear, and regret, and keeps his mind in ceaseless trepidation, which leads him perpetually to change his plans and his abode.

If in addition to the taste for physical well-being a social condition be superadded, in which the laws and customs make no condition permanent, here is a great additional stimulant to this restlessness of temper. Men will then be seen continually to change their track, for fear of missing the shortest cut to happiness.

It may readily be conceived, that if men, passionately bent upon physical gratifications, desire eagerly, they are also easily discouraged: as their ultimate object is to enjoy, the means to reach that object must be prompt and easy, or the trouble of acquiring the gratification would be greater than the gratification itself. Their prevailing frame of mind then is at once ardent and relaxed, violent and enervated. Death is often less dreaded than perseverance in continuous efforts to one end.

The equality of conditions leads by a still straighter road to several of the effects which I have here described. When all the privileges of birth and fortune are abolished, when all professions are accessible to all, and a man's own energies may place him at the top of any one of them, an easy and unbounded career seems open to his ambition, and he will readily persuade himself that he is born to no vulgar destinies. But this is an erroneous notion, which is corrected by daily experience. The same equality which allows every citizen to conceive these lofty hopes, renders all the citizens less able to realize them; it circumscribes their powers on every side, while it gives freer scope to their desires. Not only are they themselves powerless, but they are met at every step by immense obstacles, which they did not at first perceive. They have swept away the privileges of some of their fellow-creatures which stood in their way; but they have opened the door to universal competition: the barrier has changed its shape rather than its position. When men are nearly alike, and all follow the same track, it is very difficult for any one individual to walk quick and cleave a way through the dense throng which surrounds and presses him. This constant strife between the propensities springing from the equality of conditions and the means it supplies to satisfy them, harasses and wearies the mind.

It is possible to conceive men arrived at a degree of freedom which should completely content them; they would then enjoy their independence without anxiety and without impatience. But men will never establish any equality with which they can be contented. . . . When inequality of conditions is the common law of society, the most marked inequalities do not strike the eye; when everything is nearly on the same level, the slightest are marked enough to hurt it. Hence the desire of equality always becomes more insatiable in proportion as equality is more complete.

Among democratic nations men easily attain a certain equality of conditions; they can never attain the equality they desire. It perpetually retires from before them, yet without hiding itself from their sight, and in retiring draws them on. At every moment they think they are about to grasp it; it escapes at every moment from their hold. They are near enough to see its charms, but too far off to enjoy them; and before they have fully tasted its delights, they die. . . .

In democratic ages enjoyments are more intense than in the ages of aristocracy, and especially the number of those who partake in them is larger. But, on the other hand, it must be admitted that man's hopes and his desires are often blasted, the soul is more stricken and perturbed, and care itself more keen.

Contemporary Statements on the Cult of Domesticity

Mrs. A. J. Graves's Advice to American Women, 1843

To woman it belongs . . . to elevate the intellectual character of her household, to kindle the fires of mental activity in childhood, and to keep these steadily burning with advancing years . . . The men of our country, as things are constituted among us, find but little time for the cultivation of science and general literature—studies so eminently calculated to refine the mind and purify the taste, and which furnish so exhaustless a fund of elevated enjoyment to the heart. And this is the case even with those who have acquired a fondness for intellectual pursuits in early life. The absorbing passion for gain, and the pressing demands of business, engross their whole attention. Thus the merchant becomes a merchant, and nothing more; and the mind of the lawyer is little else than a library of cases and precedents, of legal records and commentaries. The physician loses sight of the scientific studies to which his profession so naturally directs him, contents himself with the same beaten track, and becomes a mere practitioner or operator. And the mechanic and agriculturist too often settle down into mere manual laborers, by suffering practical details wholly to occupy their minds as well as their bodies. The only relief to this absorbing devotion to "material interests" is found in the excitement of party politics.

These two engross the whole moral, intellectual, and physical man; and, to be convinced of this, we need not follow the American to his place of business or to political meetings—we have only to listen to his fireside conversation. It might be supposed that the few waking hours he spends at home in the bosom of his family, he would delight to employ upon such subjects as would interest and improve his wife and children, and that he would avail himself of these opportunities to refresh his wearied mind with new matters of thought. But in place of this, what is the perpetual theme of his conversation? Business and politics, six per cent bank discounts, stock-jobbing, insolvencies, assets, liabilities—cases at court, legal opinions and decisions—neuralgia, gastric irritation, fevers, etc.—Clay, Webster, the Bank bill, and other political topics of the day: these are the subjects incessantly talked about by the male members of the family when at home, and which the females, of course, are neither expected to take any special interest in nor to understand. Or perhaps the wife may take her turn in relating the history of the daily vexations she experiences in her household arrangements, while the husband's eye is gazing on vacancy, or his mind is occupied by his business cares. Woman should be made to take an intelligent interest in her husband's affairs, and may be benefited by a knowledge of the value of money, its best mode of investment; or by being instructed in the laws of physiology and of hygiene; but she can receive neither pleasure nor profit from hearing the cabalistic terms familiar only to the initiated in the mysteries of financiering, or the occult words and phrases which the professional man employs to communicate his knowledge or the results of his observations. The husband should doubtless sympathize with the wife in her domestic trials; but he cannot, nor ought he to, become interested in every trivial vexation she may meet with. There should, then, be some common ground on which both may meet with equal pleasure and advantage to themselves and to their offspring; and what is there so appropriate to this end as *intellectual pursuits?*

What a certain writer has said of sons, may also be said, with equal truth, of many husbands: "they seem to consider their homes as mere places of boarding and lodging"; and, we may add, forget that it is the dwelling-place of their wives and children. So long as they provide for the physical wants of their families, they think their duty is fulfilled; as though shelter, food, and clothing could satisfy the necessities of immortal minds. They are liberal, perhaps, even to profusion, in surrounding their families with all that can minister to physical comfort, and the indulgence of vanity and pride, but they neglect to excite or to satisfy the more exalted desire for intellectual adorning and spiritual improvement. It is here our men are wanting; and female influence must supply the defect. A mother should sedulously cultivate the intellectual tastes of her children, and surround them with objects calculated to stimulate and gratify their ambition for knowledge. Her own mind should not only be richly stored with the wisdom of the past, but she should keep herself familiar with the current literature of the day, with the progress of science, and the new and useful truths it is constantly bringing to light. Out of all this fullness of knowledge she should communicate freely to her children, and labor by her conversation gently to draw her husband away from his contracted sphere of thought, to enter with her upon a more extended field of observation and reflection. She should entice him to forget his business and his politics, and to devote the few hours he spends at home to those higher pleasures of the mind, which will not only yield a delightful refreshment at the time, but enable him to return with renewed vigor to the routine of his daily labors.

Letter of Abigail May Alcott to Lucretia and Samuel May, 1833

Philadelphia, June 22^d. 1833—

Dear Sam and Lu,

It is a good while since I wrote to you. I write but seldom to any one, excepting father; I frequently have an opportunity to send him a line and I always improve it . . . it costs me but little effort—but a full connected letter seems to me now a formidable undertaking—my eyes are very uncertain—and my time is abundantly occupied with my babies—It seems to me at times as if the weight of responsibility connected with these little immortal beings would prove too much for me—am I doing what is right? Am I doing enough? Am I not doing too much, is my earnest inquiry. I am almost at times discouraged if I find the result prove unfavorable—My Anna is just at that critical period when the diseases incident to her age makes her irritable and engrossing; and yet so intelligent as to her making inferences about everything which is done for her, or that I may mistake the motive which instigates many of her actions. Mr. A. aids me in general principles but nobody can aid me in the detail—credit is a theme of constant thought— an object of momentary solicitude—if I may neglect every thing else, I must be forgiven—I know—you laugh at me and think me a slave to my children and think me foolishly *anxious*—I can hear it all, better than one reproach of conscience, or one thoughtless word or look given to my Anna's inquiry.—

Well dear Lu. How do you like the fair sex—An't they dear little creatures? What's her name? How I should love to take my Louisa (who is all smiles and love) and stand the day with you, and tend baby. I hope dear you get sympathy and care and kindness and tender love from all about you—. These are moments when tenderness and love are our best instrument and support. I hear that John is a "noble boy" and has made a visit to Boston—can't he make a visit to Phil^d with father—I'll take the best care of him—If I talk long about you I shall cry and then good bye letter . . . Am just as tearful as ever when I think of the few dear ones left me on earth—but when I stick to my little family and my round of little duties I am brave and invincible as a lion. . . .

Abba

Impressions of the Lowell Mills, 1833, 1844, 1845

Regulations of the Appleton Company, 1833

REGULATIONS

TO BE OBSERVED BY ALL PERSONS EMPLOYED IN THE FACTORIES OF THE

APPLETON COMPANY.

THE Overseers are to be punctually in their rooms at the starting of the mill, and not to be absent unnecessarily during working hours. They are to see that all those employed in their rooms are in their places in due season. They may grant leave of absence to those employed under them, when there are spare hands in the room to supply their places; otherwise they are not to grant leave of absence, except in cases of absolute necessity.

ALL persons in the employ of the APPLETON COMPANY are required to observe the regulations of the overseer of the room where they are employed. They are not to be absent from their work, without his consent, except in case of sickness, and then they are to send him word of the cause of their absence.

THEY are to board in one of the boarding houses belonging to the Company, and conform to the regulations of the house where they board.

A regular attendance on public worship on the Sabbath is necessary for the preservation of good order. The Company will not employ any person who is habitually absent.

ALL persons entering into the employment of the Company are considered as engaging to work twelve months, and those who leave sooner will not receive a discharge unless they had sufficient experience when they commenced, to enable them to do full work.

ALL persons intending to leave the employment of the Company, are to give two weeks' notice of their intention to their overseer; and their engagement with the Company is not considered as fulfilled, unless they comply with this regulation.

PAYMENTS will be made monthly, including board and wages, which will be made up to the last Saturday in every month, and paid in the course of the following week.

THESE regulations are considered part of the contract with all persons entering into the employment of the APPLETON COMPANY.

G. W. LYMAN, Agent.

Tompe & Press, Gorham Street.

Letters from "Susan," a Mill Worker, 1844

I went into the mill to work a few days after I wrote to you. It looked very pleasant at first, the rooms were so light, spacious, and clean, the girls so pretty and neatly dressed, and the machinery so brightly polished or nicely painted. The plants in the windows, or on the overseer's bench or desk, gave a pleasant aspect to things. You will wish to know what work I am doing. I will tell you of the different kinds of work.

There is, first, the carding-room, where the cotton flies most, and the girls get the dirtiest. But this is easy, and the females are allowed time to go out at night before the bell rings—on Saturday night at least, if not on all other nights. Then there is the spinning-room, which is very neat and pretty. In this room are the spinners and doffers. The spinners watch the frames; keep them clean, and the threads mended if they break. The doffers take off the full bobbins, and put on the empty ones. They have nothing to do in the long intervals when the frames are in motion, and can go out to their boardinghouses, or do any thing else that they like. In some of the factories the spinners do their own doffing, and when this is the case they work no harder than the weavers. These last have the hardest time of all— or can have, if they choose to take charge of three or four looms, instead of the one pair which is the allotment. And they are the most constantly confined. The spinners and dressers have but the weavers to keep supplied, and then their work can stop. The dressers never work before breakfast, and they stay out a great deal in the afternoons. The drawers-in, or girls who draw the threads through the harnesses, also work in the dressing-room, and they all have very good wages—better than the weavers who have but the usual work. The dressing-rooms are very neat, and the frames move with a gentle undulating motion which is really graceful. But these rooms are kept very warm, and are disagreeably scented with the "sizing," or starch, which stiffens the "beams," or unwoven webs. There are many plants in these rooms, and it is really a good green-house for them. The dressers are generally quite tall girls, and must have pretty tall minds too, as their work requires much care and attention.

I could have had work in the dressing-room, but chose to be a weaver; and I will tell you why. I disliked the closer air of the dressing-room, though I might have become accustomed to that. I could not learn to dress so quickly as I could to weave, nor have work of my own so soon, and should have had to stay with Mrs. C. two or three weeks before I could go in at all, and I did not like to be "lying upon my oars" so long. And, more than this, when I get well learned I can have extra work, and make double wages, which you know is quite an inducement with some.

Well, I went into the mill, and was put to learn with a very patient girl—a clever old maid. I should be willing to be one myself if I could be as good as she is. You cannot think how odd every thing seemed to me. I wanted to laugh at every thing, but did not know what to make sport of first. They set me to threading shuttles, and tying weaver's knots, and such things, and now I have improved so that I can take care of one loom. I could take care of two if I only had eyes in the back part of my head, but I have not got used to "looking two ways of a Sunday" yet.

At first the hours seemed very long, but I was so interested in learning that I endured it very well; and when I went out at night the sound of the mill was in my ears, as of crickets, frogs, and jewsharps, all mingled together in strange discord. After that it seemed as though cotton-wool was in my ears, but now I do not mind at all. You know that people learn to sleep with the thunder of Niagara in their ears, and a cotton mill is no worse, though you wonder that we do not have to hold our breath in such a noise.

It makes my feet ache and swell to stand so much, but I suppose I shall get accustomed to that too. . . . I never saw so many pretty looking girls as there are here. Though the number of men is small in proportion there are many marriages here, and a great deal of courting. I will tell you of this last sometime. . . .

You ask if the girls are contented here: I ask you, if you know of *any one* who is perfectly contented. Do you remember the old story of the philosopher, who offered a field to the person who was contented with his lot; and, when one claimed it, he asked him why, if he was so perfectly satisfied, he wanted his field. The girls here are not contented; and there is no disadvantage in their situation which they do not perceive as quickly, and lament as loudly, as the sternest opponents of the factory system do. They would scorn to say they were contented, if asked the question; for it would compromise their Yankee spirit—their pride, penetration, independence, and love of "freedom and equality" to say that they were *contented* with such a life as this. Yet, withal, they are cheerful. I never saw a happier set of beings. They appear blithe in the mill, and out of it. If you see one of them, with a very long face, you may be sure that it is because she has heard bad news from home, or because her beau has vexed her. But, if it is a Lowell trouble, it is because she has failed in getting off as many "sets" or "pieces" as she intended to have done; or because she had a sad "break-out," or "break-down," in her work, or something of that sort.

You ask if the work is not disagreeable. Not when one is accustomed to it. It tried my patience sadly at first, and does now when it does not run well; but, in general, I like it very much. It is easy to do, and does not require very violent exertion, as much of our farm work does.

A Lowell Woman Worker's Protest, 1845

. . . For the purpose of illustration, let us go with that light-hearted, joyous young girl who is about for the first time to leave the home of her childhood, that home around which clusters so many beautiful and holy associations, pleasant memories, and quiet joys; to leave, too, a mother's cheerful smile, a father's care and protection; and wend her way toward this far famed "city of spindles," this promised land of the imagination, in whose praise she has doubtless heard so much.

Let us trace her progress during her first year's residence, and see whether she indeed realizes those golden prospects which have been held out to her. Follow her now as she enters that large gloomy looking building— she is in search of employment, and has been told that she might here obtain an eligible situation. She is sadly wearied with her journey, and withal somewhat annoyed by the noise, confusion, and strange faces all around her. So, after a brief conversation with the overseer, she concludes to accept the first situation which offers; and reserving to herself a sufficient portion of time in which to obtain the necessary rest after her unwonted exertions, and the gratification of a stranger's curiosity regarding the place in which she is now to make her future home, she retires to her boarding house, to arrange matters as much to her mind as may be.

From "Voices from Lowell," 1845, in Philip Foner, ed., *The Factory Girls*, 1977, pp. 135–138 (Urbana: University of Illinois Press, 1977).

The intervening time passes rapidly away, and she soon finds herself once more within the confines of that close noisy apartment, and is forthwith installed in her new situation—first, however, premising that she has been sent to the Counting-room, and receives therefrom a Regulation paper, containing the rules by which she must be governed while in their employ; and lo! here is the beginning of mischief; for in addition to the tyrannous and oppressive rules which meet her astonished eyes, she finds herself compelled to remain for the space of twelve months in the very place she then occupies, however reasonable and just cause of complaint might be hers, or however strong the wish for dismission; thus, in fact, constituting herself a slave, a very slave to the caprices of him for whom she labors. Several incidents coming to the knowledge of the writer, might be somewhat interesting in this connection, as tending to show the prejudicial influence exerted upon the interests of the operative by this unjust requisition. The first is of a lady who has been engaged as an operative for a number of years, and recently entered a weaving room on the Massachusetts Corporation: the overseers having assured her previous to her entrance, that she should realize the sum of $2.25 per week, exclusive of board; which she finding it impossible to do, appealed to the Counting-room for a line enabling her to engage elsewhere but it was peremptorily refused. . . .

But to return to our toiling Maiden,—the next beautiful feature which she discovers in this *glorious* system is, the long number of hours which she is obliged to spend in the above named close, unwholesome apartment. It is not enough, that like the poor peasant of Ireland, or the Russian serf who labors from sun to sun, but during one half of the year, she must still continue to toil on, long after Nature's lamp has ceased to lend its aid—nor will even this suffice to satisfy the grasping avarice of her employer; for she is also through the winter months required to rise, partake of her morning meal, and be at her station in the mill, while the sun is yet sleeping behind the eastern hills; thus working on an average, at least twelve hours and three fourths per day, exclusive of the time allotted for her hasty meals, which is in winter simply one half hour at noon,—in the spring is allowed the same at morn, and during the summer is added 15 minutes to the half hour at noon. Then too, when she is at last released from her wearisome day's toil, still may she not depart in peace. No! her footsteps must be dogged to see that they do not stray beyond the corporation limits, and she *must,* whether she will or no, be subjected to the manifold inconveniences of a large crowded boarding-house, where too, the price paid for her accommodation is so utterly insignificant, that it will not ensure to her the common comforts of life; she is obliged to sleep in a small comfortless, half ventilated apartment containing some half a dozen occupants each; but no matter, *she is an operative*—it is all well enough for her; there is no "abuse" about it; no, indeed; so think our employers,—but do we think so? time will show. . . .

Reader will you pronounce this a mere fancy sketch, written for the sake of effect? It is not so. It is a real picture of "Factory life"; nor is it one half so bad as might truthfully and justly have been drawn. But it has been asked, and doubtless will be again, why, if these evils are so aggravating, have they been so long and so peacefully borne? Ah! and why have they? It is a question well worthy of our consideration, and we would call upon every operative in *our* city, aye, throughout the length and breadth of the land, to awake from the lethargy which has fallen upon them, and assert and maintain their rights. We call upon you for action—*united and immediate action*. But, says one, let us wait till we are stronger. In the language of one of old, we ask, when shall we be stronger? Will it be the next week, or the next year? Will it be when we are reduced to the service conditions of the poor operatives of England? for verily we shall be and that right soon, if matters be suffered to remain as they are. Says another, how shall we act? we are but one amongst a thousand, what shall we do that our influence may be felt in this vast multitude? We answer there is in this city an Association called the Female Labor Reform Association, having for its professed object, the amelioration of the condition of the operative. Enrolled upon its records are the names of five hundred members—come then, and add thereto five hundred or rather five thousand more, and in the strength of our united influence we will soon show these *drivelling* cotton lords, this mushroom aristocracy of New England, who so arrogantly aspire to lord it over God's heritage, that our rights cannot be trampled upon with impunity; that we will no longer submit to that arbitrary power which has for the last ten years been so abundantly exercised over us. . . .

On the Lives of Big-City Craftsmen, 1845

A British Cabinetmaker Describes His Life in New York City, 1845

I was a cabinet-maker by trade, and one of the many who, between the years 1825–35, expatriated themselves in countless thousands, drawn by the promise of fair wages for faithful work, and driven by the scanty remuneration offered to unceasing toil at home, and the overpowering pressure of the burthens imposed by the state, at a time when none of that sympathy which now occupies so large a portion of the public mind was shown to or felt for the working classes. Many an anxious look did poor parents at that day cast on the expectant faces of their little ones when seated round the table, on comparing the demand for bread with the small and uncertain supply, and with a shudder of horror half anticipated the piteous cry of hunger and misery. Work they did, work unceasingly; but apparently to no good; the wolf would never go away from the door, and was always heard scratching on the outside. . . . I had always read in books and letters on America, that work was ever abundant, and to be obtained without difficulty; but all my experience proves the contrary, at least as regards New York. At the first place I entered, the proprietor informed me that trade was "pretty well used up," and "no hands were wanted." Another gave as a reason for not requiring any addition to his number of workmen that "General Jackson had tinkered the constitution too successfully for business to be what it ought to be for a pretty considerable time." At a third place, a lad waiting in the store, in reply to my query, hailed a companion working at the back of the house, "Hiram, call the boss:" the boss came, and on repeating my inquiry, he observed, "My stock of furniture is going off, that's a fact; but I can't take hands on for want of the pewter."

It would be tedious to detail all the reasons given by the "bosses" on whom I called during my walks, which were continued unsuccessfully for a week. In only a single instance did I hear any thing like an expression of jealousy of strangers; one manufacturer remarked in an angry tone, that "the city was overcrowded with foreigners who took away work that by right belonged to the citizens." "Go west," was the general observation, "go west; the city's too full; any quantity of work out west." My means, however, did not admit of my undertaking another long journey; and on the eighth day I was fortunate enough to find employment from a master tradesman who had emigrated from England twenty years previously; he now lived in his own house, had a capital business, and was worth many thousand dollars. On telling him that I had been advised to go to the country, he said, "Don't do any such thing; if you can't get a living in New York, you can't in any part of the Union; I have tried both, and know it."

This was cheering. I went to work the next morning; and in the course of the same week had the good luck to meet with two rooms and a pantry to let, in a small farmhouse, which I hired for sixty-five dollar yearly rent. During my first day's work I found my shopmates were from many different countries; two were Americans, one Irish, one English, two Germans, and one Frenchman. On my first entrance, the foreman, an American, called out to the representative of the emerald isle, "Look here, Paddy; here's another Johnny Bull come over to be civilized." John Bull, however, can afford to be laughed at. After we became acquainted we went on very pleasantly together: the superior skill of the Germans and Frenchman was of the highest service to me, who had much to learn, never having worked but in a provincial town in England; and as the Frenchman could not speak a word of English, and worked at the next bench to mine, my French studies were materially benefited by the conversations I had with him, and the more so as he was a remarkably intelligent workman. . . .

The markets of New York teem with a rich supply of vegetables and fruits in the fine season: the duty of going to market is not confined exclusively to females; most of it is done by the men. I have often started for the market as early as five o'clock in the morning, in order to be ready for work at six, as well as to take advantage of the cool hours for the buying of meat, which in the hot months must be cooked soon after it is killed, to prevent putrefaction. What a tempting sight to an Englishman is the display of pine-apples, melons, peaches, and profusion of tropical fruits! I have frequently bought a large and juicy melon for three cents, and a peck of the most delicious peaches for ten cents, whose flavour, ripened by the glowing sun of an American sky, far exceeds all that I have ever tasted in this country. He only who has panted under that sultry sky can have any adequate conception of the luxury and enjoyment of cutting open a rich cool melon, and suffering its pulpy substance to dissolve in the mouth. It is then we gratefully feel how bountifully Nature compensates for all her apparent annoyances and inconveniences.

To one who has been accustomed to see meat sold, as in England, by ounces—to weigh the loaf against the appetite—the abundance and cheapness of an American market are very gratifying. Instead of buying a chop, wherewith to flavour a large mass of potatoes, he will carry home a quarter of a sheep or a lamb, or a solid rib of beef, with as many vegetables as he can well stagger under, pleased with the anticipation that the tender frames of his little growing family will receive due development under the generous nourishment. In such a case there is no stint; no uneasy thoughts about the coming day's supply; no impending dread of hungry looks or hungry stomachs among those who claim his best affections. This, I have often thought, is the chief cause of the firmer tone and manner which soon becomes apparent in the person of newly-arrived emigrants: shadowed forth in glowing colours in the letters which they write to their friends at home. Unfortunately it too often ends here:—the physical is fostered, but the moral is neglected. . . .

These prices are, however, subject to great fluctuations: the severe winters cause a general rise in all kinds of vegetable produce; at such times twelve or eighteen cents will be charged for a cabbage; from the month of January to May, the scarcity of green food is universal. The price of bread also is not less uncertain: I have often paid six cents for a loaf, which a few weeks earlier in the season would not have cost more than half that sum. For more than half of the five years that we lived in New York, the prices of provisions were, with very slender exceptions, as high as those in the large towns of [England]. . . .

On landing in New York I made up my mind to lose none of the advantages it offered by want of diligence on my part. During the first two years I took but one holiday, and that was passed in company with a French shopmate, in a glorious stroll on the wave-beaten sands, and among the breezy woods of Staten Island. In summer we began work at six; at eight took half an hour for breakfast, and then worked till twelve, when came an hour for dinner; after which we kept on till six, seven, or eight, as we pleased, deferring our third meal until the close of our daily labour. In the winter we took breakfast before daylight, so as to arrive at the workshop by the time that we could see to work, thereby gaining time, and saving ourselves a walk in unpleasant weather. On leaving at eight in the evening, I carried with me a portion of my tools, and set myself to make up such articles of furniture as we most needed; and frequently have I found myself still busy, impatient for the completion of the object that would afford us at once convenience and ornament, at the striking of the "wee short hour ayont the twal." At other times, after laying down my load of tools, I would find it difficult to resist the feeling of weariness induced by eleven hours of previous labour, and sinking instinctively into a chair, take up a book, and soon forget my mechanical duties. It will show how far I was possessed by the utilitarian feeling that, on such occasions, I thought on going to bed that I had lost an evening. I did not then know that this was one of the methods made use of by nature for restoring her balance, compensating for the tension of muscular exertion.

It took another form in the workshop: there it frequently happened about the middle of the afternoon of some sultry summer's day, or of a stormy day in winter, after several weeks of real hard work unrelieved by any change, that a simultaneous cessation from work took place, no one could tell why, though no surprise was manifested that, in the one case, we placed ourselves near an open window, or in the other that we drew round the stove. Then, as it were by tacit agreement, every hand held out its contribution of "loose change;" the apprentice was sent on his errand, and speedily returned laden with wine, brandy, biscuits, and cheese. The appropriation of these refreshments was sure to call forth songs from those who felt musical; after which came a proposition for a further supply, which provoked a more noisy vocalization, while the conversation which had been animated became excited. With a third instalment we concluded the day, and went home half in wonder at our folly, half vexed at our loss of time, feelings which the dizziness of our heads and the uneasiness of our limbs rendered more acute the next day. . . .

In the summer of 1836, when the inflated state of commerce and speculation had reached its height, when prices and rents were increasing in a like proportion, a strike took place among the cabinet-makers. They were dissatisfied with the wages then paid for their labour; and having compiled a new price-book as the basis of their claims, they held meetings; appointed committees; and on a given day, with very few exceptions, ceased working in all the shops of the city. The Americans of our workshop were among the noisiest of the strike, and naturally expected that I should join them; but to this, for several reasons, I was disinclined. First, I considered that I was receiving quite as high wages as my manual skill deserved; next, I felt disposed to attach more importance to the claims of my family than to the ill-considered demands of a body of men, of which the greater part were but the stepping-stones for a few selfish individuals; and last, my "turning out" would have been but an ill return for the kindness of my employer, who had given me work in the anxious time immediately following our arrival, and befriended me in various ways afterwards. Two or three deputations were sent to argue with me on the subject; in vain I expressed my belief that the unsatisfactory rate of wages was rather to be attributed to the unprecedented influx of workmen from abroad, than to any other circumstance; they silenced, without convincing me; and finding me firm, they resorted to threats, and promised to waylay and "hammer" me on my way home from work, and concluded their arguments with a highflown and frothy exposition of the rights of man—of the bounden duty of the minority to yield to whatever the majority may enact. Threats succeeded no better than arguments; I kept on working during the whole of the strike, and in the six weeks that it lasted earned forty-eight dollars; while the others, although in a few instances they obtained a rise, were, at the end of a month after, working at the old wages, having lost nearly half of the best season, and in many cases were supplanted by other artisans which the continued tide of emigration poured into the city. A year or two afterwards I accidentally met one of the members of the deputations, who, recognising me, stopped for a few minutes to speak of his recollections of the event, and added, with a laugh, "You were the toughest customer we had; but I guess it would have been better for us had we all done as you did."

A Newspaper Exposé of Labor in New York, 1845

THE CABINET-MAKERS

A great falling off in the earnings of Cabinet-Makers has taken place during the last ten years. In 1836 an average hand could make by the piece from $12 to $15 per week, and the pay to those who worked by the week was about the same. In 1840 wages fell to about $8 per week, and now probably a majority of the Journeymen in this Trade do not make more than $5 per week. Smart hands who work in establishments where the very best kind of work is turned out are paid $8.

The cause of the great decrease in the wages of Cabinet-Makers is in a great measure the immense amount of poor Furniture manufactured for the Auction-Stores. This is mostly made by Germans, who work rapidly, badly and for almost nothing. There are persons who are constantly on the watch for German emigrants who can work at Cabinet-Making—going on board the ships before the emigrants have landed and engaging them for *a year* at $20 or $30 and their board, or on the best terms they can make. The emigrants of course know nothing of the state of the Trade, prices, regulations, &c. &c. and become willing victims to any one who offers them immediate and permanent employment. This it is which has ruined the Cabinet-Making business, and the complaints on the part of the Journeymen are incessant. There is, however, no remedy for the evil, as we see. So pervading is the idea among the great purchasing classes, the housekeepers, that it must of course be good economy to buy *cheap* things, that good work and good prices must of necessity go a-begging.

Thomas Skidmore on the Rights of Man to Property, 1829

. . . One thing must be obvious to the plainest understanding; that as long as property is unequal; or rather, as long as it is so enormously unequal, as we see it at present, that those who possess it, *will* live on the labor of others, and themselves perform none, or if any, a very disproportionate share, of that toil which attends them as a condition of their existence, and without the performance of which, they have no *just* right to preserve or retain that existence, even for a single hour.

It is not possible to maintain a doctrine to the contrary of this position, without, at the same time, maintaining an absurdity no longer tolerated in enlightened countries; that a part, and that a very great part, of the human race, are doomed, of right, to the slavery of toil, while others are born, only to enjoy.

I, for one, disavow every such doctrine. . . .

We live near to a great epoch, in the history of our own country—the Revolution that separated us from England—we are acquainted with the distinguished men, who performed a prominent part, as well in the separation of the two countries, as in erecting the new governments that succeeded. We are able to know their minds, and to judge for ourselves, how far they were adequate to institute government, on principles of original right; for it was on such principles *as they understood them,* that they supported the Revolution and erected the political edifices that in consequence became necessary.

Of all these, no man, more than Mr. Jefferson, deserves to be considered, as possessing in his own mind, not only "the standard of the man," but the standard of the age. If there was any one capable of ascending to first principles, it was he; and if it was not to be expected of him, how was it to be expected of any one else? Yet Mr. Jefferson speaks of the rights of man, in terms, which when they come to be investigated closely, appear to be very defective and equivocal. I do not mean, that he thought or meant them so; for it is evident that the contrary was the fact. Let us quote him, however; let us weigh his expressions; let us arrive at his intentions in the most legitimate manner: and then see, if I am borne out, in my declaration. If I am, I shall be sustained. If I am not, I shall fail, and deserve to do so. He says:—

"We hold these truths to be self-evident; that all men are created equal; that they are endowed by their Creator with certain unalienable rights; that among these are life, liberty, and the *pursuit of happiness.*" These are his words in the declaration of American Independence.

Whoever looks over the face of the world, and surveys the population of all countries; our own, as well as any and every other; will see it divided into rich and poor; into the hundred who have every thing, and the million who have nothing. If, then, Mr. Jefferson, had made use of the word *property,* instead of *"the pursuit of happiness,"* I would have agreed with him. Then his language would have been clear and intelligible, and strictly conformable to natural right. For I hold, that man's natural right to *life* or *liberty,* is not more sacred or unalienable, than his right to property. But if property is to descend only to particular individuals from the previous generation, and if the many are born, having neither parents nor any one else, to give them property, equal in amount to that which the sons of the rich receive from their fathers and other testators, how is it established that they are created equal? In the pursuit of happiness, is property of no consequence? Can any one be as happy without property of any kind, as with it? Is even liberty and life to be preserved without it? Do we not every day, see multitudes, in order to acquire property in the very pursuit of that happiness which Mr. Jefferson classes among the unalienable rights of man, obliged to sacrifice both liberty and health and often ultimately life, into the bargain? If then property be so essential and indispensable in the pursuit of happiness, as it appears to be, how can it be said, that I am created with an equal right to this happiness—with another, when I must purchase property of him, with labor and suffering—and when he is under no necessity to purchase the like of me at the same costly price? If we are created equal—how has he the right to monopolize all, or even an undue share of the property of the preceding generation? If, then, even the rights of liberty and life, are so insecure and precarious, without property—how very essential to *their* preservation is it, that "the pursuit of happiness"—should be so construed, as to afford title to that, without which, the rights of life and liberty are but an empty name? . . .

Mankind have enquired *too little* after their rights, their interests, and their happiness. If it had not been so, such enormities could not have been allowed to take place, daily and forever before our eyes, without having been remedied. They could not have been plunged into such deep distress and degradation as we now see them. The high and the lofty, those who have become so, from the inevitable operation of causes, which they did not bring into being; and which neither they have had, nor could have had the power to control; would have been tumbled from their elevations, and seated on a level with their fellow-beings. Then would they have enjoyed their equal chance of acquiring property; for then, would they have had only their equal share of it, to begin with; and with this, they could have had only their proper opportunity to employ their industry and talents; others would have been in the same enviable situation; and no one would then be found, in such necessitous condition, that he must work or die; and work, too *on such terms, that a very great share of the value of his labor must go to the employer,* or to him, who, no matter how, affords the means of employment!

It is not long since a member of the Common Council of this city, I do not now recollect his name, and on some occasion of which I do not remember exactly the nature, indulged in a strain of feeling and invective against the poor, [and] . . . launched out into some intemperate expressions against those, whose lot, as society is now modelled, it is to perform THE LABOR THAT SUPPORTS US ALL; such as this, "that he who would not work *ought* to starve." There is no occasion to question the general truth of the observation; but the barbarous *feeling* with which, it struck me, it was uttered, could not fail to raise my indignation. I could not but resent it in the name of my fellow-beings, as an insult to that class who now perform all the work that is done in our support, as well of the honorable member, as of all others, implying an unwillingness to work, which there is no kind of propriety in laying to their charge. But it implied also more. It implied, that *it is right enough* for a certain description of men, among us, to live without labor of their own; while others are called upon to labor, not only enough to support themselves, but to support also, these DRONES in the hive into the bargain. . . . Why is it, that men, at our Hall, or elsewhere, should not be called upon to perform the labor that supports them, as well as other men? If a man will not work, why should he not starve? This is a question which may well be asked, if it is intended to mean, that *all* men, shall be called upon to work alike; and to depend solely upon the labor of their own hands, and draw nothing from the labor of others, but what they are willing to pay for with an equal return in labor of their own hands, I agree to it. . . . Is it not quite as reasonable for a poor man to eat a good dinner, without having labored to earn it, as for a rich man to do it? Is there a difference in rights? Is there one sort of rights for one class of men, and another for another? May one do lawfully what the other will do criminally; have we two codes of law among us? Have we a law for the Lilliputians and another for the Brobdingnaggians? We have been told, in the Declaration of Independence, that "all men are created equal"; but if one man must work for his dinner, and another need not, and does not, how are we equal? If the gentleman shall say, the rich man has property, and the poor man has not; then the question is only changed for another; what is his *right* to such property? . . .

Under the present unequal distribution of property, where labor is the sole resource the poor have, by which to maintain their existence, degraded as it is, by the slavery in which they are plunged, it is not wonderful that they have been found to be opposed to the introduction of improvements. Fruitless and unavailing as such opposition is, it is yet less unreasonable than at first sight it may appear to be. It is true, that one consequence of such improvement, as we have already shown, is, that a poor man even, may obtain 4,800 times as much as he could obtain without it; yet, it may be asked, may he not be an ultimate loser? May not improvement extend to such a degree, that there will be no demand for his labor? Or if it does not reach this point, will it not approach so near it, as to make him an extreme sufferer? . . .

The Steam-Engine is not injurious to the poor, when they can have the benefit of it; and this, on supposition, being *always* the case, instead of being looked upon, as a curse, would be hailed as a blessing. If, then, it is seen that the Steam-Engine, for example, is likely to greatly impoverish, or destroy the poor, what *have* they to do, but TO LAY HOLD OF IT, AND MAKE IT THEIR OWN? LET THEM APPROPRIATE ALSO, in the same way, THE COTTON FACTORIES, THE WOOLEN FACTORIES, THE IRON FOUNDERIES, THE ROLLING MILLS, HOUSES, CHURCHES, SHIPS, GOODS, STEAM-BOATS, FIELDS OF AGRI-CULTURE, &c. &c. &c. in manner as proposed in this work, AND AS IS THEIR RIGHT; and they will never have occasion any more to consider that as an evil which never deserved that character; which, on the contrary, is all that is good among men; and of which, we cannot, under these new circumstances, have too much. It is an equal division of property that MAKES ALL RIGHT, and an equal transmission of it to posterity, KEEPS IT SO.

Reverend Alonzo Potter Defends Wage Labor, 1841

[T]he chief motive to labour, freely exercised, must be the result accruing to the labourer. This is technically called his *wages*. And, since the more productive labour is rendered by machinery, by subdivision of employments, and facilitation of exchanges, the greater must be the aggregate quantity of the good things of life produced, it seems self-evident that the share falling to the lot of each individual labourer, as his recompense or wages, *ought* to be proportionately augmented. And such doubtless would be the case were the labourer, his employer, and other joint partners in the work of production left free to apportion among themselves their respective shares, untrammelled on the one hand by unwise laws, and on the other by unfair combinations; it being supposed, of course, that each party is honest and moderately intelligent. The great principles, in short, of *free labour, and free disposal of its produce,* would seem, in such case, amply sufficient to secure an equitable distribution of property among the several classes who contribute to its creation; and the benefits they thence derive would so stimulate their exertions as to cause a continued increase, not merely in the wealth of the society, but also in the share of that wealth falling to the lot of any individual member. . . .

[U]nder a system of free and equitable exchange, the recompense (wages) of every labourer will be by no means equal, nor even exactly proportioned to the severity or duration of his employment. It must be determined by the *value* of his produce in the market. And this will increase in proportion to the talent, skill, and application of the labourer, or any other circumstances which may render his labour more *productive* than that of another. A man whose natural powers of body or mind enable him to contribute more efficiently to the general work of production than another, may equitably expect, and will, under the system of free exchange, receive a larger share of the gross general produce. The same is true of one who, by advantages of education or continued application, has acquired a superior degree of skill or knowledge in any of the arts of industry, and of one, too, whose reputation for integrity and vigilance in his employer's service secures him peculiar confidence. The increased reward thus obtained by increased productiveness is the motive and necessary stimulus to most of those efforts for rendering labour more productive, which have carried mankind forward from the savage to the civilized state, and must be depended upon for inciting him to yet farther advances. Every attempt to equalize the wages of different employments or individuals by compulsory arrangements has the certain effect of damping the ardour of industry, putting a stop to improvement, and thus checking the march of production. . . .

All this seems so obvious to the most ordinary capacity as hardly to be worth dwelling upon. And yet there are persons who still—in the present light of civilization, in the nineteenth century, and in the midst of all the evidence which is afforded, wherever we turn our eyes, of the prodigious part which capital is playing in the production of the necessaries, comforts, and luxuries of human life—declaim against capital as the poison of society, and the taking of interest on capital by its owners as an abuse, an injustice, a robbery of the class of labourers! Such blindness is to me truly unaccountable. That those who observe the prevalence of great misery among the inferior classes of workmen in some wealthy countries—who witness and deplore the fact, that, in spite of all the manifold improvements which are continually adding to the productiveness of labour, the share of the gross production which falls to the common labourer does not increase, perhaps even diminishes—that, on viewing this anomaly, they should conclude *something* to be wrong, is no source of astonishment to me, for I arrive at the same necessary conclusion from the same observation. But that any sane person should attribute the evil to *the existence of capital*—that is, to the employment of wealth in aiding the production of farther wealth, instead of being unproductively consumed, almost, if not quite, as fast as it is created, or unproductively hoarded to satisfy the lust of the miser—is indeed wonderful. Why, without capital, the Island of Great Britain would not afford subsistence to a hundredth part of its present population. Destroy the *security* for the free enjoyment or disposal of capital, deny its owner the privilege of accepting what any one may find it for his advantage to give for its use, and every individual will soon be reduced to his unaided resources. He will find nowhere any store of food on which to live while he is digging, and sowing, and protecting his immature crop; no stock of tools with which to work, or of clothes and other necessaries of existence. All trades would stop at once, for every trade is carried on by means of capital. Men would at once be reduced to the isolation and helplessness of barbarism.

But perhaps it is in the imagination of these schemers that there should not be a general destruction, but only *a general division,* of the capital now existing among the present race of labourers; so that each, it is thought, would for some time, at least, be provided with a stock of food, clothes, and tools, with which to continue the business of production. We suppose something like this is contemplated. But, putting out of sight the injustice, confusion, and attendant horrors of the frightful scramble which is here disguised under the smooth name of a general division of property (a scramble which, in the extremely complicated and artificial state of society characterizing a country like ours, must be attended with infinitely more violence, convulsion, and disturbance than any political catastrophe on record), how, we must beg to ask, is production to go on afterward? In a very short time, a large part of the population—*all the idle*—and in such a crisis there can be but little industry—will have consumed their share of the plunder in riot and excess. Admitting that others have gone to work industriously in the production of the things they require, each for himself; have ploughed and sown, and spun and wove; have stored corn in their granaries, and cattle in their homesteads, and fuel, and clothing, and comforts of various kinds in their lofts, and cellars, and warehouses, what is to become of all that large body who, having squandered away their share of the general booty, will have left no means of maintenance? It is clear that one of two things must occur. Either they will, if sufficiently numerous and strong, call for *another division of property,* that is, *once more* plunder the barns, granaries, homesteads, and warehouses of the industrious; or, if they are not strong enough to attempt this, they will humble themselves to the owners of these same barns and warehouses, and petition for food and clothing in return for all they have to offer, *their labour;* that is to say, they will apply to them for *employment and wages.* If the owners of property refuse their petition, starvation and disease must rapidly carry them off; not, however, before they have robbed, and plundered, and done all the injury to the remainder of society which their despair and destitution will prompt. If their request *is* acceded to, the old system of masters and men, *capitalists and labourers,* will recommence; and the society—at least whatever portion of it we can suppose to have survived the shock of such a convulsion—will be reconstituted on its old and natural principles, to recommence the difficult march of improvement, and with the feeble hope of regaining, after the lapse of years, perhaps of ages, the elevated position we are at present so fortunate as to occupy, as yet unscathed; to reproduce slowly and painfully the vast stock of accumulated capital which it once possessed, but which, in a fit of popular insanity, had been broken down and scattered to the winds.

The security of property, and the liberty of consuming or employing it in whatever way the owner pleases or finds most for his interest, is, as has been truly observed, the first of the *rights of industry*, and the essential condition of its progressive activity. But of all modes of employing property, the very last which it would occur to an enlightened friend of humanity to obstruct, is its employment *in aiding production*—that is, as *capital*. It is quite clear that the profit or interest to be gained by the employment of capital is the principal motive to its accumulation, and the *only* one to its employment in furthering production. It is quite clear that, if the owner of capital is not allowed to make what profit he can upon it by lending it to others, no one will accumulate more capital than he can use himself; and nearly all savings would thenceforward be hoarded in cellars and closets, instead of aiding industry and facilitating production.

From the Artisan's Republic to the Factory System

When Philadelphians celebrated the newly ratified U.S. Constitution in 1791, masters, journeymen, and apprentices marched through the streets under banners that announced the unity reigning within each craft; only seventy years later, in the era when northern men rallied in support of the Union, urban workmen no longer felt it possible to march in the same ranks with merchants and manufacturers, who now employed them. In 1865 most Americans were farmers, and artisans working in traditional ways still produced most manufactured goods. But the egalitarianism of the early-nineteenth-century workshop had been replaced by a gaping social chasm that divided wage laborers in almost every trade from the factory owners and great merchants of the Civil War era.

The artisanal world had been characterized by small-scale production, local markets, skilled craftsmanship, and a self-reliant sense of community and citizenship. Early-nineteenth-century workmen thought of themselves as masters both in their household and in their trade, the upholders of an equal-rights tradition whose roots stretched back to the American Revolution. White women, blacks, and unskilled immigrants would obviously have an ambiguous relationship to this tradition. However, many historians have found in republicanism, the ideology that links civil virtue and personal independence to self-government, a powerful standard by which nineteenth-century workers judged and rejected the new men of wealth and power, who seemed to rise so quickly and to challenge so dramatically the values and livelihood of America's producing classes.

Factories, banks, railroads, and mines did not appear overnight. In nineteenth-century America, as in many underdeveloped nations today, large, mechanized enterprises existed alongside extensive systems of home production and the craft-based trades. In fact, the process of industrialization had a patchwork quality that deskilled and depressed some trades and skipped others entirely. In New York and Philadelphia, a process of ''metropolitan industrialization'' created a marvelously heterogeneous working class divided by skill, race, sex, and nationality. In contrast, the textile industry, which put its mills on isolated sites along the New England rivers, generated a more homogeneous class of workers. At the famous Lowell, Massachusetts mills, Boston capitalists recruited thousands of young farm women and housed them in dormitory-like boarding houses. The textile factories of Rhode Island and Pennsylvania more typically employed whole families, relying heavily on a brutal system of child labor.

To what extent did these textile operatives share the same outlook as the more skilled artisans? Could women share with their menfolk the equal-rights ideology that sustained antebellum workingmen? Or was the republicanism of these artisans an obstacle to gender equality and class consciousness?

The rise of the factory system revolutionized the shoemaking trade in the pre–Civil War era. The first four documents offer a glimpse of the work culture and protest traditions of Lynn, Massachusetts, workers in the shoe industry. In sketching apprenticeship life during the days of the old-time shoe workshop, David Johnson, a Lynn resident, re-creates in the first document the masculine work culture that members of the Mutual Benefit Society of Journeymen Cordwainers celebrated in the 1844 "Cordwainer's Song," reprinted here as the second document. Their proud republican world view had little meaning for female shoebinders like "Constance," who, in the third document, from the pages of the *Awl*, the newspaper of Lynn's artisan shoemakers, complains of her exclusion from the male fraternity. The fourth document, a reporter's account of a mass meeting of Lynn women during the Great Strike of 1860, demonstrates that both men and women drew upon the equal-rights tradition to attack wage slavery, but it also exposes persistent and deep gender divisions within the shoemaking work force.

The fifth document, testimony from the Pennsylvania State Senate, uncovers some of the horrors of the early textile mills and shows that their workers sought state regulation of excessive hours, child labor, and other exploitive conditions. Finally, in the sixth document, a voice from the Lowell Female Labor Reform Association demonstrates how women made their own ideologically charged attack upon wage slavery.

Why might workers have chosen to turn to the state rather than to their own organizations to fight the factory system? What roles did the increasing division of labor, and employer-hiring practices, play in the inability of so many workers to find common ground?

David Johnson Remembers Apprenticeship Life in the Artisan Shoe Shop, 1830

. . . A boy while learning his trade was called a "seamster"; that is, he sewed the shoes for his master, or employer, or to use one of the technicalities of the "craft," he "worked on the seam." Sometimes the genius of one of these boys would outrun all limits. One of this kind, who may be called Alphonzo, worked on the seam for a stipulated sum. He seemed to regard his work as an incidental circumstance. When he left the shop at night he might be expected back the next morning: but there were no special grounds for the expectation. He might drop in the next morning, or the next week. He left one Saturday night and did not make his appearance again until the following Thursday morning. On entering the shop he proceeded to take off his jacket as though there had been no hiatus in his labor. His master watched him with an amused countenance to see whether he would recognize the lapse of time. At length he said, "Where

---

David N. Johnson, *Sketches of Lynn* (Lynn: Thomas P. Nichols, 1880), pp. 30, 32–35, 59–62.

have you been, Alphonzo?'' Alphonzo turned his head in an instant, as if struck with the preposterousness of the inquiry, and exclaimed, "Me? I? O, I've been down to Nahant.'' The case was closed. . . .

In almost every one of these shops there was one whose mechanical genius outran that of all the rest. He could "temper wax,'' "cut shoulders,'' sharpen scrapers and cut hair. The making of wax was an important circumstance in the olden time. To temper it just right so that it would not be too brittle and "fly'' from the thread, or too soft and stick to the fingers, was an art within the reach of but few, or if within reach, was attained only by those who aspired to scale the heights of fame, and who, "while their companions slept, were toiling upward in the night.'' Such a one eyed his skillet of melted rosin as the alchemist of old viewed his crucible wherein he was to transmute the baser metals into gold. When the rosin was thoroughly melted, oil or grease was added until the right consistency was supposed to be nearly reached, the compound being thoroughly stirred in the meantime. Then the one having the matter in charge would first dip his finger in cold water and then into the melted mass, and taking the portion that adhered to his finger, would test its temper by pulling it, biting it, and rolling it in his hands. If found to be too hard, more oil or grease would be added, but very cautiously, as the critical moment was being reached. Then the test would be again applied. When the right result was supposed to be nearly gained, a piece of wax would be passed around among the crew for a confirmatory verdict. If the judgment of the master of ceremonies was indorsed, the experiment ended, and the mixture was poured into a vessel of cold water—usually the "shop-tub''—to cool sufficiently to be "worked.'' . . .

The shop-tub was an indispensable article in every shop. In early times, before the manufactures of wooden ware had become plenty and cheap, some rudely-constructed wooden vessel of home manufacture served the purpose. Afterwards a paint-keg or a firkin with the top sawed off, and still later a second-hand water-pail, was made to do service.

The theory was that the water of the shop-tub was to be changed every day. As this water was used for *wetting* the "stock''—which meant all the sole leather put into the shoe—and also often used for washing hands, it was somewhat necessary that it should be changed occasionally. The shifting of the "tub'' often devolved upon the boy of the shop, except when he was too bright. In that case he "shirked'' with the rest of the crew. This was the sort of boy that looked out of the attic window of the dormitory where he slept, to see if the smoke was gracefully curling from the shop's chimney, in the gray of the morning as he stretched himself for a supplementary snooze.

The man who had an "eye'' for cutting "shoulders'' occupied a niche of distinction among his fellow-craftsmen. If it was not necessary that he should have a "microscopic eye''—which Mr. Pope [the eighteenth-century English poet] tells us man does not need because he "is not a fly,''—it was needful that he should have a "geometric eye'' when called upon to adjust the "shoulder'' to "convex'' and "concave'' edges. To do this successfully required little less than a stroke of genius. Two cents was the usual price for cutting a "shoulder," and an experienced cutter would gather in each week quite a pile of the larger-size coppers of those days, whose purchasing power of many things was twice as great as at present. . . .

Perhaps one of the sorest experiences a boy had in old times in learning the "craft," was that which came from *breaking awls*. In order to fully appreciate the situation, the reader must take a survey of the whole field. It was a period of low wages. Awls were the most expensive "kit" used by the shoemaker. . . .

The awls were of two kinds, diamond and round, so called from the shape of their points. The diamond-shaped were usually preferred, as they were thought to be less liable to become dulled by use; but the so-called round awls—these were rather flatted at their points—were often used by "don" workmen, as they were less liable to "cut" the "upper." The awls first in use in this country were of English manufacture. The name of the manufacturer was stamped upon each awl, and there were three kinds, more or less in use, some fifty or more years ago when those of American make began to take their place. These were known as the Allerton, Wilson, and Titus awls, respectively. After the introduction of the American awl, the English article was not held in very high esteem by workmen employed upon ladies' shoes. They were badly shaped, and the points were left unfinished. The Allerton and Wilson had usually too long a crook, while the Titus was faulty in the opposite direction, being too straight, especially for certain kinds of work. They had, however, two important recommendations—they were better tempered, and therefore less liable to break, and their cost was only one-half, or less, that of the American awl.

Before the English awl was used, it was necessary to finish the points. This was sometimes done by grinding, sometimes by filing, and sometimes by sandpaper; and the points were smoothed off on a "whet-board," or by rubbing them on the pine floor. The man who could do this job skillfully was considered something of a genius. As already intimated, a boy could spoil a day's wages by breaking a few awls. If he was working on the seam on "long reds," and had a lot of extra hard soles on hand—some *hemlock tanned leather* for instance,—he had gloomy forebodings of the peril of the situation. If the master was a "hard" one, and the boy somewhat careless, there would most likely be an appeal to the "stirrup," whenever accidents of this kind rose above the average in frequency. . . .

"Cordwainers' Song," 1844

(Tune—"My Bible Leads to Glory")

The cause of labor's gaining,
The cause of labor's gaining,
The cause of labor's gaining,

Throughout the town of Lynn.

Chorus

Onward! onward! ye noble-hearted working men;
Onward! onward! and victory is yours.

Arouse the working classes, &c.
Unite the free cordwainers, &c.
Let JUSTICE be our motto, &c.
Come, join us, all true hearted, &c.
Our prices are advancing, &c.
The WOMEN, too, are *rising*, &c.
New members daily join us, &c.
Our victory is certain, &c.
We'll *stitch* our SOLES still closer, &c.
Let all protect free labor, &c.
There'll soon be joy and gladness, &c.

Constance, "On the Art of Shoemaking," 1845

Great was his genius, and *inventive* thought!
Who first the curious *shoe* so nicely wrought,
Before this trade, others must soon retreat;
None will forego, this covering for their feet.

Without her shoe, what lady would be *seen*?
Take them away, what woman could be *Queen*?
Even the *Chinese* skill, in all the arts;
Will find this competition in these parts.

The town of Lynn in history is found:
Let all her sons be proud to have her named,
The very rocks with legions, rife are crowned;
And all the place with romance, still abound.

The lack of knowledge *see,* we cannot plead;
Our public schools give all the chance to *read,*
And learned men and great, with *faces* wise,
Will from the land of shoes, henceforth arise.

And now the Awl and Needle are combined,
Ladies your talent show, with intellect refined;
Though *men* still take the lead in politics and shoes,
Yet, when they ask our aid, oh! let us not refuse!

But help them in this work, with willing heart and hand,
And let not man be left alone, within this happy land;
Yet when we own this claim, (let not despotic sway,)
Arouse the woman's wrath, (and that *old* term, Obey.)

A Reporter's Account of Lynn Women's Mass Meeting During the Great Strike, 1860

. . . About noon, the procession from Lynn, consisting of about 3,500 men, preceded by a brass band, entered the village green, escorted by 500 Marbleheaders. The sight from the hotel steps was a very interesting one. Four thousand men, without work, poor, depending partially upon the charities of their neighbors and partially upon the generosity of the tradesmen of their town, giving up a certainty for an uncertainty, and involving in trouble with themselves many hundreds of women and children, while to a certain extent the wheels of trade are completely blocked, and no immediate prospect of relief appears. Their banners flaunted bravely. Their inscriptions of "Down with tyranny," "We are not slaves," "No sympathy with the rich," "Our bosses grind us," "We work and they ride," "No foreign police," and many others of like import, read very well and look very pretty, but they don't buy dinners or clothing, or keep the men at work or the women at home about their business. By this strike $25,000 *weekly is kept from circulation in Lynn alone,* and who can say what the effect will be on the storekeepers, dealers in articles of home consumption, if such a state of drainage is kept up for any great length of time? . . .

The most interesting part of the whole movement took place last evening, and will be continued tonight. I refer to the mass meeting of the binders and stitchers held by the female strikers at Liberty Hall. . . .

There are two classes of workers—those who work in the shops and those who work at home—the former use the machines and materials of the bosses, while the latter work on their own machines, or work by hand, furnishing their own materials. It is evident that the latter should receive higher pay than the former, and the report not having considered this fact, was subjected to severe handling. The discussion which followed was rich beyond description—the jealousies, piques and cliques of the various circles being apparent as it proceeded. One opposed the adoption of the report because, "the prices set were so high that the bosses wouldn't pay them." Cries of "Put her out," "Shut up," "Scabby," and "Shame" arose on all sides; but, while the reporters were alarmed, the lady took it all in good part, and made up faces at the crowd. The Chairman stated that, hereafter, Pickleeomoonia boots were to be made for three cents a pair less, which announcement was received with expressions of dismay, whereupon he corrected himself, and said they were to be three cents higher; and this announcement drew forth shouts and screams of applause. "There, didn't I *say* so?" said an old lady behind me. "You shut up," was the response of her neighbor; "you think because you've got a couple of machines you're some; but you ain't no more than anybody else." At this point some men peeped in at the window—"Scat, scat, and put 'em out," soon drove them away, and the meeting went into a Committee of the Whole, and had a grand chabbering for five minutes. Two ladies, one representing the machine

---

Howard, "The Bay State Strike," *New York Times,* Feb. 29, 1860, p. 3.

400

interest, and the other the shop girls, became very much excited, and were devoting themselves to an *exposé* of each other's habits, when the Chairman, with the perspiration starting from every pore, said in a loud and authoritative tone of voice: "Ladies! look at me; stop this wranglin'. Do you care for your noble cause? Are you descendants of old Molly Stark or not? Did you ever hear of the spirit of '76? [Yes, yes, we've got it.] Well, then, do behave yourselves. There ain't nobody nowhere who will aid you if you don't show 'em that you're regular built Moll Starks over agin." [Cheers, clappings, &c.] . . .

A proposition to march in the procession was the next topic which drew forth discussion. Some thought that proper minded women would better stay at home than be gadding about the streets following banners and music. To this there was some assent, but when a younger girl asked the last speaker what she meant by talking that way, when everybody in Lynn knew that she had been tagging around on the sidewalk after the men's processions the last week. . . .

Some of the statements were quite interesting. A Mrs. Miller said that she hired a machine on which she was able to make $6 per week—out of that she paid—for the machine, $1; for the materials, $1.50; for her board, $2; for bastings, $1;—making $5.50 in all, which left her a clear profit of only fifty cents a week. One of the bosses says, however, that if a woman is at all smart she can make $10 per week with her machine, which would be clear $3, sure. In fact, from remarks which were dropped around I judge that Mrs. Miller's estimate is rather low. The leading spirit of the meeting, Miss Clara Brown, a very bright, pretty girl, said that she called at a shop that day and found a friend of hers hard at work on a lot of linings. She asked what she was getting for them, and was told *eight cents for sixty*. "Girls of Lynn," said Clara, "*Girls* of Lynn, do you hear that and will you stand it? Never, Never, NEVER. Strike, then—strike at once; demand $8\frac{1}{2}$ cents for your work when the binding isn't closed and you'll get it. Don't let them make niggers of you; [Shame, there are colored persons here.] I meant Southern niggers:—keep still; don't work your machines; let 'em lie still till we get all we ask, and then go at it, as did our Mothers in the Revolution."

This speech was a good one; it seemed to suit all parties, and they proposed to adjourn to Tuesday night, when they would have speeches and be more orderly. Canvassing Committees were appointed to look up female strikers and to report female "scabs." And with a vote of thanks to the Chairman, the meeting adjourned to meet in Lyceum Hall. . . .

Textile Operative William Shaw's Testimony on Child Labor in Pennsylvania's Textile Mills, 1838

. . . The greatest evils known are, first, the number of hours of labor, and the number of young children employed. Has worked in four different factories in nine years; in John P. Crozier's, nearly three years; Samuel

Riddle's, nearly two years; Joseph Dean, nearly two, and Jonathan Hatch, nearly one year, and now at Jos. Fleming's; is twenty-six years old. At Fleming's, about fifty persons employed; about eighteen females; about four children under twelve years old; about fifteen under eighteen years old. The proportion of children varies in different establishments; has known more than one-fourth to be children under twelve years of age; under twenty years, would include, in many cases, three-fourths; not many are apprenticed; they are usually hired to employers by parents and guardians. The hours vary in different establishments; in some I have worked fourteen and a-half hours. I have known work to commence as early as twenty minutes past four o'clock, in the summer season, and to work as late as half an hour before eight, P.M., an hour and a-half allowed for breakfast and dinner, when the hands all leave to go to dinner—children and all; the ringing of the bell was the notice to begin, and docking wages the penalty; the foreman rings the bell and stops the machinery. In the cities, the engineer rings the bell and stops the machinery.

The period of labor is not uniform; in some cases, from sun to sun. It is most common to work as long as they can see; in the winter they work until eight o'clock, receiving an hour and a-half for meals; an hour and a half is the entire time allowed for going, eating and returning; and that time is often shortened by the ringing of the bell too soon.

The labor of the children is, in some cases, excessive—in others it is not. The children are employed at spinning and carding. The question of excessive labor is more upon the kind of work; carding is the hardest work; their work is regulated by the operation of the machinery, at carding; and they must stand during the whole time; considers twelve or fourteen hours labor excessive at either branch for a child. I have known children of nine years of age to be employed at spinning—at carding, as young as ten years. Punishment by whipping, is frequent; they are sometimes sent home and docked for not attending punctually; never knew both punishments to be inflicted; generally the children are attentive, and punishments are not frequent. The carder, or person having charge of the children, inflicts the chastisement.

Boys and girls work together; no attention is paid by the manufacturer, or others in the factory, to the personal cleanliness of the children. Rules, sometimes printed, are posted in some of the factories, for the government.

The children are tired when they leave the factory; has known them to sleep in corners and other places, before leaving the factory, from fatigue. The younger children are generally very much fatigued particularly those under twelve years of age; has not heard frequent complaints of pain; more of being worried; has known the children to go to sleep on arriving at home, *before* taking supper; has known great difficulty in keeping children awake at their work; has known them to be struck, to keep them awake.

The children *are* more healthy when they first enter the factories, than afterwards; they lose colour, loss of appetite, and sometimes, not frequently, complain themselves; has known them to be compelled in some instances, to quit the factories, in consequence of ill health, particularly females. Boys quit frequently to go to trades; has known no deformity produced by the labor.

Parents are favorable to a reduction of hours; I think no attention is paid to education during the time they are employed in factories, except what they receive from Sabbath schools, and some few at night schools, when they are in an unfit condition to learn; the children attend Sabbath school with great reluctance; many will not attend in consequence of the confinement of the week.

No particular attention is paid to morals; the boys and girls are not kept separate in the factories; they have different water closets; generally separated only by a partition; obscene language is frequently used; not often by females; profane language is frequently used; care is seldom taken to prevent these things; if their work is done, it is all that is required; girls and boys work together and talk together; no pains are taken to ventilate factories; sometimes the windows are nailed down; sometimes fifty are employed in one room; in small factories, as few as ten; has never known a thermometer to be kept in the rooms; in the winter they are generally kept too cold. The machinery is propelled in the city by steam, in the country by water. In the carding room, the air is frequently filled with flyings. The only instance of a contageous disease being generated in a factory, was near Baltimore, some years ago, when the yellow fever broke out 'in the factory of the Messrs Buchanan's, when it was not in the city. The superintendents are generally careful in their language, not to set a bad example.

The wages of children are not regulated by the number of hours they labor; I have known some to get no more than fifty cents per week; I have known some to get as much as $1.25; the common rate is $1.00; oftener less than greater; most of the children are boys.

Amelia, a Woman Worker, Protests
Lowell Wage Slavery, 1845

. . . For the purpose of illustration, let us go with that light-hearted, joyous young girl who is about for the first time to leave the home of her childhood, that home around which clusters so many beautiful and holy associations, pleasant memories, and quiet joys; to leave, too, a mother's cheerful smile, a father's care and protection; and wend her way toward this far famed "city of spindles," this promised land of the imagination, in whose praise she has doubtless heard so much.

Let us trace her progress during her first year's residence, and see whether she indeed realizes those golden prospects which have been held out to her. Follow her now as she enters that large gloomy looking building—she is in search of employment, and has been told that she might

From "Voices from Lowell," 1845, in Philip Foner, ed., *The Factory Girls*, 1977, pp. 135–138, (Urbana: University of Illinois Press, 1977).

here obtain an eligible situation. She is sadly wearied with her journey, and withal somewhat annoyed by the noise, confusion, and strange faces all around her. So, after a brief conversation with the overseer, she concludes to accept the first situation which offers; and reserving to herself a sufficient portion of time in which to obtain the necessary rest after her unwonted exertions, and the gratification of a stranger's curiosity regarding the place in which she is now to make her future home, she retires to her boarding house, to arrange matters as much to her mind as may be.

The intervening time passes rapidly away, and she soon finds herself once more within the confines of that close noisy apartment, and is forthwith installed in her new situation—first, however, premising that she has been sent to the Counting-room, and receives therefrom a Regulation paper, containing the rules by which she must be governed while in their employ; and lo! here is the beginning of mischief; for in addition to the tyrannous and oppressive rules which meet her astonished eyes, she finds herself compelled to remain for the space of twelve months in the very place she then occupies, however reasonable and just cause of complaint might be hers, or however strong the wish for dismission; thus, in fact, constituting herself a slave, a very slave to the caprices of him for whom she labors. Several incidents coming to the knowledge of the writer, might be somewhat interesting in this connection, as tending to show the prejudicial influence exerted upon the interests of the operative by this unjust requisition. The first is of a lady who has been engaged as an operative for a number of years, and recently entered a weaving room on the Massachusetts Corporation: the overseers having assured her previous to her entrance, that she should realize the sum of $2.25 per week, exclusive of board; which she finding it impossible to do, appealed to the Counting-room for a line enabling her to engage elsewhere but it was peremptorily refused. . . .

But to return to our toiling Maiden,—the next beautiful feature which she discovers in this *glorious* system is, the long number of hours which she is obliged to spend in the above named close, unwholesome apartment. It is not enough, that like the poor peasant of Ireland, or the Russian serf who labors from sun to sun, but during one half of the year, she must still continue to toil on, long after Nature's lamp has ceased to lend its aid— nor will even this suffice to satisfy the grasping avarice of her employer; for she is also through the winter months required to rise, partake of her morning meal, and be at her station in the mill, while the sun is yet sleeping behind the eastern hills; thus working on an average, at least twelve hours and three fourths per day, exclusive of the time allotted for her hasty meals, which is in winter simply one half hour at noon,—in the spring is allowed the same at morn, and during the summer is added 15 minutes to the half hour at noon. Then too, when she is at last released from her wearisome day's toil, still may she not depart in peace. No! her footsteps must be dogged to see that they do not stray beyond the corporation limits, and she *must,* whether she will or no, be subjected to the manifold inconveniences of a large crowded boarding-house, where too, the price paid for her accommodation is so utterly insignificant, that it will not ensure to her the common comforts of life; she is obliged to sleep in a small comfortless, half ventilated apartment containing some half a dozen occupants each; but no matter, *she is an operative*—it is all well enough for her; there is no "abuse" about it; no, indeed; so think our employers,—but do we think so? time will show. . . .

Reader will you pronounce this a mere fancy sketch, written for the sake of effect? It is not so. It is a real picture of "Factory life"; nor is it one half so bad as might truthfully and justly have been drawn. But it has been asked, and doubtless will be again, why, if these evils are so aggravating, have they been so long and so peacefully borne? Ah! and why have they? It is a question well worthy of our consideration, and we would call upon every operative in *our* city, aye, throughout the length and breadth of the land, to awake from the lethargy which has fallen upon them, and assert and maintain their rights. We call upon you for action—*united and immediate action*. But, says one, let us wait till we are stronger. In the language of one of old, we ask, when shall we be stronger? Will it be the next week, or the next year? Will it be when we are reduced to the service conditions of the poor operatives of England? for verily we shall be and that right soon, if matters be suffered to remain as they are. Says another, how shall we act? we are but one amongst a thousand, what shall we do that our influence may be felt in this vast multitude? We answer there is in this city an Association called the Female Labor Reform Association, having for its professed object, the amelioration of the condition of the operative. Enrolled upon its records are the names of five hundred members—come then, and add thereto five hundred or rather five thousand more, and in the strength of our united influence we will soon show these *drivelling* cotton lords, this mushroom aristocracy of New England, who so arrogantly aspire to lord it over God's heritage, that our rights cannot be trampled upon with impunity; that we will no longer submit to that arbitrary power which has for the last ten years been so abundantly exercised over us.

One word ere we close, to the hardy independent yeomanry and mechanics, among the Granite Hills of New Hampshire, the woody forests of Maine, the cloud capped mountains of Vermont, and the busy, bustling towns of the old Bay State—ye! who have daughters and sisters toiling in these sickly prison-houses which are scattered far and wide over each of these States, we appeal to you for aid in this matter. Do you ask how that aid can be administered? We answer through the Ballot Box. Yes! if you have one spark of sympathy for our condition, carry it there, and see to it that you send to preside in the Councils of each Commonwealth, men who have hearts as well as heads, souls as well as bodies; men who will watch zealously over the interests of the laborer in every department; who will protect him by the strong arm of the law from the encroachments of arbitrary power; who will see that he is not deprived of those rights and privileges which God and Nature have bestowed upon him—yes,

> From every rolling river,
>   From mountain, vale and plain.
>
> We call on you to deliver
>   Us, from the tyrant's chain:

And shall we call in vain? We trust not. More anon.

Work and Protest in
Antebellum New England

The great paradox of the early nineteenth century is that the same period that witnessed the development of the cult of domesticity also saw the first movement by American white women into industrial employment—seemingly the very antithesis of domesticity. The first factories in the United States were the cotton textile mills of New England, and their labor force was largely female. As the production of cloth increasingly became mechanized, the farmers' daughters who had worked in their own homes producing clothing for their families moved into factories to take on the same tasks on a much larger scale. Rather than spinning wheels and hand looms, they now worked with spinning jennies and weaving equipment run by water power.

Yet in this early phase of industrialization, not all work for wages took place in large factories in mill towns. Some New England industries greatly expanded production not by building such manufacturing centers but rather by incorporating traditional work performed in the household, like shoemaking or straw-hat weaving, into a more efficient system through the use of what was called "putting out." In such a system of production, a boss sent materials to individual contractors, who then made items in their homes, returning the finished product to the supplier. Although in preindustrial America the work of artisans had been largely the province of men, the new system, especially in shoemaking, led to the increasing involvement of women in the manufacturing process.

These developments did not take place without protest and resistance from the workers involved. Historians have long been intrigued by the beginnings of industrial capitalism in the United States and by the nearly simultaneous origins of protest against the new system. Although it was once thought that women took little part in these processes, it is now apparent that their participation was central to both industrialization and resistance. What were some of the advantages of industrialization that propelled women into the work force? What conditions led them to protest? How did the values and circumstances of female factory workers versus those of home workers influence the protest movement?

⁂ DOCUMENTS

The Lowell Offering, a magazine produced by the women who worked in the textile mills, often carried essays written by young women about their experiences. The first document consists of two such essays from the issue of December 1840. Mary Paul, an operative at Lowell in the 1840s, wrote letters home describing her life in the mills; excerpts from them constitute the second selection. In the third document, a description of the work of female shoebinders precedes extracts from the laconic diary of one of the shoebinders, Sarah Trask, of Lynn, Massachusetts. These documents illustrate the wide range of women's responses to the economic changes influencing their lives.

Two Essays from *The Lowell Offering*, 1840

Defence of Factory Girls

"She has worked in a factory, is sufficient to damn to infamy the most worthy and virtuous girl."

So says Mr. Orestes A. Brownson; and either this horrible assertion is true, or Mr. Brownson is a slanderer. I assert that it is *not* true, and Mr. B. may consider himself called up to prove his words, if he can. . . .

And whom has Mr. Brownson slandered? A class of girls who in this city alone are numbered by thousands, and who collect in many of our smaller towns by hundreds; girls who generally come from quiet country homes, where their minds and manners have been formed under the eyes of the worthy sons of the Pilgrims, and their virtuous partners, and who return again to become the wives of the free intelligent yeomanry of New England, and the mothers of quite a proportion of our future republicans. Think, for a moment, how many of the next generation are to spring from mothers doomed to infamy! "Ah," it may be replied, "Mr. Brownson acknowledges that you may still be worthy and virtuous." Then we must be a set of worthy and virtuous idiots, for no virtuous girl of common sense would choose for an occupation one that would consign her to infamy. . . .

Whence has arisen the degree of prejudice which has existed against factory girls, I cannot tell; but we often hear the condition of the factory population of England, and the station which the operatives hold in society there, referred to as descriptive of *our* condition. As well might it be said, as say the *nobility* of England, that *labor itself* is disgraceful, and that all who work should be consigned to contempt, if not to infamy. And again: it has been asserted that to put ourselves under the influence and restraints of corporate bodies, is contrary to the spirit of our institutions, and to that love of independence which we ought to cherish. There is a spirit of independence which is averse to social life itself; and I would advise all who wish to cherish it, to go far beyond the Rocky Mountains, and hold communion with none but the untamed Indian, and the wild beast of the forest. We are under restraints, but they are voluntarily assumed; and we are at liberty to withdraw from them, whenever they become galling or irksome.

Neither have I ever discovered that any restraints were imposed upon us, but those which were necessary for the peace and comfort of the whole, and for the promotion of the design for which we are collected, namely, to get money, as much of it and as fast as we can; and it is because our toil is so unremitting, that the wages of factory girls are higher than those of females engaged in most other occupations. It is these wages which, in spite of toil, restraint, discomfort, and prejudice, have drawn so many worthy, virtuous, intelligent, and well-educated girls to Lowell, and other factories; and it is the wages which are in a great degree to decide the characters of the factory girls as a class. . . . The avails of factory labor are now greater than those of many domestics, seamstresses, and school-teachers; and strange would it be, if in money-loving New England, one of the most lucrative female employments should be rejected because it is toilsome, or because some people are prejudiced against it. Yankee girls have too much *independence* for *that*.

But it may be remarked, "You certainly cannot mean to intimate, that all factory girls are virtuous, intelligent," &c. No, I do not; and Lowell would be a stranger place than it has ever been represented, if among eight thousand girls there were none of the ignorant and depraved. Calumniators have asserted, that *all* were vile, because they knew *some* to be so; and the sins of *a few* have been visited upon *the many*. While the mass of the worthy and virtuous have been unnoticed, in the even tenor of their way, the evil deeds of a few individuals have been trumpeted abroad, and they have been regarded as specimens of factory girls. It has been said, that factory girls are not thought as much of any where else as they are in Lowell. If this be true, I am very glad of it; it is quite to our credit to be most respected where we are best known. Still, I presume, there are girls here who are a disgrace to the city, to their sex, and to humanity. But *they* do not fix the tone of public sentiment, and their morals are not the standard. . . . Our well filled churches and lecture halls, and the high character of our clergymen and lecturers, will testify that the state of morals and intelligence is not low.

Mr. Brownson, I suppose, would not judge of our moral characters by our church-going tendencies; but as many do, a word on this subject may not be amiss. That there are many in Lowell who do not regularly attend any meeting; is as true as the correspondent of the Boston Times once represented it; but for this there are various reasons. There are many who come here for but a short time, and who are willing for a while to forego every usual privilege, that they may carry back to their homes the greatest possible sum they can save. There are widows earning money for the maintenance and education of their children; there are daughters providing for their aged and destitute parents; and there are widows, single women, and girls, endeavoring to obtain the wherewithal to furnish some other home than a factory boarding-house. Pew rent, and the dress which custom has wrongly rendered essential, are expenses which they cannot afford, and they spend their Sabbaths in rest, reading, and meditation. There may also be many other motives to prevent a regular attendance at church, besides a disinclination to gratify and cultivate the moral sentiments.

There have also been nice calculations made, as to the small proportion which the amount of money deposited in the Savings Bank bears to that earned in the city; but this is not all that is saved. Some is deposited in Banks at other places, and some is put into the hands of personal friends. Still, much that is earned is immediately, though not foolishly, spent. Much that none but the parties concerned will ever know of, goes to procure comforts and necessaries for some lowly home, and a great deal is spent for public benevolent purposes. The fifteen hundred dollars which were collected in one day for Missionary purposes by a single denomination in our city, though it may speak of what Mrs. Gilman calls the "too great tendency to overflow in female benevolence," certainly does not tell of hearts sullied by vice, or souls steeped in infamy. And it is pleasing to view the interest which so many of the factory girls take in the social and religious institutions of this place, who do not call Lowell aught but a temporary home. Many of them stay here longer than they otherwise would, because these institutions have become so dear to them, and the letters which they send here after they do leave, show that the interest was too strong to be easily eradicated. I have known those who left homes of comfort and competence, that they might here enjoy religious privileges which country towns would not afford them. And the Lowell Offering may prove to all who will read it, that there are girls here whose education and intellect place them above the necessity of pursuing an avocation which will inevitably connect them with the ignorant and vicious. . . .

Pleasures of Factory Life

Pleasures there are, even in factory life; and we have many, known only to those of like employment. To be sure it is not so convenient to converse in the mills with those unaccustomed to them; yet we suffer no inconvenience among ourselves. But, aside from the talking, where can you find a more pleasant place for contemplation? There all the powers of the mind are made active by our animating exercise; and having but one kind of labor to perform, we need not give all our thoughts to that, but leave them measurably free for reflection on other matters.

The subjects for pleasurable contemplation, while attending to our work, are numerous and various. Many of them are immediately around us. For example: In the mill we see displays of the wonderful power of the mind. Who can closely examine all the movements of the complicated, curious machinery, and not be led to the reflection, that the mind is boundless, and is destined to rise higher and still higher; and that it can accomplish almost any thing on which it fixes its attention!

In the mills, we are not so far from God and nature, as many persons might suppose. We cultivate, and enjoy much pleasure in cultivating flowers and plants. A large and beautiful variety of plants is placed around the walls of the rooms, giving them more the appearance of a flower garden than a workshop. It is there we inhale the sweet perfume of the rose, the lily, and geranium; and, with them, send the sweet incense of sincere gratitude to the bountiful Giver of these rich blessings. And who can live with such a rich and pleasant source of instruction opened to him, and not be wiser and better, and consequently more happy.

Another great source of pleasure is, that by becoming operatives, we are often enabled to assist aged parents who have become too infirm to provide for themselves; or perhaps to educate some orphan brother or sister, and fit them for future usefulness. And is there no pleasure in all this? No pleasure in relieving the distressed and removing their heavy burdens? And is there no pleasure in rendering ourselves by such acts worthy of the confidence and respect of those with whom we are associated?

Another source is found in the fact of our being acquainted with some person or persons that reside in almost every part of the country. And through these we become familiar with some incidents that interest and amuse us wherever we journey; and cause us to feel a greater interest in the scenery, inasmuch as there are gathered pleasant associations about every town, and almost every house and tree that may meet our view.

Let no one suppose that the 'factory girls' are without guardian. We are placed in the care of overseers who feel under moral obligations to look after our interests; and, if we are sick, to acquaint themselves with our situation and wants; and, if need be, to remove us to the Hospital, where we are sure to have the best attendance, provided by the benevolence of our Agents and Superintendents.

In Lowell, we enjoy abundant means of information, especially in the way of public lectures. The time of lecturing is appointed to suit the convenience of the operatives; and sad indeed would be the picture of our Lyceums, Institutes, and scientific Lecture rooms, if all the operatives should absent themselves.

And last, though not least, is the pleasure of being associated with the institutions of religion, and thereby availing ourselves of the Library, Bible Class, Sabbath School, and all other means of religious instruction. Most of us, when at home, live in the country, and therefore cannot enjoy these privileges to the same extent; and many of us not at all. And surely we ought to regard these as sources of pleasure.

Mary Paul's Letters, 1845–1848

[Woodstock, Vt.] Saturday Sept. 13th 1845

Dear Father . . .

I want you to consent to let me go to Lowell if you can. I think it would be much better for me than to stay about here. I could earn more to begin with than I can any where about here. I am in need of clothes which I cannot get if I stay about here and for that reason I want to go to Lowell or some other place. We all think if I could go with some steady girl that I might do well. I want you to think of it and make up your mind. Mercy Jane Griffith is going to start in four or five weeks. Aunt Miller and Aunt Sarah think it would be a good chance for me to go if you would consent—which I want you to do if possible. I want to see you and talk with you about it. . . .

Mary

Lowell Nov 20th 1845

Dear Father

An opportunity now presents itself which I improve in writing to you. I started for this place at the time I talked of which was Thursday. . . . On Saturday after I got here Luthera Griffith went round with me to find a place but we were unsuccessful. On Monday we started again and were more successful. We found a place in a spinning room and the next morning I went to work. I like very well have 50 cts first payment increasing every payment as I get along in work have a first rate overseer and a very good boarding place. I work on the Lawrence Corporation. Mill is No 2 spinning room. . . .

Thomas Dublin, ed., "Letters of Mary Paul, 1845–1848," in *Farm to Factory*, 1981, 100–109, copyright © 1981 Columbia University Press. Used by permission.

It cost me $3.25 to come. Stage fare was $3.00 and lodging at Windsor, 25 cts. Had to pay only 25 cts for board for 9 days after I got here before I went into the mill. Had 2.50 left with which I got a bonnet and some other small articles. . . .

excuse bad writing and mistakes
This from your own daughter
Mary

Lowell Dec 21st 1845

Dear Father

I received your letter on Thursday the 14th with much pleasure. I am well which is one comfort. My life and health are spared while others are cut off. Last Thursday one girl fell down and broke her neck which caused instant death. She was going in or coming out of the mill and slipped down it being very icy. The same day a man was killed by the [railroad] cars. Another had nearly all of his ribs broken. Another was nearly killed by falling down and having a bale of cotton fall on him. Last Tuesday we were paid. In all I had six dollars and sixty cents paid $4.68 for board. With the rest I got me a pair of rubbers and a pair of 50.cts shoes. Next payment I am to have a dollar a week beside my board. We have not had much snow the deepest being not more than 4 inches. It has been very warm for winter.

Perhaps you would like something about our regulations about going in and coming out of the mill. At 5 o'clock in the morning the bell rings for the folks to get up and get breakfast. At half past six it rings for the girls to get up and at seven they are called into the mill. At half past 12 we have dinner are called back again at one and stay till half past seven. I get along very well with my work. I can doff as fast as any girl in our room. I think I shall have frames before long. The usual time allowed for learning is six months but I think I shall have frames before I have been in three as I get along so fast. I think that the factory is the best place for me and if any girl wants employment I advise them to come to Lowell. . . .

This from
Mary S Paul

Lowell April 12th 1846

Dear Father

You wanted to know what I am doing. I am at work in a spinning room and tending four sides of warp which is one girls work. The overseer tells me that he never had a girl get along better than I do and that he will do the best he can by me. I stand it well, though they tell me that I am growing very poor. I was paid nine shillings a week last payment and am to have more this one. . . .

I have a very good boarding place have enough to eat and that which is good enough. The girls are all kind and obliging. The girls that I room with are all from Vermont and good girls too. Now I will tell you about our rules at the boarding house. We have none in particular except that we have to go to bed about 10. o'clock. At half past 4 in the morning the bell rings for us to get up and at five for us to go into the mill. At seven we are called out to breakfast are allowed half an hour between bells and the same at noon till the first of May when we have three quarters [of an hour] till the first of September. We have dinner at half past 12 and supper at seven. . . .

Yours affectionately
Mary S Paul

Lowell Nov 5th 1848

Dear Father

Doubtless you have been looking for a letter from me all the week past. I would have written but wished to find whether I should be able to stand it—to do the work that I am now doing. I was unable to get my old place in the cloth room on the Suffolk or on any other corporation. I next tried the dressrooms on the Lawrence Cor[poration], but did not succe[e]d in getting a place. I almost concluded to give up and go back to Claremont, but thought I would try once more. So I went to my old overseer on the Tremont Cor. I had no idea that he would want one, but he *did,* and I went to work last Tuesday—warping—the same work I used to do.

It is *very* hard indeed and sometimes I think I shall not be able to endure it. I never worked so hard in my life but perhaps I shall get used to it. I shall try hard to do so for there is no other work that I can do unless I spin and that I shall not undertake on any account. I presume you have heard before this that the wages are to be reduced on the 20th of this month. It is *true* and there seems to be a good deal of excitement on the subject but I can not tell what will be the consequence. The companies pretend they are losing immense sums every *day* and therefore they are obliged to lessen the wages, but this seems perfectly absurd to me for they are constantly making *repairs* and it seems to me that this would not be if there were really any danger of their being obliged to *stop* the mills.

It is very difficult for any one to get into the mill on any corporation. All seem to be very full of help. I expect to be paid about two dollars a week but it will be dearly earned. I cannot tell how it is but never since I have worked in the mill have I been so very tired as I have for the last week but it may be owing to the long rest I have had for the last six months. . . .

(Monday Eve) I have been to work today and think I shall manage to get along with the work. I am not so tired as I was last week. I have not yet found out what wages I shall get but presume they will be about $2.00 per week exclusive of board. . . .

Write soon. Yours affectionately
Mary S Paul

David Johnson's Description of Shoebinding, 1880

The shoe-binder of Lynn performed a very important part in the domestic economy of the household thirty, or more, years ago. The shoemaker's wife and daughters—if he had any—were often his best bowers, enabling him to weather many a financial tempest—on a small scale—and were often the chief reliance when the head of the family, through sickness, or other causes, could no longer work to support the family. As the wife and daughters "bound" the shoes made by the workmen of the family, the "uppers," all ready to "bind," with the needful silk, cotton and thread, and sometimes beeswax, made part of the load carried home in the "little cart," or in some other way, from the boss' shop. Then there would be a little delay, perhaps, until a shoe was bound, with which to start off the new lot.

But, generally, before the "jour" got his "stock" seasoned, one or two "uppers" were ready, and enough were usually bound ahead to keep all hands at work. And so, now and then, the order would be heard—"Come, John, go and see if your mother has got a shoe bound; I 'm all ready to last it." It may be well to notice here that the "jours" often called the "uppers" *shoes,* and the soles *"stuffs."* Accordingly, one would hear the remark—"The 'boss' did n't give me 'stuffs' enough"—meaning soles—or, "Come, William, go over to Isaiah's and get me a lot of shoes and 'stuffs.' " The dictionaries do not recognize this use of the word "stuffs," but the shoemakers did.

The style of "uppers" in vogue some forty years ago, and later, was a "foxed" boot. This foxing was of kid, with lasting top, and the boot laced in front. A few years later the "gaiter boot" came into fashion, which usually had a lower foxing, and the "lace" on the side. These were usually made "right" and "left." The binding of these boots, when it was done well, was quite a nice job. The price of binding ranged from seventeen to twenty-five cents a pair, and a smart woman could bind four pairs a day, and sometimes even more.

It will be seen that such help was no small item in maintaining the family. Many a little home was earned by "all hands," father and mother, boys and girls, who worked for years, cheered by the hope of paying off the mortgage, so that they could have a "house of their own."

Sarah Trask's Diary, 1849

Jan 25   Stay down to C. [Sarah's friend Catherine], all night for her to show me about my shoes, but did not do much, but I will try and see what I can do, for I cannot afford to make a coat for, 33, Cts. for, L. O. Hale, if I can get anny thing else to do.

Mary H. Blewett, "I Am Doom to Disapointment: The Diaries of a Beverly, Massachusetts, Shoebinder, Sarah E. Trask, 1849–51" *Essex Institute Historical Collections,* CXVII (1981), 200–204. Reprinted by permission of the Essex Institute, Salem, Massachusetts.

Jan 26   Stitched on three pairs of shoes, have I not done bravely, hope I shall do more than that, tomorrow, or I shall have to go to California, to seek my fortune, oh California for that all I hear, most every one is going there and I fear many will go that will never come back to their friends again. I am glad that I have not anny friends gone there.

Jan 31   . . . winter seem so dull. At home all day and in the evening. Oh my shoes they do go of so slow only four pairs and a half today, I wish they were all done, but what is the use of that it will not get them done anny sooner; so I must not despair. . . .

Feb 20   . . . Just for fun I counted the stiches in a shoe, the size was fives, 719 in the whole, 250 on the top, 173 in the filling, 120, on the side seams or 65 in one side, 69 in the closeing or 23 on a seam, 58 in the lineing, or 29, on a side, 99 on the surgeing. . . .

March 7   At home all day, in the evening went down to Hannah, and Mary Ellen, for it seem as though I must see her before I went to [prayer meeting], she was binding shoes four Cts. a pair and thread found, that is very good I think for thoes kind.

March 14   Another wedding last night one of our shop girls, all getting married. Mr. Shale will not have anny to work for him, if they go [off] so fast as they have done, this two or three years. It is three years last Novemeber [*sic*] since I went [to work binding shoes], there as been 20 Married. . . .

April 10   My shoes are not done yet, I begin to think that I am Lazy, and yet I try to do all I can, Mother tells that I run about [too] much, to do anny work, I can't think so, but I suppose I shall have to. . . .

April 17   today I have had another lot of shoes come, although I have not got my others done, but I hope I shall soon. . . .

April 21   This day I have been trying to finish my shoes, and have got them done and I am so glad. . . .

April 23   This day I have begun my gaiter boots, I have not finish anny tonight but hope I shall tomorrow. L.A.B. came in with her work a little while, and we saw a large bark come down the Southern way and go into Salem, we like so well to look at it, that we did not so much work as we ought to. . . .

April 26   This day [I] have finished four pairs of boots, just fifty cents this week, I hope I shall do four pair more before Saterday.

April 28   At home today, finishing my week work eight pairs of boots one dollar; how smart, beside my housework, and last tuesday I work for Lizzy, so there the duty of the week. I almost think I shall make my fortune soon. . . .

May 10   At home all day, housework and shoes have been my work to-day. . . .

Slavery and
the Old South

Artisans' struggle against the factory system proved to be a central theme in northern industrial society, while slavery and emancipation defined southern economic and social life. Historians now recognize that cotton pickers, cane cutters, household servants, and slave carpenters were also part of working-class America. So too were the tenant farmers, sharecroppers, and farm laborers who emerged from the southern agricultural economy after the Civil War. Black labor had built the antebellum southern economy, and its cotton exports generated the single greatest source of capital that industrialized America.

But was the slave system of the American South merely a more exploitative form of northern "wage slavery"? Were plantation owners simply agricultural capitalists who availed themselves of a particularly low-cost class of laborers? And what did the slaves think of their own servitude? How did they resist, and how did they accommodate the will of their masters? Historians have debated these issues for years. Many now think of the antebellum South as a society quite different from that of the North, and one characterized by its own peculiar set of social relations. Some masters did hire out their slaves by the month or year to mines, docks, and workshops, but most considered plantation agriculture the highest and best use of their human property because it insured their political and social dominance in a society fundamentally at odds with that of the bourgeois, capitalist North.

The plantation ruling class could hardly be expected to relinquish its power voluntarily, and it took a war of revolutionary proportions to abolish slavery in the American South once and for all. Although the Union armies freed the slaves, the labor question formed the heart of Reconstruction politics in the years immediately after the war. A bitter conflict over the character and control of agricultural labor became central to the meaning of blacks' freedom and emancipation. Would the former slaves become peasant proprietors cultivating their own land, or rural wage laborers supervised by old-regime slavemasters? Would women be forced to work in the fields, as they had under slavery, or would their labor be of a more domestic sort? And finally, would the former slaves

have access to education, the franchise, and political organizations that repre-
sented their own interests? The outcome of this intensely fought struggle, in
which northern capital and the federal government had a significant stake,
would prove decisive in shaping the class structure and the political life of the
southern states for generations afterward.

✢ D O C U M E N T S

Plantation management was a complicated task, involving the coordination of
many types of labor. Planters often kept detailed operational records in diary and
account books. A page from such a log, listing slaves, animals, and other tools of
production, appears as the first document. In the second document, Solomon
Northup, a free black kidnapped into slavery, describes cotton planting and
harvesting on the Bayou Boeuf in Avoyelles Parish, Louisiana. While both sexes
engaged in such field work, planters designated some jobs as "women's work,"
as is seen in the third document, which comprises selections from the oral
histories that elderly ex-slaves offered federal historians in the 1930s. The fourth
document, a planter's advice on rearing slave children, sustains abolitionists'
charges that masters bred slaves for the market in the Old South. But not all
slaves worked on plantations; the black abolitionist Frederick Douglass had been
hired out as a shipyard apprentice while still a slave. In the last document, he
shows how competition with slave laborers kindled a racist response among
those white workers whose wages they undercut.

A Record of Plantation Management, 1850

Daily Records of Passing Events on _Pleasant Hill_ Plantation During the Week Commencing on _22_ Day of _Sept._, 185_0_, _Jones_ Overseer*

Sunday

Monday
A very dry time and verry warm. Waggon went to Clinton with 6 Bales Cotton & 5 Mules & Back

Tuesday
A verry warm and dry day wanting rain verry much. Finished cutting Hay in Orchard to day verry healthy in Country

Wednesday

Thursday
A verry warm dry dusty day, Cotton wanting rain verry much, opening two fast, I had my Cogs put away in oat house, Put one Man to David Jacksons Jack I hear of but little Sickness

Friday
A shower of rain after noon with a good deal of Thunder. I went to saw Mill with one waggon after plank for fences, 3 Boys pressed 6 Bales & broke the ferrale. The Cotton pickers lossed about two hours by the rain

Saturday

* Handwritten entries appear in italics.

Daily Records of Cotton Picked on _Pleasant Hill_ Plantation During the Week Commencing on _21st_ Day of _Octr._, 1850_, _Jones_ Overseer

NAME	NO.	MONDAY	TUESDAY	WEDNESDAY	THURSDAY	FRIDAY	SATURDAY	Week's Picking Brought Forward
Sandy	1	Ginning	Pressing	Ginning	Ginning	Ginning	Ginning	
Scott	2	Clearing	Pressing	Clearing	Clearing	Hauling corn		64
Solomon	3	Clearing	Hauling rails	Clearing	Gone to Clinton	Hauling		54
Bill	4	Clearing	Do	Clearing	Clearing	Hauling		30
Jerry	5	Clearing	Clearing	Clearing	Clearing	Do Do		90
Isaac	6	Clearing	Clearing	Clearing	Clearing	Do Do		70
Jim	7	Sick	Sick	Sick	Sick	Sick		Sick
Dotson	8	Gone after shoes	Clearing	Clearing	Clearing	Ho corn		60

The Planter's Annual Record of his Negroes upon *Pleasant Hill* Plantation, During the year 1850, *E. J. Capell* Overseer

MALES

NAME	AGE	VALUE AT COMMENCEMENT OF THE YEAR	VALUE AT END OF THE YEAR
John	70	$ 50.00	75.00
Tom	49	1000.00	1200.00
Sandy	38	600.00	800.00
Edmund	35	1000.00	1300.00
Jerry	40	700.00	950.00
Solomon	38	700.00	950.00
William	24	1000.000	1100.00
Charles	10	500.00	650.00
Tom	5	250.00	275.
Monroe	4	200.00	225.
Aaron	3	175.00	200
Jerry	1	75.00	100

FEMALES

NAME	AGE	VALUE AT COMMENCEMENT OF THE YEAR	VALUE AT END OF THE YEAR
Hannah	60	$100.00	125.00
Mary	34	800.00	900.00
Fanny	23	800.00	900.00
Rachel Sen.	32	675.00	750.00
Lucy	28	600.00	750.00
Azaline	13	600.00	700.00
Sarah	9	350.00	450.00
Harriet	8	300.00	400.00
Melissa	3	100.00	125.00
Carolina	3	150.00	150.00
Laura	1	100.00	125.00

The Planter's Statement of the Expenses of _Pleasant Hill_ Plantation, During the Year 185_0_, ——— Overseer

	TO WHOM, HOW, WHEN AND WHERE PAID, &C.	SUM
Overseer's wages,	To Tom, Cash, Febry 1st Paid at home	10.00
	To R. M. Jenkins at Thickwood Precinct on	
Taxes,	27th of January 1851 for 1850	53.00
Pork, bacon, &c.,	None purchased	
	To 3 Barrels of Molasses @ 21¢ To Clauss	
Corn, flour, &c.,	& McCombs	25.20
	B Sara on the 7th Feby	
	To 10 New Plows part in Centi & part at	
Implements & tools,	home Jan 1st	51.00
	1 Two horse Waggon 1 Cart & Sundries	
	Septr 30th	140.00
	1 Sett Harness 1 Sett Cart Do	
	1 Bellows for Shop Oct. 30th	60.00
Bale rope & bagging,	To Cash paid for 477½ yds Rope	33.14
	" for 445 yds. Bagging	56.60
Blacksmith, carpenter		
&c.,	To Cash paid Carpenter	190.00
	Cash paid Blacksmith	7.25
Physician and		
apothecary,	To Cash paid J. R. Caulfield & Drug Store	21.00

The Slave Solomon Northup's View of Cotton Planting and Harvesting, 1854

. . . The ground is prepared by throwing up beds or ridges, with the plough—back-furrowing, it is called. Oxen and mules, the latter almost exclusively, are used in ploughing. The women as frequently as the men perform this labor, feeding, currying, and taking care of their teams, and in all respects doing the field and stable work, precisely as do the ploughboys of the North.

The beds, or ridges, are six feet wide, that is, from water furrow to water furrow. A plough drawn by one mule is then run along the top of the ridge or center of the bed, making the drill, into which a girl usually drops the seed, which she carries in a bag hung round her neck. Behind her comes a mule and harrow, covering up the seed, so that two mules, three slaves, a plough and harrow, are employed in planting a row of cotton. This is done in the months of March and April. Corn is planted in February. When there are no cold rains, the cotton usually makes its appearance in a week. In the course of eight or ten days afterwards the first hoeing is commenced. This is performed in part, also, by the aid of the plough and mule. The plough passes as near as possible to the cotton on both sides, throwing the furrow from it. Slaves follow with their hoes, cutting up the grass and cotton, leaving hills two feet and a half apart. This is called scraping cotton. In two weeks more commences the second hoeing. This time the furrow is thrown towards the cotton. Only one stalk, the largest, is now left standing in each hill. In another fortnight it is hoed the third time, throwing the furrow towards the cotton in the same manner as before, and killing all the grass between the rows. About the first of July, when it is a foot high or thereabouts, it is hoed the fourth and last time. Now the whole space between the rows is ploughed, leaving a deep water furrow in the center. During all these hoeings the overseer or driver follows the slaves on horseback with a whip. . . . The fastest hoer takes the lead row. He is usually about a rod in advance of his companions. If one of them passes him, he is whipped. If one falls behind or is a moment idle, he is whipped. In fact, the lash is flying from morning until night, the whole day long. The hoeing season thus continues from April until July, a field having no sooner been finished once, than it is commenced again.

In the latter part of August begins the cotton picking season. At this time each slave is presented with a sack. A strap is fastened to it, which goes over the neck, holding the mouth of the sack breast high, while the bottom reaches nearly to the ground. Each one is also presented with a large basket that will hold about two barrels. This is to put the cotton in when the sack is filled. The baskets are carried to the field and placed at the beginning of the rows.

When a new hand, one unaccustomed to the business, is sent for the first time into the field, he is whipped up smartly, and made for that day to pick as fast as he can possibly. At night it is weighed, so that his capability in cotton picking is known. He must bring in the same weight each night following. If it falls short, it is considered evidence that he has been laggard, and a greater or less number of lashes is the penalty.

An ordinary day's work is two hundred pounds. A slave who is accustomed to picking, is punished, if he or she brings in a less quantity than that. There is a great difference among them as regards this kind of labor. Some of them seem to have a natural knack, or quickness, which enables them to pick with great celerity, and with both hands, while others, with whatever practice or industry, are utterly unable to come up to the ordinary standard. Such hands are taken from the cotton field and employed in other business. Patsey, of whom I shall have more to say, was known as the most remarkable cotton picker on Bayou Bœuf. She picked with both hands and with such surprising rapidity, that five hundred pounds a day was not unusual for her.

Each one is tasked, therefore, according to his picking abilities, none, however, to come short of two hundred weight. I, being unskillful always in that business, would have satisfied my master by bringing in the latter quantity, while on the other hand, Patsey would surely have been beaten if she failed to produce twice as much. . . .

The hands are required to be in the cotton field as soon as it is light in the morning, and, with the exception of ten or fifteen minutes, which is given them at noon to swallow their allowance of cold bacon, they are not permitted to be a moment idle until it is too dark to see, and when the moon is full, they often times labor till the middle of the night. They do not dare to stop even at dinner time, nor return to the quarters, however late it be, until the order to halt is given by the driver.

The day's work over in the field, the baskets are "toted," or in other words, carried to the gin-house, where the cotton is weighed. No matter how fatigued and weary he may be—no matter how much he longs for sleep and rest—a slave never approaches the gin-house with his basket of cotton but with fear. If it falls short in weight—if he has not performed the full task appointed him, he knows that he must suffer. And if he has exceeded it by ten or twenty pounds, in all probability his master will measure the next day's task accordingly. So, whether he has too little or too much, his approach to the gin-house is always with fear and trembling. Most frequently they have too little, and therefore it is they are not anxious to leave the field. After weighing, follow the whippings; and then the baskets are carried to the cotton house, and their contents stored away like hay, all hands being sent in to tramp it down. If the cotton is not dry, instead of taking it to the gin-house at once, it is laid upon platforms, two feet high, and some three times as wide, covered with boards or plank, with narrow walks running between them.

This done, the labor of the day is not yet ended, by any means. Each one must then attend to his respective chores. One feeds the mules, another the swine—another cuts the wood, and so forth; besides, the packing is all done by candle light. Finally, at a late hour, they reach the quarters, sleepy and overcome with the long day's toil. Then a fire must be kindled in the cabin, the corn ground in the small hand-mill, and supper, and dinner for the next day in the field, prepared. All that is allowed them is corn and bacon, which is given out at the corncrib and smoke-house every Sunday morning. Each one receives, as his weekly allowance, three and a half pounds of bacon, and corn enough to make a peck of meal. That is all— no tea, coffee, sugar, and with the exception of a very scanty sprinkling now and then, no salt. . . .

Twentieth-Century Women Recall
Their Work Lives in Slavery, 1930s

. . . I had to do everythin' dey was to do on de outside. Work in de field, chop wood, hoe corn, till sometime I feels like my back surely break. I done everythin' 'cept split rails. I never did split no rails.

This race coming up now don't know nothing 'bout hard work. Over there, see a road all turned up and you would see men and women both throwing up dirt and rocks; the men would haul it off and the women would take picks and things and get it up. You could, any day see a woman, a whole lot of 'em making on a road. Could look up and see ten women up over dar on the hill plowing and look over the other way and see ten more. I have done ever thing on a farm what a man done 'cept cut wheat.

I split rails like man. I used a iron wedge drove into the wood with a maul.

Marster Boles didn't have many slave on de farm, but lots in brickyard. I toted bricks and put 'em down where dey had to be. Six bricks each load all day. I fired de furnace for three years. Standin' front wid hot fire on my face. Hard work, but God was with me.

At night de men chops wood and hauls poles to build fences and de women folks has to spin four cuts of thread and make all de clothes. Some has to card cotton to make quilts and some weave and knits stockin's. Marse give each one a chore to do at night and iffen it warn't did when we went to bed, we's whipped. One time I fells plumb asleep befo' I finished shellin' some corn.

My young mistress name Catherine. When her marry, I was give to them for a housemaid, 'cause I was trim and light complected lak you see I is dis very day. Young missie say, "You come in my room Delia, I wants to see if I can put up wid you." I goes in dat room, winter time mind you, and Miss Charlotte sets down befo' de fire. Well, she allowed to me, "Delia, put kettle water on de fire." So I does in a jiffy. Her next command was: "Would you please be so kind as to sweep and tidy up de room?" I do all dat, then she say, "You is goin' to make maid, a good one!" She give a silvery giggle and says, "I just had you put on dat water for to see if you was goin' to make any slop. No, No! You didn't spill a drop, you ain't goin' to make no sloppy maid, you just fine." Then her call her mother in. "See how pretty Delia's made dis room, look at them curtains, draw back just right, observe de pitcher, and de towels on de rack of de washstand, my I'm proud of her!" She give old mistress a hug and a kiss and thank her for de present. Dat present was me. De happiness of dat minute is on me to dis day.

Dey was a big weavin' room where de blankets was wove, and cloth for de winter clothes. Linda Herndon and Milla Edwards was de head weavers; dey looked after de weavin' of de fancy blankets. De cardin' and spinnin' room was full of niggers. I can hear dem spinnin' wheels now turnin' round and saying hum-m-m-m, hum-m-m-m.

Mammy Rachel stayed in de dyein' room. She knew every kind of root, bark, leaf, and berry dat made red, blue, green, or whatever color she wanted. Dey had a big shelter where de dye pots set over de coals. Mammy Rachel would fill de pots with water, den she put in de roots, bark and stuff and boil de juice out. Den she strain it and put in de salt and vinegar to set de color. After de wool and cotton done been carded and spun to thread, Mammy take de hanks and drop dem in de pot of boilin' dye. She stir dem round and lift dem up an down with a stick, and when she hang dem up on de line in de sun, dey was every color of de rainbow. When dey dripped dry dey was sent to de weavin' room.

When I was 13 years old my ol' mistress put me wid a doctor who learned me how to be a midwife. Dat was 'cause so many women on de plantation was catchin' babies. I stayed wid dat doctor, Dr. McGill his name was, for 5 years. I got to be good. Got so he'd sit down an' I'd do all de work.

When I come home, I made a lot o' money for old miss. Lots of times, didn't sleep regular or git my meals on time for three–four days. Cause when dey call, I always went. Brought as many white as culled children. I's brought lots of 'em an' I ain't never lost a case. You know why. It's cause I used my haid. When I'd go in, I'd take a look at de women, an' if it was beyond me, I'd say, "Dis is a doctor case. Dis ain't no case for a midwife. You git a doctor." An' dey'd have to get one. I'd jes' stan' before de lookin' glass, an I wouldn't budge. Dey couldn't make me.

A Planter on Child Rearing, 1836

I have a nurse appointed to superintend all my little negroes, and a nursery built for them. If they are left to be protected by their parents, they will most assuredly be neglected. I have known parents take out an allowance for their children and actually steal it from them, to purchase articles at some shop. Besides, when they would be honest to their offspring, from their other occupations, they have not the time to attend to them properly. The children get their food irregularly, and when they do get it, it is only half done. They are suffered, by not having one to attend to them, to expose themselves; and hence many of the deaths which occur on our plantations.

I have just stated that I have a nursery for my little negroes, with an old woman or nurse to superintend and cook for them, and to see that their clothes and bedding are well attended to. She makes the little ones, generally speaking, both girls and boys, mend and wash their own clothes, and do many other little matters, such as collecting litter for manure, &c. In this they take great pleasure, and it has the tendency to bring them up to industrious habits. The nurse also cooks for them three times a day; and she always has some little meat to dress for them, or the clabber or sour milk from the dairy to mix their food. In *sickness* she sees that they are well attended to; and from having many of them together, one is taught to wait upon the other. My little negroes are consequently very healthy; and from pursuing the plan I have laid down, I am confident that I raise more of them, than where a different system is followed.

Frederick Douglass Confronts Working-Class Racism, 1836

. . . Very soon after I went to Baltimore to live, Master Hugh succeeded in getting me hired to Mr. William Gardiner, an extensive ship-builder on Fell's Point. I was placed there to learn to calk, a trade of which I already had some knowledge, gained while in Mr. Hugh Auld's ship-yard. Gardiner's, however, proved a very unfavorable place for the accomplishment of the desired object. Mr. Gardiner was that season engaged in building two large man-of-war vessels, professedly for the Mexican government. These vessels were to be launched in the month of July of that year, and in failure thereof Mr. Gardiner would forfeit a very considerable sum of money. So, when I entered the ship-yard, all was hurry and driving. There were in the yard about one hundred men; of these, seventy or eighty were regular carpenters—privileged men. There was no time for a raw hand to learn anything. Every man had to do that which he knew how to do, and in entering the yard Mr. Gardiner had directed me to do whatever the carpenters told me to do. This was placing me at the beck and call of about seventy-five men. I was to regard all these as my masters. Their word was to be my law. My situation was a trying one. I was called a dozen ways in the space of a single minute. I needed a dozen pairs of hands. Three or four voices would strike my ear at the same moment. It was "Fred, come help me to cant this timber here,"—"Fred, come carry this timber yonder,"—"Fred, bring that roller here,"—"Fred, go get a fresh can of water,"—"Fred, come help saw off the end of this timber,"—"Fred, go quick and get the crow-bar,"—"Fred, hold on the end of this fall,"— "Fred, go to the blacksmith's shop and get a new punch,"—"Halloo, Fred! run and bring me a cold-chisel,"—"I say, Fred, bear a hand, and get up a fire under the steam-box as quick as lightning,"—"Hullo, nigger! come turn this grindstone,"—"Come, come; move, move! and *bowse* this timber forward,"—"I say, darkey, blast your eyes! why don't you heat up some pitch?"—"Halloo! halloo! halloo! (three voices at the same time)"—"Come here; go there; hold on where you are. D—n you, if you move I'll knock your brains out!" Such, my dear reader, is a glance at the school which was mine during the first eight months of my stay at Gardiner's ship-yard. At the end of eight months Master Hugh refused longer to allow me to remain with Gardiner. The circumstance which led to this refusal was the committing of an outrage upon me, by the white apprentices of the ship-yard. The fight was a desperate one, and I came out of it shockingly mangled. I was cut and bruised in sundry places, and my left eye was nearly knocked out of its socket. The facts which led to this brutal outrage upon me illustrate a phase of slavery which was destined to become an important element in the overthrow of the slave system, and I may therefore state them with some minuteness. That phase was this—the conflict of slavery with the interests of white mechanics and laborers. In the country this conflict was not so apparent; but in cities, such as Baltimore, Richmond, New Orleans, Mobile, etc., it was seen pretty clearly. The slaveholders, with a craftiness peculiar to themselves, by encouraging the enmity of the poor laboring white man against the blacks, succeeded in making the said white man almost as much a slave as the black slave himself. . . .

Until a very little while before I went there, white and black carpenters worked side by side in the ship-yards of Mr. Gardiner, Mr. Duncan, Mr. Walter Price and Mr. Robb. Nobody seemed to see any impropriety in it. Some of the blacks were first-rate workmen and were given jobs requiring the highest skill. All at once, however, the white carpenters swore that they would no longer work on the same stage with negroes. Taking advantage of the heavy contract resting upon Mr. Gardiner to have the vessels for Mexico ready to launch in July, and of the difficulty of getting other hands at that season of the year, they swore that they would not strike another blow for him unless he would discharge his free colored workmen. Now, although this movement did not extend to me in *form,* it did reach me in *fact.* The spirit which it awakened was one of malice and bitterness toward colored people *generally,* and I suffered with the rest, and suffered severely. My fellow-apprentices very soon began to feel it to be degrading to work with me. They began to put on high looks and to talk contemptuously and maliciously of "the niggers," saying that they would take the "country," and that they "ought to be killed." Encouraged by workmen who, knowing me to be a slave, made no issue with Mr. Gardiner about my being there, these young men did their utmost to make it impossible for me to stay. They seldom called me to do anything without coupling the call with a curse, and Edward North, the biggest in everything, rascality included, ventured to strike me, whereupon I picked him up and threw him into the dock. Whenever any of them struck me I struck back again, regardless of consequences. I could manage any of them *singly,* and so long as I could keep them from combining I got on very well. In the conflict which ended my stay at Mr. Gardiner's I was beset by four of them at once—Ned North, Ned Hayes, Bill Stewart, and Tom Humphreys. Two of them were as large as myself, and they came near killing me, in broad daylight. One came in front, armed with a brick; there was one at each side and one behind, and they closed up all around me. I was struck on all sides; and while I was attending to those in front I received a blow on my head from behind, dealt with a heavy hand-spike. I was completely stunned by the blow, and fell heavily on the ground among the timbers. Taking advantage of my fall they rushed upon me and began to pound me with their fists. With a view of gaining strength, I let them lay on for awhile after I came to myself. They had done me little damage, so far; but finally getting tired of that sport I gave a sudden surge, and despite their weight I rose to my hands and knees. Just as I did this one of their number planted a blow with his boot in my left eye, which for a time seemed to have burst my eye-ball. When they saw my eye completely closed, my face covered with blood, and I staggering under the stunning blows they had given me, they left me. As soon as I gathered strength I picked up the hand-spike and madly enough attempted to pursue them; but here the carpenters interfered and compelled me to give up my pursuit. It was impossible to stand against so many.

Dear reader, you can hardly believe the statement, but it is true and therefore I write it down; that no fewer than fifty white men stood by and saw this brutal and shameful outrage committed, and not a man of them all interposed a single word of mercy. There were four against one, and that one's face was beaten and battered most horribly, and no one said, "that is enough"; but some cried out, "Kill him! kill him! kill the d—n nigger! knock his brains out! he struck a white person!" I mention this inhuman outcry to show the character of the men and the spirit of the times at Gardiner's ship-yard; and, indeed, in Baltimore generally, in 1836. As I look back to this period, I am almost amazed that I was not murdered outright, so murderous was the spirit which prevailed there. On two other occasions while there I came near losing my life. On one of these, I was driving bolts in the hold through the keelson, with Hayes. In its course the bolt bent. Hayes cursed me and said that it was my blow which bent the bolt. I denied this and charged it upon him. In a fit of rage he seized an adze and darted toward me. I met him with a maul and parried his blow, or I should have lost my life.

After the united attack of North, Stewart, Hayes, and Humphreys, finding that the carpenters were as bitter toward me as the apprentices, and that the latter were probably set on by the former, I found my only chance for life was in flight. I succeeded in getting away without an additional blow. To strike a white man was death by lynch law, in Gardiner's ship-yard; nor was there much of any other law toward the colored people at that time in any other part of Maryland. . . .

After learning to calk, I sought my own employment, made my own contracts, and collected my own earnings—giving Master Hugh no trouble in any part of the transactions to which I was a party. . . .

I was living among *freemen,* and was in all respects equal to them by nature and attainments. *Why should I be a slave?* There was *no* reason why I should be the thrall of any man. Besides, I was now getting . . . a dollar and fifty cents per day. I contracted for it, worked for it, collected it; it was paid to me, and it was *rightfully* my own; and yet upon every returning Saturday night, this money—my own hard earnings, every cent of it,—was demanded of me and taken from me by Master Hugh. He did not earn it; he had no hand in earning it; why, then should he have it? I owed him nothing. He had given me no schooling, and I had received from him only my food and raiment; and for these, my services were supposed to pay from the first. The right to take my earnings was the right of the robber. He had the power to compel me to give him the fruits of my labor, and this *power* was his only right in the case. . . .

In December 1852 a northerner, Frederick Law Olmsted, embarked on a fourteen-month southern tour, the object of which was to produce articles for the *New York Daily Times*, whose editor was an antislavery Whig. The excerpts in the first document describe parts of Virginia and Mississippi he visited. The status of free blacks was always controversial in the Old South, as the petitions in the second and third documents, from Virginia and South Carolina, illustrate. In general, free blacks were regarded as a dangerous class and many states had laws requiring them to leave shortly after their emancipation.

Frederick Law Olmsted's Observations on the South, 1852–1854

The Wilderness

I have described, perhaps with tedious prolixity, what adventures befell me, and what scenes I passed through in my first day's random riding, for the purpose of giving an idea of the uncultivated and unimproved—rather, sadly worn and misused—condition of some parts, and I judge, of a very large part, of all Eastern Virginia, and of the isolated, lonely and dissociable aspect of the dwelling places of a large part of the people.

Much the same general characteristics pervade the Slave States everywhere, except in certain rich regions, or on the banks of some rivers, or in the vicinity of some great routes of travel and transportation, which have occasioned closer settlement or stimulated public spirit. For hours and hours one has to ride through the unlimited, continual, all-shadowing, all-embracing forest, following roads in the making of which no more labor has been given than was necessary to remove the timber which would obstruct the passage of wagons; and even for days and days he may sometimes travel and see never two dwellings of mankind within sight of each other, only at long distances often several miles asunder these isolated plantation patriarchates. If a traveler leaves the main road to go any distance, it is not to be imagined how difficult it is for him to find his way from one house to any other in particular; his only safety is in the fact that, unless there are mountains or swamps in the way, he is not likely to go many miles upon any wagon or horse track without coming to some white man's habitation.

The Meeting-House

The country passed through, in the early part of my second day's ride, was very similar in general characteristics to that I have already described, only that a rather larger portion of it was cleared, and plantations were more frequent. About eleven o'clock I crossed a bridge and came to the meeting-house I had been expecting to reach by that hour the previous day. It was in the midst of the woods, and the small clearing around it was

From Frederick Law Olmsted, *The Slave States*, edited by Harvey Wish. New York: Capricorn Books, 1959.

still dotted with the stumps of the trees out of whose trunks it had been built; for it was a log structure. In one end there was a single square port, closed by a sliding shutter; in the other end were two doors, both standing open. In front of the doors, a rude scaffolding had been made of poles and saplings, extending out twenty feet from the wall of the house, and this had been covered with boughs of trees, the leaves now withered; a few benches, made of split trunks of trees, slightly hewn with the axe, were arranged under this arbor, as if the religious service was sometimes conducted on the outside in preference to the interior of the edifice. Looking in, I saw that a gallery or loft extended from over the doors, across about one-third the length of the house, access to which was had by a ladder. At the opposite end was a square, unpainted pulpit, and on the floor were rows of rude benches. The house was sufficiently lighted by crevices between the upperlogs.

A Tobacco Plantation

Half an hour after this I arrived at the negro-quarters—a little hamlet of ten or twelve small and dilapidated cabins. Just beyond them was a plain farm-gate, at which several negroes were standing; one of them, a well-made man, with an intelligent countenance and prompt manner, directed me how to find my way to his owner's house. It was still nearly a mile distant; and yet, until I arrived in its immediate vicinity, I saw no cultivated field, and but one clearing. In the edge of this clearing, a number of negroes, male and female, lay stretched out upon the grounds near a small smoking charcoal pit. Their master afterwards informed me that they were burning charcoal for the plantation blacksmith, using the time allowed them for holidays—from Christmas to New Year's—to earn a little money for themselves in this way. He paid them by the bushel for it. When I said that I supposed he allowed them to take what wood they chose for this purpose, he replied that he had five hundred acres covered with wood, which he would be very glad to have any one burn, or clear off in any way. Cannot some Yankee contrive a method of concentrating some of the valuable properties of this old-field pine, so that they may be profitably brought into use in more cultivated regions? Charcoal is now brought to New York from Virginia; but when made from pine it is not very valuable, and will only bear transportation from the banks of the navigable rivers, whence it can be shipped, at one movement, to New York. Turpentine does not flow in sufficient quantity from this variety of the pine to be profitably collected, and for lumber it is of very small value.

Mr. W.'s house was an old family mansion, which he had himself remodeled in the Grecian style, and furnished with a large wooden portico. An oak forest had originally occupied the ground where it stood; but this having been cleared and the soil worn out in cultivation by the previous proprietors, pine woods now surrounded it in every direction, a square of a few acres only being kept clear immediately about it. A number of the old oaks still stood in the rear of the house, and, until Mr. W. commenced his improvements, there had been some in its front. These, however, he had cut away, as interfering with the symmetry of his grounds, and in place of them had planted ailanthus trees in parallel rows.

On three sides of the outer part of the cleared square there was a row of large and comfortable-looking negro-quarters, stables, tobacco-houses, and other offices, built of logs.

Mr. W. was one of the few large planters, of his vicinity who still made the culture of tobacco their principal business. He said there was a general prejudice against tobacco in all the tidewater region of the State, because it was through the culture of tobacco that the once fertile soils had been impoverished; but he did not believe that, at the present value of negroes, their labor could be applied to the culture of grain with any profit, except under peculiarly favorable circumstances. Possibly, the use of guano might make wheat a paying crop, but he still doubted. He had not used it, himself. Tobacco required fresh land, and was rapidly exhausting, but it returned more money for the labor used upon it than anything else, enough more, in his opinion, to pay for the wearing out of the land. If he was well paid for it, he did not know why he should not wear out his land.

His tobacco-fields were nearly all in a distant and lower part of his plantation; land which had been neglected before his time in a great measure, because it had been sometimes flooded, and was, much of the year, too wet for cultivation. He was draining and clearing it, and it now brought good crops.

He had had an Irish gang draining for him, by contract. He thought a negro could do twice as much work in a day as an Irishman. He had not stood over them and seen them at work, but judged entirely from the amount they accomplished: he thought a good gang of negroes would have got on twice as fast. He was sure they must have "trifled" a great deal, or they would have accomplished more than they had. He complained much, also, of their sprees and quarrels. I asked why he should employ Irishmen, in preference to doing the work with his own hands. "It's dangerous work [unhealthy?], and a negro's life is too valuable to be risked at it. If a negro dies, it's a considerable loss, you know."

He afterwards said that his negroes never worked so hard as to tire themselves—always were lively, and ready to go off on a frolic at night. He did not think they ever did half a fair day's work. They could not be made to work hard: they never would lay out their strength freely, and it was impossible to make them do it.

This is just what I have thought when I have seen slaves at work—they seem to go through the motions of labor without putting strength into them. They keep their powers in reserve for their own use at night perhaps.

Mr. W. also said that he cultivated only the coarser and lower-priced sorts of tobacco, because the finer sorts required more pains-taking and discretion than it was possible to make a large gang of negroes use. "You can make a nigger work," he said, "*but you cannot make him think.*"

Although Mr. W. was very wealthy (or, at least, would be considered so anywhere at the North), and was a gentleman of education, his style of living was very farmerlike, and thoroughly Southern. On their plantations, generally, the Virginia gentlemen seem to drop their full-dress and constrained town-habits, and to live a free, rustic, shooting-jacket life. We dined in a room that extended out, rearwardly, from the house, and which, in a Northern establishment, would have been the kitchen. The cooking was done in a detached log-cabin, and the dishes brought some distance, through the open air, by the servants. The outer door was left constantly open, though there was a fire in an enormous old fire-place, large enough, if it could have been distributed sufficiently, to have lasted a New York seamstress the best part of the winter. By the door, there was indiscriminate admittance to negro-children and fox-hounds, and, on an average, there were four of these, grinning or licking their chops, on either side of my chair, all the time I was at the table. A stout woman acted as head waitress, employing two handsome little mulatto boys as her aids in communicating with the kitchen, from which relays of hot corn-bread, of an excellence quite new to me, were brought at frequent intervals. There was no other bread, and but one vegetable served—sweet potato, roasted in ashes, and this, I thought, was the best sweet potato, also, that I ever had eaten; but there were four preparations of swine's flesh, besides fried fowls, fried eggs, cold roast turkey, and opossum, cooked I know not how, but it somewhat resembled baked sucking-pig. The only beverages on the table were milk and whisky.

I was pressed to stay several days with Mr. W., and should have been glad to have accepted such hospitality, had not another engagement prevented. . . .

"Swell-heads"

. . . The farce of the vulgar-rich has its foundation in Mississippi, as in New York and in Manchester, in the rapidity with which certain values have advanced, especially that of cotton, and, simultaneously, that of cotton lands and negroes. Of course, there are men of refinement and cultivation among the rich planters of Mississippi, and many highly estimable and intelligent persons outside of the wealthy class, but the number of such is smaller in proportion to that of the immoral, vulgar, and ignorant newly-rich, than in any other part of the United States. And herein is a radical difference between the social condition of this region and that of the sea-board slave States, where there are fewer wealthy families, but where, among the people of wealth, refinement and education are much more general.

I asked how rich the sort of men were of whom he spoke.

"Why, sir, from a hundred thousand to ten million."

"Do you mean that between here and Natchez there are none worth less than a hundred thousand dollars?"

"No, sir, not beyond the ferry. Why, any sort of a plantation is worth a hundred thousand dollars; the niggers would sell for that."

"How many negroes are there on these plantations?"

"From fifty to a hundred."

"Never over one hundred?"

"No; when they've increased to a hundred they always divide them; stock another plantation. There are sometimes three or four plantations adjoining one another, with an overseer for each, belonging to the same man; but that isn't general—in general, they have to strike off for new land.''

"How many acres will a hand tend here?"

"About fifteen—ten of cotton, and five of corn; some pretend to make them tend twenty."

"And what is the usual crop?"

"A bale and a half to the acre on fresh land and in the bottom. From four to eight bales to a hand they generally get; sometimes ten and better, when they are lucky."

"A bale and a half on fresh land? How much on old?"

"Well, you can't tell—depends on how much it's worn and what the season is, so much. Old land, after a while, isn't worth bothering with."

"Do most of these large planters who live so freely anticipate their crops as the sugar planters are said to—spend the money, I mean, before the crop is sold?"

"Yes, sir, and three and four crops ahead generally."

"Are most of them the sons of rich men? are they old estates?"

"No, sir; many of them were overseers themselves once."

"Well, have you noticed whether it is a fact that these large properties seldom continue long in the same family? Do the grandsons of wealthy planters often become poor men?"

"Generally the sons do; almost always their sons are fools, and soon go through with it."

"If they don't kill themselves before their fathers die," said the other.

"Yes; they drink hard and gamble, and of course that brings them into fights."

This was while they were smoking on the gallery after supper. I walked to the stable to see how my horse was provided for; when I returned they were talking of negroes who had died of yellow fever while confined in the jail at Natchez. Two of them were spoken of as having been thus "happily released," being under sentence of death, and unjustly so, in their opinion. . . .

Review of a First-Rate Cotton Plantation

We had a good breakfast in the morning, and immediately afterward mounted and rode to a very large cottonfield, where the whole field-force of the plantation was engaged.

It was a first-rate plantation. On the highest ground stood a large and handsome mansion, but it had not been occupied for several years, and it was more than two years since the overseer had seen the owner. He lived several hundred miles away, and the overseer would not believe that I did not know him, for he was a rich man and an honorable, and had several times been where I came from—New York.

The whole plantation, including the swamp land around it, and owned with it, covered several square miles. It was four miles from the settlement to the nearest neighbor's house. There were between thirteen and fourteen hundred acres under cultivation with cotton, corn, and other hoed crops, and two hundred hogs running at large in the swamp. It was the intention that corn and pork enough should be raised to keep the slaves and cattle. This year, however, it has been found necessary to purchase largely, and such was probably usually the case, though the overseer intimated the owner had been displeased, and he "did not mean to be caught so bad again."

There were 135 slaves, big and little, of which 67 went to field regularly—equal, the overseer thought, to 60 able-bodied hands. Beside the field-hands, there were 3 mechanics (blacksmith, carpenter and wheelwright), 2 seamstresses, 1 cook, 1 stable servant, 1 cattle-tender, 1 hog-tender, 1 teamster, 1 house servant (overseer's cook), and one midwife and nurse. These were all first-class hands; most of them would be worth more, if they were for sale, the overseer said, than the best of field-hands. There was also a driver of the hoe-gang who did not labor personally, and a foreman of the plow-gang. These two acted as petty officers in the field, and alternately in the quarters.

There was a nursery for sucklings at the quarters, and twenty women at this time who left their work four times each day, for half an hour, to nurse their young ones, and whom the overseer counted as half-hands—that is, expected to do half an ordinary day's work.

Deserters and Detectives

He had no runaways out at this time, but had just sold a bad one to go to Texas. He was whipping the fellow, when he turned and tried to stab him—then broke from him and ran away. He had him caught almost immediately by the dogs. After catching him, he kept him in irons till he had a chance to sell him. His niggers did not very often run away, he said, because they were almost sure to be caught. As soon as he saw that one was gone he put the dogs on, and if rain had not just fallen, they would soon find him. Sometimes, though, they would outwit the dogs, but if they did they almost always kept in the neighborhood, because they did not like to go where they could not sometimes get back and see their families, and he would soon get wind of where they had been; they would come round their quarters to see their families and to get food, and as soon as he knew it, he would find their tracks and put the dogs on again. Two months was the longest time any of them ever kept out. They had dogs trained on purpose to run after niggers, and never let out for any thing else.

Driving

We found in the field thirty plows, moving together, turning the earth from the cotton plants, and from thirty to forty hoers, the latter mainly women, with a black driver walking about among them with a whip, which he often cracked at them, sometimes allowing the lash to fall lightly upon their shoulders. He was constantly urging them also with his voice. All worked very steadily, and though the presence of a stranger on the plantation must have been rare, I saw none raise or turn their heads to look at me. Each gang was attended by a "water-toter," that of the hoe-gang being a straight, sprightly, plump little black girl, whose picture, as she stood balancing the bucket upon her head, shading her bright eyes with one hand, and holding out a calabash with the other to maintain her poise, would have been a worthy study for Murillo.

Days and Hours of Labor

I asked at what time they began to work in the morning. "Well," said the overseer, "I do better by my niggers than most. I keep 'em right smart at their work while they do work, but I generally knock 'em off at 8 o'clock in the morning Saturdays, and give 'em all the rest of the day to themselves, and I always gives 'em Sundays, the whole day. Pickin' time, and when the crap's bad in grass, I sometimes keep 'em to it till about sunset, Satudays, but I never work 'em Sundays."

"How early do you start them out in the morning, usually?"

"Well, I don't never start my niggers 'fore daylight except 'tis in pickin' time, then maybe I got 'em out a quarter of an hour before. But I keep 'em right smart to work through the day." He showed an evident pride in the vigilance of his driver, and called my attention to the large area of ground already hoed over that morning; well hoed, too, as he said.

"At what time do they eat?" I asked. They ate "their snacks" in their cabins, he said, before they came out in the morning (that is before daylight—the sun rising at this time at a little before five, and the day dawning, probably, an hour earlier); then at 12 o'clock their dinner was brought to them in a cart—one cart for the plow-gang and one for the hoe-gang. The hoe-gang ate its dinner in the field, and only stopped work long enough to eat it. The plow-gang drove its teams to the "weather houses"—open sheds erected for the purpose in different parts of the plantation, under which were cisterns filled with rain water, from which the water-toters carried drink to those at work. The mules were fed as much oats (in straw), corn and fodder as they would eat in two hours; this forage having been brought to the weather houses by another cart. The plowmen had nothing to do but eat their dinner in all this time. All worked as late as they could see to work well, and had no more food nor rest until they returned to their cabin. At half past nine o'clock the drivers, each on an alternate night, blew a horn, and at ten visited every cabin to see that its occupants were at rest, and not lurking about and spending their strength in fooleries, and that the fires were safe—a very unusual precaution; the negroes are generally at liberty after their day's work is done till they are called in the morning. When washing and patching were done, wood hauled and cut for the fires, corn ground, etc., I did not learn: probably all chores not of daily necessity, were reserved for Saturday. Custom varies in this respect. In general, with regard to fuel for the cabins, the negroes are left to look out for themselves, and they often have to go to "the swamp" for it, or at least, if it has been hauled, to cut it to a convenient size, after their day's work is done. The allowance of food was a peck of corn and four pounds of pork per week, each. When they could not get "greens" (any vegetables) he generally gave them five pounds of pork. They had gardens, and raised a good deal for themselves; they also had fowls, and usually plenty of eggs. He added, "the man who owns this plantation does more for his niggers than any other man I know. Every Christmas he sends me up a thousand or fifteen hundred dollars' [equal to eight or ten dollars each] worth of molasses and coffee, and tobacco, and calico, and Sunday tricks for 'em. Every family on this plantation gets a barrel of molasses at Christmas." (Not an uncommon practice in Mississippi, though the quantity is very rarely so generous. It is usually made somewhat proportionate to the value of the last crop sold.)

Beside which, the overseer added, they are able, if they choose, to buy certain comforts for themselves—tobacco for instance—with money earned by Saturday and Sunday work. Some of them went into the swamps on Sunday and made boards—"puncheons" made with the ax. One man sold last year as much as fifty dollars' worth.

Opportunities for frank testimony by slaves about their bondage were rare, but one such opportunity arose during the Civil War. The American Freedmen's Inquiry Commission was established in 1863 to gather information and report to the secretary of war with recommendations on the future of the slaves. The frank accounts that Harry McMillan and Alexander Kenner gave the commission about their differing experiences of bondage appear in the first selection. Many decades later, in the 1930s, the Federal Writers' Project interviewed former slaves. The recollections of the men and women interviewed, who were then quite elderly, provide valuable insights into the slave's experience. Two of these accounts are provided in the second document. Talented and trusted slaves sometimes were permitted to manage their owner's plantation in his absence, as the third document shows. The slave George Skipwith did so on an Alabama plantation of John Hartwell Cocke, an absentee landlord who resided at his Virginia plantation, Bremo. Letters to Cocke from Lucy Skipwith, George's daughter, reveal her intensely religious nature, which developed in adulthood. The photograph from the Library of Congress in the fourth selection shows five generations of a South Carolina slave family and suggests the importance of family ties to those in bondage. R. Henry Gaston was a white man who agreed to assume the duties of overseer on a farm in the North Carolina piedmont. His letter to a relative, reprinted as the fifth document, lays bare the type of contests that frequently ensued between slaves and their overseers. Additional insight on what was known as the "management" of slaves, and the daily realities of slavery, can be gained from the advice that planters gave to one another in southern agricultural journals and other periodicals. A number of these appear in the sixth selection. Successful free blacks in Charleston, South Carolina, did not have to deal with overseers, but they faced a different threat on the eve of the Civil War. Affluent and frequently well known to a few high-status whites, these free people suddenly confronted a rising popular demand that free blacks be reenslaved or made to furnish strict legal proof (often difficult to obtain) of their free status. James M. Johnson, a tailor, describes these frightening developments to his brother-in-law, Henry Ellison, in the last selection. (Henry's father, William Ellison, was the successful manufacturer of high-quality cotton gins; see Chapter 6.)

Freedmen Describe Their Bondage, 1863

Harry McMillan, South Carolina

I am about 40 years of age, and was born in Georgia but came to Beaufort when a small boy. I was owned by General Eustis and lived upon his plantation.

Q. Tell me about the tasks colored men had to do?

A. In old secesh times each man had to do two tasks, which are 42 rows or half an acre, in "breaking" the land, and in "listing" each person had to do a task and a half. In planting every hand had to do an acre a day; in hoeing your first hoeing where you hoe flat was two tasks, and your second hoeing, which is done across the beds, was also two tasks. After going through those two operations you had a third which was two and a half tasks, when you had to go over the cotton to thin out the plants leaving two in each hill.

Q. How many hours a day did you work?

A. Under the old secesh times every morning till night—beginning at daylight and continuing till 5 or 6 at night.

Q. But you stopped for your meals?

A. You had to get your victuals standing at your hoe; you cooked it over night yourself or else an old woman was assigned to cook for all the hands, and she or your children brought the food to the field.

Q. You never sat down and took your food together as families?

A. No, sir; never had time for it.

Q. The women had the same day's work as the men; but suppose a woman was in the family way was her task less?

A. No, sir; most of times she had to do the same work. Sometimes the wife of the planter learned the condition of the woman and said to her husband you must cut down her day's work. Sometimes the women had their children in the field.

Q. Had the women any doctor?

A. No, sir; There is a nurse on the plantation sometimes—an old midwife who attended them. If a woman was taken in labor in the field some of her sisters would help her home and then come back to the field.

Q. Did they nurse their children?

A. Yes, sir; the best masters gave three months for that purpose.

Q. If a man did not do his task what happened?

A. He was stripped off, tied up and whipped.

Q. What other punishments were used?

A. The punishments were whipping, putting you in the stocks and making you wear irons and a chain at work. Then they had a collar to put round your neck with two horns, like cows' horns, so that you could not lie down on your back or belly. This also kept you from running away for the horns would catch in the bushes. Sometimes they dug a hole like a well with a door on top. This they called a dungeon keeping you in it two or three weeks or a month, and sometimes till you died in there. This hole was just big enough to receive the body; the hands down by the sides. I have seen this thing in Georgia but never here. I know how they whip in the Prisons. They stretch out your arms and legs as far as they can to ring bolts in the floor and lash you till they open the skin and the blood trickles down. . . .

Q. Suppose a son of the Master wanted to have intercourse with the colored women was he at liberty?

A. No, not at liberty, because it was considered a stain on the family, but the young men did it. There was a good deal of it. They often kept one girl steady and sometimes two on different places; men who had wives did it too sometimes, if they could get it on their own place it was easier but they would go wherever they could get it.

Q. Do the colored people like to go to Church?

A. Yes, Sir; They are fond of that; they sing psalms, put up prayers, and sing their religious songs.

Q. Did your Masters ever see you learning to read?

A. No, Sir; You could not let your Masters see you read; but now the colored people are fond of sending their children to school.

438

Q. What is the reason of that?

A. Because the children in after years will be able to tell us ignorant ones how to do for ourselves.

Q. How many children have you known one woman to have?

A. I know one woman who had 20 children. I know too a woman named Jenny, the wife of Dagos, a slave of John Pope, who has had 23 children. In general the women have a great many children[;] they often have a child once a year.

Q. Are the children usually obedient?

A. There are some good and some bad, but in general the children love their parents and are obedient. They like their parents most but they stand up for all their relations.

Q. Suppose a boy is struck by another boy what does he do?

A. If he is injured bad the relations come in and give the boy who injured him the same hurt. I would tell my boy to strike back and defend himself.

Q. How about bearing pain—do you teach your children to bear pain?

A. Yes, sir.

Q. When a colored man was whipped did he cry out?

A. He would halloa out and beg, but not cry for pain but for vexation.

Q. Did they try to conceal their whippings and think it a disgrace?

A. Yes, sir; they tried to conceal it; a great many are marked all over and have not a piece of skin they were born with.

Alexander Kenner, Kentucky

Mr. Kenner said he was born in Louisiana. His father was the Hon. George R. Kenner. His father had seven children by his mother, and then married a white woman, but told his mother she might go away. She went away, and took with her four of her children. Another was subsequently born. Mr. Kenner intended to make her free, but did not give her free papers. They went to St. Louis, and the mother worked for several years at washing, and he (Alexander) carried out the clothes. She throve exceedingly well. After seven years, Mr. George Kenner sold out the plantation, with all its rights, to his brother, Hon. Duncan F. Kenner, and his mother bought three of her children, including Alexander, for $1800. The oldest brother had remained on the plantation, and became valuable to Mr. Kenner as a rider of his race horses, and he would not let him go. They were very anxious indeed to buy him, and having prospered, they offered Mr. Kenner $2000 for him, which he refused to take. The mother, in the mean time, had rented some apartments and furnished them, and let them out to single men, and made a good deal of money. When she died, she was 53 years old, & her property was appraised at $7000. He and his brothers wanted Mr. Kenner to sell their oldest brother to them, but he had become valuable to him there as a trainer of race horses, & therefore he said he would not sell him unless they would give him the whole of the mother's property. Alexander would not consent to this, but the other brothers were exceedingly anxious to have their oldest brother, and they offered to give their shares, amounting to $2500, for his freedom; but the master insisted that besides this, the brother should serve three years, at $15 a month, to pay the balance, so that the whole amount would be $3400—and he a million-aire. When the mother died, this Kenner got himself made executor, and the three children being under age, he received the property. When Alexander became of age, he demanded his share, but Kenner refused it to him, then Alexander sued him in the court, and recovered the amount. Alexander had gone before this to the plantation, and offered to give Mr. Kenner all his share if he would free William, but he wouldn't do so. Besides, William was very much devoted to his master. He lingered on the plantation, and felt himself bound to remain until he had paid all the money which he had agreed to. When the war broke out, Alexander came away; William is still on the plantation.

On most of the plantations, the blacks have small patches of land, which they fence in, and take a great deal of care of. They raise poultry and hogs, and take the money they get from the sale of these to buy themselves tea, clothes and little comforts, and are very fond of dressing out in their clothes to go to the log churches. They are so anxious to make money that they work upon their little patches at night. On the plantation where he lived, he has known them to raise a thousand dozen chickens in a year; but their master obliged them to sell the chickens to him, instead of selling them to the hucksters, because he wanted to know how much money they had, and didn't want them to have too much; and besides, he wanted to get the advanced price from the hucksters. He would give them twenty cents a pair, and sell them to the hucksters for thirty cents. The masters didn't wish the slaves to accumulate any property, but to spend whatever money they got. Sometimes, however, they did accumulate property. He knew one man, old Cudjo, on a neighboring plantation, who used to get him (Alexander) to come and count his dollars. He stated that he had counted for him over five hundred silver dollars. Cudjo himself couldn't count over thirty or forty, but nobody could take any of the money without his knowing it, for he knew by the appearance or weight whether it was all right or not, but he wanted to know the exact number. His (Alexander's) mother, although an intelligent woman, could never count over one hundred, & certainly did not know how many hundred there were in a thousand. The negroes on the river, he thinks, are intelligent, and certainly take care of themselves. Those in the interior, away from the river, are stupid; they see nothing, know nothing, and are very like cattle. The negroes in Mississippi are more stupid than those in Louisiana, on account of the masters being more cruel and oppressive. The masters in Mississippi are sometimes bloody and cruel; they may kill their negroes, and there is no law to punish them.

Ex-Slaves Recall Slavery, 1936, 1937

Nancy Boudry, Thomson, Georgia

"If I ain't a hunnerd," said Nancy, nodding her white-turbaned head, "I sho' is close to it, 'cause I got a grandson 50 years old."

Nancy's silky white hair showed long and wavy under her headband. Her gingham dress was clean, and her wrinkled skin was a reddish-yellow color, showing a large proportion of Indian and white blood. Her eyes were a faded blue.

"I speck I is mos' white," acknowledged Nancy, "but I ain't never knowed who my father was. My mother was a dark color."

The cottage faced the pine grove behind an old church. Pink ramblers grew everywhere, and the sandy yard was neatly kept. Nancy's paralyzed granddaughter-in-law hovered in the doorway, her long smooth braids hanging over Indian-brown shoulders, a loose wrapper of dark blue denim flowing around her tall unsteady figure. She was eager to take part in the conversation but hampered by a thick tongue induced, as Nancy put it, "by a bad sore throat she ain't got over."

Nancy's recollections of plantation days were colored to a somber hue by overwork, childbearing, poor food and long working hours.

"Master was a hard taskmaster," said Nancy. "My husband didn' live on de same plantation where I was, de Jerrell place in Columbia County. He never did have nuthin' to give me 'cause he never got nuthin'. He had to come and ask my white folks for me. Dey had to carry passes everywhar dey went, if dey didn't, dey'd git in trouble.

"I had to work hard, plow and go and split wood jus' like a man. Sometimes dey whup me. Dey whup me bad, pull de cloes off down to de wais'—my master did it, our folks didn' have overseer.

"We had to ask 'em to let us go to church. Went to white folks church, 'tell de black folks got one of dere own. No'm, I dunno how to read. Never had no schools at all, didn't 'low us to pick up a piece of paper and look at it."

"Nancy, wasn't your mistress kind to you?"

"Mistis was sorta kin' to me, sometimes. But dey only give me meat and bread, didn' give me nothin' good—I ain' gwine tell no story. I had a heap to undergo wid. I had to scour at night at de Big House—two planks one night, two more de nex'. De women peoples spun at night and reeled, so many outs a night. Us had to git up befo' daybreak be ready to go to de fiel's.

"My master didn' have but three cullud people, dis yuh man what I stayed wid, my young master, had not been long married and dus' de han's dey give him when he marry was all he had.

"Didn' have no such house as dis," Nancy looked into the open door of the comfortable cottage, "sometimes dey have a house built, it would be daubed. Dus' one family, didn' no two families double up."

"But the children had a good time, didn't they? They played games?"

"Maybe dey did play ring games, I never had no time to see what games my chillun play, I work so hard. Heap o' little chillun slep' on de flo'. Never had no frolics neither, no ma'm, and didn' go to none. We would have prayer meetings on Saturday nights, and one night in de week us had a chairback preacher, and sometimes a regular preacher would come in."

Nancy did not remember ever having seen the Patterollers [patrollers].

"I hearn talk of 'em you know, heap o' times dey come out and make out like dey gwine shoot you at night, dey mus' been Patterollers, dey was gettin' hold of a heap of 'em."

"What did you do about funerals, Nancy?"

"Dey let us knock off for funerals, I tell de truth. Us stay up all night, singin' and prayin'. Dey make de coffin outter pine boards."

"Did you suffer during the war?"

"We done de bes' we could, we et what we could get, sometimes didn' have nothin' to eat but piece of cornbread, but de white folks allus had chicken."

"But you had clothes to wear?"

"Us had clothes 'cause we spun de thread and weaved 'em. Dey bought dem dere great big ole brogans where you couldn' hardly walk in 'em. Not like dese shoes I got on." Nancy thrust out her foot, easy in "Old Ladies' Comforts."

"When they told you were free, Nancy, did the master appear to be angry?"

"No'm, white folks didn' 'pear to be mad. My master dus' tole us we was free. Us moved right off, but not so far I couldn' go backwards and forwards to see 'um." (So it was evident that even if Nancy's life had been hard, there was a bond between her and her former owners.) "I didn' do no mo' work for 'um, I work for somebody else. Us rented land and made what we could, so we could have little somethin' to eat. I scoured and waited on white people in town, got little piece of money, and was dus' as proud!"

Nancy savored the recollection of her first earned money a moment, thinking back to the old days.

"I had a preacher for my second marriage," she continued. "Fo' chillun died on me—one girl, de yuthers was babies. White doctor tended me."

Asked about midwifery, Nancy smiled.

"I was a midwife myself, to black and white, after freedom. De Thomson doctors all liked me and tole people to 'git Nancy.' I used 'tansy tea'— heap o' little root—made black pepper tea, fotch de pains on 'em. When I would git to de place where I had a hard case, I would send for de doctor, and he would help me out, yes, doctor holp me out of all of 'em."

Asked about signs and superstitions, Nancy nodded.

"I have seed things. Dey look dus' like a person, walkin' in de woods. I would look off and look back to see it again and it be gone." Nancy lowered her voice mysteriously, and looked back into the little room where Vanna's [her paralyzed granddaughter-in-law] unsteady figure moved from bed to chair. "I seed a coffin floatin' in de air in dat room . . ." she shivered, "and I heard a heap o' knockings. I dunno what it bees—but de sounds come in de house. I runs ev'y squeech owl away what comes close, too." Nancy clasped her hands, right thumb over left thumb, "does dat—and it goes on away—dey quite hollerin', you chokin' 'em when you does dat."

"Do you plant by the moon, Nancy?"

"Plant when de moon change, my garden, corn, beans. I planted some

442

beans once on de wrong time of de moon and dey didn' bear nothin'—I hated it so bad, I didn' know what to do, so I been mindful ever since when I plant. Women peoples come down on de moon, too. I ain't know no signs to raise chillun. I whup mine when dey didn' do right, I sho' did. I didn' 'low my chillun to take nothin'—no aigs and nothin' 'tall and bring 'em to my house. I say 'put dem right whar you git 'em.' "

"Did you sing spirituals, Nancy?"

"I sang regular meetin' songs," she said, "like 'lay dis body down' and 'let yo' joys be known'—but I can't sing now, not any mo'."

Nancy was proud of her quilt-making ability.

"Git 'um, Vanna, let de ladies see 'um," she said; and when Vanna brought the gay pieces made up in a "double-burst" (sunburst) pattern, Nancy fingered the squares with loving fingers. "Hit's pooty, ain't it?" she asked wistfully, "I made one for a white lady two years ago, but dey hurts my fingers now—makes 'em stiff."

Delia Garlic, Montgomery, Alabama

Delia Garlic lives at 43 Stone Street, Montgomery, and insists she is 100 years old. Unlike many of the old Negroes of the South, she has no good words for slavery days or the old masters, declaring: "Dem days was hell."

She sat on her front porch and assailed the taking of young children from mothers and selling them in different parts of the country.

"I was growed up when de war come," she said, "an' I was a mother befo' it closed. Babies was snatched from dere mother's breas' an' sold to speculators. Chilluns was separated from sisters an' brothers an' never saw each other ag'in.

"Course dey cry; you think dey not cry when dey was sold lak cattle? I could tell you 'bout it all day, but even den you couldn't guess de awfulness of it.

"It's bad to belong to folks dat own you soul an' body; dat can tie you up to a tree, wid yo' face to de tree an' yo' arms fastened tight aroun' it; who take a long curlin' whip an' cut de blood ever' lick.

"Folks a mile away could hear dem awful whippings. Dey was a turrible part of livin'."

Delia said she was born at Powhatan, Virginia, and was the youngest of thirteen children.

"I never seed none of my brothers an' sisters 'cept brother William," she said. "Him an' my mother an' me was brought in a speculator's drove to Richmon' an' put in a warehouse wid a drove of other niggers. Den we was all put on a block an' sol' to de highes' bidder.

"I never seed brother William ag'in. Mammy an' me was sold to a man by de name of Carter, who was de sheriff of de county.

"No'm, dey warn't no good times at his house. He was a widower an' his daughter kept house for him. I nursed for her, an' one day I was playin' wid de baby. It hurt its li'l han' an' commenced to cry, an' she whirl on me, pick up a hot iron an' run it all down my arm an' han'. It took off de flesh when she done it.

443

"Atter awhile, marster married ag'in; but things warn't no better. I seed his wife blackin' her eybrows wid smut one day, so I thought I'd black mine jes' for fun. I rubbed some smut on my eyebrows an' forgot to rub it off, an' she kotched me. She was powerful mad an' yelled: 'You black devil, I'll show you how to mock your betters.'

"Den she pick up a stick of stovewood an' flails it ag'in' my head. I didn't know nothin' more 'till I come to, lyin' on de floor. I heard de mistus say to one of de girls: 'I thought her thick skull and cap of wool could take it better than that.'

"I kept on stayin' dere, an' one night de marster come in drunk an' set at de table wid his head lollin' aroun'. I was waitin' on de table, an' he look up an' see me. I was skeered, an' dat made him awful mad. He called an overseer an' tol' him: 'Take her out an' beat some sense in her.'

"I begin to cry an' run an' run in de night; but finally I run back by de quarters an' heard mammy callin' me. I went in, an' raght away dey come for me. A horse was standin' in front of de house, an' I was took dat very night to Richmon' an' sold to a speculator ag'in. I never seed my mammy any more.

"I has thought many times through all dese years how mammy looked dat night. She pressed my han' in bofe of hers an' said: 'Be good an' trus' in de Lawd.'

"Trustin' was de only hope of de pore black critters in dem days. Us jest prayed for strength to endure it to de end. We didn't 'spect nothin' but to stay in bondage 'till we died.

"I was sol' by de speculator to a man in McDonough, Ga. I don't ricolleck his name, but he was openin' a big hotel at McDonough an' bought me to wait on tables. But when de time come aroun' to pay for me, his hotel done fail. Den de Atlanta man dat bought de hotel bought me, too. 'Fo' long, dough, I was sol' to a man by de name of Garlic, down in Louisiana, an' I stayed wid him 'till I was freed. I was a regular fiel' han', plowin' an' hoein' an' choppin' cotton.

"Us heard talk 'bout de war, but us didn't pay no 'tention. Us never dreamed dat freedom would ever come."

Delia was asked if the slaves ever had any parties or dances on her plantation.

"No'm," she replied, "us didn't have no parties; nothin' lak dat. Us didn't have no clothes for goin' 'roun. I never had a undershirt until jest befo' my first chil' was borned. I never had nothin' but a shimmy an' a slip for a dress, an' it was made out'en de cheapes' cloth dat could be bought; unbleached cloth, coarse, but made to las'.

"Us didn't know nothin' 'cept to work. Us was up by three or four in de mornin' an' everybody got dey somethin' to eat in de kitchen. Dey didn't give us no way to cook, nor nothin' to cook in our cabins. Soon as us dressed us went by de kitchen an' got our piece of cornbread. Dey wan't even no salt in dem las' years. Dat piece of cornbread was all us had for breakfus', an' for supper, us had de same.

"For dinner us had boiled vittles; greens, peas an' sometimes beans. Coffee? No'm, us never knowed nothin' 'bout coffee.

"One mornin' I 'members I had started to de fiel', an' on de way I los' my piece of bread. I didn't know what to do. I started back to try to fin' it, an' it was too dark to see. But I walk back raght slow, an' had a dog dat walked wid me. He went on ahead, an' atter awhile I come on him lyin' dere guardin' dat piece of bread. He never touched it, so I gived him some of it.

"Jus' befo' de war I married a man named Chatfield from another plantation; but he was took off to war an' I never seed him ag'in. Atter awhile I married a boy on de plantation named Miles Garlic.

"Yas'm, Massa Garlic had two boys in de war. When dey went off de Massa an' missis cried, but it made us glad to see dem cry. Dey made us cry so much.

"When we knowed we was free, everybody wanted to git out. De rule was dat if you stayed in yo' cabin you could keep it, but if you lef', you los' it. Miles was workin' at Wetumpka, an' he slipped in an' out so us could keep on livin' in de cabin.

"My secon' baby soon come, an' raght den I made up my min' to go to Wetumpka where Miles was workin' for de railroad. I went on down dere an' us settled down.

"Atter Miles died, I lived dere long as I could an' den come to Montgomery to live wid my son. I'se eatin' white bread now an' havin' de best time of my life. But when de Lawd say, 'Delia, well done; come up higher,' I'll be glad to go."

George and Lucy Skipwith Write Their Master, 1847, 1857, 1859

may the 11 [1847] green County Ala

Sir

I imbrace this oppertunity to write you a few lines. I Reseved your letter and should have anserd it before now but master John was from home on busness and I could not write untel he returned wich was last Sunday. You told me in your letter that you was glad that I had the management of the farm my self, and you said that you noed that I was able to do as you and master John wish providing that I would not make use of ardent spirits, but I am convinced that it has been my greatest enemy and I shall consider it so as long as I live. We have not been able to do any thing towards marling our land our team could not be spared from farming except wet spells and it would be too wet for hauling, and master

Cocke Family Papers (#2433-b, #5685, #1480), Manuscripts Division, Special Collections Department, University of Virginia Library.

John thougt we could do as good busines by toating leaves to put on the poorest partes of the land by the spare hands and we put down two thousand and five hndred baskets full weighing from thirty five to forty, and thirty cart load out of the farm pen, and ninety out of the horse lot. We have a very good stand of cotton, but it has been so cold that it does not grow but our corn cannot be beaten and about three days from now we will finish plowing our corn the second time and our peas. we will be then reddy to commence plowing our cotton the second time. it has been about a week since the hoes started over the second time. our oats crop hav been somwhat backward but we had a very fine rane and I am in hopes they will start to growing again. Lee and archa hav been working with us for sum time building a screw whiat looks very fine I have not herd any thing from brother peyton sence you was out here I should be very glad to hear when you herd from him We are all well and hav had no call for a docter this year and I hope that you will reseve this letter in good helth my self and master John gets on very smooth together he have not given me a cross worde this year. give my love to every boddy boath white and black and beleave me to be your umble servant

George Skipwith

June the 17 1847

Sir

I would hav written to you a few days suner but i was wating to see if you found any fault in my letter or not I hav nothing perticulerly to say more than how we have spent our time sence i wrote to you. I mentioned in my letter that i could not write untel mas John returned but i signed no reason. I will now sign my reason I wanted mas John to see my letters so that you may knoe that what I write is so. I hav ploued my cotten over the second time putting four furrows in a roe with the sweeps and we will finish in three days from to day the hoes will also finish the last of this week or the first of next the third time in the cotten. then you may considder your cotten crop out of the danger of grass, tho we have had grass and a plenty of it and so has every boddy in green County for grass hav never growed so before. the Lice hav ingured the cotten cropes in our naberhood very much. they hav been very plentyful with us but hav not done us no great damage. mas John told me to chop it out in large bunches and that was all that saved it. it is now growing and ses it is the best cotten he has seen. I hav also ploued my corn the third time and hav laid it by and i dont see any thing to pervent us from makine an elogent crop of corn for it [is] much such a crop as we made the first year that we come into the country and it is praised by every boddy that speakes about it. there was about thirty acers of sandy land corn that was too thick, and mas John told me to thin it out and give it the second working over with the hoes and i hav don so and it is improveing every day. we expect rane every

446

day and if we can get it in eight or ten days I shall not dought it for a moment. I Thought at one time that our oats would not be worth cutting but they mend very fast and I think that we will make a pretty good crope. I think that our last years crope will last us untel the new crope comes. our potatoes looks better this year than any we hav had since we hav been into this country   our muls stands well after hard driven and i can shoe them all with second sholders except too. I hav ten regelar worke muls but I hav been oblige to worke the three mares and the horse utill, but i can spell them in a few days. we hav six young coalts   amonge them are four horse coalts two of them which will be three years old this coming spring   they are boath very likely coalts. the other too, one is about ten days old and the other about a year old. we also hav two filies among them one is two years old and the other is one year old, and the one at one year old is the finest colt I ever saw. I hav sixty hogs for this years killing. our fouls hav failed this year   we have hatched hundreds of turkeys and chickins but the Rats destroied them all so that we have not raised none. we are all well and hav had no sickness since i wrote except Spencer he is got a risen hand, and i am in hopes that this letter will fine them all as well there as they are here. Lee and Archa are done ther Job at home (haveing Quitt cotton Prep) and are hierd out. Remember me to the family boath black and white a[nd] Beleave me your servant

George Skipwith

hopewell   July the 8 1847

Sir

on the forth day of July I reseved your letter dated may the 25. I wrote to yo the 15 of June the second time giveing you a true statement of the crops, horses, hogs, and chickeins but I am sorry that I shall have to write yo princerble about other matters. I hav a good crop on hand for you, boath of cotten and corn. this you knoe could not be don without hard worke. I have worked the people but not out of reason, and I have whiped none without a caus   the persons whome I have correct I will tell you thir name and thir faults.

Suky who I put to plant som corn and after she had been there long anuf to hav been done I went there and she had hardly began it   I gave her som four or five licks over her clothes   I gave isham too licks over his clothes for covering up cotton with the plow.

I put frank, isham, violly, Dinah Jinny evealine and Charlott to Sweeping cotten going twice in a roe, and at a Reasonable days worke they aught to hav plowed seven accers a peice, and they had been at it a half of a day, and they had not done more than one accer and a half and I gave them ten licks a peace upon thir skins   I gave Julyann eight or ten licks for misplacing her hoe. that was all the whiping I hav done from the time that I pitched the crop untell we comenced cutting oats.

my Dear Master

I would have writen to you before this but for eight or ten days I have been sick. I feels better at this time tho not well. Maria also has been very sick but is up again. mrs Carters Baby also has been very sick but it is now a little better. it has fallen off a great deal. mrs Carters health is not very good. the Children all seem to be suffering with very bad Colds. the old ones seem to stand very well. we have two very fine young Babies. one is Jinneys, and the other Bettias. Matilda also had one but it died. I do not think that our sweet potatoe patch will make us many potatoes. they were planted so late I think that the frost will catch them. the Cotton seem to be opening very fast   they will start to picking it out before very long. the Carpenters are still workeing at the low place   mr Powell told Archa to try to get the Buildeings done by the first of November any how. mr Powell left this place on the 27th. he wrote to you from this place. you have heard I supose of his wifes sickness   he expects to be here again the middle of November   Mr Bendon visited him while he was here. mrs Avery and miss mary was here a few days ago   they were well. miss Fanny has not yet returned from North Carolina. mr Ben Carter is still liveing with them, and expect to live there next year. the Topp mare has a very fine horse colt. it is a very pretty Male. I am in hopes that you will soon be makeing ready to start out here and spend a longer time than ever with us, and should any thing pervent you comeing I hope that master Charles will come. I send you these verses which I have taken from the 10 Commandments. I wish you would have them printed for me in a small track. I will now bring my letter to a close   hopeing soon to hear from you I remane your servant

Lucy Skipwith

The 10 Commandments

1st

Thou no god shalt have but me
This Command I give to Thee
love me then with all thy heart
Never from my words depart

2nd

Thou no golden gods shalt have
gods of silver do not love
Seek the true the liveing Lord
For I am a Jealous god

3rd

Thou shalt not take my name in vain
Sinful words thou shalt disdain
guiltless live before my face
And I will be thy hideing place

Remember thou the Sabbath day
Never work nor even play
The god of Heaven will ever bless
The man who keeps the day of rest

5th

Honour thou thy Mothers words
Never break they Fathers laws
They who does their Parents will
Long upon this earth shall live

6th

Thou no murder shall commit
With the murders do not set
Lest thou learn his wicked ways
And live in Sorrow all thy days

7th

Thou no wicked deed shall do
Righteousness shalt thou persue
Let your actions all be right
And like the morning star be bright

8th

Thou shalt see by this Command
Honesty do I demand
Every human being should feel
That it is a sin to steal

9th

Thou shalt always speak the truth
To the aged and the youth
False witnesses do I despise
Ile drag them downwards from the sky

10th

Covetousness here thou see
Is a great offence to me
Thy neighbours goods thou shalt not crave
Thy neighbours goods thou shalt not have

Hopewell   June the 9th 1859

my Dear Master

I received your message by mr Powell, also the one by mr Lawrence about not writeing to you, and I am sorry that you had to remind me of it. I would have writen to you before this but I have been waiteing to hear of your safe arival at home. as we had not heard a word from you we did not know but what you was sick on the road. we are much releaved by hearing from you and will try to let you hear from us as often as necessary, and keep you informed of our movements here.

I knoe that you will be mortified to hear of the troble that my little girl Betsey has got into at mr Joe Bordens by being perswaded by one of their servants to steal money for him, and I lear[ne]d that this is the second time that he has made her do it. she says that she had no thought of it being so much monney neither did he. he saw that she did not dress up like the other girls did and he tempted her with such things as he knew she wanted. I do not know what master Joe will do with the man. he belongs to mr Ben Borden but he lives with master Joe. he has a wife and four Children at master Joes. he also has Brothers and Sisters there, and I heard mas Joe say to day that they were good hands to work, but they would steal, and that girl is growing up among them and if she continue there they will bring her to everlasting destruction. her mistress has taken very little pains to bring her up right. the girl has had the raising of her self up. she has been left down there among those people four and six weeks at a time with not as much as a little sewing to do, and now they complains of her being so lazy. It seems to be almost Imposeing upon you to ask the faver of you to let the Child come home, but I would thank you a thousand time If you would do so. I want to give her religious instructions and try to be the means of saving her soul from death. master Joe says he rather that she would come home. mr Powell says he thinks she had better come home and work in Williams place and let him work out. I hope that you will not sell her if you can posuble do any thing else with her. if you do sell her, have you any objection of my trying to get mr Powell to bye her, providing he is willing to do so, as I think that he could make a woman of her. let me hear from you on the Subject by the first of July. if it was not for the grace of god I would sink beneath such a load as this, but I have a preasant help in the time of troble. I have not seen the girl but once in twelve months. We are all geting along very well at this time. the people are all well, and in good Spirits, and I hope that we may continue to do well. mr Lawrence still holds family Prayers with us every Sunday morning, and explains the scriptures to us. we have had preaching at the Chapple three times this year. we have mr Duboise and Dr Mears the school teacher from greensboro. they will preach every second and fourth sunday in the month. we have Just received a letter from mr Crains sister. she wants his things to be sent to her by mr Powells wagon when it comes down after his goats next monts. we have seven beautiful little kids since you went away, and two very pretty Coalts. we have a very nice garden but every thing is suffering very much for rain.

I have seen nothing of the Japan plum seed in the flower pots nor the garden. only one of the Chessnuts have come up. I will write to you again soon. the people Joines me in love to you. nothing more at preasant from your servant

Lucy Skipwith

To Gen John H Cocke

Five Generations of a South Carolina Slave Family

R. Henry Gaston on His Contests with Slaves, 1850

I have scarcely enough to write to make a letter but I will write all I can think of and "praps" I can fill up.

First I must tell you of a "criminary" I got into with those negroes. On the Monday morning after I came here [Gibsons Quarter, Concord, North Carolina] I called them all up (the men of them) and told them how I intended to be governed here and allotted off their work they would have to do of evenings and mornings feeding +c. and told one of them named Rob to make a fire for me at night and morning.

But instead of coming to make my fire he goes to Concord (where his master lives) to know of him if he should make fires for me. Gibson told him he must do what I told him. The next day I Rec^d. a note from Gibson

---

Letter from R. Henry Gaston reprinted with permission of Rachel Kirksey Abernathy.

directing me to whip all that disobeyed me. Next morning I call up Rob + commence on him with my cowhide (wich I intended to do any how). I give him a stripe or two + he run saying I shouldn't whip him a dam lick.

I concluded I would wait until he thought I would forget it before I would attack him again. On Saturday following I told Aaron (a young lad just grown) to make fire for me + he also failed to do it. I spoke to Gen. Means who lives $\frac{1}{4}$ mile of here to assist me to whip them. He said if he came they would suspicion something at once. I got Dr. Gibson here on Monday morning last + we went to the clearing where they were all choping + I called Rob + Aaron up and made them take their coats off + I thrashed them in good style. This I thought would make them obey me but the same evening Rob failed again. (I told him when I whiped him that he had to make a fire for me that week out + then I intended to make Aaron do it as Rob has a house of his own + 2 sisters to attend to). I went down where Rob was choping his wood and asked him if he intended making my fire. Says he "didn't master say I had to curry the mules" (This was mentioned when I whiped them but he got no such orders). I told him to lay down his axe + go make me a fire on. He sidled around the wood pile + didn't seem like he was going to do it.

I then drew my Pistol with a full determination to shoot him let the consequences have been as they may. As soon as he saw what was coming he dashed off like lightning + fell over some gullies. I could have caught him easily when he fell but I knew it wouldn't do to shoot.

After my passion cooled a little I came to the House without saying a word. The following morning he was sick (or pretended to be). I went to his bed + told him in as determined a tone as I could that he could have his choice either to make my fire or be beaten to death because I was determined to make him do it or take his life. Also that he or any of them need not expect to trifle with me.

That evening he was up here in due time + made the fire and has been doing it ever since.

You can Judge from this what kind of Negroes I have to deal with. I don't blame the negroes as much as I do the former overseers for from all I can learn they have had their own way all the while and the overseer had to knock under.

I don't think I will have much more trouble with them for they are beginning to find that they cant get over me. I put it on one to make a fire for me because there is more of them than has any thing to do of evenings + mornings + I thought they may as well do that as nothing and I havent time to do it myself. There is a great many Negroes about here the most I ever saw in any neighbourhood + they think themselves about as good as any common poor people if not better.

There is nine grown men here and about the same no. of women + 3 boys and lots of children

Enough about Negroes.

Slaveowners on the Management of Blacks, 1828–1860

Good Management

South Carolina, 1838, Young Planter

There is no employment I am acquainted with that requires more constant and unremitted attention than a plantation when profitably managed. The master must have a thorough knowledge of every part of his business. It is not alone his duty to plan every thing, but he must see that every plan is executed properly, and as he intended it; no profits can be obtained without it. I care not what may be said to the contrary. The first thing that presents itself to his most serious consideration is the management of his negroes; and upon this depends every thing, but how wretchedly is it often neglected! I will readily acknowledge the difficulties to be encountered in reducing to a system and order the complicated operations of a plantation where nothing like system or order ever prevailed. But the difficulties are at the beginning alone, and you are soon remunerated ten fold. Where negroes have been well fed and clothed and strict, even-handed justice has been meted out both to them and their master, tempered with kindness and humanity, you will as surely obtain the two great principles in their government, *fear and love,* as effect follows cause. Their attachment frequently reaches enthusiasm, and I am inclined to repose much confidence in it. To effect so desirable a state of things, the master should make himself thoroughly acquainted with their habits, character and disposition. He should invariably give a willing ear to all their complaints, put them to the test of investigation and apply an efficient remedy. They will then look up to him as their great arbiter and protector in all their difficulties, which will inspire both respect and confidence, and he will find them much more true to his interest than they are generally supposed to be. He should never suffer them to be degraded either in the manner of inflicting punishment or in any other way. They should be punished in moderation and without passion. The overseer should be a man of fair moral character, of good sense, mild temper and great firmness. What difficulty could be found in introducing the strictest order and discipline in a plantation that had been so managed? Not the least. But, when they have been treated with injustice and falsehood, and a deaf ear turned to their complaints, the master knowing nothing except through the medium of an overseer, probably as trifling and contemptible as the negroes, the worst consequences must be anticipated, and it would be a Herculean task to introduce any thing like system or order. Nothing is more common or more pernicious than to invest your overseer with discretionary powers in inflicting punishment. Passion, prejudice, or ignorance often makes him grossly abuse it. The negro does not go to his master for protection, for he will find none there, but must quietly submit to the despotic will of one but little his superior. It would be almost impossible to organize any regular system under such government. The laws necessary for the regular and proper management of a plantation should be few and simple, operating alike upon overseer and negro, and as immutable and inviolable as those of the Medes and Persians. There should be a certain and definite penalty imposed upon both immediately following their violation. The penalty imposed upon the overseer should be pecuniary, that upon the negro corporeal. The overseer that would not submit to this is not worth having, for if he has intelligence and honesty enough efficiently and faithfully to discharge his duty the advantages both to himself and employer would be presented in so strong a light that they could not be misunderstood.

South Carolina, 1840, Young Planter

There are, in all concerns of life, extremes much to be regretted and avoided, and to an alarming extent is this the case in not using a proper, close, uncompromising discipline over negroes, keeping in mind at all times the line of distinction between master and servant and prohibiting entirely the association of any and all white persons from intercourse with them who do not observe the same rule rigidly, and all innovations to said rule should be fearlessly, instantly, and promptly punished. Upon the other hand, however, there are many, very many, weighty responsibilities due from masters to slaves—and it is a source of just satisfaction to the exalted citizens of our own State, and the South generally, to know that many of these obligations they daily acquit themselves of most honourably, as in the daily allowance of food, clothing, and comfortable cabins—and of at least paramount importance only a moderate service is required; all of which, in the eye of the humane, or even judicious owner, are necessary, scrupulously so, for his own advancement, if not to satisfy the risings of a benevolent heart—which is, with but few exceptions, the prompter to good deeds. But there are exceptions to this rule of conduct which deserve our attention and action from its source being diametrically opposed to both the laws of God, and man, and to reason, common sense, and self-interest. The more to be regretted, too, from the fact that such inhuman owners of slaves frequently perturb whole neighborhoods and inflict, measureably, disgrace upon whole districts, yea States.

Plantation Order

Mississippi, 1851, Planter, 150 slaves

"Rules and Regulations for the Government of a Southern Plantation"

1. THERE SHALL BE A PLACE FOR EVERY THING, AND EVERY THING SHALL BE KEPT IN ITS PLACE.

2. On the first days of January and July, there shall be an account taken of the number and condition of all the negroes, stock, and farming utensils of every description on the premises, and the same shall be entered in the plantation book.
3. It shall be the duty of the overseer to call upon the stockminder once each day to know if the cattle, sheep, and hogs have been seen and counted, and to find out if any are dead, missing, or lost.
4. It shall be the duty of the overseer, at least once in every week, to see and count the stock himself, and to inspect the fences, gates, and water-gaps on the plantation and see that they are in good order.
5. The wagons, carts, and all other implements are to be kept under the sheds and in the houses where they belong, except when in use.
6. Each negro man will be permitted to keep his own axe, and shall have it forthcoming when required by the overseer. No tools shall be taken or used by any negro without the permission of the overseer. . . .
12. It shall be the duty of the driver, at such hours of the night as the overseer may designate, to blow his horn and go around and see that every negro is at his proper place, and to report to the overseer any that may be absent; and it shall be the duty of the overseer, at some hour between that time and daybreak, to patrol the quarters himself and see that every negro is where he should be.

Workdays

Georgia, 1860, Farmer

EDITORS *SOUTHERN CULTIVATOR*—As I am a new beginner, and a *small farmer,* and am disposed to do my own overseeing, I find it very inconvenient and troublesome on account of not knowing the amount of work a hand ought to do per day, and am consequently often much imposed on. Will you, or some one of your many subscribers, be so kind as to answer the following questions:

1. What is a task, in hoeing or hilling Corn?
2. Chopping out Cotton?
3. Hoeing and bringing Cotton to a stand?
4. Hoeing Rice (not subject to irrigation) in its different stages?
5. Hoeing Potatoes, &c.?
6. Ditching?
7. Turning up land with a hoe?
8. Listing ground?
9. Bedding up with a hoe?
10. Trenching for Rice?
11. Splitting Pine Rails, &c.?

Adapted to Pine and Bay Lands.
Yours, very respectfully,

SMALL FARMER
Scriven Co., Ga., June, 1860.

REPLY.—We find answers to most of the above inquiries in Holmes' "Southern Farmer," and proceed to give them in order—

1. From one half to a full acre.
2. Half an acre.
3. From half an acre to an acre.
4. On inland from 1/4 to 1/2 acre.
5. From 1/2 an acre to an acre.
6. About 600 square feet.
7. Say 1/4 of an acre.
8. From 1/4 to 1/2 acre.
9. From 1/4 to 1/2 acre.
10. A square of 150 feet each way, or about 1/2 an acre.
11. From 100 to 125 heavy rails, 12 feet long.

It will be necessary to modify these tasks in accordance with the nature of the soil, obstructions by stumps, rocks, &c., but in the main they will be found nearly correct.—EDS. *So. Cult.*

Discipline

South Carolina, 1828, Overseer

More punishment is inflicted on every plantation by the men in power from private pique than from a neglect of duty. This I assert as a fact; I have detected it often. . . . When I pass sentence myself, various modes of punishment are adopted; the lash least of all.—Digging stumps or clearing away trash about the settlements in their own time; but the most severe is confinement at home six months to twelve months, or longer. . . . The lash is, unfortunately, too much used; every mode of punishment should be devised in preference to that, and when used, never to lacerate—all young persons will offend. A Negro at twenty-five years old, who finds he has the marks of a rogue inflicted when a boy (even if disposed to be orderly) has very little or no inducement to be otherwise.

South Carolina, 1830, Planter

The proper management and discipline of slaves subjects the man of care and feeling to more dilemmas than perhaps any other vocation he could follow. To keep a diary of their conduct would be a record nothing short of a series of violations of the laws of God and man. To moralize and induce the slave to assimilate with the master and his interest has been and is the great desideratum aimed at; but I am sorry to say that I have long since desponded in the completion of this task. But, however true this picture may be, of those servile creatures, we are bound under many sacred obligations to treat them with humanity at all times and under all circumstances. Although compelled to use coercive measures for their good discipline, yet we should never lose sight of humanity in its strictest sense. Under all these considerations, it requires for the good management and discipline of those people a man of steady habits, connected with sobriety, fortitude, energy, and humanity, and a passion for enterprise. To clothe the naked, feed the hungry, and soothe the sick should be our ceaseless duty toward the slave; and to compel them to theirs should be the order of the day.

Virginia, 1834, Planter

In the management of negroes there should always be perfect uniformity of conduct toward them; that is, you should not be too rigid in your discipline at one time and too lax at another. They should understand that real faults will not go unpunished; but at the same time, moderate punishment, with a certainty of its succeeding a fault, is much more efficient in producing good conduct than severe punishment irregularly inflicted—that is, sometimes inflicted for an offence and at others omitted when the same or a worse [one] is committed; for the ill disposed will always risk the chances of escaping punishment altogether. It is the certainty of punishment, and not its severity, which deters from misconduct and, in fact, after awhile, on a well regulated plantation, that certainty will prevent the necessity of inflicting punishments almost entirely. The best evidence of the good management of slaves is the impartiality of treatment to be used towards them all, unless for particular good conduct, and then it should be understood as such.

South Carolina, 1836, Overseer

For the breach of every rule, *certainty of punishment* is every thing. If a negro is permitted to go once unpunished for a fault, he will at any time afterwards do the same and risk being flogged. I have always discovered that where the overseer is positive that the negroes are better disciplined, more mildly treated, and consequently more happy; once, however, a negro has been punished, the fault should be overlooked, and his spirits should not be broken down by continually reminding him of his past misconduct. Not observing this rule has very often ruined some of the very best negroes. I have frequently met with negroes, whom the whip would ruin, with whom a little flattery could do everything.

Tennessee and Arkansas, 1860, Planter

Allow me [A. T. Goodloe] to place before your readers a few important facts in reference to the management of negroes. When I was a boy (and it has not been many years since) negroes, as far as my knowledge extends, were kept under strict discipline. But since Mrs. [Harriet Beecher] Stowe and others of a like stripe have, from pecuniary motives (for I have no idea they fancy black more than any other color), sent out their vile publications to the world, many at the South have thought proper, perhaps from similar motives, to write books and newspaper articles in answer to those abolition works. Most of these Southern writers have, in my opinion, done more injury than good to the institution which they pretend to defend, for the plan of management which they generally lay down is such as to render a slave unhappy and very unprofitable property.

The general published opinion seems to be that negroes should be managed with great lenity and encouraged to labor by kind words.

Now, I speak what I know when I say it is like "casting pearls before swine" to try to *persuade* a negro to work. He must be *made* to work, and should always be given to understand that if he fails to perform his duty he will be punished for it.

There was an article published last fall in the Nashville *Christian Advocate* on this subject, and the writer tried to prove that the only humane and profitable way to manage negroes was to allow them to have patches of such sizes as they wished, and be permitted to work them every time they worked over their master's crop. To prove that to be the right way, some Senator from Georgia I believe (who has devoted his life to the study of politics) owning a great many slaves let them have patches, and the annual income of their crops was good wages for a white man. Can such stuff be called management? No sir. What do slaves want with money? What good can it possibly do them? I can tell you what becomes of most of it. The proprietors of road-side groceries get it. There are several such filthy institutions in the country, and they are considered by the good neighbors to be great nuisances; but these neighbors, with scarcely an exception, allow their negroes to make what money they can for themselves, and give them the privilege of going wherever their inclinations may lead them at night and on Sunday. Tell me, if you please, who is responsible for the existence of whiskey-venders on the road-side in a moral neighborhood? I will take the liberty of saying that, if the negroes were kept at home, as they should be, such characters would go somewhere else to seek a support. Every managing farmer can well afford to buy such things for their negroes as he wishes them to have. Take his negroes to the nearest dry goods store, or send the overseer with them (do not let them go alone), and let them select such things as suit their fancies, within a certain limit, and pay for the goods himself, always rewarding more liberally those that have performed their duty best.

I read an article in the *Southern Cultivator* some time last year (I don't recollect now what number it was in) written by a rich Southern planter, in which he said he always took negro evidence against an overseer. Negroes are weak-minded, unprincipled creatures, and at the same time will frequently evince a great deal of shrewdness in fixing up a "tale" on an overseer they do not like. I had an evidence of that on my plantation last year. The negroes had become tired of the overseer, and concluded to fix up a plan to have him turned off [fired]. They assembled in counsel near the cabins one night, after they thought he had gone to bed and was asleep;

but he, ever on the watch, as an overseer should be who regards the interests of his employer, concealed himself near where they were, and learned all they said. He told me of it next morning and requested that I should hear it all from their own lips before I punished them, for it has always been a rule with me to whip any negro that tries to tell me anything about the overseer. I think I can find out without their assistance whether he is a gentleman or not. Their plans were well laid, and they, no doubt, would have succeeded in their measures if they had belonged to such a man as the rich Southern planter. In compliance with the request of my overseer, I heard them with my own ears, and they acknowledged their "tale" was entirely false, that their only object was to get the overseer turned off. The impropriety and absurdity of listening to what negroes have to say about their overseer is perfectly evident to any one who will reflect a minute on the subject.

Abolitionists and their books can never affect the institution of slavery, but managing negroes in the way I have referred to will. It will make them a reckless, dissatisfied population and expense to their owners. People adopting such government with their negroes are laboring against their own interests, the interests of their slaves, and the interests of the South.

I have a plantation in Arkansas on which I have been living six years and have been quite successful for a beginner. In order to gain information, when I first went out, I observed very closely and made many inquiries about the management of negroes. Most of the neighbors (clever people) allowed their negroes to visit about through the country, and cultivated small crops to the land. The land was rich and they always made enough to live on, which was all they cared for. I went there to make money, and soon found out that I could not make anything by following their example. I, therefore, after consulting the most successful planters, arrived at the following conclusions, viz: Negroes should have as much as they can eat and a sufficient quantity of comfortable clothing. They should be made to go to bed early at night and be up in time next morning to get breakfast and be at their places in the field as soon as it is light enough to see to work, and remain diligently at work till dark. They should not be permitted to visit away from the plantation, nor negroes from the neighborhood allowed to visit them. Rigid discipline should always be observed with them, for it is the only way to make them contented and profitable.

Charleston's Free Blacks on Fear of Reenslavement, 1859–1860

Charleston, Decr 23d/59

Dear Henry,

I hope this will find you relieved from your cold. I am annoyed with one. The wedding came off in style. Nat Fuller was the caterer. He had

From *No Chariot Let Down: Charleston's Free People on the Eve of the Civil War*, edited by Michael P. Johnson and James L. Roark, pp. 41, 101–102. © 1984 The University of North Carolina Press.

oysters served for E Ann at 9 o'clock. We left soon after. We had two bottles of champagne broached before leaving & did not even eat a piece of cake. The crowd was a large & respectable one. Mr Gadsden performed the ceremony, Dr Hanckel being sick. There were 10 attending of each sex. Some of the bridesmaids left before we did for Savannah. Beard went down with them but took care to get back before supper. The bride & groom are gone on a Tour in the country.

Matilda was at Home today for the first time. She is well. Mrs Bonneau is quite feeble. R Kinloch gets married shortly, also Miss Gourdin, an apprentice of Mrs. Lee.

Do tender my congratulations to your Father on the adjournment of the Legislature. He ought to read Col Memminger's speech against Moore's bill. It is in the Courier of 16th. I prophesied from the onset that nothing would be done affecting our position.

We have sent some little nick nacks for the children, not having room for the grown folks. You must come down & follow the fashion. I heard a few days ago my cotton was sold, but did not learn the rates. I will be able to settle up with your Father for Bagging, Rope, &c. Do see that Sarah behaves herself & salts the creatures regularly. We have not heard from Charley for some days. Father, Mother, Gabriella, & E Ann unite with me in wishing you & all at Wisdom Hall a Merry Christmas. As ever, I am yrs truly

J M J

Charleston Aug 28th 1860

Dear Henry,

Yours is recd. I am sorry to hear of Wm & Charlotte's indisposition. We are not very well. The heat is oppressive.

The stir has subsided, but arrests are still made & the people are leaving. It is vain for us to hope that if it is not the *will* of God he will not permit it. The bible tells us He is not the minister of Sin, & again the wicked shall flourish &c. In that model prayer we are taught to pray that His will may be done on earth as it is in heaven, & yet as free agents we are free to obey or reject. Hence it is that on earth wicked rule prevails, while in Heaven His will is done by the Just. I have implicit Faith in Providence & recognize its doing in directing those who seek His guidance, by over-ruling what is a present calamity to the future good of the virtuous. But I very much doubt that He wills or sanctions unrighteous acts, although in answer to prayer He often overthrows them & converts them into an engine of good provided we will act in accordance with His will as suggested by His Spirit & not supinely wait for the working of a miracle by having a Chariot let down to convey us away.

The magistrates boast of the good it has done them & Trusted that they did not know they were so rich. Slaves have come by magic. It is evident that the movement is intended for their emolument. On the other hand it must prove the Death of many & the loss of earthly goods, the hard earnings of a life time, to others. And yet those who put their trust in God may derive benefits spiritually & temporally.

Our Friends sympathise & express indignation which has checked it, but they are not in power & cant put down the majority. Nothing more is heard of the suits. Fordham had to comply with the Law. Gen. Schnierlie placed himself in the stead of a Man he holds & defied them to touch him. He would beat the one to Death who did. And Col. Whaley says he will stand a lawsuit before complying, but the majority has succumbed. The money has to come out of the purses of those held in Trust.

Hicks had his watch & chain taken from him in a Mob raised in Market St.

Col. Seymour stood in front of our House speaking to an Irish carter on the subject & pointed to No 7 & 9 as being for sale. And you can see Hand bills on property held by cold. people in every quarter, which will have the effect of depreciation. The action of the people has taken them by surprise & the originators blame the Mayor for being so rash. They say All must leave but they did not want them ran off thus.

As it regards the Miss D's I expected you to select for yourself first, which would be a good recommendation. They wont leave before their Father except entrusted to better hands. He is not disposed to move quick enough for them.

Father has been to Niagara Falls with Charley & to Love Feast & class meetings with Marshall & R. Clark & to pic nics with Gabriella & Charlotte & is enjoying the sights with a zest. Charley begs to join with Father in Love to you & to assure you that you have never been forgotten.

Jas Glover was taken to the Guard House at the instance of Dr Dessausure for standing in a Drug store with his Hat on. I have not heard the sentence. Beard has closed his school & is about to leave before he is pounced upon.

Dr. Dereef is flourishing in Washington yet. He has written about 30 Letters home since he left. They come daily. If the one I saw is a sample he must have more constant employment than the Secry of State.

I cant write your Father for the present. I suppose the H & G affair has attained the result. I fancy I see them in a Fond embrace.

W. P. Dacoster appears to be circumspect. De Large has got back to fret a few. Sasportas has Returned from Aiken with his daughter. They tried to prevail on him to make his abode there. The Family joins me in Love.

Yours,
J M J

The Civil War

The Secession Crisis

As President-elect Abraham Lincoln journeyed from Springfield, Illinois, to Washington in February 1861, negotiations and conferences were still taking place in the capital to stall and reverse the movement for southern secession. Even if they failed, contemporaries believed, war was not the only possible outcome. So the situation remained quite fluid; or was this perception just an illusion? Perhaps too much had already transpired—not only in the few months following Lincoln's election but in the previous quarter-century of sectional wrangling—for the momentum to be stopped.

Secession had been urged for roughly a decade by a group of southern politicians who recognized that there was no permanent security within the Union for the South's way of life, based as it was on the "peculiar institution." They had maneuvered and organized to prepare the South for the break that had now arrived as a result of the disintegration of the Democratic party and the attainment of the presidency by the antislavery Republicans. But most southern voters were not convinced. Secession was closely contested in Texas as well as in Alabama and Georgia, with many in those states feeling that withdrawal was completely ill advised, or else that it was premature until Lincoln demonstrated hostile intentions with an overt act.

Meanwhile, in the Upper South—Virginia, Tennessee, North Carolina, and Arkansas—secession had been voted down or not even put to a vote at all. These Upper South states were less committed to slavery than the Deep South, while they also had valuable economic ties to the North. Their inhabitants concluded that secession not only was a risky undertaking but also might jeopardize their own interests.

When Lincoln took office, only the seven Lower South states had seceded. A conciliatory approach might therefore have confined the Confederacy to a remnant that was not likely to survive as an independent nation. But what could the president offer without undermining his party and betraying the voters who had elected him? Historians continue to debate whether an opportunity was lost during the secession crisis or whether the die had already been cast.

462

With the Deep South states in the process of seceding, the new Republican administration, headed by Abraham Lincoln, deliberated over the course it should pursue. The documents reprinted here represent the options that were considered. In the first selection, Henry Adams (the future historian and novelist who was in Washington with his father, Charles Francis Adams, Lincoln's designated ambassador to London) describes the competing approaches of Secretary of State William H. Seward and President Lincoln to the secession crisis. Like his father, the young Adams preferred Seward's policy, a position evident in the extract from his essay entitled "The Great Secession Winter of 1860–61," written just after the war began. The second document is President-elect Lincoln's firm statement to Senator Lyman Trumbull of Illinois on December 10, 1860, that he would not back down from his party's campaign position on slavery in the territories.

While the Upper South states were deciding whether or not to secede, Congressman John A. Gilmer of North Carolina became an important spokesman for the Unionists there. Lincoln's reply of December 15, 1860, to an inquiry from Gilmer about the incoming president's likely policy toward the Upper South appears here as the third document. The fourth is Gilmer's letter to Seward of March 8, 1861, imploring that a strategy of delay and conciliation be pursued to keep the remaining states, particularly Virginia, from seceding. And the final selection is from Seward's memorandum of March 15, 1861, to Lincoln on the resupply of Fort Sumter; the president had asked the entire cabinet for their written advice, and Seward still urged avoidance of confrontation.

Henry Adams Later Describes the Policy Options, 1861

. . . Rather through the faults and mistakes of their opponents than through their own skill, the Republicans managed to maintain their ground tolerably well. Their first fear had been that the North would again yield to some compromise by which the old state of things would be brought back and a new struggle become necessary. Probably their fears would have been justified if the southern States had not, by withdrawing, thrown the whole power into the hands of the firmer anti-slavery men. But when it became evident that the danger did not now lie on this side, but was rather lest all the slave States should be dragged out and thus involve the whole country in a common ruin, a difference of opinion, as to the policy to be pursued, soon showed itself. One wing of the party declared for a strong policy by which the seceding States should be compelled to submit to the laws. Many of these really underrated the danger and difficulty, or, if they saw it, yet could not conscientiously take any steps to avoid it. Others confounded the conspirators with the slave-holders, placing all on the same footing, which was exactly what the disunionists were straining every nerve to bring about. Thus these practically played into the hands of the traitors by doing all in their power to combine the southern States. Others were perhaps conscientiously not unwilling that all the slave States should secede, believing that to be the shortest and surest way of obtaining the destruction of the slave power, as it was certainly a very sure way of obtaining the destruction of their own, if their policy should lead to civil war and a revulsion of feeling in the North. On the other hand, an influential portion of the party urged temporizing till the height of the fever was over, and were in favor of shaping their policy in such a way as to secure the border States and prevent bloodshed. Mr. Seward declared himself very early in the winter a favorer of conciliation in this way. He felt that something must be done, not only to resist disunion in the South, where it was every day acquiring more strength, but to sustain himself and his party in the North, where they were not strong enough to sustain the odium of a dissolution and civil war. For it is a fact, and it is right that it should be so, that with the people the question of the nation's existence will in the end override all party issues, no matter what they may be, and Mr. Seward foresaw that if the new administration was to prove a success it must shape its course so as to avoid the responsibility of the convulsion, and obtain the confidence of a large majority of the people. . . .

Mr. Lincoln arrived in Washington and took up the reins of control. It soon became very evident that, so far as the Republican party is concerned, secession if properly managed is rather a benefit than a misfortune. Anti-slavery was the only ground on which it could act with anything like unanimity. In ordinary times the tariff bill would have broken it down, and even under the tremendous pressure of disunion, the struggle over the Cabinet shook it to its very centre. On all questions except that of slavery it can never act together with any reliable degree of concert, made up as it is of incongruous elements freshly and roughly joined together. Under these circumstances the task of Mr. Lincoln was one which might well have filled with alarm the greatest statesman that ever lived. He had to deal with men and measures that would have taxed the patience of Washington and required the genius of Napoleon. It was therefore not to be expected, nor indeed wished, that on his arrival he would instantly throw himself into the arms of either set of his friends before judging for himself the merits of the case; nor was it possible that all the dangers and pressing necessities of the time should be wholly apparent to him. The matter of the passage of the Corwin measures [essentially, an amendment protecting slavery in the states] became one of secondary interest, the result of those measures depending as they did on the influence which was to prevail in the Cabinet. This influence became now the great feature of the day, and the struggle was vehement between the two wings of the party. The mere fact that the Cabinet had not yet been agreed upon was sufficient to prove that Mr. Lincoln, while placing Mr. Seward in the chief place in his councils, did not intend to allow his influence to rule it, and the result of the contest between the friends of Mr. [Henry] Winter Davis and Mr. [Montgomery] Blair soon decided this question beyond a doubt. Mr. Seward's policy had been to go outside of the party in selecting members of the Cabinet from southern States, and to choose men whose influence would have strengthened the administration. The fact that Mr. Blair, a strict Republican, was preferred over any other man to represent Maryland and Virginia in the Cabinet, was decisive of the policy of Mr. Seward.

When once this question was settled it was of little consequence what became of the proposed measures of conciliation, which were worth nothing, except as one weak link in the chain by which the border States were to be held to the Union. . . .

President-Elect Lincoln Explains What Is at Stake, December 1860

I.

Private, & confidential

Springfield, Ills. Dec. 10, 1860

Hon. L. Trumbull.

My dear Sir: Let there be no compromise on the question of *extending* slavery. If there be, all our labor is lost, and, ere long, must be done again. The dangerous ground—that into which some of our friends have a hankering to run—is Pop. Sov. Have none of it. Stand firm. The tug has to come, & better now, than any time hereafter. Yours as ever,

A. Lincoln

II.

Strictly confidential.

Springfield, Ill. Dec 15, 1860.

Hon. John A. Gilmer:

My dear Sir—Yours of the 10th is received. I am greatly disinclined to write a letter on the subject embraced in yours; and I would not do so, even privately as I do, were it not that I fear you might misconstrue my silence. Is it desired that I shall shift the ground upon which I have been elected? I cannot do it. You need only to acquaint yourself with that ground, and press it on the attention of the South. It is all in print and easy of access. May I be pardoned if I ask whether even you have ever attempted to procure the reading of the Republican platform, or my speeches, by the Southern people? If not, what reason have I to expect that any additional production of mine would meet a better fate? It would make me appear as if I repented for the crime of having been elected, and was anxious to apologize and beg forgiveness. To so represent me, would be the principal use made of any letter I might now thrust upon the public. My old record cannot be so used; and that is precisely the reason that some new declaration is so much sought.

Now, my dear sir, be assured, that I am not questioning *your* candor;

I am only pointing out, that, while a new letter would hurt the cause which I think a just one, you can quite as well effect every patriotic object with the old record. Carefully read pages 18, 19, 74, 75, 88, 89, & 267 of the volume of Joint Debates between Senator Douglas and myself, with the Republican Platform adopted at Chicago, and all your questions will be substantially answered. I have no thought of recommending the abolition of slavery in the District of Columbia, nor the slave trade among the slave states, even on the conditions indicated; and if I were to make such recommendation, it is quite clear Congress would not follow it.

As to employing slaves in Arsenals and Dockyards, it is a thing I never thought of in my life, to my recollection, till I saw your letter; and I may say of it, precisely as I have said of the two points above.

As to the use of patronage in the slave states, where there are few or no Republicans, I do not expect to inquire for the politics of the appointee, or whether he does or not own slaves. I intend in that matter to accommodate the people in the several localities, if they themselves will allow me to accommodate them. In one word, I never have been, am not now, and probably never shall be, in a mood of harassing the people, either North or South.

On the territorial question, I am inflexible, as you see my position in the book. On that, there is a difference between you and us; and it is the only substantial difference. You think slavery is right and ought to be extended; we think it is wrong and ought to be restricted. For this, neither has any just occasion to be angry with the other.

As to the state laws, mentioned in your sixth question, I really know very little of them. I never have read one. If any of them are in conflict with the fugitive slave clause, or any other part of the constitution, I certainly should be glad of their repeal; but I could hardly be justified, as a citizen of Illinois, or as President of the United States, to recommend the repeal of a statute of Vermont, or South Carolina.

With the assurance of my highest regards I subscribe myself

Your obt. Servt.,

A. Lincoln

A North Carolina Unionist Urges Delay and Conciliation, March 1861

Confidential.

Greensboro, N.C., March 8th

Since the defeat of the secessionists on the 28th in this state they have become furious. Our Governor went down to Wilmington on last Saturday among his fellow disunionists, was called, and made a speech to a large crowd of disunionists. He was bold, and defiant. He said that circumstances would soon occur, which would induce N.C. to retrace her steps, and that she would be out of the Union soon.

The only hope of the secessionists now is that some sort of collision will be brought about between federal and state forces in one of the seceding states. I have full confidence that you in some way wiser and better than I can devise or suggest can prevent this.

If you can do this, I believe I can say that Virginia can be kept from secession. You can do much to quiet Virginia. If the Virginia convention can adjourn without harm to the peace of the country, a great point will be gained. If the border states can be retained, Mississippi, Louisiana and Texas will soon be back. If the others never come back, there will be no great loss. But I believe Georgia and Alabama will also soon want to return.

If for any decent excuse the Govt. could withdraw the troops from all the southern fortifications, the moment this is known N.C., Va., Md., Del., Ky., Tenn., Md. and I believe Arkansas are certainly retained. The only thing now that gives the secessionists the advantage of the conservatives is the cry of coercion—that the whipping of a slave state, is the whipping of slavery.

When these states come back as many of them will they will come with the fortifications. If they do not find it to their interest to return let them keep their plunder—or if any whipping is to be done let it be after the other slave states have certainly determined to remain.

The present excitement should be allowed to pass away as soon as possible without fighting.

Secretary of State Seward Advises Restraint, March 1861

. . . The policy of the time, therefore, has seemed to me to consist in conciliation, which should deny to disunionists any new provocation or apparent offence, while it would enable the Unionists in the slave states to maintain with truth and with effect that the alarms and apprehensions put forth by the disunionists are groundless and false.

I have not been ignorant of the objections that the administration was elected through the activity of the Republican party; that it must continue to deserve and retain the confidence of that party; while conciliation toward the slave states tends to demoralize the Republican party itself, on which party the main responsibility of maintaining the Union must rest.

But it has seemed to me a sufficient answer—first, that the administration could not demoralize the Republican party without making some sacrifice of its essential principles, while no such sacrifice is necessary, or is anywhere authoritatively proposed; and secondly, if it be indeed true that pacification is necessary to prevent dismemberment of the Union and civil war, or either of them, no patriot and lover of humanity could hesitate to surrender party for the higher interests of country and humanity.

Partly by design, partly by chance, this policy has been hitherto pursued by the late administration of the Federal government, and by the Republican party in its corporate action. It is by this policy, thus pursued, I think, that the progress of dismemberment has been arrested after the seven Gulf states had seceded, and the border states yet remain, although they do so uneasily, in the Union.

It is to a perseverance in this policy for a short time longer that I look as the only peaceful means of assuring the continuance of Virginia, Maryland, North Carolina, Kentucky, Tennessee, Missouri, and Arkansas, or most of those states in the Union. It is through their good and patriotic offices that I look to see the Union sentiment revived and brought once more into activity in the seceding states, and through this agency those states themselves returning into the Union. . . .

The fact, then, is that while the people of the border states desire to be loyal, they are at the same time sadly, though temporarily, demoralized by a sympathy for the slave states, which makes them forget their loyalty whenever there are any grounds for apprehending that the Federal government will resort to military coercion against the seceding states, even though such coercion should be necessary to maintain the authority, or even the integrity, of the Union. This sympathy is unreasonable, unwise, and dangerous, and therefore cannot, if left undisturbed, be permanent. It can be banished, however, only in one way, and that is by giving time for it to wear out, and for reason to resume its sway. Time will do this, if it be not hindered by new alarms and provocations. . . .

The question submitted to us, then, practically is: Supposing it to be possible to reinforce and supply Fort Sumter, is it wise now to attempt it, instead of withdrawing the garrison?

The most that could be done by any means now in our hands would be to throw two hundred and fifty to four hundred men into the garrison, with provisions for supplying it five or six months. In this active and enlightened country, in this season of excitement, with a daily press, daily mails, and an incessantly operating telegraph, the design to reinforce and supply the garrison must become known to the opposite party at Charleston as soon at least as preparation for it should begin. The garrison would then almost certainly fall by assault before the expedition could reach the harbor of Charleston. But supposing the secret kept, the expedition must engage in conflict on entering the harbor of Charleston; suppose it to be overpowered and destroyed, is that new outrage to be avenged, or are we then to return to our attitude of immobility? Should we be allowed to do so? Moreover, in that event, what becomes of the garrison?

I suppose the expedition successful. We have then a garrison in Fort Sumter that can defy assault for six months. What is it to do then? Is it to make war by opening its batteries and attempting to demolish the defences of the Carolinians? Can it demolish them if it tries? If it cannot, what is the advantage we shall have gained? If it can, how will it serve to check or prevent disunion?

In either case, it seems to me that we will have inaugurated a civil war by our own act, without an adequate object, after which reunion will be hopeless, at least under this administration, or in any other way than by a popular disavowal both of the war and of the administration which unnecessarily commenced it. Fraternity is the element of union; war is the very element of disunion. Fraternity, if practised by this administration, will rescue the Union from all its dangers. If this administration, on the other hand, take up the sword, then an opposite party will offer the olive branch, and will, as it ought, profit by the restoration of peace and union. . . .

Fighting the War:
The Experience of the Soldiers

In recent years, the field of history has been transformed by the blossoming of an awareness of and concern about the doings of ordinary people. Military history has also been affected by this interest in the masses—"history from the bottom up" instead of "from the top down." Beginning perhaps with John Keegan, in his Face of Battle *(1976), which explored the experience of combat by British soldiers in three major battles—Agincourt in 1415, Waterloo in 1815, and the Somme in 1916—many military historians have become social historians of battles and wars. This kind of attention is also being directed toward American military history, especially in the Civil War era. Studies of how battles were fought from the ground up are appearing, as are analyses of the combat experience of the rank and file.*

The sources for this kind of account and analysis are particularly rich for the American Civil War, because the participants left an immense array of memoirs and recollections, a large number of which were published. This unusual outpouring of accounts by ordinary soldiers occurred for several reasons besides the high level of literacy among the combatants. First, there was a great deal of interest among the civilian populations in a war that was fought on their own soil rather than in a foreign land. And second, those who fought were greeted with respect, even awe, when they returned home, since both sides—even the defeated Confederates—regarded the struggle as worthy and heroic. So there was an audience eager to read the reminiscences of Civil War soldiers.

The existence of such a valuable resource will undoubtedly facilitate the writing of the military history of the Civil War from the bottom up. But it will have to be used with care, since the writers of most of these memoirs either stressed the adventure and bravery in the experience or else narrated in great detail what happened without revealing their own feelings and emotions while under fire or in the hospitals and camps. The historian's task of discovering the inner thoughts and experiences of common soldiers is therefore likely to be more difficult than it first seemed, and it will require considerable insight and imagination. Moreover, the outcome of these kinds of studies will almost certainly be a greater awareness of the seamy side of this war—its horror, drudgery, and incompetence. From the foot soldier's point of view, a war that has been treated almost with reverence by subsequent generations may begin to look rather less grand.

The experience of combat is the main focus of the documents that follow, but other aspects, particularly religion, are also illustrated. The first selection presents two songs from among the many that were composed during the war and sung by the soldiers. Both are northern, but one is religious and sentimental, while the other is worldly and impudent. A letter to his father written by Eugene Blackford of the 5th Alabama Volunteer Infantry Regiment on July 22, 1861, recounting his first battlefield experience, is the second document. The third selection offers a rather different view of courage in combat; it is from a book of wartime memoirs published by John Dooley, an Irish infantryman in the Confederate Army of Northern Virginia who went into battle on numerous occasions.

The fourth selection captures the frustration, and often anger, that soldiers felt about the war. In it, Frank Wilkeson, a northern private, approves of his colleagues' unwillingness to fight at one point during the siege at Petersburg, Virginia, in June 1864. Similarly, the fifth extract, which is from the letters of Tully McCrea, an officer in the Army of the Potomac, to his wife, reveals how commanders' actions were often ridiculed by their soldiers, usually with good reason, as was the case in this incident before Chancellorsville in January 1863. The grisly horrors of combat are depicted vividly in the sixth selection, an account by General Carl Schurz of what he witnessed in the Federal field hospitals after Gettysburg in July 1863.

The last two documents illustrate the role of religion in the Confederacy. Jefferson Davis's Proclamation of October 26, 1864, calling for a Day of Prayer, is one instance of many official invocations of God's aid, indicating how much the Confederate cause was imbued with religious sentiment. And the eighth and last selection is a postwar account of the religious revivals in the 19th Alabama Regiment from its chaplain, Reverend Dr. John J. D. Renfroe. This description is just one of a host of eyewitness reports collected by John William Jones in his *Christ in the Camp; or, Religion in Lee's Army* (1887).

Songs the Soldiers Sang—Sentimental and Secular

Just Before the Battle, Mother

> Just before the battle, mother,
> I am thinking most of you;
> While upon the field we are watching,
> With the enemy in view.
> Comrades brave are 'round me lying,
> Filled with thoughts of home and God;
> For well they know upon the morrow
> Some will sleep beneath the sod.

> *Chorus:* Farewell, mother, you may never
> Press me to your heart again;
> But, oh, you'll not forget me, mother,
> If I'm numbered with the slain.

Oh! I long to see you, mother,
And the loving ones at home;
But I'll never leave our banner
'Till in honor I can come.
Tell the enemy around you
That their cruel words, we know,
In every battle kill our soldiers
By the help they give the foe.—*Chorus*

—George F. Root

We Are the Boys of Potomac's Ranks

We are the boys of Potomac's ranks,
  Hurrah! Hurrah!
We are the boys of Potomac's ranks,
We ran with McDowell, retreated with Banks,
And we'll all drink stone blind—
Johnny, fill up the bowl.

We fought with McClellan, the Rebs, shakes, and fever,
  Hurrah! Hurrah!
We fought with McClellan, the Rebs, shakes, and fever,
But Mac joined the navy on reaching James River,
And we'll all drink stone blind—
Johnny, fill up the bowl.

They gave us John Pope, our patience to tax,
  Hurrah! Hurrah!
They gave us John Pope, our patience to tax,
Who said that out West he'd seen naught but *gray backs,*
And we'll all drink stone blind—
Johnny, fill up the bowl.

He said his headquarters were in the saddle,
  Hurrah! Hurrah!
He said his headquarters were in the saddle,
But Stonewall Jackson made him skedaddle—
And we'll all drink stone blind—
Johnny, fill up the bowl.

Then Mac was recalled, but after Antietam,
  Hurrah! Hurrah!
Then Mac was recalled, but after Antietam
Abe gave him a rest, he was too slow to beat 'em,
And we'll all drink stone blind—
Johnny, fill up the bowl.

Oh, Burnside, then he tried his luck,
  Hurrah! Hurrah!

Oh, Burnside, then he tried his luck,
But in the mud so fast got stuck,
And we'll all drink stone blind—
Johnny, fill up the bowl.

Then Hooker was taken to fill the bill,
   Hurrah! Hurrah!
Then Hooker was taken to fill the bill,
But he got a black eye at Chancellorsville,
And we'll all drink stone blind—
Johnny, fill up the bowl.

Next came General Meade, a slow old plug,
   Hurrah! Hurrah!
Next came General Meade, a slow old plug,
For he let them get away at Gettysburg,
And we'll all drink stone blind—
Johnny, fill up the bowl.

—Authur Unknown

A Federal Soldier Deals with Combat, July 1861

Bivouac Camp of the Advanced Guard,
on the railroad near Union Mills
Above Manassas

22nd July, 1861

My Dear Father:

We are very much fatigued and jaded by our late movements. I must relieve your anxiety by letting you know that I am alive and well. I was in the great battle of yesterday, tho our regt. arrived too late to take any considerable part in the action. But I will go back and let you know what I have been doing since this day a week.

Last Monday the enemy advanced their lines considerably and caused our pickets to fall back some two miles. We were up all Tuesday night expecting to march down to the battery to defend it. At 8 o'clock Wednesday, the advance guard of the enemy appeared, and we went out to give battle. We all took our positions behind our entrenchments, and remained there some time while parties of our men were skirmishing in front.

At last they were driven in, and the firing commenced upon our line. The enemy, having minie muskets, could fire upon us long before we could think of returning the compliment, and so we had to take it coolly. No wound was sustained by our men (in my company) except one pretty badly wounded. The balls make a very loud singing noise when they pass near you, and at first caused me to duck my head, but I soon became used to it. I never expected to be alarmed or excited in battle, but really it is a very different affair from what I thought it. I never was cooler in my life, and have ever since been very much pleased therefore, as I shall have no trouble hereafter.

Just as we were about to make our fire general, news was brought that the [Illinois] had retreated from Fairfax Court House and thus had exposed our flank. Of course there was nothing to be done but to retreat. This we barely had time to do, the enemy was almost in sight of the crossroads when we passed at double quick. Had we been twenty minutes later, we would have been cut off utterly. As I said before, we marched quick time for twenty miles to this place, my company being deployed as skirmishers on the side next to the enemy. The part was one of honor and implied trust, but it was at a great cost, as the country was awfully rough, and we suffered very much. . . .

We then came right about and set off to reinforce our men in the great battle (not yet named) about ten miles from us. This distance we marched at double time and came on the field about five o'clock, too late as I said to do much service, but early enough to smell a little gunpowder and receive a little of the enemy's fire. We went over the battlefield several miles in extent. T'was truly awful, an immense cloud of smoke and dust hung over the whole country, and the flashing of the artillery was incessant tho none of the balls struck my company. One bomb burst a little above me, and killed and wounded several. This was our only loss. Had we been an hour earlier, many would not have lived to tell of it.

I shan't attempt to describe the appearance of the field, literally covered with bodies, and for five miles before reaching it I saw men limping off, more or less wounded. We met wagon loads of bodies coming off to Manassas, where they are now piled in heaps. While we were looking over the field, an order came for us to go back to our batteries ten miles off, and defend them from the enemy who were advancing upon them, so we had to go back, tired as we were, to our holes, where we arrived half dead at twelve o'clock last night, having marched twenty-six miles heavily loaded. We have no protection against the rain, which has been falling all day. I have no blanket, not having seen my baggage since leaving Fairfax; I never was so dirty before in my life and besides I have scurvy in my mouth, not having anything but hard bread and intensely salty meat to eat, and not enough of that.

I do not however complain, nor do my men, tho I never thought that such hardships were to be endured. We have our meat in the blaze, and eat it on our bread. A continual firing is now going on around us.

Your affectionate son,

Eugene Blackford

A Confederate Soldier Acknowledges Fear, (Undated)

The Psychology of Soldiers' Fear

We know how straight into the very jaws of destruction and death leads this road of Gettysburg; and none of us are yet aware that a battle is before us; still there pervades our ranks a solemn feeling, as if some unforeseen danger was ever dropping darksome shadows over the road we unshrinkingly tread.

For myself, I must confess that the terrors of the battlefield grew not less as we advanced in the war, for I felt far less fear in the second battle of Manassas than at South Mountain or even at Fredericksburg; and I believe that soldiers generally do not fear death less because of their repeated escape from its jaws. For, in every battle they see so many new forms of death, see so many frightful and novel kinds of mutilation, see such varying fortunes in the tide of strife, and appreciate so highly their deliverance from destruction, that their dread of incurring the like fearful perils unnerves them for each succeeding conflict, quite as much as their confidence in their oft tried courage sustains them and stimulates them to gain new laurels at the cannon's mouth.

An Officer Laments the Inadequacy of Northern Generals, January 1863

. . . Tomorrow the army is going to cross the river again and attack the enemy. The attack this time is going to be made upon their right, instead of the center. This movement has been in contemplation for a week past and everyone has been praying for a rain or a snow to stop it. No one seems to have any confidence in what we attempt to do. The movement began today. The left and center Grand Divisions commanded by Generals Franklin and Hooker moved up the river today, ready to commence the crossing in the morning. General Sumner's Grand Division, which is the right, is to act as reserve. General Sumner is as mad as he can be because he could not have the advance. Whenever there is a fight he wants to be in the thickest of it, which accounts for his old corps (the Second) being now reduced so low by the severe losses that they have sustained. He never spares himself either, but rides wherever the bullets are thickest and takes his whole staff with him. It did not rain in time to prevent the movement, but now that the movement has begun, it has commenced to rain. . . . About eighty thousand men are now marching or standing shivering in the rain. On the Rebel side I suppose that they are equally busy, for no doubt they are by this time fully informed where the attack is to be made and are preparing to meet it. (January 20, 1863.)

. . . General Sumner was today relieved from command and his splendid staff, with nearly all of whom I was acquainted and intimate, is broken up. Two of them were just here. One is going home on a leave of absence, the other, MacKenzie, is going to Acquia Creek tomorrow to lay fortifications and will not be back for some time. I am not the only one who feels blue. A feeling of despondency hangs over this whole army. Burnside was liked, although none had much confidence in his ability to command this large army. General Franklin, who is regarded as the most able of the generals with the army, has been ordered to Washington like General Sumner, and Joe Hooker takes command. Dear me! This army is fast going to ruin. It is hard indeed after all the hardships, gallant fighting, and long service that it has seen that it should at last be disgraced, all for no fault of its own, but merely through the meddling of the officials at Washington. (January 26, 1863.)

A Federal Private Applauds a Refusal to Fight, June 1864

. . . In the morning I saw that there had been some advance of the line. The Second Corps had gained a little ground at great cost, and we heard that Burnside had also gained ground and captured a redoubt. The dead soldiers of the Second Corps lay thickly in front of us, placed in long trenches by their comrades.

That afternoon the battery quartermaster-sergeant, goaded to desperation by the taunts of the artillery privates, nerved himself with whiskey and came to the battery to display his courage. The Confederate sharp-shooters had attacked us about noon, and our works were hot. I, snugly seated under the earthworks, looked at this representative of the staff with all the intense dislike privates have for the gold-laced officers. I was wicked enough to wish that he would get shot. He swaggered up and down behind the guns, talking loudly, and ignorant of the danger. I, with high-beating heart, looked eagerly at him, hungrily waiting for him to jump and howl. I was disappointed. A sharp-shooter's bullet struck him on the throat. It crashed through his spine at the base of the brain, and he neither jumped nor howled—simply fell on his back dead.

Early on the morning of June 18th, some of our pickets brought word to the battery that the Confederates had abandoned their front line during the night, and that they had moved back to their interior line, which was shorter and stronger and more easily defended. The infantry soldiers moved forward, and occupied the works they had been unable to capture. My battery moved to another position, and again the guns opened on the Confederate line, and again they husbanded their ammunition. But their sharp-shooters fairly made us howl with anguish. I heartily wished that Lee had not abandoned his front line. Our infantry moved to and fro, getting ready to assault the new line of intrenchments. The soldiers were thoroughly discouraged. They had no heart for the assault. It was evident that they had determined not to fight staunchly, not to attempt to accomplish the impossible. At about four o'clock in the afternoon the infantry was sent to the slaughter, and the Confederates promptly killed a sufficient number of them to satisfy our generals that the works could not be taken by assaults delivered by exhausted and discouraged troops. In many places our battle line did not advance to the line of rifle-pits held by the Confederate pickets. We had lost about 12,000 men in the attempts to capture Petersburg. The Second Corps could have taken the city on the night of June 15th without losing more than 500 men. This fact disheartened the enlisted men of the Army of the Potomac. They were supremely disgusted with the display of military stupidity our generals had made.

We marched somewhere at night. The road was lined with sleeping infantry. I was hungry. As I look back at those bloody days it seems to me that I was always hungry. Men to the right of us, to the left of us, lay as though dead—they slept so soundly; but their haversacks were not in sight. They were veterans who knew enough to hide their haversacks when they slept on roads. We came to a heavy double line of men, who looked as if they had opened ranks and then fallen over asleep. Soon we light-artillery men recognized them as 100-day men from Ohio. Their haversacks stood at their heads. Wickedly we all went to plundering the 100-day men as they slept. We exchanged our empty haversacks for full ones, and every man of us had a spare haversack filled with food hanging on the guns or caissons. At the time I thought it a capital joke on the Ohio men; but I now think that some of those men were very hungry before they got any thing to eat. They must have bitter recollections of the night march of some of the Second Corps' artillery. . . .

General Carl Schurz Describes the Horror of the Field Hospitals after Gettysburg, July 1863

. . . There were more harrowing experiences in store for me that day. To look after the wounded of my command, I visited the places where the surgeons were at work. At Bull Run, I had seen only on a very small scale what I was now to behold. At Gettysburg the wounded—many thousands of them—were carried to the farmsteads behind our lines. The houses, the barns, the sheds, and the open barnyards were crowded with moaning and wailing human beings, and still an unceasing procession of stretchers and ambulances was coming in from all sides to augment the number of the sufferers. A heavy rain set in during the day—the usual rain after a battle—and large numbers had to remain unprotected in the open, there being no room left under roof. I saw long rows of men lying under the eaves of the buildings, the water pouring down upon their bodies in streams. Most of the operating tables were placed in the open where the light was best, some of them partially protected against the rain by tarpaulins or blankets stretched upon poles. There stood the surgeons, their sleeves rolled up to the elbows, their bare arms as well as their linen aprons smeared with blood, their knives not seldom held between their teeth, while they were helping a patient on or off the table, or had their hands otherwise occupied; around them pools of blood and amputated arms or legs in heaps, sometimes more than man-high. Antiseptic methods were still unknown at that time. As a wounded man was lifted on the table, often shrieking with pain as the attendants handled him, the surgeon quickly examined the wound and resolved upon cutting off the injured limb. Some ether was administered and the body put in position in a moment. The surgeon snatched his knife from between his teeth, where it had been while his hands were busy, wiped it rapidly once or twice across his blood-stained apron, and the cutting began. The operation accomplished, the surgeon would look around with a deep sigh, and then—"Next!"

And so it went on, hour after hour, while the number of expectant patients seemed hardly to diminish. Now and then one of the wounded men would call attention to the fact that his neighbor lying on the ground had given up the ghost while waiting for his turn, and the dead body was then quietly removed. Or a surgeon, having been long at work, would put down his knife, exclaiming that his hand had grown unsteady, and that this was too much for human endurance—not seldom hysterical tears streaming down his face. Many of the wounded men suffered with silent fortitude, fierce determination in the knitting of their brows and the steady gaze of their bloodshot eyes. Some would even force themselves to a grim jest about their situation or about the "skedaddling of the rebels." But there were, too, heart-rending groans and shrill cries of pain piercing the air, and despairing exclamations, "Oh, Lord! Oh, Lord!" or "Let me die!" or softer murmurings in which the words "mother" or "father" or "home" were often heard. I saw many of my command among the sufferers, whose faces I well remembered, and who greeted me with a look or even a painful smile of recognition, and usually with the question what I thought of their chances of life, or whether I could do anything for them, sometimes, also, whether I thought the enemy were well beaten. I was sadly conscious that many of the words of cheer and encouragement I gave them were mere hollow sound, but they might be at least some solace for the moment.

There are people who speak lightly of war as a mere heroic sport. They would hardly find it in their hearts to do so, had they ever witnessed scenes like these, and thought of the untold miseries connected with them that were spread all over the land. He must be an inhuman brute or a slave of wild, unscrupulous ambition, who, having seen the horrors of war, will not admit that war brought on without the most absolute necessity, is the greatest and most unpardonable of crimes.

President Davis Seeks God's Aid and Mercy, October 1864

A Proclamation

It is meet that the people of the Confederate States should, from time to time, assemble to acknowledge their dependence on Almighty God, to render devout thanks to his holy name, to bend in prayer at his footstool, and to accept, with fervent submission, the chastening of his all-wise and all-merciful providence.

Let us, then, in temples and in the field, unite our voices in recognizing, with adoring gratitude, the manifestations of his protecting care in the many signal victories with which our arms have been crowned; in the fruitfulness with which our land has been blessed, and in the unimpaired energy and fortitude with which he has inspired our hearts and strengthened our arms in resistance to the iniquitous designs of our enemies.

And let us not forget that, while graciously vouchsafing to us his protection, our sins have merited and received grievous chastisement; that many of our best and bravest have fallen in battle; that many others are still held in foreign prisons; that large districts of our country have been devastated with savage ferocity, the peaceful homes destroyed, and helpless women and children driven away in destitution; and that with fiendish malignity the passions of a servile race have been excited by our foes into the commission of atrocities from which death is a welcome escape.

Now, therefore, I, Jefferson Davis, President of the Confederate States of America, do issue this my proclamation, setting apart Wednesday, the 16th day of November next, as a day to be specially devoted to the worship of Almighty God; and I do invite and invoke all the people of these Confederate States to assemble on the day aforesaid, in their respective places of public worship, there to unite in prayer to our Heavenly Father that he bestow his favor upon us; that he extend over us the protection of his almighty arm; that he sanctify his chastisement to our improvement, so that we may turn away from evil paths and walk righteously in his sight; and that he may restore peace to our beloved country, healing its bleeding wounds, and securing to us the continued enjoyment of our own right to self-government and independence, and that he will graciously hearken to us while we ascribe to him the power and glory of our independence.

Given under my hand and the seal of the Confederate States at Richmond, this 26th day of October, in the year of our Lord 1864.

Jefferson Davis.

By the President:

J. P. Benjamin, *Secretary of State.*

A Confederate Chaplain Recounts His Experience of the Revivals (1863–1864), January 1867

[From Rev. Dr. Renfroe, Baptist, Chaplain Tenth Alabama Regiment.]

Talladega, Alabama, January 31, 1867.

Dear Brother Jones: In attempting to give you some account of the religious character of Wilcox's old brigade, in the army of Northern Virginia, I find that I am entirely dependent upon my memory. I loaned my "notes" of events to a brother, who now informs me that he cannot lay his hand on them, having mislaid them.

The Tenth Alabama was the regiment of which I was chaplain. The brigade was composed of the Eighth, Ninth, Tenth, Eleventh and Fourteenth Alabama Regiments. I reckon this brigade comprised as noble a body of men as ever served in any army. I reached my post of duty while the army was in winter-quarters at Fredericksburg, in the early part of the year 1863. There were then three other chaplains in that brigade, but they were all then absent but one. Very little preaching had been done in the brigade up to that time. Many Christian soldiers and other good-disposed men told me that I could do no good in preaching to soldiers, but all seemed glad to welcome me among them. I was acquainted with a large number of the regiment before the war. The first Sabbath after I got there I preached twice, and from that time until I left them, I had a large attendance upon worship, and as good order in my congregations as I ever had at home. About that time the Rev. Mr. Bell, of Greenville, Alabama, visited the Eighth, which had no chaplain. He and I preached daily for two weeks. He baptized a Mr. Lee, of Marion, Alabama, the first profession that I saw in the army; though there were many men in the brigade who were Christians before they went to the army, and who maintained their religion. The chaplains of the brigade soon returned. We built arbors, and preached regularly to large and attentive congregations—on through the spring this continued—only interrupted by the battle of Chancellorsville. Then came the campaign to Gettysburg. I preached thirteen sermons on that campaign, but not more than half of them to our own brigade. I preached several sermons in line of battle. After we returned to the south side of the Potomac, at Bunker's Hill, we had several sermons in the brigade. Two of the chaplains (Mr. Rains, of the Fourteenth, and Mr. Whitten, of the Ninth) remained at Gettysburg with the wounded. Up to this time I saw but few signs of the good work—I saw no evidences of revival—I heard of no conversions in our brigade. Then we fell back to Orange Court House. There we at once established arbors—one in the Fourteenth, one in the Tenth, and began to preach. Rev. Mr. Johnson, chaplain of the Eleventh, and Mr. Cumbie, Lieutenant in the Fourteenth, did the preaching at the Fourteenth's preaching place. Their labors were blessed, and many were converted. At the preaching place of the Tenth I did the preaching for the most part. This lasted for about six weeks, in which time I was visited and aided by Rev. A. E. Dickinson, of Richmond, who preached for me a week; then by Rev. J. B. F. Mays, of Alabama, who preached nearly a week for me. God greatly blessed our efforts. I have stood at that place at night and on Sabbaths and preached, as it seemed to me, to a solid acre of men. I think I have seen as many as five or six hundred men, in one way and another, manifest at one time a desire to be prayed for. I have never seen such a time before or since. There were as many evidences of genuine penitence as I ever noticed at home—yes, more. Almost every day there would be a dozen conversions, and there were in the six weeks in the brigade, not less than five hundred who professed conversion. Not all of our brigade, for there was a battalion of artillery camped near us, and other brigades, who attended our preaching, many of whom professed religion. We estimated the conversions then at five hundred and fifty. I baptized about one hundred, Brother Cumbie about fifty, and most of the others joined the Methodists. This work, as you know, prevailed nearly all through the army. But it was partially interrupted by the fall campaign, when we drove Meade back to Bull Run. But the army returned from that campaign to Orange, went into winter-quarters and spent the winter there. Part of this winter I was at home on furlough. But prayer-meetings, Bible-classes and preaching were successfully kept up through the winter. And the revival also, in a less degree, continued. The Young Men's Christian Association was largely attended, many went to exhorting, and a great many prayed in public, some of whom were greatly gifted. A most interesting feature was the large number who would retire after the evening "roll-call" in groups, to pray. Walk out from camp at that hour in any direction and you would find them, two, three, half-dozen and a dozen, in a place, all bowed in the dark, earnestly praying for themselves and the conversion of their comrades; they nearly always took some unconverted ones with them.

Through the awful campaign of 1864 there were very limited opportunities to preach to this brigade. It was almost constantly under fire or on the march. From the Wilderness to Petersburg and around Petersburg, this was the case. Though I preached to them as often as I could, yet most of my preaching was to other commands. I have several times preached when shot and shell were flying over our heads, and also several times I had minnie-balls to strike in my congregation while preaching. We often had prayer-meetings in the trenches, where God did greatly bless and comfort our hearts. In the winter-quarters at Petersburg there was much faithful preaching, and regular prayer-meetings kept up in this brigade.

1. I believe that the conversions were genuine. There were exceptions of course. But I received candidates for baptism just as I do at home, *i. e.,* I assembled the Baptists of the regiment, heard a relation of the applicants' Christian experience, took the vote, etc. All other Baptist ministers, I think, did the same. And their statements of the work of grace were clear and satisfactory.

2. So far as my knowledge extended, these converts maintained their professions with astonishing faithfulness. Up to the time that I left them, I knew of but two or three exceptions.

3. The character of the brigade was decidedly moral and religious, compared with what it was before this good work began. The worship of God became a fixed part of the regular duties of the brigade. The religious element was as well defined, as well organized and as constant, as in any congregation to whom I have preached. Christians were recognized as such, ministers were respected and kindly treated and loved. I have never had a congregation at home that seemed to esteem me more, and certainly I never loved a congregation so much. I never was treated disrespectfully by a soldier or officer while I was in the army—not in one instance. They preserved a tender regard for my feelings. None of them ever gambled or swore in my immediate presence; if any did swear in my immediate presence in a moment of unguarded levity or haste or passion, they always followed it with a becoming apology. Card-playing and the like ceased to be public in this brigade, except among the Irish Catholics, of whom there were three companies, who seemed "neither to fear God nor regard man"; only they were very good soldiers.

4. The officers of my regiment, to a man, were respectful to me and to my position. They always attended preaching. There was no exception. Some of them were good Christians, while all believed that there was no officer in the regiment worth more to it than a good chaplain, and no part of their daily duties of so much importance as that of religious services. The men who commanded the regiment for the most part of the time that I was with them, were: Colonel W. H. Forney, Episcopalian; Lieutenant-

Colonel Shelley, Methodist inclined; Major Joseph Truss, Baptist; Captain Brewster, of seemingly no fixed denominational preference. There never was a time that any one of these noble spirits would not do any and every thing that I desired to further the interests of public worship, preaching, prayer-meetings, etc. They did not allow anything that they could control to interfere with our hours of worship. And Colonel Shelley, who commanded most of the time (Colonel Forney being a prisoner), often said that the work of the chaplain was essential to the welfare of the regiment, essential to its efficiency, etc. The officers of the brigade, nearly all of them, were similar in conduct and disposition to those of my own regiment. And so I found the officers throughout the army, so far as I had opportunity to test the matter. No one of any rank ever treated me other than respectfully and kindly.

5. There were some very efficient Christians in the brigade. Lieutenant Cumbie, of the Fourteenth Regiment, was a most useful man. He was pious, devoted and active, a very good preacher, a brave soldier and an efficient officer. Privates E. B. Hardie, of the Tenth, and Jacob Nelson, of the same regiment, were both most excellent young men, faithful and zealous in the service of the Lord, and brave soldiers. Both of them were young ministers. These three men were Baptists, and are pastors at home now, and successful. There were many others who were not preachers, that were in every way faithful and true.

6. So far as I have been able to observe, those who professed religion in the army and lived to get home, are as faithful, constant and zealous now, as any other part of the religious community. I am pastor of several of them, and I know many others. Some of them are splendid church-members; but some have made shipwreck of the faith, or never had any faith. Yet I think three-fourths are maintaining a good profession, and proving that they were truly converted.

7. I believe it was generally conclusive that religious men made the best soldiers. And I know that officers frequently expressed themselves as believing thus. Religious soldiers complained less at army regulations, hard service and short rations. They did their duty more generally and more willingly, and I never knew one of them to disgrace himself in battle. Many of them died at their posts. They straggled less on marches, and committed fewer depredations on the rights of citizens.

8. The religious *status* of this brigade remained firm and decided to the surrender of the army.

Brother Jones, I am aware that this letter is a very poor and indifferent account of the religious standing of my old brigade. Maybe, however, that you can get something out of it. I baptized about two hundred while I was in the army, two years, but nearly half of them were men of other brigades than my own, and converted under the ministry of other men. The Lord bless you in your good work,

Yours fraternally,

J. J. D. Renfroe

Emancipation and Its Aftermath

As the war began, Frederick Douglass lamented that, since the North was anti-slavery but opposed to abolition, the outcome of the contest was of little concern to the slaves themselves. Whichever side won, they would still remain in slavery. Nevertheless, pressure to widen the scope of the conflict to include abolition as a war aim was constantly brought to bear on the Lincoln administration by the abolitionists and their political allies, the radical wing of the Republican party.

The president resisted these demands, however. He feared that any advocacy of emancipation would stiffen Confederate resistance and, quite likely, scare slaveholders in Union areas like Missouri and Kentucky into carrying their states over to the Confederacy. Besides giving comfort to the enemy, sympathy for abolition would certainly frighten northern whites, who widely feared the consequence of slave liberation and would hesitate to support or fight in a war to free millions of blacks.

By midsummer 1862, after the border states had rejected his offer of financial compensation in return for gradual abolition, President Lincoln was compelled to move against slavery more forcefully. In September he announced his intention of proclaiming emancipation on January 1, 1863. This was a courageous and radical step. It made the destruction of slavery a certain consequence of northern victory, while it also confronted the nation with the eventual yet disturbing prospect of assimilating a vast population of black people. In the meantime, slaves within the Union lines could be conscripted into the Federal army and, with guns in their hands, fight to secure their freedom. Other aspects of Lincoln's initiative were less bold, however. The proclamation applied only to the slaves currently located inside the Confederacy, so in practice it freed no slaves at all. Moreover, emancipation would not be officially achieved until 1865, when the Thirteenth Amendment was ratified. Also, the tenor of Lincoln's announcement was rather grudging. He did not grandly proclaim liberation. Rather, he indicated that he was embarking upon it primarily out of military necessity.

The revolutionary implications of the decision for emancipation were, in effect, tempered by the cautious manner of its execution. Similarly mixed was the experience of emancipation by the slaves themselves. After the exhilaration of the first months of liberation, the former slaves soon discovered that their freedom was to be severely limited. Gains were made, but frequently they turned out to be more fleeting and insubstantial than had been hoped. The freedmen must therefore have wondered, as have historians ever since, how radical and transforming emancipation really was.

Emancipation was both a question of policy at the highest levels of the Federal government and a matter of practical experience for the liberated slaves on the lowest rungs of southern society. The documents reflect both aspects of this episode.

The first document is President Lincoln's much-quoted reply of August 22, 1862, to Horace Greeley, the antislavery editor of the *New York Tribune,* explaining to him that saving the Union was his "paramount object." A short time later, Lincoln decided that emancipation had become a necessary means to that end, and he defended his action in the second selection, a long letter of August 26, 1863, to James C. Conkling and other Illinois Republicans who had called a mass meeting in Springfield and invited Lincoln to attend. The third extract, from the preliminary report of the American Freedmen's Inquiry Commission, issued on June 30, 1863, reveals the way that sympathetic members of a government commission initially approached the question of the free blacks' future status in society. In the fourth document, Frederick Douglass, the most influential African-American spokesman at the time, gives an impatient answer in April 1865 to the very same inquiry about the social status of the former slaves.

As for the freedmen themselves, the fifth selection provides some information, since it is a report of August 23, 1863, from Adjutant-General Lorenzo Thomas, the official responsible for those slaves in the Mississippi Delta who had fled to the Union lines from nearby plantations. An affidavit sworn by a black soldier named Joseph Miller, recounting his and his family's grim experiences after he enlisted in the Union army, is the sixth selection. His testimony was given to a Freedmen's Bureau agent on November 26, 1864. The seventh and final document is a long extract from a perceptive official report submitted on November 14, 1867, by a Freedmen's Bureau agent, Charles Raushenberg, who was stationed at Cuthbert in southern Georgia. His report focuses on how the freedmen were faring as laborers within his rural jurisdiction.

President Lincoln Discusses War Aims, August 1862

Executive Mansion,
Washington, August 22, 1862.

Hon. Horace Greely [*sic*]:

Dear Sir

I have just read yours of the 19th. addressed to myself through the New-York Tribune. If there be in it any statements, or assumptions of fact, which I may know to be erroneous, I do not, now and here, controvert them. If there be in it any inferences which I may believe to be falsely drawn, I do not now and here, argue against them. If there be perceptable [*sic*] in it an impatient and dictatorial tone, I waive it in deference to an old friend, whose heart I have always supposed to be right.

As to the policy I "seem to be pursuing" as you say, I have not meant to leave any one in doubt.

I would save the Union. I would save it the shortest way under the Constitution. The sooner the national authority can be restored; the nearer the Union will be "the Union as it was." If there be those who would not save the Union, unless they could at the same time *save* slavery, I do not agree with them. If there be those who would not save the Union unless they could at the same time *destroy* slavery, I do not agree with them. My paramount object in this struggle *is* to save the Union, and is *not* either to save or to destroy slavery. If I could save the Union without freeing *any* slave I would do it, and if I could save it by freeing *all* the slaves I would do it; and if I could save it by freeing some and leaving others alone I would also do that. What I do about slavery, and the colored race, I do because I believe it helps to save the Union; and what I forbear, I forbear because I do *not* believe it would help to save the Union. I shall do *less* whenever I shall believe what I am doing hurts the cause, and I shall do *more* whenever I shall believe doing more will help the cause. I shall try to correct errors when shown to be errors; and I shall adopt new views so fast as they shall appear to be true views.

I have here stated my purpose according to my view of *official* duty; and I intend no modification of my oft-expressed *personal* wish that all men every where could be free. Yours,

A. Lincoln

President Lincoln Defends Emancipation, August 1863

Executive Mansion,
Washington, August 26, 1863.

Hon. James C. Conkling

My Dear Sir:

. . . To be plain, you are dissatisfied with me about the negro. Quite likely there is a difference of opinion between you and myself upon that subject. I certainly wish that all men could be free, while I suppose you do not. Yet I have neither adopted, nor proposed any measure, which is not consistent with even your view, provided you are for the Union. I suggested compensated emancipation; to which you replied you wished not to be taxed to buy negroes. But I had not asked you to be taxed to buy negroes, except in such way, as to save you from greater taxation to save the Union exclusively by other means.

You dislike the emancipation proclamation; and, perhaps, would have it retracted. You say it is unconstitutional—I think differently. I think the constitution invests its commander-in-chief, with the law of war, in time of war. The most that can be said, if so much, is, that slaves are property. Is there—has there ever been—any question that by the law of war, property, both of enemies and friends, may be taken when needed? And is it not needed whenever taking it, helps us, or hurts the enemy? Armies, the world over, destroy enemies' property when they cannot use it; and even destroy their own to keep it from the enemy. Civilized belligerents do all in their power to help themselves, or hurt the enemy, except a few things regarded as barbarous or cruel. Among the exceptions are the massacre of vanquished foes, and non-combatants, male and female.

But the proclamation, as law, either is valid, or is not valid. If it is not valid, it needs no retraction. If it is valid, it cannot be retracted, any more than the dead can be brought to life. Some of you profess to think its retraction would operate favorably for the Union. Why better *after* the retraction, than *before* the issue? There was more than a year and a half of trial to suppress the rebellion before the proclamation issued, the last one hundred days of which passed under an explicit notice that it was coming, unless averted by those in revolt, returning to their allegiance. The war has certainly progressed as favorably for us, since the issue of the proclamation as before. I know as fully as one can know the opinions of others, that some of the commanders of our armies in the field who have given us our most important successes, believe the emancipation policy, and the use of colored troops, constitute the heaviest blow yet dealt to the rebellion; and that, at least one of those important successes, could not have been achieved when it was, but for the aid of black soldiers. Among the commanders holding these views are some who have never had any affinity with what is called abolitionism, or with republican party politics; but who hold them purely as military opinions. I submit these opinions as being entitled to some weight against the objections, often urged, that emancipation, and arming the blacks, are unwise as military measures, and were not adopted, as such, in good faith.

You say you will not fight to free negroes. Some of them seem willing to fight for you; but, no matter. Fight you, then, exclusively to save the Union. I issued the proclamation on purpose to aid you in saving the Union. Whenever you shall have conquered all resistance to the Union, if I shall urge you to continue fighting, it will be an apt time, then, for you to declare you will not fight to free negroes.

I thought that in your struggle for the Union, to whatever extent the negroes should cease helping the enemy, to that extent it weakened the enemy in his resistance to you. Do you think differently? I thought that whatever negroes can be got to do as soldiers, leaves just so much less for white soldiers to do, in saving the Union. Does it appear otherwise to you? But negroes, like other people, act upon motives. Why should they do any thing for us, if we will do nothing for them? If they stake their lives for us, they must be prompted by the strongest motive—even the promise of freedom. And the promise being made, must be kept. . . .

Peace does not appear so distant as it did. I hope it will come soon, and come to stay; and so come as to be worth the keeping in all future time. It will then have been proved that, among free men, there can be no successful appeal from the ballot to the bullet; and that they who take such appeal are sure to lose their case, and pay the cost. And then, there will be some black men who can remember that, with silent tongue, and clenched teeth, and steady eye, and well-poised bayonet, they have helped mankind on to this great consummation; while, I fear, there will be some white ones, unable to forget that, with malignant heart, and deceitful speech, they have strove to hinder it.

Still let us not be over-sanguine of a speedy final triumph. Let us be quite sober. Let us diligently apply the means, never doubting that a just God, in his own good time, will give us the rightful result. Yours very truly,

A. Lincoln

A Federal Commission Considers Policy Toward the Ex-Slaves, June 1863

. . . The commission here desire to record their profound conviction, that upon the judicious selection of department superintendents and of super-intendent general of freedmen will mainly depend the successful practical workings of the . . . plan of organization. The African race, accustomed to shield itself by cunning and evasion, and by shirking of work, whenever it can be safely shirked, against the oppression which has been its lot for generations, is yet of genial nature, alive to gratitude, open to impressions of kindness, and more readily influenced and led by those who treat it well and gain its confidence than our race, or perhaps than any other. The wishes and recommendations of government, if they are not harshly en-forced, but quietly communicated by those who understand and sympathize with the African nature, will be received and obeyed as commands in almost every instance. It is highly important, therefore, that those who have in charge the interests of these freedmen shall be men not only of adminis-trative ability, but also of comprehensive benevolence and humanitarian views.

On the other hand, it is equally desirable that these refugees, as readily spoiled as children, should not be treated with weak and injurious indulg-ence. Evenhanded justice, not special favor, is what they need. Mild firm-ness is the proper spirit in which to control them. They should find them-selves treated, not as children of preference, fostered by charity, dependent for a living on government or on benevolent associations, but as men from whom, in their new character of freedmen, self-reliance and self-support are demanded. . . .

Frederick Douglass States the Freedmen's Demands, April 1865

. . . I have had but one idea for the last three years to present to the American people, and the phraseology in which I clothe it is the old abolition phraseology. I am for the "immediate, unconditional, and universal" enfranchisement of the black man, in every State in the Union. Without this, his liberty is a mockery; without this, you might as well almost retain the old name of slavery for his condition; for in fact, if he is not the slave of the individual master, he is the slave of society, and holds his liberty as a privilege, not as a right. He is at the mercy of the mob, and has no means of protecting himself.

It may be objected, however, that this pressing of the Negro's right to suffrage is premature. Let us have slavery abolished, it may be said, let us have labor organized, and then, in the natural course of events, the right of suffrage will be extended to the Negro. I do not agree with this. The constitution of the human mind is such, that if it once disregards the conviction forced upon it by a revelation of truth, it requires the exercise of a higher power to produce the same conviction afterwards. The American people are now in tears. The Shenandoah has run blood—the best blood of the North. All around Richmond, the blood of New England and of the North has been shed—of your sons, your brothers and your fathers. We all feel, in the existence of this Rebellion, that judgments terrible, widespread, far-reaching, overwhelming, are abroad in the land; and we feel, in view of these judgments, just now, a disposition to learn righteousness. This is the hour. Our streets are in mourning, tears are falling at every fireside, and under the chastisement of this Rebellion we have almost come up to the point of conceding this great, this all-important right of suffrage. I fear that if we fail to do it now, if abolitionists fail to press it now, we may not see, for centuries to come, the same disposition that exists at this moment. Hence, I say, now is the time to press this right.

It may be asked, "Why do you want it. Some men have got along very well without it. Women have not this right." Shall we justify one wrong by another? This is a sufficient answer. Shall we at this moment justify the deprivation of the Negro of the right to vote, because some one else is deprived of that privilege? I hold that women, as well as men, have the right to vote, and my heart and my voice go with the movement to extend suffrage to women; but that question rests upon another basis than that on which our right rests. We may be asked, I say, why we want it. I will tell you why we want it. We want it because it is our *right*, first of all. No class of men can, without insulting their own nature, be content with any deprivation of their rights. We want it again, as a means for educating our race. Men are so constituted that they derive their conviction of their own possibilities largely from the estimate formed of them by others. If nothing is expected of a people, that people will find it difficult to contradict that expectation. By depriving us of suffrage, you affirm our incapacity to form an intelligent judgment respecting public men and public measures; you declare before the world that we are unfit to exercise the elective franchise, and by this means lead us to undervalue ourselves, to put a low estimate upon ourselves, and to feel that we have no possibilities like other men. Again, I want the elective franchise, for one, as a colored man, because ours is a peculiar government, based upon a peculiar idea, and that idea is universal suffrage. If I were in a monarchial government, or an autocratic or aristocratic government, where the few bore rule and the many were subject, there would be no special stigma resting upon me, because I did not exercise the elective franchise. It would do me no great violence. Mingling with the mass I should partake of the strength of the mass; I should be supported by the mass, and I should have the same incentives to endeavor with the mass of my fellow-men; it would be no particular burden, no particular deprivation; but here where universal suffrage is the rule, where that is the fundamental idea of the Government, to rule us out is to make us an exception, to brand us with the stigma of inferiority, and to invite to our heads the missiles of those about us; therefore, I want the franchise for the black man. . . .

I ask my friends who are apologizing for not insisting upon this right, where can the black man look, in this country, for the assertion of his right, if he may not look to the Massachusetts Anti-Slavery Society? [Douglass was addressing a meeting of this society.] Where under the whole heavens can he look for sympathy, in asserting this right, if he may not look to this platform? Have you lifted us up to a certain height to see that we are men, and then are any disposed to leave us there, without seeing that we are put in possession of all our rights? We look naturally to this platform for the assertion of all our rights, and for this one especially. I understand the anti-slavery societies of this country to be based on two principles,—first, the freedom of the blacks of this country; and, second, the elevation of them. Let me not be misunderstood here. I am not asking for sympathy at the hands of abolitionists, sympathy at the hands of any. I think the American people are disposed often to be generous rather than just. I look over this country at the present time, and I see Educational Societies, Sanitary Commissions, Freedmen's Associations, and the like,—all very good: but in regard to the colored people there is always more that is benevolent, I perceive, than just, manifested towards us. What I ask for the Negro is not benevolence, not pity, not sympathy, but simply *justice*. The American people have always been anxious to know what they shall do with us. Gen. Banks [the federal commander in Louisiana, 1863–1864] was distressed with solicitude as to what he should do with the Negro. Everybody has asked the question, and they learned to ask it early of the abolitionists, "What shall we do with the Negro?" I have had but one answer from the beginning. Do nothing with us! Your doing with us has already played the mischief with us. Do nothing with us! If the apples will not remain on the tree of their own strength, if they are wormeaten at the core, if they are early ripe and disposed to fall, let them fall! I am not for tying or fastening them on the tree in any way, except by nature's plan, and if they will not stay there, let them fall. And if the Negro cannot stand on his own legs, let him fall also. All I ask is, give him a chance to stand on his own legs! Let him alone! If you see him on his way to school, let him alone, don't disturb him! If you see him going to the dinner-table at a hotel, let him go! If you see him going to the ballot-box, let him alone, don't disturb him! If you see him going into a work-shop, just let him alone,—your interference is doing him a positive injury. . . .

The U.S. Adjutant General Describes the Condition of Fleeing Slaves, August 1863

Adjutant General of the Army to the Secretary of War

Cairo, Illinois, Aug' 23. 1863.

Sir, I arrived at this place this morning with General Grant, and shall return with him to-day or tomorrow to Vicksburg.

I have delayed making a report of the condition of affairs until I visited the several positions on the river. I was disappointed at finding but few negroes at Vicksburg, as they had been either absorbed by the several Departments as laborers, or taken to fill up the regiments previously organized. Of these regiments I get good accounts and some of them are in a high state of discipline. I visited Natchez, which at the present time is the best place for obtaining negroes, and gave orders for the immediate organization of two regiments, one as heavy Artillery to garrison Vicksburg, and also a Cavalry regiment to be mounted on mules. These animals can be obtained in great abundance.

I was fortunate in arriving at Memphis before General Steele left Helena for the interior of Arkansas as I was enabled to have him instructed to bring back all the blacks he could possibly gather, and sent recruiting officers with him. This expedition must give me a large number of men. A force also goes up Red River, and another from Goodrich's Landing back to bayou Macon, and their commanders are also instructed to collect the able bodied men, and in future such will be the standing orders. All the surplus blacks employed by the troops, or hovering round the Camps will be gathered up, General Grant having at my request issued such an order. He gives me every assistance in my work.

On arriving at Lake Providence on my way to Vicksburg, I found upwards of a thousand negroes, nearly all women and children, on the banks of the river, in a most helpless condition, who had left the plantations in consequence of the withdrawal of the troops on account of sickness. They had successfully sustained one attack of guerillas, aided by a gunboat, but expected another attack. I took them all to Goodrich's Landing where there is a garrison of negro troops. The number of this helpless class in the various camps is very large and daily increasing, and altho' everything is done for their well being, I find that sickness prevails to an alarming extent, and the bills of mortality are very high. This results from their change of life and habits, from daily work to comparative idleness, and also from being congregated in large numbers in camps, which is a matter of necessity. Besides, they will not take care of themselves much less of those who are sick. I have therefore after much reflection and consultation with officers, come to the conclusion that the old men, women and children should be advised to remain on the plantations, especially on those within our lines where we can have an oversight of them. Besides, it is important that the crops on the plantations within our lines should be gathered. A number of those now in our camps express a desire to return to their old homes, and indeed many have already done so. All such will be encouraged to do so, in cases where we are satisfied their former masters will not run them off or sell them. I have conversed with a number of planters, several strong union men at Natchez especially, and they all express the opinion that slavery has received its death blow, and cannot again exist in regions passed over by our armies. They are perfectly willing to hire the negroes and adopt any policy the Government may dictate. Many citizens of Mississippi, Louisiana and Arkansas are desirous that their States should resume their position in the Union with laws providing for the emancipation of slaves in a limited number of years. This feeling is constantly increasing, even among those who were strong advocates of secession. They now see it is vain to resist our arms, and only see utter ruin to themselves as the war goes on.

It is important that woodyards should be established on the river, and General Grant is encouraging the measure. I will permit persons duly authorized to cut wood for steamboats, to hire wood-choppers from those who are unfit for military service, including the women. It will be far more for their benefit to support themselves than to sit in idleness in camps depending on the Government for subsistence.

I have issued an order for general distribution in the armies of Generals Grant and Rosencrans [sic] setting forth some of the above points, a copy of which is enclosed—special Order No 45.—

I should be pleased to receive your instructions if my action is in any respect not in accordance with your views. The subject is now assuming vast proportions, and while I will do every thing in my power to carry out the policy of the administration and support the Government, I feel that my responsibilities are great and need the advice of my superiors. . . .

L. Thomas

A Black Union Soldier Protests His Mistreatment, November 1864

Camp Nelson Ky November 26, 1864

Personally appered before me E. B. W. Restieaux Capt. and Asst. Quartermaster Joseph Miller a man of color who being duly sworn upon oath says

I was a slave of George Miller of Lincoln County Ky. I have always resided in Kentucky and am now a Soldier in the service of the United

States. I belong to Company I 124 U.S.C. Inft now Stationed at Camp Nelson Ky. When I came to Camp for the purpose of enlisting about the middle of October 1864 my wife and children came with me because my master said that if I enlisted he would not maintain them and I knew they would be abused by him when I left. I had then four children ages respectively ten nine seven and four years. On my presenting myself as a recruit I was told by the Lieut. in command to take my family into a tent within the limits of the Camp. My wife and family occupied this tent by the express permission of the aforementioned Officer and never received any notice to leave until Tuesday November 22 when a mounted guard gave my wife notice that she and her children must leave Camp before early morning. This was about six O'clock at night. My little boy about seven years of age had been very sick and was slowly recovering My wife had no place to go and so remained until morning. About eight Oclock Wednesday morning November 23 a mounted guard came to my tent and ordered my wife and children out of Camp The morning was bitter cold. It was freezing hard. I was certain that it would kill my sick child to take him out in the cold. I told the man in charge of the guard that it would be the death of my boy I told him that my wife and children had no place to go and I told him that I was a soldier of the United States. He told me that it did not make any difference. he had orders to take all out of Camp. He told my wife and family that if they did not get up into the wagon which he had he would shoot the last one of them. On being thus threatened my wife and children went into the wagon My wife carried her sick child in her arms. When they left the tent the wind was blowing hard and cold and having had to leave much of our clothing when we left our master, my wife with her little one was poorly clad. I followed them as far as the lines. I had no Knowledge where they were taking them. At night I went in search of my family. I found them at Nicholasville about six miles from Camp. They were in an old meeting house belonging to the colored people. The building was very cold having only one fire. My wife and children could not get near the fire, because of the number of colored people huddled together by the soldiers. I found my wife and children shivering with cold and famished with hunger They had not recieved a morsel of food during the whole day. My boy was dead. He died directly after getting down from the wagon. I Know he was Killed by exposure to the inclement weather I had to return to camp that night so I left my family in the meeting house and walked back. I had walked there. I travelled in all twelve miles Next morning I walked to Nicholasville. I dug a grave myself and buried my own child. I left my family in the Meeting house—where they still remain And further this deponent saith not

his
(Signed) Joseph   Miller
mark

A Freedmen's Bureau Agent Discusses
Labor Relations, November 1867

Office Agent Bur. R. F. A. Lds.
Division of Cuthbert
Cuthbert, Ga. Novbr. 14, 1867.

Lieut O. H. Howard,
Sub. Asst Commnr Bur R. F. A. Lds
Albany, Ga.

Sir,

In obedience to the instructions received from you I have the honor to submit this Report on the General Condition of Affairs in my division.

When I entered upon my duties as Agent in this Division the Bureau of R. F. A. Lds [Bureau of Refugees, Freedmen and Abandoned Lands] seemed to be generally considered by the community, a substitute for overseers and drivers and to take up and return run away laborers and to punish them for real or imaginary violations of contract by fines, imprisonment and some times by corporeal punishment seemed to be the principal occupation of its agents.

The idea that a planter or employer of any kind should in case of dissatisfaction with his freedmen, instead of driving him [off] often without paying him his wages, first establish a complaint before the Bureau and let that tribunal decide wether a sufficient violation of contract existed to justify the discharge of the laborer or not, was then considered quite unreasonable; while every employer thought it perfectly proper that a Bureau agent, when notified of a freedmans leaving his employment should immediately issue an order for the arrest of the same and have him brought back—in chains if possible. The fairness of the principle that either party must submit its complaints to the Bureau for adjustment and that the white man can not decide the case a priori and only use the agent of the bureau as his executive organ and that employer as well as employee must submit to its decision wether the laborer ought to be discharged or ought to remain is just beginning to gain ground amongst both races and the negroes have ceased to a great extent to leave their employers as they used to do and employers are not as apt to run them off at will as they used to do. The common bulk of the population is just beginning to suspect that nothing else but what is justice and equity to a white man under certain circumstances would be justice and equity to a negro under the same circumstances and while they begin to feel the truth of this fact their moral courage and conscientiousness is generally not sufficient to overcome their prejudices and passions to a sufficient extent to give life and practical execution to this principle in their conduct towards and treatment of the negro in every day life.

The number of complaints made at this office is very large and increasing continually as the time of settlements is drawing nearer. The white man complains generally that the freedman is lazy, impudent and unreliable, that he will not fulfill his contract any further than it suits his convenience, that he claims the right to loose as much time as he pleases and when he pleases but wants full rations all the time, that he owes for goods and provisions more than his wages or his part of the crop amount to and that he wants to quit his employment on account of it; the freedman on the other hand generally complains that the white man has made him sign a contract, which he does not understand to mean what the white man says it does mean, that the white man wants him to do work which he did not contract to do, that the employer does not want to furnish him rations; that he charges him [too] much for lost time, that he curses him, threatens to whip him or has really struck him or shot at him. This is about the usual purport of the complaints of the two races and these complaints are frequently well established by each party and inevitably lead to the conclusion that a great deal of bad material exists in both races and that both in reality have much cause to complain of each other.

The freedpeople generally have worked better this year than last year and have adhered more faithfully to their contracts by staying out their time and a large number certainly at least one half of them have got along with their employers without serious dissatisfaction and trouble.

The majority of complaints that have been made at this Office by both races have found their origin in contracts, where freedmen received as compensation for their labor a certain share in the crop. The majority of the plantations in my division were worked under such contracts. The freedman claims under such contracts frequently that he has no other work to do but to cultivate and gather the crop, that being a partner in the concern he ought to be allowed to exercise his own judgement in the management of the plantation, that he ought to be permitted to loose time, when it suits his convenience to do so and when according to his judgement his labor is not needed in the field, that he ought to have a voice in the manner of gathering and dividing the corn and cotton and in the ginning, packing and selling of the latter product—while the employer claims that the labor of the employee belongs to him for the whole year, that he must labor for him six days during the week and do all kinds of work required of him wether directly connected with the crop or not, that he must have the sole and exclusive management of the plantation and that the freedman must obey his orders and do all work required as if he was receiving money wages, the part of the crop standing in the place of money, that the laborer must suffer deduction for lost time, that if he does not work all the time for him, he is not bound to furnish him provisions all the time, that the crop must be gathered, divided and housed to suit the convenience and judgement of the employer and that the share of the employee must be held responsible for what he has received in goods & provisions during the year. Taking in consideration that often quite a number of freedmen are employed on one plantation under such contracts, who frequently not only become discontented with the employer but with each other, accusing each other of loosing [sic] time unnecessarily and of not working well enough to be entitled to an equal share in the crop, it is easily understood to what amount of implicated difficulties and vexations questions these contracts furnish the material. . . .

The present aspect of the two races in their relations to each other therefore warrants no just expectation that they will get along amically with each other for any length of time but insures the belief that after the removal of the military authority the freedmen when allowed to exercise all the rights & privileges of citizens with their want of knowledge and experience in business and law, will generally fail to obtain justice from the hands of the white race in the daily relations of life as well as in the courts. They would generally come out the loosers, factors liens and mortgages being pushed in before their claims, frequently before they even suspected a danger of any loss, would yearly take away thousands of Dollars of their wages, all kinds of frauds would be practiced on them in making contracts, all kinds of impediments and obstacles would be put in the way of their complaints even reaching the courts and when there they would often fail to receive the necessary attention as the ignorance of the freedmen would often furnish opportunities to take advantage of them and to let them go by default or have them nol' pros.'d etc. This all would exasperate the freedmen more and more he would feel the wrong and still not be able to mend the matter and so, many outbreaks and at least local troubles would certainly take place. . . .

Charles Raushenberg

Two Views of the War's Meaning

Mary Boykin Chesnut 1823–1886

Historians and literary critics alike have praised Mary Boykin Chesnut's "diary" for its vivid and sweeping narrative of Confederate life during the Civil War. As her editor C. Vann Woodward points out, the enduring value of Chesnut's autobiographical writing lies not so much in the information it contains, but "in the life and reality with which it endows people and events and with which it evokes the chaos and complexity of a society at war." A politically astute, well-educated, and gregarious woman whose father and husband were southern political figures, Mary Chesnut was in an ideal position to observe and record the intricacies of her society and her era. Born in Statesburg, South Carolina, she was the oldest daughter of Mary Boykin and Stephen Miller. Her father was, at various periods, a U.S. Congressman and Senator, governor and state senator.

According to her biographer Elisabeth Muhlenfeld, young Mary Miller received an unusually solid education for a nineteenth-century southern woman. She attended Madame Talvande's French School for Young Ladies in Charleston where she excelled in a course of study which stressed foreign language, history, rhetoric, literature, and science, as well as traditional female "accomplishments." While in attendance at Madame Talvande's, she met James Chesnut Jr., whom she married when she was barely seventeen. From a wealthy Camden family, her husband, a Princeton graduate and law-

yer, served in various political positions before the war, including a U.S. Senate seat which he gave up in 1860 when differences between the North and South became insurmountable. His connections with such figures as Jefferson Davis during the war years opened windows of opportunity for his wife's observations of and relationships with key figures in the national drama, as did her own enjoyment of friendships with a broad spectrum of the Confederacy's most prominent men and women. After the war the Chesnuts' land and plantation near Camden were lost to debt; and after James's death in 1884, Mary was left with a struggling dairy farm and a strong desire to complete her memoirs. Always in danger from heart trouble, she died of an attack before seeing her work published.

Like many other southern autobiographers writing about the Civil War, many of them women who struggled through the vicissitudes of a war on home territory, Chesnut created her "diary" out of a complexly rendered combination of an actual diary written during the war and her memories of the past. The 1984 publication of *The Private Mary Chesnut,* edited by Woodward and Muhlenfeld, makes the original, and highly personal, diary available for the first time. This actual diary, which she kept under lock and key, was not meant for publication; and the autobiographical book known as her "diary" was actually written twenty years after the war, in 1881–1884. Woodward's 1981 edition,

[7] Edward Bissell Hunt, an army engineer killed during the Civil War, and husband of Helen

Hunt Jackson, author of *Ramona.*

entitled *Mary Chesnut's Civil War*, incorporates part of the original diary with the retrospective memoirs. Mary Chesnut's writing was first published in 1905 and later in 1949 in an edition by Ben Ames Williams with the title (not one of Chesnut's choosing) *A Diary from Dixie*. Unlike Williams's *Diary*, Woodward's edition provides a synthesis of the two forms of autobiography, the diary and the memoir, in a responsibly edited combination of what Chesnut actually wrote during the war and twenty years later. One of her stated purposes in her revision of the eighties, Woodward discovers through her correspondence, was what she called "leaving myself out." To whatever extent she succeeded, Woodward attempts to right the balance by reinserting personal comments which the previous editions have left unpublished. In the selections reprinted below from Woodward's edition, deleted passages have been indicated by brackets. *Mary Chesnut's Civil War* thus captures the sweep and chaos of a society at war, as did Williams's *A Diary from Dixie*, but the more recent edition also allows an intimate picture of the woman as writer of her own story of that society.

Chesnut describes herself as writing "like a spider, spinning [her] own entrails." This web of self, like Chesnut's sense of history, is complexly attached to and woven out of a keen awareness of the white woman's position in a patriarchal slave society. At a personal level Chesnut, who was childless and married to the only son of a wealthy planter family, was painfully cognizant of white woman's role as the bearer of legitimate heirs. Her attitude toward slavery and patriarchal ideology has been seen as radically feminist for the times, and it has become commonplace to point out that Chesnut saw miscegenation as the embodiment of the evil of slavery and of the double standard that allowed the white southern male sexual freedom and marital infidelity while his wife and daughter were bound by the prohibitions of chastity. In her frequently quoted diatribes against this aspect of slavery, such as the one reproduced below, though, Chesnut seems so intent on pitying the white women whose husbands are involved in philanderings in the slave quarters that she has no sympathy left for the black women who became their victims. She views black women instead as symbols of sexuality, ironically with freedoms not allowed "respectable" white women. Moreover, she seems to blame black women for a sexual coercion only white men could instigate or force, thereby focusing her bitterness at the victims of slavery, not the victimizers.

Thus Chesnut, a member of the wealthy planter class, abhorred slavery and its sexual vices; but, like many white women of her time and position, seemed to remain blind, or at least myopic, concerning the intersections of gender and race with the power structures of the system in which she lived much of her life. Yet, despite her limited critique of the patriarchal underpinnings of slavery, Mary Boykin Chesnut's massive volume paints a valuable portrait, interior as well as exterior, of the Old South's physical and ideological struggle to survive, its ultimate failure to do so, and perhaps some of the reasons behind that failure.

Minrose C. Gwin
Virginia Polytechnic Institute
and State University

PRIMARY WORKS

Mary Chesnut's Civil War, ed. C. Vann Woodward, 1981; *The Private Mary Chesnut: The Unpublished Civil War Diaries*, ed. Woodward and Elisabeth Muhlenfeld, 1984.

SECONDARY WORKS

Mary Boykin Chesnut: A Biography, Muhlenfeld, 1981.

from Mary Chesnut's Civil War

March 18, 1861

. . . ⟨⟨I wonder if it be a sin to think slavery a curse to any land. Sumner said not one word of this hated institution which is not true. Men and women are punished when their masters and mistresses are brutes and not when they do wrong—and then we live surrounded by prostitutes. An abandoned woman is sent out of any decent house elsewhere. Who thinks any worse of a negro or mulatto woman for being a thing we can't name? God forgive us, but ours is a *monstrous* system and wrong and iniquity. Perhaps the rest of the world is as bad—this *only* I see. Like the patriarchs of old our men live all in one house with their wives and their concubines, and the mulattoes one sees in every family exactly resemble the white children—and every lady tells you who is the father of all the mulatto children in everybody's household, but those in her own she seems to think drop from the clouds, or pretends so to think. Good women we have, *but* they talk of all *nastiness*—tho' they never do wrong, they talk day and night of [*erasures illegible save for the words* "all unconsciousness"] my disgust sometimes is boiling over—but they are, I believe, in conduct the purest women God ever made. Thank God for my countrywomen—alas for the men! No worse than men everywhere, but the lower their mistresses, the more degraded they must be.

⟨⟨My mother-in-law told me when I was first married not to send my female servants in the street on errands. They were then tempted, led astray—and then she said placidly, so they told *me* when I came here, and I was very particular, *but you see with what result.*

⟨⟨Mr. Harris said it was so patriarchal. So it is—flocks and herds and slaves—and wife Leah does not suffice. Rachel must be *added,* if not *married.*[1] And all the time they seem to think themselves patterns—models of husbands and fathers.

⟨⟨Mrs. Davis told me everybody described my husband's father as an odd character—"a millionaire who did nothing for his son whatever, left him to struggle with poverty, &c." I replied—"Mr. Chesnut Senior thinks himself the best of fathers—and his son thinks likewise. I have nothing to say—but it is true. He has no money but what he makes as a lawyer." And again I say, my countrywomen are as pure as angels, tho' surrounded by another race who are the social evil!⟩⟩

August 26, 1861

. . . Now, this assemblage of army women or Confederate matrons talked pretty freely today. Let us record. . . .

"You people who have been everywhere, stationed all over the U.S.—states, frontiers—been to Europe and all that, tell us homebiding ones: are our men worse than the others? Does Mrs. Stowe know? You know?"

---

[1] In Genesis 29–30, Jacob, unhappy with his wife Leah, also marries her sister Rachel. He has children by both women and by their handmaidens as well. M.B.C. apparently believed old Mr. Chesnut had children by a slave whom she calls "Rachel" (p. 72). She confesses no such suspicions of her husband.

"No, Lady Mary Montagu did. After all, only men and women—everywhere.[2] But Mrs. Stowe's exceptional cases may be true. You can pick out horrors from any criminal court record or newspaper in any country."

"You see, irresponsible men, county magnates, city millionaires, princes, &c do pretty much as they please. They are above law and morals."

Russell once more, to whom London and Paris and India have been an everyday sight—and every night, too, streets and all—for him to go on in indignation because there are women on negro plantations who were not vestal virgins! Negro women are married and after marriage behave as well as other people. Marrying is the amusement of their life. They take life easily. So do their class everywhere. Bad men are hated here as elsewhere.

"I hate slavery. I hate a man who—You say there are no more fallen women on a plantation than in London, in proportion to numbers. What do you say to this? A magnate who runs a hideous black harem and its consequences under the same roof with his lovely white wife and his beautiful and accomplished daughters? He holds his head as high and poses as the model of all human virtues to these poor women whom God and the laws have given him. From the height of his awful majesty he scolds and thunders at them, as if he never did wrong in his life.

"Fancy such a man finding his daughter reading *Don Juan*.[3] 'You with that unmoral book!' And he orders her out of his sight.

"You see, Mrs. Stowe did not hit the sorest spot. She makes Legree[4] a bachelor. Remember George II and his like."[5]

"Oh, I knew half a Legree, a man said to be as cruel as Legree—but the other half of him did not correspond. He was a man of polished manners. And the best husband and father and member of the church in the world."

"Can that be so?"

"Yes, I know it. Exceptional case, that sort of thing, always."

"And I knew the dissolute half of Legree well. He was high and mighty. But the kindest creature to his slaves—and the unfortunate results of his bad ways were not sold, had not to jump over ice blocks. They were kept in full view and provided for handsomely in his will.

"His wife and daughters in the might of their purity and innocence are supposed never to dream of what is as plain before their eyes as the sunlight, and they play their parts of unsuspecting angels to the letter. They prefer to adore their father as model of all earthly goodness."

"Well, yes. If he is rich, he is the fountain from whence all blessings flow."

"The one I have in my eye—my half of Legree, the dissolute half—was so furious in his temper and thundered his wrath so at the poor women they were glad to let him do as he pleased in peace, if they could only escape his everlasting faultfinding and noisy bluster. Making everybody so uncomfortable."

"*Now*. Now, do you know any woman of this generation who would stand that sort of thing?"

---

[2] "This world consists of men, women, and Herveys." Lady Mary (Wortley) Montagu, *Letters* (1763), volume 1. Lady Montagu, the wife of an adviser to George I, chronicled the scandals of London society.

[3] Lord Byron, *Don Juan* (1824).

[4] Simon Legree of *Uncle Tom's Cabin*.

[5] The ten-year relationship of George II with Mrs. Henrietta Howard was an open secret, as were several more casual liaisons.

"No, never—not for one moment. The make-believe angels were of the last century. We know—and we won't have it."

"Condition of women is improving, it seems. These are old-world stories."

"Women were brought up not to judge their fathers or their husbands. They took them as the Lord provided—and were thankful."

"If they should not go to heaven, after all—think of what lives most women lead."

"No heaven, no purgatory, no ——, the other thing—never. I believe in future rewards and punishments."

"How about the wives of drunkards? I heard a woman say once to a friend of her husband, tell it as a cruel matter of fact, without bitterness, without comment: 'Oh, you have not seen him. He is changed. He has not gone to bed sober in thirty years.' She has had her purgatory—if not what Mrs. —— calls 'the other thing'— here in this world. We all know what a drunken man is. To think, *for no crime* a person may be condemned to live with one thirty years."

"You wander from the question I asked. Are Southern men worse because of the slave system and the—facile black women?"

"Not a bit. They see too much of them. The barroom people don't drink. The confectionary people loathe candy. They are sick of the black sight of them."

"You think a nice man from the South is the nicest thing in the world."

"I know it. Put him by any other man and see!"

"And you say no saints and martyrs now—those good women who stand by bad husbands? Eh?"

"No use to mince matters—no use to pick words—everybody knows the life of a woman whose husband drinks."

"Some men have a hard time, too. I know women who are—well, the very devil and all his imps."

"And have you not seen girls cower and shrink away from a fierce brute of a father? Men are dreadful animals."

"Seems to me those of you who are hardest on men here are soft enough with them when they are present. Now, everybody knows I am 'the friend of man,' and I defend them behind their backs, as I take pleasure in their society—well—before their faces." . . .

October 13, 1861

Went to hear Tom Davis[6] preach. It was a political sermon. He ended it by commenting on a remark made by a celebrated person from Washington who said he was bored with politics all the week. And if he could not hear a little pure religion, undefiled, on Sunday, he would not go to church.

Nudged me: "That's you. You are always grumbling at political sermons." "But I am not the least celebrated." However, the whispered dispute was soon settled. Henry Clay was the man who hoped to eschew politics one day in seven.

Our parson cited Lord Nelson as a case of good prayer from a bad man. At the

---

[6] Thomas Frederick Davis, Jr., was associate pastor of the Grace Episcopal Church in Camden. His wife was M.B.C.'s first cousin.

battle of Trafalgar he prayed fervently, and his prayer was answered. And there he died, saying, "Thank God I die doing my duty." Again my whisper: "He prayed, too, for Lady Hamilton, and he left her a legacy to his country—ungrateful country would not accept the bequest."[7]

At Mulberry we went in the afternoon to the negro church on the plantation. Manning Brown,[8] Methodist minister, preached to a very large black congregation. Though glossy black, they were well dressed—some very stylishly gotten up. They were stout, comfortable-looking Christians. The house women in white aprons and white turbans were the nicest looking. How snow-white the turbans on their heads appeared. But the youthful sisters flaunted in pink and sky blue bonnets which tried their complexions. For *the family* they had a cushioned seat near the pulpit, neatly covered with calico.

Manning Brown preached hell fire—so hot I felt singed, if not parboiled, though I could not remember any of my many sins worthy of an eternity in torment. But if all the world's misery, sin, and suffering came from so small a sin as eating that apple, what mighty proportions mine take.

Jim Nelson, the driver—the stateliest darky I ever saw. He is tall and straight as a pine tree, with a fair face—not so very black, but full-blooded African. His forefathers must have been of royal blood over there.

This distinguished gentleman was asked to "lead in prayer." He became wildly excited. Though on his knees, facing us, with his eyes shut, he clapped his hands at the end of every sentence, and his voice rose to the pitch of a shrill shriek. Still, his voice was strangely clear and musical, occasionally in a plaintive minor key that went to your heart. Sometimes it rung out like a trumpet. I wept bitterly. It was all sound, however, and emotional pathos. There was literally nothing in what he said. The words had no meaning at all. It was the devotional passion of voice and manner which was so magnetic. The negroes sobbed and shouted and swayed backward and forward, some with aprons to their eyes, most clapping their hands and responding in shrill tones, "Yes, my God! Jesus!" "Aeih! Savior! Bless de Lord, amen—&c."

It was a little too exciting for me. I would very much have liked to shout, too. Jim Nelson, when he rose from his knees, trembled and shook as one in a palsy. And from his eye you could see the ecstasy had not left him yet. He could not stand at all—sunk back on his bench.

Now, all this leaves not a trace behind. Jim Nelson is a good man—honest and true. And so he continues. Those who stole before steal on, in spite of sobs and shouts on Sunday. Those who drink continue to drink when they can get it. Except that for any open, *detected* sin they are turned out of church. A Methodist parson is practical—no mealy-mouth creature. He requires them to keep the commandments. If they are not married and show they ought to be, out of the church they go. If married members are not true to their vows and it is made plain to him by their conduct, he has them up before the church. They are devoted to their church membership. And it is a keen police court.

---

[7] The night before his death at the battle of Trafalgar, Horatio Nelson added a codicil to his will, leaving his mistress Lady Emma Hamilton and their daughter Horatia "a legacy to my king and country" and asking that they be given a pension. The will was not made public, and no such grant was ever made.

[8] A nephew of Old Colonel Chesnut who lived in Sumter District.

Suddenly, as I sat wondering what next, they broke out into one of those soul-stirring negro camp-meeting hymns. To me this is the saddest of all earthly music—weird and depressing beyond my powers to describe.

> The wrestling of the world asketh a fall;
> Here is no home: here is a wildernesse.
> Forth Pilgrim! forth! Oh! beast out of thy stall!
> Look up on high—And thank thy God for all.
>
> —Chaucer

October 20, 1861

. . . Hume says, "Mighty governments are built up by a great deal of accident with a very little of human foresight and wisdom."[9]

We have seen the building of one lately with no end of Jefferson and a constant sprinkling of Calhoun, &c&c&c. Which is the wisdom—where the accident or foresight? Somebody said Jefferson and Calhoun were the stern lights and did not help us to see what is before us.

One thing Mrs. Browne and I discussed. There were in Richmond and in Montgomery the safe, sober, second thoughts of the cool, wise morning hours. There in that drawing room after dinner—how much more in the smoking congresses where women were not—came what we called ideas preserved in alcohol. The self-same wild schemes, mad talk, exaggerated statements, inflamed and irrational views—our might and the enemies' weakness, &c&c. If "in vino veritas," God help us. After all it was not, could not be, unadulterated truth—it was truth, alcoholized.

I care no more for alcoholized wisdom than I do for the chattering of blackbirds—[*remainder of page cut off*].

Hard on the poor innocent birds! They were made so. And the great statesmen and soldiers deliberately drink down their high inheritance of reason and with light hearts become mere gabbling geese. *Alcools*—

Hume, after his kind, talks of *accident*. Lamartine says, "Dieu est Dieu—ce que les hommes appellent *rencontre,* les anges l'appellent Providence."[10]

Thank God for pine knots. Gas and candles and oil are all disappearing in the Confederacy. Lamb thinks for social purposes candles so much better than the garish light of the sun.[11] The unsocial nights of our ancestors in their dark caves. They must have laid about and abused one another in the dark. No, they went to sleep. And women then were too much slaves to dream of curtain lectures—which is one form of lying about and abusing one another in the dark. "What repartees

[9] David Hume, *History of England* (1754–62), volume 2, chapter 23.

[10] A paraphrase from *Geneviève*, part 116. "God is God—what people call meeting, the angels call Providence."

[11] Paraphrased from Charles Lamb, "Popular Fallacies, XV.—That We Should Lie Down with the Lamb," in *The Last Essays of Elia* (1833). The quotation at the end of this paragraph derives from the same essay, although M.B.C. does not reproduce Lamb's wording exactly.

could have passed, when you had to feel around for a smile and had to handle your neighbor's cheek to see if he understood you?"

> Fool enough to attempt to advise.
>   Ah, gentle dames! It gars me greet,
> To think how many counsels sweet,
>   How many lengthened sage advices
> The husband from the wife despises.[12]

⟨⟨poor me—⟩⟩

January 16, 1865

My husband is at home once more—for how long, I do not know. And his aides fill the house, and a group of hopelessly wounded haunt the place. And the drilling and the marching goes on—and as far as I can see, for. bats. happily forgotten.

It rains a flood—freshet after freshet. The forces of nature are befriending us, for our enemies have to make their way through swamps.

A month ago my husband wrote me a letter which I promptly suppressed after showing it to Mrs. McCord. He warned us to make ready—for the end had come. Our resources were exhausted—and the means of resistance could not be found.

It was what we could not bring ourselves to believe. And now—he thinks, with the RR all blown up, the swamps impassable by freshets which have no time to subside, so constant is the rain. The negroes are utterly apathetic (would they be so, if they saw us triumphant!), and if we had but an army to seize the opportunity. No troops—that is the real trouble. Dr. Gibbes took it on himself to send a telegram. Some people are cool enough—and fools enough for anything.

"Does Jeff Davis so hate South Carolina that he means to abandon her to her fate?" I wonder if they showed Mr. Davis this.

The answer has come.

"No. Jeff Davis loves South Carolina—only Yankees hate her. He will do all he can to save her."

Hardee—he of Hardee's *Tactics*[13]—he has a head for tactics, but it is not large enough to plan a campaign. He can only fight well when under orders.

We seem utterly without a head down here—utterly at sea. If some heavenborn genius would rush in and take command—

The pilot in calm weather lets any sea boy toy with his rudder—but when the winds howl and the waves rise, he seizes the helm himself.

And our pilot? Where is he?

"Napoleon had to go to St. Helena when he had exhausted his levies. No more soldiers until France could grow them."

"Suppose we try Stephen Elliott—everybody trusts him."

Today Mrs. McCord exchanged 16,000 dollars, Confederate bills, for gold— 300 dollars. Sixteen thousand—for three hundred.

The bazaar will be a Belshazzar affair.[14] The handwriting is on the wall. Bad news everywhere.

---

[12] Slightly misquoted from Robert Burns, "Tam o' Shanter" (1791).

[13] William Joseph Hardee was the author of a stan- dard textbook, *Rifle and Light Infantry Tactics* (1853–55).

[14] Daniel 5.

Miss Garnett was in agony.

"I fear the very worst—before they find out, those stupid Yankees, that I am Irish."

The fears of old maids increase, apparently in proportion to their age and infirmities—and hideous ugliness.

Isabella fairly white and shining—resplendent in apparel—has gone down to Millwood.

She reproved the "weary heart" for dragging so in the road of life, or as she put it:

"What do you mean to do if your father dies—or anybody that you really care for dies? You leave yourself no margin for proper affliction—when the time comes."

January 17, 1865

Bazaar opens today.

Sherman marches always—all RR's smashed.

And if I laugh at any mortal thing, it is that I may not weep.

Generals as plenty as blackberries, none in command. Beauregard with his Shiloh green sickness again. Bad time for a general seized by *melancholia*.

And this refrain is beating in my brain—

> March—March—Ettrick and Teviotdale—
>   Why the de'il do ye not march all in order,
> March—March—Teviot and Clydesdale—
>   *All* the blue bonnets are over the Border.[15]

1981

---

[15] The first lines, slightly misquoted, of a "ditty" sung to "the ancient air of 'Blue Bonnets over the Border,'" in Sir Walter Scott, *The Monastery. A Romance* (1820), volume 2, chapter 11.

Tom Lincoln, born to poverty, almost illiterate, and raised to the mastery of a limited body of farming skills, struggled to squeeze, from a succession of small farms in Kentucky, Indiana, and Illinois, a livelihood for his family. But his son Abraham, burdened with the gift of an extraordinary intelligence, sensed nothing but weary futility in what seemed to him a treadmill of squatting and moving on; and though his formal schooling was as minimal as his father's, Abraham was inspired to educate himself by the few books that came his way and by the support of his sensitive and ambitious mother and stepmother. From these resources and from his own native sensitivity he gleaned that he ought to make his life, like the books he had cherished, a story with a meaningful end.

To say that he succeeded in this would be an understatement. At twenty-one he was on his own, working as laborer, storekeeper, and postmaster in the small town of New Salem, Illinois—and teaching himself the law; by his mid-twenties he was not only a successful practicing lawyer but a member of the state legislature (in which he served four terms); at thirty-eight he was elected to Congress; at fifty-two, he was elected President of the United States; and by the time of his death by assassination—only a few weeks after the inauguration of his second Presidential term—he had made of himself so extraordinary a statesman that his end was all too painfully meaningful.

The ideals of the Republic which were celebrated in the histories he read as a child instilled in Lincoln the faith that, despite the poverty and squalor of his birth, he could determine his own destiny, and that the Constitution of his country guaranteed him the right to do so. Consequently he both revered the Constitution and labored, in his legal and political career, to assure that the Constitution's guarantees extended as far in practice as they did in ideal. That these two concerns were incompatible—that the compromise with slavery which was written into the Constitution made the United States (as he was to describe it) "a house divided against itself," a union which could not honor the rights of its southern states without making a mockery of its own Bill of Rights—occurred to him only gradually: for though he was vocal in his disapproval of slavery, throughout most of his political career he stood for free soil in the new territories but not for Abolition. When he campaigned for the Presidency in 1860 his platform emphasized not the problem of slavery, but the preservation of the Union, as his primary concern.

It seemed clear enough that the new President was not the avenging angel of liberty the abolitionists had waited for, but rather an adroit politician whose appearance of flexible moderation made him tolerable to many though satisfactory to few: not the man anyone really wanted, but the only man who could command a tentative majority among the now bitterly divided population. He was quick and resourceful in appeasing the conflicting interests of his constituents—as ready to paint himself a defender of segregation as of universal liberty, where doing either would persuade his audience to accept his vision of the Constitution.

Yet the hysterical dread and outrage with which his opponents—both North and South—viewed his candidacy, which caused them to brand him the "blackest" of the "black Republicans," and which caused seven southern states to secede from the Union in response to his election in 1861, was not unfounded. Adherents of slavery had good reason to fear him, for in Lincoln the worldly pragmatism that made him a skillful manipulator of men was coupled with an extraordinary intellectual independence. He had demonstrated in Congress his willingness to jeop-ardize his own political future by taking an unpopular stand on principle, once the reins of power were in his hands; and the stand he had taken then indicated that as President he would be the enemy of slave-holders, despite his protestations of mod-eration. During his Presidency he was be-sieged as much by the defenders of slavery as by its enemies, but in 1862, at a criti-cally unstable moment in the war, he cast the weight of his administration with im-mediate emancipation of the slaves in the Confederate states, against the wishes of what seemed an overwhelming majority of the people. In his efforts to preserve the Union, he was willing to appease, and re-luctant to offend, the powerful adherents of slavery—a posture which dictated a number of half-measures and dubious compromises. But the Union he envi-sioned was one in which slavery—and all artificial perpetuation of inequality among men—should have no lasting place.

Lincoln's rhetorical posture shifted with the needs of the moment much as his policies did; but like his policies, the lan-guage of Lincoln's Presidential speeches has about it a ring of enlightened purpo-siveness which seems to reach beyond the merely strategic dimension of rhetoric. In early speeches he employed the precise language and humorous illustrative fables appropriate to an attorney arguing a case in law, but in the later speeches—of which the selections offered here are the most famous examples—he turned stead-ily toward the rhetoric of the Bible, both in style and reference. This shift from the legal to the religious parallels Lincoln's shift from the legislative to the executive branches of government and from a pos-ture of legislative compromise to one of military force; his Biblical rhetoric, which had characterized the speeches of aboli-tionists for decades, appeals as they did to an authority that could not finally be found in the Constitution, but which might be counted on to unite a politically divided people under the banner of the Christianity they still shared.

The *Address at the Dedication of the Gettysburg National Cemetery* and the *Sec-ond Inaugural Address* are remarkable, however, not for their employment of Bib-lical cadence and reference but for the simplicity and clarity with which that rhet-oric is fused with the self-educated law-yer's measured concern for justice in the affairs of men. Two addresses were given on November 19, 1863, at the dedication of the national cemetery at Gettysburg—site, only three months before, of the bloodiest battle of the War—and *both* ap-pealed to the Christian sentiments of the fifteen thousand Americans who gathered for the ceremonies: but it was Edward Everett's two-hour paean to the forces of armed righteousness which met the public standard for eloquence and piety. Lin-coln's two-minute speech, over almost before the crowd could gather that the President was speaking, seemed a failure—for it was concise and simple, barren of the florid language which would demon-strate the speaker's passionate response to the occasion. The piece, however, like Lincoln himself, gained after a time the regard of a people who (as Lincoln once jested) could be fooled some of the time but not forever; and his little speech has gradually come to seem more eloquent than any less restrained or more complex statement could have been. The author seems to speak from a place above narrow rational self-interest yet below blind ad-herence to an extrarational authority, so that these pleas for unity and support be-come reassertions of faith in the rational humanist principles on which his pre-cious, precarious Republic had been founded.

Elaine Sargent Apthorp
San Jose State University

PRIMARY WORKS

Roy Basler, ed., *The Collected Works of Abraham Lincoln,* 9 volumes, 1953–1955; *Supplement 1832–1865,* 1974.

SECONDARY WORKS

Steven B. Oates, *With Malice Toward None,* 1978; Jacques Barzun, *Lincoln the Literary Genius,* 1960; Charles B. Strozier, *Lincoln's Quest for Union: Public and Private Meanings,* 1982, 1987.

Address at the Dedication of the Gettysburg National Cemetery

Four score and seven years ago our fathers brought forth on this continent, a new nation, conceived in Liberty, and dedicated to the proposition that all men are created equal.

Now we are engaged in a great civil war; testing whether that nation, or any nation so conceived and so dedicated, can long endure. We are met on a great battlefield of that war. We have come to dedicate a portion of that field as a final resting-place for those who here gave their lives that that nation might live. It is altogether fitting and proper that we should do this.

But, in a larger sense, we cannot dedicate—we cannot consecrate—we cannot hallow—this ground. The brave men, living and dead, who struggled here have consecrated it, far above our poor power to add or detract. The world will little note, nor long remember, what we say here, but it can never forget what they did here. It is for us the living, rather, to be dedicated here to the unfinished work which they who fought here have thus far so nobly advanced. It is rather for us to be here dedicated to the great task remaining before us—that from these honored dead we take increased devotion to that cause for which they gave the last full measure of devotion; that we here highly resolve that these dead shall not have died in vain; that this nation, under God, shall have a new birth of freedom; and that government of the people, by the people, for the people, shall not perish from the earth.

Second Inaugural Address

FELLOW-COUNTRYMEN:

At this second appearing to take the oath of the presidential office, there is less occasion for an extended address than there was at the first. Then a statement, somewhat in detail, of a course to be pursued, seemed fitting and proper. Now, at the expiration of four years, during which public declarations have been constantly called forth on every point and phase of the great contest which still absorbs the attention and engrosses the energies of the nation, little that is new could be presented. The progress of our arms,[1] upon which all else chiefly depends, is as well known to the public as to myself; and it is, I trust, reasonably satisfactory and encouraging to all. With high hope for the future, no prediction in regard to it is ventured.

On the occasion corresponding to this four years ago, all thoughts were anxiously directed to an impending civil war. All dreaded it—all sought to avert it. While the inaugural address was being delivered from this place, devoted altogether to saving the Union without war, insurgent agents were in the city seeking to destroy it without war—seeking to dissolve the Union, and divide effects, by negotiation. Both parties deprecated war; but one of them would make war rather than let the nation survive; and the other would accept war rather than let it perish. And the war came.

One-eighth of the whole population were colored slaves, not distributed generally over the Union, but localized in the Southern part of it. These slaves constituted a peculiar and powerful interest. All knew that this interest was, somehow, the cause of the war. To strengthen, perpetuate, and extend this interest was the object for which the insurgents would rend the Union, even by war; while the government claimed no right to do more than to restrict the territorial enlargement of it.

Neither party expected for the war the magnitude or the duration which it has already attained. Neither anticipated that the cause of the conflict might cease with, or even before, the conflict itself should cease.[2] Each looked for an easier triumph, and a result less fundamental and astounding. Both read the same Bible, and pray to the same God; and each invokes his aid against the other. It may seem strange that any men should dare to ask a just God's assistance in wringing their bread from the sweat of other men's faces; but let us judge not, that we be not judged.[3] The prayers of both could not be answered—that of neither has been answered fully.

The Almighty has his own purposes. "Woe unto the world because of offences! for it must needs be that offences come; but woe to that man by whom the offence cometh."[4] If we shall suppose that American slavery is one of those offences which, in the providence of God, must needs come, but which, having continued through His appointed time, He now wills to remove, and that He gives to both North and South this terrible war, as the woe due to those by whom the offence came, shall we

---

[1] The success of our armies. At the time of Lincoln's second inaugural, the Civil War was essentially over, the Union forces victorious.

[2] That the slaves would be freed before the war to decide their future was ended. Lincoln's Emancipation Proclamation went into effect on January 1, 1863.

[3] Reference to the Book of Matthew, 7:1.

[4] Reference to the Book of Matthew, 17:7.

discern therein any departure from those divine attributes which the believers in a Living God always ascribe to Him? Fondly do we hope—fervently do we pray—that this mighty scourge of war may speedily pass away. Yet, if God wills that it continue until all the wealth piled by the bondman's two hundred and fifty years of unrequited toil shall be sunk, and until every drop of blood drawn with the lash shall be paid by another drawn with the sword, as was said three thousand years ago, so still it must be said, "The judgments of the Lord are true and righteous altogether."[5]

With malice toward none; with charity for all; with firmness in the right, as God gives us to see the right, let us strive on to finish the work we are in; to bind up the nation's wounds; to care for him who shall have borne the battle, and for his widow, and his orphan—to do all which may achieve and cherish a just and lasting peace, among ourselves, and with all nations.

[5] Reference to the Book of Psalms 9:9.

Diplomatic Issues
in the
Civil War Era

Manifest Destiny and
the War with Mexico

*The 1840s witnessed an expansionist surge that netted the United States new
territories. Texas, Oregon, and the California territory, after the use or threat of
force and much debate, became parts of the expanding American empire. Expansionism was certainly not new to the United States in the 1840s. From infancy the nation had been expansionist and, between the Louisiana Purchase of
1803 and the treaty ending the war with Mexico in 1848, the United States had
moved steadily westward, enlarging its territory, pushing out its boundaries,
and removing Native Americans. The 1840s, however, were particularly active.
What explains this burst of territorial acquisitiveness? James K. Polk as President? a cumulative and traditional American expansionism? idealism? racism?
commercial interest? The answers vary, as the selections in this chapter make
evident.*

✳ D O C U M E N T S

John L. O'Sullivan is credited with having popularized the idea of Manifest Destiny. As editor of the *Democratic Review*, he flamboyantly sketched an unbounded American future of democratic mission and territorial expansion. The
first document is selected from his "The Great Nation of Futurity," published in
1839. James K. Polk became President in 1845. An avowed expansionist, he
eyed Mexican lands and disputed territories in the Southwest and Northwest.
His Inaugural Address of March 4, 1845, made the case for absorbing Texas and
Oregon. The third document is Polk's War Message of May 11, 1846, in which
he asked Congress to declare war against Mexico and presented United States
grievances against its southern neighbor.

The outbreak of war, American territorial ambitions, and the ultimate American triumph aroused considerable debate. The fourth selection, the Wilmot
Proviso, drafted by Representative David Wilmot of Pennsylvania, was an attempt to keep slavery out of any territory won from Mexico. Although the

House passed this amendment to an appropriations bill in 1846 and 1847, the Senate turned it down, exposing deep differences over whether limits ought to be placed on expansion. The fifth document is a strongly worded anti-war resolution penned by Charles Sumner and passed in 1847 by the Massachusetts legislature. The final selection is a statement by some Mexican editors who believed that a rapacious United States provoked war and wronged the Mexican people.

John L. O'Sullivan on Manifest Destiny, 1839

The American people having derived their origin from many other nations, and the Declaration of National Independence being entirely based on the great principle of human equality, these facts demonstrate at once our disconnected position as regards any other nation; that we have, in reality, but little connection with the past history of any of them, and still less with all antiquity, its glories, or its crimes. On the contrary, our national birth was the beginning of a new history, the formation and progress of an untried political system, which separates us from the past and connects us with the future only; and so far as regards the entire development of the natural rights of man, in moral, political, and national life, we may confidently assume that our country is destined to be the great nation of futurity.

It is so destined, because the principle upon which a nation is organized fixes its destiny, and that of equality is perfect, is universal. It presides in all the operations of the physical world, and it is also the conscious law of the soul—the self-evident dictates of morality, which accurately defines the duty of man to man, and consequently man's rights as man. Besides, the truthful annals of any nation furnish abundant evidence, that its happiness, its greatness, its duration, were always proportionate to the democratic equality in its system of government. . . .

What friend of human liberty, civilization, and refinement, can cast his view over the past history of the monarchies and aristocracies of antiquity, and not deplore that they ever existed? What philanthropist can contemplate the oppressions, the cruelties, and injustice inflicted by them on the masses of mankind, and not turn with moral horror from the retrospect?

America is destined for better deeds. It is our unparalleled glory that we have no reminiscences of battle fields, but in defence of humanity, of the oppressed of all nations, of the rights of conscience, the rights of personal enfranchisement. Our annals describe no scenes of horrid carnage, where men were led on by hundreds of thousands to slay one another, dupes and victims to emperors, kings, nobles, demons in the human form called heroes. We have had patriots to defend our homes, our liberties, but no aspirants to crowns or thrones; nor have the American people ever suffered themselves to be led on by wicked ambition to depopulate the land, to spread desolation far and wide, that a human being might be placed on a seat of supremacy.

We have no interest in the scenes of antiquity, only as lessons of avoidance of nearly all their examples. The expansive future is our arena, and for our history. We are entering on its untrodden space, with the truths of God in our minds, beneficent objects in our hearts, and with a clear conscience unsullied by the past. We are the nation of human progress, and who will, what can, set limits to our onward march? Providence is with us, and no earthly power can. We point to the everlasting truth on the first page of our national declaration, and we proclaim to the millions of other lands, that "the gates of hell"—the powers of aristocracy and monarchy—"shall not prevail against it."

The far-reaching, the boundless future will be the era of American greatness. In its magnificent domain of space and time, the nation of many nations is destined to manifest to mankind the excellence of divine principles; to establish on earth the noblest temple ever dedicated to the worship of the Most High—the Sacred and the True. Its floor shall be a hemisphere—its roof the firmament of the star-studded heavens, and its congregation an Union of many Republics, comprising hundreds of happy millions, calling, owning no man master, but governed by God's natural and moral law of equality, the law of brotherhood—of "peace and good will amongst men." . . .

Yes, we are the nation of progress, of individual freedom, of universal enfranchisement. Equality of rights is the cynosure of our union of States, the grand exemplar of the correlative equality of individuals; and while truth sheds its effulgence, we cannot retrograde, without dissolving the one and subverting the other. We must onward to the fulfilment of our mission—to the entire development of the principle of our organization—freedom of conscience, freedom of person, freedom of trade and business pursuits, universality of freedom and equality. This is our high destiny, and in nature's eternal, inevitable decree of cause and effect we must accomplish it. All this will be our future history, to establish on earth the moral dignity and salvation of man—the immutable truth and beneficence of God. For this blessed mission to the nations of the world, which are shut out from the life-giving light of truth, has America been chosen; and her high example shall smite unto death the tyranny of kings, hierarchs, and oligarchs, and carry the glad tidings of peace and good will where myriads now endure an existence scarcely more enviable than that of beasts of the field. Who, then, can doubt that our country is destined to be *the great nation* of futurity?

James K. Polk on Texas and Oregon, 1845

I regard the question of annexation as belonging exclusively to the United States and Texas. They are independent powers competent to contract, and foreign nations have no right to interfere with them or to take exceptions to their reunion. Foreign powers do not seem to appreciate the true character of our Government. Our Union is a confederation of independent States, whose policy is peace with each other and all the world. To enlarge its limits is to extend the dominions of peace over additional territories and increasing millions. The world has nothing to fear from military ambition in our Government. While the Chief Magistrate and the popular branch of Congress are elected for short terms by the suffrages of those millions who must in their own persons bear all the burdens and miseries of war, our Government can not be otherwise than pacific. Foreign powers should therefore look on the annexation of Texas to the United States not as the conquest of a nation seeking to extend her dominions by arms and violence, but as the peaceful acquisition of a territory once her own, by adding another member to our confederation, with the consent of that member, thereby diminishing the chances of war and opening to them new and ever-increasing markets for their products.

To Texas the reunion is important, because the strong protecting arm of our Government would be extended over her, and the vast resources of her fertile soil and genial climate would be speedily developed, while the safety of New Orleans and of our whole southwestern frontier against hostile aggression, as well as the interests of the whole Union, would be promoted by it.

In the earlier stages of our national existence the opinion prevailed with some that our system of confederated States could not operate successfully over an extended territory, and serious objections have at different times been made to the enlargement of our boundaries. These objections were earnestly urged when we acquired Louisiana. Experience has shown that they were not well founded. The title of numerous Indian tribes to vast tracts of country has been extinguished; new States have been admitted into the Union; new Territories have been created and our jurisdiction and laws extended over them. As our population has expanded, the Union has been cemented and strengthened. As our boundaries have been enlarged and our agricultural population has been spread over a large surface, our federative system has acquired additional strength and security. It may well be doubted whether it would not be in greater danger of overthrow if our present population were confined to the comparatively narrow limits of the original thirteen States than it is now that they are sparsely settled over a more expanded territory. It is confidently believed that our system may be safely extended to the utmost bounds of our territorial limits, and that as it shall be extended the bonds of our Union, so far from being weakened, will become stronger.

None can fail to see the danger to our safety and future peace if Texas remains an independent state or becomes an ally or dependency of some foreign nation more powerful than herself. Is there one among our citizens who would not prefer perpetual peace with Texas to occasional wars, which so often occur between bordering independent nations? Is there one who would not prefer free intercourse with her to high duties on all our products and manufactures which enter her ports or cross her frontiers? Is there one who would not prefer an unrestricted communication with her citizens to the frontier obstructions which must occur if she remains out of the Union? Whatever is good or evil in the local institutions of Texas will remain her own whether annexed to the United States or not. None of the present States will be responsible for them any more than they are for the local institutions of each other. They have confederated together for certain specified objects. Upon the same principle that they would refuse to form a perpetual union with Texas because of her local institutions our forefathers would have been prevented from forming our present Union. Perceiving no valid objection to the measure and many reasons for its adoption vitally affecting the peace, the safety, and the prosperity of both countries, I shall on the broad principle which formed the basis and produced the adoption of our Constitution, and not in any narrow spirit of sectional policy, endeavor by all constitutional, honorable, and appropriate means to consummate the expressed will of the people and Government of the United States by the reannexation of Texas to our Union at the earliest practicable period.

Nor will it become in a less degree my duty to assert and maintain by all constitutional means the right of the United States to that portion of our territory which lies beyond the Rocky Mountains. Our title to the country of the Oregon is "clear and unquestionable," and already are our people preparing to perfect that title by occupying it with their wives and children. But eighty years ago our population was confined on the west by the ridge of the Alleghanies. Within that period—within the lifetime, I might say, of some of my hearers—our people, increasing to many millions, have filled the eastern valley of the Mississippi, adventurously ascended the Missouri to its headsprings, and are already engaged in establishing the blessings of self-government in valleys of which the rivers flow to the Pacific. The world beholds the peaceful triumphs of the industry of our emigrants. To us belongs the duty of protecting them adequately wherever they may be upon our soil. The jurisdiction of our laws and the benefits of our republican institutions should be extended over them in the distant regions which they have selected for their homes. The increasing facilities of intercourse will easily bring the States, of which the formation in that part of our territory can not be long delayed, within the sphere of our federative Union. In the meantime every obligation imposed by treaty or conventional stipulations should be sacredly respected.

Polk's War Message, 1846

The existing state of the relations between the United States and Mexico renders it proper that I should bring the subject to the consideration of Congress. . . .

The strong desire to establish peace with Mexico on liberal and honorable terms, and the readiness of this Government to regulate and adjust our boundary and other causes of difference with that power on such fair and equitable principles as would lead to permanent relations of the most friendly nature, induced me in September last to seek the reopening of diplomatic relations between the two countries. . . . An envoy of the United States repaired to Mexico with full powers to adjust every existing difference. But though present on the Mexican soil by agreement between the two Governments, invested with full powers, and bearing evidence of the most friendly dispositions, his mission has been unavailing. The Mexican Government not only refused to receive him or listen to his propositions, but after a long-continued series of menaces have at last invaded our territory and shed the blood of our fellow-citizens on our own soil.

It now becomes my duty to state more in detail the origin, progress, and failure of that mission. In pursuance of the instructions given in September last, an inquiry was made on the 13th of October, 1845, in the most friendly terms, through our consul in Mexico, of the minister for foreign affairs, whether the Mexican Government "would receive an envoy from the United States intrusted with full powers to adjust all the questions in dispute between the two Governments," with the assurance that "should the answer be in the affirmative such an envoy would be immediately dispatched to Mexico." The Mexican minister on the 15th of October gave an affirmative answer to this inquiry. . . . On the 10th of November, 1845, Mr. John Slidell, of Louisiana, was commissioned by me as envoy extraordinary and minister plenipotentiary of the United States to Mexico, and was intrusted with full powers to adjust both the questions of the Texas boundary and of indemnification to our citizens. The redress of the wrongs of our citizens naturally and inseparably blended itself with the question of boundary. The settlement of the one question in any correct view of the subject involves that of the other. I could not for a moment entertain the idea that the claims of our much-injured and long-suffering citizens, many of which had existed for more than twenty years, should be postponed or separated from the settlement of the boundary question.

Mr. Slidell arrived at Vera Cruz on the 30th of November, and was courteously received by the authorities of that city. But the Government of General Herrera was then tottering to its fall. The revolutionary party had seized upon the Texas question to effect or hasten its overthrow. Its determination to restore friendly relations with the United States, and to receive our minister to negotiate for the settlement of this question, was violently assailed, and was made the great theme of denunciation against it. The Government of General Herrera, there is good reason to believe, was sincerely desirous to receive our minister; but it yielded to the storm raised by its enemies, and on the 21st of December refused to accredit Mr. Slidell upon the most frivolous pretexts. These are so fully and ably exposed in the note of Mr. Slidell of the 24th of December last to the Mexican minister of foreign relations, herewith transmitted, that I deem it unnecessary to enter into further detail on this portion of the subject.

Five days after the date of Mr. Slidell's note General Herrera yielded the Government to General Paredes without a struggle, and on the 30th of December resigned the Presidency. This revolution was accomplished solely by the army, the people having taken little part in the contest; and thus the supreme power in Mexico passed into the hands of a military leader.

Determined to leave no effort untried to effect an amicable adjustment with Mexico, I directed Mr. Slidell to present his credentials to the Government of General Paredes and ask to be officially received by him. There would have been less ground for taking this step had General Paredes come into power by a regular constitutional succession. In that event his administration would have been considered but a mere constitutional continuance of the

Government of General Herrera, and the refusal of the latter to receive our minister would have been deemed conclusive unless an intimation had been given by General Paredes of his desire to reverse the decision of his predecessor. But the Government of General Paredes owes its existence to a military revolution, by which the subsisting constitutional authorities had been subverted. The form of government was entirely changed, as well as all the high functionaries by whom it was administered.

Under these circumstances Mr. Slidell, in obedience to my direction, addressed a note to the Mexican minister of foreign relations, under date of the 1st of March last, asking to be received by that Government in the diplomatic character to which he had been appointed. This minister in his reply, under date of the 12th of March, reiterated the arguments of his predecessor, and in terms that may be considered as giving just grounds of offense to the Government and people of the United States denied the application of Mr. Slidell. Nothing therefore remained for our envoy but to demand his passports and return to his own country.

Thus the Government of Mexico, though solemnly pledged by official acts in October last to receive and accredit an American envoy, violated their plighted faith and refused the offer of a peaceful adjustment of our difficulties. Not only was the offer rejected, but the indignity of its rejection was enhanced by the manifest breach of faith in refusing to admit the envoy who came because they had bound themselves to receive him. Nor can it be said that the offer was fruitless from the want of opportunity of discussing it; our envoy was present on their own soil. Nor can it be ascribed to a want of sufficient powers; our envoy had full powers to adjust every question of difference. Nor was there room for complaint that our propositions for settlement were unreasonable; permission was not even given our envoy to make any proposition whatever. Nor can it be objected that we, on our part, would not listen to any reasonable terms of their suggestion; the Mexican Government refused all negotiation, and have made no proposition of any kind.

In my message at the commencement of the present session I informed you that upon the earnest appeal both of the Congress and convention of Texas I had ordered an efficient military force to take a position "between the Nueces and the Del Norte." This had become necessary to meet a threatened invasion of Texas by the Mexican forces, for which extensive military preparations had been made. The invasion was threatened solely because Texas had determined, in accordance with a solemn resolution of the Congress of the United States, to annex herself to our Union, and under these circumstances it was plainly our duty to extend our protection over her citizens and soil.

This force was concentrated at Corpus Christi, and remained there until after I had received such information from Mexico as rendered it probable, if not certain, that the Mexican Government would refuse to receive our envoy.

Meantime Texas, by the final action of our Congress, had become an integral part of our Union. The Congress of Texas, by its act of December

19, 1836, had declared the Rio del Norte to be the boundary of that Republic. Its jurisdiction had been extended and exercised beyond the Nueces. The country between that river and the Del Norte had been represented in the Congress and in the convention of Texas, had thus taken part in the act of annexation itself, and is now included within one of our Congressional districts. Our own Congress had, moreover, with great unanimity, by the act approved December 31, 1845, recognized the country beyond the Nueces as a part of our territory by including it within our own revenue system, and a revenue officer to reside within that district has been appointed by and with the advice and consent of the Senate. It became, therefore, of urgent necessity to provide for the defense of that portion of our country. Accordingly, on the 13th of January last instructions were issued to the general in command of these troops to occupy the left bank of the Del Norte. This river, which is the southwestern boundary of the State of Texas, is an exposed frontier. From this quarter invasion was threatened; upon it and in its immediate vicinity, in the judgment of high military experience, are the proper stations for the protecting forces of the Government. In addition to this important consideration, several others occurred to induce this movement. Among these are the facilities afforded by the ports at Brazos Santiago and the mouth of the Del Norte for the reception of supplies by sea, the stronger and more healthful military positions, the convenience for obtaining a ready and a more abundant supply of provisions, water, fuel, and forage, and the advantages which are afforded by the Del Norte in forwarding supplies to such posts as may be established in the interior and upon the Indian frontier.

The movement of the troops to the Del Norte was made by the commanding general under positive instructions to abstain from all aggressive acts toward Mexico or Mexican citizens and to regard the relations between that Republic and the United States as peaceful unless she should declare war or commit acts of hostility indicative of a state of war. He was specially directed to protect private property and respect personal rights.

The Army moved from Corpus Christi on the 11th of March, and on the 28th of that month arrived on the left bank of the Del Norte opposite to Matamoras, where it encamped on a commanding position, which has since been strengthened by the erection of fieldworks. A depot has also been established at Point Isabel, near the Brazos Santiago, 30 miles in the rear of the encampment. The selection of his position was necessarily confided to the judgment of the general in command.

The Mexican forces at Matamoras assumed a belligerent attitude, and on the 12th of April General Ampudia, then in command, notified General Taylor to break up his camp within twenty-four hours and to retire beyond the Nueces River, and in the event of his failure to comply with these demands announced that arms, and arms alone, must decide the question. But no open act of hostility was committed until the 24th of April. On that day General Arista, who had succeeded to the command of the Mexican forces, communicated to General Taylor that "he considered hostilities commenced and should prosecute them." A party of dragoons of 63 men and officers were on the same day dispatched from the American camp up the Rio del Norte, on its left bank, to ascertain whether the Mexican troops had crossed or were preparing to cross the river, "became engaged with a large body of these troops, and after a short affair, in which some 16 were killed and wounded, appear to have been surrounded and compelled to surrender."

The grievous wrongs perpetrated by Mexico upon our citizens throughout a long period of years remain unredressed, and solemn treaties pledging her public faith for this redress have been disregarded. A government either unable or unwilling to enforce the execution of such treaties fails to perform one of its plainest duties.

Our commerce with Mexico has been almost annihilated. It was formerly highly beneficial to both nations, but our merchants˙have been deterred from prosecuting it by the system of outrage and extortion which the Mexican authorities have pursued against them, whilst their appeals through their own Government for indemnity have been made in vain. Our forbearance has gone to such an extreme as to be mistaken in its character. Had we acted with vigor in repelling the insults and redressing the injuries inflicted by Mexico at the commencement, we should doubtless have escaped all the difficulties in which we are now involved.

Instead of this, however, we have been exerting our best efforts to propitiate her good will. Upon the pretext that Texas, a nation as independent as herself, thought proper to unite its destinies with our own she has affected to believe that we have severed her rightful territory, and in official proclamations and manifestoes has repeatedly threatened to make war upon us for the purpose of reconquering Texas. In the meantime we have tried every effort at reconciliation. The cup of forbearance had been exhausted even before the recent information from the frontier of the Del Norte. But now, after reiterated menaces, Mexico has passed the boundary of the United States, has invaded our territory and shed American blood upon the American soil. She has proclaimed that hostilities have commenced, and that the two nations are now at war.

As war exists, and, notwithstanding all our efforts to avoid it, exists by the act of Mexico herself, we are called upon by every consideration of duty and patriotism to vindicate with decision the honor, the rights, and the interests of our country.

The Wilmot Proviso, 1846

Provided, That, as an express and fundamental condition to the acquisition of any territory from the Republic of Mexico by the United States, by virtue of any treaty which may be negotiated between them, and to the use by the Executive of the moneys herein appropriated, neither slavery nor involuntary servitude shall ever exist in any part of said territory, except for crime, whereof the party shall first be duly convicted.

Massachusetts Protests the Mexican War, 1847

Resolves. Concerning the Mexican War, and the Institution of Slavery.

Resolved, That the present war with Mexico has its primary origin in the unconstitutional annexation to the United States of the foreign state of Texas while the same was still at war with Mexico; that it was unconstitutionally commenced by the order of the President, to General Taylor, to take military possession of territory in dispute between the United States and Mexico, and in the occupation of Mexico; and that it is now waged ingloriously—by a powerful nation against a weak neighbor—unnecessarily and without just cause, at immense cost of treasure and life, for the dismemberment of Mexico, and for the conquest, of a portion of her territory, from which slavery has already been excluded, with the triple object of extending slavery, of strengthening the "Slave Power," and of obtaining the control of the Free States, under the Constitution of the United States.

Resolved, That such a war of conquest, so hateful in its objects, so wanton, unjust, and unconstitutional in its origin and character, must be regarded as a war against freedom, against humanity, against justice, against the Union, against the Constitution, and against the Free States; and that a regard for the true interests and the highest honor of the country, not less than the impulses of Christian duty, should arouse all good citizens to join in efforts to arrest this gigantic crime, by withholding supplies, or other voluntary contributions, for its further prosecution; by calling for the withdrawal of our army within the established limits of the United States; and in every just way aiding the country to retreat from the disgraceful position of aggression which it now occupies towards a weak, distracted neighbor and sister republic.

Resolved, That our attention is directed anew to the wrong and "enormity" of slavery, and to the tyranny and usurpation of the "Slave Power," as displayed in the history of our country, particularly in the annexation of Texas and the present war with Mexico.

A Mexican Perspective, 1849

To explain then in a few words the true origin of the war, it is sufficient to say that the insatiable ambition of the United States, favored by our weakness, caused it. But this assertion, however veracious and well founded, requires the confirmation which we will present, along with some former transactions, to the whole world. This evidence will leave no doubt of the correctness of our impressions.

In throwing off the yoke of the mother country, the United States of the North appeared at once as a powerful nation. This was the result of their excellent elementary principles of government established while in colonial subjection. The Republic announced at its birth, that it was called upon to represent an important part in the world of Columbus. Its rapid advancement, its progressive increase, its wonderful territory, the uninterrupted augmentation of its inhabitants, and the formidable power it had gradually acquired, were many proofs of its becoming a colossus, not only for the feeble nations of Spanish America, but even for the old populations of the ancient continent.

The United States did not hope for the assistance of time in their schemes of aggrandizement. From the days of their independence they adopted the project of extending their dominions, and since then, that line of policy has not deviated in the slightest degree. . . .

The American Minister, Mr. Shannon, whether from his really believing that the war was positively to be undertaken, or because a pretext was sought to compel Mexico to declare hostilities against the United States, and to make us appear as aggressors, transmitted an official note. In it he made known in the name of his government, that its policy had always been directed to the incorporation of Texas into the American Union, and the invasion which was proposed by Mexico against that Department would now be deemed an offence to the United States.

In this celebrated communication, which will disgrace for ever the diplomatist who subscribed it, a protest was entered against a war with Texas, while the project of annexation was pending. Here the confession had been made, important for us, that the scheme to obtain this part of our territory had been invariably pursued by all parties, and nearly all the administrations of the Republic of North America, for the space of twenty years. The facts which we have mentioned, with others, passed in silence, being less interesting, and, for the sake of brevity, prove by good evidence that this plan existed, and was of longer standing than had been said. But the explicit avowal of the Minister Shannon, not denied nor contradicted by the authorities of his country—this avowal, we say, is of the greatest importance, coming from the very mouths of the usurpers who style themselves the most honest before all civilized nations.

Again, Mexico ought at this time to have broken completely with her deceitful neighbor, and made war wherever her forces would have permitted. Temporizing, however, throughout, our government, in conformity with the justice on which it is founded and guided, hoped that the American Senate would decide upon the project of annexation. As the decision of this body had then been favorable, it continued an intercourse disturbed at present, but still existing, between our Republic and the one at Washington. The most that was done was to protest that annexation would be considered as a declaration of war, for it would come to this extremity if it should thereby heap upon us contempt and degradation.

At this time, more properly than before, it would have been exact justice to have immediately made war on a power that so rashly appropriated what by every title belonged to us. This necessity had increased to a point, that the administrations which had successively been intrusted with our affairs, upon consideration, had all agreed in the principle, that a decree of annexation should be viewed as a *casus belli*—a cause of war. But while this new injury was being suffered, without deciding anything, but keeping diplomatic relations suspended between both countries, our minister, General

Almonte, retired from Washington, and the one from the United States did the same from Mexico.

At the close of the year 1844, a new revolution having overturned the government of General Santa Anna, intrusted in the interim to General Canaliso, elevated to power D. José Joaquin de Herrera, the President of the Council. The famous decree of the 29th of November of that year had ended in disgracing the public officers who had framed it. It had established an unlimited dictatorship, and the war with Texas was, as it had been at other times, the gloss of justice with which they tried to conceal the attack directed against the constitution. A majority of the people distrusted the sincerity of the government, recollecting that the national and indispensable war which they ought to have made in that separate Department had not been preferred to Yucatan, which, without any beneficial result, had been the sacrifice of so many men and so with it, the decree of the 6th of July was passed. By it the government was authorized to use the natural defences of the country to repel aggression committed against many of the departments, and to make known to friendly nations the justifiable causes which obliged it to defend its rights by repelling force by force.

While the United States seemed to be animated by a sincere desire not to break the peace, their acts of hostility manifested very evidently what were their true intentions. Their ships infested our coasts; their troops continued advancing upon our territory, situated at places which under no aspect could be disputed. Thus violence and insult were united: thus at the very time they usurped part of our territory, they offered to us the hand of treachery, to have soon the audacity to say that our obstinacy and arrogance were the real causes of the war. . . .

From the acts referred to, it has been demonstrated to the very senses, that the real and effective cause of this war that afflicted us was the spirit of aggrandizement of the United States of the North, availing itself of its power to conquer us. Impartial history will some day illustrate for ever the conduct observed by this Republic against all laws, divine and human, in an age that is called one of light, and which is, notwithstanding, the same as the former—one of *force and violence*.

Civil War Diplomacy

American expansionism faltered in the 1850s and 1860s when sectionalism bedeviled the nation. After Union and Confederate armies began to bloody themselves and ravage the countryside, expansionists on both sides worried more about their survival than about extending empire. Southern diplomats busied themselves with the task of winning European favor for their secession and independence. Northern diplomats threw their energy into preventing European interference. Whereas Confederate leaders worked to internationalize the internecine conflict, Union leaders strove to contain the conflagration and to warn Europeans—including the French who meddled in Mexico—against taking advantage of American weakness to enlarge their interests in the western hemisphere.

The competition centered on Britain and cotton. Jefferson Davis's Confederacy sought to woo the British with "King Cotton" arguments, believing that British industry was dependent upon Southern cotton exports and could be persuaded to back Confederate independence because of economic self-interest. Abraham Lincoln's Union tried to foil such arrangements with a blockade of Southern ports, sparking controversy with London over maritime rights. The British building of war vessels for the confederacy particularly angered the people of the North and rekindled Anglophobia. Whether Britain chose to limit itself to only recognition of belligerency and small amounts of military supplies because of Northern diplomatic skills, dependency on American foodstuffs, Southern ineptitude, the political influence of pro-American British citizens, or a cautious respect for Northern military power is the stuff of debate among historians.

✳ DOCUMENTS

Secretary of State William H. Seward was such an ardent nationalist that he advised President Lincoln, in the first document, dated April 1, 1861, to take the drastic action of fighting either Spain or France so as to cause Southern secessionists to rally around the flag and rejoin the Union. Lincoln discreetly buried the proposal and reminded his impertinent secretary that the president was in charge. The second document is Lincoln's controversial proclamation of blockade, April 19, 1861. In the third document, Seward instructs Minister to England Charles Francis Adams to warn the British not to deal with the Confederate commissioners in London—"fraternize with our domestic enemy"—unless they wish an Anglo-American war. The Confederate faith in cotton as an inducement to a favorable British policy is illustrated well by the next document, a September 23, 1861, letter from Confederate Secretary of State R. M. T. Hunter to Confederate agent James M. Mason. In the fall of 1861, Mason and another Confederate agent were boldly seized from the British vessel *Trent* by Captain Charles Wilkes of the United States Navy. The British howled in protest, while Americans cheered Wilkes for his audacity. In the end, the agents were set free. On January 9, 1862, Senator Charles Sumner of Massachusetts made the best of it by slamming the Confederates, applauding Wilkes's noble if mistaken act, and ribbing the British for finally endorsing a traditional American principle against boarding neutral ships. The last document is Charles Francis Adams's firm protest to the British against their delivery of an "iron-clad" to the Confederate Navy: "This is war."

William H. Seward's Call for a Foreign War, 1861

I would demand explanations from *Spain* and France, categorically, at once.

I would seek explanations from Great Britain and Russia, and send agents into *Canada, Mexico* and *Central America,* to rouse a vigorous continental *spirit of independence* on this continent against European intervention.

And if satisfactory explanations are not received from Spain and France, Would convene Congress and declare war against them

But whatever policy we adopt, there must be an energetic prosecution of it.

For this purpose it must be somebody's business to pursue and direct it incessantly.

Either the President must do it himself, and be all the while active in it; or

Devolve it on some member of his Cabinet. Once adopted, debates on it must end, and all agree and abide.

It is not in my especial province.

But I neither seek to evade nor assume responsibility.

Abraham Lincoln's Blockade Proclamation, 1861

Whereas an insurrection against the Government of the United States has broken out in the States of South Carolina, Georgia, Alabama, Florida, Mississippi, Louisiana, and Texas, and the laws of the United States for the collection of the revenue cannot be effectually executed therein conformably to that provision of the Constitution which requires duties to be uniform throughout the United States:

And whereas a combination of persons engaged in such insurrection, have threatened to grant pretended letters of marque to authorize the bearers thereof to commit assaults on the lives, vessels, and property of good citizens of the country lawfully engaged in commerce on the high seas and in waters of the United States:

And whereas an Executive Proclamation has been already issued, requiring the persons engaged in these disorderly proceedings to desist therefrom, calling out a militia force for the purpose of repressing the same, and convening Congress in extraordinary session, to deliberate and determine thereon:

Now, therefore, I, Abraham Lincoln, President of the United States, with a view to the same purposes before mentioned, and to the protection of the public peace, and the lives and property of quiet and orderly citizens pursuing their lawful occupations, until Congress shall have assembled and deliberated on the said unlawful proceedings, or until the same shall have ceased, have further deemed it advisable to set on foot a blockade of the ports within the States aforesaid, in pursuance of the laws of the United States, and of the law of Nations in such case provided. For this purpose a competent force will be posted so as to prevent entrance and exit of vessels from the ports aforesaid. If, therefore, with a view to violate such blockade, a vessel shall approach, or shall attempt to leave either [sic] of the said ports, she will be duly warned by the Commander of one of the blockading vessels, who will endorse on her register the fact and date of such warning, and if the same vessel shall again attempt to enter or leave the blockaded port, she will be captured and sent to the nearest convenient port, for such proceedings against her and her cargo as prize, as may be deemed advisable.

And I hereby proclaim and declare that if any person, under the pretended authority of the said States, or under any other pretense, shall molest a vessel of the United States, or the persons or cargo on board of her, such person will be held amenable to the laws of the United States for the prevention and punishment of piracy.

Seward's Warning to the British, 1861

. . .This government considers that our affairs in Europe have reached a crisis, in which it is necessary for it to take a decided stand, on which not only its immediate measures, but its ultimate and permanent policy can be determined and defined. At the same time it neither means to menace Great Britain nor to wound the susceptibilities of that or any other European nation. That policy is developed in this paper. . . .

Mr. Dallas, in a brief dispatch of May 2, tells us that Lord John Russell recently requested an interview with him on account of the solicitude which his lordship felt concerning the effect of certain measures represented as likely to be adopted by the President. In that conversation the British Secretary told Mr. Dallas that the three representatives of the Southern Confederacy were then in London, that Lord John Russell had not yet seen them, but that he was not unwilling to see them unofficially. He further informed Mr. Dallas that an understanding exists between the British and French governments which would lead both to take one and the same course as to recognition. . . .

Intercourse of any kind with the so-called commissioners is liable to be construed as a recognition of the authority which appointed them. Such intercourse would be none the less hurtful to us for being called unofficial, and it might be even more injurious, because we should have no means of knowing what points might be resolved by it. Moreover, unofficial intercourse is useless and meaningless if it is not expected to ripen into official intercourse and direct recognition. . . . You will, in any event, desist from all intercourse whatever, unofficial as well as official, with the British government, so long as it shall continue intercourse of either kind with the domestic enemies of this country. When intercourse shall have been arrested for this cause, you will communicate with this department and receive further directions. . . .

As to the blockade, you will say that by our own laws and the laws of nature, and the laws of nations, this government has a clear right to suppress insurrection. An exclusion of commerce from national ports which have been seized by insurgents, in the equitable form of blockade, is a proper means to that end. You will not insist that our blockade is to be respected, if it be not maintained by a competent force; but passing by that question as not now a practical or at least an urgent one, you will add that the blockade is now, and it will continue to be, so maintained, and therefore we expect it to be respected by Great Britain. You will add that we have already revoked the *exequatur* of a Russian consul who had enlisted in the military service of the insurgents, and we shall dismiss or demand the recall of every foreign agent, consular or diplomatic, who shall either disobey the Federal laws or disown the Federal authority.

As to the recognition of the so-called Southern Confederacy, it is not to be made a subject of technical definition. It is, of course, direct recognition to publish an acknowledgment of the sovereignty and independence of a new power. It is direct recognition to receive its ambassadors, ministers, agents or commissioners, officially. A concession of belligerent rights is liable to be construed as a recognition of them. No one of these proceedings will pass unquestioned by the United States in this case.

Hitherto, recognition has been moved only on the assumption that the so-called Confederate States are *de facto* a self-sustaining power. Now, after long forbearance, designed to soothe discontent and avert the need of civil war, the land and naval forces of the United States have been put in force to suppress insurrection. The true character of the pretended new state is at once revealed. It is seen to be a power existing in *pronunciamento* only. It has never won a field. It has obtained no forts that were not virtually betrayed into its hands or seized in breach of trust. It commands not a single port on the coast nor any highway out from its pretended capital by land. Under these circumstances, Great Britain is called upon to intervene and give it body and independence by resisting our measures of suppression. British recognition would be British intervention, to create within our territory a hostile state by overthrowing this Republic itself. . . .

As to the treatment of privateers in the insurgent service, you will say that this is a question exclusively our own. We treat them as pirates. They are our own citizens, or persons employed by our citizens, preying on the commerce of our country. If Great Britain should choose to recognize them as lawful belligerents, and give them shelter from our pursuit and punishment, the laws of nations afford an adequate and proper remedy.

Happily, however, her Britannic Majesty's government can avoid all these difficulties. It invited us in 1856 to accede to the declaration of the Congress of Paris, of which body Great Britain was herself a member, abolishing privateering everywhere in all cases and forever. You already have our authority to propose to her our accession to that declaration. If she refuse it, it can only be because she is willing to become the patron of privateering when aimed at our devastation.

These positions are not elaborately defended now, because to vindicate them would imply a possibility of our waiving them.

We are not insensible of the grave importance of this occasion. We see how, upon the result of the debate in which we are engaged, a war may ensue between the United States and one, two, or even more European nations. War in any case is as exceptional from the habits as it is revolting from the sentiments of the American people. But if it come it will be fully seen that it results from the action of Great Britain, not our own; that Great Britain will have decided to fraternize with our domestic enemy either without waiting to hear from you our remonstrances and our warnings, or after having heard them. War in defence of national life is not immoral, and war in defence of independence is an inevitable part of the discipline of nations.

The Confederacy Lures the British with Cotton, 1861

The enemy, with greatly superior numbers, have been routed in pitched battles at Bethel and at Manassas (in Virginia), and their recent defeat at Springfield, Mo., was almost as signal as that of Manassas. The comparatively little foothold which they have had in the Confederate States is gradually being lost, and after six months of war, in which they employed their best resources, it may be truly said they are much farther from the conquest of the Southern States than they seemed to be when the struggle commenced. The Union feeling supposed to exist largely in the South, and which was known to us to be imaginary, is now shown in its true light to all mankind. Never were any people more united than are those of the Confederate States in their purpose to maintain their independence at any cost of life and treasure, nor is there a party to be found anywhere in these States which professes a desire for a reunion with the United States.

Nothing could prove this unanimity of feeling more strongly than the fact that this immense army may be said to have taken the field spontaneously, and faster almost than the Government could provide for its organization and equipment. But the voluntary contributions of the people supplied all deficiencies until the Government could come to their assistance, as it has done with the necessary military establishments.

And what is perhaps equally remarkable, it may be said with truth that there has been no judicial execution for a political offense during the whole of the war, and, so far as military offenses are concerned, our prisons would be empty if it were not for a few captured spies. Under these circumstances it would seem that the time has arrived when it would be proper in the Government of Great Britain to recognize our independence. If it be obvious that the Confederate States cannot be conquered in this struggle, then the sooner the strife be ended the better for the cause of peace and the interests of mankind. Under such circumstances, to fail to throw the great moral influence of such a recognition into the scale of peace, when this may be done without risk or danger, may be to share in the responsibility for the longer continuance of an unnecessary war. This is a consideration which ought, perhaps, to have some weight with a nation which leads so largely as does that of Great Britain in the progress of Christian civilization. That the British people have a deep political and commercial interest in the establishment of the independence of the Confederate States must be obvious to all. Their real interest in that event is only a little less than our own. The great question of cotton supply, which has occupied their attention so justly and so anxiously for some years past, will then be satisfactorily settled. Whilst the main source of cotton production was in the hands of such a power as that of the United States, and controlled by those who were disposed to use that control to acquire the supremacy in navigation, commerce, and manufactures over all rivals, there was just cause for anxiety on the part of nations who were largely dependent upon the source of supply for the raw material of important manufactures. But the case will be far different when peace is assured and the independence of the Confederate States is acknowledged. Within these States must be found for years to come the great source of cotton supply. So favorable a combination of soil, climate, and labor is nowhere else to be found. Their capacity for increased production has so far kept pace with the increased demand, and in time of peace it promises to do so for a long while to come. In the question of the supply of this great staple there is a worldwide interest; and if the nations of the earth could choose for themselves a single depository for such an interest, perhaps none could be found to act so impartially in that capacity as the Confederacy of Southern States.

Their great interest is, and will be for a long time to come, in the production and exportation of the important staples so much sought by the rest of the world.

It would be long before they would become the rivals of those who are largely concerned in navigation, manufactures, and commerce. On the contrary, these interests would make them valuable customers and bind them to the policy of free trade. Their early legislation, which has thrown open their navigation, foreign and coasting, to the free competition of all nations, and which has imposed the lowest duties on imports consistent with their necessary revenue wants, proves the natural tendency of their commercial policy. Under such circumstances the supply of cotton to Great Britain would be as abundant, as cheap, and as certain as if these States were themselves her colonies.

The establishment of such an empire, committed as it would be to the policy of free trade by its interests and traditions, would seem to be a matter of primary importance to the progress of human industry and the great causes of human civilization. It would be of the deepest interest to such a Government to preserve peace and to improve its opportunities for the pursuit of the useful arts. The residue of the world would find here, too, sources of supply of more than the great staples in which manufactures and commerce are most deeply interested, and these sources would probably prove to be not only constant, as being little likely to be troubled by the chances of war, but also of easy access to all who might desire to resort to them. In presenting the great importance of this question to the Government of Great Britain in its connection with their material interests, you will not omit its bearing upon the future political relations between the Old and the New World.

With a balance of power established between the great Confederacies of the North American Continent, the fears of a disturbance of the peace of the world from the desire for the annexation of contiguous territory on the part of a vast and overshadowing political and military organization will be dissipated. Under the former Union the slaveholding States had an interest in the acquisition of territory suitable to their institutions, in order to establish a balance of power within the Government for their own protection. This reason no longer exists, as the Confederate States have sought that protection by a separation from the Union in which their rights were endangered. It is manifest, from the nature of its interests, that the Southern Confederacy, in entering as a new member in the family of nations, would exercise not a disturbing but a harmonizing influence on human society; for it would not only desire peace itself, but to some extent become a bond of peace amongst other.

Charles Sumner on the *Trent* Affair, 1862

Two old men and two younger associates, recently taken from the British mail packet Trent on the high seas by order of Captain Wilkes of the United States Navy, and afterwards detained in custody at Fort Warren, have been liberated and placed at the disposition of the British Government. This has been done at the instance of that Government, courteously conveyed, and founded on the assumption that the original capture of these men was an act of violence which was an affront to the British flag, and a violation of international law. This is a simple outline of the facts. But in order to appreciate the value of this precedent, there are other matters which must be brought into view.

These two old men were citizens of the United States, and for many years Senators. One was the author of the fugitive slave bill, and the other was the chief author of the filibustering system which has disgraced our national name and disturbed our national peace. Occupying places of trust and power in the service of their country, they conspired against it, and at last the secret traitors and conspirators became open rebels. The present rebellion, now surpassing in proportions and also in wickedness any rebellion in history, was from the beginning quickened and promoted by their untiring energies. That country to which they owed love, honor, and obedience, they betrayed and gave over to violence and outrage. Treason, conspiracy, and rebellion, each in succession, have acted through them. The incalculable expenditures which now task our national resources, the untold derangement of affairs not only at home but also abroad, the levy of armies almost without an example, the devastation of extended regions of territory, the plunder of peaceful ships on the ocean, and the slaughter of fellow-citizens on the murderous battle-field; such are some of the consequences proceeding directly from them. To carry forward still further the gigantic crime of which they were so large a part, these two old men, with their two younger associates, stole from Charleston on board a rebel steamer, and, under cover of darkness and storm, running the blockade and avoiding the cruisers in that neighborhood, succeeded in reaching the neutral island of Cuba, where, with open display and the knowledge of the British consul, they embarked on board the British mail packet the Trent, bound for St. Thomas, whence they were to embark for England, in which kingdom one of them was to play the part of ambassador of the rebellion, while the other was to play the same part in France. The original treason, conspiracy, and rebellion of which they were so heinously guilty, were all continued on this voyage, which became a prolongation of the original crime, destined to still further excess, through their embassadorial pretensions, which, it was hoped, would array two great nations against the United States, and enlist them openly in behalf of an accursed slaveholding rebellion. While on their way, the ambassadors were arrested by Captain Wilkes, of the United States steamer San Jacinto, an accomplished officer, already well known by his scientific explorations, who, on this occasion, acted without instructions from his Government. If, in this arrest, he forgot for a moment the fixed policy of the Republic, which has been from the beginning like a frontlet between the eyes, and transcended the law of nations, as the United States have always declared it, his apology must be found in the patriotic impulse by which he was inspired, and the British examples which he could not forget. They were the enemies of his country, embodying in themselves the triple essence of worst enmity—treason, conspiracy, and rebellion; and they wore a pretended embassadorial character, which, as he supposed, according to high British authority, rendered them liable to be stopped. . . .

If this transaction be regarded exclusively in the light of British precedents; if we follow the seeming authority of the British admiralty, speaking by its greatest voice; and especially if we accept the oft-repeated example of British cruisers, upheld by the British Government against the oft-repeated protests of the United States, we shall not find it difficult to vindicate it. The act becomes questionable only when brought to the touchstone of these liberal principles, which, from the earliest times, the American Government has openly avowed and sought to advance, and which other European nations have accepted with regard to the sea. Indeed, Great Britain cannot complain except by now adopting those identical principles; and should we undertake to vindicate the act, it can be done only by repudiating those identical principles. Our two cases will be reversed. In the struggle between Laertes and Hamlet, the two combatants exchanged rapiers; so that Hamlet was armed with the rapier of Laertes and Laertes was armed with the rapier of Hamlet. And now on this sensitive question a similar exchange has occurred. Great Britain is armed with American principles, while to us is left only those British principles which, throughout our history, have been constantly, deliberately, and solemnly rejected. . . .

The seizure of the rebel emissaries on board a neutral ship cannot be justified according to our best American precedents and practice. There seems to be no single point where the seizure is not questionable, unless we choose to invoke British precedents and practice, which beyond doubt led Captain Wilkes to the mistake which he committed. In the solitude of his ship he consulted familiar authorities at hand, and felt that in following Vattel and Sir William Scott, as quoted and affirmed by eminent writers, reinforced by the inveterate practice of the British navy, he could not err. He was mistaken. There was a better example; it was the constant, uniform, unhesitating practice of his own country on the ocean, conceding always the greatest immunities to neutral ships, unless sailing to blockaded ports— refusing to consider dispatches as contraband of war—refusing to consider persons, other than soldiers or officers, as contraband of war; and protesting always against an adjudication of personal rights by the summary judgment of a quarter-deck. Had these well-attested precedents been in his mind, the gallant captain would not, even for a moment, have been seduced from his allegiance to those principles which constitute a part of our country's glory.

Mr. President, let the rebels go. Two wicked men, ungrateful to their country, are let loose with the brand of Cain upon their foreheads. Prison doors are opened; but principles are established which will help to free other men, and to open the gates of the sea. Never before in her active history has Great Britain ranged herself on this side. Such an event is an epoch. *Novus saeclorum nascitur ordo.* To the liberties of the sea this Power is now committed. To a certain extent this cause is now under her tutelary care. If the immunities of passengers, not in the military or naval service, as well as of sailors, are not directly recognized, they are at least implied; while the whole pretension of impressment, so long the pest of neutral commerce, and operating only through the lawless adjudication of a quarter-deck, is made absolutely impossible. Thus is the freedom of the seas enlarged, not only by limiting the number of persons who are exposed to the penalties of war, but by driving from it the most offensive pretension that ever stalked upon its waves. To such conclusion Great Britain is irrevocably pledged. Nor treaty nor bond was needed. It is sufficient that her late appeal can be vindicated only by a renunciation of early, long-continued tyranny. Let her bear the rebels back. The consideration is ample; for the sea became free as this altered Power went forth upon it, steering westward with the sun, on an errand of liberation.

In this surrender, if such it may be called, our Government does not even "stoop to conquer." It simply lifts itself to the height of its own original principles. The early efforts of its best negotiators—the patriot trials of its soldiers in an unequal war—have at length prevailed, and Great Britain, usually so haughty, invites us to practice upon those principles which she has so strenuously opposed. There are victories of force. Here is a victory of truth. If Great Britain has gained the custody of two rebels, the United States have secured the triumph of their principles.

Charles Francis Adams's Protest
Against the Ironclads, 1863

At this moment, when one of the iron-clad vessels is on the point of departure from this kingdom, on its hostile errand against the United States, I am honored with the reply of your lordship to my notes of the 11th, 16th and 25th of July, and of the 14th of August. I trust I need not express how profound is my regret at the conclusion to which her Majesty's government have arrived. I can regard it no otherwise than as practically opening to the insurgents free liberty in this kingdom to execute a policy described in one of their late publications in the following language:

"In the present state of the harbor defences of New York, Boston, Portland, and smaller northern cities, such a vessel as the Warrior would have little difficulty in entering any of these ports and inflicting a vital blow upon the enemy. The destruction of Boston alone would be worth a hundred victories in the field. It would bring such a terror to the 'blue-noses,' as to cause them to wish eagerly for peace, despite their overweening love of gain which has been so freely administered to since the opening of this war. Vessels of the Warrior class would promptly raise the blockade of our ports, and would even, in this respect, confer advantages which would soon repay the cost of their construction."

It would be superfluous in me to point out to your lordship that this is war. No matter what may be the theory adopted of neutrality in a struggle, when this process is carried on in the manner indicated, from a territory and with the aid of the subjects of a third party, that third party to all intents and purposes ceases to be neutral. Neither is it necessary to show, that any government which suffers it to be done fails in enforcing the essential conditions of national amity towards the country against whom the hostility is directed. In my belief it is impossible that any nation, retaining a proper degree of self-respect, could tamely submit to a continuance of relations so utterly deficient in reciprocity. I have no idea that Great Britain would do so for a moment.

The Era
of
Reconstruction

The Republican Party and
the Reconstruction Party

Reconstruction was, in a real sense, what the war was all about. After putting down the southerners' attempted secession and liberating their slaves in the process, the Federal government now had to decide what kind of society should emerge in the South. Simply ending slavery and terminating hostilities were not enough. The freed slaves now had to be protected and given the opportunity to enjoy and develop their new status. This meant guaranteeing their legal rights and economic security, perhaps even giving them access to the vote or to land. At the same time, the leaders of the rebellion had to be punished and their political influence curbed, if not eliminated altogether. Since most of these men were also slaveholders, their economic power might be reduced, especially if some of their land was to be made available to the former slaves. All of these possibilities had to be considered as part of a final settlement of the issues and problems raised by the sectional conflict and the war that had ensued.

In the seven months between Andrew Johnson's sudden accession to the presidency in April 1865 and December of that year, when the new Thirty-ninth Congress convened, the president's approach to Reconstruction was to impose minimal demands on the South. He required the former Confederates to make only minor concessions before being allowed to resume their political rights and retain their lands. As for the freedmen, he seemed to think that they needed no further protection beyond the fact of their emancipation. The Republican-dominated Congress disagreed, however. The terms for southern readmission were, in its view, to be determined by the legislative branch—a position that had already brought Congress into a confrontation with Lincoln over the Wade-Davis bill and its veto in 1864. The Republican majority in Congress also rejected the specifics of Johnson's terms as far too conciliatory.

But exactly what alternative did the party have in mind? Some Republicans recognized that the former Confederates needed firmer restrictions and the freedmen greater protection, but they were concerned about causing further disruption in southern society and politics and about involving the Federal government in the internal affairs of states now that the war was over. Other Republicans, however, saw the moment of southern defeat as a vital opportunity to reorganize the region's politics and economy, and move it in a new, more democratic and egalitarian direction.

From early 1866 until March 1867, the congressional Republicans struggled to establish a policy to replace that of the president. Their first proposal, the Fourteenth Amendment, met with resistance from both Johnson, who vetoed it, and the South, which rejected it. The Republicans then proposed a plan to reorganize the southern state governments and enfranchise the freedmen. This measure was called the Reconstruction Act, and its terms were mandatory.

This lengthy and difficult struggle revealed the dimensions of Republican thought on the problem of reunion and Reconstruction. What was the general thrust of the party's thinking and policymaking? Was the party radical and innovative in its approach, or was it, in reality, rather cautious? Historians have debated this question almost as vigorously as the Republicans debated Reconstruction policy.

✎ D O C U M E N T S

The testimony about the Republican party's Reconstruction policy in the documents that follow comes from congressmen involved in the formulation and passage of the legislation or from others who were affiliated with the party. The first selection is the angry manifesto drawn up on August 5, 1864, by the two authors of the Wade-Davis bill, Senator Benjamin F. Wade and Representative Henry Winter Davis, after Lincoln had pocket-vetoed their proposed measure. The second document contains extracts from the "Grasp of War" speech given in Boston on June 21, 1865, by Richard Henry Dana, Jr., a prominent Republican lawyer, in which he outlined an important constitutional theory about Reconstruction—a theory that is later discussed in the two essays of this chapter. In the third selection, Senator Lyman Trumbull's view of the scope of his Civil Rights bill is presented. His remarks are from two speeches in the Senate—the first on January 29, 1866, when the bill was initially introduced, and the second on April 4, 1866, when the Senate was about to override President Johnson's veto of it.

The remaining documents relate to the Reconstruction Act of 1867, which embodied the Republican-dominated Congress's final terms for southern readmission. The fourth selection is from a speech of January 3, 1867, by Representative Thaddeus Stevens on an early version of the bill in which he stated his radical views about Reconstruction. The specifics of a radical approach to Reconstruction are enumerated in the fifth extract, which is from a speech of January 28, 1867, called "Regeneration Before Reconstruction" by George W. Julian, a radical Republican congressman from Indiana. The position of a more conservative Republican is presented in the sixth document—Senator John Sherman of Ohio raises objections to some of the proscriptive terms of the bill in a Senate speech on February 19, 1867. The seventh selection contains text from the Reconstruction Act of March 2, 1867, as well as the Fourteenth Amendment that the South had already rejected in the fall of 1866 but which was now part of the terms required for readmission under the Reconstruction Act. The eighth and last selection is from the 1879 novel *A Fool's Errand*, by Albion W. Tourgee, an Ohioan who had been a leading figure in the Republican party of North Carolina during Reconstruction but who regarded the provisions of the Reconstruction Act as quite inadequate for the task at hand.

The Wade-Davis Manifesto Denounces
Lincoln's Reconstruction Policy, August 1864

. . . [T]he President persists in recognizing those shadows of governments in Arkansas and Louisiana [formed under Lincoln's presidential Proclamation of Amnesty and Reconstruction, December 8, 1863] which Congress formally declared should not be recognized—whose representatives and senators were repelled by formal votes of both Houses of Congress—which it was declared formally should have no electoral vote for President and Vice-President.

They are mere creatures of his will. They are mere oligarchies, imposed on the people by military orders under the form of election, at which generals, provost marshals, soldiers and camp-followers were the chief actors, assisted by a handful of resident citizens, and urged on to premature action by private letters from the President. . . .

Mark the contrast! The bill requires a majority, the [president's Reconstruction] proclamation is satisfied with one-tenth; the bill requires one oath, the proclamation another; the bill ascertains voters by registering, the proclamation by guess; the bill exacts adherence to existing territorial limits, the proclamation admits of others; the bill governs the rebel States *by law,* equalizing all before it, the proclamation commits them to the lawless discretion of Military Governors and Provost Marshals; the bill forbids electors for President, the proclamation and defeat of the bill threaten us with civil war for the admission or exclusion of such votes; the bill exacted exclusion of dangerous enemies from power and the relief of the nation from the rebel debt, and the prohibition of slavery forever, so that the suppression of the rebellion will double our resources to bear or pay the national debt, free the masses from the old domination of the rebel leaders, and eradicate the cause of the war; the proclamation secures neither of these guaranties.

It is silent respecting the rebel debt and the political exclusion of rebel leaders; leaving slavery exactly where it was by law at the outbreak of the rebellion, and adds no guaranty even of the freedom of the slaves he undertook to manumit.

It is summed up in an illegal oath, without sanction, and therefore void.

The oath is to support all proclamations of the President, during the rebellion, having reference to slaves.

Any government is to be accepted at the hands of one-tenth of the people not contravening that oath.

Now that oath neither secures the abolition of slavery, nor adds any security to the freedom of the slaves the President declared free.

It does not secure the abolition of slavery; for the proclamation of freedom merely professed to free certain slaves while it recognized the institution.

Every constitution of the rebel States at the outbreak of the rebellion may be adopted without the change of a letter: for none of them contravene that proclamation; none of them establish slavery.

It adds no security to the freedom of the slaves; for their title is the proclamation of freedom.

If it be unconstitutional, an oath to support it is void. Whether constitutional or not, the oath is without authority of law, and therefore void.

If it be valid and observed, it exacts no enactment by the State, either in law or constitution, to add a State guaranty to the proclamation title; and the right of a slave to freedom is an open question before the State courts on the relative authority of the State law and the proclamation.

If the oath binds the one-tenth who take it, it is not exacted of the other nine-tenths who succeed to the control of the State government, so that it is annulled instantly by the act of recognition.

What the State courts would say of the proclamation, who can doubt?

But the master would not go into court—he would seize his slaves.

What the Supreme Court would say, who can tell?

When and how is the question to get there?

No *habeas corpus* lies for him in a United States Court; and the President defeated with this bill the extension of that writ to his case.

Such are the fruits of this rash and fatal act of the President—a blow at the friends of his Administration, at the rights of humanity, and at the principles of Republican Government.

The President has greatly presumed on the forbearance which the supporters of his Administration have so long practised, in view of the arduous conflict in which we are engaged, and the reckless ferocity of our political opponents.

But he must understand that our support is of a cause and not of a man; that the authority of Congress is paramount and must be respected; that the whole body of the Union men of Congress will not submit to be impeached by him of rash and unconstitutional legislation; and if he wishes our support, he must confine himself to his Executive duties—to obey and execute, not make the laws—to suppress by arms armed rebellion, and leave political reorganization to Congress.

If the supporters of the Government fail to insist on this, they become responsible for the usurpations which they fail to rebuke, and are justly liable to the indignation of the people whose rights and security, committed to their keeping, they sacrifice.

Let them consider the remedy of these usurpations, and, having found it, fearlessly execute it.

B. F. Wade,
Chairman Senate Committee.

H. Winter Davis,
Chairman Committee
House of Representatives
on the Rebellious States.

Republican Richard H. Dana, Jr., Presents
His "Grasp of War" Theory, June 1865

. . . A war is over when its purpose is secured. It is a fatal mistake to hold that this war is over, because the fighting has ceased. [Applause.] This war is not over. We are in the attitude and in the *status* of war to-day. There is the solution of this question. Why, suppose a man has attacked your life, my friend, in the highway, at night, armed, and after a death-struggle, you get him down—what then? When he says he has done fighting, are you obliged to release him? Can you not hold him until you have got some security against his weapons? [Applause.] Can you not hold him until you have searched him, and taken his weapons from him? Are you obliged to let him up to begin a new fight for your life? The same principle governs war between nations. When one nation has conquered another, in a war, the victorious nation does not retreat from the country and give up possession of it, because the fighting has ceased. No; it holds the conquered enemy in the grasp of war until it has secured whatever it has a right to require. [Applause.] I put that proposition fearlessly—*The conquering party may hold the other in the grasp of war until it has secured whatever it has a right to require.*

But what have we a right to require? We have no right to require our conquered foe to adopt all our notions, our opinions, our systems, however much we may be attached to them, however good we may think them; but we have a right to require whatever the public safety and public faith make necessary. [Applause.] That is the proposition. Then, we come to this: *We have a right to hold the rebels in the grasp of war until we have obtained whatever the public safety and the public faith require.* [Applause, and cries of "good."] Is not that a solid foundation to stand upon? Will it not bear examination? and are we not upon it to-day?

. . . Now, we have got to choose between two results. With these four millions of negroes, either you must have four millions of disfranchised, disarmed, untaught, landless, thriftless, non-producing, non-consuming, degraded men, or else you must have four millions of land-holding, industrious, arms-bearing, and voting population. [Loud applause.] Choose between these two! Which will you have? It has got to be decided pretty soon which you will have. The corner-stone of those institutions will not be slavery, in name, but their institutions will be built upon the mud-sills of a debased negro population. Is that public safety? Is it public faith? Are those republican ideas or republican institutions? Some of these negros have shed their blood for us upon the public faith. Ah! there are negro parents whose children have fallen in battle; there are children who lost fathers, and wives who lost hubands, in our cause. Our covenant with the freedman is sealed in blood! It bears the image and superscription of the republic! Their freedom is a tribute which we must pay, not only to Cæsar, but to God! [Applause.]

We have a right to require, my friends, that the freedmen of the South shall have the right to hold land. [Applause.] Have we not? We have a right to require that they shall be allowed to testify in the state courts. [Applause.] Have we not? We have a right to demand that they shall bear arms as soldiers in the militia. [Applause.] Have we not? We have a right to demand that there shall be an impartial ballot. [Great applause.]. . .

One step further. Suppose the states do not do what we require—what then? I have not heard that question answered yet. Suppose President Johnson's experiment in North Carolina and Mississippi fails, and the white men are determined to keep the black men down—what then? Mr. President, I hope we shall never be called upon to answer, practically, that question. It remits us to an ultimate, and, you may say, a fearful proposition. But if we come to it, though I desire to consider myself the humblest of the persons here, I, for one, am prepared with an answer. I believe that if you come to the ultimate right of the thing, the ultimate law of the case, it is this: that this war—no, not the war, *the victory in the war*—places, not the person, not the life, not the private property of the rebels—they are governed by other considerations and rules—I do not speak of them— *but the political systems of the rebel states, at the discretion of the republic.* [Great applause.] Secession does not do this. Treason does not do this. The existence of civil war does not do this. It is the necessary result of conquest, with military occupation, in a war of such dimensions, such a character, and such consequences as this. . . .

When a man accepts a challenge to a duel, what does he put at stake? He puts his life at stake, does he not? And is it not childish, after the fatal shot is fired, to exclaim, "Oh, death and widowhood and orphanage are fearful things!" They were all involved in that accepted challenge. When a nation allows itself to be at war, or when a people make war, they put at stake their national existence. [Applause.] That result seldom follows, because the nation that is getting the worst of the contest makes its peace in time; because the conquering nation does not always desire to incorporate hostile subjects in its dominions; because neutral nations intervene. The conqueror must choose between two courses—to permit the political institutions, the body politic, to go on, and treat with it, or obliterate it. We have destroyed and obliterated their central government. Its existence was treason. As to their states, we mean to adhere to the first course. We mean to say the states shall remain, with new constitutions, new systems. We do not mean to exercise sovereign civil jurisdiction over them in our Congress. Fellow citizens, it is not merely out of tenderness to them; it would be the most dangerous possible course for us. Our system is a planetary system; each planet revolving round its orbit, and all round a common sun. This system is held together by a balance of powers—centripetal and centrifugal forces. We have established a wise balance of forces. Let not that balance be destroyed. If we should undertake to exercise sovereign civil jurisdiction over those states, it would be as great a peril to our system as it would be a hardship upon them. We must not, we will not undertake it, except as the last resort of the thinking and the good—as the ultimate final remedy, when all others have failed.

I know, fellow citizens, it is much more popular to stir up the feelings of a public audience by violent language than it is to repress them; but on this subject we must think wisely. We have never been willing to try the experiment of a consolidated democratic republic. Our system is a system of states, with central power; and in that system is our safety. [Applause.] State rights, I maintain; State sovereignty we have destroyed. [Applause.] Therefore, although I say that, if we are driven to the last resort, we may adopt this final remedy; yet wisdom, humanity, regard for democratic principles, common discretion, require that we should follow the course we are now following. Let the states make their own constitutions, but the constitutions must be satisfactory to the Republic [applause], and—ending as I began—by a power which I think is beyond question, the Republic holds them in the grasp of war until they have made such constitutions. [Loud applause.]

Senator Lyman Trumbull of Illinois Explains His Civil Rights Bill, January and April 1866

I. January 29, 1866

. . . With this bill passed into a law and efficiently executed we shall have secured freedom in fact and equality in civil rights to all persons in the United States. There will be no objection to this bill that it undertakes to confer judicial powers upon some other authority than the courts. It may be assailed as drawing to the Federal Government powers that properly belong to "States"; but I apprehend, rightly considered, it is not obnoxious to that objection. It will have no operation in any State where the laws are equal, where all persons have the same civil rights without regard to color or race. It will have no operation in the State of Kentucky when her slave code and all her laws discriminating between persons on account of race or color shall be abolished. . . .

II. April 4, 1866

. . . This bill in no manner interferes with the municipal regulations of any State which protects all alike in their rights of person and property. It could have no operation in Massachusetts, New York, Illinois, or most of the States of the Union. How preposterous, then, to charge that unless some State can have and exercise the right to punish somebody, or to deny somebody a civil right on account of his color, its rights as a State will be destroyed. It is manifest that unless this bill can be passed, nothing can be done to protect the freedmen in their liberty and their rights.

Whatever may have been the opinion of the President at one time as to "good faith requiring the security of the freedmen in their liberty and their property" it is now manifest from the character of his objections to this bill that he will approve no measure that will accomplish the object. That the second clause of the constitutional amendment [the Thirteenth, abolishing slavery] gives this power there can be no question. Some have contended that it gives the power even to confer the right of suffrage. I have not thought so, because I have never thought suffrage any more necessary to the liberty of a freedman than of a non-voting white, whether child or female. But his liberty under the Constitution he is entitled to, and whatever is necessary to secure it to him he is entitled to have, be it the ballot or the bayonet. If the bill now before us, and which goes no further than to secure civil rights to the freedman, cannot be passed, then the constitutional amendment proclaiming freedom to all the inhabitants of the land is a cheat and a delusion. . . .

Representative Thaddeus Stevens of Pennsylvania Sets out His Terms, January 1867

. . . It is to be regretted that inconsiderate and incautious Republicans should ever have supposed that the slight amendments [embodied in the pending Fourteenth Amendment] already proposed to the Constitution, even when incorporated into that instrument, would satisfy the reforms necessary for the security of the Government. Unless the rebel States, before admission, should be made republican in spirit, and placed under the guardianship of loyal men, all our blood and treasure will have been spent in vain. I waive now the question of punishment which, if we are wise, will still be inflicted by moderate confiscations, both as a reproof and example. Having these States, as we all agree, entirely within the power of Congress, it is our duty to take care that no injustice shall remain in their organic laws. Holding them "like clay in the hands of the potter," we must see that no vessel is made for destruction. Having now no governments, they must have enabling acts. The law of last session with regard to Territories settled the principles of such acts. Impartial suffrage, both in electing the delegates and ratifying their proceedings, is now the fixed rule. There is more reason why colored voters should be admitted in the rebel States than in the Territories. In the States they form the great mass of the loyal men. Possibly with their aid loyal governments may be established in most of those States. Without it all are sure to be ruled by traitors; and loyal men, black and white, will be oppressed, exiled, or murdered. There are several good reasons for the passage of this bill. In the first place, it is just. I am now confining my argument to negro suffrage in the rebel States. Have not loyal blacks quite as good a right to choose rulers and make laws as rebel whites? In the second place, it is a necessity in order to protect the loyal white men in the seceded States. The white Union men are in a great minority in each of those States. With them the blacks would act in a body; and it is believed that in each of said States, except one, the two united would form a majority, control the States, and protect themselves. Now they are the victims of daily murder. They must suffer constant persecution or be exiled. The convention of southern loyalists, lately held in Philadelphia, almost unanimously agreed to such a bill as an absolute necessity.

Another good reason is, it would insure the ascendency of the Union party. Do you avow the party purpose? exclaims some horror-stricken demagogue. I do. For I believe, on my conscience, that on the continued ascendency of that party depends the safety of this great nation. If impartial suffrage is excluded in rebel States then every one of them is sure to send a solid rebel representative delegation to Congress, and cast a solid rebel electoral vote. They, with their kindred Copperheads of the North, would always elect the President and control Congress. While slavery sat upon her defiant throne, and insulted and intimidated the trembling North, the South frequently divided on questions of policy between Whigs and Democrats, and gave victory alternately to the sections. Now, you must divide them between loyalists, without regard to color, and disloyalists, or you will be the perpetual vassals of the free-trade, irritated, revengeful South. For these, among other reasons, I am for negro suffrage in every rebel State. If it be just, it should not be denied; if it be necessary, it should be adopted; if it be a punishment to traitors, they deserve it.

But it will be said, as it has been said, "This is negro equality!" What is negro equality, about which so much is said by knaves, and some of which is believed by men who are not fools? It means, as understood by honest Republicans, just this much, and no more: every man, no matter what his race or color; every earthly being who has an immortal soul, has an equal right to justice, honesty, and fair play with every other man; and the law should secure him those rights. The same law which condemns or acquits an African should condemn or acquit a white man. The same law which gives a verdict in a white man's favor should give a verdict in a black man's favor on the same state of facts. Such is the law of God and such ought to be the law of man. This doctrine does not mean that a negro shall sit on the same seat or eat at the same table with a white man. That is a matter of taste which every man must decide for himself. The law has nothing to do with it. . . .

Representative George W. Julian of Indiana Outlines the Scope of Reconstruction, January 1867

. . . Mr. Speaker, I further object to the measure [the proposed Reconstruction bill] before us that it is a mere enabling act, looking to the early restoration of the rebellious districts to their former places in the Union, instead of a well-considered frame of government contemplating such restoration at some indefinite future time, and designed to fit them to receive it. They are not ready for reconstruction as independent States, on any terms or conditions which Congress might impose; and I believe the time has come for us to say so. We owe this much to their misguided people, whose false and feverish hopes have been kept alive by the course of the Executive and the hesitating policy of Congress. I think I am safe in saying that if these districts were to-day admitted as States, with the precise political and social elements which we know to exist in them, even with their rebel population disfranchised and the ballot placed in the hands of radical Union men only, irrespective of color, the experiment would be ruinous to the best interests of their loyal people and calamitous to the nation. The withdrawal of federal intervention and the unchecked operation of local supremacy would as fatally hedge up the way of justice and equality as the rebel ascendency which now prevails. Why? Simply because no theory of government, no forms of administration, can be trusted, unless adequately supported by public opinion. The power of the great landed aristocracy in these regions, if unrestrained by power from without, would inevitably assert itself. Its political chemistry, obeying its own laws, would very soon crystallize itself into the same forms of treason and lawlessness which to-day hold their undisturbed empire over the existing loyal element. What these regions need, above all things, is not an easy and quick return to their forfeited rights in the Union, but *government,* the strong arm of power, outstretched from the central authority here in Washington, making it safe for the freedmen of the South, safe for her loyal white men, safe for emigrants from the Old World and from the Northern States to go and dwell there; safe for Northern capital and labor, Northern energy and enterprise, and Northern ideas to set up their habitation in peace, and thus found a Christian civilization and a living democracy amid the ruins of the past. That, sir, is what the country demands and the rebel power needs. To talk about suddenly building up independent States where the material for such structures is fatally wanting, is nonsense. States must *grow,* and to that end their growth must be fostered and protected. The political and social regeneration of the country made desolate by treason is the prime necessity of the hour, and is preliminary to any reconstruction of States. Years of careful pupilage under the authority of the nation may be found necessary, and Congress alone must decide when and upon what conditions the tie rudely broken by treason shall be restored. Congress, moreover, is as solemnly bound to deny to disloyal communities admission into our great sisterhood of States as it is to deny the rights of citizenship to those who have forfeited such rights by treason. . . .

Senator John Sherman of Ohio Urges Caution and Moderation, February 1867

. . . We sweep from our legislation all tests for voting except such as each State may prescribe. We build reconstruction upon the broadest humanity and invite all men to take part in the work. So far as voting is concerned we proclaim universal amnesty in exchange for universal suffrage, and yet the Senator [Sumner] is not satisfied. What more did he ask a year ago? Nothing. If we exclude from voting the rebels of the South, who compose nearly all the former voting population, what becomes of the republican doctrine that all governments must be founded on the consent of the governed? I invoke constitutional liberty against such a proposition. Beware, sir, lest in guarding against rebels you destroy the foundation of republican institutions. I like rebels no better than the Senator from Massachusetts; but, sir, I will not supersede one form of oligarchy in which the blacks were slaves by another in which the whites are disfranchised outcasts. Let us introduce no such horrid deformity into the American Union. Our path has been toward enfranchisement and liberty. Let us not turn backward in our course, but after providing all necessary safeguards for white and black, let us reconstruct society in the rebel States upon the broad basis of universal suffrage.

This bill does not proclaim universal amnesty except as to voting. On the contrary, it requires these States to adopt a constitutional amendment [the Fourteenth] by which the leading men disable themselves from holding office. Six thousand or perhaps ten thousand of the leading men of the South are embraced in the restriction of the constitutional amendment, and are forever excluded from holding office until two thirds of both Houses of Congress relieve them from that restriction. Is not that enough? Is it not enough that they are humiliated, conquered, their pride broken, their property lost, hundreds and thousands of their best and bravest buried under their soil, their institutions gone, they themselves deprived of the right to hold office, and placed in political power on the same footing with their former slaves? Is not that enough? I say it is, and a generous people will not demand more.

But, sir, when the attempt is made to defeat a measure of this kind, which yields all that the Senator has ever openly demanded in the Senate, all that has ever been demanded by any popular community in this great country, all that has been demanded by any Legislature, more than we claimed at the last election, I have the right to characterize this opposition as unusual and unnatural. Sir, let us issue this call to the people of the southern States. We have given here our deliberate judgment on a legal proposition: we say that the State governments organized by the President of the United States were without authority of law, because they were without the sanction of Congress. We therefore sweep them away, not for all purposes, but for all State purposes. We deny their validity as State governments. They only have the same force and effect as the local Mexican law had in California after we conquered California, the same effect that the local law of Maryland would have if the British should overrun the whole of Maryland; no more, no less. The State communities are swept out of existence, and the people are required to proceed in their own way to form State governments. What objection can there be to this? . . .

Congress's Terms for Readmission and Reconstruction, June 1866 and March 1867

I. 14th Constitutional Amendment

Joint Resolution proposing an Amendment to the Constitution of the United States.

Be it resolved by the Senate and House of Representatives of the United States of America, in Congress assembled, (two-thirds of both Houses concurring,) That the following article be proposed to the Legislatures of the several States as an amendment to the Constitution of the United States, which, when ratified by three-fourths of said Legislatures, shall be valid as part of the Constitution, namely:

Article XIV.

Section 1.   All persons born or naturalized in the United States, and subject to the jurisdiction thereof, are citizens of the United States and of the State wherein they reside. No State shall make or enforce any law which shall abridge the privileges or immunities of citizens of the United States; nor shall any State deprive any person of life, liberty, or property, without due process of law, nor deny to any person within its jurisdiction the equal protection of the laws.

Sec. 2.   Representatives shall be apportioned among the several States according to their respective numbers, counting the whole number of persons in each State, excluding Indians not taxed. But when the right to vote at any election for the choice of electors for President and Vice President of the United States, representatives in Congress, the executive and judicial officers of a State, or the members of the Legislature thereof, is denied to any of the male inhabitants of such State, being twenty-one years of age, and citizens of the United States, or in any way abridged, except for participation in rebellion or other crime, the basis of representation therein shall be reduced in the proportion which the number of such male citizens shall bear to the whole number of male citizens twenty-one years of age in such State.

Sec. 3.   No person shall be a Senator or Representative in Congress, or elector of President and Vice President, or hold any office, civil or military, under the United States, or under any State, who, having previously taken an oath as a member of Congress, or as an officer of the United States, or as a member of any State Legislature, or as an executive or judicial officer of any State, to support the Constitution of the United States, shall have engaged in insurrection or rebellion against the same, or given aid or comfort to the enemies thereof. But Congress may, by a vote of two thirds of each House, remove such disability.

Sec. 4.   The validity of the public debt of the United States, authorized by law, including debts incurred for payment of pensions and bounties for services in suppressing insurrection or rebellion, shall not be questioned. But neither the United States nor any State shall assume or pay any debt or obligation incurred in aid of insurrection or rebellion against the United States, or any claim for the loss or emancipation of any slave; but all such debts, obligations, and claims shall be held illegal and void.

Sec. 5. That Congress shall have power to enforce, by appropriate legislation, the provisions of this article.

Passed June 13, 1866.

II. Reconstruction Act of Thirty-Ninth Congress

An act to provide for the more efficient government of the rebel States.

Whereas no legal State governments or adequate protection for life or property now exists in the rebel States of Virginia, North Carolina, South Carolina, Georgia, Mississippi, Alabama, Louisiana,· Florida, Texas, and Arkansas; and whereas it is necessary that peace and good order should be enforced in said States until loyal and republican State governments can be legally established: Therefore

Be it enacted, &c., That said rebel States shall be divided into military districts and made subject to the military authority of the United States, as hereinafter prescribed, and for that purpose Virginia shall constitute the first district; North Carolina and South Carolina the second district; Georgia, Alabama, and Florida the third district; Mississippi and Arkansas the fourth district; and Louisiana and Texas the fifth district.

Sec. 2. That it shall be the duty of the President to assign to the command of each of said districts an officer of the army, not below the rank of brigadier general, and to detail a sufficient military force to enable such officer to perform his duties and enforce his authority within the district to which he is assigned.

Sec. 3. That it shall be the duty of each officer assigned as aforesaid to protect all persons in their rights of person and property, to suppress insurrection, disorder, and violence, and to punish, or cause to be punished, all disturbers of the public peace and criminals, and to this end he may allow local civil tribunals to take jurisdiction of and to try offenders, or, when in his judgment it may be necessary for the trial of offenders, he shall have power to organize military commissions or tribunals for that purpose; and all interference under color of State authority with the exercise of military authority under this act shall be null and void.

Sec. 4. That all persons put under military arrest by virtue of this act shall be tried without unnecessary delay, and no cruel or unusual punishment shall be inflicted; and no sentence of any military commission or tribunal hereby authorized, affecting the life or liberty of any person, shall be executed until it is approved by the officer in command of the district, and the laws and regulations for the government of the army shall not be affected by this act, except in so far as they conflict with its provisions: *Provided,* That no sentence of death under the provisions of this act shall be carried into effect without the approval of the President.

Sec. 5. That when the people of any one of said rebel States shall have formed a constitution of government in conformity with the Constitution of the United States in all respects, framed by a convention of delegates elected by the male citizens of said State twenty-one years old and upward, of whatever race, color, or previous condition, who have been resident in said State for one year previous to the day of such election, except such as may be disfranchised for participation in the rebellion, or for felony at common law, and when such constitution shall provide that the elective franchise shall be enjoyed by all such persons as have the qualifications herein stated for electors of delegates, and when such constitution shall be ratified by a majority of the persons voting on the question of ratification who are qualified as electors for delegates, and when such constitution shall have been submitted to Congress for examination and approval, and Congress shall have approved the same, and when said State, by a vote of its legislature elected under said constitution, shall have adopted the amendment to the Constitution of the United States, proposed by the Thirty-ninth Congress, and known as article fourteen, and when said article shall have become a part of the Constitution of the United States, said State shall be declared entitled to representation in Congress, and Senators and Representatives shall be admitted therefrom on their taking the oaths prescribed by law, and then and thereafter the preceding sections of this act shall be inoperative in said State: *Provided,* That no person excluded from the privilege of holding office by said proposed amendment to the Constitution of the United States shall be eligible to election as a member of the convention to frame a constitution for any of said rebel States, nor shall any such person vote for members of such convention.

Sec. 6. That until the people of said rebel States shall be by law admitted to representation in the Congress of the United States, any civil governments which may exist therein shall be deemed provisional only, and in all respects subject to the paramount authority of the United States at any time to abolish, modify, control, or supersede the same; and in all elections to any office under such provisional governments all persons shall be entitled to vote, and none others, who are entitled to vote under the provisions of the fifth section of this act; and no person shall be eligible to any office under any such provisional governments who would be disqualified from holding office under the provisions of the third article of said constitutional amendment.

Passed March 2, 1867.

A Southern Republican Later Condemns
Congress's Reconstruction Policy, 1879

So it must have been well understood by the wise men who devised this short-sighted plan of electing a President beyond a peradventure of defeat, that they were giving the power of the re-organized, subordinate republics, into the hands of a race unskilled in public affairs, poor to a degree hardly to be matched in the civilized world, and so ignorant that not five out of a hundred of its voters could read their own ballots, joined with such Adullamites among the native whites as might be willing to face a proscription which would shut the house of God in the face of their families, together with the few men of Northern birth, resident in that section since the close of the war,—either knaves or fools, or partaking of the nature of both,—who might elect to become permanent citizens, and join in the movement.

Against them was to be pitted the wealth, the intelligence, the organizing skill, the pride, and the hate of a people whom it had taken four years to conquer in open fight when their enemies outnumbered them three to one, who were animated chiefly by the apprehension of what seemed now about to be forced upon them by this miscalled measure of "Reconstruction"; to wit, the equality of the negro race.

It was done, too, in the face of the fact that within the preceding twelvemonth the white people of the South, by their representatives in the various Legislatures of the Johnsonian period, had absolutely refused to recognize this equality, even in the slightest matters, by *refusing to allow the colored people to testify in courts of justice* against white men, or to protect their rights of person and property in any manner from the avarice, lust, or brutality of their white neighbors. It was done in the very face of the "Black Codes," which were the first enactments of Provisional Legislatures, and which would have established a serfdom more complete than that of the Russian steppes before the *ukase* of Alexander.

And the men who devised this plan called themselves honest and wise statesmen. More than one of them has since then hugged himself in gratulation under the belief, that, by his co-operation therein, he had cheaply achieved an immortality of praise from the liberty-lovers of the earth! After having forced a proud people to yield what they had for more than two centuries considered a right,—the right to hold the African race in bondage,—they proceeded to outrage a feeling as deep and fervent as the zeal of Islam or the exclusiveness of Hindoo caste, by giving to the ignorant, unskilled, and dependent race—a race who could not have lived a week without the support or charity of the dominant one—equality of political right! Not content with this, they went farther, and, by erecting the rebellious territory into self-regulating and sovereign States, they abandoned these parties like cocks in a pit, to fight out the question of predominance without the possibility of national interference. They said to the colored man, in the language of one of the pseudo-philosophers of that day, "Root, hog, or die!"

It was cheap patriotism, cheap philanthropy, cheap success!

The African-American Experience
in the Reconstruction South

The promise of emancipation to the slaves and the enlistment of 180,000 blacks in the United States armed forces had helped the Union win the war and, in the process, guaranteed the demise of slavery. The contribution of southern blacks was also crucial to the success of Reconstruction, since the Republican governments in the South relied on the support of the newly enfranchised black voters to gain power as well as keep it. For the African-Americans themselves, the triumph of Reconstruction was, needless to say, an outcome they devoutly wished for, just like victory in the war. And this convergence of aims simply confirmed how dependent upon each other the Federal government and southern blacks were in their parallel struggles against the slaveholders and their allies.

African-Americans' needs and demands lay at the center of the contest over Reconstruction. From the beginning, blacks insisted on equal rights before the law, military protection, economic security, and even the vote. They made their demands known through petitions to the Federal government and the state conventions and legislatures. Once some of these goals were obtained, they then kept up the pressure for their enforcement. Meanwhile, African-Americans voted Republican and began to hold office in increasingly large numbers at all levels of government. And this occurred despite the unrelenting vilification and violence that was employed to deter black voters and officials.

The status of African-Americans as laborers was also a major question during Reconstruction. Landownership was the overriding objective of the liberated slaves because it would give them autonomy from white control as well as a stake in the economy. When they were denied land, however, the freedmen refused to work as laborers in gangs under supervision, as in slavery, and demanded instead to rent land and work it independently as tenants. A number of blacks did manage to pool their resources and buy land, and some even formed self-governing and self-sufficient communities. Meanwhile, they established their own churches and self-help and benevolent societies. Also, black children went to school for the first time when volunteer teachers and the Freedmen's Bureau set up schools after the war, and later when systems of public education were introduced by the Reconstruction governments. Finally, black women ceased working in the fields and began to assume new roles at work and in the family.

With the end of Reconstruction in the mid-1870s, however, these changes and gains were in jeopardy. Some even claimed that they had been ephemeral and pretty insignificant all along. Later on, historians wondered how much blacks had gained during Reconstruction—was it a period of achievement or an opportunity denied? They have also questioned whether Reconstruction collapsed because Federal policy was tied so closely to black interests and advancement or whether it would have failed in any case.

These documents illuminate the diversity of the African-American role and contribution in the Reconstruction of the South. In the first selection, John W. DeForest, a Freedmen's Bureau agent who later became a well-known novelist, reveals how prejudiced even educated and sympathetic northern officials could be. The comments are from his reminiscences, which first appeared in *Harper's, Atlantic Monthly,* and *Putnam's Magazine* in 1868 and 1869 and were later published as *A Union Officer in the Reconstruction* (1949). The second document, a petition to Congress of the Colored People's Convention of South Carolina on November 24, 1865, shows that from the outset African-Americans were calling public meetings to present demands. In the third selection, Richard H. Cain, an African-American who would later be elected to Congress, tries to convince the Constitutional Convention of South Carolina to endorse his petition to Congress for a loan of $1 million to purchase land for the freedmen. His forceful speech of February 17, 1868, was, however, unsuccessful. In the same convention, Francis L. Cardozo, a black soon to become state treasurer, wrestled with the question of mixed schools on March 4, 1868; the fourth document presents his conclusions.

The fifth selection features a speech by Representative Robert B. Elliott of South Carolina on January 6, 1874, in which he demands that the House pass the Civil Rights bill that was finally enacted the following year. In the sixth extract a freed slave, Mattie Curtis, recalls how she fared in the post-emancipation years. Finally, the seventh document contains a report by an African-American observer named Henry Adams on black women's response to working in the fields after they were freed.

A Freedmen's Bureau Agent Predicts a Grim Future for the Freed Slaves, 1868–1869

. . . What is to become of the African in our country as a race? Will he commingle with the Caucasian, and so disappear? It is true that there are a few marriages, and a few cases of illegal cohabitation, between Negro men and the lowest class of white women. For example, a full-blooded black walked twenty miles to ask me if he could have a white wife, assuring me that there was a girl down in his "settlement" who was "a-teasin' every day about it."

He had opened his business with hesitation, and he talked of it in a tremulous undertone, glancing around for fear of listeners. I might have told him that, as it was not leap year, the woman had no right to propose to him; but I treated the matter seriously. Bearing in mind that she must be a disreputable creature, who would make him a wretched helpmeet, I first informed him that the marriage would be legal and that the civil and military authorities would be bound to protect him in it, and then advised him against it, on the ground that it would expose him to a series of underhanded persecutions which could not easily be prevented. He went away evidently but half convinced, and I presume that his Delilah had her will with him, although I heard no more of this odd love affair.

Miscegenation between white men and Negresses diminished under the new order of things. Emancipation broke up the close family contact in which slavery held the two races, and, moreover, young gentlemen did not want mulatto children sworn to them at a cost of three hundred dollars apiece. In short, the new relations of the two stocks tended to separation rather than to fusion. There will be no amalgamation, no merging and disappearance of the black in the white, except at a period so distant that it is not worth while now to speculate upon it. So far as we and our children and grandchildren are concerned, the Negro will remain a Negro and must be prophesied about as a Negro.

But will he remain a Negro, and not rather become a ghost? It is almost ludicrous to find the "woman question" intruding itself into the future of a being whom we have been accustomed to hear of as a "nigger," and whom a ponderous wise man of the East [the British writer Thomas Carlyle] always persisted in abusing as "Quashee." There was a growing disinclination to marriage among the young freedmen, because the girls were learning to shirk out-of-door work, to demand nice dresses and furniture, and, in short, to be fine ladies. The youths had, of course, no objection to the adornment itself; indeed, they were, like white beaux, disposed to follow the game which wears the finest feathers; but they were getting clever enough to know that such game is expensive and to content themselves with looking at it. Where the prettiest colored girls in Greenville were to find husbands was more than I could imagine.

There are other reasons why the blacks may not increase as rapidly as before the emancipation. The young men have more amusements and a more varied life than formerly. Instead of being shut up on the plantation, they can spend the nights in frolicking about the streets or at drinking-places; instead of the monotony of a single neighborhood, they can wander from village to village and from South Carolina to Texas. The master is no longer there to urge matrimony and perhaps other methods of increasing population. Negroes, as well as whites, can now be forced by law to support their illegitimate offspring and are consequently more cautious than formerly how they have such offspring.

In short, the higher civilization of the Caucasian is gripping the race in many ways and bringing it to sharp trial before its time. This new, varied, costly life of freedom, this struggle to be at once like a race which has passed through a two-thousand-years' growth in civilization, will probably diminish the productiveness of the Negro and will terribly test his vitality.

It is doubtless well for his chances of existence that his color keeps him a plebeian, so that, like the European peasant held down by caste, he is less tempted to destroy himself in the struggle to become a patrician.

What judgment shall we pass upon abrupt emancipation, considered merely with reference to the Negro? It was a mighty experiment, fraught with as much menace as hope.

To the white race alone it was a certain and precious boon.

South Carolina Blacks Assert Their Demands, November 1865

Memorial to the Senate and House of Representatives
of the United States in Congress Assembled

Gentlemen:

We, the colored people of the State of South Carolina, in Convention assembled, respectfully present for your attention some prominent facts in relation to our present condition, and make a modest yet earnest appeal to your considerate judgment.

We, your memorialists, with profound gratitude to almighty God, recognize the great boon of freedom conferred upon us by the instrumentality of our late President, Abraham Lincoln, and the armies of the United States.

"The fixed decree, which not all Heaven can move,
Thou, Fate, fulfill it; and, ye Powers, approve."

We also recognize with liveliest gratitude the vast services of the Freedmen's Bureau together with the efforts of the good and wise throughout the land to raise up an oppressed and deeply injured people in the scale of civilized being, during the throbbings of a mighty revolution which must affect the future destiny of the world.

Conscious of the difficulties that surround our position, we would ask for no rights or privileges but such as rest upon the strong basis of justice and expediency, in view of the best interests of our entire country.

We ask first, that the strong arm of law and order be placed alike over the entire people of this State; that life and property be secured, and the laborer free to sell his labor as the merchant his goods.

We ask that a fair and impartial instruction be given to the pledges of the government to us concerning the land question.

We ask that the three great agents of civilized society—the school, the pulpit, the press—be as secure in South Carolina as in Massachusetts or Vermont.

We ask that equal suffrage be conferred upon us, in common with the white men of this State.

This we ask, because "all free governments derive their just powers from the consent of the governed"; and we are largely in the majority in this State, bearing for a long period the burden of onerous taxation, without a just representation. We ask for equal suffrage as a protection for the hostility evoked by our known faithfulness to our country and flag under all circumstances.

We ask that colored men shall not in every instance be tried by white men; and that neither by custom nor enactment shall we be excluded from the jury box.

We ask that, inasmuch as the Constitution of the United States explicitly declares that the right to keep and bear arms shall not be infringed and the Constitution is the Supreme law of the land—that the late efforts of the Legislature of this State to pass an act to deprive us of arms be forbidden, as a plain violation of the Constitution, and unjust to many of us in the highest degree, who have been soldiers, and purchased our muskets from the United States Government when mustered out of service.

We protest against any code of black laws the Legislature of this State may enact, and pray to be governed by the same laws that control other men. The right to assemble in peaceful convention, to discuss the political questions of the day; the right to enter upon all the avenues of agriculture, commerce, trade; to amass wealth by thrift and industry; the right to develop our whole being by all the appliances that belong to civilized society, cannot be questioned by any class of intelligent legislators.

We solemnly affirm and desire to live orderly and peacefully with all the people of this State; and commending this memorial to your considerate judgment.

Thus we ever pray.

Charleston, S. C., November 24, 1865
Zion Presbyterian Church.

Richard H. Cain of South Carolina Stresses the Importance of Land, February 1868

... *Mr. R. H. Cain.* I may be mistaken, but I watched very closely the arguments made by the gentleman last Saturday, and I distinctly understood him to say he was in favor of taxing the lands so as to compel the sale of them, and throw them into the market. The poor would then have a chance to buy. I am unqualifiedly opposed to any measure of taxation for the simple purpose of compelling the owners to sell their lands. I believe the best measure to be adopted is to bring capital to the State, and instead of causing revenge and unpleasantness, I am for even-handed justice. I am for allowing the parties who own lands to bring them into the market and sell them upon such terms as will be satisfactory to both sides. I believe a measure of this kind has a double effect: first, it brings capital, what the people want; second, it puts the people to work; it gives homesteads, what we need; it relieves the Government and takes away its responsibility of feeding the people; it inspires every man with a noble manfulness, and by the thought that he is the possessor of something in the State; it adds also to the revenue of the country. By these means men become interested in the country as they never were before. It was said that five and one-seventh acres were not enough to live on. If South Carolina, in its sovereign power, can devise any plan for the purchase of the large plantations in this State now lying idle, divide and sell them out at a reasonable price, it will give so many people work. I will guarantee to find persons to work every five acres. I will also guarantee that after one year's time, the Freedman's Bureau will not have to give any man having one acre of land anything to eat. This country has a genial clime, rich soil, and can be worked to advantage. The man who can not earn a living on five acres, will not do so on twenty-five. I regret that another position taken by gentlemen in the opposition, is that they do not believe that we will get what we ask for. I believe that the party now in power in the Congress of the United States, will do whatever they can for the welfare of the people of this State and of the South. I believe that the noble men who have maintained the rights of the freedmen before and since their liberation, will continue to do everything possible to forward these great interests. I am exceedingly anxious, if possible, to allay all unpleasant feeling—I would not have any unpleasant feeling among ourselves.

I would not have any unpleasant feelings between the races. If we give each family in the State an opportunity of purchasing a home, I think they will all be better satisfied.

But it is also said that it will disturb all the agricultural operations in the State. I do not believe if the Congress of the United States shall advance one million of dollars to make purchase of lands, the laborers will abandon their engagement and run off. I have more confidence in the people I represent. I believe all who have made contracts will fulfill those contracts, and when their contracts have expired, they will go on their own lands, as all freemen ought to go. I claim it would do no harm. It would be a wonderful concatenation of circumstances indeed, to find that because the Government had appropriated one million of dollars for the purchase of lands, to see all of four hundred thousand people, rushing pell mell down to Charleston to get a homestead. I know the ignorance of the people with whom I am identified is great. I know that four hundred years of bondage has degraded them, but I have more confidence in humanity than to believe the people will leave their homes and their families to come to Charleston just to get five acres of land.

If I understood the speaker in the opposition this morning, he offered it because he said it was simply a scheme for colored men. I wish to state this question right. If there was one thing on which I thought I had been specific, it was on that point. The clock had struck two and I had dashed down my pen when the thought struck me it might be misunderstood. I retraced my steps and so shaped the petition as simply to state the poor of any class. I bore in mind the poor whites of the upper districts. I saw, not long ago, a poor white woman walk eighteen miles barefooted to receive a bag of corn and four pounds of meat, resting all night on the roadside, eating one-half and then go away, living on roots afterwards and half starved. I desire that class of people to have homes as well as the black man. I have lost long since that hateful idea that the complexion of a man makes any difference as far as rights are concerned. The true principle of progress and civilization is to recognize the great brotherhood of man, and a man's wants, whatever he may be, or whatever clime he comes from, are as sacred to me as any other class of men. I believe this measure will advance the interests of all classes.

Francis L. Cardozo of South Carolina Discusses
Mixed Schooling, March 1868

. . . Before I proceed to discuss the question, I want to divest it of all false issues, of the imaginary consequences that some gentlemen have illogically thought will result from the adoption of this section with the word compulsory. They affirm that it compels the attendance of both white and colored children in the same schools. There is nothing of the kind in the section. It means nothing of the kind, and no such construction can be legitimately placed upon it. It simply says all the children shall be educated; but how is left with the parents to decide. It is left to the parent to say whether the child shall be sent to a public or private school. The eleventh section has been referred to as bearing upon this section. I will ask attention to this fact. The eleventh section does not say, nor does the report in any part say there shall not be separate schools. There can be separate schools for white and colored. It is simply left so that if any colored child wishes to go to a white school, it shall have the privilege to do so. I have no doubt, in most localities, colored people would prefer separate schools, particularly until some of the present prejudice against their race is removed.

We have not provided that there shall be separate schools; but I do not consider these issues as properly belonging to the question. I shall, therefore, confine myself to the more important matter connected with this subject.

My friend yesterday referred to Prussia and Massachusetts as examples that we should imitate, and I was much surprised to hear some of the members who have spoken, ridicule that argument. It was equivalent to saying we do not want the teachings of history, or the examples of any of those countries foremost in civilization.

It was said that the condition of affairs in Prussia and Massachusetts was entirely different. But they are highly civilized countries, with liberty-loving, industrious citizens, and the highest social order exists there. I want South Carolina to imitate those countries, which require the compulsory attendance of all children of certain ages for fixed periods, at some school. If you deem a certain end worthy of being attained, it must be accompanied by precisely the same means those countries have attained it. . . .

Another argument was that this matter had better be left to the Legislature. I have been charged with appealing to the prejudices and feelings of the colored delegates to this Convention. It is true to a certain extent. I do direct their attention to matters concerning their peculiar interests, but if it is meant to charge me with appealing to their passions as against the white people, I respectfully deny the charge, and stamp the assertion as gratuitous. But I do desire we shall use the opportunities we now have to our best advantage, as we may not ever have a more propitious time. We know when the old aristocracy and ruling power of this State get into power, as they undoubtedly will, because intelligence and wealth will win in the long run, they will never pass such a law as this. Why? Because their power is built on and sustained by ignorance. They will take precious good care that the colored people shall never be enlightened. . . .

Representative Robert B. Elliott of South Carolina Demands Federal Civil Rights, January 1874

. . . Sir, it is scarcely twelve years since that gentleman [Alexander H. Stephens of Georgia] shocked the civilized world by announcing the birth of a government which rested on human slavery as its corner-stone. The progress of events has swept away that *pseudo*-government which rested on greed, pride, and tyranny; and the race whom he then ruthlessly spurned and trampled on are here to meet him in debate, and to demand that the rights which are enjoyed by their former oppressors—who vainly sought to overthrow a Government which they could not prostitute to the base uses of slavery—shall be accorded to those who even in the darkness of slavery kept their allegiance true to freedom and the Union. Sir, the gentleman from Georgia has learned much since 1861; but he is still a laggard. Let him put away entirely the false and fatal theories which have so greatly marred an otherwise enviable record. Let him accept, in its fullness and beneficence, the great doctrine that American citizenship carries with it every civil and political right which manhood can confer. Let him lend his influence, with all his masterly ability, to complete the proud structure of legislation which makes this nation worthy of the great declaration which heralded its birth, and he will have done that which will most nearly redeem his reputation in the eyes of the world, and best vindicate the wisdom of that policy which has permitted him to regain his seat upon this floor.

To the diatribe of the gentleman from Virginia, [Mr. Harris,] who spoke on yesterday, and who so far transcended the limits of decency and propriety as to announce upon this floor that his remarks were addressed to white men alone, I shall have no word of reply. Let him feel that a negro was not only too magnanimous to smite him in his weakness, but was even charitable enough to grant him the mercy of his silence. [Laughter and applause on the floor and in the galleries.] I shall, sir, leave to others less charitable the unenviable and fatiguing task of sifting out of that mass of chaff the few grains of sense that may, perchance, deserve notice. Assuring the gentleman that the negro in this country aims at a higher degree of intellect than that exhibited by him in this debate, I cheerfully commend him to the commiseration of all intelligent men the world over—black men as well as white men.

Sir, equality before the law is now the broad, universal, glorious rule and mandate of the Republic. No State can violate that. Kentucky and Georgia may crowd their statute-books with retrograde and barbarous legislation; they may rejoice in the odious eminence of their consistent hostility to all the great steps of human progress which have marked our national history since slavery tore down the stars and stripes on Fort Sumter; but, if Congress shall do its duty, if Congress shall enforce the great guarantees which the Supreme Court has declared to be the one pervading purpose of all the recent amendments, then their unwise and unenlightened conduct will fall with the same weight upon the gentlemen from those States who now lend their influence to defeat this bill, as upon the poorest slave who once had no rights which the honorable gentlemen were bound to respect.

But, sir, not only does the decision in the Slaughter-house cases [a Supreme Court decision of 1873 limiting federal jurisdiction over the citizens of individual states] contain nothing which suggests a doubt of the power of Congress to pass the pending bill, but it contains an express recognition and affirmance of such power. I quote now from page 81 of the volume:

> "Nor shall any State deny to any person within its jurisdiction the equal protection of the laws."
>
> In the light of the history of these amendments, and the pervading purpose of them, which we have already discussed, it is not difficult to give a meaning to this clause. The existence of laws in the States where the newly emancipated negroes resided, which discriminated with gross injustice and hardship against them as a class, was the evil to be remedied by this clause, and by it such laws are forbidden.
>
> If, however, the States did not conform their laws to its requirements, then, by the fifth section of the [fourteenth] article of amendment, Congress was authorized to enforce it by suitable legislation. We doubt very much whether any action of a State not directed by way of discrimination against the negroes as a class, or on account of their race, will ever be held to come within the purview of this provision. It is so clearly a provision for that race and that emergency, that a strong case would be necessary for its application to any other. But as it is a State that is to be dealt with, and not alone the validity of its laws, we may safely leave that matter until Congress shall have exercised its power, or some case of State oppression, by denial of equal justice in its courts shall, have claimed a decision at our hands.

No language could convey a more complete assertion of the power of Congress over the subject embraced in the present bill than is here expressed. If the States do not conform to the requirements of this clause, if they continue to deny to any person within their jurisdiction the equal protection of the laws, or as the Supreme Court had said, "deny equal justice in its courts," then Congress is here said to have power to enforce the constitutional guarantee by appropriate legislation. That is the power which this bill now seeks to put in exercise. It proposes to enforce the constitutional guarantee against inequality and discrimination by appropriate legislation. It does not seek to confer new rights, nor to place rights conferred by State citizenship under the protection of the United States, but simply to prevent and forbid inequality and discrimination on account of race, color, or previous condition of servitude. Never was there a bill more completely within the constitutional power of Congress. Never was there a bill which appealed for support more strongly to that sense of justice and fair-play which has been said, and in the main with justice, to be a characteristic of the Anglo-Saxon race. The Constitution warrants it; the Supreme Court sanctions it; justice demands it.

Sir, I have replied to the extent of my ability to the arguments which have been presented by the opponents of this measure. I have replied also to some of the legal propositions advanced by gentlemen on the other side; and now that I am about to conclude, I am deeply sensible of the imperfect manner in which I have performed the task. Technically, this bill is to decide upon the civil status of the colored American citizen; a point disputed at the very formation of our present Government, when by a short-sighted policy, a policy repugnant to true republican government, one negro counted as three-fifths of a man. The logical result of this mistake of the framers of the Constitution strengthened the cancer of slavery, which finally spread its poisonous tentacles over the southern portion of the body-politic. To arrest its growth and save the nation we have passed through the harrowing operation of intestine war, dreaded at all times, resorted to at the last extremity, like the surgeon's knife, but absolutely necessary to extirpate the disease which threatened with the life of the nation the overthrow of civil and political liberty on this continent. In that dire extremity the members of the race which I have the honor in part to represent—the race which pleads for justice at your hands to-day, forgetful of their inhuman and brutalizing servitude at the South, their degradation and ostracism at the North—flew willingly and gallantly to the support of the national Government. Their sufferings, assistance, privations, and trials in the swamps and in the rice-fields, their valor on the land and on the sea, is a part of the ever-glorious record which makes up the history of a nation preserved, and might, should I urge the claim, incline you to respect and guarantee their rights and privileges as citizens of our common Republic. But I remember that valor, devotion, and loyalty are not always rewarded according to their just deserts, and that after the battle some who have borne the brunt of the fray may, through neglect or contempt, be assigned to a subordinate place, while the enemies in war may be preferred to the sufferers.

The results of the war, as seen in reconstruction, have settled forever the political status of my race. The passage of this bill will determine the civil status, not only of the negro, but of any other class of citizens who may feel themselves discriminated against. It will form the cap-stone of that temple of liberty, begun on this continent under discouraging circumstances, carried on in spite of the sneers of monarchists and the cavils of pretended friends of freedom, until at last it stands in all its beautiful symmetry and proportions, a building the grandest which the world has ever seen, realizing the most sanguine expectations and the highest hopes of those who, in the name of equal, impartial, and universal liberty, laid the foundation stones. . . .

A Freed Slave Remembers Her Struggle
After Emancipation, (Undated)

I got married before de war to Joshua Curtis. I always had craved a home an' plenty to eat, but freedom ain't give us notin' but pickled hoss meat an' dirty crackers an' not half enough of dat. Josh ain't really care 'bout no home but through dis land corporation I buyed dese fifteen acres on time. I cut down de big trees dat wus all over dese fields an' I hauled out de wood an sold hit, den I plowed up de fields an' planted dem. Josh did help to build de house an' he worked out some. All of dis time I had nineteen chilluns an' Josh died, but I kep' on.

I'll never fergit my first bale of cotton an' how I got hit sold. I was some proud of dat bale of cotton, an' atter I had hit ginned I set out wid hit on my steercart for Raleigh. De white folks hated de nigger den, 'specially de nigger what was makin' something so I dasen't ax nobody whar de market wus. I rid all day an' had to take my cotton home wid me dat night 'case I can't find no place to sell hit at. But dat night I think hit over an' de next day I axes a policeman 'bout de market.

I done a heap of work at night too, all of my sewin' and such and de piece of lan' near de house over dar ain't never got no work cept at night. I finally paid for de land.

A Black Observer Reports on Women and Fieldwork, 1867

I seen on some plantations on Red River where the white men would drive colored women out in the fields to work, when the husbands would be absent from their home, and would tell colored men that their wives and children could not live on their places unless they work in the fields. The colored men would tell them they wanted their children to attend school; and whenever they wanted their wives to work they would tell them themselves; and if he could not rule his own domestic affairs on that place he would leave it and go somewhere else. So the white people would tell them if he expected for his wife and children to live on their places without working in the field they would have to pay house rent or leave it; and if the colored people would go to leave, they would take everything they had, chickens, hogs, horses, cows, mules, crops, and everything and tell them it was for what his damn family had to eat, doing nothing but sitting up and acting the grand lady and their daughters acting the same way, for I will be damn if niggers ain't got to work on my place or leave it.

Walt Whitman Remembers President Lincoln

Walt Whitman 1819–1892

The publication of *Leaves of Grass* on or about July 4, 1855, represented a revolutionary departure in American literature. Printed at Whitman's expense, the green, quarto-sized volume bore no author's name. Opposite the title page appeared a daguerreotype engraving of the poet, dressed in workingman's trowsers, a shirt unbuttoned to reveal his undershirt, and a hat cocked casually upon his head. In a rousing Preface, the poet declared America's literary independence, and in verse that rolled freely and dithyrambically across the page, he presented himself as "Walt Whitman, an American, one of the roughs, a kosmos,/Disorderly fleshy and sensual . . . . eating drinking and breeding." Like his poet as common man, Whitman's act of self-naming represented an assault on literary decorum and the Puritan pieties of the New England literary establishment. "It is as if the beasts spoke," wrote the otherwise sympathetic Thoreau.

In the six editions of *Leaves of Grass* that were published between 1855 and 1881, Whitman opened the field of American and ultimately of modern poetry. His subject was not "the smooth walks, trimm'd hedges, poseys and nightingales of the English poets, but the whole orb, with its geologic history, the Kosmos, carrying fire and snow." He was the poet not only of Darwinian evolution, but of the city and the crowd, science and the machine. Presenting himself as a model democrat who spoke as and for rather than apart from the people, Whitman's poet was a breaker of bounds: he was female and male, farmer and factory worker, prostitute and slave, citizen of America and citizen of the world; shuttling between past, present, and future, he was "an acme of things accomplished" and an "encloser of things to be." His songs were songs not only of occupations but of sex and the body. He sang of masturbation, the sexual organs, and the sexual act; he was one of the first poets to write of the "body electric," of female eroticism, homosexual love, and the anguish of repressed desire.

Puzzled by Whitman's sudden emergence at age 36 in 1855 as the American bard, critics have proposed several explanations: a reading of Emerson, a love affair, a mystic experience, an Oedipal crisis. Considered within the context of his time, however, Whitman's emergence seems neither mystifying nor particularly disconnected from his family background and his early life as radical Democrat, political journalist, and sometime dandy. His mother was an ardent follower of the mystical doctrines of the Quaker preacher Elias Hicks, whom Whitman later described as "the democrat in religion as Jefferson was the democrat in politics." His father was a carpenter who embraced the radical political philosophy of Tom Paine and subscribed to the *Free Enquirer,* edited by Frances Wright and Robert Dale Owen, which sought through the rhetoric of class warfare to unite the grievances of New York City workers in an anticapitalist and anticlerical platform. Raised among eight brothers and sisters whose very names—Andrew Jackson, George Washington, and Thomas Jefferson—bore the inscription of the democratic ideals of his family, Whitman early began to develop a sense of self that was inextricably bound up with the political identity of America.

Although Whitman attended school between 1825 and 1830, he was largely self-educated. During the thirties he served as a printer's apprentice, engaged in local politics, and taught for a few years in Long Island schools. He read voraciously but erratically, attended the theater and the opera, and poked about the antiquities at Dr. Abbott's Egyptian Museum. As editor of the *Aurora* in 1842 and later of the Brooklyn *Daily Eagle* (1846–47), Whitman placed himself at the very center of the political battles over slavery, territorial expansion, the Mexican War, sectionalism, free trade, states' rights, worker strife, and the new market economy. His support for David Wilmot's proposal to forbid the extension of slavery into the new territory led to his being fired as editor of the *Eagle*. Perhaps disillusioned by party politics, he began to experiment with the idea of using poetry as a form of political action. When in his earliest notebook, dated 1847, Whitman breaks for the first time into lines approximating the free verse of *Leaves of Grass,* the lines bear the impress of the slavery issue:

I am the poet of slaves, and of the
    masters of slaves
I am the poet of the body
And I am

Similarly, Whitman's first free verse poems, "Blood Money," "House of Friends," and "Resurgemus," which were published in 1850, emerged out of the political passions aroused by slavery, free soil, and the European revolutions of 1848.

Although Whitman continued to support the cause of Free Soil, in the early fifties he withdrew from party politics. Working part-time as a house builder in Brooklyn, he completed his 1855 edition of *Leaves of Grass.* The poems are propelled by the desire to enlighten and regenerate the people in the ideals of the democratic republic. The drama of identity in the initially untitled "Song of Myself," the first and longest poem in the 1855 *Leaves,* is rooted in the political drama of a nation in crisis. The poet's conflict between separate person and en masse, between pride and sympathy, individualism and equality, nature and the city, the body and the soul, symbolically enacts the larger political conflicts in the nation, which grew out of the controversies over industrialization, wage labor, women's rights, finance, immigration, slavery, territorial expansion, technological progress, and the whole question of the relation of individual and state, state and nation.

Whitman sent a copy of the 1855 *Leaves of Grass* to Ralph Waldo Emerson, whose response was immediate and generous: "I find it the most extraordinary piece of wit and wisdom that America has yet contributed." Spurred by Emerson's words of praise, Whitman published a second edition of *Leaves of Grass* with several new poems in 1856. While he was planning a third edition of *Leaves* as a kind of "New Bible" of democracy, Whitman had an unhappy love affair with a man. This tale of love and loss is the subject of a small sheaf of twelve poems, initially titled "Live Oak with Moss," which was later incorporated into the "Calamus" cluster in the 1860 *Leaves of Grass.* Whitman's homosexual love crisis along with the impending dissolution of the Union caused him to become increasingly doubtful about the future of America and his own future as the bard of democracy.

This doubt is evident in the 1860 edition of *Leaves of Grass,* particularly in the "Chants Democratic" and "Calamus" groupings, and in such individual poems as "Out of the Cradle Endlessly Rocking" and "As I Ebb'd with the Ocean of Life." In the poems of "Calamus," Whitman draws upon the language of democracy and phrenology to name his erotic feeling for men as both comradeship and "adhesiveness" (the phrenological term which Whitman defined as "the personal attachment of man to man"). The love poems of "Calamus" are paired with the procreation poems of "Children of Adam," which focus upon "amative" love, the phrenological term for the love between men and women. Although the press and the literary establishment immediately focused upon the "sex" poems of "Children of Adam" as Whitman's most provocative grouping, the love poems of "Calamus" were in fact his most radical sequence sexually and politically. Whitman infused the abstractions of democracy with the intensity of erotic passion, giving literature some of its first and most potent images of democratic comradeship; and by linking homoeroticism with a democratic breaking of bounds, he presents one of the most tender and moving accounts of homosexual love in Western literature.

For Whitman, as for the nation, the Civil War was a period of major crisis. Uncertain of the role of a national poet during a time of fratricidal war, Whitman published little during the war years. In 1862, when he went to the front in search of his brother George, he found the role he would play: he would become a kind of spiritual "wound-dresser" by visiting the sick and dying soldiers in the hospital wards of Washington. Like Lincoln's "Gettysburg Address," the poems of *Drum-Taps and Sequel* (1865–66) and the prose of *Memoranda During the War* (1875–76) were attempts to come to terms with the massive carnage of the war by placing its waste and apparent unreason within some larger providential design. In these volumes Whitman turns from romance to realism, vision to history, anticipating the naturalistic war writings of Stephen Crane, Ernest Hemingway, and Norman Mailer.

Whitman remained in Washington during and after the war, working first as a clerk in the Indian Bureau and then, after being dismissed in 1865 for moral turpitude by Secretary of the Interior James Harlan, in the Attorney General's office. For all Whitman's effort to (re)present the war as testing ground for democracy, the Civil War unleashed a hoard of psychic and socio-economic demons that would continue to haunt his dream of America in the postwar period.

In his incisive political essay *Democratic Vistas* (1871), which was initially composed as a response to Carlyle's attack on the "democratic rabble" in "Shooting Niagara," Whitman seeks to come to terms with the gilded monsters of post-Civil War America. Even before the worst scandals of the Grant administration were exposed, he presents an image of America saturated in corruption and greed from the national to the local level. In "reconstructing, democratizing society" Whitman argues, the true "revolution" would be of the "interior life"; and in bringing about this democratic revolution, the poet would play the leading role by overhauling the "Culture theory" of the past and by providing the language, commonality, and myths by which America named itself. Like *Leaves of Grass, Democratic Vistas* works dialectically, as Whitman seeks to reconcile self and other, state and nation, North and South, country and city, labor and capital, money and soul. He arrives at no final synthesis of the values he seeks to juggle. Amid the modernizing, standardizing, and capitalizing whirl of America, where "with steam-engine speed" generations of humanity are turned out "like uniform iron castings," Whitman recognizes that the road to the future might be the road of the "fabled damned."

Whereas Whitman's war poems were merely tagged onto the end of the fourth edition of *Leaves*, which was published in 1867, in the 1871 *Leaves* these poems were incorporated into the main body of his work. By 1872, Whitman came to regard *Leaves of Grass* as essentially complete. In his 1872 "Preface" to "As a Strong Bird on Pinions Free," he announced his intention of turning away from his former emphasis on "a great composite *democratic individual,* male or female" toward an increased emphasis on "an aggregated, inseparable, unprecedented, vast, composite, electric *democratic nationality."* His plan was cut short by a paralytic stroke which he suffered at the beginning of 1873. The seizure left him bedridden for several weeks and paralyzed for the rest of his life.

Whitman made a trip to Camden, New Jersey a few days before his mother's death in May, 1873, and never returned to Washington. He spent the remainder of his life in Camden, first at his brother George's house and finally, beginning in 1884, in his own home at 328 Mickle Street. Struggling with occasional spells of dizziness and a prematurely aging body, Whitman mustered enough strength to publish a dual volume of poetry and prose on the occasion of the American centennial in 1876. Invigorated by the visits to the New Jersey farm of Susan and George Stafford that he began making in 1876, by the economic recovery of the nation under the new political regime of Rutherford B. Hayes (1877–81), and by the attention his work was beginning to receive in England and abroad, Whitman revised, reinte-grated, and reordered all of his poems into the final 1881 edition of *Leaves of Grass.* In 1882, he published a prose companion to his poems titled *Specimen Days,* in which he refigures the events of his life and times as a narrative of personal, national, and cosmic restoration.

The poems that Whitman wrote in the last two decades of his life, such as "Passage to India" and "Prayer of Columbus," are characterized by a leap away from the physical landscape of America toward a more traditionally religious vision of God's providence and spiritual grace. Despite his apparent disillusionment with the material conditions of America, however, Whitman continued to name the possibility of an *other* America. Figuring himself in the image of a new-world Columbus, he continued to imagine the possibility of a democratic golden world which, like the dream of a passage to India and a world in round, might bloom in some future transformation of vision into history.

Betsy Erkkila
University of Pennsylvania

PRIMARY WORKS

Leaves of Grass 1855–1881; *Drum-Taps and Sequel* 1865–66; *Democratic Vistas* 1871; *Memoranda During the War* 1875–76; *Specimen Days and Collect* 1882.

SECONDARY WORKS

Gay Wilson Allen and Sculley Bradley, eds., *The Collected Writings of Walt Whitman,* 1961; Sculley Bradley and Harold W. Blodgett, eds., *Leaves of Grass,* 1973; Library of America, Justin Kaplan, ed., *Whitman: Poetry and Prose,* 1982; Malcolm Cowley, ed., *Leaves of Grass,* 1959; Roy Harvey Pearce, ed., *Leaves of Grass,* 1961; Gay Wilson Allen, *The Solitary Singer,* 1955. *The New Walt Whitman Handbook,* 1975; Roger Asselineau, *The Evolution of Walt Whitman,* 1962; James E. Miller, *A Critical Guide to Leaves of Grass,* 1957; F.O. Matthiessen, *The American Renaissance,* 1941; Richard Chase, *Walt Whitman Reconsidered,* 1955; Betsy Erkkila, *Whitman the Political Poet,* 1988. *Walt Whitman and the Critics* 1900–1978, 1980.

from Memories of President Lincoln[1]

When Lilacs Last in the Dooryard Bloom'd[2]

1

When lilacs last in the dooryard bloom'd,
And the great star early droop'd in the western sky in the night,[3]
I mourn'd, and yet shall mourn with ever-returning spring.

Ever-returning spring, trinity sure to me you bring,
5 Lilac blooming perennial and drooping star in the west,
And thought of him I love.

2

O powerful western fallen star!
O shades of night—O moody, tearful night!
O great star disappear'd—O the black murk that hides the star!
10 O cruel hands that hold me powerless—O helpless soul of me!
O harsh surrounding cloud that will not free my soul.

3

In the dooryard fronting an old farm-house near the white-wash'd
palings,
Stands the lilac-bush tall-growing with heart-shaped leaves of rich
green,
With many a pointed blossom rising delicate, with the perfume
strong I love,
15 With every leaf a miracle—and from this bush in the dooryard,
With delicate-color'd blossoms and heart-shaped leaves of rich
green,
A sprig with its flower I break.

4

In the swamp in secluded recesses,
A shy and hidden bird is warbling a song.

20 Solitary the thrush,
The hermit withdrawn to himself, avoiding the settlements,
Sings by himself a song.

---

[1] This is the only place that Lincoln is specifically
named as the subject of these poems.
[2] "Lilacs" was written immediately following Lincoln's death. He was shot on Good Friday,
April 14, 1864 by John Wilkes Booth; he died the
next morning. In a long procession through various American cities, his body was carried by train
back to Springfield, Illinois, where he was buried
on May 4, 1864.
[3] The "great star" is the Western star, Venus.

Song of the bleeding throat,
Death's outlet song of life, (for well dear brother I know,
25   If thou wast not granted to sing thou would'st surely die.)

5

Over the breast of the spring, the land, amid cities,
Amid lanes and through old woods, where lately the violets peep'd
    from the ground, spotting the gray debris,
Amid the grass in the fields each side of the lanes, passing the
    endless grass,
Passing the yellow-spear'd wheat, every grain from its shroud in
    the dark-brown fields uprisen,
30   Passing the apple-tree blows of white and pink in the orchards,
Carrying a corpse to where it shall rest in the grave,
Night and day journeys a coffin.

6

Coffin that passes through lanes and streets,
Through day and night with the great cloud darkening the land,
35   With the pomp of the inloop'd flags with the cities draped in
    black,
With the show of the States themselves as of crape-veil'd women
    standing,
With processions long and winding and the flambeaus[4] of the
    night,
With the countless torches lit, with the silent sea of faces and the
    unbared heads,
With the waiting depot, the arriving coffin, and the sombre faces,
40   With dirges through the night, with the thousand voices rising
    strong and solemn,
With all the mournful voices of the dirges pour'd around the
    coffin,
The dim-lit churches and the shuddering organs—where amid
    these you journey,
With the tolling tolling bells' perpetual clang,
Here, coffin that slowly passes,
45   I give you my sprig of lilac.

7

(Nor for you, for one alone,
Blossoms and branches green to coffins all I bring,
For fresh as the morning, thus would I chant a song for you O
    sane and sacred death.

---

[4]Large candlesticks.

All over bouquets of roses,
50 O death, I cover you over with roses and early lilies,
But mostly and now the lilac that blooms the first,
Copious I break, I break the sprigs from the bushes,
With loaded arms I come, pouring for you,
For you and the coffins all of you O death.)

8

55 O western orb sailing the heaven,
Now I know what you must have meant as a month since I
    walk'd,
As I walk'd in silence the transparent shadowy night,
As I saw you had something to tell as you bent to me night after
    night,
As you droop'd from the sky low down as if to my side, (while the
    other stars all look'd on,)
60 As we wander'd together the solemn night, (for something I know
    not what kept me from sleep,)
As the night advanced, and I saw on the rim of the west how full
    you were of woe,
As I stood on the rising ground in the breeze in the cool
    transparent night,
As I watch'd where you pass'd and was lost in the netherward
    black of the night,
As my soul in its trouble dissatisfied sank, as where you sad orb,
65 Concluded, dropt in the night, and was gone.

9

Sing on there in the swamp,
O singer bashful and tender, I hear your notes, I hear your call,
I hear, I come presently, I understand you,
But a moment I linger, for the lustrous star has detain'd me,
70 The star my departing comrade holds and detains me.

10

O how shall I warble myself for the dead one there I loved?
And how shall I deck my song for the large sweet soul that has
    gone?
And what shall my perfume be for the grave of him I love?

Sea-winds blown from east and west,
75 Blown from the Eastern sea and blown from the Western sea, till
    there on the prairies meeting,
These and with these and the breath of my chant,
I'll perfume the grave of him I love.

11

O what shall I hang on the chamber walls?
And what shall the pictures be that I hang on the walls,
80 To adorn the burial-house of him I love?

Pictures of growing spring and farms and homes,
With the Fourth-month eve at sundown, and the gray smoke lucid
    and bright,
With floods of the yellow gold of the gorgeous, indolent, sinking
    sun, burning, expanding the air,
With the fresh sweet herbage under foot, and the pale green leaves
    of the trees prolific,
85 In the distance the flowing glaze, the breast of the river, with a
    wind-dapple here and there,
With ranging hills on the banks, with many a line against the sky,
    and shadows,
And the city at hand with dwellings so dense, and stacks of
    chimneys,
And all the scenes of life and the workshops, and the workmen
    homeward returning.

12

Lo, body and soul—this land,
90 My own Manhattan with spires, and the sparkling and hurrying
    tides, and the ships,
The varied and ample land, the South and the North in the light,
    Ohio's shores and flashing Missouri,
And ever the far-spreading prairies cover'd with grass and corn.

Lo, the most excellent sun so calm and haughty,
The violet and purple morn with just-felt breezes,
95 The gentle soft-born measureless light,
The miracle spreading bathing all, the fulfill'd noon,
The coming eve delicious, the welcome night and the stars,
Over my cities shining all, enveloping man and land.

13

Sing on, sing on you gray-brown bird,
100 Sing from the swamps, the recesses, pour your chant from the
    bushes,
Limitless out of the dusk, out of the cedars and pines.

Sing on dearest brother, warble your reedy song,
Loud human song, with voice of uttermost woe.

O liquid and free and tender!
105 O wild and loose to my soul—O wondrous singer!
You only I hear—yet the star holds me, (but will soon depart,)
Yet the lilac with mastering odor holds me.

14

Now while I sat in the day and look'd forth,
In the close of the day with its light and the fields of spring, and
the farmers preparing their crops,
110 In the large unconscious scenery of my land with its lakes and
forests,
In the heavenly aerial beauty, (after the perturb'd winds and the
storms,)
Under the arching heavens of the afternoon swift passing, and the
voices of children and women,
The many-moving sea-tides, and I saw the ships how they sail'd,
And the summer approaching with richness, and the fields all busy
with labor,
115 And the infinite separate houses, how they all went on, each with
its meals and minutia of daily usages,
And the streets how their throbbings throbb'd, and the cities pent—
lo, then and there,
Falling upon them all and among them all, enveloping me with the
rest,
Appear'd the cloud, appear'd the long black trail,
And I knew death, its thought, and the sacred knowledge of death.
120 Then with the knowledge of death as walking one side of me,
And the thought of death close-walking the other side of me,
And I in the middle as with companions, and as holding the hands
of companions,
I fled forth to the hiding receiving night that talks not,
Down to the shores of the water, the path by the swamp in the
dimness,
125 To the solemn shadowy cedars and ghostly pines so still.

And the singer so shy to the rest receiv'd me,
The gray-brown bird I know receiv'd us comrades three,
And he sang the carol of death, and a verse for him I love.

From deep secluded recesses,
130 From the fragrant cedars and the ghostly pines so still,
Came the carol of the bird.

And the charm of the carol rapt me,
As I held as if by their hands my comrades in the night,
And the voice of my spirit tallied the song of the bird.

Come lovely and soothing death,
Undulate round the world, serenely arriving, arriving,
In the day, in the night, to all, to each,
Sooner or later delicate death.

Prais'd be the fathomless universe,
140 *For life and joy, and for objects and knowledge curious,*
And for love, sweet love—but praise! praise! praise!
For the sure-enwinding arms of cool-enfolding death.

Dark mother always gliding near with soft feet,
Have none chanted for thee a chant of fullest welcome?
145 *Then I chant it for thee, I glorify thee above all,*
I bring thee a song that when thou must indeed come, come
unfalteringly.

Approach strong deliveress,
When it is so, when thou hast taken them I joyously sing the dead,
Lost in the loving floating ocean of thee,
150 *Laved in the flood of thy bliss O death.*

From me to thee glad serenades,
Dances for thee I propose saluting thee, adornments and feastings for
thee,
And the sights of the open landscape and the high-spread sky are
fitting,
And life and the fields, and the huge and thoughtful night.
155 *The night in silence under many a star,*
The ocean shore and the husky whispering wave whose voice I
know,
And the soul turning to thee O vast and well-veil'd death,
And the body gratefully nestling close to thee.

Over the tree-tops I float thee a song,
160 *Over the rising and sinking waves, over the myriad fields and the*
prairies wide,
Over the dense-pack'd cities all and the teeming wharves and ways,
I float this carol with joy, with joy to thee O death.

15

To the tally of my soul,
Loud and strong kept up the gray-brown bird,
165 With pure deliberate notes spreading filling the night.

Loud in the pines and cedars dim,
Clear in the freshness moist and the swamp-perfume,
And I with my comrades there in the night.

While my sight that was bound in my eyes unclosed,
170 As to long panoramas of visions.

And I saw askant the armies,
I saw as in noiseless dreams hundreds of battle-flags,
Borne through the smoke of the battles and pierc'd with missiles I
saw them,
And carried hither and yon through the smoke, and torn and
bloody,
175 And at last but a few shreds left on the staffs, (and all in silence,)
And the staffs all splinter'd and broken.

I saw battle-corpses, myriads of them,
And the white skeletons of young men, I saw them,
I saw the debris and debris of all the slain soldiers of the war,
180 But I saw they were not as was thought,
They themselves were fully at rest, they suffer'd not,
The living remain'd and suffer'd, the mother suffer'd,
And the wife and the child and the musing comrade suffer'd,
And the armies that remain'd suffer'd.

16

185 Passing the visions, passing the night,
Passing, unloosing the hold of my comrades' hands,
Passing the song of the hermit bird and the tallying song of my
soul,
Victorious song, death's outlet song, yet varying ever-altering song,
As low and wailing, yet clear the notes, rising and falling, flooding
the night,
190 Sadly sinking and fainting, as warning and warning, and yet again
bursting with joy,
Covering the earth and filling the spread of the heaven,
As that powerful psalm in the night I heard from recesses,
Passing, I leave thee lilac with heart-shaped leaves,
I leave thee there in the door-yard, blooming, returning with
spring.

195 I cease from my song for thee,
From my gaze on thee in the west, fronting the west, communing
with thee,
O comrade lustrous with silver face in the night.
Yet each to keep and all, retrievements out of the night,
The song, the wondrous chant of the gray-brown bird,
200 And the tallying chant, the echo arous'd in my soul,
With the lustrous and drooping star with the countenance full of
woe,

With the holders holding my hand nearing the call of the bird,
Comrades mine and I in the midst, and their memory ever to
    keep, for the dead I loved so well,
For the sweetest, wisest soul of all my days and lands—and this
    for his dear sake,
205 Lilac and star and bird twined with the chant of my soul,
There in the fragrant pines and the cedars dusk and dim.

1865–66